FROM LEFT: KAVALENKAVA/SHUTTERSTOCK, TUUL & BRUNO MORANDI/GETTY IMAGES, FARION_O/SHUTTERSTOCK

Kotor (p295), Montenegro

Bled Island, Lake Bled (p426), Slovenia

lonely planet

Eastern Europe

Estonia
p175

Latvia
p234

Lithuania
p253

Belarus
p72

Russia
p373

Poland
p317

Ukraine
p435

Czechia
p146

Slovakia
p397

Moldova
p272

Hungary
p196

Romania
p346

Slovenia
p416

Croatia
p119

Bosnia &
Hercegovina
p79

Serbia
p378

Bulgaria
p96

Montenegro
p291

Kosovo
p223

North
Macedonia
p304

Albania
p55

Mark Baker, Joel Balsam, Marc Di Duca, Peter Dragicevich, Anthony Ham, Kata Fári, Anna Kaminski, Vesna Maric, Owen Morton, Anja Mutić, Leonid Ragozin, Brana Vladisavljević, Luke Waterson, Angelo Zinna

CONTENTS

Zlatni Rat (p135), Croatia

**Alexander Nevsky Cathedral
(p180), Tallinn, Estonia**

GELIA/SHUTTERSTOCK

Bratislava (p400), Slovakia

Toolkit

Storybook

ZGPHOTOGRAPHY/SHUTTERSTOCK

Liberty Bridge (p205), Budapest, Hungary

EASTERN EUROPE
THE JOURNEY BEGINS HERE

Venture to the continent's eastern side and you'll be rewarded with an adventure that's authentic, quirky, affordable and wild in all the best ways. This is a region where history hits hard: think medieval old towns, million-year-old caves, reborn cosmopolitan capitals and socialist hangovers. The people are warm, unpretentious and unapologetically real – and many think 11am is a perfectly reasonable time to offer you a shot of homemade alcohol. The hearty food nurtures both the body and the soul, and while the public transport may not always be on time, it will definitely take you to some incredible places. Eastern Europe may still be a little rough around the edges but it's oh-so-loveable. Come hungry, expect a little bit of chaos, a whole lot of culture and be sure to mingle, for it's in the people where the true spirit of Eastern Europe resides.

My favourite experience is pausing halfway across the sage-green **Liberty Bridge** (p205) to marvel at Budapest's incredible beauty.

Kata Fári

@ *@kata.fari*

Kata is a Budapest-based writer who sings the praises of the world's best places online and in print. Kata wrote the Hungary, Plan Your Trip and Toolkit chapters.

WHO GOES WHERE

Our writers and experts choose the places which, for them, define Eastern Europe.

My favourite place in Prague is **Charles Bridge** (p155). I love to wander the old town's closed-in, cobbled streets and then emerge onto the open bridge – hopefully on a sunny day.

Mark Baker

markbakerprague.com

Mark is based in Prague and writes frequently about Central Europe. He curated the Czechia, Romania and Slovenia chapters.

I love to wander around the Ottoman-era stone alleyways in **Berat** (p60), snapping photos as the light strikes its cherished windows.

Joel Balsam

@joelbalsam

Joel is a Canadian freelance journalist based in Rio de Janeiro and the author of more than a dozen Lonely Planet guidebooks. He curated the Albania chapter.

Gdańsk's (p337) blend of 20th-century history, compelling museums, windswept beaches and filling Baltic food make the capital of the north my favourite place in Poland.

Marc Di Duca

@marcdiduca

Marc has written travel guides for over two decades. He curated the Poland chapter.

Montenegro claimed a special place in my heart the first time I crossed the border from Croatia and took a drive around the astonishingly beautiful **Bay of Kotor** (p295). The same thrill hits me each time I return.

Peter Dragicevich

@peterdragnz

Born in New Zealand but with family roots in the former Yugoslavia, Peter curated the Montenegro chapter.

My perfect day in North Macedonia centres on the timeworn villages of **Trpejca** (p310) and Vevčani at Lake Ohrid – truly the medieval Balkans the world forgot.

Anthony Ham

@AnthonyHamWrite

Anthony travels the world in search of stories, taking readers into the forgotten back roads of the world. He curated the Kosovo and North Macedonia chapters.

For nearly 20 years, the Curonian Spit has been one of my happy places: I've come back to Nida, time and again to walk in solitude along pine-scented forest trails and up the **Parnidis Dune** (p265) to recapture the silence that's missing from my daily life.

Anna Kaminski

@ *@anna.cohen.kaminski*

Anna writes about travel and culture, and is the author of Eyeball Tacos and Kangaroo Stew, *a food-driven travel memoir. She curated the Lithuania chapter.*

My favourite place in Eastern Europe is Sarajevo, where the Ottoman quarter of **Baščaršija** (p82) and the medley of historic architecture is coupled with great food and warm and wonderful locals.

Vesna Maric

@ *@vesnamarx*

Vesna writes literary fiction and nonfiction. She is the author of a memoir, Bluebird, *and a novel,* The President Shop. *She curated the Bosnia and Hercegovina chapter.*

When I climbed the stairs of the **Candle of Gratitude** (p284), a cloudburst erupted just as I reached the top. Seconds later, a beautiful rainbow appeared in the sky, stretching across the Dniester River from Moldova to Ukraine.

Owen Morton

@ *@owenmortonmanul*

Owen loves exploring the post-Soviet world, which made curating the Moldova chapter a delight.

I love driving along the back roads of **Hvar** (p135) and exploring the unsung spots of the island's interior, with its olive groves, fields of aromatic herbs and half-abandoned stone hamlets.

Anja Mutić

@ *@everthenomad*

Zagreb-based Anja Mutić writes about travel and runs Storyline Studio, a creative-content agency for tourism and hospitality. She curated the Croatia chapter.

FROM LEFT: MATYAS REHAK/SHUTTERSTOCK, LMSPENCER/SHUTTERSTOCK

Walking aimlessly around **Sofia's old town** (p100) is one of my favourite pastimes in Bulgaria. The area is teeming with unique restaurants, bars and cafes, many of which are soulful family-run businesses. Everything is outdoors in good weather and – bonus – the weather is good most of the time.

Leonid Ragozin

X @leonidragozin

Leonid Ragozin is a travel writer and political journalist focusing on the Russo-Ukrainian conflict. He curated the Belarus, Bulgaria, Latvia, Russia and Ukraine chapters.

In Đerdap (p391), it's as if the Danube casts a spell on all those who enter the formidable Iron Gates – even the name evokes a fantasy world. Whether you traverse the gorge by bicycle, car or boat, that sense of awe is a constant companion.

Brana Vladisavljević

🖊 lonelyplanet.com/authors/brana-vladisavljevic

A freelance editor and translator based in Belgrade, Brana writes about her native Western Balkans region for Lonely Planet. She curated the Serbia chapter.

FROM LEFT: MARTINA STRIHOVA/SHUTTERSTOCK, MO WU/SHUTTERSTOCK

Slovakia is filled with marvels but it's the **Malé Karpaty** (Small Carpathians; p404) in particular that hold me in thrall. Dense, untrammelled forest means you can traipse across Western Slovakia and scarcely cross a road.

Luke Waterson

lukeandhiswords.com

Luke is an adventure writer specialising in Slovakia, Scandinavia, the UK and Latin America. He curated the Slovakia chapter.

The impressive remains of the Lootsi cog, a Hanseatic shipwreck, is visible outside of **Seaplane Harbour** (p183), one of Europe's great maritime museums. Take a peek before entering the Soviet-era hangar housing the museum to learn more about Estonia's long relationship with the sea.

Angelo Zinna

@angelo_zinna

Angelo Zinna is an Italian-Finnish writer and photographer based in Florence. He curated the Estonia chapter.

22PLAN YOUR TRIP

0 500 km
0 250 miles

FINLAND

NORWAY   SWEDEN

HELSINKI
TALLINN
ESTONIA

OSLO

RĪGA
LATVIA

SCOTLAND

North
Sea

LITHUANIA

Kraków, Poland
Picturesque streets, intriguing history and pierogi (p326)

High Tatras, Slovakia
Well-marked hiking trails in the **Carpathians** (p409)

ENGLAND

NETHERLANDS   AMSTERDAM

LONDON

Prague, Czechia
Historic city and the best beer in Europe (p150)

BERLIN

GERMANY

WARSAW

POLAND

Kraków

PRAGUE

CZECHIA

SLOVAKIA

BRATISLAVA

Budapest, Hungary
Grandiose architecture and splendid thermal **spas** (p200)

PARIS

VIENNA

AUSTRIA

BUDAPEST

HUNGARY

SLOVENIA

Lake Bled, Slovenia
Serene islet crowned by a **church** (p426)

FRANCE

LJUBLJANA

ZAGREB

BOSNIA & HERCEGOVINA

BELGRADE

SERBIA

CROATIA

SARAJEVO

PRISTI

Dubrovnik, Croatia
Spectacular walls that hug the city's historic **core** (p136)

ITALY

Adriatic
Sea

Mostar

MONTENEGRO

PODGORICA

TIRANA

SPAIN

ROME

Kotor, Montenegro
1350 steps up the city walls lead to glorious **views** (p295)

ALBANIA

10

SARDINIA

Mediterranean Sea

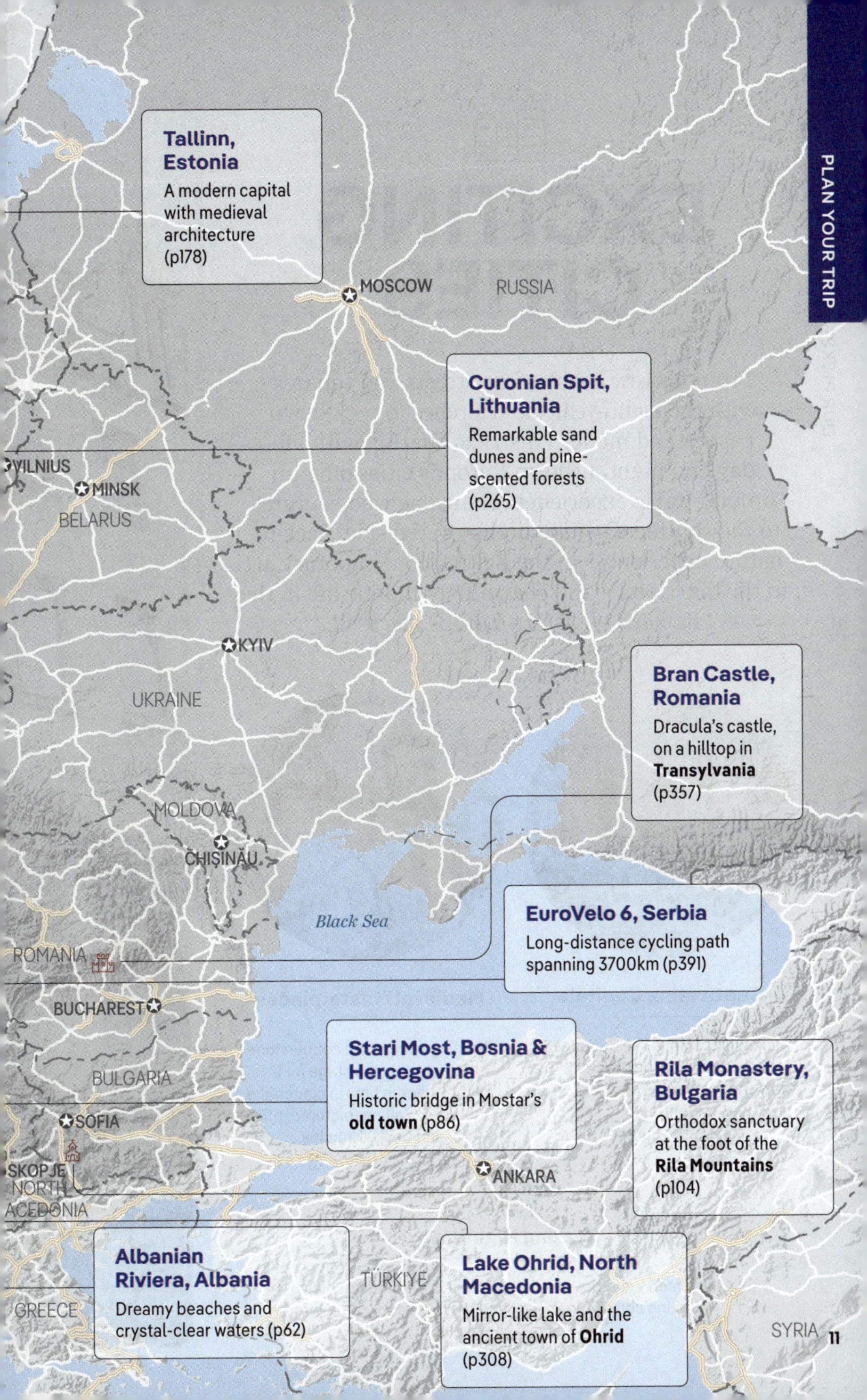

Tallinn, Estonia

A modern capital with medieval architecture (p178)

MOSCOW   RUSSIA

Curonian Spit, Lithuania

Remarkable sand dunes and pine-scented forests (p265)

VILNIUS

MINSK

BELARUS

KYIV

UKRAINE

Bran Castle, Romania

Dracula's castle, on a hilltop in **Transylvania** (p357)

MOLDOVA

CHIŞINĂU

Black Sea

EuroVelo 6, Serbia

Long-distance cycling path spanning 3700km (p391)

ROMANIA

BUCHAREST

BULGARIA

Stari Most, Bosnia & Hercegovina

Historic bridge in Mostar's **old town** (p86)

Rila Monastery, Bulgaria

Orthodox sanctuary at the foot of the **Rila Mountains** (p104)

SOFIA

SKOPJE

NORTH
MACEDONIA

ANKARA

Albanian Riviera, Albania

Dreamy beaches and crystal-clear waters (p62)

Lake Ohrid, North Macedonia

Mirror-like lake and the ancient town of **Ohrid** (p308)

GREECE

TÜRKIYE

SYRIA

11

EXCITING CITIES

From narrow cobblestone streets and squares with thousand-year-old churches to rock-hewn castles and modern districts buzzing with life day and night, Eastern Europe's cities offer an unforgettable experience for anyone who ventures to the continent's more undiscovered side. Back-to-nature experiences in the Baltics, contemporary art in the big capitals and charmingly chaotic life in the Balkans – Eastern Europe has it all.

Captivating Capitals

Exciting capitals like Budapest (pictured), Prague and Warsaw are the perfect places to transition from Central to Eastern Europe.

Medieval Masterpieces

Strolling along worn cobblestone streets sets the stage for a journey back in time in places like Dubrovnik, Tallinn (pictured; p178) and Český Krumlov.

Buzzing Nightlife

Making merry into the wee hours is best in Belgrade's *splavs* (floating clubs), Riga's bars and Kraków's cool clubs.

BEST URBAN EXPERIENCES

Climb to the dome of Budapest's splendid ❶ **St Stephen's Basilica** (p207; pictured far left) for gorgeous views of the city.

Czech out the medieval ❷ **Astronomical Clock** (p156) built into the tower on the southern side of Prague's Old Town Hall.

Tour the world's largest ❸ **parliament building** (p351), the infamous creation of former dictator Nicolae Ceaușescu, in Romania's capital Bucharest.

Dance the night away in ❹ **Belgrade** (p386), whether at a floating club on the river, atop a fortress or in a former slaughterhouse.

Have coffee on ❺ **Town Hall Square** (p178) in Tallinn's exceptionally well-preserved Old Town.

GLACIER BLUES & SECRET SHORES

Some lakes glisten with icy beauty, while others invite you to dive in for a refreshing swim. And then there are those so perfect that they're almost too beautiful to touch. Whether you're exploring remote glacial wonders or soaking in the sun on a beach, Eastern Europe's lakes invite both adventure and awe.

BEST LAKESIDE EXPERIENCES

Explore a small islet with a lovely church on **❶ Lake Bled** (p426) – the turquoise waters are just as lucid in real life.

Paddle in the famously shallow waters of Central Europe's largest lake, **❷ Lake Balaton** (p215), surrounded by rolling green hills.

Marvel at Europe's oldest and one of its deepest lakes, **❸ Lake Ohrid** (p308), a natural treasure shared by North Macedonia and Albania.

Jump into Montenegro's **❹ Lake Skadar** (p298; pictured far left), the biggest lake in the Balkans and a wild wonder.

Hike by the prettiest lake in Slovakia's High Tatras, **❺ Štrbské pleso** (p410; pictured left), with one of the country's best hotels on the shores.

FROM LEFT: JAROSLAV SEKERES/SHUTTERSTOCK, ALEXANDRE ROSA/SHUTTERSTOCK

For Your Eyes Only

Though the clear mountain lakes in the High Tatras or the Plitvice Lakes near Zagreb look inviting, you can't always take the plunge. Check ahead.

Water Sports

Many lakes are ideal for kayaking, canoeing and kite surfing. Budget enough time to get the most out of a visit.

Superlatives

Some of the region's lakes hold impressive titles: Central Europe's largest, Europe's oldest and the world's largest swimmable thermal lake are all here.

OTAVIOCOSTA/SHUTTERSTOCK

Sarmales, Budapest (p200)

BEST CULINARY EXPERIENCES

Fill up with goulash and a shot of *pálinka* at one of Budapest's many ❶ **restaurants** (p206).

Don't count how many pierogi you eat while sampling Polish vodka at a milk bar (*bar mleczny*) in ❷ **Kraków** (p328).

Enjoy a flaky *burek* pastry in the Balkans – ❸ **Sarajevo** (p82) has plenty of bakeries – and share some homemade *raki* with locals.

Savour *sarmale* (stuffed cabbage) in Romania's less-explored capital, ❹ **Bucharest** (p350).

Try some fresh fish at the ❺ **Curonian Spit** (p265) in Lithuania and wash it down with local beer or cider.

EAT, DRINK, REPEAT

The hearty, rich and flavourful meals here have a distinct homemade feel. Though beer and wine are part of social life, hardly any Eastern European household is without an innocent-looking water bottle in the fridge, containing the most fiery alcohol you've ever had – which they'll warmly insist you try.

Hearty Cuisine

Eastern Europe has a variety of culinary traditions, but one similarity is that meals tend to be filling, flavourful and meaty.

Feisty Spirits

The region welcomes you with shots of liquid fire disguised as harmless drinks. Try vodka, *pálinka* or *raki*.

15

TIMELESS TREASURES

Eastern Europe's eventful and turbulent history manifests in its monumental buildings and ruins. Many a castle, medieval fortification and ancient ruin tells the tale of victory, defeat, resilience and undying spirit. Dedicate time to understand all that has transpired over the centuries through the various cultures that coexist together – sometimes peacefully, other times not – in the many small, geographically diverse and colourful nations.

Castles Everywhere

From robust fortresses and crumbling piles of bricks to grandiose Renaissance residences, Eastern Europe has a castle on pretty much every hilltop.

Thousand-Year-Old Ruins

History buffs will enjoy Eastern Europe's ancient ruins – Roman, Greek, Byzantine and Venetian – found in cities and small towns alike.

City Wall Workouts

Climbing a medieval city wall is a great way to leap into history and gain marvellous views from a unique perspective.

BEST HISTORICAL EXPERIENCES

Climb the ❶ **Kotor City Walls** (p295) that zigzag up a mountain for splendid views.

Walk the historic walls of ❷ **Dubrovnik** (p136; pictured far left), which hug the old medieval centre and provide unobstructed views of the Adriatic Sea.

Head to ❸ **Butrint** (p63; pictured left) to see a 2800-year-old city with architecture from the Greeks, Romans, Byzantines and Venetians.

Discover the Old Town of Český Krumlov, where the massive ❹ **fortress** (p162) rivals Prague Castle.

Experience the history, the myths and the intrigue of Romania's ❺ **Bran Castle** (p357) of Dracula fame.

KOVOP/SHUTTERSTOCK

High Tatras (p409), Slovakia

AWESOME SCENERY

The landscape of the continent's eastern half is as varied as it is breathtaking. Majestic mountain ranges from the Julian Alps to the Urals are interspersed with numerous rivers, lakes and a variety of coastlines along the Baltic, Black and Adriatic Seas. Inland, pristine forests and quaint villages await.

Magnificent Mountains

The Carpathian Mountains, the Julian Alps, the Accursed Mountains and many other jagged peaks make Eastern Europe beautifully bumpy.

Lakes, Rivers & Seas

Between the Baltic and Ionian Seas, marvellous lakes and serpentine rivers await. Paddle the rapids or float peacefully in pristine waters.

BEST NATURE EXPERIENCES

Explore Slovenia's ❶ **Soča Valley** (p427), from the frothy rapids to the placid streams.

Enjoy a combination of wild coastal nature and cultural landmarks in Estonia's ❷ **Lahemaa National Park** (p181).

Save money at the beach towns of Sarandë or ❸ **Ksamil** (p63) on the Albanian Riviera, where turquoise water is just steps away.

Hike on the many marked trails of Slovakia's ❹ **High Tatras** (p409), the highest range in the Carpathians.

Explore lesser trod paths at North Macedonia's ❺ **Mavrovo National Park** (p311) for deep canyons and dense forests.

CULTURAL MARVELS

Sure, you may have seen the Slav squat meme or imagine life in the East as centred around drab housing blocks from the Soviet era. But the real culture here is a diverse tapestry that's characterised by strong family and community values, deep religious and folk traditions, and a vast historical heritage that is reflected in the region's architecture.

❶

❷

❸

❹ ❺

BEST CULTURAL EXPERIENCES

Brutalist Architecture

Most of Eastern Europe was behind the Iron Curtain for decades. Many socialist and brutalist buildings from this era survive in cities and towns.

Sombre Museums

Many museums dwell on sombre topics like Soviet oppression, independence struggles and the heartrending Yugoslavian war.

See Warsaw's tallest and most iconic building, the ❶ **Palace of Culture & Science** (p322; pictured far left), a controversial gift from Stalin.

Visit Budapest's ❷ **Great Synagogue** (p208), the largest Jewish house of worship in Europe.

Learn about the fascinating, tumultuous history of socialism in the Balkans at Belgrade's ❸ **Museum of Yugoslavia** (p383; pictured left).

Wonder how on earth the ❹ **Ostrog Monastery** (p299) was built within two large cliffside caves in Montenegro.

Quiet Religious Sights

From Eastern Orthodox monasteries to synagogues and mosques, Eastern Europe has many contemplative religious sites.

Visit the ❺ **Rila Monastery** (p104) in Bulgaria, known for its striking black-and-white archways and vivid exterior frescoes.

INTO THE WILD

Feeling on top of the world after summiting a mountain? Is your heart pounding after running a canyon's rapids? Are you straining to find your way through a pitch-black subterranean chamber? These are just some of the many adventures that await in Eastern Europe. But it isn't just for the wild at heart – pristine lakes, low-key cycling routes and walks in the park are perfect for anyone ready to breathe some fresh air.

Epic Hikes

The region's mountain ranges and rugged peaks are laced with well-marked trails, leading to amazing flora, fauna and views.

Go Spelunking

Subterranean karst landscapes, dripstone formations and unique underground rivers and lakes can be seen on stunning caving excursions.

Two-Wheeled Fun

Eastern Europe has many cycling routes to explore. Some lead up mountains, others follow rivers, but they all offer something exciting.

BEST OUTDOOR EXPERIENCES

Explore the jaw-dropping ❶ **Postojna Cave system** (p428; pictured left) in Slovenia, some of which is toured on an underground mini train.

Trek through Albania's Accursed Mountains via the ❷ **Valbonë Pass** (p66) on a multi-day circuit that also includes a ferry ride.

Cycle the EuroVelo 6 through the Iron Gates gorge in ❸ **Đerdap National Park** (p391) for a challenging but rewarding experience.

Find glacial lakes and perfect views on Bulgaria's ❹ **Seven Rila Lakes hike** (p104; pictured far left).

Paddle furiously through the white-water rapids of ❺ **Tara National Park** (p389) in Serbia.

REGIONS & CITIES

Find the places that tick all your boxes.

Estonia

A CULTURAL CROSSROADS

The northernmost Baltic state, Estonia is a small country that has long fought for independence. Apart from its rich history, Estonia is famous for its natural landscapes. Half of the country is covered by vast forests, and over 2000 islands lie off its coast. Inland, charming towns like Tallinn and Tartu await.

Lithuania

UNSPOILED NATURE MEETS MILLENNIAL HISTORY

The largest of the Baltic states is filled with vast natural beauty and it takes good care of it, too. In 2025, Vilnius was named Europe's Green Capital. There's hardly been a better time to explore its protected forests, lakes, sandy dunes and exciting towns.

Poland

A WARM, WELCOMING AND RESILIENT NATION

The home of Chopin has a turbulent history marked by both triumph and tragedy. Warsaw was painstakingly and wonderfully rebuilt after World War II, while colourful Kraków is known for its medieval old town, cultural riches and modern nightlife. Elsewhere, woods, rivers and lakes offer fresh-air fun.

Estonia p175

Lithuani p253

Poland p317

Czechia p146

Czechia

BREATHTAKING CASTLES AND EVEN BETTER BEER

Prague is home to iconic historic sites like Charles Bridge and Prague Castle, as well as an exciting urban centre with cool clubs and chic museums. Outside the capital, castles and palaces abound. Wherever you go, be sure to grab a glass, as hardly anyone does beer better than the Czechs.

Latvia

DUNES AND BALTIC FORESTS

Nestled between Estonia and Lithuania, Latvia is known for its dense forests and white sand beaches. Its capital, Riga, endears with art nouveau architecture and a vibrant cultural scene. Latvia is a small stunner, and with a population of under 2 million you're never far away from unspoiled serenity.

Belarus

EUROPE'S ODDEST POLITY

At the time of writing, travel to Belarus was not recommended. The war in Ukraine, president Alexander Lukashenko's repressive rule and anti-Lukashenko protests are all reasons to give it a miss. Visiting Belarus on a politically motivated mission may result in arrest or deportation.

Latvia
p234

Russia
p373

Belarus
p72

Russia

THE WORLD'S LARGEST COUNTRY AT WAR

The world's largest country has it all: from dense, snow-covered boreal forests and semi-deserts to splendid cities with rich histories like St Petersburg and Moscow. That said, you need a pressing reason to travel to Russia these days due to the ongoing war with Ukraine.

Ukraine
p435

Moldova
p272

Ukraine

A COUNTRY UNDER BRUTAL ATTACK

At the time of writing, Ukraine was a war zone. Though a glimmer of hope had appeared in the form of peace talks, it's safe to say that once Ukraine becomes safe to explore again, it will be an entirely different country than the one it was before.

Moldova

UNDERGROUND WINE LABYRINTHS AND SOVIET MEMORABILIA

Often overlooked, Moldova draws those looking for authentic Eastern European experiences. Transnistria, a self-declared country where socialism lives on in statues of Lenin and blocky architecture, has become an unlikely star in this regard. Moldova is also home to the world's largest winery and the lively capital of Chișinău.

Slovakia

MAJESTIC MOUNTAINS, CASTLES AND MEDIEVAL MARVELS

Epic hikes in the High Tatras, caving in the Slovak Karst and cycling through primeval beech forests are reasons why most travellers add Slovakia to their travel lists. While Slovakia appeals most to lovers of the outdoors, don't sleep on Bratislava: its Old Town is filled with medieval and baroque gems.

Hungary

STUNNING ARCHITECTURE AND THERMAL SPAS

A landlocked country with an undying love for water, Hungary is home to healing thermal spas, the world's largest swimmable thermal lake and Central Europe's largest lake. Budapest is one of the most stunning capitals in Europe with astonishing architecture and exciting nightlife.

Slovenia

RELAXING TOWNS AND PRISTINE NATURE

Tucked between the Alps and the Adriatic, Slovenia has everything under the sun when it comes to the great outdoors. Hiking, swimming, cycling, skiing, horse riding, ballooning, caving and canyoning are all possible. Lake Bled looks like something straight out of a fairytale, but don't skip the sleepy capital, Ljubljana.

Croatia

LIVING UP TO THE HYPE

With a 1778km-long coastline and some 1185 islands dotting turquoise waters, Croatia has long been a favourite of beachgoers. Inland, national parks protect lush forests, mountains, rivers, lakes and waterfalls. Apart from nature, Croatia's medieval towns have been preserved for over a thousand years.

Bosnia & Hercegovina

RICH HISTORY, WILD NATURE, WARM WELCOME

Many still associate Bosnia & Hercegovina with the heartbreaking war of the 1990s and are consequently surprised by how much the country has to offer. Mountains, wild swimming, white-water rafting, impressive waterfalls, skiing and even a rainforest are all major draws, as are the historical centres of Sarajevo and Mostar.

Montenegro

MOUNTAINS, COAST AND ANCIENT TOWNS

A tiny country with a compact but impressive coastline, rugged mountains and historic towns, Montenegro draws thousands of tourists every year. The picturesque Bay of Kotor is a must-see, but away from the obvious attractions are great hikes, rafting, canyoning, skiing and wild corners.

Romania

RURAL CHARM, UNSPOILT NATURE, ENERGETIC CITIES

The largest of the Balkan countries, Romania has dramatic mountain scenery and a Black Sea coastline. Though Transylvania has long lured travellers interested in its mysticism and Dracula eeriness, elsewhere the country consists of rolling hills, a pristine landscape and the buzzy capital of Bucharest.

Bulgaria

ANCIENT MONUMENTS, GREAT OUTDOORS, BEACHES GALORE

A beguiling blend of history, wild landscapes and endless adventure, Bulgaria is one of the most affordable destinations in Eastern Europe. From the laid-back capital of Sofia to the stunning beaches on the Black Sea and all sorts of outdoor fun, Bulgaria is a fascinating mix of tradition and modernity.

North Macedonia

WILD NATURE, ANCIENT HISTORY

Beyond famed Lake Ohrid and its namesake town, North Macedonia offers amazing off-the-beaten-path adventures thanks to its dramatic mountains, lakes and national parks like Mavrovo, Galičica and Pelister. Don't expect swanky hotels and Michelin-starred restaurants – the country's charm lies in its undiscovered beauty.

Serbia

DIVERSITY OFF THE BEATEN PATH

In the heart of the Balkans, Serbia is a country of complex history and strong cultural identity. Belgrade's historic architecture and lively nightlife fuelled by that feisty Serbian spirit is world-famous, but the country also has unsullied outdoors crowned by the Carpathian mountain ranges, grand river gorges and ancient caves ripe for exploration.

Kosovo

A YOUNG AND BEAUTIFUL NATION

Having gained independence from Serbia in 2008, Kosovo is Europe's youngest country. The capital Pristina is a growing urban centre with a mix of modern and historical landmarks, while the country's rugged terrain and natural beauty make it a true hidden gem – at least for now.

Albania

MYSTERIOUS NO LONGER

Albania remained mostly off-limits throughout much of the 20th century, but now the secret is out. Its dreamy beaches rival any in the Mediterranean, its spectacular mountains are threaded with hiking trails and its authentic towns are the home of many a Greek and Roman ruin.

Essential Cities

Allow: 14 days
Distance: 2130km

From the charming streets of Kraków to the majestic castles of Prague, and the thermal baths of Budapest to the grand architecture of Sofia, this journey takes you on a whirlwind adventure through five Eastern European countries. Consider overnight trains so you can wake with the sun in an entirely new place.

Charles Bridge (p155), Prague

① WARSAW ⏱ 2 DAYS

Start off by staying in the Polish capital **Warsaw** (p320; pictured below) for one night. Take it easy during your gentle introduction to Eastern Europe – explore the beautifully restored Old Town, take pictures in Castle Square with Sigismund's Column and the Royal Castle, and eat pierogi (dumplings) to your heart's content before taking a train south to colourful Kraków.

② KRAKÓW ⏱ 3 DAYS

Stay for two nights to take in the atmosphere of one of Poland's most beautiful and historic cities, **Kraków** (p326). See the Old Town, Wawel Royal Castle and wander around the famous Jewish Quarter, Kazimierz, before taking an overnight train to Prague.

🚂 **Detour:** *Take a day trip to harrowing* **Oświęcim** *(Auschwitz; p331) or the spectacular* **Wieliczka Salt Mine** *(p331).*

③ PRAGUE ⏱ 2 DAYS

Spend another two days exploring medieval architecture in **Prague** (p150). Walk across the famous Charles Bridge, explore Prague Castle and grab a drink on the Old Town Square. Don't forget to try some tantalising Czech beer in a local pub.

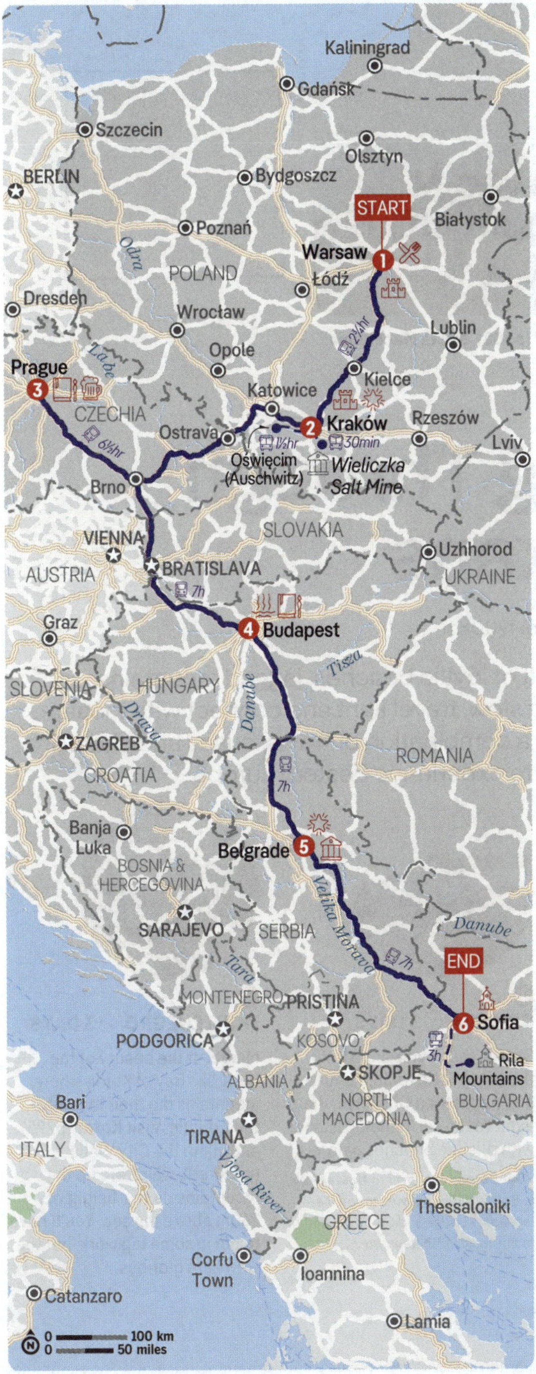

4

BUDAPEST ⏱ 3 DAYS

Brace yourself for beauty and get your camera ready: the architecture in **Budapest** (p200) is astonishing. Spend your time wandering the historic Castle District, soak your muscles at the splendid Széchenyi Baths, take a sightseeing cruise on the Danube River and enjoy Budapest's buzzing nightlife in District VII. Keleti Railway Station is an elegant place to bid farewell.

5

BELGRADE ⏱ 2 DAYS

Two days will be plenty to cover the main sights in Serbia's **cool capital** (p382), including the Kalemegdan Fortress and the Nikola Tesla Museum, dedicated to the life and inventions of the great futurist. In the evening, explore the riverside cafes and shops and party with the locals at *splavs*, Belgrade's floating nightclubs.

6

SOFIA ⏱ 2 DAYS

Explore the glamour of the **Bulgarian capital** (p100; pictured above), in particular the golden-domed Aleksander Nevski Cathedral and the Ancient Serdica Complex.

🚂 *Detour:* Take a day trip through the Rila Mountains to the country's spiritual nucleus. The thousand-year-old **Rila Monastery** (p104) is Bulgaria's holiest site, its setting as spine-tingling as its apocalyptic frescoes.

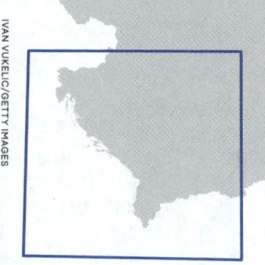

IVAN VUKELIC/GETTY IMAGES

Lake Ohrid (p308), North Macedonia

ITINERARIES

Breezing Through the Balkans

Allow: 15 Days   **Distance:** 1900km

This exciting region is full of idyllic beaches, jagged mountains and quirky towns. Take it slow, travel light and connect with locals. You can drive, but using a combination of trains, buses and shared minivans is the real way to experience Eastern Europe.

① SLOVENIA ⏱ 2 DAYS

Start in the capital **Ljubljana** (p420) and check out the castle, beautiful buildings and bridges before heading south to Croatia's Dalmatian Coast.

🔜 *Detour: Head north to explore two splendid lakes: Lake Bled (p426), with its postcard-like church on an islet, and the less crowded and more authentic Lake Bohinj (p427). Indulge in superb scenery and adrenaline sports in the surrounding Julian Alps.*

② CROATIA ⏱ 3 DAYS

Stop in Dubrovnik and stroll the **City Walls** (p136; pictured) and pedestrian Old Town, then explore the surrounding islands with pristine beaches galore.

🔜 *Detour: Pop over to Mostar (p86) in Bosnia & Hercegovina to see the legendary bridge and Old Town. Return to the coast in Montenegro.*

③ MONTENEGRO ⏱ 3 DAYS

Marvel at the beauty of the fjord-like Bay of Kotor, where mountains dip their toes into the Adriatic. Visit **Kotor** (p295) and climb the City Walls (pictured), which arc up the mountainside to a height of 260m above the sea. You'll have to put in some leg work, but the views are glorious.

AUSTRIA
Graz
BUDAPEST
Lake Bled
Lake Bohinj
1½hr
SLOVENIA
HUNGARY
START
1 Ljubljana
Trieste
Venice
ZAGREB
CROATIA
Novi Sad
1¼hr
END
ROMANIA
SAN MARINO
Banja Luka
Belgrade 6
BOSNIA & HERCEGOVINA
7hr
Ancona
SARAJEVO
4½hr
SERBIA
Mostar
2½hr
L'Aquila
MONTENEGRO
Dubrovnik 2
2½hr
3 Kotor
PODGORICA
PRISTINA
Sofia
ITALY
KOSOVO
3½hr
4½hr
SKOPJE
BULGARIA
NORTH MACEDONIA
Bari
Tirana 4
3hr
3hr
Naples
5 Ohrid
2hr
Berat
Komotini
3hr 20min
Thessaloniki
Sarandë
Ksamil
Corfu Town
Larissa
GREECE
Catanzaro
Lamia
0 100 km
0 50 miles

4

ALBANIA 2 DAYS

Explore the up-and-coming capital **Tirana** (p58). Start at its bustling epicentre, Skanderbeg Sq (pictured), then see where dictator Enver Hoxha coordinated a network of spies at the House of Leaves.

***Detour:** Head southeast to the Ottoman town of **Berat** (p60), then continue on to the **Albanian Riviera** (p62) for serene beach towns like Sarandë and Ksamil.*

5

NORTH MACEDONIA 3 DAYS

Enter North Macedonia to reach pretty **Ohrid** (p208). Spend at least two days here, visiting the ancient churches and swimming in the lake. Make your way to the capital, **Skopje** (p309; pictured), where an abundance of modern Italianate structures are redefining the city.

***Detour:** Bulgaria is just across the border, if you fancy visiting the laid-back capital of **Sofia** (p100).*

6

SERBIA 2 DAYS

Take a train to Serbia's capital, **Belgrade** (p382). Don't miss the ancient Kalemegdan Fortress (pictured) and the restaurant and clubbing scenes.

***Detour:** Check out **Novi Sad** (p387) for neoclassical buildings and Danube views. In summer, head to the Štrand, a 700m-long sandy beach that throngs with bars and stalls. When the tide is low, cross to Fisherman's Island.*

FROM LEFT: SAATON/SHUTTERSTOCK TIM E WHITE/GETTY IMAGES, MYKHAILO BRODSKYI/SHUTTERSTOCK

Baltic Blast

Allow: 13 days   **Distance:** 860km

The Baltic states are small, but they pack a big punch when it comes to nature. Their golden sand dunes and beaches complement the region's cool capitals and quirky towns, and thick forest covers much of the inland area. Expect a scenic, outdoorsy type of trip here.

Pärnu beach (p190), Estonia

TALLINN ⏱2 DAYS

Explore the **Estonian capital** (p178) for two days. Wander the chocolate-box streets and stone towers of the Old Town. Admire the Town Hall, one of the oldest municipal buildings in northern Europe, and seek traces left behind by the Hanseatic League at the Great Guild Hall before heading to Estonia's second city, the university town of Tartu.

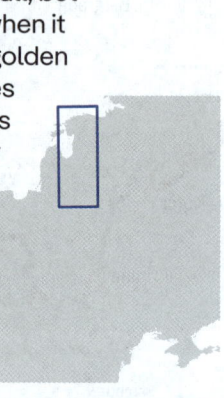

② TARTU ⏱1 DAY

European Capital of Culture in 2024, **Tartu** (p184) is packed with museums, parks and handsome wooden buildings. It's a friendly place that stays vibrant thanks to its seasonal student population. Walk through the Old Town and climb up Toomemägi to admire the remains of Tartu Cathedral (pictured above). Around Tartu, religious and linguistic minorities keep ancient traditions alive.

③ PÄRNU ⏱3 DAYS

Duck west to the Baltic coast to find the inviting Estonian beach resort of **Pärnu** (p188), approximately midway between Riga and Tallinn on Estonia's western coast. Rest here for a few days to indulge in the pleasures of summer holiday-making: mud baths, Bacchanalian nightlife and golden-sand beaches. You can rent kayaks and SUP boards or join a windsurfing course.

4

RIGA ⏱ 3 DAYS

Continue on to Latvia's delightful capital, **Riga** (p238), where you can take in fantastic art nouveau architecture, plus bleak history and a contrastingly friendly Old Town over two days, including an excursion to the opulent Rundāle Palace to see how the aristocrats lived. Add a day-trip to the beaches of Jūrmala.

5

KAUNAS ⏱ 2 DAYS

In Lithuania's second city, **Kaunas** (p261), you'll find a medieval castle, a handsome square and numerous restaurants and churches in the Old Town. The New Town, meanwhile, has superb museums and art deco architecture.

🚌 **Detour:** *Lithuania's astounding* **Hill of Crosses** *(p263) in Šiauliai is a pilgrimage site and symbol of national identity.*

6

VILNIUS ⏱ 2 DAYS

End your journey in beautiful **Vilnius** (p256; pictured above), Lithuania's crowning glory and the European Green Capital of 2025. Wander the cobbled streets and stumble upon charming courtyards, churches and historic buildings. Don't miss Vilnius Cathedral and belfry for views of the city. Learn about the Soviet occupation at the Museum of Occupations and Freedom Fights.

ITINERARIES

Seas, Lakes & Coastlines

Allow: 20 Days   **Distance:** 3600km

Azure waters in the Ionian and Adriatic Seas, Central Europe's largest lake and a natural thermal lake, followed by the Baltic Coast – it's time for some beachside fun! Swimming, kayaking, canoeing, stand-up paddleboarding, rafting and jet-skiing are just some of the ways to stay cool in summer.

Diocletian's Palace (p132), Split

❶ ALBANIA ⏱ 3 DAYS

Start in Sarandë and pop over to nearby Ksamil for the best beaches of the **Albanian Riviera** (p62). The ruins of Butrint, UNESCO-listed Gjirokastër and **Berat** (p60), the city of a thousand windows, are all good places to stop before reaching the capital, **Tirana** (p58).

🚗 *Detour: North Macedonia's **Lake Ohrid** (p308) combines history and a gorgeous landscape.*

❷ MONTENEGRO ⏱ 3 DAYS

Begin in **Budva** (p296; pictured above), with its atmospheric Old Town and Adriatic beaches, then discover walled **Kotor** (p295) and its extraordinarily picturesque bay. Climb the Kotor City Walls that arc up the mountain to a height of 260m above sea level.

🚗 *Detour: Head inland to the cliff-hugging **Ostrog Monastery** (p299), a wondrous sight.*

❸ CROATIA ⏱ 4 DAYS

From Montenegro, head to neighbouring Croatia and wend your way up the 1778km-long coast, dotted with splendid towns like medieval **Dubrovnik** (p136) and **Split** (p132). Up north is the Adriatic's largest peninsula, Istria, crowned by seaside **Pula** (p128) and the country's largest island, Krk.

🚗 *Detour: On your way to Hungary, consider exploring Slovenia's two splendid lakes, **Bled** (p426) and **Bohinj** (p427)*

4 HUNGARY ⏱ 3 DAYS

Central Europe's largest lake, **Lake Balaton** (p215), awaits in western Hungary. Nearby is **Lake Hévíz** (p215), the world's largest swimmable natural thermal lake, where the water remains comfortably warm even in winter and is believed to cure a variety of ills. The capital, **Budapest** (p200), offers famous thermal spas like Széchenyi and Gellért Baths.

5 SLOVAKIA ⏱ 3 DAYS

Slovakia's **High Tatras** (p409) are home to a number of pristine alpine lakes, such as Popradské pleso, Štrbské pleso and Skalnaté pleso. All have fresh, clear waters hugged by majestic mountains. Break up the long drive to Jūrmala by stopping in Warsaw to see the pretty Old Town and enjoy some pierogi.

6 LATVIA ⏱ 4 DAYS

One of the best beach towns in the Baltics is **Jūrmala** (p242; pictured above): an elegant ensemble of white sand beaches, art nouveau villas and pine forests. The beach in Jūrmala doubles as Latvia's longest and flashiest promenade. The oldest area is near the Dzintari, Majori and Dubulti stations; the heart of the action is the 1km-long pedestrian street, Jomas iela.

33

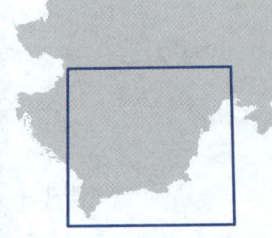

OLGA KOT PHOTO/SHUTTERSTOCK

Tara National Park (p389), Serbia

ITINERARIES

Off the Beaten Track

Allow: 18 Days   **Distance**: 1500km

Discover the heart of the Balkans and beyond on a tour of some less-visited sights. From the lively streets of Belgrade to the serene landscapes of Moldova, this journey will take you through six fascinating countries, each with its own unique blend of history, culture and natural beauty.

❶ SERBIA ⏱ 4 DAYS

Start in the laid-back capital of **Belgrade** (p382; pictured), famous for its rowdy nightlife. Then head south to discover Serbia's most impressive scenery found within the 250-sq-km **Tara National Park** (p389), set along the Bosnian border with densely forested slopes and the dramatic Drina River Canyon. Hikers will enjoy Tara's 30 marked trails, while the emerald Drina creates a stunning background for water-based activities.

❷ KOSOVO ⏱ 2 DAYS

Spend a day enjoying **Pristina** (p226), Europe's youngest capital city full of optimism and potential. Get a taste for traditional Kosovar cooking and explore the Serbian Orthodox **Visoki Dečani Monastery** (p229; pictured) for superb medieval frescoes. Then head to the country's most appealing town, **Prizren** (p228), to explore the old town. Climb up to Prizren Fortress to watch the sunset.

❸ NORTH MACEDONIA ⏱ 2 DAYS

Spend a day or two in **Skopje** (p308). For the best views of the city, take the cable car to Mt Vodno (pictured).

🔷 *Detour: Head to **Ohrid** (p308) to swim in the eponymous lake, stroll the waterside villages and explore frescoed medieval churches at Sveti Naum Monastery. Don't miss **Mavrovo National Park** (p311) on the way back to Skopje.*

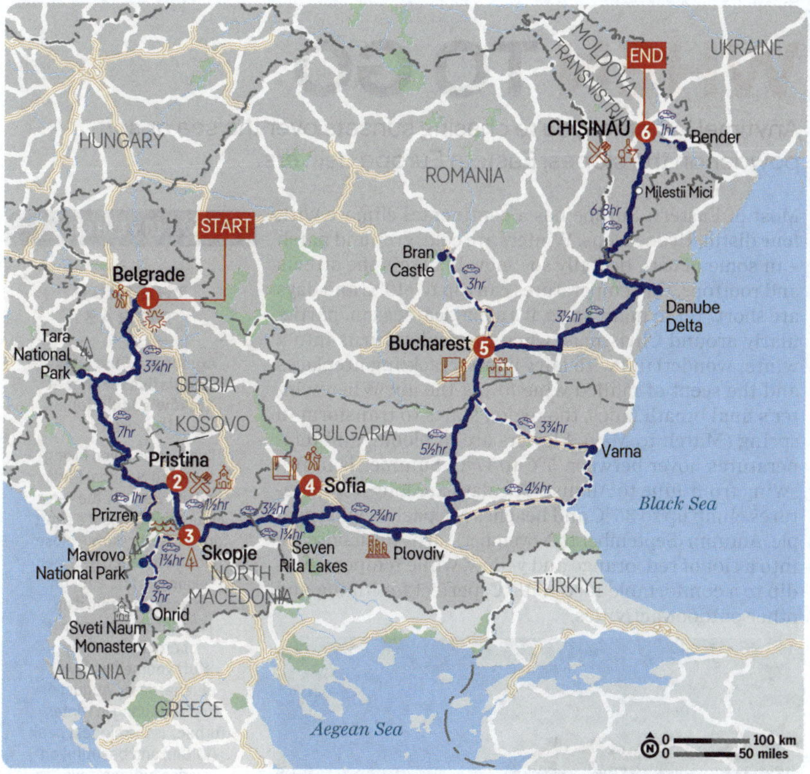

Map annotations:

UKRAINE

MOLDOVA / TRANSNISTRIA

END

CHIȘINĂU **6** 1hr Bender

ROMANIA

6-8hr

Milestii Mici

HUNGARY

START

Belgrade **1**

Bran Castle 3hr

Danube Delta

Tara National Park 3¾hr

Bucharest **5** 3½hr

SERBIA

KOSOVO

BULGARIA 5½hr 3¾hr

Varna

Pristina **2** 1hr Prizren

1½hr 3½hr **4** Sofia 4½hr

Black Sea

3 Skopje 1¼hr

Mavrovo National Park 1¾hr

Seven Rila Lakes

Plovdiv 2¾hr

TÜRKIYE

NORTH MACEDONIA

3hr Ohrid

Sveti Naum Monastery

ALBANIA

GREECE

Aegean Sea

N 0 ——— 100 km / 0 ——— 50 miles

4 BULGARIA ⏱ 4 DAYS

Visit **Sofia** (p100) and see landmarks like the Alexander Nevsky Cathedral and the Ancient Serdica Complex. The **Seven Rila Lakes hike** (p104) down south is a popular day trip. Afterwards, head to **Plovdiv** (p111), known for its Roman theatre (pictured) and Old Town.

🐾 *Detour: Bulgaria's Black Sea coast, with resorts like **Varna** (p107), has both beaches and historical sites.*

5 ROMANIA ⏱ 4 DAYS

Start in **Bucharest** (p350) and check out the grand Parliament Palace (pictured), the second-largest national assembly in the world, and stroll through the Old Town's vibrant streets. Continue east to the **Danube Delta** (p365), a wonderful wildlife hotspot.

🐾 *Detour: Venture north to Transylvania to see **Bran Castle** (p357), famously linked to Dracula.*

6 MOLDOVA ⏱ 2 DAYS

The capital city **Chișinău** (p276; pictured) hosts Moldova's best restaurants and bars, and is also a convenient base for day trips to the countryside. Don't miss Moldova's underground wine cellars: the most impressive is **Milestii Mici** (p280), holding the world's biggest wine collection.

🐾 *Detour: Visit **Transnistria** (p284), a breakaway state where the Soviet Union seems to live on.*

WHEN TO GO

Anytime! Whether you're chasing sunsets over the sea or soft powder on the slopes, Eastern Europe delivers.

Most of Eastern Europe has a continental climate with four distinctive seasons. Winters are cold, grey and harsh – in some places, brutally so. Snow blankets the streets and rooftops, the temperatures can dip to –10°C and days are short. Yet in many ways, it's a magical season, particularly around Christmas, when the region turns into a winter wonderland with fairy lights, crackling fireplaces and the scent of mulled wine filling the air. When winter's final breath fades, the region starts to transform in spring (March to May). Flowers are in bloom, and temperatures hover between 5°C to 17°C. Summer is in full swing from June to August. The days are long, temperatures climb up to 35°C and beaches are packed with people. Autumn (September to November) turns the landscape into a riot of red, orange and yellow, while temperatures dip to a comfortable 10°C to 18°C, perfect for hiking and other outdoor activities.

FROM LEFT: PAWEL KAZMIERCZAK/SHUTTERSTOCK, PHOTOPANK.PL/SHUTTERSTOCK

High Tatras (p409), Slovakia

⊚ I LIVE HERE

THE HIGH TATRAS

Agnieszka Guspiel is a linguistics teacher at Kraków's Jagiellonian University.

I've always loved hiking in Gorce National Park, with its views of the Tatra Mountains. It's just a short drive from Kraków – close enough to reach between exams but far enough to get away from it all. Hike through meadows of crocuses in May, stuff yourself with wild blueberries in August or try ski touring in winter. Turbacz is the highest peak (1310m) and beautiful on crisp autumn days.

WHAT'S THE TIME?

Eastern Europe spans three time zones: Central European Time (GMT+1), Eastern European Time (GMT+2) and Further-Eastern European or Moscow Time (GMT+3). When it's noon in New York, it's 6pm in Warsaw, 7pm in Sofia and 8pm in Moscow. Most countries use daylight savings.

Weather through the Year

JANUARY	 FEBRUARY	MARCH	APRIL	MAY	JUNE
Avg. daytime max: **2°C**	Avg. daytime max: **5°C**	Avg. daytime max: **10°C**	Avg. daytime max: **16°C**	Avg. daytime max: **21°C**	Avg. daytime max: **24°C**
Days of rainfall: **6**	Days of rainfall: **6**	Days of rainfall: **6**	Days of rainfall: **7**	Days of rainfall: **9**	Days of rainfall: **8**

EMBRACE THE SHOULDER SEASONS

The shoulder seasons are the best time to travel in Eastern Europe. Crowds and prices drop off, while the weather remains pleasant. If you're on a shoestring, November, January and February offer the cheapest rates, but be ready for limited daylight and attraction closures.

Major Festivals

Symphony orchestras and chamber-music ensembles around the world perform at the **Prague Spring International Music Festival**, which is one of Central Europe's premier classical-music events. ☀ **May**

One of the world's largest choral-music events, the **Song Festival** (p182) brings tens of thousands of people to the Estonian capital of Tallinn every five years. ☀ **July**

Held annually in Bosnia and Hercegovina, the globally acclaimed **Sarajevo Film Festival** provides a crucial platform for filmmakers from the region and beyond, screening commercial and art-house movies side by side. ☀ **August**

Around the winter holidays, every major city in Eastern Europe sets up a **Christmas Market** selling mulled wine, sweet treats and fabulous gifts. The best ones are in Gdańsk (Poland), Budapest (Hungary), Tallinn (Estonia), Zagreb (Croatia) and Prague (Czechia). ❄ **December**

Music, Folk & Arts Festivals

Dating back to the 17th century, the **Kaziukas Crafts Fair** in Lithuania is a charming annual arts-and-crafts fair. 🌥 **March**

Folk-music artists from across Europe step on a spectacular stage set amid the ruins of the Viljandi Castle during Estonia's **Viljandi Folk Festival**. ☀ **July**

Offering a relaxed and friendly atmosphere, a multi-cultural lineup and diverse events beyond music, the **Pohoda Festival** at Trenčín Airport is Slovakia's biggest music festival. ☀ **July**

The world's largest annual celebration of Balkan brass music is Serbia's **Guča Festival** (p389), complete with lively street parties, traditional food and a unique atmosphere of intense music and celebration. ☀ **August**

Guča Festival (p389), Serbia

WHITE NIGHTS IN THE BALTICS

In summer, Estonia, Latvia, Lithuania and parts of Russia offer an enchanting 'white nights' experience, when darkness barely descends on the land. In June and July, daylight fades to twilight, but never goes pitch black.

JULY	AUGUST	 SEPTEMBER	OCTOBER	NOVEMBER	DECEMBER
Avg. daytime max: **27°C**	Avg. daytime max: **26°C**	Avg. daytime max: **21°C**	Avg. daytime max: **16°C**	Avg. daytime max: **10°C**	Avg. daytime max: **3°C**
Days of rainfall: **8**	Days of rainfall: **6**	Days of rainfall: **6**	Days of rainfall: **6**	Days of rainfall: **7**	Days of rainfall: **7**

FROM LEFT: NATALIA DERIABINA/SHUTTERSTOCK; HBO MAX/ALBUM

Lake Bled (p426), Slovakia

GET PREPARED FOR EASTERN EUROPE

Useful things to load in your bag, your ears and your brain.

Clothes

Smart casual Eastern Europeans wear casual clothes, but tend to dress up for going out, so bring at least one nice outfit.
Swimsuits A must for the beautiful beaches of Eastern Europe. Don't forget them in winter if headed to Hungary's breathtaking thermal baths.
Footwear Bring waterproof snow boots for winter and hiking boots if you're planning on hitting the trails. The rest of the time, trainers and sandals will do.
Layers Bring a sweater and a waterproof jacket for all seasons, since downpours and cold nights can happen at any time. For winter, thermal underlayers and a warm coat come in handy.

Manners

Punctuality Being on time is highly appreciated, especially in formal settings.

Don't get mixed up The region is diverse and cultures and attitudes vary widely. Don't assume Eastern Europeans are all the same. Remember that Budapest and Bucharest are very different.

Clinking glasses During a toast, especially with Eastern Europe's famous spirits, maintain eye contact.

Modesty You'll have to cover up when visiting religious sights – legs and shoulders should not show. In rural areas and small towns, avoid revealing clothes.

📖 READ

The Bridge on the Drina (Ivo Andrić; 1945) Historical tale from the 1961 Nobel laureate; delves into Bosnia's cultural complexities.

Sátántangó (László Krasznahorkai; 1985) Postmodern debut novel from the 2025 Nobel laureate; set in rainy, rural Hungary.

I Must Betray You (Ruta Sepetys; 2022) A gripping historical thriller about a boy's struggle for freedom in Romania.

The Joke (Milan Kundera; 1967) Kundera's debut follows the repercussions of a joke in Soviet-occupied Czechoslovakia.

Words

Learning the basics of the Cyrillic alphabet is highly beneficial in Bosnia, Bulgaria, Kosovo, North Macedonia, Montenegro, Macedonia and Serbia.

Albanian
Tungjatjeta (toon-dya-*tye*-ta) Hello.
Faleminderit (fa-le-meen-*de*-reet) Thank you.
Po (po) Yes.
Jo (yo) No.

BCMS (Bosnian, Croatian, Montenegrin, Serbian)
Zdravo (*zdra*-vo) Hello.
Hvala (*hva*-la) Thank you.
Da (da) Yes.
Ne (ne) No.

Bulgarian
Здравейте (zdra-*vey*-te) Hello.
Благодаря (bla-go-dar-*ya*) Thank you.
Да (da) Yes.
Не (ne) No.

Czech
Ahoj (*uh*-hoy) Hello.
Děkuji (*dye*-ku-yi) Thank you.
Ano (*uh*-no) Yes.
Ne (ne) No.
Pivo (pee-voh) Beer.

Hungarian
Jó napot (yoh nah-pot) Hello.
Köszönöm (*kew*-sew-newm) Thank you.
Igen (*i*-ghen) Yes.
Nem (Nehm) No.

Polish
Cześć (cheshch) Hello.
Dziękuję (jyen-*koo*-ye) Thank you.
Tak (tak) Yes.
Nie (nye) No.

Romanian
Bună ziua (*boo*-nuh zee-wa) Hello.
Mulțumesc (mool-tsoo-mesk) Thank you.
Da (da) Yes.
Nu (noo) No.

📺 WATCH

Pelikan Blue (László Csáki; 2023) Incredible true story of three Hungarian friends who decide to travel to the West after communism.

Chernobyl (HBO; 2019) Miniseries that tells the story of one of the worst nuclear disasters in the history of humankind.

The Informant (HBO; 2022; pictured) The story of Budapest university students in communist Hungary, one of whom is an informant.

20 Days in Mariupol (Mstyslav Chernov; 2023) Documentary about the early months of Russia's war against Ukraine.

🎧 LISTEN

Papp László Aréna Live (2023) Live album of Gen Z icon Azahriah, currently Hungary's hottest singer-songwriter.

Paket Aranžman (1981) Pivotal compilation album of Yugoslav new wave, featuring three Belgrade bands.

Atvadas nav skumjas, ja zinām, ka drīz tiksimies (Chris Noah; 2024) Debut album from prominent Latvian indie singer.

Fantaisie-Impromptu (Chopin; 1834) Poland's greatest composer and virtuoso pianist at his best.

HERACLES KRITIKOS/SHUTTERSTOCK

Memento Park (p206), Budapest

TRIP PLANNER

THE LEGACY OF THE SOVIET UNION

Monumental Soviet-era architecture, eerie leftovers of Cold War military sites and declassified secret bunkers – many places in Eastern Europe still whisper tales of repression and resistance. But exploring communist sites isn't only about looking back, but understanding a past that's still very much alive in the present.

Brief History

WORKERS OF THE WORLD, UNITE!

After Lenin, red was all the rage in the Union of Soviet Socialist Republics (USSR), but the Soviet Union's 'golden age' only really started after World War II, when it extended its influence throughout much of Eastern Europe. A sphere of satellite states, known as the Eastern Bloc, were politically, economically and culturally aligned with the USSR and encompassed Poland, Czechoslovakia, East Germany, Hungary, Romania and Bulgaria. The Baltic states of Estonia, Latvia and Lithuania were annexed and became Soviet republics, while Yugoslavia and Albania also fell under Soviet influence and control to varying degrees.

Even while the Soviet Union was governed by infamous leaders like Joseph Stalin, Eastern European countries also had their own iron-fisted, heartless dictators, including Albania's Enver Hoxha, Romania's Nicolae Ceaușescu and Hungary's Mátyás Rákosi.

LIFE BEHIND THE IRON CURTAIN

In the post-war years, a red haze settled over most of Eastern Europe. The hammer and sickle was emblazoned on everything, and towering statues of Stalin, Lenin and

Exploring Eastern Europe's Soviet history offers a unique glimpse into a turbulent period that shaped the modern world, but it's important to understand its complexities and approach the subject with sensitivity.

Although many younger people may not have personal memories of the era and now also approach the topic with curiosity, older generations may still carry the trauma of Soviet occupation. The history of

repression, forced labour camps and political purges is still alive in cultural memory.

The hammer-and-sickle motif may appear on souvenirs, but in some countries it has actually been banned or is seen as deeply offensive, similar to Nazi symbols.

For many countries, the fall of communism didn't immediately result in democracy or prosperity. Understanding the challenges faced by countries

transitioning from communism to capitalism can provide context for current political situations.

Communism in Eastern Europe wasn't a monolithic experience – it varied across countries, regions and even specific time periods. Expect complexity, nuance and even contradictions in what you learn.

homegrown heroes filled the streets. The era of communism was characterised by central planning, mass housing, free education and healthcare, but also strict censorship, travel restrictions, oppression, food shortages and surveillance. The secret police maintained such tight control that you never knew if your close friend, colleague or neighbour was an informant, and a few mispoken words could land you in serious trouble. In most cases, people who were declared an enemy of the state were never seen again.

CRACKS IN THE SYSTEM

In the decades following World War II, Eastern Europe saw repeated uprisings, most notably the bloody 1956 Freedom Fights in Hungary and the Prague Spring in 1968. The latter was brought to a violent end by troops from the Warsaw Pact (the USSR's collective defence alliance that served as a military counterbalance

House of Leaves (p59), Tirana

FROZEN IN TIME

Transnistria

Statues of Lenin on the streets, eternal flames and coins stamped with a hammer and sickle – no, this isn't a movie set but a breakaway, self-governed state within Moldova. Transnistria, occupying the land east of the Dnister River, is infamous for its apparent refusal to accept the fall of the Soviet Union. Except for Bender (p284), the UK FCDO advises against travelling to Transnistria, as the region is outside the control of the Moldovan government. That said, many travellers still visit the area trouble-free, and there are numerous tour operators and Young Pioneers who arrange trips. Travelling independently is also possible by taking a bus from Chişinău or driving.

Pripyat

Time appears to have stopped in the town of Pripyat, Ukraine, following the harrowing 1986 Chernobyl Nuclear Plant disaster. Previously home to nearly 50,000 people, Pripyat was a typical Soviet town complete with apartment blocks, schools and socialist posters – though many communist monuments and symbols have since been removed. Following the disaster the entire town was evacuated, and what remains is an eerie snapshot of late Soviet life with personal belongings still scattered about. Though it was once possible to visit the Chernobyl Exclusion Zone on a guided tour, because of the war in Ukraine all travel here is strongly discouraged.

to NATO). After much political unrest, Mikhail Gorbachev introduced a reform policy of *glasnost* (openness) and *perestroika* (restructuring) in the late 1980s, which gradually weakened the Soviet grip.

THE FALL OF THE WALL

The year 1989 was a turbulent one for oppressed countries. The previously banned Solidarity Trade Union captured seats in parliament in Poland; Hungarians dismantled 240km of barbed wire along the border with Austria; and Estonia, Latvia and Lithuania organised the so-called Singing Revolution, forming a 600km-human chain calling for independence.

On 9 November 1989, the Berlin Wall fell, triggering domino revolutions across the region. In 1991, the USSR collapsed and Eastern Europe began to slowly break free of repression and heal.

The Former Eastern Bloc Today

Though the huge thud caused by the fall of the Berlin Wall was decades ago, its echoes still reverberate across Eastern Europe. Communist history is never too far away, and its legacy is embedded in the architecture, political systems and memories of the people.

Endless rows of grey tower blocks built in the 1960s, '70s and '80s still dominate many cityscapes and house millions of people – though some are being modernised with bright colours. Brutalist buildings abound, and the lavishly designed stations of the Moscow Metro, a propaganda triumph intended to display Soviet power, are still in use today. Vintage cars like Trabants (East Germany) and Ladas (USSR), once completely unaffordable and a dream for most households, are now used for nostalgia tours.

Societies still bear the scars. It's often argued that under communism, people learned to keep their heads down and distrust authority, which still influences attitudes today. In poorer regions, some older people miss the security of communism (job guarantees, cheap housing), despite the lack of freedom. This is called Ostalgie (nostalgia for the East), which is a complex and complicated phenomenon.

As for political systems, while Eastern Europe has largely transitioned to democracy and market economies following the collapse of the Soviet Union, in some countries, the weak institutions that communist regimes left behind have made it easier for populist leaders to centralise power.

Explore with Care

Today, many relics of the communist years still whisper tales of a past that left an indelible imprint on the region. Moving museums, tours and retro-themed restaurants offer a glimpse of life behind the Iron Curtain, and communist memorabilia features at every flea market. But remember: what feels quirky or kitsch to you may be remembered as traumatic or oppressive to locals. Whenever you're using speedy Wi-Fi in a retro cafe or watching people commute from Soviet-era apartment blocks to high-tech offices, bear in mind that the past is never far away – now, it simply coexists alongside modern Eastern European life.

BEST PLACES TO DISCOVER COMMUNIST HISTORY

Memento Park, Budapest (p206) A huge open-air museum home to humongous Soviet statues removed from the streets of Budapest.

House of Leaves, Tirana (p59) Albania's Museum of Secret Surveillance documents state control during Enver Hoxha's dictatorship.

Palace of Parliament, Bucharest (p351) A great representation of the sheer megalomania, folly and waste of resources that characterised the 25-year rule of Nicolae Ceaușescu.

KGB Atomic Bunker, Kaunas (p263) A KGB spy museum in a nuclear bunker; one of Lithuania's most unique museums.

Children's Railway, Budapest (p205) A communist hand-me-down, the Children's Railway is operated almost entirely by kids.

SASHKO/SHUTTERSTOCK

Belgrade–Bar train, Montenegro (p291)

Explore Eastern Europe by Train

There's something truly magical about watching the landscape slide by as it gradually shifts from the gentle coastline of the Baltics to the chaotic, colourful Balkans. Eastern Europe's varied terrain is perfect for slow travel. Whether you're drawn to baroque city centres, Soviet-era nostalgia or dramatic mountain vistas, consider the following to build your perfect route.

The Advantages of Rail Travel

Trains are efficient, affordable, charmingly unpredictable and often take you straight to the centre of a city. Along the way you'll get to interact with locals, the heart and soul of the region. Overnight trains are also an efficient way to travel to another country – you'll be there by the time you wake up. And it's a greener way to travel, so why not?

Ticket or Pass?

Consider whether you want an Interrail/Eurail pass (best for visiting multiple countries quickly) or point-to-point tickets – surprisingly, the latter might be cheaper. Book key legs ahead of time and note that some overnight trains will fill up.

Plan Your Route

It's best to plan your route around your interests. If you love big cities, include Kraków, Budapest, Prague, Sofia and Bucharest. Prefer trains that carve through mountains and hug coastlines? Consider Ljubljana, Lake Bled, Zagreb, Sarajevo, Mostar, Podgorica and Bar. For a deep dive into history, put Vilnius, Warsaw, Bucharest, Iasi, Chișinău and a possible detour to Transnistria on your itinerary.

Set Your Schedule

Eastern European trains range from efficient, punctual and modern to charmingly outdated and always late, so build some flexibility into your schedule. Useful websites are Rail Europe (raileurope.com), Interrail (interrail.eu) and Deutsche Bahn (int.bahn.de/en). The Man in Seat 61 (seat61.com) includes useful tips from a devoted train traveller.

What to Bring

Pack layers, snacks, water, a power bank (some trains lack outlets) and toilet paper and sanitizer as older trains may lack supplies. Keep your passport ready, as some trains stop for passport checks, especially outside the Schengen Area. Carry local currency, as stations may not accept cards. Finally, remember that trains are more than just transport, they're part of the adventure.

SCENIC ROUTES IN EASTERN EUROPE

Belgrade–Bar The ultimate Balkans train trip with magical scenery.

Mostar–Sarajevo Witnesses the beautiful landscapes of Neretva Canyon.

Bohinj Railway Connects the Slovenian town of Jesenice with Trieste in Italy, running through the Julian Alps and along the Soča River.

Kraków–Zakopane Chugs through the Tatra foothills to Poland's 'winter chapel'.

Bucharest–Brașov–Sighișoara–Cluj Napoca Transylvania's castles, fortified churches and mountains.

43

BRENT HOFACKER/SHUTTERSTOCK

Pierogi

THE **FOOD** SCENE

Eastern Europe welcomes travellers with flavourful, hearty food and knock-out (sometimes literally) spirits.

Eastern Europe takes food seriously: eating isn't just about sustenance but also about family, community and celebrating life through shared meals, which are often long and involve several courses. From the shores of the Baltic to the windswept plains of the Balkans, the region offers a wide palate of flavours. The rustic, robust dishes are shaped by centuries of tradition, diverse culinary landscapes and a deep connection to the land's resources. Think thick, slow-cooked stews, earthy root vegetables, meats and grains. An Eastern European plate is designed to comfort and nourish at the same time. And the drinks...well, the region's world-famous spirits will bring tears to your eyes even as the locals insist they're good for your health. One thing is for sure,

Eastern Europe excels in homestyle cooking and potent liquor, so get ready to loosen your belt, because this will be one flavourful journey you won't want to miss.

Meaty Marvels

Historically, meat has been a central part of the Eastern European diet, especially during the long, cold winters when protein-rich food was necessary for survival. And people do wonders with it – the region has a wide range of meaty dishes, each with its own twist. Hungarian goulash soup – a rich ensemble of cubed beef, vegetables and lots of paprika – is heavenly. Poland takes pride in *kielbasa* (sausage) that comes in many varieties, from smoked to garlic and herb. Czechia has *svíčková,* a hearty beef stew

Best Eastern European Dishes	GOULASH, HUNGARY	PIEROGI, POLAND	LAKROR, ALBANIA	VEPŘO-KNEDLO-ZELO, CZECHIA
	Rich soup of beef cubes, vegetables and paprika.	Crescent-shaped dumplings with a variety of fillings.	Doughy pie stuffed with spinach, baked under an open fire.	Roast pork with bread dumplings and sauerkraut.

with creamy vegetable gravy and dumplings. And in the Balkans, *ćevapi* – small minced-meat sausages made of a blend of beef, pork and lamb – are widespread. The coastal areas in both the Baltics and Balkans have plenty of fresh fish.

For vegetarians, Eastern European dining can sometimes present a challenge, especially in more rural areas. However, plant-based options have become increasingly common in major cities and modern restaurants, allowing everyone to enjoy the delicious flavours of the region, no matter their dietary preferences.

Wine, Beer & Spirits

Eastern Europe has been quietly producing excellent wines for centuries. From the fertile soils of Hungary to the historic vineyards of Moldova, the region has a wide range of unique and bold wines. Hungary's sweet dessert wine, Tokaji Aszú, is referred to as 'the wine of kings and the king of wines' (p216). Moldova is one of the world's oldest wine-producing countries, and its wines are surprisingly diverse, from crisp whites to rich reds. Romania makes excellent reds from Fetească Neagră grapes, which produce wines with notes of dark fruit and spices. The Tămâioasă Românească grape is best

for aromatic whites that often have a touch of sweetness.

Beer is an essential part of the drinking culture in Eastern Europe, and nobody does it better than the Czechs – they excel in lager-style beers with a crisp, refreshing finish that pairs well with many dishes. The Baltic states, meanwhile, are known for cider, but when it comes down to it, Eastern Europe will always be best known for its fiery spirits (often homemade), which are strong enough to knock out a horse. Spirits are often potato-based (vodka) or fruit brandies like *pálinka* or *raki*.

MATT MUNRO/LONELY PLANET

Vodka

KNOW THE BIG SHOTS

Most Eastern European countries pride themselves on their own unique liquor, and knowing the difference will put you ahead of most travellers. Poland and Russia love potato-based vodka. The word is a diminutive of *voda* (water), literally meaning 'little water'. Hungarians have *pálinka*, a fruit brandy typically made from plums, apricots or cherries. The nectar in the Balkans is *raki*, a fruit brandy typically made of plum, grape or fig – Serbia, Bulgaria, Bosnia, Croatia, Montenegro and North Macedonia all claim they do it best. In Serbia, *šljivovica* (plum *raki*) is considered to be so important that it was inscribed on UNESCO's Intangible Cultural Heritage of Humanity list in 2022. These drinks traditionally consist of 40% to 60% alcohol, though homemade bottles can push well past that.

YESPHOTOGRAPHERS/SHUTTERSTOCK

Prekmurska gibanica

PREKMURSKA GIBANICA, SLOVENIA	MULGIPUDER, ESTONIA	BRYNDZOVÉ HALUŠKY, SLOVAKIA	JAGNJETINA ISPOD SAČA, BALKANS	TOCHITURĂ, ROMANIA
Layered pastry, today a national treasure.	A filling porridge made from mashed potatoes and barley.	Dumplings with sheep's cheese and smoked bacon.	Lamb, slow-cooked with vegetables under a metal dome.	Hearty stew of pan-fried pork in a spicy tomato or wine sauce.

Specialities

Street Food

Lángos A Hungarian deep-fried, disc-shaped dough with a variety of toppings – traditionally sour cream and cheese.

Burek A flaky pastry filled with meat or cheese, common across the Balkans.

Kranjska Klobasa Majestic Slovenian pork sausage.

Covrigi Somewhere between a pretzel and a bagel and always delicious.

Ćevapi/ćevapčići Small minced beef, lamb or pork sausages, common throughout the Balkans.

Kibinai Karaite savoury pastries, filled with meat, mushrooms or cheese. They're best in Lithuania.

Kürtőskalács

Sweet Treats

Kürtőskalács Called chimney cake in English, this cylindrical dough is baked over an open fire and rolled in cinnamon, vanilla sugar or other sweet toppings. Common in Hungary and Transylvania.

Ovocné knedlíky Sweet dumplings, stuffed with berries, plums or apricots, and drizzled with butter and a sprinkle of sugar. A Czech treasure.

Koláč Sweet Czech pastries, filled with fruit or poppy seeds.

Baklava Flaky phyllo dough, filled with crushed walnuts and sweetened with honey or syrup. Find it all throughout the Balkans.

Szarlotka This beloved Polish dessert is made with sweet apples and has a buttery, flaky crust.

Szarlotka

MEALS OF A LIFETIME

Modrá Hviezda, Slovakia (p403) On the way to Bratislava Castle, this restaurant features high-end takes on traditional Slovak food.

420 Restuarant, Czechia (p156) Directly across from Prague's Astronomical Clock, but it feels like a find. The original baroque statues are hard to forget. Reserve.

JAZ by Ana Roš, Slovenia (p422) A young, lively vibe and Mediterranean flavours from Michelin-starred chef Ana Roš.

Iva New Balkan Cuisine, Serbia (p384) Local gastronomy reinvented by head chef Vanja Puškar in a fusion of flavours and organic ingredients.

Stand25, Hungary (p206) Freestyle Hungarian cuisine, overseen by Bocuse d'Or Europe–winning chef Tamás Széll.

THE YEAR IN FOOD

SPRING

Upon awakening from winter, food becomes lighter, brighter and greener in spring. Colourful vegetables, soft fruit and fresh herbs abound, and Eastern Europe takes its Easter feast seriously.

SUMMER

Lots of grilling and cooking outside. Meals become social gatherings. People start preserving by pickling, drying, fermenting and jarring everything that grows.

AUTUMN

The pantry is stocked and tables are full. Warm, rich dishes and soups start to return. After the harvest season in September, wine festivals feature and cheeses and cold cuts become prominent.

WINTER

Slow-cooked, hearty dishes take centre stage. Meals are made to fill and nourish both body and spirit. Ferments, smoked meats and pickles rule the table, balanced by meat from hunting season.

BOROVSKA OLGA/SHUTTERSTOCK

Pálinka

HOW TO...

Enjoy Eastern Europe's Spirits

Travelling in Eastern Europe? It won't be long before you're offered a glass of the region's famous fiery spirits. The following is a crash course in raising a toast, surviving the night and perhaps even remembering it all the next morning

A Daily Ritual

Whether it's a wedding, a celebration, a funeral or just a regular Tuesday, Eastern Europeans need no excuse to pull out a bottle of their favourite drink. Some may even start the morning with a shot, as it's strongly believed that fiery spirits are a cure-all and good for health. Locals are generous with their spirits, especially if they're homemade, in which case it's considered impolite to refuse. Try to take at least a sip; if you really can't, just wet your lips.

Liquid Fire

Vodka is enjoyed ice cold and straight – prepare for serious side-eyes if you add some orange juice on top. Though the Russians down it, the Polish sometimes sip. Make sure to eat lots of *zakuski*: an assortment of cold appetisers including smoked fish, cured meats and pickles. Hungarian *pálinka* is served at room temperature in a tulip-shaped glass – round at the bottom, narrow at the rim. Full glasses are sipped and savoured, although locals may challenge you to gulp it in one go. *Pálinka* tastings are a serious art form in Hungary.

All around the Balkans, *raki* is generally served in a small glass at room temperature. Forget bottoms up and take small sips instead. The fiery rush will warm you up from the inside out as you enjoy your meal.

Get Ready to Toast

Though customs vary by region, it's typical to toast before a drink. These can be long, heartfelt and sentimental – especially in the later rounds – but other times it's just a few words. Glasses are almost always raised and clinked before drinking. Eye contact is important – some places, like Serbia, take this more seriously than others. Say *'Egészségedre!'* in Hungary, *'Živeli!'* in Serbia or Bulgaria and *'Na zdrowie!'* in Poland. Cheers!

THE SPIRIT OF EASTERN EUROPE

Eastern Europe's real spirit is not in the bottle, but in the people who pour and share the drinks. Toasts aren't just about boozing but about connections, and each bottle hides centuries of history in liquid form. These drinks warmed soldiers on frozen frontlines, sealed marriages, comforted mourners and turned long winter nights into something bearable. If you accept a glass, you'll get a taste of a centuries-old circle of hospitality and resilience. A word of advice: never try to drink someone under the table. They've been training since birth; this is not a competition you're likely to win.

47

NIGLAYNIK/SHUTTERSTOCK

Canyon Matka (p311), North Macedonia

THE OUTDOORS

If you're after an outdoor experience that feels authentic, raw and still undiscovered, Eastern Europe is an adventure waiting to happen.

From the Alps to the Urals, spanning the wild terrain of the Carpathian Mountains, the pristine Baltic coastline, the rugged Balkans and the High Tatras and Albanian Alps, Eastern Europe not only has stunning natural beauty but also thrills without the crowds. The secret? The region is still relatively untouched by mass tourism. Whether you're keen to hike through thick forests, cycle along ancient rivers, ski down less-crowded slopes or dive into crystal clear waters, Eastern Europe delivers all of that and more.

Walking & Hiking

Eastern Europeans love to hike, and trails crisscross the region. Routes tend to be well marked but less groomed than in the Western Alps, giving them a more authentic and rugged appeal. Some of the most dramatic and popular hikes are provided by the compact but mighty mountain range of the High Tatras – the highest point of the Carpathian Mountains – which is full of alpine lakes and challenging peaks. For long-distance trekking, the snow-dusted summits, deep green valleys and thick forests of the evocatively named Accursed Mountains, or Albanian Alps, are a big draw. Lovers of pristine lakes will be mesmerised in the Rila Mountains, located in southwest Bulgaria, with a stunning view of seven glacial lakes nestled in the heart of the mountains.

Underground Experiences

POSTOJNA CAVE
Explore this 24km-long **cave system** (p428) in Slovenia, a series of two-million-year-old caverns, halls and passages.

HOSPITAL IN THE ROCK
Walk around a maze of hospital wards in this underground **hospital** (p204) turned secret nuclear bunker in Budapest.

BRNO'S UNDERGROUND
Find your way through the **Labyrinth under the Vegetable Market** (p166), situated 8m beneath cabbage vendors.

Enjoy the famously shallow waters of Hungary's **Lake Balaton** (p215), which is suitable even for little kids. Heaps of fun for the whole family.

Cruise the flat, scenic routes of the **Danube Cycle Path** (p389) through Hungary, Slovakia and Serbia. Along

the way, historical cities and pretty riverfronts await.

Row across Lake Bled (p426) to a magic island that's a blast to explore; parents will appreciate the serene atmosphere.

Swim beneath Hercegovina's incredible **Kravica Waterfall**

(p89) and escape the scorching summer heat.

Go kayaking in the natural paradise of **Canyon Matka** (p311) near North Macedonia's capital Skopje.

Watch for bears on a tour or go dog sledding at Slovakia's **Tatras National Park** (p09).

Skiing & Snow Sports

Eastern Europe's ski resorts offer an experience that is both affordable and authentic, and with fewer crowds than in Western Europe. The resorts are generally smaller and less commercial, but they definitely punch above their weight in terms of value, quality and the sheer beauty of their surroundings. Most are family-friendly, making them perfect for those after a relaxed atmosphere. Bansko in Bulgaria has gained a reputation as one of the best-value ski resorts in Europe, with well-maintained slopes and a charming Old Town. Sarajevo's two main ski resorts,

Jahorina and Bjelašnica, were home to alpine skiing events in the 1984 Winter Olympics, while Romania's Poiana Brașov offers modern lifts and a variety of slopes – it's also the gateway to the medieval city of Brașov, adding cultural appeal to your skiing experience. If you like donning skates and gliding around gracefully instead, frozen lakes are perfect for practising your pirouettes, while major cities also have ice-skating rinks in winter. Don't miss skating in Warsaw's Old Town or Budapest's Városliget Lake – the latter is Europe's largest outdoor ice-skating rink.

Water Sports

Peaceful rivers, warm seas and pristine lakes: Eastern Europe's crystal clear and often untouched waters offer thrilling opportunities for rafting, kayaking, canoeing, jet skiing, sailing, diving and peaceful paddleboarding. Whether you want to tackle the white-water rapids of Montenegro or paddle across Slovenia's Lake Bled, the region has plenty of inviting waterways. You might find shipwrecks while diving in the Adriatic, raise your heart rate while rafting Europe's deepest river canyon (the Tara River Canyon) or let your imagination roam wild while lying on a paddleboard and gazing up at the cotton-ball-like clouds above Central Europe's largest lake, Lake Balaton.

ACTION AREAS

For the best outdoor locations, see p50

GUBERNAT/GETTY IMAGES

Tatras National Park (p409), Slovakia

BUNK'ART1
Dive into the paranoid mind of Albanian dictator Enver Hoxha as you explore five **subterranean floors** (p59) in Tirana.

MILESTII MICI
Embark on the **winery tour** (p280) in Moldova to visit the world's largest underground wine collection – about 1.5 million bottles!

DOMICA CAVE
Take a trip on the underground River Styx in this bat-inhabited **cave** (p412) as part of your Slovakian spelunking adventure.

WIELICZKA SALT MINE
Marvel at the stunning beauty of the huge underground **salt mine** (p331) in Kraków, where even the chandeliers are made of salt.

ACTION AREAS

Where to find Eastern Europe's best outdoor activities.

Walking/Hiking

1. Carpathian Mountains (p410)
2. Julian Alps (p426)
3. Kotor City Walls (p295)
4. Rila Mountains (p104)
5. Accursed Mountains (p66)
6. Slovenský Raj National Park (p411)
7. Dubrovnik City Walls (p138)

Skiing/Snowboarding

1. Bansko (p105)
2. Jahorina Olympic Centre (p85)
3. Bjelašnica (p85)
4. Mavrovo National Park (p311)
5. Vratna Valley Ski Area (p408)
6. Ski Resort Tatranská Lomnica (p410)
7. Vogel Ski Centre (p427)

Swimming & Water Sports

1. Lake Balaton (p215)
2. Albanian Riviera (p62)
3. Lake Bled (p426)
4. Dalmatian Islands (p132)
5. Nida (p265)
6. Bay of Kotor (p295)
7. Lake Bohinj (p427)

500 km

250 miles

MOSCOW

RUSSIA

VILNIUS

MINSK

BELARUS

KYIV

UKRAINE

MOLDOVA

CHIŞINĂU

ROMANIA

BUCHAREST

Black Sea

BULGARIA

SOFIA

SKOPJE

NORTH
MACEDONIA

ANKARA

TÜRKIYE

GREECE

Vineyards/Wineries

❶ Tokaj (p216)
❷ Milestii Mici (p280)
❸ Eger (p216)
❹ Župa Wine Region (p290)
❺ Istria & Kvarner (p128)

National Parks

❶ Aukštaitija National Park (p260)
❷ Kiskunság National Park (p216)
❸ Sutjeska National Park (p85)
❹ Tara National Park (p389)
❺ Lahemaa National Park (p181)
❻ Mavrovo National Park (p311)

EASTERN EUROPE

THE GUIDE

Chapters in this section are organised by countries, with each country split into hubs and their surrounding areas. Each hub includes unique experiences, local insights, insider tips and expert recommendations. It's also your gateway to the surrounding area, where you'll see what and how much you can do from there.

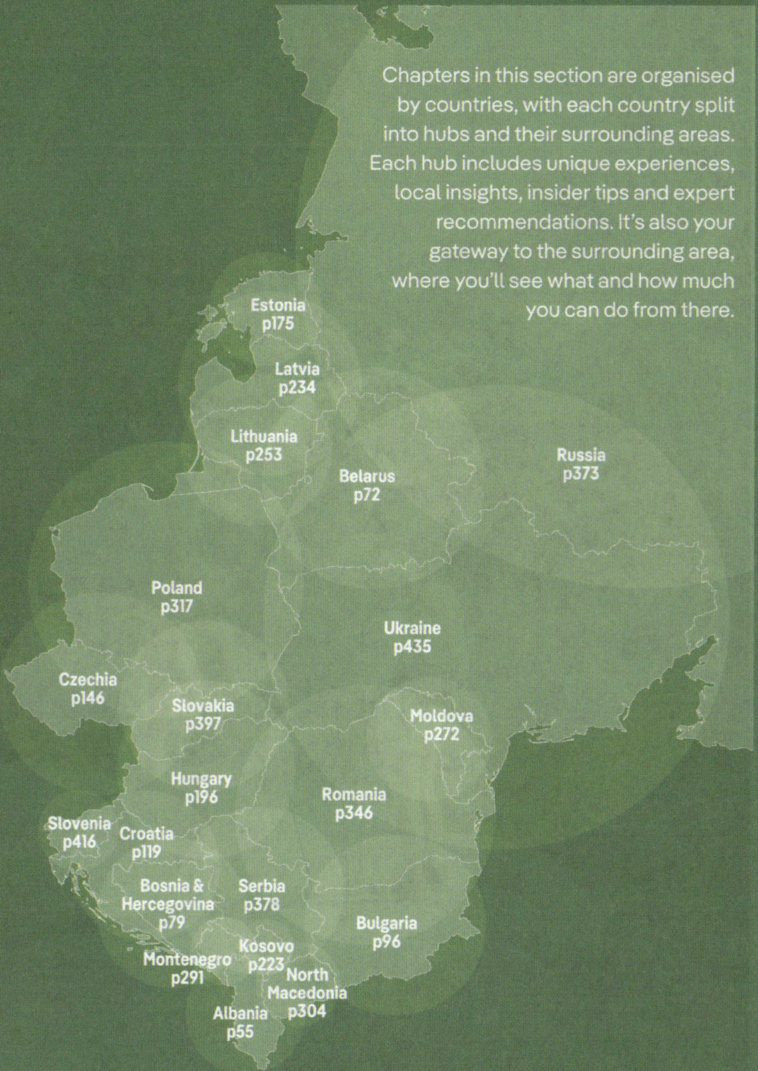

Estonia p175
Latvia p234
Lithuania p253
Belarus p72
Russia p373
Poland p317
Ukraine p435
Czechia p146
Slovakia p397
Moldova p272
Hungary p196
Romania p346
Slovenia p416
Croatia p119
Bosnia & Hercegovina p79
Serbia p378
Bulgaria p96
Kosovo p223
Montenegro p291
North Macedonia p304
Albania p55

Lake Skadar National Park (p298), Montenegro

ART2.0/SHUTTERSTOCK

For places to stay
in Albania, see
p68

ANDRII MARUSHCHYNETS/SHUTTERSTOCK

Above: Accursed Mountains (p66), Shkodër; Right: Berat (p60)

Curated by
Joel Balsam

Albania

MYSTERIOUS NO LONGER

Cotton-candy-blue waters, spectacular mountain hiking
and thousands of years of history etched into crumbling
ruins. It's hard to understand why some still skip Albania.

Albania's borders were shut for much of the 20th century due to a brutal strain of communism steered by the iron fist of dictator Enver Hoxha. Even its own residents couldn't get out. But in 1991, communism fell and Albania's doors swung open. What travellers discovered was an enchanting country where the wind whistled through shattered remnants of half-forgotten Roman and Greek ruins and azure water lapped gently at empty beaches. These days, the secret's out, as Instagram reels of dreamy beaches rivalling any in the Mediterranean have put Albania at the top of many a travel list.

Albanians, for the most part, haven't changed. They're still as curious and warm as ever. The prices aren't close to nearby Greece or Croatia. And you can still find quiet beaches and authentic towns. In Tirana, construction cranes and stylish bars are evidence that this European capital is on the upswing, while the Albanian Riviera's cool water is a refreshing respite from the summer heat. Inland, Berat and Gjirokastër's genius Ottoman architecture and alleyways graciously remain intact, and bike-friendly Shkodër is a perfect gateway to breathtaking trails in the Albanian Alps.

Strangely, some still avoid Albania due to the infamous reputation of its overseas mafia, memories of communism and ethnic discrimination. Ignore them and go now before this amazing country gets well and truly swarming.

MILOSK50/SHUTTERSTOCK

THE MAIN AREAS

TIRANA & CENTRAL ALBANIA
Up-and-coming capital and
UNESCO city. **p58**

THE ALBANIAN RIVIERA
Turquoise water and stone
castles. **p62**

**THE ALBANIAN ALPS &
NORTHERN ALBANIA**
Mountain hikes and mysterious
history. **p66**

Find Your Way

There are no easy options when it comes to getting around. Public transport is unpredictable and mountain roads are dramatic. Your budget and available time are the main factors.

The Albanian Alps & Northern Albania, p66

Hike to villages in the Accursed Mountains, cruise a high-altitude lake and tour an artsy town.

Tirana & Central Albania, p58

Albania's capital is the place to delve into the country's history, gastronomy and culture. To the south, visit Ottoman-era Berat's wonderful windows.

CAR

Cars provide the most flexibility, especially for exploring lesser-visited destinations. However, roads off the major highways can be dicey. City driving is also a challenge, with narrow streets and drivers who park in the middle of the road.

The Albanian Riviera, p62

Aquamarine water and gorgeous viewpoints along the Ionian coast, plus amazing archaeological sites and a mystical stone city.

FURGON

Albania's main public transport is the *furgon* – a shared van, minibus or car. *Furgons* don't have schedules and make plenty of stops as they go, making arrival times unpredictable.

0 — 50 km
0 — 25 miles

JANA JANINA/SHUTTERSTOCK

Himarë (p64)

Plan Your Time

Albania's main cities can be visited in a day or two, but you should leave extra time for delays and infrequent *furgon* if taking public transport.

The Capital & the Coast in a Week

● Start in Tirana to learn about communism at **subterranean bunkers** (p59) and sample *raki* in trendy **Blloku** (p59). Then it's off to the Ottoman town of **Berat** (p60) for winding alleyways. Pick a beach on the Albanian Riviera: there are plenty around **Ksamil** (p63) and **Himarë** (p64). Leave time for ancient **Butrint** (p63).

The Albanian Alps in a Week

● After **Tirana** (p58), head up to cooler climes in **Shkodër** (p66). The city has a young vibe and several excellent museums. Follow up with the multi-day **Valbonë to Theth loop** (p66) over a mountain pass. In Theth, hike to an electric-blue **natural pool** (p67) before returning to Shkodër.

SEASONAL HIGHLIGHTS

SPRING
Albania starts to warm up after Dita e Verës (Summer's Day) on 14 March, though it's often still cloudy and rainy.

SUMMER
Peak season, especially around Sarandë and Ksamil. Make sure to book accommodation ahead of time.

AUTUMN
The best time to travel, with milder temperatures and fewer crowds. September is ideal for hiking in the Alps.

WINTER
Warm up with a *raki* in Tirana then go to the city that makes the masks for Venice during the **Shkodër Carnival** (p67).

Tirana & Central Albania

COMMUNIST HISTORY | CUISINE | NIGHTLIFE

Places

 TOP TIP

Albanians are firmly committed to cash payments; few businesses accept credit cards. Both lekë and euros are accepted (except the bus, which only takes lekë), so there's no need to change money. ATMs dispense lekë: Credins and Tirana Bank usually have the lowest fees.

Lively Tirana (Tiranë) has come a long way from its decades of brutal dictatorship, which lasted from 1944 to 1991. The Albanian capital today is bursting with colour, from parks and thoroughfares flourishing with foliage to Soviet-style apartment buildings painted with vibrant murals. Busy traffic rolls past captivating mosque minarets and church domes in this secular though still faithful city, while Tirana's chic locals stroll through clean, safe streets to sprawling patios for an espresso, *raki* (fruit brandy) or fancy cocktail in the dapper Blloku neighbourhood. Look at the modern skyscrapers popping up everywhere, especially around Skanderbeg Sq, for more evidence that this aspiring European Union capital is on the rise.

Then punch the numbers into your time machine and travel back to life under the Ottoman Empire in beautiful Berat. With a story that dates back 2400 years, this UNESCO city is a mountain town with a special kind of magic.

Tirana

Explore the city's heart

Start exploring the Albanian capital at its bustling epicentre: **Skanderbeg Sq**. Walk in a circle to see the epic socialist-realist facade outside the **National History Museum** *(mhk.gov.al; closed for repairs until 2028)*, the **statue** of national

---

🧭 **GETTING AROUND**

An airport bus (400L) runs every hour from near Skanderbeg Sq and takes 30 minutes. Tirana also has more than 20 municipal bus lines (traditional buses, not *furgon*). Electric taxis like Lux Taxi *(069 844 4487)* are cheaper than official cabs and can pick you up wherever you are. The **Berat Bus**

Terminal is nearly 3km from the historic centre. There are occasional public buses into town, or you can take a taxi. Historic Berat is walkable, although it may be challenging for those with mobility issues.

IS ALBANIA SAFE?

Many who've never been to Albania will warn you not to visit. Ignore them. Albania is as safe as anywhere in Europe, if not safer, with a crime rate lower than Canada's. Pickpocketing isn't common and locals are friendly, curious and welcoming. Stereotypes stem from centuries-old ethnic conflicts between Slavs and Illyrians as well as Christians and Muslims. They also derive from Albania's long communist period and the Albanians' mafia-like crime presence elsewhere in Europe. As the country develops and cracks down on corruption in an effort to join the European Union, this discrimination will inevitably decline. In the meantime, it's travellers' responsibility to share the truth about this friendly country.

hero Skanderbeg and prayer sites for Tirana's large populations of Muslims and Christians: the 19th-century **Et'hem Bey Mosque** (*entry by donation*) and **Resurrection of Christ Orthodox Cathedral**. Around the corner, see where Enver Hoxha (1908–85), a tyrant who ruled Albania during one of Europe's most oppressive dictatorships, coordinated a vast network of spies at **House of Leaves** (*muzeugjethi.gov.al; entry 700L*).

A short taxi or bus ride will take you further into the paranoid logic of Hoxha and his regime. **Bunk'Art 1** (*bunkart.al; entry 500L*) is a vast network of tunnels spread out over five subterranean floors. It's one of 175,000 bunkers built during the communist period as a backup in case enemies (pretty much everyone except North Korea) attacked. There's also **Bunk'Art 2** (*bunkart.al; entry 500L*) near Skanderbeg Sq, though the lengthy texts are incomprehensible in English.

Capital nightlife

The stylish **Blloku** neighbourhood south of the Lana River is the place to be seen in Tirana. Blocked off for nearly half a century as a heavily guarded home for Communist Party

EATING IN TIRANA: OUR PICKS

Lakror TeEla: Sample the Korça speciality *lakror* (spinach pie) swigged down with *dhallë* (a salted yoghurt drink). *5am-3pm Mon-Fri, to 2pm Sat & Sun* €

Te Met Kodra: There's just one thing to order here: freshly grilled *qofte* (meatballs) made with meat straight from the farm. *8am-10pm Mon-Sat, to 4.30pm Sun* €

Era: Widely considered Tirana's best restaurant for traditional dishes like *dollma* (stuffed grape leaves), with excellent service and reasonable prices. *11am-midnight* €€

Mullixhiu: Fine dining and bakery in the park from Bledar Kola (a former footballer), who helped kickstart Albania's slow-food movement. *noon-4pm & 6-10pm* €€

GESTUR GISLASON/SHUTTERSTOCK

officials, Blloku's gates were thrown open in 1991 and quickly started filling up with trendy bars and restaurants. Our favourites are **Komiteti** for its many flavours of *raki* (fruit brandy) and **Radio** for creative cocktails with an Albanian twist.

Or attend a wedding performance at **Albanian Night** *(albaniannight.com; entry 3800L)*. There's singing, traditional clothing (you'll wear vibrant clothing collected and made by Albanian artisans) and, like any good wedding, plenty of gossip.

Berat

TIME FROM TIRANA: **2HR**

Visit an ancient castle

Imagine life under the Ottoman Empire in beautiful Berat. With a story that dates back 2400 years, this UNESCO World Heritage site and mountain town in central Albania, recognised as a rare example of an architectural character typical of the Ottoman period, has a special kind of magic. Look up and you can't miss **Berat Castle** *(Kalaja e Beratit; 300L)* peeking over the mountain. The castle dates back to the 4th century BCE and was added to by various empires as recently

---

 EATING IN BERAT: OUR PICKS

Eni: Small spot jutting out of the cliffside (the mountain rock is visible) on the Goricë side. An affordable menu, with dishes made from the heart. *11.30am-10.30pm* €

Klea: Castle-top restaurant with a lovely courtyard and fresh Albanian dishes. Breakfast for guests only. *noon-10pm* €

Amalia: Candlelit Goricë alleyway restaurant with an Albanian cuisine tasting menu (€28 for two). Great place to try Berati wine. *11.30am-11.30pm* €€

Lili: Leave with a smile on your face, a full belly and a new friend in English-speaking owner Lili. Reserve ahead. *5.30-10pm Mon-Fri* €€

Berat Castle

WHY I LOVE BERAT

Joel Balsam, Lonely Planet writer
Berat might only occupy a day or two on your trip, and it's clearly not off the beaten track, but it's a guaranteed highlight. There was a chance that multi-faith Berat could have been destroyed under the communists. But it wasn't, which is a huge win for humanity. I love wandering through Berat's stone alleyways, picturing what it might've been like 300 years ago. No matter how many times I visit, I always notice something different. And while I can appreciate a bare stone wall as much as the next world traveller, seeing the Ottoman villas painted in white, with their enchanting wooden windows and roofs, really makes it feel like you've been transported back in time.

as the 19th century. It's a town in and of itself, with more than 100 residential buildings, dozens of towers and church ruins, two mosques and a stone wall that stretches 1.4km. Don't miss the **Onufri Museum** *(Muzeu Kombëtar Ikonografik Onufri; muzeumet-berat.al; 400L)*, a medieval art gallery located inside Cathedral Assumption of Saint Mary (1797).

Ottoman-era neighbourhoods

Below the castle, wander Ottoman-era neighbourhoods for a glimpse at life in Berat from the 16th to 19th centuries. There's **Mangalem**, a neighbourhood of winding stone alleyways, mosques and picturesque windows, earning Berat the nickname 'one above the other windows' or, as it's more commonly known, 'town of a thousand windows'. On the other side of the Osum River is **Goricë**. It has a few stone thoroughfares, a couple of pretty churches and a romantic ambience.

Taste Albanian wine

Say *gëzuar* (cheers) to Albanian wines with grape varieties only found at vineyards located a short 30-minute drive from Berat's historic centre. On the way into Berat, **Çobo Winery** *(cobowine.com; standard/premium €25/45)* does tastings inside its beautiful family-built cottage and in its peaceful garden. Or visit **Alpeta Agrotourism** *(alpeta.al; tastings 2000L)*, located in Roshnik village. It's one of the first agrotourism operations in Albania, with vineyards tumbling down a verdant hillside consisting of 37,000 sq m of land received from the government after the fall of communism. As well as tastings, it does delicious meals and three-hour cooking classes *(per person €50)*.

The Albanian Riviera

SEAFRONT | CASTLE SUNSETS | SEAFOOD

Places

☑ TOP TIP

If beaches are your target, fly to the Greek island of Corfu and take a ferry to Sarandë. Finikas Lines *(finikas-lines.com)* and Ionian Seaways *(ionianseaways.com)* run several daily trips between the two by Flying Dolphin high-speed hydrofoil *(30 minutes, per person €30)* or car ferry *(1¼ hours, per person €20)*.

The Albanian Riviera was a revelation roughly two decades ago, when backpackers discovered the last virgin stretch of coast in Europe and proceeded to flock here in droves, setting up ad-hoc campsites and exploring scores of little-known beaches fronting the out-of-this-world turquoise Ionian Sea. Since then, things have become a lot busier, especially around Sarandë and Ksamil.

But worry not: the water is still a dream to swim in, and if you drive north you'll find plenty of space to throw down a towel and while away the day under a beaming sun, or hire a boat to take you to remote beaches. And all the better if you're looking for fun vibes, as electronic music festivals and beach clubs keep the party popping throughout the summer.

Aside from beach life, the Albanian Riviera has some worthwhile archaeological sites built by various empires, including Hellenistic tribes, the Romans, Venetians and the Albanian-Ottoman despot Ali Pasha.

Sarandë

TIME FROM CORFU: **30MIN** ⛴

Seaside strolls and sunsets

Stroll Sarandë's busy boardwalk, stopping at buzzing roof-top bars, or board a pirate ship for a booze cruise – *yaaarr!* Boat tour operators *(per person 2500L)* can take you to secluded beaches.

 GETTING AROUND

Sarandë is the main hub, where it's easy to walk and catch a bus down the coast to Ksamil (150L) and Butrint (200L), or northbound. Riviera Bus *(rivierabus.com/ albania; €50)*, a seven-person air-con minivan, drives from Tirana to Sarandë and back three days a week in summer. The van stops at all major beach towns and also runs from Vlorë to Sarandë for €30 on weekdays in July and August.

Ksamil

SHIMMERING WATER ON THE ALBANIAN RIVIERA

Pulëbardha Beach: Climb down to this amazing beach at the foot of steep cliffs. It's less busy than the main Ksamil beaches.

Blue Eye: It's not a beach and you can't swim here, but the natural phenomenon that creates electric-blue water 30 minutes from Sarandë is a must-see.

Gjipe Beach: Hike 20 minutes to get here from the parking lot near Himarë; arguably Albania's most stunning beach.

Aquarium Beach: Hike or 4WD drive down to this tiny, hidden beach, where crystal-clear turquoise water splashes under the rocks.

Dhërmi Beach: Electronic music festivals in early June attract those who like to shake it; there's wellness mixed in, too.

At sunset, climb to the ruins of **Lekursi Castle**, an Ottoman castle built in 1537, or the 6th-century **Monastery of the 40 Saints**.

Ksamil

TIME FROM SARANDË: 30MIN 🚗

Find your beach bliss

If you've seen photos or videos on social media of the tantalisingly turquoise water on the Albanian Riviera, they were probably taken in **Ksamil**. The beach town is lined with breathtaking beaches backed by stark cliffs and stylish bars playing melodic deep house. Bliss out in a beach chair at **Ksamil Beach**, then paddle to the uninhabited islands (**Tre Ishujt**) just offshore. Or go underwater to see WWII and communist-era shipwrecks with **Saranda Diving** (*saranda diving.com; per dive 7000L*).

An ancient 2800-year-old city

The most romantic of Albania's ancient sites, **Butrint** (*butrint.al; entry adult/teen/child 800/500L/free*), has been inhabited for 2800 years. In the 8th century BCE, Hellenist (Greek) tribes built the first *polis* (city) and later Butrint's celebrated site: the

 EATING IN KSAMIL & SARANDË: OUR PICKS

Ftelea Fish Taverna: Serves only the freshest fish and seafood, grilled, fried or served tucked into pasta or risotto. A Ksamil highlight. *noon-11.30pm* €€

Guvat: On a hill's edge in Ksamil with some of the best views around and often live music at sunset. Service can be slow. *7am-11.30pm* €€€

Taverna Labëria: This family-run restaurant off the Sarandë boardwalk serves terrific portions of steak and seafood at its two busy terraces. *8am-midnight* €€

Manxuranë: Inspired by his mother's cooking, Fatmir's carefully prepared plates are a knockout – as are the Sarandë views. One of Albania's best. *10am-11pm* €€€

ZDENEK MATYAS PHOTOGRAPHY/SHUTTERSTOCK

Gjirokastër Bazaar

Theatre. The Romans followed, building a **Forum**, thermal **Baths** with mosaic wall patterns and more. Then came the Byzantines, who built the well-kept 6th-century **Great Basilica**, and Venetians, responsible for a 16th-century **Tower** and **Triangular Castle**.

Himarë

TIME FROM SARANDË: 1½HR

Budget friendly vibes

Himarë (Himara) is the biggest town on the Riviera and has a less bougie vibe than some other beach resorts along the coast, though the beaches are just as magnificent. Those on a budget will feel especially at home here.

Amazing castles

Taxi up to the ruins of **Himarë Castle** *(entry 300L)*, an enchanting citadel that has existed in some form for 3500 years, with the earliest fortifications dating back to the Hellenistic Chaonians. South of town is the triangular **Porto Palermo Castle** *(entry 300L)*, likely built by the Venetians and expanded upon by Albanian-Ottoman despot Ali Pasha of Tepelenë.

 EATING IN HIMARË: OUR PICKS

Taverna Lefteri:
This town has lots of delicious seafood, but Lefteri stands out for its presentation and quality. *noon-4pm & 7pm-midnight* €€

To Steki sti Gonia:
Himarë's Hellenistic heritage shines at this Greek restaurant on the seafront. The menu ventures beyond *souvlaki*. *11.30am-midnight* €€

Fig and Olive: With views over Livadhi Beach and twinkly-lit evening meals, this place has a romantic vibe to go along with its seafood dishes. *5.30-10pm* €€

Manolo Beach Bar:
Tried-and-true beach bar without the trendiness of some of its competitors. Open year-round. *7.30am-3am* €€

Gjirokastër

Stroll through a stone city

Go for a walk around Gjirokastër to see its fascinating metre-thick stone walls that hold up roofs layered with heavy stone slabs. Start by shopping and eating at the **Bazaar**, found at the top of Gjirokastër's old town at a five-point intersection. Nearby is the 18th-century **Bazaar Mosque**, and beneath it is the atmospheric stone-walled cafe, **Te Kubé**, which doubles as a mini-museum with a communist-bunker tunnel exhibit dedicated to Albanian iso-polyphony music. This chilling vocal art is recognised by UNESCO as a Masterpiece of the Oral and Intangible Heritage of Humanity and celebrates sadness through song. Alternatively, see the 80-room **Cold War Tunnel** (entry 200L) on a guided tour led every hour during high season.

Also check out **Gjirokastër Castle** (entry 400L), a medieval fortress dating to the 4th century that later operated as a base for Italian soldiers during the WWII occupation.

Visit historic house museums

Gjiorkastër happens to be the birthplace of many of Albania's most important 20th-century figures, and it has museums dedicated to the lot of them. **Kadare House** (entry 500L) celebrates the life of Albania's most famous writer, Ismail Kadare (1936–2024), while **Muza Ime Musine Kokalari** (entry 500L) is dedicated to Musine Kokalari (1918–83), a feminist writer and social democratic politician. Enver Hoxha was also born here, but his former house has been rebuilt into an interesting **Ethnographic Museum** (entry 500L).

While its former inhabitants aren't as well-known, tour **Zekate House** (entry 250L) and **Skenduli House** (entry 300L) to see how wealthy families lived during the Ottoman days.

ALBANIAN DISHES TO TRY

Tavë kosi: Lamb baked in a cast-iron pan with yoghurt and rice.

Lakror: Doughy Korçan pie usually stuffed with spinach, and sometimes also cheese, leeks or meat.

Specë/patëllxhan të mbushur: Baked peppers or aubergines stuffed with rice, tomatoes and herbs.

Fërgesë: Dip made with red peppers and ricotta cheese.

Flia (also flija or fli): Layered crepes that can be sweet or sour; from Kosovo and the northern regions.

EATING IN GJIROKASTËR: OUR PICKS

Odaja: Delightful, honest Albanian cooking since 1937 in an upper-floor restaurant. Plenty of vegetarian options. *10am-11pm* €

Kardhashi: A tad pushy, though eminently generous top-of-the-hill restaurant with plenty of outdoor seating. *8.30am-10.30pm* €

Furra: Recently opened spot in the Bazaar with top-quality Albanian casseroles and pizzas. Good vibes, too. *noon-10.30pm* €€

The Barrels: Farm-to-table cuisine beside a vineyard at this wildly popular agritourism destination across the valley. Reserve. *noon-11pm* €€

The Albanian Alps & Northern Albania

MOUNTAIN HIKES | MYSTERIOUS HISTORY | GRILLED CARP

Places

Shkodër p66
Theth p67

☑ TOP TIP

Hikes in the Albanian Alps, including the ever-popular Valbonë-to-Theth circuit, take at least two nights – one in Valbonë after taking the Lake Koman Ferry and another in Theth. Allow extra time for a blissful escape from society, and even more if you want to explore Shkodër.

Names don't come much more evocative than the Accursed Mountains (Bjeshkët e Namuna), also known as the Albanian Alps. And the dramatic peaks of northern Albania truly live up to their name. Sure, at under 3000m they might not be as high as the peaks in Switzerland, but the snow-sprinkled mountain pinnacles, deep green valleys and thick forests northeast of the area's only major city, Shkodër, are nothing to scoff at.

Many come here to hike from Valbonë to Theth, a nifty circuit that also includes a three-hour ferry ride. But this popular excursion is far from the only hiking option, and if you ask in-the-know locals, it's not even the best. So find your own favourite mountain trail followed by a plunge into a turquoise blue-eye pool near Theth. And leave time to cycle around Shkodër: it's a lovable, colourful city with historic architecture and a carp-filled lake.

Shkodër

TIME FROM TIRANA: 2HR 🚌

Hike the Accursed Mountains

Many people come to the Albanian Alps for a single reason: the spectacular three- or four-day circuit from Shkodër, which includes hiking along a section of the multinational **Peaks of the Balkans Trail**. The 14.7km hike over the **Valbonë Pass** (1795m) to Theth takes roughly five to seven hours. The rest of the time will be spent winding over mountain roads in a *furgon*, crossing Lake Koman by ferry and relaxing in mountain tranquillity. Book a self-guided tour that includes transport

---

🧭 GETTING AROUND

The most popular way to get around Shkodër is on a bicycle. Most accommodations rent them. Official taxis and public buses (40L), many of which stop at Democracy Sq, can take you to the lake or the castle. The road to Theth and other roads in the Alps can be rough, windy and covered in snow or black ice as late as June, so take public or private minibuses rather than drive.

and places to stay along the way with any Shkodër accommodation. Alternatively, reserve transport via the **Koman Ferry** website *(komanilakeferry.com)* and pick your own stays.

Understand Albanian culture

See early images of Albanians at the **Marubi National Photography Museum** *(marubi.gov.al; entry 700L)*, which celebrates the work of Pietro Marubi (1832–1903) and his heirs, who documented Albanian life in the late 19th and early 20th centuries. Continue learning about Albanian history at the **Site of Witness & Memory Museum** *(instagram.com/siteofwitnessandmemory; entry 200L)*, which was an interrogation centre and prison for political detainees during the communist era.

Outside the centre, **Rozafa Fortress** *(entry 400L)* was founded in the 4th century BCE during Illyrian times and rebuilt much later by the Venetians and then the Turks. The fortress takes its name from a woman who was allegedly walled into the ramparts as an offering to the gods.

Another key Shkodër spot is the **Venice Art Mask Factory** *(tour €3)*, which is the leading producer of the papier-mâché masks used during Venice's Carnival as well as, of course, **Shkodër's**. Fun fact: the mask worn by Tom Cruise in *Eyes Wide Shut* was made by the artist who founded the Mask Factory.

Theth

TIME FROM SHKODËR: **2HR**

Hike to a waterfall and blue eye

The mountain village of Theth has the most dramatic setting in Albania. Just getting here is quite incredible, whether you cross the mountains on foot from Valbonë or drive from Shkodër. Come to explore **Theth National Park** by hiking to the gushing **Grunas Waterfall**, just 30 minutes from town. Or continue on a six- to seven-hour round-trip to **Blue Eye Kaprre**, an electric-blue natural pool that you can swim in.

See a blood-feud tower

You'll see plenty of stone *kullas* (towers) across Albania, but the one in Theth has a particularly fascinating story. **Reconciliation Tower** *(entry 150L)* dates back 400 years and was used as a 'lock-in tower' during blood feuds – long-standing cycles of violence that were intended to restore honour through vengeance. A tower like this one was meant to protect a family member from an enemy; climb the stairs for an idea of what life was like inside.

KANUN

Northern Albanians traditionally lived according to the Kanun, a legal and moral code from the 1400s (or possibly earlier) that wasn't written down until the early 20th century. This extensive code – 12 books and over 1200 articles – governs everything from what to do when your goat crosses into a neighbour's yard to how to avenge family murders through blood feuds. The Kanun also created the role of 'sworn virgins', women who pledged celibacy in order to benefit from men's social privileges. Despite being declared illegal under Ottoman rule and the Hoxha regime, the Kanun endures to this day: as of 2022, around a dozen sworn virgins remain, and thousands of people escaping blood feuds have sought asylum in Europe over the last two decades.

EATING & DRINKING IN SHKODËR: OUR PICKS

Fisi: Hearty portions and fair prices for mixed grilled meats and friendly service. A Shkodër classic. *11am-10.30pm* €€

Pelikani Kaçurrel: Cycle along Lake Shkodër and have grilled carp at this lovely lakeside restaurant that has its own beach. *8am-11.30pm* €€

Tradita Hotel: Restored 17th-century mansion that once belonged to a local writer; delivers one of the city's finest restaurant experiences. *noon-11.30pm* €€

n'Odë: This bohemian spot gets everyone singing on Saturday nights when a live band takes the stage. It's smack in the centre. *7am-11pm*

Places We Love to Stay

€ Budget €€ Midrange €€€ Top End

Tirana & Central Albania

MAP p59

Tirana

Tirana Backpacker Hostel € Albania's oldest hostel is still going strong, with a vibrant decor reminiscent of the glory days of backpacking. Vegetarian communal breakfast.

Bujtina e Gjelit €€ Tirana's most charming hotel has Ottoman-era vibes with brick archways centred around a pool courtyard. The drawback is that it's far from the centre.

The Plaza €€€ The first of many stylish skyscrapers to open near Skanderbeg Sq was finished in 2016. Modernist design and a great option.

Berat

Berat Backpackers € The best hostel in Berat, and also the oldest, is on the Goricë side. It has dorms, camping, a garden and a fun atmosphere.

Klea Hotel €€ Hilltop hideaway inside the castle, with five compact rooms, pretty patios and a lovely restaurant terrace.

Mangalemi Hotel €€ Built over the pasha's 1764 palace, this is Berat's first post-communist hotel, with beautiful traditional furnishings.

The Albanian Riviera

Sarandë

Central Boutique Hostel € Everything's fresh in this backpacker spot that opened in 2025 – beds with curtains, clean bathrooms and a kitchen that serves a simple breakfast.

Harmony Hotel €€ Minimalist Mediterranean decor away from the loud promenade is a great pick for couples looking for a romantic retreat.

Vila Kalcuni €€€ Watch the boats pass this white mansion on a beachy corner close to Sarandë port.

Ksamil

Ksamil Caravan Camping € Save some cash for the beach by parking your van or pitching a tent at this campground. Open year-round.

Meta Hotel €€ The closest you'll get to the beach at the midrange price point. The stone-shaped headboard cushions might have you feeling like you've woken up in a much comfier Butrint.

Arameras Beach Resort €€€ Go all-out at this beach resort on the far side of Ksamil, with an infinity pool and private beach.

Himarë

Camping Himara € Set up a tent under the olive trees at this camping ground across the main road from Livadhi Beach. Best access to the Aquarium Beach cove.

Vila Kosteli €€ Cliffside apartments run by a friendly couple between Himarë's two beaches. Some rooms have terraces with sun loungers overlooking the sea.

Gjirokastër

Stone City Hostel € Dutch owner Wouter runs Albania's best hostel, with modern-meets-traditional decor and daily activities including fascinating history walks and 4WD tours.

Old Bazaar 1790 €€ Immerse yourself in 18th-century Gjirokastër at this 11-room boutique hotel close to the Bazaar. Rooms have ornate handcrafted bed frames and cute windows with views of the town.

Kerculla Resort €€€ Sleep like a sultan in this palatial hotel overlooking Gjirokastër. Intricate wooden carvings, a relaxing pool area and exquisite views.

The Albanian Alps & Northern Albania

Shkodër

Mi Casa Es Tu Casa € Beautiful mansion that's now a chill, colourful backpackers hostel for all ages. It's not a party vibe.

InTown € Behind the bright orange facade is a lovely B&B with freshly renovated rooms and a tranquil garden steps from the action.

Tradita Hotel €€ Painstakingly restored 17th-century mansion that once belonged to a famous Shkodran writer, now a museum-like boutique hotel with comfortable rooms and locally woven bed linens.

Theth

Molla €€ Have your breakfast in front of a grand mountain amphitheatre and sleep on a comfy bed in a cosy wooden guesthouse. What the Albanian Alps are all about.

Marashi €€€ Recently renovated guesthouse facing the water with an eye-catching standalone tub in the penthouse suite.

Practicalities

LGBTIQ+ Travellers
Albania is often targeted as one of the worst places in Europe for LGBTIQ+ people. The truth is, it isn't great – but it could be worse. Same-sex relationships are legal and discrimination is prohibited. However, LGBTIQ+ people can't get married, adopt or undergo a gender change. Avoid PDA, especially outside of Tirana.

TRABANTOS/SHUTTERSTOCK

Tirana (p58)

Safe Travel
Stereotypes painting Albania as dangerous date back to historic religious tensions, a brutal dictatorship and the admittedly violent organised crime network. But travelling here is as safe as anywhere in Western Europe, if not more so. Albania has low crime rates and pickpocketing is relatively rare.

Opening Hours
Most businesses in tourist hubs outside of Tirana shut down from October through May.
Banks 8am–4pm Monday to Friday
Cafes 7am–10pm
Bars noon–midnight
Restaurants 11am–10pm
Shops 9am–8pm
Supermarkets 7am–10pm

Electricity & Connectivity
Albania uses Type F 230V/50Hzv plugs. Local SIM cards and tourist packages are available inside the Tirana airport. Internet connection is spotty in the Alps. Wi-fi is usually decent.

Water
Tap water is not drinkable anywhere in Albania, but it's safe enough for brushing your teeth and washing produce.

Public Holidays
New Year's Day 1 January
Dita e Verës (Summer Day) 14 March
Ramadan Bajram/Eid al-Fitr February & March (2026–28)
Sultan Nevruz 22 March
Easter March or April
Labour Day 1 May
Eid al-Adha May (2026–28)
Independence Day 28 November
Liberation Day 29 November
Youth Day 8 December
Christmas 25 December

Visas
Citizens of European Schengen Zone countries and nearly 60 other nations can enter Albania without a visa for up to 90 days within a 180-day period. US citizens can stay up to one year.

Language

In Albanian – also understood in Kosovo and North Macedonia – *ew* is pronounced as 'ee' with rounded lips, *uh* as the 'a' in 'ago', *dh* as the 'th' in 'that', *dz* as the 'ds' in 'adds', and *zh* as the 's' in 'pleasure'. Also, *ll* and *rr* are pronounced stronger than when they are written as single letters.

Basics

Hello. Tungjatjeta. *toon·dya·tye·ta*
Goodbye. Mirupafshim. *mee·roo·paf·sheem*
Yes. Po. *po*
No. Jo. *yo*
Please. Ju lutem. *yoo loo·tem*
Thank you. Faleminderit. *fa·le·meen·de·reet*
What's your name? Si quheni? *see choo·he·nee*
My name is ... Unë quhem ... *oo·nuh choo·hem ...*
Do you speak English? A flisni anglisht? *a flees·nee ang·leesht*
I don't understand. Unë nuk kuptoj. *oo·nuh nook koop·toy*

Emergencies

Help! Ndihmë! *ndeeh·muh*
Go away! Ik! *eek*
I'm ill. Jam i/e sëmurë. (m/f) *yam ee/e suh·moo·ruh*

Call the doctor/police! Thirrni doktorin/policinë! *theerr·nee dok·to·reen/po·lee·tsee·nuh*

Eating & Drinking

What would you recommend? Çfarë më rekomandoni? *chfa·ruh muh re·ko·man·do·nee*
I'll have... Dua... *doo·a*
Cheers! Gëzuar! *guh·zoo·ar*
I'd like the bill/menu, please. Më sillni faturën/menunë, ju lutem. *muh seell·nee fa·too·ruhn/me·noo·nuh yoo loo·tem*

Shopping & Services

I'm looking for ... Po kërkoj për ... *po kuhr·koy puhr ...*
How much is it? Sa kushton? *sa koosh·ton*
Cheers! Gëzuar! *guh·zoo·ar*
That's too expensive. Është shumë shtrenjtë. *uhsh·tuh shoo·muh shtreny·tuh*

NUMBERS

1
një *nyuh*

2
dy *dew*

3
tre *tre*

4
katër *ka·tuhr*

5
pesë *pe·suh*

6
gjashtë *dyash·tuh*

7
shtatë *shta·tuh*

8
tetë *te·tuh*

9
nëntë *nuhn·tuh*

10
dhjetë *dhye·tuh*

English & Other Tourist Languages

While most people dealing with tourists on a daily basis speak English extremely well, that's not true of the entire population. English is taught in schools, but the older generations are more likely to know some German, Russian or, along the coast, Italian.

FROM LEFT: PPT14TH/SHUTTERSTOCK, TUPUNGATO/SHUTTERSTOCK

Nënë Tereza International Airport

Arriving & Getting Around

Albania has frequent flights to Tirana. If the beach is your priority, consider taking a ferry from the Greek island of Corfu. Albania also has bus connections to neighbouring Greece, Montenegro, North Macedonia and Kosovo.

By Air
Tirana's **Nënë Tereza International Airport**, 17km from the city centre, is a seamless experience for EU, Canadian and US passport holders. The new **Vlorë International Airport** opened in summer 2025.

By Boat
The best way to get to the Albanian Riviera is via the Flying Dolphin ferry, running from Corfu (Greece) to Sarandë. Ferries also run to Durrës and Vlorë from Bari and Brindisi (Italy).

Furgon
Furgon is the main form of public transport in Albania. Fares are low and you either pay the conductor when you board or before you hop off, which can be anywhere along the route. *Furgon* only leave when full.

Car Hire
Driving in Albania has plenty of issues (aggressive drivers, narrow roads, potholes) but it's the only way to see much of the country and the roads are gorgeous. There are plenty of private car-hire agencies, but few international brands. Speed limits are 40km/h in towns and cities, and 90 to 110km/h on highways. Maps.me is more accurate than Google Maps. Traffic stops are common.

MONEY
Currency: Albanian Lek (L) & Euro (€)

CASH
Cash is still king in Albania. Both Albanian lekë and euros are accepted, and most businesses will give you the actual conversion rate (it's usually 100 lekë to €1). You'll find ATMs dispensing lekë in all major towns and cities; expect a 600L to 850L fee and possibly a conversion percentage in addition to what your home bank charges. Keep smaller bills and change handy, especially if taking the bus.

CARD
Bank and credit cards are almost never accepted in Albania outside of upscale hotels. Even car hire agencies want cash or a bank transfer, and online bookings won't require a credit card if you used one to reserve. If cards are accepted, expect a transaction minimum.

Curated by
Leonid Ragozin

Belarus

EUROPE'S ODDEST POLITY

One man has defined Belarus for more than 30 years, and
he is not going away.

Belarus has been one of Europe's political oddities ever since President Aleksandr Lukashenko came to power in 1994 under the slogans of restoring the Soviet way of life – in which he partly succeeded – as well as the Soviet Union per se, in which he didn't. 'Communism with cappuccino' is how this guidebook series described Belarus in the early 2000s.

Routinely branded as a dictator in the international media, Lukashenko brutally suppressed a peaceful popular uprising against his rule in 2021–22 and allowed Russian troops to launch an attack on Ukraine's capital, Kyiv, in February 2022. However, since Russia withdrew troops from the vicinity of Kyiv the same year, it didn't use Belarusian territory for further attacks on Ukraine and the Belarusian army has never participated in the conflict (though given its unpredictable trajectory, this could change at any time).

Although Lukashenko makes attempts to distance himself from Russia's war in Ukraine and mend relations with the West, Belarus remains under Western sanctions, levied on the country for its role in the war on top of the previous sanctions that punished it for mass human rights violations.

Partly because Belarus began sliding back towards authoritarian rule long before Russia, it has never been on the radar of international travellers. It has few obvious natural or historical attractions, except for Belavezhskaya Pushcha National Park – a piece of primeval forest that's home to a large population of European bison.

Its current geography, demography and urban landscapes were defined by WWII, in which it lost over a quarter of its population – the highest percentage among all European nations. Main Belarusian cities, most notably Minsk, were rebuilt from scratch in the post-war years, giving the country its idiosyncratic hyper-Soviet feel.

ANASTASIA PETROVA/SHUTTERSTOCK

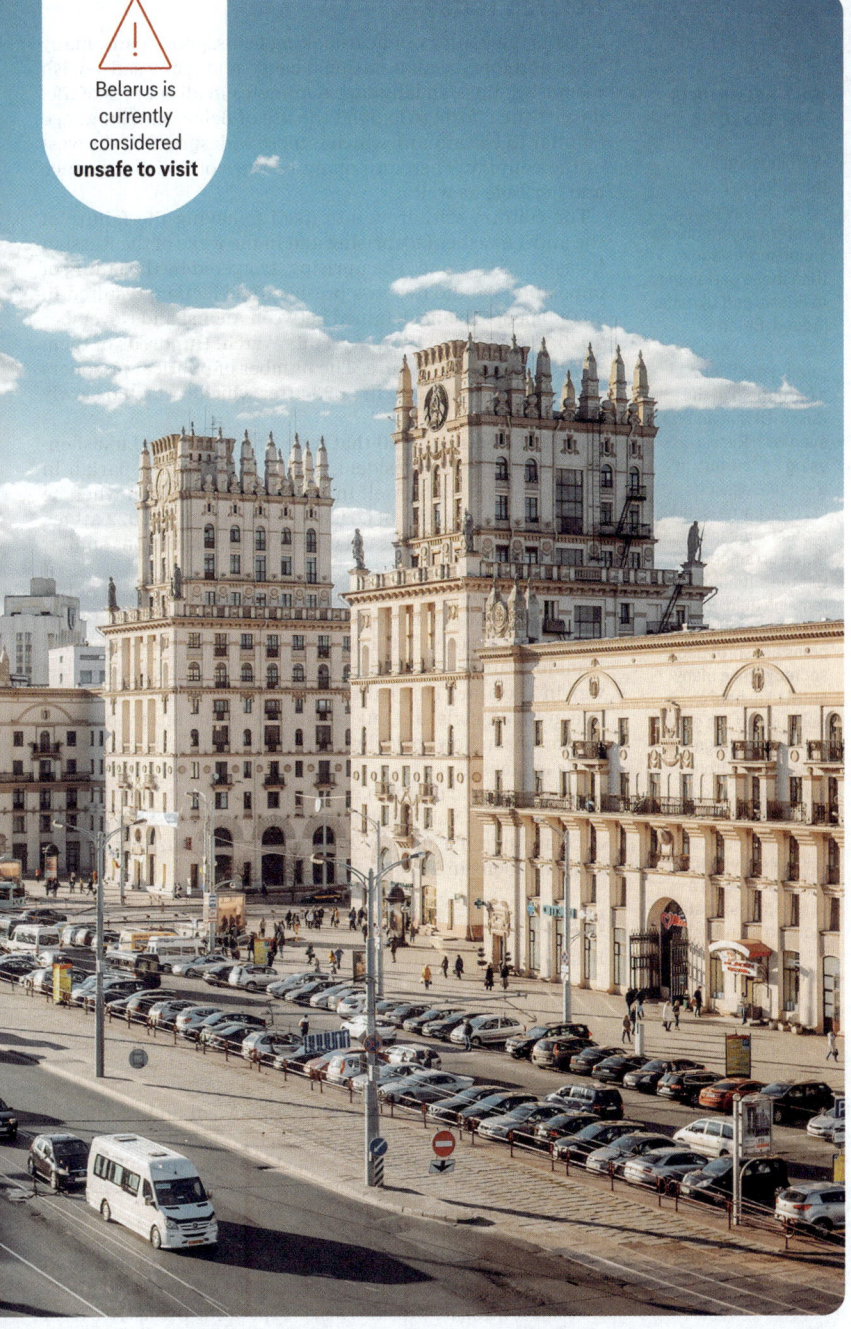

Belarus is currently considered **unsafe to visit**

Left: Obelisk, Belarusian Great Patriotic War Museum; Above: Station Square, Minsk

Belarus Today

Belarus is a country of neat-looking fields, good roads, many lakes and forests, an occasional castle and many sad Jewish memories. Russian language dominates in all spheres of life, despite the efforts to expand the use of Belarusian language (similar to Ukrainian), which is more widespread in the west of the country. There are many vestiges of Polish influence and heritage as well.

The country withdrew into itself following the failure of the anti-Lukashenko uprising and in the wake of the Russian invasion of Ukraine. The uprising, triggered by the jailing of opposition candidates in a presidential election, resulted in 25,000 people being detained between August and November 2020, according to Human Rights Watch. Hundreds of them were subjected to torture. The number of political prisoners peaked at around 1500 in 2023 after which it started slowly diminishing.

The EU stated in 2020 that it doesn't recognise Lukashenko as a legitimate president, which left him as a pariah in Europe. He found himself in even greater isolation when he allowed Russia to use Belarusian territory in its 2022 attack on Ukraine, and Belarus fell under Western sanctions similar to those slapped on Russia.

But things have changed since then. Belarus stayed out of the Ukraine war after 2022, while Lukashenko tried to sell himself as a potential mediator. His efforts paid off when Donald Trump, re-elected in 2024, attempted to stop the war in Ukraine. This led to a frenzy of communication between US officials and Lukashenko, with the latter coaching the former in how to deal with President Putin, according to *Time* magazine.

Ordinary Belarusians have been going about their lives in the meantime. Nobody challenged Lukashenko when he was once again 're-elected' in 2025. Few will be surprised if the same happens in 2030.

History

Belarus means 'White Rus' in Slavic languages, a reference to the fact that its statehood stems from the same root as Russia's and Ukraine's – Kyivan Rus. Its national awakening has been subdued from the outset and remains so today.

Kyivan Rus and Polish-Lithuanian rule

Eastern Slavs from the Krivichi, Dregovichi and Radimichi tribes arrived in what is now Belarus in the 6th to 8th centuries CE. The principalities of Polatsk, Turau, Pinsk and Minsk were formed, all falling under the suzerainty of Prince Vladimir's Kyivan Rus by the late 10th century.

In the 14th century the territory of modern-day Belarus – along with much of today's Ukraine – became part of the Grand Duchy of Lithuania. In the 400 years before Belarus fell under Russian control, Belarusians began separating themselves from Russians and Ukrainians linguistically and culturally.

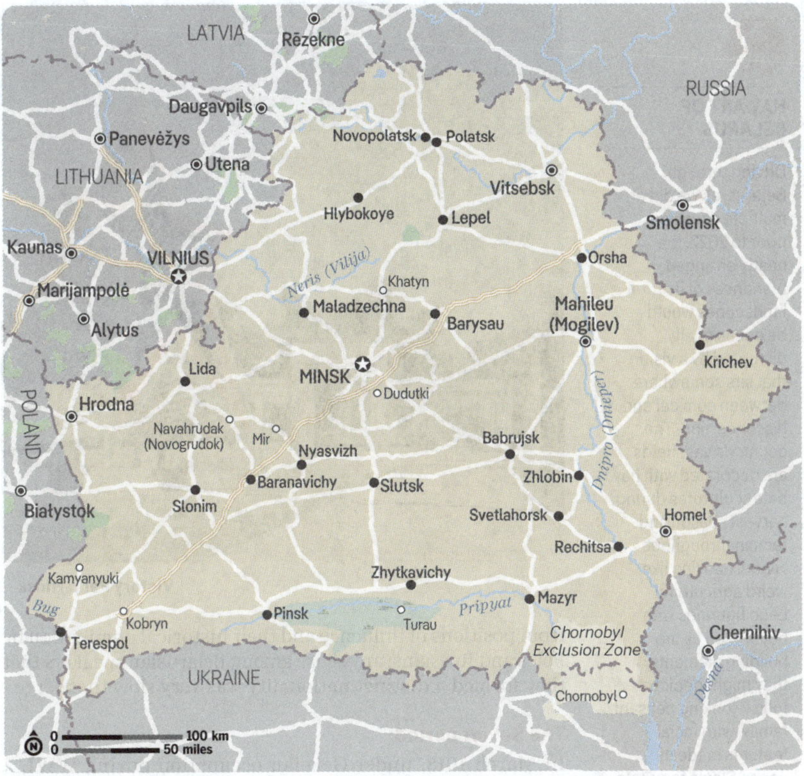

After Lithuania united with Poland and became Roman Catholic in 1386, the Belarusian peasantry remained in the Orthodox Church. Lithuania permitted its subjects a fair degree of autonomy, even using their emerging language, yet to be called Belarusian, as the official language.

In 1596 the Polish authorities arranged the Union of Brest, which set up the Uniate Church, bringing much of the Orthodox Church in Belarus under the authority of the Vatican.

Over the next two centuries of Polish rule, Poles and Jews controlled trade and most Belarusians remained peasants. Only after the three Partitions of Poland (in 1772, 1793 and 1795–96) was Belarus absorbed into Russia.

The Russian Empire

Under Russian rule, a policy of Russification was pursued. In 1839 the Uniate Church was abolished, with most Belarusian parishes absorbed by the Russian Church.

During the 19th century Belarus was part of the Pale of Settlement, the area where Jews in the Russian Empire were required to settle. The percentage of Jews in many Belarusian cities and towns before WWII was between 35% and 75%.

The vast majority of Belarusians remained on the land, poor and illiterate. Due to their cultural stagnation, their absence

FAST FACTS

Capital Minsk

Population 9.5 million

Area 207,595 sq km

Official languages Russian & Belarusian

Time zone GMT+3

Currency Belarusian rouble (BYN)

HAY ART OF BELARUS

Driving through Belarus, as we did on multiple occasions prior to 2022, the neatly arranged blandness of its rural landscapes would be occasionally disrupted by a vision that sits somewhere between comical and disconcerting. The country's vast fields are decorated with hay bale sculptures during harvest season and remain throughout winter. Looking like weird agricultural Lego figurines with bales used as the building elements, they might depict a folksy-looking peasant family, with facial features made of paper, Slavic fairy-tale characters or a toy train, with bales arranged as carriages.

This is the kind of aesthetic promoted by and in many ways embodied by Aleksandr Lukashenko, who headed a Soviet collective farm shortly before becoming national leader. A vivid example of political paternalism, he enjoys being called Batka (Daddy) and does so himself – he loves talking about himself in the third person. His political brand might come across as exotic, but in an East European context it is also somewhat typical.

ALENA ZHARAVA/SHUTTERSTOCK

Victory Park, Minsk

from positions of influence and their historical domination by Poles and Russians, any sense among Belarusian speakers that they formed a distinct nationality was very slow to emerge.

The Soviet period

In March 1918, under German occupation during WWI, a short-lived independent Belarusian Democratic Republic was declared, but the land was soon under the control of the Red Army and the Belarusian Soviet Socialist Republic (BSSR) was formed. The 1921 Treaty of Riga allotted roughly the western half of modern Belarus to Poland, which launched a programme of Polonisation. These lands would be annexed by the USSR when Hitler and Stalin divided Poland in 1939.

The eastern half was left to the Bolsheviks and the redeclared BSSR became a founding member of the USSR in 1922. The 1930s also saw industrialisation, agricultural collectivisation and purges in which hundreds of thousands were executed – most in the Kurapaty Forest, outside Minsk.

When Nazi Germany invaded the USSR in 1941, Belarus was at the epicentre of the catastrophe and suffered more than any current European nation. The German occupation was savage and partisan resistance widespread until the Red Army drove the Germans out in 1944, with massive destruction on both sides.

Hundreds of villages were destroyed and much of Minsk was flattened. The Nazis and their auxiliaries locked villagers in their churches and burnt them alive, as happened in Khatyn, now the site of a Soviet-era memorial. At least 25% (over two million people) of the Belarusian population died between 1939 and 1945. At the concentration camp of Maly

Trostenets alone, more than 200,000 people were executed.

In the post-war years, the Soviet authorities reinvented Belarus as the 'assembly shop' of the USSR, transforming it into a major manufacturing and machine-building hub. By the 1980s, Belarus was one of the Soviet Union's most prosperous republics by the 1980s and the wartime population loss was compensated for by the influx of Russian-speaking immigrants.

The 1986 Chornobyl disaster, just over the border in Ukraine, was profoundly felt by the people of Belarus. The radiation cloud released left about a quarter of the country seriously contaminated and it still has effects today.

The Lukashenko decades

Belarus proclaimed itself an independent country after the collapse of the August 1991 coup in Moscow. With no history whatsoever as a politically or economically independent entity, the country of Belarus was one of the oddest outcomes of the disintegration of the USSR.

In July 1994, Aleksandr Lukashenko came to power and has ruled Belarus with an iron grip ever since. His initial promise was reunification with Russia but his relations with Moscow were never ideal and over the years he grew staunchly pro-independence. He has altered the constitution on several occasions to allow himself to remain in office. Resistance to Lukashenko's reign has been muted, though protests have flared up around the time of elections, which all major international observers, including the United Nations Human Rights Council, denounced for failing to meet free and fair standards. These protests occurred when Lukashenko won the presidential vote in 2006 and again in 2010, when he won again with almost 80% of the vote. When the conflict in Ukraine began in 2014, he went on to host peace talks between Russia, Ukraine, France and Germany, which resulted in the Minsk Agreements, which put an end to the initial hot phase of the conflict. Lukashenko's confidence and international clout grew accordingly.

However, his new election bid in 2020 was countered by a united opposition, who made a coordinated attempt at nominating several candidates and launching powerful election campaigns for each of them, despite knowing full well that they would most likely be barred from running. This is exactly what happened, and the candidates and their staffers were arrested. The only opposition personality Lukashenko allowed to run was the last-minute nominee Sviatlana Tsikhanouskaya, the wife of a jailed candidate. Although Lukashenko claimed he won, with 81% voting for him and 10% for Tsikhanouskaya, many believe that she was the real winner. Several EU countries recognise the government in exile she formed after fleeing to Lithuania as the only legitimate body in Belarus. But its influence waned in the years that followed and Lukashenko's confidence grew again. After 'winning' another election in 2025, he released Tsikhanouskaya's husband Siarhei from jail in a prisoner swap organised by the Trump administration.

ZUBR'S COMEBACK

The rescue of the European bison (or *zubr* in Slavic languages) as a species was one of the greatest stories of European cross-border cooperation during the worst periods of the 20th century, in which Belarus played no small part.

The last remaining piece of primeval forest in Central Europe, Belavezhskaya Pushcha was also the last home of European bison before they became extinct in the wild in the 1920s. But 52 bison from Belovezhskaya Pushcha, as well as from the Caucasus, were still living in European zoos. The return of the bison into the wild was championed by pre-war Poland, who controlled the forest in its entirety. The first bison was released in 1929. After WWII, Belavezhskaya Pushcha found itself divided between the USSR and Poland, with no bison on the Soviet side. But almost immediately the Soviet authorities began populating the Belarusian part of the forest with several bison provided by Poland. There were 6244 free-roaming bison in the world by 2020: of these, 2269 were in Poland and 2101 in Belarus.

For places to stay in Bosnia & Hercegovina, see p92

BOSNIA & HERCEGOVINA

CAYO SEMPERE/SHUTTERSTOCK

Above: Stari Most (p86), Mostar; Right: Sebilj Fountain (p82), Sarajevo

Curated by
Vesna Maric

Bosnia & Hercegovina

RICH HISTORY, WILD NATURE, WARM WELCOME

Bosnia and Hercegovina has stunning natural beauty, charming cities and a fascinating history. Make sure you engage with its friendly people.

Bosnia and Hercegovina's dramatic natural beauty is only matched by its history. Over the centuries, the region has been the meeting point of Byzantine and Roman Christianity, Islam and Judaism, and the Ottoman and Austro-Hungarian Empires – all followed by Yugoslavia's socialism. Most people still associate the country with the heartbreaking war of the 1990s, but while the scars from that time are real, today's visitors will be impressed by the genuine and unassuming human warmth, incredible mountains, wild swimming and rafting, impressive waterfalls and bargain-value skiing.

Major attractions include the historical centres of Sarajevo and Mostar, which counterpoint splendid Ottoman stone architecture with quirky bars, inviting street-terrace cafes, traditional barbecue restaurants and vibrant arts scenes. Nature abounds here, in places like eastern Bosnia's Sutjeska National Park just outside Sarajevo. Hercegovina's incredible Kravica Waterfall and the Ottoman mini-towns of Počitelj and Blagaj are like tiny gems on the horizon, while Jajce in western Bosnia combines cascades, lakes and rivers with fascinating historical sights in its town centre. Rafting and swimming on the gorgeous River Una is an unforgettable experience. According to the *Guardian*, flights from the UK to Bosnia and Hercegovina increased by 284% in 2025, so hurry and visit while the country is still relatively crowd-free and the prices are affordable. This is one of Europe's best-value destinations.

TRABANTOS/SHUTTERSTOCK

THE MAIN AREAS

SARAJEVO
Bustling Ottoman centre and the nation's best food. **p82**

MOSTAR
Celebrity bridge, magnificent Old Town. **p86**

WESTERN BOSNIA
Incredible waterfalls, rivers and verdant towns. **p90**

80

Find Your Way

Hiring your own car is the best way to explore Bosnia & Hercegovina. For those not wishing to drive, the bus network is reasonably priced and efficient. Trains are limited but pleasant.

BUS & TRAIN

Reasonably priced, with comprehensive coverage and frequent departures. Bus stations pre-sell tickets. Trains are less frequent and with a limited network. ŽFBH (*zfbh.ba*) has an online rail timetable search.

CAR

Hiring a car is the best way to travel at your own pace and to visit regions with minimal public transport. Car rental is easy to organise.

Sarajevo, p82

Stroll around Baščaršija's fascinating Ottoman alleyways, sip Bosnian coffee and savour the nation's best *burek* and *ćevapi*.

Mostar, p86

Gawp at the magnificently rebuilt Mostar bridge, wander the cute Old Town and see one of the most spectacular remnants of Yugoslav architecture.

Western Bosnia, p90

Watch the waterfall tumble photogenically past Jajce's castle-crowned Old Town and raft down one of Bosnia & Hercegovina's fast-flowing rivers.

CROATIA

Novi Grad
Bosanska Dubica
Bosanska Gradiška
Prijedor
Bosanski Petrovac
Bosanska Krupa
Kulen Vakuf
Bihać

Sremska Mitrovica
Bijeljina
Brčko
Tuzla
Doboj
Zvornik
Kladanj
Vlasenica
Srebrenica
SERBIA

Drina
Sava
Bosna

Banja Luka
Kotor Varoš
Jajce
Tešanj
Žepče
Zenica
Travnik
Bugojno
Vareš

Glamoč
Mrkonjić Grad
Ključ
Bosansko Grahovo

Vrbas

Livno
Tomislav Grad
Posušje
Široki Brijeg

Jablanica
Konjić

SARAJEVO
Sarajevo City Hall
Jahorina

Nerreva

★ Stari Most
Mostar
Pocitelj
Stolac

Goražde
Višegrad
Šćepan Polje
Gacko

MONTENEGRO

Nikšić
Trebinje
PODGORICA

Split
BRAČ
HVAR
KORČULA
Dubrovnik

Adriatic Sea

N

100 km
50 miles

NIGLAYNIK/SHUTTERSTOCK

Buna River (p89), Blagaj

Plan Your Time

Explore Sarajevo and Mostar, but make sure you go into the mountains and river valleys to do some hiking and rafting. This is where the real charm of Bosnia and Hercegovina lies.

If You Only Do One Thing

● In **Sarajevo** (p82), stroll the Ottoman city centre, drink coffee, eat local food and go out with the locals. Alternatively, in **Mostar** (p86), meander around the Old Town and admire the Stari Most and the turquoise Neretva River. Add a visit to nearby **Blagaj** (p89) for beautiful architecture and local trout.

Four Days to Travel Around

● After a day in **Sarajevo** (p82), stop in **Mostar** (p86) on the way to the spectacular **Kravica Waterfall** (p89), where you can spend a few hours and take a dip. Follow this with the hilltop gem of **Počitelj** (p89). The next day, choose between a stop in **Blagaj** (p89) or **Stolac** and the **Radimlja Necropolis** (p89).

SEASONAL HIGHLIGHTS

SPRING
Beat the heat in Hercegovina and see flowers bloom in Bosnia. Rivers are at peak flow. The best time for hiking.

SUMMER
Hot and sweaty, but great for swimming in rivers. The **Sarajevo Film Festival** happens in August.

AUTUMN
The heat is less intense, the nights are cooler and the rains have yet to begin – the ideal time to visit.

WINTER
Skiing gets cheaper after the New Year holidays and the snow usually lasts until mid-March.

81

Sarajevo

UNIQUE ATMOSPHERE | HISTORY | STREET LIFE

GETTING AROUND

Sarajevo has trams, buses, trolleybuses and minibuses, all operated by GRAS *(gras.ba)*. You can pre-purchase tickets from kiosks or buy them from the driver. They must be stamped once aboard; inspections are common. Tram 3 leaves from Ilidža, passes the National Museum then loops one way (anticlockwise) around Baščaršija. Tram 1 starts at the railway station, then does the same loop as Tram 3.

For reliable on-the-meter fares (2KM plus about 1KM per kilometre) download the Moj Taxi app *(mojtaxi.ba)*. Avoid the taxis waiting outside the airport.

☑ **TOP TIP**

The best way to get a feel for the city is to stroll the Old Town's lanes and avenues, then climb the picturesque slopes of Vratnik for sweeping views..

Ringed by mountains, Sarajevo is a singular city with an atmosphere all its own. Meander around the Ottoman quarter of Baščaršija and enjoy a meal or local coffee at the smoking barbecue restaurants and cafes. Peek into the mosques, churches and synagogues, and marvel at the dilapidating socialist architecture. Then it's time to join the locals in the lively and stylish bars and restaurants. The 20th century thrust Sarajevo into the world's consciousness, from the assassination that precipitated WWI to the successful 1984 Winter Olympics to the brutal almost-four-year siege of the city in the 1990s. Once renowned as the Jerusalem of Europe for its religious diversity, Sarajevo is now a largely divided place, with most of the Serb population living in Istočno Sarajevo (East Sarajevo) on the Republika Srpska side. But the scars are fading with each passing year and Sarajevo has become a wonderful destination to visit. Enjoy its intriguing architectural medley, vibrant street life and irrepressible spirit.

Explore Baščaršija, the Heart of Sarajevo

Atmospheric alleys and architecture

Centred on **Sebilj Fountain**, **Baščaršija** ('barsh-char-shi-ya') is the heart of old Sarajevo. The name for the city's Ottoman-era market is derived from the Turkish for 'main market' and it's still lined with stalls, grand Ottoman mosques and inviting cafes. Splendid 16th-century buildings include the 1531 **Gazi Husrev-beg Mosque** *(vakuf-gazi.ba; 3KM)*, with its 45m minaret, and **Brusa Bezistan**, a former silk-trading bazaar. It now houses a branch of the **Museum of Sarajevo 1878–1918** *(muzejsarajeva.ba; entry 5KM)*.

Religious Harmony Throughout the Centuries

From synagogues to Orthodox cathedrals

Sarajevo has been home to Muslims, Jews and Christians for centuries and it remains so to a lesser degree to this day. The

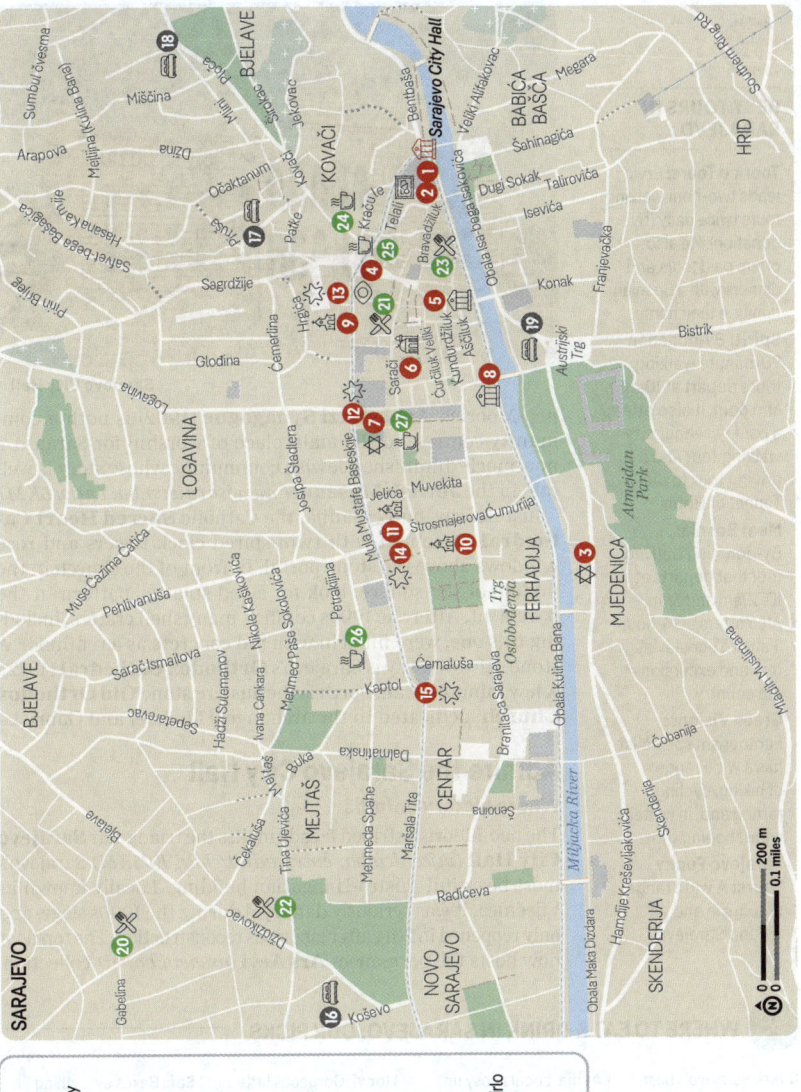

SARAJEVO

HIGHLIGHTS
1 Sarajevo City Hall

SIGHTS
2 Ars Aevi
3 Ashkenazi Synagogue
4 Baščaršija
5 Brusa Bezistan
6 Gazi Husrev-beg Mosque
7 Jewish Museum
8 Museum of Sarajevo 1878–1918
9 Old Orthodox Church
10 Orthodox Cathedral
11 Sacred Heart Cathedral
see 4 Sebilj Fountain

ACTIVITIES
12 Meet Bosnia
13 Sarajevo Funky Tours
14 Spirit
15 Toorico Tours

SLEEPING
16 Colors Inn
17 Halvat Guest House
18 Hotel Aziza
19 Isa-begov Hamam Hotel

EATING
20 Avlija
21 Dveri
22 Noovi
23 Sač

DRINKING & NIGHTLIFE
24 Čajdžinica Džirlo
25 Dibek
26 Kawa
27 Slatko ćoše

BEST TOURS IN SARAJEVO

Toorico Tours: Ervin leads two-hour walking tours twice daily (by donation). He also offers paid tours and dinners with a Bosnian family in their home.

Spirit: By-donation 90-minute walking tours depart at 10am and 6pm. It also offers a paid two-hour city walking tour and a driving tour to the Tunnel of Hope.

Meet Bosnia: By-donation walking tour that departs at 10.30am and 3pm. Also offers a 3½-hour 'Fall of Yugoslavia' tour and excursions to the country.

Green Visions: Ecotourism specialist has a wide range of hiking, cycling, rafting and, in winter, snowshoeing trips.

Sarajevo Funky Tours: A wide range of tours in and around Sarajevo.

Sarajevo City Hall

neo-Moorish **Ashkenazi Synagogue** (1902) is both a community centre and the main place of worship for Sarajevo's now much-diminished Jewish community, whose story is well told in the **Jewish Museum** *(muzejsarajeva.ba; entry 5KM)*.

Just nearby, on Ferhadija, the Catholic **Sacred Heart Cathedral** is fronted with twin-spired clock towers and rose windows above the stone portal. In front of the church in the middle of the square, look for a red splatter pattern in the pavement. After the 1990s conflict, many shell craters, including this one, were filled in with red concrete as a reminder. A stone's throw away is Sarajevo's **Orthodox Cathedral** (1872). A few minutes' walk north is the austere stone **Old Orthodox Church**, dedicated to the archangels Michael and Gabriel.

Admire the Sarajevo City Hall

Where history unfolds

The neo-Moorish striped facade makes the triangular **Sarajevo City Hall** *(vijecnica.ba; entry adult/child 10/5KM)* Sarajevo's most beautiful Austro-Hungarian building. Locally known as Vijećnica, it was seriously damaged during the 1990s siege, and only reopened in 2014 after laborious reconstruction. The top floor now hosts the permanent **Ars Aevi** *(arsaevi.ba)* art collection.

 WHERE TO EAT & DRINK IN SARAJEVO: OUR PICKS

Dveri: Sarajevo's best restaurant is this 'country cottage' spot with an enchanting atmosphere. Serves goulash, Bosnian specialities and inky risottos. *8am-11pm* €€	**Avlija**: Locals cosy up here for home cooking in a buzzing covered yard, dangling with trailing pot plants, strings of peppers and the odd birdcage. *8am-11pm* €€	**Noovi**: Gorgeous little courtyard with a small but eclectic menu of steaks, pizzas and vegetarian dishes, plus a good wine list. Local favourite. *noon-11pm Tue-Sun* €€	**Sač**: Bakes everything *ispod sača*-style – under a domed metal lid covered with charcoal. Our pick for Sarajevo's best *burek* and *sirnica*. *8.30am-11pm* €
Kawa: A popular neighbourhood cafe on a hill overlooking the city, yet close to the centre. The views are amazing and the coffee is excellent. *8am-11pm*	**Dibek**: The place to try Bosnian coffee and taste *tucana kahva* (coffee ground in a mortar and pestle) on low stools beneath a central plane tree. *8am-2am*	**Slatko čoše**: Baščaršija's favourite coffee and cake spot, where you can try Bosnian coffee and Turkish tea, and sweeten it up with a Bosnian dessert. *6.30am-10pm*	**Čajdžinica Džirlo**: Minuscule but brimming with character, Džirlo brews 29 types of tea, many of them made from distinctive Bosnian herbs. *8.30am-11pm*

Beyond Sarajevo

The area around Sarajevo is a patchwork of gorgeous landscapes, interesting towns and good skiing.

Sarajevo is surrounded by some amazing mountains. Make sure you get out and explore them, summer or winter. Aside from the capital, however, eastern Bosnia is largely off the radar for most travellers. The sad legacy of ethnic cleansing has cast a pall over much of the region, although many stop to pay their respects at Srebrenica, the most notorious site of all. The main places of interest include the magnificent Sutjeska National Park and skiing at Jahorina and Bjelašnica. Most sights can be easily reached on a day trip from Sarajevo.

Places

Jahorina p85

Bjelašnica p85

Sutjeska National Park p85

GETTING AROUND

You'll need your own car to get to Sutjeska National Park and the ski slopes.

Jahorina

TIME FROM SARAJEVO: **40MIN** 🚗

Ski Olympic slopes

Of Sarajevo's two Olympic skiing resorts, **Jahorina Olympic Centre** (*oc-jahorina.com; entry adult day pass 86KM*), 26km southeast of the city on the Republika Srpska side, has the widest range of hotels. Stay at the upmarket **Termag Hotel** (p92). **Rajska Vrata** is a charming ski-in alpine chalet off of Jahorina's longest run.

Bjelašnica

TIME FROM SARAJEVO: **1¼HR** 🚗

Winter sports & hiking trails

The modest ski resort of **Bjelašnica** (*ocbjelasnica.com; entry adult day pass 47KM*), around 25km south of Sarajevo, has eight runs and there's usually enough snow to ski by Christmas. February usually has the best snow. Love competitive mountain walking? Check out the Vučko Trail (*vuckotrail.ba*).

Sutjeska National Park

TIME FROM SARAJEVO: **2HR** 🚗

Tjentište: A magnificent monument

Tjentište is the site of the **Memorial Complex to the Battle of Sutjeska**. Built in honour of one of the bloodiest WWII battles in Yugoslavia, it was designed by sculptor Miodrag Živković in 1971 and is considered one of the most complex memorials in the former Yugoslav region.

Mostar

OLD BRIDGE | OLD TOWN | MAGNIFICENT RIVER

GETTING AROUND

Mostar has its own airport, with flights to Belgrade, Zagreb and beyond. However, many use Dubrovnik and Split airports (both in Croatia) to reach Mostar.

The one railway line runs from Ploče (in Croatia) to Mostar and on to Sarajevo through the Neretva Canyon. The main centres are all well connected by bus.

☑ TOP TIP

Many visitors find crossing the Old Bridge a slippery experience – rather than floundering and sliding around on the smooth stone surface, make sure you step firmly on the protruding 'treads' that line the arc of the bridge, like a true Mostarian.

Mostar is the largest city in Hercegovina and the country's biggest tourist attraction. It has a small but thoroughly enchanting Old Town, which is where you'll find the fittingly named Old Bridge, which forms a majestic stone arc between medieval towers and crosses the rushing turquoise waters of the Neretva River below. At dusk the lights of numerous millhouse restaurants twinkle across the gushing streams, while narrow Kujundžiluk bustles with trinket sellers.

After the summer day trippers have departed, savvy travellers who have chosen to base themselves here can enjoy memorable regional attractions as well as ponder the city's darker side. Beyond the cobbled lanes of the attractively restored Ottoman quarter are entire blocks of bombed-out buildings, a poignant legacy of the 1990s conflict. Between November and April most tourist facilities are in hibernation, while summer is scorchingly hot. Spring and autumn are ideal times to visit.

Admire the Splendid Old Bridge

The Balkans' most celebrated span

The world-famous **Stari Most** (meaning 'Old Bridge') is the indisputable heart of Mostar and its pale stone magnificently reflects the golden glow of sunset. The bridge's swooping arch was originally built between 1557 and 1566 on the orders of Suleiman the Magnificent. An engineering marvel in its time, it was pounded into the river during a deliberate Croatian artillery attack in November 1993. The current structure is a faithful 21st-century rebuild.

Don't miss Mostar's best shopping experience, on either sides of the bridge, at the bustling **Kujundžiluk Bazaar**.

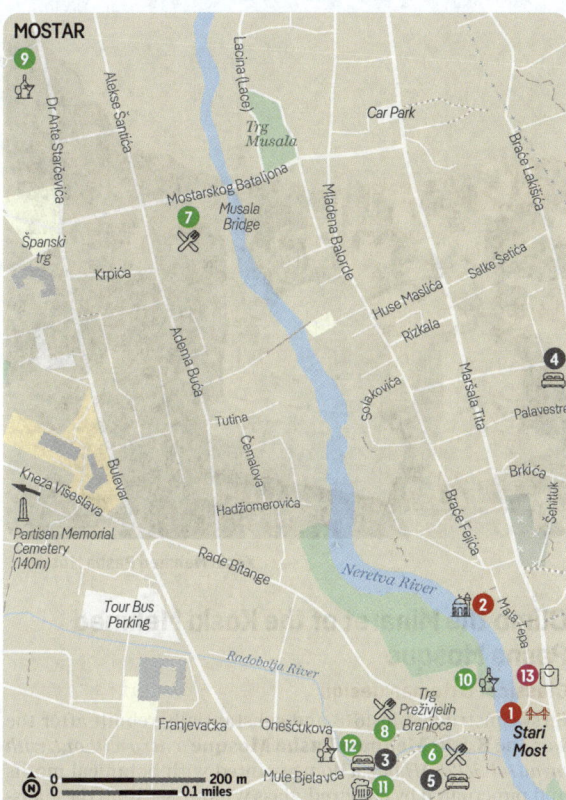

MOSTAR

★ **HIGHLIGHTS**
1 Stari Most

● **SIGHTS**
2 Koski Mehmed Pasha
  Mosque

● **SLEEPING**
3 Kriva Ćuprija 1
4 Muslibegović House
5 Villa Čardak

● **EATING**
6 Hindin Han
see 3 Konoba Taurus
7 Nacionalni Restoran
  MM
8 Podrum

● **DRINKING &
NIGHTLIFE**
9 Club Calamus
10 Duradžik
11 Ima i Može Craft Beer
  Garden
12 Ljetna Bašta Oscar

● **SHOPPING**
13 Kujundžiluk Bazaar

Watch Divers on the Stari Most

Cold river plunge

Every summer, young men leap from the parapet of Stari Most, plummeting more than 20m into the freezing cold Neretva River. Divers won't leap until 50KM has been collected (in winter it's double). If you want to see professionals compete, watch the **annual diving competition** in late July. In September, the **Red Bull Cliff Diving** (*cliffdiving.redbull.com*) competition attracts international divers and an audience of thousands.

 WHERE TO EAT IN MOSTAR: OUR PICKS

Konoba Taurus: One of Mostar's best, with a terrace next to the Crooked Bridge. Chef Amnerisa cooks traditional food and Dalmatian specialities. *11am-11pm* €€

Podrum: Right at the entrance to the Old Town with a little terrace on the cobbled street, this place is great for *ćevapi* and all kinds of grilled meat. *11am-11pm* €€

Hindin Han: This atmospheric old mill cottage serves a mixture of local dishes. Aim for a table on one of the terraces above the Radobolja River. *11am-midnight* €€

Nacionalni Restoran MM: The perfect place to taste homemade Bosnian food. Try the local favourite, *buredžici – burek* covered in garlicky yoghurt. *8am-6pm* €€

MOSTAR'S HISTORY

Mostar means 'bridge-keeper' and the 16th-century construction of the Stari Most marks an era of prosperity for Mostar during the Ottoman Empire. Under Austro-Hungarian rule in the 19th century, the city's centre of gravity shifted north to Trg Musala, with its lovely neo-Moorish buildings. Before the 1990s conflict, Mostar had one of Yugoslavia's largest proportions of mixed marriages. When the Yugoslav army started bombarding Mostar in April 1992, the city's Bosniaks and Croats banded together, but on 9 May 1993 a conflict erupted between the former allies. A front line emerged north–south along the Bulevar, with Croats to the west and Bosniaks to the east. Every building in the city suffered damage; around 2000 people lost their lives.

GIRAFFE VIDEO STUDIO/SHUTTERSTOCK

Koski Mehmed Pasha Mosque

Climb the Minaret of the Koski Mehmed Pasha Mosque

Classical Ottoman design

First constructed in 1618 and substantially rebuilt after the war, the **Koski Mehmed Pasha Mosque** *(entry without/with minaret 6/12KM)* has a dome painted with botanical motifs and punctuated by coloured-glass windows. Climb the claustrophobic minaret for sweeping town views.

Visit a Fascinating Partisan Memorial

Awe-inspiring architecture

Although sadly neglected and badly vandalised, the **Partisan Memorial Cemetery** is nonetheless a must-visit in Mostar for fans of 20th-century socialist architecture. It was designed by leading Yugoslav-era architect Bogdan Bogdanović and completed in 1965. Paths wind up to the upper section, which contains the gravestones of 810 Mostar partisans who died fighting fascism during WWII.

WHERE TO DRINK IN MOSTAR: OUR PICKS

Duradžik: This rock-edged bar spills into the central courtyard of the Tabhana (former tannery). There's live music most evenings at midnight. *6pm-3am Mon-Sat*

Club Calamus: Perched on top of an inauspicious-looking office building, this urbane rooftop bar offers cocktails and engrossing city views. It stages live music. *7am-2am*

Ima i Može Craft Beer Garden: Craft-beer lovers will enjoy this open-sided wooden pavilion above the Radobolja River; it has frequent live music and DJ nights. *9am-11pm*

Ljetna Bašta Oscar: Set in a large shady garden, this cafe-bar and chill-out place creates an exotic feel with giant cushions, hammocks and colourful fabrics. *10am-2am*

Beyond
Mostar

This is Hercegovina, the sun-scorched south, home to lovely waterfalls and small towns.

Hercegovina's arid Mediterranean landscape encompasses a distinctive beauty punctuated by barren mountain ridges and photogenic river valleys. Famed for its fine wines and sun-kissed fruit, the region is sparsely populated but features historic towns and a toehold on the Adriatic coast. Visit old Ottoman Blagaj and Počitelj, and swim beneath Kravica Waterfall. Hercegovina ('hair-tse-go-vi-na') takes its name from 15th-century Duke Stjepan Vukčić Kosača (*herceg* is 'duke' in the local lingo), under whose rule it became a semi-independent duchy of the Kingdom of Bosnia.

Places

Blagaj p89
Kravica Waterfall p89
Počitelj p89
Stolac p89

Blagaj

TIME FROM MOSTAR: **20MIN**

Relax by the Buna River

Pretty Blagaj hugs the turquoise Buna River at its source, where it gushes out of a cave to flow past a historical **tekke** (*tekijablagaj.ba/en; entry 10KM*) and Ottoman-era homesteads.

Kravica Waterfall

TIME FROM MOSTAR: **1HR**

Take a dip in emerald pools

In spring, the gorgeous **Kravica Waterfall** (*kravica.ba; entry adult/child 20/10KM*) pounds the water below with a dramatic, steamy fury. In summer it's a more gentle cascade, and the basin offers an idyllic respite from the sweltering heat.

Počitelj

TIME FROM MOSTAR: **40MIN**

An architectural ensemble

This medieval fortified village is one of the most beautiful spots in the country. Cupped in a steep rocky amphitheatre, it's a warren of stairways, stone-roofed houses and pomegranate bushes.

Stolac

TIME FROM MOSTAR: **45MIN**

Admire ancient tombstones

Stolac is one of Hercegovina's prettiest castle towns, with a history going back to Roman times. In the vicinity of Stolac are two sets of classic *stećci* (grave carvings). Beside the Mostar road, 3km west of Stolac, is the famous **Radimlja Necropolis**, a group of around 110 intricately carved white stone tombstones dating back to medieval times.

GETTING AROUND

The only railway line runs from Čapljina to Mostar and on to Sarajevo, though the main towns are all well connected by bus. The best way to see the area is to hire a car.

Western Bosnia

GUSHING RIVERS | GREEN FORESTS | LOVELY TOWNS

GETTING AROUND

Banja Luka is the region's biggest city and transport hub, though Bihać is also well connected.

Bus-hopping from Sarajevo via Visoko, Travnik and Jajce to Banja Luka is relatively straightforward.

Visiting the Una River valley is best done by car. Various Una rafting companies offer client pick-ups from Bihać.

☑ **TOP TIP**

Renting a car is recommended in order to really see the best of this wonderful region.

Travelling through this little-trodden region of green wooded hills, river canyons, lakes and historical towns is a rewarding experience. In the west, the Una River gushes flamboyantly over a series of waterfalls before joining the Sava on its rush to the Danube and, ultimately, the Black Sea. You can hop between the old Ottoman administrative capital Travnik and the gorgeous hilltop settlement of Jajce, with its town-centre cascades and gorgeous lakes for swimming. Make a stop in Visoko to see the weird and wonderful world of the alleged pyramids. Banja Luka is another good pit stop if you're passing through. You'll find yourself passing in and out of Bosniak-Croat Federation territory and the Republika Srpska. You'll know when you're in the latter by the profusion of Serbian flags.

Swim in Jajce's Gorgeous Lakes

Two rivers and a waterfall

Jajce is a historical gem, with a highly evocative walled Old Town clinging to a steep rocky knoll with rivers on two sides. The Pliva River tumbles into the Vrbas River by way of the impressive 21m-high **Jajce Waterfall**, right at the foot of the town walls. Immediately to the west, the Pliva is dammed to form two pretty lakes that are popular with swimmers, strollers, bikers and boaters. Between them lie the Mlinčići, a cute collection of 20 tiny wooden watermills. At the bottom of the lower, smaller lake, boardwalks cross a pretty set of rivulets spilling into a dam basin, which is a popular swimming spot.

Raft, Swim & Admire the Una River

A lush waterway of greens and opals

The adorable Una River has a variety of moods. In the green gorges to the northeast, some sections are as calm as mirrored opal, while others gush over widely fanned rapids. The **Una Aqua rafting centre** *(una-aqua.com; raft trip 100KM per person)* is an attraction in itself, comprising five small islands interlinked with wooden bridges. There's a good swimming

WESTERN BOSNIA

spot, a restaurant, a campsite and a treehouse cabin raised on stilts above a comfy waterside hammock.

The river broadens and gurgles over a series of shallow falls as it passes through the unassuming town of Bihać. Occasionally it leaps over more impressive falls, notably at **Štrbački Buk**, which forms the centrepiece of the 198-sq-km **Una National Park** (*nationalpark-una.ba; entry adult/child 12/8KM*). A strong contender for the title of the nation's most impressive waterfall, this is a dramatic 40m-wide cascade, pounding 23.5m down three travertine sections, including a superbly photogenic 18m drop-off, overlooked by a network of viewing platforms. The easiest access is 8km along a graded but potholed and unpaved section from Orašac on the Kulen Vakuf road. There are swimming holes to stop at along the way.

Amble Around Pretty Travnik

Castle, cheese and a Nobel laureate

Once the seat of Bosnia's viziers (Ottoman governors), the castle town of **Travnik** is now best known for its sheep's cheese and for being the birthplace of Nobel Prize–winning author Ivo Andrić. Travnik's 15th-century **Old Town Fortress** (*adult/child 3/1.50KM*) surveys the city from a shoulder of hillside. The stone walls gleam so brightly in the sun that they appear to have been scrubbed. The fortress looks over **Plava Voda** (Blue Water), a convivial gaggle of restaurants flanking a gurgling stream, crisscrossed by small bridges. You should definitely have your lunch here.

In the centre of town is the Sulejmanija Mosque, although everyone in Travnik calls it the **Many-Coloured Mosque** (*Šarena Džamija; free*), a longstanding nickname that references its famous frescoed facade.

TRAVNIK'S LITERARY PRODIGY

Travnik is the hometown of Yugoslav author Ivo Andrić, who won the Nobel Prize in Literature in 1961. The town is the setting of one of his most famous novels, *Bosnian Chronicle*. Although Travnik was under Austo-Hungarian rule when Andrić was born (1892), the author focused mainly on life under the Ottomans, and his lyrical style and perennial theme of the melancholy of passing time earned him the Nobel over authors such as JRR Tolkien, Robert Frost, John Steinbeck and EM Forster, all of whom were in the running that year.

Places We Love to Stay

€ Budget €€ Midrange €€€ Top End

Sarajevo
MAP p83

Halvat Guest House €€ The six rooms at this friendly, family-run guesthouse are clean and spacious, and surprisingly quiet for such a central location. Baščaršija is just down the road.

Colors Inn €€€ Modernist decor is given a dramatic twist with vast, wall-sized black-and-white photos of 20th-century Sarajevo. The 37 comfortable, stylish rooms have a kettle, coffee and chocolates. The breakfast is abundant.

Isa-begov Hamam Hotel €€€ An ornate 19th-century hammam and hotel (originally founded in 1492) has 15 delicious rooms designed to evoke the spirit of the age, with lashings of handcrafted dark-wood furniture. Guests get free use of the hammam.

Hotel Aziza €€€ This comfortable family-run hotel has 17 spacious, light-filled rooms that pay homage to the love story of its owners Mehmed and Aziza Poričanin. A daily sauna is included in the rates.

Jahorina

Termag Hotel €€ Traditional ideas and open fireplaces are given a stylish modern twist, and the rooms have excellent beds and sturdy woodwork. There's an excellent spa centre.

Bjelašnica

Hotel Han €€ Ski-in, ski-out access at the Bjelašnica resort, with stylishly appointed rooms that have been decorated like bleached Mondrian abstracts. In summer, the hotel rents bikes.

Mostar
MAP p87

Muslibegović House €€ An extremely charming boutique hotel, with a variety of room sizes and styles. The excellent modern bathrooms contrast with traditional Bosnian, Turkish and Moroccan design.

Kriva Ćuprija 1 €€ Inhabiting a cluster of stone buildings set around a millhouse restaurant in the heart of old Mostar, this atmospheric place has boutique-style bedrooms and immaculate bathrooms.

Villa Čardak €€ This old stone house on a central lane has been thoroughly modernised and now has seven spacious en-suite rooms; accent walls are emblazoned with forest scenes. There's also a small guest kitchen.

Blagaj

Hotel Blagaj €€ A professional 27-room hotel that has white and lavender walls and a nice terrace. It's just beyond the main car park en route to Blagaj Tekke.

Jajce

Hotel Stari Grad € Heavy beams, wood panelling and a heraldic fireplace give this comfortable place a sense of suavely modernised antiquity. The six standard rooms are somewhat cramped, but nicely decorated and clean.

Una River Valley

Kostelski Buk €€ Set beside a triple set of rapids, this luxurious hotel has stylish rooms with some of the most comfortable mattresses you could hope to sleep on. Some rooms have river views. The restaurant is excellent, too.

Opal Exclusive €€ Hidden away but only 300m north of central Bihać, the Opal's spacious rooms are modern and comfortable. The best have lovely views over the rapids. There's a terrace overlooking the river.

SENAD KOSTIC/SHUTTERSTOCK

Kostelski Buk

Practicalities

LGBTIQ+ Travellers

Homosexuality was decriminalised in 1998, but attitudes remain conservative. Although Bosnia and Hercegovina's gay community still faces many obstacles and prejudice, it is well organised. Pride Festivals have taken place annually since 2019 (with the exception of 2020). Check @bh.povorkaponosa on Instagram. LGBTIQ+ advocacy organisation Sarajevo Open Centre *(soc.ba)* is active in fighting sexuality-based discrimination.

SERGII FIGURNYI/SHUTTERSTOCK

Sacred Heart Cathedral (p84), Sarajevo

Dangers & Annoyances

Landmines and unexploded ordnance still affect 2% of Bosnia and Hercegovina's land area. For your safety, stick to paved surfaces or well-worn paths in affected areas, and avoid exploring war-damaged buildings. If you're going hiking, make sure you go with a professional guide.

Accessible Travel

Bosnia's steep townscapes are full of stairways and rough streets that can prove awkward if you have mobility issues. A few places have wheelchair ramps to serve those wounded in the war, but smaller hotels won't have lifts and disabled toilets remain rare.

Smoking

Some consider smoking to be Bosnia's Olympic sport. It is prevalent indoors and out, although new laws mean that there are now designated non-smoking areas in most establishments.

Opening Hours

Banks 8am–6pm Monday to Friday, 8.30am–1.30pm Saturday
Bars and Cafes 8am–11pm
Restaurants 7am–10.30pm, or until the last customer
Shops 8am–6pm daily; many stay open later

Etiquette

It's polite to remove footwear before entering a home or guesthouse. If entering a mosque or church, cover legs and shoulders. In mosques, women should cover their hair with a scarf (usually provided).

Public Holidays

New Year's Day 1 and 2 January
Orthodox Christmas 7 January
Republika Day (Srpska) 9 January
Orthodox New Year 14 January
Independence Day 1 March
Easter & Easter Monday (Catholic/Orthodox) March or April
May Day 1 and 2 May
Ramazan Bajram June
Kurban Bajram August or September
All Saints Day 1 November
Statehood Day 25 November
Catholic Christmas 25 December

Language

The official languages are Bosnian, Croatian and Serbian; the guide below is for Bosnian. The official writing system uses both the Roman and Cyrillic alphabets.

Basics

Hello. Zdravo/Здраво. *zdra·vo*
Goodbye. Doviđenja/Довиђења. *do·vee·dje·nya*
Yes. Da/Да. *da*
No. Ne/Не. *ne*
Please. Molim/Молим. *mo·lim*
Thank you. Hvala/Хвала. *hva·la*
Excuse me. Izvinite/Извините. *iz·vee·nee·te*
Sorry. Žao mi je/Жао ми. *zha·o mi ye*

What's your name?
Kako se zovete/zoveš? (pol/inf)
Како се зовете/зовеш?
ka·ko se zo·ve·te/zo·vesh

My name is ...
Zovem se .../ Зовем се ... *zo·vem se*

Do you speak English?
Govorite/Govoriš li engleski? (pol/inf)
Говорите/Говориш ли енглески?
go·vo·ri·te/go·vo·rish li en·gle·ski

I don't understand.
Ne razumijem./Не разумијем. *ne ra·zu·mi·yem*

Shopping & Services

I'm looking for...
Tražim ... / Тражим... *tra·zhim*

How much is it?
Koliko košta ...? / Колико кошта ...? *ko·li·ko kosh·ta*

That's too expensive.
To je preskupo. / То је прескупо. *to ye pre·sku·po*

Emergencies

Help! Upomoć!/Упомоћ! *u·po·moch*
Go away! Idite!/Идите! *i·di·te*
Call ...! Zovite ...!/Зовите ...! *zo·vi·te*

  a doctor ljekara/љекара *lye·ka·ra*

  the police policiju/полицију *po·li·tsi·yu*

I'm lost.
Izgubljen/Izgubljena sam. (m/f)
Изгубљен/Изгубљена сам. (m/f)
iz·gub·lyen/iz·gub·lyena sam

I'm ill.
Ja sam bolestan/bolesna. (m/f)
Ја сам болестан/болесна. (m/f)
ya sam bo·le·stan/bo·le·sna

Eating & Drinking

What would you recommend?
Šta biste preporučili?
Шта бисте препоручили?
shta bi·ste pre·po·ru·chi·li

Do you have vegetarian food?
Da li imate vegetarijanski obrok?
Да ли имате вегетаријански оброк?
da li i·ma·te ve·ge·ta·ri·yan·ski o·brok

Cheers! Živjeli!/Живјели! *zhi·vye·li*

Can I have the bill/menu please?
Mogu li dobiti račun/jelovnik, molim?
Могу ли добити рачун/јеловник, молим?
mo·gu li do·bi·ti ra·chun/ye·lov·nik mo·lim

NUMBERS

1
jedan
један
ye·dan

2
dva/два *dva*

3
tri/три *tri*

4
četiri
четири
che·ti·ri

5
pet/пет *pet*

6
šest/шест
shest

7
sedam/
седам
se·dam

8
osam/осам
o·sam

9
devet/девет
de·vet

10
deset/десет
de·set

Tram (p82), Sarajevo

MONEY

Currency: Bosnian Convertible Mark (KM)

ATMS

ATMs accepting Visa and MasterCard are ubiquitous in city centres and towns, but will charge around 10KM for withdrawals. Before withdrawing money, compare the different ATM fees to find the cheapest option.

CREDIT CARDS

Top-end hotels, airline offices and upmarket boutiques generally accept major credit cards. You should be able to pay by card at most restaurants (bar the cheapest ones). Pay by cash in the budget category, whether you are at a hotel, restaurant or bar.

DIGITAL PAYMENTS

You can use digital payments in fancier restaurants, hotels and shops. Outside of major cities, always carry cash.

Arriving & Getting Around

Transport is reasonably priced and generally efficient. Bus services are excellent and inexpensive, while trains are slower, less extensive and cheaper. Driving is the best way to explore the country.

Arriving By Air
Sarajevo International Airport is Bosnia's busiest, with flights connecting to Europe and the Middle East. **Tuzla International Airport** is tiny but a hub for budget airline WizzAir. Mostar also has international flights.

Train
Trains are slower and less frequent than buses, but also slightly cheaper. ŽFBH (*zfbh. ba*) has an online rail timetable. The main routes are Sarajevo–Visoko–Bihać and Sarajevo–Konjic–Mostar–Ploče (in Croatia).

Car
Driving makes sense in more remote areas. There are a few toll roads in the centre of the country; collect your ticket where you enter, then pay at the toll booths when you exit.

Bus
Bus services are excellent and relatively inexpensive. There are often different companies handling each route, so prices can vary substantially. Luggage stowed in the baggage compartment under the bus costs extra (around 2KM a piece). Bus stations pre-sell tickets.

95

Curated by
Leonid Ragozin

Bulgaria

ANCIENT MONUMENTS, GREAT OUTDOORS, BEACHES GALORE

The only country in the EU that uses the Cyrillic alphabet is just one of the many things that makes Bulgaria special.

Occupying a large chunk of the Balkans, Bulgaria is a land of sombre mountains ranges, some of Europe's most ancient cities, lovely countryside, the beautiful (if overdeveloped) Black Sea coast and rose shrubs on every corner. It was at the centre of action in Europe through much of antiquity and into the Middle Ages, with succeeding empires and kingdoms each leaving an architectural and cultural footprint, starting with Rome. The supranational structure it now finds itself a part of is the EU: Bulgaria joined the Schengen Area in 2025 and replaced its currency with the euro in 2026.

The capital, Sofia, is a city that has some of the best features of southeastern Europe: an easygoing atmosphere, a lively and increasingly sophisticated restaurant and cafe scene, and plenty of historical monuments, from Roman to communist. Two other major historical hubs, Plovdiv and Veliko Târnovo, are also filled with millennia-old stories and monuments. The mountains south of Sofia are the country's outdoor nexus, with multiple opportunities for skiing and hiking. The Black Sea coast is also steeped in ancient history, with settlements like Nesebâr tracing its roots back to ancient Greece. Although it's endowed with beautiful sandy beaches, this region does suffer from overtourism.

ROSSHELEN/SHUTTERSTOCK

THE MAIN AREAS

SOFIA
Bulgaria's historic but youthful capital. **p100**

BLACK SEA COAST
Sandy beaches, ancient Greek legacy. **p107**

CENTRAL BULGARIA
Roman ruins and Bulgarian heritage. **p111**

For places to stay
in Bulgaria, see
p115

JOVAN M/SHUTTERSTOCK

Left: Stadium of Philippopolis (p112), Plovdiv; Above: Aleksander Nevski Cathedral (p101), Sofia

Find Your Way

International airports at Sofia, Burgas and Varna serve as the main entry points for travellers. An extensive network of bus routes and ramshackle trains connect most places around the country.

BUSES & TRAINS

Travelling around Bulgaria means combining buses and trains. Buses (book tickets on *obilet.com*) are often faster and the network is more extensive. Trains (book tickets on *bileti.bdz.bg*) provide more leg space, but little else.

CAR

Renting a car is a fun and rewarding way to explore Bulgaria. The main rental hubs around the country are Sofia, Varna and Burgas. To avoid unexpected charges, it's best to book directly from local operators, such as *toprentacar.bg*.

Sofia, p100

Bulgaria's capital is full of life and youthful energy, and peppered with architectural monuments from different epochs.

Central Bulgaria, p111

Plovdiv and Veliko Tărnovo are quintessentially Bulgaria and have heaps of cultural heritage.

Black Sea Coast, p107

Bulgaria's beaches are wide, sandy and filled to the brim during a rather short season. But there are also ancient treasures to explore.

Dobrich

Varna

Archaeological Museum

Nesebăr

Burgas

Sozopol

Sredets

Black Sea

Shumen

Razgrad

Yambol

Targovishte

Sliven

Ruse

Stara Zagora

Veliko Tărnovo

Kazanlăk

ROMANIA

Haskovo

Pleven

Lovech

Centralen Balkan

Troyan

Kărdzhali

Cherven Bryag

Panagyurishte

Plovdiv

Evros (Marítsa)

Pazardzhik

Shiroka Lăka

Komotini

Vratsa

Montana

Velingrad

Gotse Delchev

Rilski Rila manastir

Kalotina

Rilski Rila manastir

Aleksander Nevski Cathedral

Sveta Sofia Church

SOFIA

Pernik

Dupnitsa

Bansko

Pirin National Park

Sandanski

Kyustendil

Blagoevgrad

Strumica

Petrich

GREECE

SERBIA

NORTH MACEDONIA

100 km

50 miles

N

Veliko Târnovo (p114)

Plan Your Time

Distances are large and trains are slow, so factor in extra time to get around. It's best to plan your trip in advance.

Three Days

● Spend two days in **Sofia** (p100) and explore its numerous monuments and museums; enjoy the city's easygoing ambience. Take a hike up **Mt Vitosha** (p103) and make sure you visit the ancient **Boyana Church** (p103). On day three, take a tour to the **Rila Monastery** (p104) and try to fit a visit to the **Seven Rila Lakes** (p104) into your itinerary.

With More Time

● Follow the three-day itinerary, then head to **Veliko Târnovo** (p114) and immerse yourself in the essence of Bulgaria. Make your way to **Varna** (p107) and begin exploring the **Black Sea coast** (p107), moving south to **Burgas** (p108) via **Nesebār** (p108). Return to Sofia via **Plovdiv** (p111), where you can visit the Roman ruins and the wonderful Old Town.

SEASONAL HIGHLIGHTS

SPRING

The Black Sea is too cold for swimming, but everything is in bloom. An ideal time for hiking and exploring culture.

SUMMER

As the temperatures climb, locals seek refuge in the mountains and by the sea. Beaches fill up with sunseekers.

AUTUMN

September is prime festival season in seaside cities, but the mercury drops soon after, most in the mountains.

WINTER

Snow blankets the mountain peaks: time to get out the skis and enjoy a white Christmas.

Sofia

ROMAN RUINS | MEDIEVAL CHURCHES | MOUNTAIN AIR

GETTING AROUND

Sofia has a convenient public transit system: the three metro lines are supplemented by multiple bus and tram routes going in all directions from the metro stations. Electronic tickets are available at metro stations, and the metro also conveniently connects the city to the airport.

While you don't need a car in the city, it is a good place to pick one up for further travels. Rental agencies, like *greenrentacar.bg*, are located at the airport and in shopping malls. A bike-share network exists, but leaves much to be desired.

☑ TOP TIP

Sofia has its own nature park on Mt Vitosha, with dozens of hiking trails in summer and ski slopes in winter.

The chef who prepared this spicy cultural stew chose to throw a bit of everything into the mix. Tramlines and fin-de-siècle buildings give Sofia a measure of Central European charm with more than a whiff of imperial grandeur. Mosques and Turkish baths provide a strong Levantine flavour. Communist-era neoclassicism and Cyrillic script add an air of political intrigue. Sundrenched streets, Roman ruins, cafe tables scattered in squares and mountains in the distance remind travellers that they are within the Mediterranean cultural universe. And the best time to visit Sofia is now: it's fairly well organised, easy to get around and increasingly cosmopolitan, but thankfully still devoid of the slick sterility of richer European capitals. Its captivating ambience feels organic, deriving from the natural charm of its friendly and energetic inhabitants.

Central Sofia

Roman foundations

The heart of Sofia is a peculiar organism that lives above and below ground: the **Ancient Serdica Complex** *(entry free)*, plus two medieval churches, all wrapped up in a subway transfer hub and topped with a massive Soviet-style government compound known as the **Largo**.

The Serdi, the Celtic tribe that lived here in antiquity, gave its name to Ulpia Serdica, a Roman settlement and the precursor of today's Sofia. The two connected metro stations, **Serdika** and **Serdika II**, envelope two large Roman ruins from this era. You'll see fragments of eight streets, an early Christian basilica, and baths and houses dating from the 4th to 6th centuries.

Surrounded on all sides by the Serdica site, the quaint **Sveta Petka Samardzhiiska Church** hails from another era. It was built during the early years of Ottoman rule (late 14th century), hence its subterranean position and inconspicuous exterior. Inside are some 16th-century murals.

The vast courtyard formed by the Largo complex conceals an ancient gem: the **Sveti Georgi Rotunda**. This red-brick church was built in the 4th century CE, which makes it Sofia's oldest preserved building. It was initially designed as a Roman bath house but was repurposed as a church in the Roman or early Byzantine times. The murals inside were painted between the 10th and 14th centuries.

Dig into Bulgarian history

If you only get to visit one museum in Sofia, make it the **National Museum of Archaeology** (*Национален археологически музей; naim.bg; entry adult/concession €6/1.50*). Housed in a former mosque built in 1496, it displays a wealth of Thracian, Roman and medieval artefacts. Highlights include a mosaic floor from the Church of Sveta Sofia, a Thracian gold burial mask (4th century BCE) and a magnificent bronze head, thought to represent a Thracian king. Also look out for the heart-warmingly cute zoomorphic figurines from the prehistoric Chalcolithic period.

The original Sofia

Believed to be a contemporary of the Hagia Sophia in Istanbul, the **Sveta Sofia Church** (*Света София*) was built on the foundations of four earlier churches – as well as a Roman amphitheatre. The church dates back to the 4th century, during the reign of Roman emperor Constantine. In the 14th century, it gave the city its current name. A **subterranean museum** (*sofiahistory museum.bg; entry adult/concession €4/1.50*) houses an ancient necropolis, with 56 tombs and the remains of four other churches.

Church of fallen soldiers

One of the symbols not just of Sofia but of Bulgaria itself, the awe-inspiring **Aleksander Nevski Cathedral** (*Свети*

RED DECADES

Bulgaria was ruled by the Communist Party for 43 years. Memories of this period range from total resentment to deep nostalgia. Vestiges of the communist past are scattered around Sofia, with the **Largo complex** presiding over the centre and monuments on display at the **Museum of Socialist Art**. The main legacy is the sea of apartment blocks. Check out the **Red Flat** museum if you're curious about life during the communist era.

ANCIENT SERDICA

In addition to the main Largo ruins, remnants of ancient Serdica pop up throughout the centre. Excavated sites include the following:

Western Gate: Remains of two towers, by the St Joseph Catholic Cathedral at Tsar Boris 1.

Amphitheatre: Incorporated into the Arena di Serdica hotel at Budapeshta 2.

Roman Thermal Baths: Remnants of a Roman spa and temples by the Turkish Mineral Baths.

Konstantinov Quarter: Sophisticated Roman residential complexes in the courtyard of the President's Office.

Remains of Northern Wall: Stones from a 6th-century wall, built during the reign of Emperor Justinian.

BORYANA MANZUROVA/SHUTTERSTOCK

Mt Vitosha

Александър Невски; cathedral.bg) was built between 1882 and 1912 in memory of the 200,000 Russian soldiers who died fighting for Bulgaria's independence during the Russo-Turkish War (1877–78). It was named in honour of a 13th-century Russian warrior-prince. The crypt houses the **Museum of Christian Art** *(nationalgallery.bg; entry adult/concession €4/1.50),* Bulgaria's biggest and best collection of icons, stretching back to the 5th century.

Cafe culture and mountain views

The attraction of Sofia's main pedestrian strip, **Vitosha Boulevard**, reveals itself immediately. The magnificent view of Mt Vitosha, which the street seems to abut (but doesn't), is always there – no matter if you're strolling around or sipping on a latte. The Byzantine silhouette of **Sveta Nedelya Cathedral** at the Serdika end of the boulevard is also quite imposing.

Built in the 20th-century interwar period, Vitosha Boulevard's arcades have a predictable array of high-end fashion brands and tourist-oriented cafes. If you'd like to enjoy a glass of wine or a meal, bear in mind that the best options are located in the smaller streets that run parallel to the main drag.

WHERE TO EAT IN CENTRAL SOFIA: OUR PICKS

Dark Sister: A bohemian haunt disguised as a sidewalk cafe. Food encompasses the Balkans and the Middle East, from hummus to schnitzel. *noon-10.30pm* €€

Izbata Tavern: One of the best places in town to sample Bulgarian food. The menu comes with an intriguing vegetarian section, plus lots of meat. *11am-11pm* €€

Moma Bulgarian Food & Wine: An update on a traditional *mehana* (tavern). Try the *gozba* pork stew cooked in a bread loaf and Bulgarian wine. *12.30-11.30pm* €€

Fake French: Not at all fake, but instead a creative take on French standards (eg onion soup), with a merry brasserie ambience. *6.30-11pm* €€

Fruit of the land

The city's oldest open-air market is known as the **Ladies' Market** *(Женски пазар)*; it stretches for several blocks along bul Stefan Stambolov, ending at the **Lions' Bridge**, a prominent landmark. The name derives from the Ottoman policy that forbids women from shopping anywhere else but this area. The section of the market closer to Serdika metro has lately acquired a more gentrified look, but further on, the place morphs into a much livelier traditional East European market, where mountains of fruit and vegetables adorn simple metal stalls and sellers chat amicably with customers.

Mt Vitosha Area

A breath of fresh mountain air

Not only does **Mt Vitosha** serve as a decorative element in Sofia's cityscape, but it also happens to be the capital's favoured hiking and skiing destination. There are dozens of clearly marked trails, a handful of hotels, cafes and restaurants, and numerous huts and chalets. The sightseeing highlight is **Zlatnite Mostove** *(Златните мостове)* – a spray of large boulders (a 'stone river') that tumbles down a slope from 1700m to 1350m.

Neither of the two cable-car services that once served Mt Vitosha were operational at the time of writing. It's best to either take a taxi or bus 63, which runs from the Krasno Selo metro station to the mountaintop, terminating near Zlatnite Mostove. This is the best place to start exploring the mountain.

Medieval frescoes

A visit to Mt Vitosha can be easily combined with a serious dive into history and art. One way to access the park is to take bus 64 to the final stop, which drops you off at the UNESCO-protected **Boyana Church** *(Боянска Църква; boyanachurch.info; entry adult/concession €6/1.50)*, one the most enchanting religious structures in the country and one of the rare examples of medieval Bulgarian religious art. Inside is a hall of 90 frescoes, the most important of which was painted in 1259 and depicts biblical scenes as well as portraits of the local overlord Kaloyan and his wife Desislava, who had them commissioned.

From the church, it's an arduous 3.1km climb to the **Boyana Waterfall**, followed by a 3.2km hike to Zlatnite Mostove. Or you can take bus 63 instead; hop on at the Kv *Boyana* bus stop.

BEST HIKES ON MT VITOSHA

Boyana Church–Zlatnite Mostove: Ask for directions to Boyana Waterfall. From there, obvious paths lead to Zlatnite Mostove (three hours).

Zlatnite Mostove–Mt Cherni Vrâh: A challenging hike, via Kumata Hut and Mt Sedloto (2018m; three hours).

Aleko–Mt Cherni Vrâh: Popular but steep trail (90 minutes on foot).

Aleko–Zlatnite Mostove: Follow the trail to Goli Vrâh, skirt around Mt Sredets (1969m) and pass Hotel Bor (three hours).

Dragalevtsi–Boyana: An easy 5km low-altitude route connecting two main entry points into Vitosha Nature Park.

 WHERE TO EAT IN CENTRAL SOFIA: OUR PICKS

Yum: Feast on Chinese dumplings, noodles and delicious salads in this tiny and intimate establishment with impeccable service. *noon-10pm* €€	**Krâchme Divaka:** In an appealing old house, this is a good choice for traditional Bulgarian food. Try the signature chicken soup cooked in a bread loaf. *noon-11pm* €€	**Manastirska Magernitsa:** Enormous and entertainingly idiosyncratic menu featuring recipes collected from monasteries across the country. *noon-11pm* €€	**Made in Blue:** A blue-coloured house with art on the wall and an outdoor patio. Middle Eastern flavours and seafood stand out on the eclectic menu. *noon-11pm* €€

Beyond Sofia

South of Sofia, Bulgaria's tallest mountains rise above the country's most important monastery, top ski resort and beautiful lakes.

Places

Rila Monastery p104
Seven Rila Lakes p104
Bansko p105

GETTING AROUND

It's best to explore these areas by car, especially if you're pressed for time. Buses from Sofia's central bus station are convenient for Bansko. The tour company Traventuria (*rilamonasterybus. com*) runs shuttle buses from Sofia to Rila Monastery and Seven Rila Lakes.

Two mountain ranges east of the road that connects Sofia to Greece are home to some of Bulgaria's most popular destinations. The Rila Mountains are the first chain you'll encounter when travelling south from the capital. This is where the heart of Bulgarian cultural identity was preserved at Rila Monastery, the holiest of the country's Orthodox sites. Also here are seven gorgeous mountain lakes that are strung together at the centre of prime hiking territory. Further south are the Pirin Mountains, Bulgaria's highest range and the home of Bansko, a once traditional mountain town that's become a favourite with skiers and digital nomads.

Rila Monastery

DISTANCE FROM SOFIA: 1¾HR

The holiest ground

Ensconced within a remote wooded enclave along the Rilska River, the **Rila Monastery** (*rilskimanastir.org; entry free*) is a living testament to centuries of faith, resilience and architectural artistry. This is Bulgaria's largest and most famous Orthodox monastery, and it's hard not to be awed by its spiritual significance, imposing scale and sheer grandeur of the fortress-like sanctuary: arcaded balconies are set around a cobblestone courtyard and the surrounding residential wings can house over 300 pilgrims. Plan on spending a couple of hours here. The monastery is in the Rila Mountains at an elevation of 1147m.

Seven Rila Lakes

DISTANCE FROM SOFIA: 1¾HR

Hike Bulgaria's lake country

Alpine vistas, glistening lakes and craggy mountain peaks – hiking the **Seven Rila Lakes** is arguably the most attractive

WHERE TO EAT: RILA MONASTERY & SEVEN RILA LAKES

Bakery: Just outside the monastery walls, this bakery sells freshly baked bread and *mekitsi* (Bulgarian donuts) accompanied by buffalo milk. *9.30am-4.30pm* €

Gorski Kut Hotel & Restaurant (p115): Right on the river with gorgeous forest views, five minutes from the monastery. The fresh trout is excellent. *10am-10pm* €€

Restaurant Gayzera: Traditional Bulgarian dishes, plenty of outdoor seating and a fireplace in colder weather. Located in Sapareva Banya. *noon-11.30 pm* €€

Lovna Hut: Serves traditional Bulgarian cuisine in a forested setting and also has accommodation. Walking distance from the Panichishte Chairlift. *10am-8pm* €€

DENNIS VAN DE WATER/SHUTTERSTOCK

Rila Monastery

AN ALPINE BASE

Over the past decade, Bansko has reinvented itself as one of Europe's digital nomad hubs. What began with a single coworking space has since blossomed into an international community of remote workers, drawn by the town's affordability, scenery and nomad scene. Each summer, the Bansko Nomad Fest attracts hundreds of laptop-toting wanderers, with a full schedule of talks, workshops and activities – it's the largest digital nomad gathering in the world. Outside of the week-long celebration, Bansko retains its cosmopolitan flair with coworking spaces like Altspace (altspacecoworking. com) providing reliable infrastructure and an instant network of new connections for the constant stream of temporary residents looking for a slice of mountain paradise.

open-air adventure in Bulgaria, and delivers some of Eastern Europe's most dramatic highland scenery for comparatively little effort. Cradled in the Rila Mountains, the area is defined by its seven glacial lakes, each named after its shape and connected via a complex system of streams.

To begin, take the **Panichishte Chairlift** (*€9 return*) to the start of the trailhead just outside **Rila Lakes Hut**. From here, follow a steep and rocky path up to a moderately challenging trail that traces a high ridge on a well-marked circular route. You'll tick off each member of the crystal-clear septet as you go, from Kidney Lake (2100m) to Tear Lake (2500m), which remains frozen for nine months of the year.

Bansko

DISTANCE FROM SOFIA: 2½HR

From skiing to mountain biking

Sitting 925m above sea level in the foothills of the **Pirin Mountains**, Bansko has transformed itself from a quiet revival-era town of cobbled streets, *mehana* (traditional taverns) and timber-framed houses into the country's busiest year-round resort. In winter, its slopes buzz with high-octane energy as skiers and snowboarders race down its groomed pistes, lured by the Alpine-style terrain at Balkan prices. In summer, the slopes become the playground of hikers and mountain bikers who fan out across the UNESCO-listed wilderness, tackling the park's craggy ridges and 118 glacial lakes.

WHERE TO EAT IN BANSKO: OUR PICKS

Mehana Vodenitsata: Next to main square, this timber-and-stone *mehana* serves grilled Bulgarian classics in generous portions, with a warm welcome. *noon-late* €€

Baryakova: Cosy mountain tavern known for grilled meats, seasonal dishes, wine and slow-cooked pork knuckle. *5pm-late Mon-Fri, from 11am Sat & Sun* €€

Dedo Yonkata: Family-run, 100-year-old house near the gondola, serving Pirin specialties in clay pots over wooden embers; spacious garden for dining. *10am-late* €€

Dedo Tase: This Old Town favourite has large portions of traditional fare: smoked meats, hearty soups, local cheeses and lamb skewers. *5-11pm Fri-Wed* €€

A SANCTUARY OF SPIRIT & IDENTITY

The hermit St John of Rila founded the Rila Monastery in the first half of the 10th century and it has been an active centre of worship and devotion ever since. Beyond its spiritual significance, it also played an important role in preserving Bulgaria's national identity, especially during Ottoman rule from the 15th to 19th centuries. During this time, the monastery not only protected monks from religious persecution but also safeguarded the Bulgarian language by preserving ancient manuscripts and books. Many of these are now displayed in the Church History Museum. The current buildings, including the main church, largely date from 1834–37, and were rebuilt after earlier structures were destroyed by fire.

JULIA MOUNTAIN PHOTO/SHUTTERSTOCK

Vihren Peak

Hit the trail in Pirin National Park

There are over a dozen different trails in **Pirin National Park**, from short 30-minute treks – such as the trail from **Vihren Hut** to **Okoto Lake**, which promises stunning views with minimal physical exertion – to longer and more strenuous multi-day treks. Most hikes begin at **Vihren Hut**, which you can reach in about 30 minutes by car or taxi, or via a local shuttle (€6, one hour) from town. From the trailhead parking lot, it's a 20-minute walk past the 1300-year-old **Baykusheva Mura**, Bulgaria's oldest coniferous tree. Alternatively, you can hike up from Bansko via the ski slopes in three to four hours – less if you take the gondola to its midway station.

For a more challenging hike, summit **Vihren Peak** (2914m), Bulgaria's second-highest mountain. The trail from the Vihren Hut takes five to six hours return and involves steep, mostly continuous climbing. However, there are plenty of scenic stops to rest and admire the views and glacial lakes along the way. It's also possible to reach the summit from **Banderitsa Hut** via a wooded trail that cuts through alpine meadows and granite-filled valleys, and passes the **Snezhnika Glacieret**, the southernmost glacial mass in Europe, en route. The final section involves some scrambling; a chain helps you up some of the steepest sections. From the summit, you can continue down to Vihren Hut for lunch before heading back to Bansko.

For more experienced mountaineers seeking an even greater thrill, **Koncheto Ridge**'s famous knife-edge traverse (about 400m long and half a meter at its narrowest) awaits. Connecting Kutelo Banski and Suhodol Peaks, it has nearly vertical drops on both sides. A metal safety cable aids passage, but only those comfortable with heights should attempt it.

Black Sea Coast

ANTIQUITY | VIBRANT CITIES | BEACHES

Blessed with golden sands, ancient ruins and a near-subtropical climate, the Black Sea coast is Bulgaria's greatest asset. Unfortunately, mass tourism in its most oppressive form is now the single dominating feature of the region. But this is not a reason to pass it by, but rather to adjust your plans. Paradoxically, its two coastal cities, Burgas and Varna, now provide a more rewarding beach experience for independent travellers. Varna in particular has the perfect combination of laid-back atmosphere, ancient monuments, interesting restaurants and a nice beach (although the one in Burgas is better). The rest of the coast is best savoured outside the July and August holiday mayhem. This is particularly true when it comes to the two main destinations, Nesebâr and Sozopol, both former Greek towns with illustrious histories.

Varna

Ancient stones, precious metals

Elegant and eclectic, ancient and modern, partially spruced-up and simultaneously run-down, Varna is charmingly authentic. Despite its seaside resort feel, with a long sandy beach and vast maritime gardens, it provides a welcome respite from the holidaying crowds that occupy the rest of the Bulgarian coast.

Varna was a major hub of civilisation in prehistoric times. Archaeologists have unearthed metal objects here, including what is reputed to be the world's oldest piece of golden jewellery. These finds are the pride of the excellent **Archaeological Museum** (*Археологически музей; museumvarna.com; entry adult/student €5/1.50*) and there is more here, too: dark-coloured Thracian pottery and Roman marble, as well as touching Hellenistic items like a Greek marble plaque listing the names of the city's school graduates in 221 CE.

Other remnants of antiquity are still a part of Varna's landscape. Deep inside the historic quarter, the well-preserved

Places

Varna p107
Nesebâr p108
Burgas p108
Sozopol p110

GETTING AROUND

Varna and Burgas both have international airports, with flights to Sofia and a number of European and Turkish destinations. Trains from Varna run to Veliko Târnovo and Sofia. From Burgas, Sofia trains pass through Plovdiv. Frequent buses connect all major destinations along the coast.

☑ TOP TIP

There are a lot of seafood restaurants on the coast and many of them serve creatures that don't live in the Black Sea, like squid and octopus. Take a look at the boxed text on p109 to learn more about which fish are local.

TOURS OF VARNA

Just arrived in Varna? Sign up for a free two-hour walking tour through the **Tourist Information Centre** (*visit.varna. bg*) from June to September. Tours leave at 10.30am and cover major sights, especially churches. Tours run almost daily in July and August, and less frequently in June and September. Contact the office for dates and to book a spot. Alternatively, try a half- or full-day cycling tour of Varna run by **Plateau Cycling** (*plateucycling.com*), which also offers trips around the Black Sea coast and eastern Bulgaria. Tours include hybrid bikes and gear, as well as pick-ups, drop-offs, luggage transfers and cold drinks.

ruins of Varna's 2nd-century **Roman Thermae** (*Римски терми; museumvarna.com; entry adult/student €5/1.50*) are the largest in Bulgaria and the fourth largest of their kind in Europe (after two in Rome and one in Trier, Germany).

Nesebâr

Town of medieval crosses

On a small rocky outcrop 37km northeast of Burgas and connected to the mainland by a narrow, artificial isthmus, pretty-as-a-postcard **Nesebâr** is famous for its numerous, albeit mostly ruined, medieval churches. Bulgaria's main package-tourism hub, Sunny Beach (Slânchev Bryag), is just across the bay; hence every conceivable water sport is on hand.

Greeting visitors at the town's medieval gates, the fine **Archaeological Museum** (*Археологически музей; ancient-nesebar.com; entry adult/concession €4.60/2.30*) tells the story of Mesembria, as the place was known to the ancients. Greek and Roman pottery, statues, tombstones, Thracian gold jewellery and ancient anchors are all on display. Europe's Dark Ages were not that dark here, as suggested by the partly excavated remains of 6th-century **Byzantine baths** (*Ранновизантийски терми*), which was one of the region's biggest and best spas, renowned for its curative waters.

Burgas

Beach and gardens

A gateway to the Bulgaria seacoast for many visitors, Burgas is a beach destination in itself, with arguably better access to the sea and nature than some of the drab coastal resort towns nearby.

The pride of Burgas is its subtropical **Maritime Gardens**, which stretch along the Black Sea coast and are filled with manicured flower beds, fountains, busts of Bulgarian worthies, abstract sculptures and cafes. There are spectacular views over the sea from the terraces, and steps lead down to the 3km-long beach, which is surprisingly pretty given its urban location.

History lessons

The compact Old Town, with low-rise houses from the 19th and early 20th centuries, is enveloped in an extensive pedestrian area filled with street cafes and idle strollers. There are a couple of interesting museums to peek into. The small **Archaeological Museum** (*Археологически музей; burgasmuseums.bg;*

WHERE TO EAT & DRINK IN VARNA AND NESEBÂR

Stariya Chinar: Upmarket Balkan soul food at its best. Try the baked lamb, made to an old Bulgarian recipe, or the divine BBQ pork ribs. In Varna. *8am-midnight* €€	**Bacaro:** A stylish fusion restaurant in Varna that leans towards Asian cuisine and has a garden across the road. *5-11pm Tue-Sat* €€	**Arnautova Kâshta:** Find refuge from Nesebâr's tourist crowds in this sweet rustic courtyard. The menu is standard, but the cooking is soulful. *11am-10pm* €€	**Pri Maykla:** An idiosyncratic little bar in Nesebâr designed as a cave with fake stalagmites, turtles and waterfalls. Long list of cocktails. *noon-midnight*

Aquae Calidae

KNOW YOUR FISH

Pretty much every restaurant on the coast serves seafood, but many, if not most, offer fish and molluscs that don't even live in the Black Sea, due to its low salinity. Black Sea classics are smaller fish, especially bluefish (*chernokop*), gobies (*popcheta*), red mullet (*barbun*) and the needle-headed garfish (*zargan*), famous for its phosphorescent bones. Larger fish include sea bream (*tsipura*), sea brill (*kalkan*) and sea bass (*lavrak*). Another famous Black Sea speciality is mussels, but which mussels wind up on your plate in the EU single-market zone is anyone's guess – unless you're eating at a mussel farm.

entry adult/concession €3/1.50) houses a diverting collection of local finds, including Neolithic flint tools, a wooden canoe from the 5th century BCE, Greek statuary and the remarkably well-preserved wooden coffin of a Thracian chieftain. It's all well laid out and signposted in English. The lively **Ethnographic Museum** (*Етнографически музей; burgasmuseums.bg; entry adult/concession €3/1.50)* displays a rich collection of folk costumes, jewellery and furniture. You may notice that the people dressed in traditional garments in large photos at the entrance are museum staffers who sell tickets and provide guide services.

Bathe like a sultan

How about combining a plunge into ancient history with some 'me time' in a modern spa? Hot springs in what is now **Vetren**, off the Sofia motorway 14km from Burgas, have been known since Thracian times and associated with a cult of river nymphs. The baths were famous across the ancient world under the name of Thermopolis. In Ottoman times, Suleiman the Magnificent converted it into an opulently decorated hammam. Today, the ruins of Thermopolis are enveloped by the modern spa complex **Aquae Calidae** (*aquae-calidae.com; entry adult/child €13/7.70*). Visitors get to see the **ruins of the ancient spa** (*adult/student €8/7*) and an informative animation video inside the restored hammam. Afterwards,

---

WHERE TO EAT & DRINK IN BURGAS AND SOZOPOL

8 Mammas: You'll feel mothered by the kind women making and serving home-style Bulgarian-Turkish specialities at this tiny patio in Burgas. *11.30am-11pm* €

Ethno: An old-time Burgas favourite in a new location. The menu departs from the tourist-trap routine towards more unusual Bulgarian flavours. *11am-11pm* €€

Palikari (Doctor's House): This upmarket place in Sozopol has a perfect cliffside setting in Sozopol with postcard sea views. *11am-midnight* €€

Metalhead Brewery: Combine your spa visit to Aquae Calidae with some popular local craft produce in the immediate vicinity. *2-10pm Wed-Sun*

THERE I WAS ON A JULY MORNING

It might hark back to the solar cults of the ancient Thracians, but this tradition was nonetheless born in the communist period and it's even framed today as a subtle protest against the regime. Crowds of hippies would meet in the area of Yaylata, north of Varna, to greet the sunrise on the morning of 1 July. Why this particular date? Because of Uriah Heep – the ritual was based on listening to the British band's most famous hit, 'July Morning', while watching the sun rise from the sea. The tradition persists today, with big municipalities – like Burgas – placing it on the city calendar. In 2007, Uriah Heep's John Lawton finally made it to Bulgaria and performed the song live.

RNDMS/SHUTTERSTOCK

Church of Sveta Bogoroditsa

enjoy the modern spa and end the day with a glass of ale at the nearby Metalhead Brewery.

Sozopol

History unwrapped

Sitting atop an island-like peninsula, Sozopol was designed to provide plenty of shade and allow its residents to marvel at the surrounding beauty, sweeping views of the sea and a fishing harbour. To get an idea of what it was like to live in one of the revival period houses here, drop into the local **Ethnographic Museum** *(Етнографски музей; sozopol-museums.bg; entry adult/concession €1.5/0.50)* located in the former dwelling of a wealthy Greek merchant, who resided here until the early 20th century. Even when it's scorching hot outside, the wooden structure continues to breathe, taking in the cooling sea breeze and keeping the heat out.

Another unmissable heritage building is the 15th-century **Church of Sveta Bogoroditsa** *(Църква 'Света Богородица'),* its quaintness being the product of the Ottoman policy that limited the height of Christian temples – architects bypassed the rule by building churches below street level. Set in a courtyard with a giant fig tree, it's one of the most picturesque places in town, with an exquisite wooden iconostasis and a pulpit carved with bunches of grapes.

Having emerged as the ancient Greek polity of Apollonia, Sozopol has a long and illustrious history. Though the building itself is drab, the **Archaeological Museum** *(Археологически музей; sozopol-museums.bg; entry adult/concession €3.50/1.50)* has a small but fascinating collection of local finds from its Apollonian glory days. In addition to a wealth of Hellenic treasures, the museum occasionally exhibits the skeleton of a local 'vampire', found with a stake driven through its chest. Enter from the building's north side.

Central Bulgaria

ROMAN RUINS | BULGARIAN HERITAGE | URBAN DELIGHTS

Central Bulgaria is where you can trace the footprints of civilisations past and savour the best of Bulgaria's own civilisation, with its unique blend of ancient Slavic and Orthodox heritage, enriched with Byzantine, Ottoman, West European and Russian influences. One of Europe's oldest settlements, Plovdiv also happens to be one of contemporary Bulgaria's liveliest cities where Roman ruins and Ottoman-era quarters mix with a vibrant modern cafe and restaurant scene. Further north, Veliko Târnovo is the cradle of Bulgarian statehood and identity. It elicits the perfect blend of quintessentially Balkan elements when it comes to architecture, ambience, food and lifestyle. Venture into the heartland to walk the winding lanes of hilly Old Towns, savour the best of the country's cuisine at *mehana* taverns, and immerse yourself in a culture and history that's extremely idiosyncratic but also essential to understanding Europe as a whole.

Places
Plovdiv p111
Stara Zagora p112
Veliko Târnovo p114

☑ TOP TIP
The Free Plovdiv Tour (freeplovdivtour.com) begins at 11am outside the City Hall. Running 365 days a year and led by friendly local guides, it's a great way to get a quick overview of the city. Tips are expected: pay what you can.

Plovdiv
More ancient than most
A seductive fusion of Roman, Hellenistic and Thracian foundations with a pinch of Ottoman spice, Plovdiv is Bulgaria's cultural heart and its second-largest metropolis. First settled over 8000 years ago, it ranks among Europe's oldest cities and its rich historical legacy lies just beneath the central pedestrianised

---

 GETTING AROUND

Plovdiv is on the main railway line between Sofia and Burgas. There are also train services to Stara Zagora, from where you can embark on a spectacular rail journey to Veliko Târnovo. The latter is located 7km from Gorna Oryahovitsa on the Sofia–Varna line. Buses run between Sofia and all the cities mentioned here. Plovdiv is best explored on foot. If you need to go further, hop on a city bus, an easy and affordable way to get around. A single ride costs just €0.50, payable in cash on board. Veliko Târnovo is also walkable.

A FORGOTTEN ARENA

It boggles the mind to think that until the 1970s, people had absolutely no idea that a vast Roman stadium lay beneath Plovdiv's main commercial street. Such collective amnesia is less a mark against the people who have come and gone in the centuries since, though, and more a testament to the metropolis' continuing evolution over 6000 years, such that even the imperial triumphs of a monumental 250m-long gladiatorial arena fell into irrelevance as ever greater chapters of its historical story unfolded. As each new construction project presents a potential new twist to its legacy, Plovdiv is a city that reminds us that history is a living thing, forever in dialogue with the present.

spaces. One of the most fascinating landmarks is the ancient **Stadium of Philippopolis** (*ancient-stadium-plovdiv.eu; entry adult/child €3.50/1.50*). It was only discovered around 50 years ago, when reconstruction work revealed its curved rows, marble seating and subterranean passages. Built in the 2nd century CE under Emperor Hadrian when Plovdiv was known by its Roman name, Philippopolis, the historic stadium staged everything from chariot races to gladiatorial duels.

Regional archaeological museum

If the stadium whetted your appetite for mortal combat, continue your journey into the past at the **Archaeological Museum** (*archaeologicalmuseumplovdiv.org; entry adult/child €4/1*). One of Bulgaria's oldest cultural institutions, it opened in 1882 and houses a collection of gladiatorial artefacts that illuminate the lives of those who once battled for fame, such as funerary stelae of fallen gladiators. Beyond the arena, the museum documents the city's 8000-year-long heritage – from Neolithic settlements and Thracian rituals to Hellenistic artistry and Roman grandeur – via a rich 100,000-strong collection of artefacts.

Ottoman aromas

Though Bulgaria eventually won its freedom from nearly 500 years of Ottoman rule in the late 19th century, traces of that era still infuse Plovdiv. Not just in its architecture, culture and cuisine, but also in the lingering aroma of Turkish coffee from the cafe beside the **Dzhumaya Mosque** in the city centre. Begin your morning with a cup here, best enjoyed from the upholstered, street-facing seats that offer both shade and prime people-watching. Coffee is served with rose water, a fragrant flourish born from the country's long-standing love affair with the flower, which was first cultivated during Ottoman times. Afterwards, step inside the adjoining 14th-century mosque. Shoes come off at the door, a small but humbling act of respect. If you're here on a Friday, prayers led by the local Muslim community – today less than 5% of the population, down from 80% in the 15th century – offer a glimpse into living faith.

Stara Zagora

Return to the dawn of history

Stara Zagora is an appealing mid-sized city that also happens to be one of Europe's oldest continually inhabited settlements – and it has the archaeological pedigree to prove it. One of

WHERE TO EAT IN PLOVDIV: OUR PICKS

Rahat Tepe: Traditional cuisine paired with stunning panoramic views. Known for its sizzling hot-plate dishes, generous portions and fresh salads. *10am-late* €€

Oleander Garden Restaurant: Charming restaurant serving fresh, locally inspired dishes in a relaxed setting. *noon-4.30pm & 6.30-10pm Tue-Sat, noon-5pm Sun* €€

Restaurant Philippopolis: A must for meat lovers, featuring a spacious hidden garden and interiors adorned with Bulgarian artwork. *11am-late* €€€

Hebros Restaurant: Elegant fine-dining in a historic house and hotel. Freshly prepared, homemade-style regional dishes are on the menu. *noon-10.30pm* €€€

Roman Theatre, Stara Zagora

HISTORY OF TSAREVETS FORTRESS

Tsarevets Fortress (p114), atop strategic Tsarevets Hill, has been settled since time immemorial. Thracians and Romans used the hill as a defensive position, but the Byzantines built the first significant citadel here between the 5th and 7th centuries. The fortress was rebuilt and fortified by the Slavs and Bulgars between the 8th and 10th centuries, and again by the Byzantines in the early 12th century. When Târnovgrad became the Second Bulgarian Kingdom's capital, the fortress was truly magnificent, but it was sacked and destroyed during the Ottoman invasion in 1393. Tourists can thank the communists for returning it to a semblance of its former glory, although some archaeologists grumble about the faithfulness of the restoration.

the most stunning finds in Europe, the **Neolithic Dwellings** *(Neolitni Zhilishta; rimstz.eu; entry adult/child €3.50/2)* were discovered in 1969 on the fringes of the city hospital. Now covered by a protective shell, the museum displays a family farmstead destroyed by fire some time around 5800 BCE. At first it may look like a pile of rubble, but it gradually becomes a source of wonder once your eyes become accustomed to what's there: walls, pots and hearths are all discernible, while a millstone and storage vessels reveal its importance as a grain store. A basement room houses a compelling collection of Neolithic pots and cult figures, and an intimate museum takes you right back to the source of European civilisation. Back in the city centre, the remarkably well-kept open-air remains of a **Roman Theatre** *(entry free)* recall the town's 2nd-century CE heyday during the reign of Emperor Marcus Aurelius. Learn more about this heritage at the nearby **History Museum** *(rimstz.eu; entry adult/child €2/1)*, which preserves a stretch of Roman street lined with statues of citizens, togas neatly draped over shoulders.

Enjoy a cross-mountain rail journey

Few Bulgarian journeys are as dramatic as the train ride from **Stara Zagora to Veliko Târnovo**, which wends its way over the Stara Planina mountains before arriving at the medieval capital. The route passes through the corn and sunflowers of the Valley of the Roses before climbing into the highlands, the thickly forested hills passing by in a kaleidoscopic flash of green. Nearing the summit, the line corkscrews its way through curving tunnels to gain height. The train then descends towards Tryavna and passes through the limestone gorge of the Dryanovo River before gliding into Veliko Târnovo station. Around five trains make the trip at roughly two-hour intervals throughout the day; fare prices start at around €4.50 and the journey takes about three hours.

A 12TH-CENTURY MEGALOPOLIS

Veliko Târnovo's high-point came in the 12th century, with the decline of Byzantium and the establishment of the Second Bulgarian Kingdom (1185–1396). It was the aristocratic brothers Asen and Petâr who made Veliko Târnovo their capital. Contemporaneous accounts describe Târnovo as a bustling, handsome city with as many as 15,000 inhabitants. The sheer size of the surviving Tsarevets Fortress, where the rulers held court, speaks to this former grandeur. The old city was centred on the fortress and the adjoining district of Asenova, site of the city's oldest and most valuable churches and buildings. In the mid-14th century, the Ottoman Turks marched into the northern Balkans; within 30 years, they possessed all of Bulgaria and held it for five centuries.

VALENTIN VALKOV/SHUTTERSTOCK

Tsarevets Fortress

Veliko Târnovo
Cradle of the nation

When people mention the heartland of Bulgarian history and culture, it's Veliko Târnovo and the Central Mountains that they're talking about. This region is where the roving Bulgar khans first settled down and formed a state, the country's medieval tsars built their capitals, and the mountain-cradled monasteries and prosperous highland villages nurtured the country's 19th-century revival. If you want to come to grips with how Bulgaria became Bulgaria, this is the place you should start.

Set aside a few hours to scramble around **Tsarevets Fortress** *(museumvt.com; entry adult/child €7.50/3),* the sprawling hilltop citadel that once served as the seat of Bulgaria's tsars during the glory days of the Second Kingdom. The fortress's walls and towers have been partially reconstructed to provide an idea of what it once looked like. Although the historical accuracy of what you see is debatable, it's a hugely evocative site. Rising up from the summit of **Tsarevets Hill** is the reconstructed former patriarchate, centred on the **Cathedral of the Holy Ascension**. Heartstopping views of the city and its surroundings from the church steps are more impressive than the church itself, which contains kitschy modern murals of Bulgarian medieval leaders.

WHERE TO EAT IN VELIKO TÂRNOVO: OUR PICKS

Bey House: Upscale hotel restaurant offers a gourmet take on Bulgarian cuisine, with great wines and delicious sweets in a walled garden. *9am-11pm* €€€

Han Hadzhi Nikoli: Courtyard dining in a beautifully restored inn, with an exciting blend of Bulgarian-European cuisine. *10am-11pm* €€

Hotel-Mehana Gurko: Traditional-style tavern with great views and tasty Bulgarian specialities, washed down with local wine. *noon-9pm* €€

Bakery for Kadaif: Syrupy *kadaif,* a traditional Bulgarian sweet with Turkish roots, as well as baklava made on the premises. *10am-6pm* €

Places We Love to Stay

€ Budget €€ Midrange €€€ Top End

Central Sofia MAP p101

Hostel Mostel € A popular hostel in a renovated 19th-century house. The dorms come in all sizes; there are a couple of singles and doubles, too.

Art Hotel 158 €€ An artsy boutique hotel with a homey feel in the heart of the city. Spacious rooms and laudable breakfasts.

Pop Bogomil €€ This small hotel has 15 small but comfortable rooms, individually decorated and priced. In the Lion's Bridge area, to the north of the city.

Agora Boutique Hotel €€ In the middle of action just off Vitosha Boulevard, this mansion has comfortable rooms.

Hotel Niky €€ Funky common areas, comfortable rooms and gleaming bathrooms. The smart suites come with kitchenettes.

Hotel Les Fleurs €€€ Features gigantic blooms on the facade, a surreal interior design and a floral motif in the more stylish rooms.

Oborishte 63 Boutique Hotel €€€ In the nicest part of central Sofia, this luxurious salmon-pink 1930s home has a view over the Aleksander Nevski Cathedral.

Rila

Gorski Kut €€ Riverside hotel with mountain views, seven minutes from Rila Monastery, midway to Bansko and Seven Lakes.

RILA 6ATO Hotel & Restaurant €€ The chairlift to the Seven Lakes is 5km away. Good value with detached wooden cabins.

Bansko

Hotel Orphey € Big rooms at this family-friendly hotel opposite City Park. Free parking and shuttle to the gondola.

Velinov Boutique Hotel €€ Super cosy with mountain views and typical Bulgarian touches right next to St Trinity Church.

Amira Boutique Hotel €€€ Premium mountain hotel 400m from the lifts with an excellent restaurant, terrace views and free shuttle.

Varna

Yo Ho Hostel € This pirate-themed place has four- and 11-bed dorm rooms and private options.

Hotel Hi €€ Well-appointed rooms designed in a classical style. Location is spot on.

Graffit Gallery Hotel €€ With its own gallery and themed rooms, this is one of Varna's more colourful options.

Black Sea Coast

Boutique Hotel St Stefan €€ Art-filled rooms with views over the harbour and the Black Sea from old Nesebâr.

Guest House Tony €€ A popular oldie in an excellent location overlooking the sea in Nesebâr; it fills up quickly. No-frills but homey, with a great host.

Hotel St Nikola €€ Bland but comfortable rooms in a traditional-looking house in a superb location in Nesebâr.

Burgas & Beyond

Boutique Guest House Ruvan €€ A neat family hotel in heart of Old Town. Spacious rooms come with balconies.

Hotel Chiplakoff €€ This attractively restored art nouveau mansion features original spiral staircases.

Hotel Briz €€ Spacious rooms with sea views in a quiet location at the far end of Sarafovo. The perfect place to land before flying in or out of Burgas.

Plovdiv

Hostel Ginger House € Walking distance to attractions. Velin, the super friendly owner, makes this a highly recommended stay.

Boutique Guest House Yes For You €€ Stylish accommodation with character and a welcoming vibe. Close to sights, cafes, bars and restaurants.

Villa Flavia Boutique Hotel €€€ Steps from the Roman Theatre. Chic rooms, superb breakfast and a recently discovered ancient bath beneath the hotel.

Veliko Târnovo

Hotel-Mehana Gurko €€ On the city's oldest street, with blooms spilling over the balconies and great views. Book in advance.

Hotel Kiev €€ Much better inside than it appears at first glance. Excellent value, great central location and spotlessly clean.

Bey House Royal Hotel €€€ Fancy property in the residence of the area's last Ottoman governor.

Bridges Residence €€€ Spacious boutique hotel suites in the city's historic core; contemporary conveniences and grand views.

Practicalities

Weather

Summer heat in Bulgaria can be oppressive, and the number of days with temperatures over 33°C has been consistently rising year on year. In winter, expect cold, icy conditions, especially in the mountains.

LGBTIQ+ Travellers

Same-sex partnerships are permitted in Bulgaria, though these unions do not enjoy the full legal protections granted to hetero partnerships. Sofia and Varna are home to large LGBTIQ+ communities, though gay culture tends to stay on the down low. GLAS (glasfoundation.bg/en) is a leading NGO that protects and promotes the rights of lesbian, gay, bisexual and transgender people.

Accessible Travel

Bulgaria is a signatory to the UN Convention on Rights of Persons with Disabilities, which mandates that all new construction meet minimum standards of accessibility. The country is far behind, however, in retrofitting existing facilities. Sofia Airport is fully modernised and meets accessibility requirements.

Smoking

Smoking is banned in all indoor public spaces, including restaurants, bars, hotels, cinemas and offices, but the rule is sometimes loosely enforced. In reality, most restaurant tables are located outdoors where smoking is permitted, so brace for tobacco-scented meals on occasion.

NATALIA SILTANOV/SHUTTERSTOCK

Vitosha Boulevard (p102), Sofia

Opening Hours

Banks 9am–5pm Monday to Friday
Museums 10am–5pm
Post Offices 8am–7pm Monday to Friday
Restaurants 9am–11pm
Shops 10am–7pm Monday to Friday, 11am–5pm Sat and Su

Language

Bulgarian is a southern Slavic language. The Cyrillic alphabet was first developed here in the 9th century and later adopted by other Slavic languages.

Hello *Здравейте* zdra-vey-te
Goodbye *Довиждане* do-veezh-da-ne
Do you speak English? *Говорите ли английски?* go-vo-ree-te lee ang-lees-kee
Thank you *Благодаря* bla-go-dar-ya
Yes *Да* da
No *Не* ne

Public Holidays

New Year's Day 1 January
Liberation Day 3 March
Orthodox Easter April/May
May Day 1 May
St George's Day/Bulgarian Army Day 6 May
Cyrillic Alphabet/Culture and Literacy Day 24 May
Unification Day 6 September
Bulgarian Independence Day 22 September
Christmas 25 & 26 December

FROM LEFT: SIMON RICHMOND/LONELY PLANET, JOHNER IMAGES/GETTY IMAGES

Station, Varna (p107)

Arriving & Getting Around

Bulgaria has three main international airports: Sofia, Varna and Burgas. Plovdiv airport gets some EU flights. All airports are modern and have regular flights between one another.

MONEY

Currency: Euro (€)

CARDS

You cannot rely exclusively on credit or debit cards in Bulgaria. Cards are commonly accepted in hotels, restaurants and shops in big cities, towns and tourist resorts; less so in more rural areas.

ATMS

ATMs that accept major credit cards (Visa and MasterCard) are common in all sizable towns and cities. Choose ATMs affiliated with major banks instead of private ATMs, where the conversion rates may be much higher.

CHANGING MONEY

Foreign-exchange offices can be found in all large towns, and rates are displayed prominently. They are no longer allowed to charge commission, but that doesn't stop them trying. Always check the final amount before handing over your cash.

Bus

The most reliable transport between cities is by bus. Local buses reach most villages, though these services are infrequent, or seasonal in ski or beach destinations. Comfort levels vary wildly.

Train

Slower than buses, trains are a scenic way to cover ground in Bulgaria. Sometimes they serve some out-of-the-way places. Comfort inside the carriages is truly substandard, so pay extra for first class.

Car

The most convenient way to get around, especially if heading to small Bulgarian villages. Car hire can be arranged in the main airports. Book with local providers, such as *toprentacar.bg*.

Road Conditions

Road conditions are patchy, but generally satisfactory. There are several motorways, some of which are only partly finished. The longest connects Sofia to Burgas and serves as the main transport axis between western Bulgaria and the Black Sea coast. The north–south axis is not particularly fast, with serpentine roads crossing mountain ranges.

For places to stay in Croatia, see p141

TRAVELLINGIN/SHUTTERSTOCK

Above: City walls (p136), Dubrovnik; Right: Krk (p131)

Curated by
Anja Mutić

Croatia

LIVING UP TO THE HYPE

A must-visit destination ever since *Game of Thrones* showcased the country's magnificent architecture and coastline, Croatia is still having its moment in the sun.

Despite the bucket-list fame of recent years, Croatia's pleasures are still more timeless than trendy. Crystalline water laps gently at a 1778km-long coast and some 1185 islands. Away from the coast, eight national parks protect pristine forests, karstic mountains, rivers, lakes and waterfalls in a landscape of primeval beauty. The culture is as varied as the scenery, with a parade of Roman, Venetian, Austro-Hungarian and Italian occupiers leaving Croatia with a unique identity. Marvel at ancient treasures and medieval towns preserved over thousands of years.

Tourism to the country is nothing new. The Habsburg Empire set up shop on the coast more than 140 years ago and opened swank health resorts, many of which are still open. Later came President Josip Broz Tito's push for international guests in the 1970s, which poured funding into impressively modern hotel architecture along the coast and created Croatia's burgeoning tourism industry. This all came to a halt during the Homeland War from 1991 to 1995, when the nation was engaged in battles with its fellow ex-Yugoslavia neighbours. While the country bounced back, it took a couple of decades for travellers to return in significant numbers. But today, they're most certainly back. With an exciting gastronomy scene, an array of islands and beaches, fascinating history and culture, and spectacular nature, Croatia is a trove of delights.

ILIJA ASCIC/SHUTTERSTOCK

THE MAIN AREAS

ZAGREB
Croatia's cosy, pocket-sized capital. **p124**

ISTRIA & KVARNER
Forward-thinking port city, delightful islands and foodie delights. **p128**

SPLIT & DALMATIAN ISLANDS
Iconic Roman-palace quarter and gorgeous beaches. **p132**

DUBROVNIK
Medieval walls, scenic streetscapes and beaches. **p136**

Find Your Way

Smooth, winding seaside roads with incredible views link the mainland villages, towns and cities of this long, thin and predominantly coastal country, but the rural inland areas are just as scenic and peaceful to explore.

Istria & Kvarner, p128

A h;eart-shaped peninsula on the northern Adriatic with seaside gems, foodie enclaves and the most underrated stretch of Croatia's coast, with a forward-thinking port city.

BUS

Croatia has a vast bus network, operated by local companies such as Arriva and international fleets like FlixBus, which often travel the length of the country and are the quickest intercity option.

CAR

Driving a car is the easiest way to explore Croatia, particularly if you plan to visit some rural, off-the-beaten-path gems. The best rental prices are found in Zagreb, Split and Rijeka.

FERRY

Ferry links in Croatia are cheap and efficient, so reaching the islands is entirely doable DIY, no matter your transport situation. National ferry company Jadrolinija connects the mainland to all inhabited islands throughout the year.

HUNGARY

Čakovec

Varaždin

Koprivnica

Zagreb, p124
A laid-back little capital city, big on coffee culture and vivacious street life, with a clutch of offbeat museums, green spaces and a mountain on its doorstep.

Subotica

SERBIA

Bjelovar

Museum of Broken Relationships

Virovitica

ZAGREB

Kupa

Kutina

Slavonska Požega

Našice

Osijek

Vukovar

Bačka Palanka

Petrinja

Sisak

Sava

Nova Gradiška

Đakovo

Vinkovci

Slavonski Brod

Una

Bihać

Banja Luka

BOSNIA & HERCEGOVINA

Brčko

Bosansko Petrovac

Split & Dalmatian Islands, p132
The heart of Dalmatia, this buzzing city showcases the monumental Diocletian's Palace, while the islands sport gorgeous beaches and sweet coastal towns.

Gračac

Knin

Krka National Park

SARAJEVO

Šibenik

Sinj

Diocletian's Palace

Split

Riva

Brač

Dubrovnik, p136
With the mesmerising beauty of its walled old town featuring marbled lanes and architectural showpieces, this Adriatic city is a stunner lined with dazzling beaches.

Zlatni Rat

Bol

Mostar

Hvar

Vis

Metković

Korčula

Neum

Mljet

Nikšić

City Walls

Dubrovnik

MONTENEGRO

Herceg Novi

Plan Your Time

Timing is crucial in Croatia, a country with 48 inhabited islands and seasonal ferry and flight schedules. Outside of summer, many places along the coast shut down and transport options are limited, so plan in advance.

PILLIP/SHUTTERSTOCK

Trg Bana Jelačića (p127), Zagreb

A Quick City Break

● Top of everyone's city-break list is enchanting **Dubrovnik** (p136), which deserves all the accolades. The walled old town's wide, marble-paved streets lined with monumental baroque churches and Gothic palaces dazzle visitors, while glorious beaches make for the perfect place to rest after a few days of sightseeing.

● Off-the-radar Kvarner is a gorgeous coastal region and an up-and-coming playground for foodies. Explore the dynamic port city of **Rijeka** (p130), with its edgy arts and culture scene.

● And there's **Zagreb** (p124), Croatia's stellar capital which is fun to visit year-round, even in winter (Advent is particularly great with its happening Christmas markets). The city is packed with lively cafes, museums and galleries, and music venues to dive into.

Seasonal Highlights

Croatia gets busy in the summer. If possible, visit during spring or autumn for the same scenery but fewer travellers. The country has lots of traditional events.

FEBRUARY
The bombastic **Rijeka Carnival** (p131) is usually in early to mid-February, or head to Dubrovnik for the mighty Feast of St Blaise.

MARCH/APRIL
Good Friday processions are particularly elaborate in Dubrovnik, where the walls are lit with flame.

MAY
The last Sunday in May is Wine Day, when winemakers open their cellars and offer tastings of their vintages.

A Week to Spare

● The winning first-timers' trip to Croatia begins with a couple of nights in buzzy **Split** (p132), where you can take in the ancient Roman city centre inside **Diocletian's Palace** (p132)followed by local beach bars and cool restaurants.

● Next, hop on a ferry to one or two of the Dalmatian islands. After a couple of nights in **Hvar** (p135; for nightlife) or **Brač** (p134; for beaches), ferry onwards to spend a final few days in **Dubrovnik** (p136), the mesmerising showpiece of Croatia's coast, with its awesome architecture within the storied old town, gorgeous beaches and all-around elegance making up for the crowds.

Slow-Travel Sojourn

● If you're location-independent or travelling long term, renting a place for a month as a base from which to explore can save you a lot of euros and ease the pace of travel. **Split** (p132) is the most popular place for digital nomads on the coast of Croatia, but **Dubrovnik** (p136) also has expat scenes worth discovering.

● If you're looking for an extended break to switch off and relax, a month on an island such as **Hvar** (p135;) or at a mainland spot such as rural **Istria** (p128) rewards with quaint, less-frequented villages steeped in local culture, food and tradition, as well as incredible wineries.

JULY
Film lovers flock to Pula in July for the **Pula Film Festival** (p128) and its nighttime screenings under the stars.

AUGUST
Okolo/Around (p127) brings public art installations and urban interventions to Zagreb's streets – many in the Upper Town – for about 10 days each August.

SEPTEMBER
September is when truffle hunters in Istria go into the forest in search of the elusive Magnatum Pico.

DECEMBER
Advent festivities in Zagreb have been drawing increasing numbers of visitors, who come to explore the fun and colourful Christmas markets.

Zagreb

ANCIENT TOWN | QUIRKY MUSEUMS | VIBRANT STREET LIFE

GETTING AROUND

Zagreb is a small and compact city made for strolling. Taking one of the iconic blue trams is part of the fun and a good way to reach the highlights beyond the city centre. Buy your ticket from the driver, at a kiosk or through an app, and make sure to validate it at a yellow machine on board.

☑ TOP TIP

Noon comes with a bang in Zagreb, and locals set their watches by it, so brace yourself for a loud blast. You'll likely get startled, but fear not; it's not an explosion, but the sound of the Grič cannon from the **Lotrščak Tower**; it's been marking midday for the last 100 years.

No more a mere stopover en route to the coast, Croatia's capital is firmly on the map of small European capitals on the rise. The wintertime Advent festivities have done much to extend the season, bringing droves of visitors to Zagreb for its Christmas markets. Beyond the big events that dot the calendar, Zagreb has an understated charm: it's the type of city that grows on you in a slow-burn kind of way. Among its chief appeals? It's a laid-back micro-metropolis made for strolling. Wander through the Upper Town's red-roof and cobblestone splendour, peppered with church spires. See the domes and ornate upper-floor frippery of the Lower Town's mash-up of Secessionist, neo-baroque and art deco buildings. Check out its collection of quirky museums and dive into its small but burgeoning art scene, its vibrant street life and its many nature parks and forests.

Upper Town

As the oldest part of Zagreb, the Upper Town (Gornji Grad) is a storybook maze of cobblestone streets and squares that make for some wonderful roaming. Spread across two small hills – Gradec and Kaptol – connected by a string of steps and passageways, this is where the city originally began in medieval times. When the two settlements merged in 1850, Zagreb was born. Today, its streets are speckled with baroque palaces, neoclassical mansions, medieval towers and neo-Gothic churches. This cobblestone feast of historic architecture has dashes of vibrant life – from perennially full cafe-bars that line the buzzy Tkalčićeva to quirky museums.

Browse Dolac Market

Indulge your senses at this central farmers market dotted with iconic red parasols and countless stalls overflowing with fresh fruit and veg. With its pops of colour, the 'belly of Zagreb' offers a field day for photo ops. **Dolac Market** has been

ZAGREB

KAPTOL

SALATA

GRADEC

DONJI GRAD

Zagreb Train Station

0   500 m
0   0.25 miles

⭐ **HIGHLIGHTS**
1 Museum of Broken Relationships

🔴 **SIGHTS**
2 Cathedral of the Assumption of the Blessed Virgin Mary

3 Galerija Klovićevi Dvori
4 Lotrščak Tower
5 Museum of Illusions
6 Trg Bana Jelačića
7 Zrinjevac

⚫ **SLEEPING**
8 Esplanade Zagreb Hotel
9 Hotel Jägerhorn

10 Stay Swanky
11 Stellar Boutique Modules

🟢 **EATING**
12 BioMania Bistro
13 Broom44
14 Gostionica Ficlek
15 Heritage

16 Otto & Frank
see 14 Pod Zidom
17 Salo
18 Vinodol

🔴 **SHOPPING**
19 Dolac Market

trader-central since the 1930s, when the city authorities set up a market space on the 'border' between the Upper and Lower Towns. Today, vendors from all over Croatia descend daily to hawk their garden-fresh produce and assorted edible goods.

Cathedral glory and city icon

The twin spires of Zagreb's **Cathedral of the Assumption of the Blessed Virgin Mary**, Croatia's largest sacral building, have soared over the city for eight centuries. The original structure has been transformed and rebuilt many times due to fires and earthquakes, but its signature neo-Gothic look came about at the turn of the 20th century. The cathedral has unfortunately been closed and under lace-like scaffolding since the 2020 earthquake.

ZAGREB ADVENT

In the last 10 years, Zagreb's Christmas market has grown from a small happening to the peak of the city's calendar, drawing in crowds from across the country and the world. Hotels and restaurants book up quickly, so it's best to plan a visit way ahead. Advent put wintertime Zagreb on the map; before that, it was a sleepy city where families celebrated Christmas by getting together at home. Now, everyone heads out to the decked-out streets, squares and parks, which come alive with buzzy food stalls, craft pop-ups, live music, mulled wine, dance parties and art happenings. Held at various locations around the city centre and beyond, Advent typically runs from late November into January.

IVAN KLINDIC/SHUTTERSTOCK

Bandstand, Zrinjevac

The pastel-coloured charm of Tkalča

Strolling up and down **Tkalča**, a charming pedestrian street that winds uphill from Trg Bana Jelačića, is a favourite pastime for locals. Centuries ago, a stream lined with watermills ran in its place, separating the medieval settlements of Kaptol and Gradec. Today, Tkalča, as Tkalčićeva is called by locals, is lined with pastel-coloured townhouses and cafe terraces bustling with life day and night. Pick your pavement table for great people-watching and city-vibe-soaking, drink in hand.

See the Museum of Broken Relationships

From romances that withered to broken family connections, the wonderfully weird **Museum of Broken Relationships** (*brokenships.com; entry adult/child €7/5.50*) explores the mementoes left behind after a relationship ends. On display in the string of all-white rooms are donations from around the globe that range from the hilarious to the heartbreaking; each comes with a story attached. Check out the adjacent shop – the 'bad memories eraser' is a bestseller.

EATING IN THE UPPER TOWN: BEST BRUNCH SPOTS

Salo: This bright bistro-bakery on Opatovina doles out artisan breads, small creative plates and speciality coffee. *8am-4pm Wed-Sat, 9am-2pm Sun €*

Broom44: Right on Dolac, with tables spilling into the market, Broom44 serves world-cuisine-inspired dishes, mostly plant-based. *6.30am-3pm Mon-Sat, 8am-2pm Sun €€*

Otto & Frank: Hearty breakfasts of eggs, French toast and the like till noon; yummy burgers and bar vibes after. *8am-11pm Mon-Sat, 9am-5pm Sun €*

BioMania Bistro: Plant-based, seasonal dishes that span the usual international favourites (think burgers and pasta). Great desserts, too. *11am-11pm Tue-Sun €€*

Lower Town

The Lower Town (Donji Grad) pretty much consists of the entire city centre of Zagreb below the Upper Town – basically anything below the historic hills stretching towards the north. It has a distinct old-world flair and central European flavour, plus some of the city's most offbeat museums and contemporary art galleries, as well as fine examples of grand Habsburg-era architecture. With its leafy U-shaped series of seven parks and squares known as Lenuci's Horseshoe, it's perfect for strolling and exploring Zagreb's vibrant cafe culture. The Lower Town is also the site of many festivals and street happenings that span almost the entire year.

The buzz of Trg Bana Jelačića

Zagreb's geographic heart and the separation line between the Upper and Lower Towns is **Trg Bana Jelačića**. If you enjoy people-watching, sit in one of the cafes and watch the tramloads of people getting out, greeting each other and dispersing among the newspaper kiosks and flower stalls lining the strip towards Dolac Market. The equestrian statue of Jelačić and the nearby clock tower are the main rendezvous points.

Zrinjevac's tree-lined beauty

Officially called Trg Nikole Šubića Zrinskog, but known as **Zrinjevac**, this verdant square is a major hangout during sunny weekends and hosts pop-up stalls during spring, summer and Advent. It acts as a venue for many festivals and events, often centred on the ornate music pavilion that dates from 1891.

Amazing Museum of Illusions

Visitors of all ages are treated to heaps of fun at the **Museum of Illusions** *(muzejiluzija.com; entry adult/child €12/9)*, a fantastic little sensory adventure that started in Zagreb in 2015 and has since spread to franchises across the world, including New York, Dubai and Athens. The Tilted Room and the Mirror of Truth are among 70-plus intriguing exhibits, hologram pictures, puzzles and educational games that offer a fun mental workout.

UPPER TOWN'S BEST SUMMER FESTS

Grič Evenings: A series of concerts held every July in the atrium of the **Galerija Klovićevi Dvori**, with everything from chamber music to world tunes. *(facebook.com/VeceriNaGricu)*

Okolo/Around: This annual event brings public art installations and urban interventions to Zagreb's streets for 10 days in August. *(@okoloaround)*

Zagreb International Folklore Festival: A celebration of traditional culture every July, this festival takes place around the city centre and the Upper Town. *(msf.hr/en)*

Le Grič: For four Saturdays in August, sip wine and champagne and mingle at this seasonal event on the walkway behind the Zagreb City Museum. *(facebook.com/legric)*

 EATING IN THE LOWER TOWN: BEST CROATIAN CUISINE

Vinodol: Upscale Central European fare with a modern twist. Go for succulent lamb or veal and potatoes under a *peka* (domed baking lid). *noon-midnight* €€

Heritage: Petit snack bar and delicatessen churning out traditional Croatian finger food. Tricky to get a table. *noon-8pm* €

Gostionica Ficlek: Real-deal Zagreb mainstays served in a cosy bistro space, grandma-style. Right by Dolac Market, so as fresh as it gets. *11am-11pm* €

Pod Zidom: Upmarket bistro next to Dolac Market, with a focus on modern cuisine with market-fresh ingredients. *noon-11pm Tue-Sun* €€

Istria & Kvarner

SEASIDE TOWNS | ANCIENT HISTORY | GASTRONOMIC DELIGHTS

Places

GETTING AROUND

The main cities, towns and islands of Kvarner and Istria are well served by public transport. Arriva *(arriva.com.hr)* is the main bus carrier. The freedom of your own wheels makes exploration easiest. The highways and artillery roads here are well maintained, smooth, scenic and easy to drive.

☑ TOP TIP

Wine lovers, don't miss the last Sunday in May (Wine Day), when cellar doors swing open and you can sample Istria's local vintages.

The Kvarner region (formerly known as Liburnia) may be less famous than coastal counterparts in the south, but therein lies its appeal. Framed by Adriatic waters and separated from Dalmatia by the mountains that form its borderlands, Kvarner showcases the dynamic port city of Rijeka and a string of forest-strewn islands. The adjoining sun-drenched peninsula of Istria is tucked into the North Adriatic Sea with its heart-like shape. Its shorelines are lined with hotel complexes and pretty beach-resort towns welcoming sunseekers in summer, while the verdant interior features hilltop towns and neat rows of vineyards and olive groves, providing the excellent wine and olive oil Istria is known for, as well as black-and-white truffles growing in dense forests.

Pula

TIME FROM ZAGREB: **3HR** 🚗

Seaside Pula is Istria's largest city, occupying the southwestern tip of the peninsula. Its well-preserved 1st-century Roman amphitheatre is the main drawcard. Other remnants of its past live on in the old town's Roman street plan, from ancient arches and mosaics to temples and theatres. During Austro-Hungarian times, Pula was an important naval base, as well as a centre for shipbuilding for over 150 years. The bilingual street signs are a reminder that Pula is one of the Istrian cities where Italian is an official second language.

On the Roman trail

Any visit to Pula starts at its harbour-facing **Roman Amphitheatre** *(arenapula.hr; entry adult/child €10/5)*, known locally as the Arena. Built in the 1st century, this limestone-built landmark is one of only six remaining Roman amphitheatres in the world. Gladiators once entertained 20,000 spectators here; today it seats 5000 for open-air concerts and the annual **Pula Film Festival**.

Rovinj

THE WORLD'S BIGGEST TRUFFLE

The truffle is a tuber that grows underground in dense forests and can only be sniffed out by specially trained dogs. While the black truffle is available year-round, the pungent white truffle can only be found for a few months of the year – generally September to January – hence its status as a luxury delicacy.

It was in Istria's Motovun forest that the world's biggest truffle was dug up in 1999, fetching a price tag of US$5000. Giancarlo Zigante and his dog Diana unearthed the 1.31kg white truffle and earned themselves a Guinness World Record. Today, Giancarlo runs **Restaurant Zigante** in nearby Livade and has a line of truffle products under the brand name Zigante (*zigantetartufi.com*).

Near the amphitheatre lies the 1st-century **Small Roman Theatre**, revived in 2023 when the stage and semicircular seating area of ancient stones got a much-needed upgrade. Today it's an atmospheric venue for concerts and cultural events, seating up to 1700.

Rovinj

TIME FROM PULA: **40MIN** 🚌

Seaside Rovinj is one of Croatia's most iconic destinations and an absolute must-visit. Set on a hilly peninsula, it seems to rise out of the sea with the Church of St Euphemia above the city's rooftops. Standing cheek by jowl along the waterline are pretty buildings with their lime-plaster facades painted in pleasing pastel shades. The egg-shaped peninsula that Rovinj stands on was once an island –it was connected to the mainland in 1763. Rovinj had a strong maritime industry in the 17th century, and its fishing tradition continues today.

Tracing Rovinj's landmarks

The **Grisia** is a lane of slippery cobbles lined with artists' galleries and studios that slopes upwards to Rovinj's highest point

DINING IN ROVINJ: TOP SPOTS

Snack Bar Rio: Much more than a snack bar, this cheerful sea-facing restaurant cooks up elevated seafood, pastas and salads. *8am-10pm Tue-Sun* €€

Brasserie Adriatic: Smack on the main square with Mediterranean cuisine and Istrian specialities, including vegan options. *7am-10pm* €€

Maestral: Enjoy an alfresco meal with superb views of the old town. Fish dominates the menu, but there are plenty of other tasty options. *10am-11pm* €€

Puntulina: Feast on plates of seafood at this stunning spot on the edge of the water. Bookings are a must. *noon-10pm Thu-Tue* €€€

and most important landmark: the 18th-century **St Euphemia's Church**. Its 60m-high bell tower is topped with a bronze statue of its patron saint. For superb views over the terracotta rooftops and nearby islands, brave the 200 steps to the top.

Grisia has had its own festival since 1967: on the second Sunday of August, the **Grisia Art Fair** celebrates the city's artistic tradition with the creations of local artists covering every available nook and cranny.

Rijeka

TIME FROM ZAGREB: **2HR**

Rijeka (meaning 'river' in Croatian) is often overlooked in favour of its Dalmatian counterparts, but this underrated cultural metropolis has nothing to prove. Its left-leaning residents enjoy their coastal city without the crowds of mass tourism, making it one of the most affordable places to live like a local and enjoy the thriving music and food scenes – and it's a five-minute drive from a beach. As well as being a punk-rock hub, Croatia's third-largest city is forward-thinking, open-minded and a lot of fun to visit.

Rijeka's gritty grandeur

The Rijeka we know today is a product of town planning by the Austrian Habsburgs, who rebuilt their biggest seaport following a devastating earthquake in the 1750s. Most of the grand, ornate architecture in the town centre dates to the late 1800s, when the city was home to the Habsburg navy and cultural institutions. Look for the baroque **City Clock Tower** above the arched city gate, renovated by Filbert Bazarig in 1876, and the **Ivan Zajc Croatian National Theatre** (*hnk-zajc.hr*), which was rebuilt in 1885.

Baška Beach

Palace Modello, designed by Buro Fellner & Helmer and built in 1885, is another impressive remnant of the era, and the colossal **Palača Adria** (Adria Palace), a neo-Renaissance layer cake completed in 1897, started out as an administrative centre for the Austro-Hungarian government.

Krk Island

 TIME FROM RIJEKA: 1HR

Croatia's largest island is known for its gorgeous seaside towns, sprawling beaches and rich cultural heritage. From the ancient Liburnians and industrious Romans to dynastic Frankopan lords and Slavic priests, Krk is steeped in history. It's a hugely popular destination for both international tourists (around 100,000 visit every summer) and Croatian visitors alike. The mainland-connecting highway bridge makes for seamless travel, the island has abundant outdoor opportunities and the enchanting old towns round out Krk's intoxicating arsenal.

Baška in the sun

There's no getting around it – Krk is touristy. In July and August, sunseekers are spread towel-to-towel across many of the island's best beaches, including the fine crescent beach set below barren hills in Baška. One of the island's prettiest stretches, **Baška Beach** sits directly across from the peaks of the mainland, evoking a sense that the sea is an alpine lake enveloped by soaring highlands. The drive to the southern end of Krk is dramatic, too, passing through a fertile valley bordered by eroded mountains, before petering out in the Baška. Outside of the highest season, it's an immensely pleasant town, with a small 16th-century core of Venetian townhouses and nice hiking trails into the surrounding mountains.

RIJEKA'S WILD FIFTH SEASON: CARNIVAL

Every year on the last Sunday before Christian Lent commences, Rijeka holds the gargantuan **Rijeka Carnival** (*rijecki-karneval.hr*). A parade of 10,000 costumed people dance, march and party down the length of the Korzo, led by the city's mayor, the Carnival queen and the honorary mayor of the day, Meštar Toni, who is handed keys to the city for the duration. Not quite winter, not yet spring, it's dubbed Rijeka's 'fifth season'.

The highlight of the parade is saved for last. A group of 100 men, the *zvončari* bell ringers, wear striped shirts and are masked as imaginary but ferocious animals. The noise of their bells is said to scare away bad spirits, the winter and – as legend would have it – the Ottoman army.

Split & Dalmatian Islands

GORGEOUS BEACHES | ICONIC PALACE | HEAPS OF HISTORY

Places

GETTING AROUND

Split's compact old town is easy to explore on foot. To explore further, try **Promet** (promet-split. hr), the excellent public bus system. Local taxis tend to be overpriced – try Uber or Bolt instead. Ferry services connect Split to nearby islands, such as Hvar and Brač, but there are also private boat taxis, charters and private tours that can whisk you to any town with a port.

☑ TOP TIP

If you'd like to cycle around Split, look out for the Nextbike (nextbike.hr) bike-share stations. A handy app lets you rent bicycles and e-bikes at a budget-friendly hourly rate.

A couple of decades ago, Split was little more than a transit town to pause in before catching a ferry to the islands. Despite the magnificence of its star attraction, the World Heritage–listed Diocletian's Palace, the city stood forlorn and overlooked, with parts of it even described as a ghetto. Meanwhile the Riva, the city's now beloved seaside promenade, was a thoroughfare for car traffic.

Today, Split is one of Croatia's most visited cities, drawing crowds of tourists even during the shoulder seasons. It's a popular halt for cruise ships and a coveted destination for Croatia's growing tribe of digital nomads. The fact that many scenes from *Game of Thrones* were filmed here may also have something to do with its popularity.

No longer a mere launchpad to the islands, Split has finally attracted the attention it deserves, though the Splićani (the people of Split) are still learning to adjust to their city's new star status.

Split

Roam ancient Roman quarters

Diocletian's Palace is one of the world's largest and most complete Roman edifices. The fortress-like palace was built in the 4th century as Emperor Diocletian's swanky retirement home. The sprawling 38,700-sq-metre complex consists of roughly 200 buildings and has been inhabited for 2000 years, but only a few hundred tenants remain today.

Don't miss the handsome **Peristyle** (courtyard), the **Cathedral of St Domnius** – originally built as Emperor Diocletian's mausoleum and today's the world's oldest working Catholic cathedral that still has its original structure – the Temple of Jupiter (now the Baptistery), and the **Vestibule**, a domed rotunda that once opened onto the imperial corridor and the emperor's apartments.

Stone-slabbed Decumanus is the palace's thoroughfare. It's bookended by the **Silver Gate** at its eastern limit and the

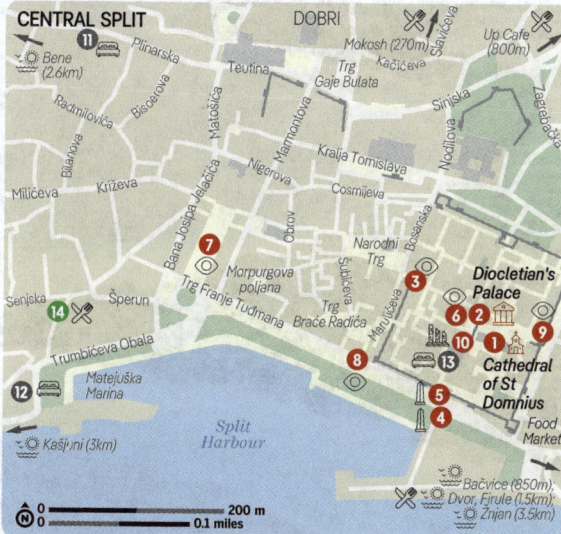

Iron Gate to the west. It separated the emperor's residence from the military quarters, and intersects with north–south Cardo at the Peristyle. Interconnecting these arteries is a labyrinth of passageways lined with ancient buildings occupied by shops, cafes and restaurants.

City life by the sea

A favourite pastime for Split residents is a relaxed stroll on the seaside promenade. The Quay of the Croatian National Revival is the official name of this 250m-long stretch of waterfront, but for the Splićani, it's the **Riva**. Come early evening, chattering swallows swoop between the Riva's neat rows of palms while families amble up and down the footpath.

At the eastern end, look for the bronze 3D **Model of Old Town** and, a few steps away, a similar **Model of Diocletian's Palace**. Ramble along the white stone walkway while browsing for wooden souvenirs, handmade jewellery, locally produced wine and honey, and a range of other goodies, including dried figs, herbal teas and natural soaps. Then do like the Splićani and sit down for a cup of coffee. On Saturday mornings, people go to town in their Sunday best, and

EATING IN SPLIT: OUR PICKS

Up Cafe: Fuel up on tofu burritos, veggie burgers, falafel wraps and plant-based cakes at this casual cafe. *7am-8pm Mon-Fri, 8am-5pm Sat* €€

Dvor: Overlooking Firule beach, this upscale restaurant delights with its shady garden and imaginative fish dishes. *noon-midnight Sun-Thu, to 1am Fri & Sat* €€

Mokosh: At this art nouveau villa set in an elegant garden, you'll find fresh fish and meat dishes, plus several vegetarian options. *8am-midnight* €€

Konoba Fetivi: A longstanding favourite for its laid-back vibe and traditional Dalmatian cuisine. Try the black risotto or octopus salad. *noon-8pm Mon-Sat* €€

SPLIT'S BEST BEACHES

Bačvice: This sandy beach with buzzing bars is also a favoured spot for players of *picigin* (a local ball game).

Firule: Popular horse-shoe-shaped sandy beach with cliffside cafes and a scene that continues way past sundown.

Žnjan: One of the bigger beaches in Split, with several bays of white pebbles and views of the mountainous coastline stretching southeast.

Kašjuni: A narrow pebble beach and sunset party spot that curves around the bay on the south side of Marjan Forest Park.

Bene: On the northern side of the Marjan Peninsula, this rocky beach has plenty of shade thanks to the many pine trees.

the long row of cafes buzzes with chitchat and the clinking of cups on saucers.

At the Riva's western end, you may catch the distinctive whiff of sulphur from the healing waters that have sprung up in this spot since Diocletian's time. Some believe these therapeutic springs are the reason he built his palatial retirement home here.

From here, venture to the handsome Venetian-inspired **Republic Square** to admire the vibrant red facades and elegant arches of its three-sided colonnade.

Brač Island

TIME FROM SPLIT: **50MIN**

Brač, Croatia's third-biggest island, is all about perfect beaches, dramatic mountain landscapes, delightful fishing villages and rustic stone hamlets locked in time. The island is also home to Vidova Gora, the highest mountain in the Adriatic archipelago, and the country's best-known beach, Zlatni Rat. The island's history has been shaped by its exceptional natural resources. The olive tree is a symbol of Brač: the rocky landscape is blanketed with groves of more than a million

EATING IN HVAR TOWN: OUR PICKS

Mediterraneo Dine & Wine: Book ahead to eat at this family-run Hvar institution. An extensive wine list complements the large menu. *noon-midnight* €€

Giaxa: Traditional Dalmatian cuisine prepared with high-quality produce. Ask about the catch of the day. *noon-11pm* €€

Štajun: A rustic restaurant offering a fine-dining menu of raw, warm and cold appetisers, with meat or fish as the main. *noon-midnight* €€€

Dalmatino: Smack in the heart of Hvar Town, this bustling dining spot serves up dishes of fish and steak. *noon-11pm Mon-Sat* €€€

SARAH SMITH 55/SHUTTERSTOCK

Zlatni Rat

HVAR'S BEST BEACHES

Mekićevica: Follow the path eastwards from Pokonji Dol to reach this small, sublime and secluded cove of white pebbles.

Malo Zaraće: This pocket-sized beach, embraced by limestone rocks lapped by cobalt-blue waters, is the perfect sunset spot.

Dubovica: After a steep, zigzagging descent, your reward is a strand of white pebbles and two-tone waters of impossible blue.

Lučišća: A magical cove carved out of a rocky cliff face with clear green-blue waters. Best reached by boat.

Jagodna: A series of tiny pebbly coves opens to shallow aquamarine waters. Arrive early.

Brusje: On the less-frequented northern coastline lies this beautiful bay with a lovely stretch of beach.

trees and neat rows of vineyards. Brač is also famous for its high-quality limestone, quarried here since Roman times and used to build many of Croatia's most notable architectural treasures.

White pebbles and turquoise water

Zlatni Rat is Croatia's best-known and most-photographed beach, and it doesn't disappoint. In the delightful town of Bol on the island's southern side, its long V shape magically shifts and changes with the waves and tides. The fine white pebbles are soft on the soles of the feet and don't stick to your skin. Then there's the astonishingly aquamarine water, as clear as a bath, making swimming a true delight. The beach can be reached from Bol along a 2km shady promenade lined with umbrella pines. A tourist train and taxi boat also make the trip from Bol's port.

Hvar Island

TIME FROM SPLIT: 1HR 🚢

Hvar has become synonymous with swank, thanks to Hvar Town's image as a posh destination for the jet set who sail in on their luxury yachts and its buzzy nightlife. But if you're not a fan of the glitterati or all-night parties, fear not, there's the rest of the island to explore. **Stari Grad**, one of the oldest Croatian towns, is charming, easier on the wallet and close to the lush Stari Grad Plain – a UNESCO World Heritage Site. Other highlights include scenic bays ribboned by gorgeous beaches, fields of fragrant lavender and superb local wines.

Dubrovnik

MEDIEVAL WALLS | HISTORIC STREETS | BEACHES

 TOP TIP

Dubrovnik suffers terribly from overtourism. June, July and August are the busiest months. If you don't need to swim, come in March, April or November. Otherwise, aim for May, September or October. Beat the busiest crowds by exploring the old town early in the morning or after dark.

Dubrovnik's extraordinary old town never fails to dazzle. Its magnificent walls enclose a romantic vision of honey-coloured stone and terracotta roofs, virtually unchanged since the 17th century. The vivid colours of the Adriatic lapping at its edges add an extra level of irreality to a scene that already appears to come straight from a fairy tale.

Dubrovnik is busier now than it has ever been, and like Venice – its one-time overlord – it's in danger of being loved to death. *Game of Thrones* is partly responsible for the upsurge in visitors, as the HBO series brought a new generation of admirers to its streets.

But there's so much more to Dubrovnik than just the old town. It's also a regional hub for education, employment and cultural events, so take your time and get to know the city outside the walls, as well as within.

Walk the City Walls

Heaps of history and dazzling views

Croatia's number-one tourist attraction, Dubrovnik's majestic **city walls** *(citywallsdubrovnik.hr; entry adult/child €40/15; 8am-7pm, reduced hours Nov-Mar)* are its defining feature. Stretching a monumental total of 1940m in length, the ramparts are among the largest and most well-preserved in Europe. Circling the old town in one unbroken loop, they're as

GETTING AROUND

The entire old town is a pedestrian zone, and **Libertas** *(libertasdubrovnik.hr)* buses will get you everywhere else you need to go. Timetables are available on the Libertas app or online. Tickets (€2.50) can be purchased on the bus, but they're slightly cheaper if bought at a *tisak* (newsstand) and free if you've

purchased a Dubrovnik Pass (p139). **Mynt** *(rentmynt.com)* is a handy pay-as-you-go app for moped (scooter) hire. Uber operates here and is considerably cheaper than regular taxis. Parking is expensive, so you're better off not hiring a car until you're ready to leave the city.

DUBROVNIK

PILE

Old Harbour

Adriatic Sea

200 m
0.1 miles

HIGHLIGHTS
★ City Walls

SIGHTS
1 City Walls
2 Fort Lovrijenac
3 Fort St John
4 Pile Gate
5 Ploče Gate
6 Rector's Palace
7 Sponza Palace

ACTIVITIES
8 Buža
9 Du Kayak Tour
10 Porporela
11 Šulić Beach
12 X-Adventure

SLEEPING
13 Karmen
Apartments

EATING
14 Gradska kavana
Arsenal
15 Lady Pi-Pi
16 Nautika
17 Nishta
18 Peppino's
19 Republic
20 Restaurant 360
21 Restaurant
Dubrovnik

DRINKING &
NIGHTLIFE
22 Beach Bar Dodo
23 Buža
24 D'vino

THE REPUBLIC OF RAGUSA

Before the Slavic name stuck, Dubrovnik was known as Ragusa. By the end of the 12th century, Ragusa had become a significant trading centre. Venice took the city in 1205, but Ragusa was able to break free in 1538 and declare itself a republic.

By the 15th century, Ragusa had extended its borders to include the entire coast from Ston to Cavtat, as well as the islands of Lastovo and Mljet. Centuries of peace and prosperity allowed art, science and literature to flourish.

The beginning of the republic's economic decline came with a major earthquake in 1667, which killed as many as 5000 people and left the city in ruins. The final coup de grâce was dealt by Napoleon, whose troops entered the city in 1808.

beautiful as they are imposing. From the sea, the juxtaposition of pinkish grey stone and azure waters is mesmerising. For those walking them, the walls provide views over the tight maze of church steeples and terracotta roofs enclosed within.

If you keep a consistent pace and don't stop for photos or refreshments at the cafes, walking the full loop of the walls will take around an hour. There are three entrance points: near the **Pile Gate**, the **Ploče Gate** and **Fort St John**. You can buy a ticket at the gate, but you're better off purchasing a Dubrovnik Pass, which grants free entry.

To avoid accidents, congestion and general confusion, the path leads in an anticlockwise loop only. Along the way are various forts and towers to explore, the highlight being **Fort Minčeta** at the highest point on the landward side. While you're walking, keep an eye out for the two basketball courts tucked away in different corners of the city.

Dubrovnik's patron and protector, St Blaise, adorns the walls of **Fort Lovrjenac**, which was constructed atop a 37m-high promontory adjacent to the old town. Built in 1301 to stand guard over the city's western approach, its walls range from 4m to 12m in thickness. It's fairly empty inside, but it's worth popping in for the incredible views of the old town over the bay. Entry is included with the city walls ticket, or you can pay €15 for just the fort.

Experience the Glory of Ragusa

Majestic palaces and history galore

Apart from its many churches, the most resplendent buildings in the old town are a pair of remarkable palaces that largely survived the earthquake of 1667. If you want to get a feel for the glory days of the Republic of Ragusa, the **Rector's Palace** (*dumus.hr; entry adult/student €15/8*) is the place to start. For nearly 400 years, the palace served as the official residence of the elected official who governed Ragusa. The palace contains his office, private chambers, public halls, administrative offices and a dungeon. It was initially built in the 1430s in Gothic style, with the Renaissance porch added later. During the rector's one-month term, he was unable to leave the building without the permission of the senate. Today, the palace has been turned into a fascinating cultural-history museum; you'll need at least an hour to do it justice. Admission for the palace is included if you've bought the Dubrovnik Pass; it's closed Mondays from November to March.

 EATING IN THE OLD TOWN: BEST CONTEMPORARY CUISINE

Nishta: Imaginative and beautifully presented vegan food incorporating Greek, Middle Eastern, Indian and Mexican flavours. *11.30am-10pm Mon-Sat* €€

Nautika: Contemporary Croatian cuisine in a romantic clifftop location just outside the city walls. The service is faultless. *6pm-midnight* €€€

Restaurant 360: Michelin-starred spot within the city walls delivering fine dining at its best, with prices to match. *6.30-10.30pm Tue-Sun* €€€

Restaurant Dubrovnik: Upmarket restaurant serving modern Mediterranean cuisine on a covered rooftop terrace. *6-11pm Easter-December* €€€

Rector's Palace

DUBROVNIK PASS

If you're planning to walk the **city walls** (p136), buying a Dubrovnik Pass *(dubrovnikpass.com; 1/3/7 days €40/50/60)* is a no-brainer, as the admission for the walls alone is the same price as the day pass.

All passes include free buses, along with admission to the city walls, **Rector's Palace**, Franciscan Monastery, Maritime Museum, Museum of Modern Art, archaeological exhibitions and five other small sights. On top of that, there are discounts to other attractions throughout the county, including **Ston Walls**.

You can buy your pass online or at various shops, sights and hotels, and at any of the official tourist offices.

The nearby **Sponza Palace** has the old town's most beautiful facade. It was completed in 1522 as a customs house and now houses the state archives. Architecturally, it's a mixture of influences. It's usually possible to pop your head in to admire the sweeping, column-lined cloister. Just inside the door is the Memorial Room of the Defenders of Dubrovnik, a moving exhibition honouring those who died during the Homeland War (1991–95).

Find a Beach for You

Swimming, suntans and glam

If the summer heat saps your enthusiasm for sightseeing, a trip to the beach is the best remedy. The main resorts are on the Lapad Peninsula, west of Gruž Harbour, but there are excellent swimming spots to be found all around Dubrovnik, including right in the shadow of the famous city walls. If you tire of the mainland options, catch a ferry to one of the nearby islands, such as Lokrum, Koločep, Lopud or Šipan.

For family fun, head to Lapad Bay, where the main beach has safe and inviting shallow waters. Close to the old town,

DRINKING IN DUBROVNIK: BEST BARS

D'vino: If you're interested in sampling top-notch local wine, this convivial and atmospheric bar in the old town is the place to go. *11am-11pm Mon-Sat*

Buža: This ramshackle cliff-edge bar by the city walls feels like a discovery, but it's often packed, especially around sunset. Cliff divers provide free entertainment. *9am-1am*

Beach Bar Dodo: Local favourite, open all day for beers, burgers and chilled vibes under the watchful eye of Fort Lovrjenac. *10am-8pm*

Cave Bar More: Choose between a seat by the water on Lapad Bay or in an actual cave with stalactites and a flooded cavern. *8am-midnight*

TOP TIPS FOR VISITING THE CITY WALLS

It makes no sense to purchase the city walls ticket separately. The one-day **Dubrovnik Pass** (p139).) is the same price and includes public transport and many other sights.

The entrance near the Pile Gate is usually the busiest. Skip the queues by entering from the Ploče side, which has the added advantage of getting the steepest climbs out of the way first.

There's little shade, so wear a hat and time your visit for the beginning or end of the day. You'll avoid the worst of the crowds, too.

Take water with you, as the stalls along the route are expensive.

GALLERY DE LABUX/SHUTTERSTOCK

Dubrovnik city walls (p136) and Lokrum

check out **Banje Beach**, Dubrovnik's busiest and most famous, just beyond the Ploče Gate, and also **Porporela**, **Buža**, **Šulić** and **Danče** beaches. For local vibes, go to **Sveti Jakov** or **Belvedere**, while the best of beach glam can be found at **Copacabana**.

Kayaking & Snorkel Tours

See the city walls from the sea

If you're an active traveller, there's lots to do on the shores of Dubrovnik. Sea kayaking is big business in the city, with tours departing from Banje Beach, Sveti Jakov Beach and little Šulić Beach under Fort Lovrjenac. **X-Adventure** (*kayak-dubrovnik.com; tours €30-40*) and **Du Kayak Tour** (*dukayaktour.com*) depart from directly beneath the walls, near Pile Gate. The views of the city walls are incredible from the sea, and most tours will take you to **Lokrum** and Betina Cave, a snorkelling spot that can only be reached from the water. Sunset tours are popular.

Outdoor Croatia (*outdoorcroatia.com; from €88*) offers a kayak and snorkel tour of the Elaphiti Islands and includes the ferry from Gruž Harbour to Lopud.

EATING IN THE OLD TOWN: BEST BREAKFASTS & SNACKS

Gradska kavana Arsenal: A top breakfast perch, with a terrace overlooking Dubrovnik's finest buildings and a Viennese-style interior. *8am-midnight* €€

Lady Pi-Pi: Start your day overlooking the old town's terracotta roofs from this little rooftop by the upper walls. *9am-9pm* €€

Republic: Gourmet burger bar on a side lane, also serving pizza, pasta and *ćevapi*. Veggie and vegan burgers available. *11am-11pm* €€

Peppino's: Dubrovnik's best and creamiest gelato, with an array of interesting, artisanal flavours and fair prices. *11am-8pm* €

Places We Love to Stay

€ Budget €€ Midrange €€€ Top End

Zagreb
MAP p125

Stay Swanky € Happening backpacker joint, with a garden bar, seasonal pool, dorms, private rooms inspired by artisans, apartments and Soi, an Asian-fusion restaurant.

Hotel Jägerhorn €€ Zagreb's oldest hotel dates back to 1827 and is a peaceful oasis in a passageway just off Ilica, with subdued, classic elegance and a terrace cafe.

Stellar Boutique Modules €€ Designer hotel along tram-lined Vlaška, with smallish all-white rooms inspired by space, artwork on the ceilings, an all-day cafe-bar serving food and a rooftop bar.

Esplanade Zagreb Hotel €€€ The grande dame of Zagreb hotels is this 100-year-old belle époque beauty with plush rooms and two restaurants, steps from the main train station.

Istria & Kvarner

Old Town Inn €€ Bang in the old town, surrounded by some of Rijeka's coolest addresses and Roman ruins, with modern rooms and historic touches.

Boutique Hotel Valsabbion €€€ Small beachside hotel in quiet Pješčana Uvala, close to Pula, with plush rooms. Perks include its own beach area, heated pool and medical spa.

Hotel Adriatic €€€ A chic design hotel on Rovinj's seafront with art-filled rooms and an elegant bar and brasserie.

Split & Dalmatian Islands

Divota Apartment Hotel €€€ A diffused hotel of apartments and rooms in multiple restored stone houses in charming Veli Varoš.

Heritage Hotel 19 €€€ An elegant boutique hotel in a heritage property with a courtyard garden and romantic vibe.

Hotel Vestibul Palace €€€ Seven rooms make up this elegant hotel with a bar and restaurant tucked just behind the palace's vestibule.

Villa Giardino Heritage Boutique Hotel €€€ A charming villa with elegant rooms in a leafy garden in the heart of Bol on Brač Island.

Maslina Resort €€€ A slice of luxury amid olive groves on a quiet bay near Stari Grad. Ingredients for the restaurant are sourced from the organic garden.

Dubrovnik
MAP p137

Karmen Apartments €€ These four character-filled apartments enjoy a great location near the harbour in Dubrovnik's old town. Book well ahead.

Guest House Biličić €€ This long-standing guesthouse is surrounded by a gorgeous subtropical garden. Bedrooms are simple and clean, with private bathrooms across the corridor.

Hotel Bellevue €€€ On a cliff at the beginning of the Lapad Peninsula, this classy hotel has modern decor, excellent facilities and a beach beneath.

Hotel Excelsior €€€ A Yugoslav-era mash-up of a 1913 hotel with a modern annex, this luxurious hotel has renovated rooms, plus indoor and outdoor pools.

Esplanade Zagreb Hotel

IVO ANTONIE DE ROOIJ/SHUTTERSTOCK

THE GUIDE

CROATIA PLACES WE LOVE TO STAY

Practicalities

LGBTIQ+ Travellers

Croatia ranked #48 on the 2025 Spartacus Gay Travel Index, which is quite low compared to other European countries. In short, Croatia is still a conservative society dominated by traditional Catholic values. Though attitudes are slowly changing, the LGBTIQ+ community prefers to stay under the radar, fearing harassment if they reveal their sexual orientation.

Digital Nomads

Croatia introduced a temporary stay permit for digital nomads in 2021. Valid for up to 18 months, any non-EU/EEA national who works remotely as an employee or is self-employed can apply for the permit as long as they do not provide services to Croatian companies.

Electricity & Connectivity

Type F plug
220V/50Hz
Free wi-fi is available at the airport and most hotels and cafes, while major cities and tourist centres have a free public wi-fi service.

Drinking Water

Croatia is known for its high-quality, abundant water resources. Tap water is perfectly safe to drink.

JULIA LAV/SHUTTERSTOCK

Rijeka (p130)

Opening Hours

Many shops close on Sundays outside of summer.
Banks 8am–6pm Monday to Friday
Bars 10am–2am
Cafes 7am–11pm
Restaurants 10am–11pm
Shopping malls 9am–10pm
Supermarkets 7am–9pm

Public Holidays

New Year's Day 1 January
Epiphany 6 January
Easter Monday March/April
Labour Day 1 May
Statehood Day 30 May
Corpus Christi 60 days after Easter
Day of Antifascist Resistance 22 June
Homeland Thanksgiving Day 5 August
Feast of the Assumption 15 August
All Saints' Day 1 November
Remembrance Day for Victims of the Homeland War 18 November
Christmas 25 & 26 December

Language

In Croatian, every letter is pronounced and its sound does not vary from word to word.

Basics

Hello. Dobar dan. *do·bar dan*
Goodbye. Zbogom. *zbo·gom*
Yes. Da. *da*
No. Ne. *ne*
Please. Molim. *mo·lim*
Thank you. Hvala vam/ti (pol/inf). *hva·la vam/ti*
Excuse me. Oprostite. *o·pro·sti·te*
Sorry. Žao mi je. *zha·o mi ye*
What's your name? Kako se zovete/zoveš? (pol/inf) *ka·ko se zo·ve·te/zo·vesh*
My name is ... Zovem se ... *zo·vem se*
Do you speak English? Govorite/Govoriš li engleski? (pol/inf) *go·vo·ri·te/go·vo·rish li en·gle·ski*
I don't understand. Ne razumijem. *ne ra·zu·mi·yem*

Directions

Where's (the station)?
Gdje je (stanica)? *gdye ye (sta·ni·tsa)*

10 Phrases to Sound Like a Local

Šta ima? – What's up?
Kužim/Ne kužim – I understand/I don't understand.
To je fora! – That's cool!
To je mrak! – That's awesome!
Idemo na cugu – Let's go for a drink.
To je puno love – That's a lot of money.
Nema šanse! – No way!
Nema veze – Never mind.
Idemo na klopu – Let's go for some food.
Nema frke – No problem.

What's the address?
Koja je adresa? *koy·a ye a·dre·sa*
Could you please write it down?
Možete li to napisati?/Možeš li to napisati? (pol/inf) *mo·zhe·te li to na·pi·sa·ti/mo·zhesh li to na·pi·sa·ti*
Can you show me (on the map)?
Možete li mi to pokazati (na karti)? *mo·zhe·te li mi to po·ka·za·ti (na kar·ti)*

Time

What time is it? Koliko je sati? *ko·li·ko ye sa·ti*
It's (10) o'clock. (Deset) je sati. *(de·set) ye sa·ti*
Half past (10). (Deset) i po. *(de·set) i po*
morning jutro. *yu·tro*
afternoon popodne. *po·pod·ne*
evening večer. *ve·cher*
yesterday jučer. *yu·cher*
today danas. *da·nas*
tomorrow sutra. *su·tra*

Emergencies

Help! Upomoć! *u·po·moch*
Go away! Maknite se! *mak·ni·te se*
Call ...! Zovite ...! *zo·vi·te*
    a doctor liječnika *li·yech·ni·ka*
    the police policiju. *po·li·tsi·yu*

Eating & Drinking

What would you recommend?
Što biste nam preporučili? *shto bi·ste nam pre·po·ru·chi·li*
Cheers! Živjeli! *zhi·vye·li*
I'd like the bill please.
Mogu li dobiti račun, molim. *mo·gu li do·bi·ti ra·chun mo·lim*

DONATIONS TO ENGLISH

Did you know that the words Dalmatian and cravat come from Croatian?

NUMBERS

1
jedan
ye·dan

2
dva *dva*

3
tri *tri*

4
četiri
che·ti·ri

5
pet *pet*

6
šest *shest*

7
sedam
se·dam

8
osam *o·sam*

9
devet *de·vet*

10
deset *de·set*

A. EMSON/SHUTTERSTOCK

Zagreb International Airport

Arriving

It's always thrilling to arrive in Croatia, whether landing at one of the nine airports, coming by sea or arriving overland as the verdant landscapes and island-dotted coastline sweep by. It's busiest during the high summer season (July and August), but with vistas this stunning, a trip any time of the year is a delight.

By Air
Zagreb International Airport (Franjo Tuđman Airport) is Croatia's main hub. During summer, additional low-cost connections from European destinations fly to Brač, Dubrovnik, Osijek, Pula, Rijeka, Split and Zadar.

By Land
With limited train services in the Balkans, many travellers find the affordable, long-haul buses run by companies such as FlixBus and Arriva to be the best way of getting to Croatia. There are regular international services to Zagreb and Rijeka.

MONEY
Currency: Euro (€)

CASH
Cash is still king in Croatia, especially in villages and smaller towns on the islands, where cafes and restaurants are likely to take cash only. Check with your accommodation in advance, particularly if staying in rural or remote spots or in a hostel.

TIPPING
Croatia doesn't have a tipping culture, but gratuities are always appreciated. Round up the bill in bars and cafes, and leave a 5% to 10% tip in restaurants. If you pay by card, leave the tip in cash.

CARDS & ATMS
You can pay by card or phone in all large chain stores in Zagreb, Zadar, Split, Dubrovnik and other urban areas. Have small change ready for small purchases, bus tickets and the like. ATMs operated by banks are widespread and reliable. Avoid Euronet ATMs – these charge high fees and offer terrible exchange rates.

Getting Around

Croatia is relatively small – it takes just seven hours to drive from one end to the other via the highways. That said, if you plan to visit the islands, a lot of your journeys will likely involve ferries, so don't rush and allow for slow travel days.

PAUL PRESCOTT/SHUTTERSTOCK

Bus
Arriva, Autotrans and FlixBus all serve Zagreb, Pula, Rijeka, Zadar, Split and Dubrovnik, where you can change to cheap, mostly punctual, local buses (Arriva and Autotrans) that journey onwards to the major islands and more rural destinations.

Ferry
Ferries connect the mainland with the islands; Jadrolinija is the biggest company. Its schedule ramps up come peak season, and other companies like Krilo serve useful routes such as Split–Dubrovnik during summer.

Train
Croatia is not well served by train. Arriving from Slovenia, Hungary, Austria and other neighbours into Zagreb Glavni Kolodvor station (pictured above), the only onward route you're likely to use is the Zagreb–Split train, which is best booked in advance.

Car
Hiring a car is undoubtedly the best way to explore Croatia. The best prices are found in Zagreb or Rijeka; expect to pay double in Split or Dubrovnik. Highways have tolls in many parts; get a ticket at the entrance and pay at the exit.

Bicycle
Long-distance cycling is popular with visitors. Nextbike is a public bike-sharing system (e-bikes too), and you can rent a bike from terminals without needing a phone. Look for docking stations in 30 locations across Croatia.

DRIVING ESSENTIALS

Drive on the right

50

Speed limit is 50km/h on urban roads, 90km/h on main roads and 130km/h on highways

While Croatians are courteous drivers, don't expect locals to stick to the speed limits

Curated by
Mark Baker

Czechia

BREATHTAKING CASTLES AND EVEN BETTER BEER

Find dramatic historical architecture, charming towns,
quirky sights and a vibrant, youthful culture.

Since the fall of communism in 1989 and the opening up of Central and Eastern Europe, Prague has evolved into one of Europe's most popular travel destinations. And for very good reason. Czechia's capital city offers an intact medieval core that transports you back – especially when strolling the hidden streets of the Old Town – some 600 years. The 14th-century Charles Bridge, linking two historic neighbourhoods across a slow-moving river – with Prague Castle pitched dramatically in the backdrop – is one of the continent's most beautiful sights. But Prague is not just about history. It's a vital urban centre with a rich array of cultural offerings, including fantastic museums, concert halls, restaurants and clubs.

Outside the capital, in the provinces of Bohemia and Moravia, castles and palaces abound – including the audacious hilltop chateau at Český Krumlov – which illuminate the stories of powerful dynasties whose influence was felt throughout Europe. Bohemia was famous in the 19th century for its regal spas, and Karlovy Vary still shows off this old-school splendour. Beer afficionados will make a beeline for Plzeň (Pilsen), where modern-day lager was first invented. Moravia lies a bit further off the beaten path. The provincial capital of Brno abounds in student-fiilled bars and cafes and ghoulish underground sights. The city of Olomouc has much of the architectural beauty of Prague, with just a fraction of the crowds.

FOTOKON/SHUTTERSTOCK

THE MAIN AREAS

PRAGUE	BOHEMIA	MORAVIA
Czechia's breathtaking and energetic capital. **p150**	Castles, historic spa resorts, beers and bones. **p159**	Underground adventure and baroque beauty. **p165**

For places to stay in Czechia, see p170

Left: Beer, Plzeň (p160); Above: Charles Bridge (p155), Prague

Find Your Way

A sampling of the best of Czechia. We've picked out some of the must-see sights in Prague, plus highlights for excursions further afield into the provinces of Bohemia and Moravia.

TRAINS & BUSES

You won't need a car to get around. The extensive train and bus network can take you to all the places covered here. We've noted where either the train or bus might be faster or cheaper.

CAR

Don't use your own vehicle to get around Prague. The city's metro and trams are much more practical. Outside the capital, a car gives you flexibility to explore the country at your own pace.

Moravia, p165

Experience Czechia without the tourists, including visiting a vibrant provincial capital and an underappreciated baroque beauty.

Prague, p150

Immerse yourself in centuries-old historic architecture, followed up with a pint at a pub or a classical concert.

Bohemia, p159

Discover castle-topped hills and charming historic towns, and then treat yourself to possibly the world's best beer tour.

GERMANY

POLAND

SLOVAKIA

AUSTRIA

Dresden · Chemnitz · Munich

Katowice

Ostrava · Opava · Olomouc · Přerov · Nový Jičín · Frýdek-Místek · Rožnov pod Radhoštěm

Šumperk · Svitavy · Blansko · Brno · Kroměříž

Hradec Králové · Ústí nad Orlicí · Chrudim · Litomyšl · Havlíčkův Brod · Třebíč · Jihlava

Mladá Boleslav · Kutná Hora · Sedlec Ossuary · Benešov · Tábor · Jindřichův Hradec · Třeboň · České Budějovice · Český Krumlov

PRAGUE · Old Town Square · Prague Castle · Kladno · Beroun · Příbram · Písek · Český Krumlov State Castle

Děčín · Ústí nad Labem · Louny · Most · Žatec · Chomutov · Karlovy Vary · Mariánské Lázně · Plzeň (Pilsen) · Klatovy · Domažlice

BOHEMIA

MORAVIA

Labyrinth under the Vegetable Market · Villa Tugendhat

Bohemian Switzerland National Park · Elbe River

Šumava National Park

Labe River · Vltava River · Morava River · Odra · Danube

100 km
50 miles

148

BORIS STROULKO/SHUTTERSTOCK

Prague (p150)

Plan Your Time

Three days is sufficient for Prague, and you can then pick and choose what you'd like to see in Bohemia or Moravia. With a car you can cover the highlights in a week.

Three Days in Prague

● Experience the exciting combination of a glorious past and energetic present in Prague. Take in the grandeur of **Prague Castle** (p151), cross **Charles Bridge** (p155) and wander Prague's Old Town. Take in the spectacle of **Old Town Square** (p156) and the **Astronomical Clock** (p156) and then explore the **Prague Jewish Museum** (p156). Spend a third day on the train going to see spectacular **Karlštejn Castle** (p158).

A Week in Czechia

● Begin in **Prague** (p150) before heading west for the spa scene at **Karlovy Vary** (p159). Balance the virtue and vice ledger with a few brews in **Plzeň** (p160), before heading south to **Český Krumlov** (p162). Take in the 'Bone Church' in **Kutná Hora** (p163) and then head east to enjoy the underground sights of **Brno** (p165). From Moravia's largest city, it's just a skip to stately **Olomouc** (p168).

SEASONAL HIGHLIGHTS

SPRING

Trees and flowers start budding in April and the country comes alive after the long winter. May and June days are often warm and sunny.

SUMMER

Hot, sunny days are perfect for escaping the city. That said, it's high season. Thousands of visitors stream through Prague daily.

AUTUMN

September and October tend to be quieter but still offer reliably good weather. Locals decamp to the forests to pick mushrooms.

WINTER

The Christmas and New Year's holidays enliven the long, cold winter. Hotel rates drop, but some attractions, including gardens, close.

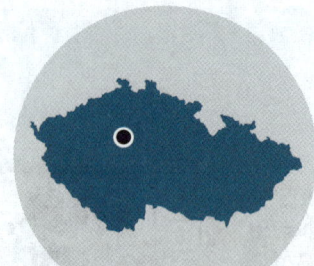

Prague

RIVETING HISTORY | STIRRING VIEWS | REGAL ARCHITECTURE

The ups and downs of centuries past, of empires, wars, plagues and prosperity, are etched into Prague's soul like the lines carved onto the facades of its Gothic towers and Renaissance palaces. Some 35 years ago, Prague re-emerged on the European stage after languishing for years under communism, and the world was agog. Those years trapped behind the Iron Curtain left the city looking neglected and rundown, but it was obvious Prague's rich history and intrinsic beauty – the hypnotic, visual tension between Charles Bridge and Prague Castle – had survived intact.

Indeed, that's the real pleasure of a trip to Prague now that the scaffolding is down and the appeal is obvious to everyone: to take in the beauty as you wander slowly from Prague Castle down through the historic Malá Strana quarter, across Charles Bridge, over the Vltava River and into the arms of the Old Town.

Prague Castle & Hradčany

The hilltop neighbourhood of Hradčany, home to Prague Castle, retains a whiff of exclusivity centuries after the emperors and kings who once lived here have gone. The main attractions include the Prague Castle complex and stately St Vitus Cathedral, which stands within the castle walls. Strahov Monastery has been here since at least 1140; the

 GETTING AROUND

Prague has an excellent public transport system of metros, trams, buses and night trams, but when it comes to moving around the relatively compact historic neighbourhoods of Staré Město (Old Town), Malá Strana and Prague Castle, it's more convenient – and more scenic – to travel by foot. Use the metro to cover longer distances or to convenient stations located near Staré Město, Malá Strana and central Wenceslas Square. Use the tram for shorter stretches. Tram 22 runs to near Prague Castle and can spare you the climb up to the castle district.

Old Royal Palace

EARLY STORY OF HRADČANY

Hradčany got its first royal residents in the 9th century. A ducal palace was built here to accommodate the early ruling Přemyslid dynasty. The 12th century saw significant expansion. A grander ducal palace was completed. In 1140, the Premonstraten-sian Monastery was founded in Strahov. In the 14th century, Emperor Charles IV rebuilt the castle to more properly represent Prague's status as seat of the Holy Roman Empire. He also embarked on construction of St Vitus Cathedral.

In 1541, a tragic fire engulfed the district and damaged many buildings, including the castle and cathedral. Yet the fire created large, empty lots that eventually gave way to today's mega-palaces, including the **Schwarzenberg Palace** and the **Archbishop's Palace**.

monks' adjoining library is one of the most beautiful in Europe. Scattered among the incredible palaces are pubs, restaurants and breathtaking views out over Malá Strana and the Old Town.

Take in sprawling Prague Castle

Looming high above the Vltava River, **Prague Castle** (*hrad.cz; tours from adult/child 300/200Kč*), with its serried ranks of spires and palaces, dominates the city. Within its walls lies a fascinating collection of historic buildings, museums and galleries, home to some of Czechia's greatest artistic and cultural treasures. The grounds of the castle complex are free to enter, though to see the interiors (including adjoining St Vitus Cathedral) requires a combined admission ticket. Buy tickets online at **Ticketportal** (*ticketportal.cz*) or at the **castle information centre**.

The high point for most visitors is the **Old Royal Palace**, situated in the castle's third courtyard. This is one of the oldest surviving parts of the castle, dating from 1135. Don't miss the **Vladislav Hall** (Vladislavský sál), which is famous for its beautiful, late-Gothic vaulted ceiling. Beyond the Old Royal Palace, the **Basilica of St George** is Czechia's best-preserved Romanesque basilica. You can also stroll **Golden Lane**, where writer Franz Kafka stayed at No 22 (from 1916 to 1917).

EATING & DRINKING NEAR PRAGUE CASTLE: OUR PICKS

Klášterní Pivovar Strahov: Convivial pub near Strahov Monastery serves its own St Norbert beers – and very good Czech food. *10am-10pm* €€

Vinobona Wine & Bistro: Tiny, romantic spot; perfect for breakfast/lunch. Dress smartly for pricier dinner tasting menu. *9am-3pm, 6-10pm Thu-Mon* €€€

Kuchyň: Book well in advance to secure one of the popular terrace tables. Excellent Czech standards. *11.30am-11pm* €€

Lobkowicz Palace Café: The best pit stop for drinks and light meals within the Prague Castle complex. Superb views from the back balcony. *10am-6pm* €€

PRAGUE

HRADČANY

Prague Castle

HRADČANY

NOVÝ SVĚT

NOVÝ SVĚT

STRAHOV

PRAHA 5

0   500 m
0   0.25 miles

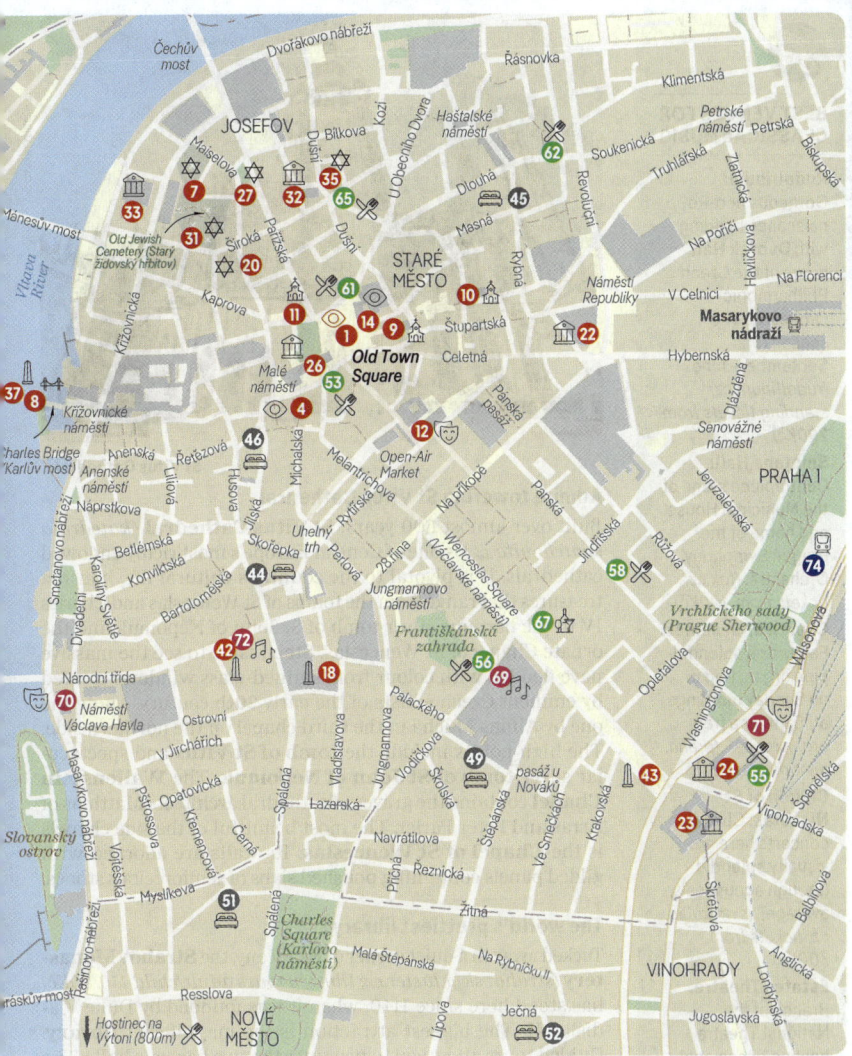

BEST VENUES FOR CLASSICAL MUSIC

Rudolfinum: Gorgeous neo-Renaissance building with **Dvořák Hall**, home of the Czech Philharmonic Orchestra. The season runs September–June. *(rudolfinum.cz; standing tickets from 200Kč)*

Smetana Hall: Centrepiece stage of the Municipal House and home of the Prague Symphony Orchestra. *(fok.cz; tickets from 400Kč)*

Church of St James: Features a splendid pipe organ. Pop in on Sunday mornings at 10am for a free organ recital. *(praha.minorite.cz; free)*

Church of St Nicholas: Chamber concerts here are visually splendid (though acoustically average). *(svmikulas.cz; tickets from 300Kč)*

Estates Theatre: Branch of the National Theatre hosting occasional baroque music concerts. *(narodni-divadlo.cz; tickets from 400Kč)*

ROSSHELEN/SHUTTERSTOCK

St Vitus Cathedral

Admire towering St Vitus Cathedral

Built over almost 600 years, **St Vitus Cathedral** *(katedrala svatehovita.cz)* is one of Central Europe's most richly endowed cathedrals. It is pivotal to the country's cultural life, housing treasures that range from the tombs of St Wenceslas and Charles IV to the baroque silver tomb of St John of Nepomuk and the ornate Chapel of St Wenceslas. Step inside to see the massive nave flooded with colour from stained-glass windows created by eminent Czech artists of the early 20th century – note the one by Alfons Mucha in the third chapel on the northern side. The high points include the **tomb of St Vitus** and spectacular silver **tomb of St John of Nepomuk**. The **Wallenstein Chapel** contains the graves of cathedral architects Matthias of Arras and Peter Parler. The most beautiful of the side chapels is the **Chapel of St Wenceslas**. Its walls are adorned with gilded panels containing polished slabs of semiprecious stones.

The world's prettiest library?

Tucked away in a quiet corner of Hradčany, the **Strahov Monastery** *(strahovskyklaster.cz; library tours adult/child 150/80Kč)* has stood here since 1140, when it was founded by Duke Vladislav II. The biggest attraction is the magnificent **library**. Guided tours allow you to peer into the two baroque halls. The stunning interior of the two-storey 'Philosophy Hall' features floor-to-ceiling walnut shelving. The older 'Theology Hall' is even more breathtaking.

Malá Strana (Lesser Town)

Visitors are often surprised to discover that Malá Strana (Lesser Town) is in some ways more beautiful than Staré Město (Old Town). In the 17th and 18th centuries, noble families built their sumptuous palaces and plotted out spacious gardens here. The neighbourhood is home to many top sights, including the impressive baroque of St Nicholass Church and the elegant Wallenstein Garden. The best way to explore is to amble along the cobblestoned backstreets, or through **Kampa Park** along the river, and admire the handsome buildings and tiny squares.

Walk across Charles Bridge

Who knew a bridge could ever be this beautiful or that mounting 30 baroque statues along its edges might elevate a handsome Gothic structure into a public work of art? **Charles Bridge** (*Karlův most, free*) is a world-class attraction. The bridge began life in 1357 when Emperor Charles IV commissioned Peter Parler (architect of St Vitus Cathedral) to replace an older, 12th-century bridge that had been washed away by floods. The new bridge was completed in 1390. The statues came three centuries later, when the bridge's first monument, the Crucifix near the eastern end, was mounted in 1657. The most famous figure is the monument to **St John of Nepomuk**. Tradition says if you rub the bronze plaque, you'll one day return to Prague.

Take in grand St Nicholas Church

Praguers generally have a love-hate affair with baroque architecture. Everyone, though, loves **St Nicholas Church** (*Kostel svatého Mikuláše; stnicholas.cz; adult/child 140/80Kč*); its big green dome can be seen from just about anywhere in the centre. The building was begun by famed baroque architect Christoph Dientzenhofer; his son Kilian continued the work and Anselmo Lurago finished the job in 1755. Mozart himself tickled the ivories on the 2500-pipe organ in 1787. Take the stairs up to the gallery to see Karel Škréta's emotive, 17th-century *Passion Cycle* paintings. On the ceiling, Johann Kracker's 1770 *Apotheosis of St Nicholas* is Europe's largest fresco.

Climb Petřín Hill

This 318m-high **Petřín** is one of Prague's largest green spaces. It's great for quiet, tree-shaded walks and fine views over the 'city of a hundred spires'. Climb up or take the **Petřín Funicular** to find the views and a handful of kid-friendly attractions. The **Petřín Lookout Tower** (*adult/child 220/150Kč*), a 60m-high Eiffel Tower lookalike (though smaller at a ratio of 1:5), offers dramatic vistas. Just near the lookout tower is a **Mirror Maze** (*adult/child 120/80Kč*). Younger children will get a kick out of the distorting funhouse mirrors and labyrinth.

Staré Město (Old Town)

Staré Město, Prague's Old Town, has been the city's beating heart for more than 1000 years. The grand buildings, churches

HOUSE SIGNS OF NERUDOVA

Steep Nerudova street leads from Malá Strana to Prague Castle. It has a long, rich history – much of it written on the playful symbols that adorn the fronts of the houses. The **House at the Three Fiddles** (Nerudova 12) once belonged, fittingly, to a family of violinmakers. **St John of Nepomuk House** (No 18) is adorned with an image of the patron saint himself. **Bretfeld Palace** (No 33) was a social hot spot, entertaining the likes of Mozart and Casanova. The **House of the Golden Horseshoe** (No 34) is named after St Wenceslas' horse, allegedly shod with gold. Czech writer and journalist Jan Neruda, after whom the street is named, lived at the **House of the Two Suns** (No 47) from 1845 to 1857.

EATING IN MALÁ STRANA: OUR PICKS

U Modré Kachničky: This feels like an old-fashioned hunting lodge, with quiet, candlelit nooks. The traditional roast duck is very good. *noon-11pm* €€€

Terasa U Zlaté Studně: Perched atop a Renaissance mansion close to the castle, the 'Golden Well' has truly fine dining. *noon-4pm & 6-11pm* €€€

Ichnusa Botega Bistro: Superb Italian food and wines ferried to Prague directly from the owner's homeland of Sardinia. *11am-10pm* €€

Café Savoy: Elegant Viennese-style coffeehouse, with terrific Czech specialties and homemade desserts. *8am-10pm Mon-Fri, from 9am Sat & Sun* €€

IN THE FOOTSTEPS OF KINGS

The **Royal Way** (Královská cesta) was the former processional route followed by the Bohemian kings on their way to St Vitus Cathedral for coronation. The first king to ride the route was the Habsburg ruler Albert II, in 1438; the last was Emperor Ferdinand I of Austria, in 1836.

The coronation route ran right through the heart of Staré Město. It began at the Powder Gate. From here, the route followed Celetná to Old Town Square and the adjacent Little Square (Malé náměstí). From the squares, the route traced Karlova street to Charles Bridge and then across to Malá Strana. On the Malá Strana side, the coronation route proceeded along Mostecká street to Malostranské náměstí (Lesser Town Square) before climbing up Nerudova to Prague Castle.

and squares, the Old Town Hall and Astronomical Clock stand as testimony to the growing wealth and influence over the centuries of Prague's merchants and artisans. This splendour came to rival that of the kings and noble families on the other side of the river. The best way to take in Staré Město's sights is to wander at will. The street plan appears to have little logic at all; perfect for getting lost in.

Explore Old Town Square

One of Europe's most beautiful and busiest urban spaces, **Old Town Square** has been Prague's principal public square since the 10th century and was its main marketplace until the beginning of the 20th century.

The most important building, the **Old Town Hall** (staromestskaradnicepraha.cz; tower adult/child 300/200Kč), was founded in 1338 to serve as Staré Město's independent seat of government. These days it no longer has a formal governing function. The main admission ticket includes entry to the tower, which affords dramatic views of the square below. The Town Hall's best-known attraction is the **Astronomical Clock** (free) on its south-facing exterior. On the hour, from 9am to 9pm, spectators are treated to a 45-second mechanised marionette display straight out of the Middle Ages.

Beyond the Old Town Hall, the most dramatic structure on the square is the twin-spired **Church of Our Lady Before Týn**, across the way, which stands incongruously behind a row of baroque facades. The 14th-century **House at the Stone Bell** is considered the square's oldest building. Find another important church, the baroque **Church of St Nicholas**, wedged into the northwestern corner.

Two pieces of statuary in the middle of the square are integral to this public space. Praguers love the dramatic art nouveau depiction of Czech religious reformer **Jan Hus** by Ladislav Šaloun. The newer **Marian Column** was only installed in 2020, and it's fair to say locals haven't quite warmed up to it yet.

Tour Prague's Jewish Museum

The **Prague Jewish Museum** (jewishmuseum.cz; from adult/child 600/400Kč) isn't simply one museum but a grouping of historic synagogues and an ancient burial ground. The holdings constitute possibly the world's biggest collection of sacred Jewish artefacts, many rescued from synagogues destroyed by Nazi Germany during WWII. The crumbling **Old Jewish Cemetery** is a must. The weatherworn headstones mark just

EATING IN STARÉ MĚSTO: OUR PICKS

420 Restaurant: Opulent dining room with baroque statues. Traditional Czech dishes given fusion upgrade. Book ahead. *11.30am-10.30pm* €€€

Mincovna: Best of an average bunch of restaurants on Old Town Square. Decent pork knee, schnitzels and duck. *11.30am-11pm* €€

Naše Maso: Tiny butcher with stand-up tables at the forefront of Prague's rush to embrace the foodie philosophy of locally sourced meat. *11am-10pm* €€

V Kolkovně: Operated by Pilsner Urquell Brewery. Stylish, modern take on traditional Prague pub; fancy-ish versions of classic Czech dishes. *11am-midnight* €€

Old Town Square

a fraction of the thousands buried here. Other important sites include the **Old-New Synagogue**, **Pinkas Synagogue**, **Maisel Synagogue**, **Spanish Synagogue**, **Klaus Synagogue** and **Ceremonial Hall**. One basic admission ticket allows entry to all of the main monuments, including the Old-New Synagogue. Buy tickets via the museum website or at the Museum Reservation Centre (Maiselova 15).

Admire art nouveau elegance

The **Municipal House** *(obecnidum.cz; guided tours adult/child 320/270Kč)* is Prague's most exuberantly art nouveau building. The building, constructed between 1906 and 1912, was a lavish joint effort by around 30 leading Czech artists, including Alfons Mucha. Every detail of its design and decoration was carefully considered. Guided tours in English can be booked via the website or at the venue box office. The tour's highlight is the octagonal Lord Mayor's Hall, the windows of which overlook the main entrance.

Nové Město (New Town)

The busy streets of Prague's main commercial area are where Prague starts to feel like a real city (and less like a living museum). Nové Město translates as 'New Town', but there's little 'new' about it. It was laid out by Emperor Charles IV in the mid-14th century to alleviate overcrowding in Staré Město.

Wenceslas Square has witnessed a great deal of Czech history. In 1848, during the revolutionary anti-Habsburg upheavals of that year, a giant mass was held here. In 1918, at the end of WWI, thousands gathered to celebrate the creation of the newly independent Czechoslovakia from the ruins of the old Austro-Hungarian Empire.

For many Czechs (and Slovaks), Wenceslas Square will forever be linked to the 1989 Velvet Revolution. Not far from the square, on Národní street, find a **memorial** to the spot where demonstrators and riot police first clashed on 17 November. In the days afterwards, angry citizens gathered on the square night after night to protest and cheer on the efforts of dissident leader Václav Havel.

 EATING IN NOVÉ MĚSTO: OUR PICKS

Kantýna: Choose your own piece of meat at the counter for the chefs to prepare, and enjoy it in an opulent former bank building. *11.30am-11pm* €€

Čestr: Splurge-worthy steakhouse behind the 'New Building' of the National Museum. Pair a meal with a trip to the museum or State Opera. *noon-11pm* €€€

Garden's: A passage opposite the entrance to the Lucerna Palace leads to a secret garden. Book ahead. *11am-10pm Mon-Sat, to 8pm Sun* €€

Hostinec na Výtoni: Duck is a beloved staple of Czech cuisine and at this picturesque inn by the river they do it better than anyone else in town. *11.30am-11pm* €€

**BEST FOR A
FUN NIGHT OUT**

**State Opera
(narodni-divado.cz):**
Prague's pre-eminent
venue for opera is
heavy on traditional
Italian opera at a very
high standard.

**National Theatre
(narodni-divadlo.
cz):** Performs virtually
anything from Czech
opera to avant-garde
dance.

**Reduta Jazz Club
(redutajazzclub.
cz):** Smartly dressed
patrons squeeze
into tiered seats and
lounges to soak up
the big-band, swing
and Dixieland.

**Lucerna Music Bar
(musicbar.cz):** Host
all kinds of live rock
bands – from Czech
superstars to visiting
indie rockers from
around the world.

**Duplex (duplex.
cz):** Visiting live
DJs, several rooms,
rooftop chillout zone.
Often considered the
best dance club
in town.

Nové Město is home to the city's most important public gathering area, Wenceslas Square, as well as many excellent museums, restaurants, hotels and concert venues. Many of the great moments of Czech history took place here.

Tour the National Museum

Nové Město's most important building looms high above Wenceslas Square. The neo-Renaissance bulk of the **National Museum** *(nm.cz; adult/child 300/200Kč)*, designed in the 1880s as an architectural symbol of the Czech National Revival, highlights not only the history of the Czech lands from the 8th to 20th centuries, but presents thorough exhibitions on natural history, the 'miracles of evolution' and much more. The holdings are divided into two buildings. In addition to the main historical building, the **annex** is home to two more attractions: the interactive Children's Museum and the Museum of the 20th Century, narrating last century's gripping events.

See Kafka's head on a swivel

Nové Město is home to two of Czech artist David Černý's *(davidcerny.cz)* most-popular installations. Don't leave Prague without checking out **K**, a giant rotating bust of Franz Kafka. The bust gives a mesmerising show, as Kafka's face rhythmically dissolves and re-emerges.

The Lucerna Palace shopping arcade holds Černý's oddest installation: **Kůň** (Horse). A giant dead horse – with St Wenceslas sitting astride – hangs from the marbled atrium. It's a wryly amusing counterpart to the more imposing equestrian statue of the Bohemian patron **St Wenceslas** on Wenceslas Square.

Outside of Prague   TIME FROM PRAGUE: 45MIN

Tour majestic Karlštejn Castle

Once you've had your fill of Prague, one fun, easy day trip is to catch the train out to Karlštejn, 35km southwest of the capital, to see magnificent **Karlštejn Castle** *(hrad-karlstejn.cz; basic tour adult/child from 300/240Kč)*. This glorious pile was conceived by Emperor Charles IV in the 14th century and wouldn't look at all out of place on Disney World's Main Street. After seeing the interior, stroll through the charming town that surrounds the structure.

Two main guided tours of the castle are available, but most visitors opt for the shorter, hourlong 'basic' tour. This option provides a good introduction. You'll get glimpses into the Knight's Hall – still daubed with the coats of arms and names of the knight-vassals – as well as views of Emperor Charles IV's bedchamber, the Audience Hall and the Jewel House.

Bohemia

HISTORIC SPA | BREATHTAKING ARCHITECTURE | BIRTHPLACE OF BEER

Czechia's western province of Bohemia, with its forests and rolling hills, surrounds Prague on all sides. The region is peppered with unique sights and UNESCO World Heritage listings. To the west, the lustrous spa region – centred on Karlovy Vary – attracted the rich and famous from all around Europe in the 19th and early 20th centuries and still has the impressive architecture to match. To the south, the medieval resplendence of Český Krumlov and its glorious Renaissance castle rival Prague in terms of wow factor. Just south of Prague, the sweet aroma of hops drifts in the air in the city of Plzeň (Pilsen), where lager was invented in the 19th century and brewing traditions are still based on Bohemia's crystal-clear water and award-winning Saaz hops. Other highlights in this incredibly varied wedge of Central Europe include the magnificent former silver-mining town of Kutná Hora. People come here not just to tour the old mines but to visit the shocking, must-be-seen-to-be-believed 'Bone Church'.

Places

☑ TOP TIP

If you've only got time for one destination in Bohemia, make it Český Krumlov, one of Europe's prettiest small towns. Plan to stay overnight, as the three-hour travel time from Prague each way can be too long for a comfortable day trip.

Karlovy Vary

TIME FROM PRAGUE: 1½HR

Karlovy Vary, or simply 'Vary' to Czechs, perhaps more than any other town in Central Europe best captures the lost glamour and elegance of 19th-century spa culture. The

---

 GETTING AROUND

Bohemia is well covered by buses and trains, though if you don't have your own wheels, the destinations listed here are probably best approached as a return trip from Prague. Whether the train or bus is best depends on the destination. For Karlovy Vary and Český Krumlov, opt for the bus, while Plzeň and Kutná Hora both lie an easy train journey away. For drivers, roads are good but get crowded on weekends. The D5 motorway whisks you from Prague to Plzeň in under an hour.

SOUVENIRS FROM KARLOVY VARY

Becherovka: This strong-tasting herbal liquor, made to a secret recipe, is available at every bar and grocery store.

Moser Glass: Visit the **Moser Glasswork Shop** at the Grandhotel Pupp for an eternal reminder of your trip.

Spa cups: Among the most popular Bohemian souvenirs are these curiously shaped sipping cups, available from spa kiosks.

Porcelain: Head to **Porcelain Pokorný** (*nábřeží J Palacha 924/6)* for a wide choice of locally produced wares.

Spa wafers: Typical Czech-spa tooth-rotters available at stalls in the spa zone.

Petrified roses: Roses left in the spring water accumulate mineral residue, essentially turning to stone; buy one from kiosks in the Vřídelní Colonnade.

promenades, colonnades and grand neoclassical buildings dazzle the eye. In the resort's heyday, royals like Russia's Peter the Great and members of the Habsburg monarchy hobnobbed here with the greatest thinkers, writers and composers of their time. These days, visitors come to admire the architecture and stroll the impressive colonnades, sipping on the health-restoring sulphurous waters from spouted ceramic drinking cups.

Stroll the colonnades

The best way to experience Karlovy Vary is to get out walking and see the magnificent colonnades up close. Start your stroll at the northern end of the spa area, whose entry is marked by the landmark communist-era **Hotel Thermal** (1976), built in the modern 'brutalist' style.

Inside, you'll find **Saunia** *(saunia.cz),* with access to the hotel's famous rooftop pool and views across the town. Walk south into the spa zone to find the cast-iron **Park Colonnade**. Then continue for 300m along the Teplá River to the biggest and most impressive colonnade, the neo-Renaissance **Mill Colonnade**, with five different springs.

Keep walking along Lázeňská street to the impressive **Market Colonnade**; one of its two springs, the pramen Karla IV (Charles IV Spring), is the spa's oldest. The street Stará Louka continues south for more splendour. At the end of the stroll stands the magnificent **Grandhotel Pupp**, the resort's choicest hotel.

Hit Vary's high points

For the best high-level views of pretty Karlovy Vary, make your way up to the **Diana lookout tower**, reached by **funicular railway** from behind the Grandhotel Pupp. The tower is free to climb and affords memorable views across the spa and the surrounding forested hills. There's a restaurant and cafe here and other attractions, including a worthwhile **Butterfly House** *(papilonia.cz).*

Plzeň (Pilsen)

TIME FROM PRAGUE: 1HR

Bohemia's second-biggest city of Plzeň (Pilsen) is a grainy, industrial place with a couple of stellar attractions that make it worth the trip from Prague. Beer drinkers will head straight for the Pilsner Urquell Brewery and Brewery Museum to pay homage to the place where modern lager was first produced (and still made to the original recipe). Parents with kids in

EATING IN KARLOVY VARY: BEST FOR A SPECIAL MEAL

La Hospoda: Upscale take on a traditional Czech pub, serving staples as well delicacies like baked goose and roast boar. *11am-10pm* €€

Ukrajina: Serves the huge, local Ukrainian refugee community, offering filling fare from their war-torn home country. *11am-10pm* €€

Tusculum: The best lunch or dinner option in town, Tusculum features organic, locally sourced ingredients. Lots of vegetarian options. *noon-10pm* €€

Embassy Restaurant: The restaurant of the Embassy Hotel plates up top-notch Czech standards for Munich prices. *noon-10pm* €€€

Pilsner Urquell Brewery

THANKS, AMERICA!

At the end of WWII, the area around Plzeň was liberated from Nazi Germany by the US army (not the Soviet Red army), and the people here have never forgotten. Throughout the communist era this was a problematic event – the communists even went so far as to claim Soviet troops in US uniforms freed Plzeň.

After the Velvet Revolution it became possible to talk more openly about how WWII ended in this part of Europe. Plzeň goes further than that, organising its May **Slavnosti Svobody** (Liberation Festival) with a dwindling number of US soldiers who were here in '45 as guests of honour. The 'General Patton' and 'Díky, Ameriko!' ('Thanks America!') monuments are permanent reminders of the US Army's greatest moment in Bohemia.

tow may bypass the brewery in favour of Techmania, a giant, hands-on science museum and arguably the best children's attraction in the country.

Learn how lager is made

The number one reason people come to Plzeň is to visit the famous **Pilsner Urquell Brewery** *(prazdroj.cz; entry 380Kč),* where Pilsner lager was first cooked up in 1842. Arguably Czechia's best known and most copied beer, it was 'invented' when a Bavarian brewer named Groll, whose task it was to upgrade the slurry the locals were forced to drink, came up with a new way of brewing. The drink – pils lager – quickly spread to Prague's pubs and the world beyond. Entry to the brewery is by guided tour. Highlights include the old cellars (dress warmly) and a glass of unpasteurised nectar (tasting far better than the Urquell you get in pubs). Get beer merch at the brewery shop.

Across the Radbuza River, close to the town's big main square, is the **Brewery Museum** *(prazdrojvisit.cz; entry 150Kč),* which offers an insight into how beer was made (and drunk) in the days before Pilsner Urquell. Highlights include a mock-up of a 19th-century pub, a huge, wooden beer tankard from Siberia and a collection of beer mats.

EATING IN PLZEŇ: OUR PICKS

Lokál pod Divadlem: The Plzeň branch of a popular pub-restaurant serving Czech standards and good beer. *11am-11.30pm* €

Na Spilce: The pub-restaurant at the Urquell Brewery is a great place to end the day in Plzeň. *11am-10pm* €€

U Salzmannů: Plzeň's oldest tavern, with a proud tradition of serving well-chilled Urquell and belly-filling Bohemian cuisine. *11am-11pm* €€

Šenk na Parkánu: At the Brewery Museum, the beer at this typically Czech pub-restaurant is tops, but so is the traditional food. *11am-late* €€

EGON SCHIELE IN ČESKÝ KRUMLOV

Art fans may be interested in knowing the celebrated Austrian expressionist painter Egon Schiele (1890–1918) loved Český Krumlov and had a deep connection to the town through his mother, Marie Soukupová, who was born here. Schiele himself lived in Krumlov in 1911, spending most of his time painting his *Dead Towns* pictures, a far cry from the explicit nudes for which he is famous. However, things did not go well when he returned to those naked female forms. He raised the ire of the townsfolk by hiring underage girls as nude models and was eventually chased out of town.

Get 'technical'

The interactive **Techmania Science Centre** *(techmania.cz; adult/child/family 280/280/1040Kč)* is one of the best ways to entertain kids that Czechia has to offer. If you arrive in the morning, you can almost guarantee you'll be dragging your reluctant-to-leave offspring out of the door at closing time eight hours later.

It's based in a huge, former heavy-engineering workshop, and kids are free to roam all day, trying out myriad experiments as they go. Sit back and relax as your little ones mess about with magnets, splash around in the water world, become TV news presenters in front of a green screen, see if they can out-run a cheetah and build towers out of thousands of wooden blocks. There are also excellent science demonstrations, a 3D planetarium and full-sized historic trains manufactured at the Škoda engineering works.

Český Krumlov

TIME FROM PRAGUE: **3HR**

Wrapped around a tight bend in the Vltava River, deep in Bohemia's south, the must-see town of Český Krumlov is a gem in every sense of the word. It's a Prague in miniature – a UNESCO World Heritage Site, with a huge castle complex, an old town, Renaissance and baroque architecture and hordes of tourists milling through the streets – but all on a smaller scale. You can walk from one end of town to the other in 20 minutes.

Lose yourself among cobbled lanes

The best way to see the town is simply to wander the Inner Town. Pass through the narrow streets packed with tiny shops and cafes to reach **Svornosti Square**, a small, painfully pretty piazza where there's always something going on – this is the focus of the Five-Petalled Rose Celebrations and the venue for the town's Christmas market. The town hall rests on six Gothic arches on the square's northeast flank, one of them providing shelter for the tourist office. There are also a few hotels and restaurants occupying prime spots. Radiating out from Svornosti are cobbled lanes, alleyways and streets that are sheer joy to explore.

Explore Krumlov's XL castle

Wherever you wander, you can't miss Český Krumlov's dramatic **Renaissance castle** *(zamek-ceskykrumlov.cz; tours adult/child from 300/90Kč)*, which stands atop a promontory high above town. The castle began life in the 13th century and acquired

EATING IN ČESKÝ KRUMLOV: OUR PICKS

Krumlovský Mlýn: This huge, heavy-beamed tavern right on the tourist trail serves Bohemian staples and has seating next to the Vltava. *11am-10pm* €€

Krčma v Šatlavské: Slightly upmarket medieval cellar with a meat-heavy menu. Reservations essential. *11am-midnight* €€

U Dwau Maryí: Old Bohemian recipes washed down with mead and ale at this tavern where time has stood still. *11am-10pm* €€

Cikánská Jizba: Raucous, tightly-packed pub-restaurant that's been around forever. Nightly gypsy music. *5pm-midnight Mon-Sat* €€

Český Krumlov

its present appearance in the 16th to 18th centuries under the stewardship of the noble Rožmberk and Schwarzenberg families. The interiors are accessible by guided tour only, though you can stroll the grounds unsupervised. Note there are over 360 rooms in the castle, though the tours examine only a small fraction.

Three tour routes are available: Tour 1, the standard tour, takes in the opulent Renaissance and baroque interiors; Tour 2 visits the Schwarzenberg portrait galleries and their 19th-century apartments. Tour 3 explores the chateau's nearly perfectly preserved baroque theatre.

Even if you don't take the tour, part of the fun here is getting lost in the passages, arcading and gangways on the south side, which lead to the **Cloak Bridge** – an amazing Renaissance structure rising incredibly high above the gorge.

Kutná Hora

TIME FROM PRAGUE: 1HR

Enriched by silver ore, the medieval city of Kutná Hora became the seat of Wenceslas II's royal mint in 1308 and once rivalled Prague in importance. By the 16th century, the mines began to run dry, and the town's demise was hastened by the Thirty Years' War. Kutná Hora became a UNESCO World Heritage Site in 1996, luring visitors with a smorgasbord of historic sights. One of those sights is the Sedlec Ossuary, aka the 'Bone Church', a chapel decorated with thousands of stacked human bones.

FIVE-PETALLED ROSE CELEBRATIONS

Bohemia's biggest medieval bash is the **Five-Petalled Rose Celebrations** (slavnostipetilister-uze.cz), a three-day Renaissance party that takes place each June. The entire historical centre is roped off (you need a ticket to get in even if you are just sightseeing) and countless events take place in every street, park and courtyard.

The biggest day is the Saturday, which sees a huge procession featuring many a silly costume somehow squeeze its way through the crooked medieval streets. In the evening, the focus is on Svornosti Square, where there are sword fights, puppeteers, medieval music and tons of food and drink. In other places there are demonstrations of horsemanship, archery, folk music, street theatre and more food.

 EATING IN KUTNÁ HORA: OUR PICKS

Restaurace V Ruthardce: Old Bohemian tavern with heavy Czech favourites and views of the St Barbara Cathedral. *11am-11pm* €€

Dačický: An old Bohemian, wood-panelled beerhall with lager and dumplings galore. *11am-8pm* €€

U Šneka Pohodáře: Enjoy a pizza and a Bernard beer at the 'Easy-going Snail'. *11am-10pm* €

Kavárna na Kozím plácku: Cute cafe with big timber beams and mismatched 1950s furniture. *9am-7pm* €

FIVE CENTURIES IN THE MAKING

It took over 500 years to complete Kutná Hora's Cathedral of St Barbara. Construction began in 1380 under Jan Parléř, son of Petr Parléř, Charles IV's favoured architect.

The Hussite Wars soon intervened and work was interrupted, but between 1489 until his death in 1506 another star architect Matěj Rejsek (of Prague's Prašná brána fame) added the cathedral's impressive vaulting, and another architectural superstar Benedikt Ried (of Old Royal Palace at Prague Castle fame) finished off the naves after that. But when the silver ran out, construction work was abandoned completely in 1558, and for over three centuries nothing much happened. It was only in the late 19th century that the cathedral was completed in neo-Gothic style.

MIKHAIL MARKOVSKIY/SHUTTERSTOCK

Sedlec Ossuary

Gasp at a ghoulish spectacle

When the Schwarzenberg royal family purchased the Sedlec Monastery (about 2.5km northeast of the town centre) in 1870 they allowed local woodcarver František Rint to get creative with the bones in the crypt (the remains of an estimated 40,000 people), resulting in the spooky **Sedlec Ossuary** *(Kostnice; sedlec.info; adult/child 220/150Kč)*, a remarkable 'bone church'. The skeletons found their way into the church when the surrounding cemetery was reduced in size. The human remains here are mostly plague victims and those who perished in the Hussite Wars of the 15th century. Garlands of skulls and femurs are strung from the vaulted ceiling, while in the centre dangles a vast chandelier containing one of each bone in the human body.

Tour the old silver mines

Originally part of the town's fortifications, the Hrádek (Little Castle) was rebuilt in the 15th century as the residence of Jan Smíšek, administrator of the royal mines, who grew rich from silver mined illegally under the building. It now houses the **Czech Silver Museum** *(cms-kh.cz; adult/concession 90/60Kč)*. There are two guided tours; the second includes a visit down an ancient silver mine.

Gaze up at the miners' cathedral

Kutná Hora's greatest monument is the Gothic **Cathedral of St Barbara** *(chramsvatebarbory.cz)*. It rivals Prague's St Vitus in size and magnificence, its soaring nave culminating in elegant, six-petalled ribbed vaulting, and the ambulatory chapels preserve original 15th-century frescoes, some of them showing miners at work. Take a walk around the outside of the church; the terrace at the eastern end enjoys the finest view in town.

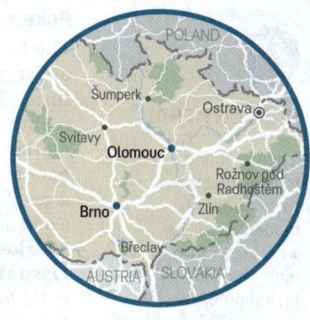

Moravia

URBAN FUN | BEAUTIFUL BAROQUE | SPOOKY UNDERGROUND

Venture into Czechia's easternmost province, Moravia, for a rurally resplendent flip on its western counterpart, Bohemia. Here, instead of industry as in the west of the country, tradition and folklore take centre stage. A dedication to vineyards and wine surpasses breweries, and big-hitter sites fill tiny towns, chronicling the former dynasties of medieval Moravia to the Habsburg Empire.

At Moravia's core is its provincial capital of Brno. The province's gateway and trendsetting student city carves a somewhat rebellious, artistic path in creating a new identity above ground, while showing off its historic cache beneath. Come here to experience the pleasures of urban Czechia – with its sights, restaurants and bars – but without the crowds of Prague.

Olomouc, to the northeast, was Moravia's first capital and a former Habsburg stronghold. This relatively sleepy city conceals its baroque beauty in a bubble – the prettiest city in the region is surprisingly overlooked. This is the place for peaceful walks through resplendent public squares while surrounded by grand churches and statues. An active student scene keeps the bar and cafe scene fresh.

Brno

TIME FROM PRAGUE: **2HR** 🚆

Prague may garner more attention, but Brno isn't trying to compete. Sure, the city isn't as pretty as Prague, but it feels somehow more authentic. Brno's vibrancy comes from its university students and start-ups that fill the city with youthful energy and creative enterprise. While Brno boasts a grand town hall and hilltop castle, many of the biggest attractions lie below ground, where history is burrowed in medieval labyrinths and subterranean cellars and crypts. Architecture buffs won't want to miss touring the early-20th-century functionalist icon, the Villa Tugendhat.

Places

Brno p165
Olomouc p168

GETTING AROUND

Both Brno and Olomouc are easily reachable by train or bus from Prague. Brno is accessible by bus or train from Vienna, Budapest and Bratislava. Long-distance and international bus companies like Flix and RegioJet use a small bus station opposite the Grandhotel Brno in the centre of the city. By car, Czechia's main D1 motorway links Prague with both Brno and Olomouc, though parking is limited. Within Moravia, fast trains run between Brno and Olomouc.

☑ TOP TIP

Guided tours of Brno's UNESCO-listed **Villa Tugendhat** (p166) are very popular and often oversubscribed. Buy tickets in advance of travelling.

MORE ON MENDEL

It's fascinating to think that the foundations of modern genetics were laid not in a high-tech lab but on a simple lawn. Between 1856 and 1863, Gregor Mendel cross-bred pea plants in a monastery garden, studying how combinations and traits like colour and size were inherited. Being a humble monk with a green-thumbed hobby, his work was largely overlooked by the scientific community at the time.

It wasn't until the mid-20th century when genetics was studied in the context of DNA and chromosomes that Mendel's pioneering research gained the recognition it deserved. His initial observations revealed the patterns of generational inheritance and predictable ratios – discoveries now known as 'Mendel's Laws'.

Poke around Brno's underground

The fun of a visit to Brno is the chance to explore the many underground passages etched into the earth over the centuries. Make your way first to the central **Vegetable Market** (Zelný trh), a fixture since the 13th century. Just next to the market find the entrance to a kilometre-long maze of chambers and passageways in a multilevel den from the Middle Ages. Tour the cellars of old city merchants and alchemists on a one-hour walk through the **Labyrinth under the Vegetable Market** (*podzemibrno.cz; adult/child 180/90Kč*). The nearby **Ossuary at the Church of St James** (*podzemibrno.cz; adult/ child 160/80Kč*) is a more sombre walk through history: find a floor-to-ceiling, bone-stacked burial shaft of some 50,000 people who perished in the Thirty Years' War of the 17th century and the plagues. For something even more ghoulish, the **Capuchin Crypt** (*hrobka.kapucini.cz; adult/child 120/70Kč*), below the Church of the Discovery of the Holy Cross on Capuchin Square, holds a truly macabre encounter. For over 100 years, until 1784, the Friars of the Christian Capuchin Order were given a simple – respectful – burial here as mummified remains.

Climb up for Old Town vistas

Brno's medieval **Old Town Hall** (Stará radnice) features a 13th-century vaulted treasury and 16th-century judicial-themed, fresco-daubed hall, but be sure to climb the 173 wooden stairs through the clocktower centriole to the 63m-high panoramic **Renaissance pavilion** (*gotobrno.cz; adult/child 90/50Kč*), and take in the city spires and pastel veneers.

Wander the halls of spooky Špilberk Castle

The mid-13th-century fortification of **Špilberk Castle** (*spilberk.cz; adult/child 160/95Kč*) turned 18th-century notorious Habsburg lockup is today a museum complex. Top exhibitions include the **Prison of Nations** with dungeon and torture exhibits; the eight-part, artefact-packed **Brno on Špilberk** timeline from medieval stronghold to the Capital of Moravia; and a preserved 18th-century **Baroque Pharmacy** set-up. Other rooms are chock-full of artworks from Austrian Moravia to the modern day.

Tour the UNESCO-listed Villa Tugendhat

Brno was no exception to the 1920s interwar boom in modern architecture, with **Villa Tugendhat** being its greatest example of functionalist architecture. This simple, purist-style living

EATING IN BRNO: OUR PICKS

Bucheck: Teeming food truck tucked off the side of the Vegetable Market (Zelný trh) serving banging pulled-pork burgers. *11.30am until sold out Tue-Sun* €

Lokál U Caipla: Traditional Czech eats from goulash soup to grilled meats served with a perfectly poured beer. *11am-midnight Mon-Thu, to 1am Fri & Sat, to 1pm Sun* €€

Eggo Truck Brno: Punk rock tunes with your mimosa or coffee-fuelled breakfast or brunch at this uber-cool bistro. *9am-1pm Mon, 8am-2pm Tue-Sat, 9am-1pm Sun* €

Cà Phê Cô: Of all the Vietnamese restaurants in Brno, this trendy joint has the tastiest street-food style pho, rolls, rice and banh mi. *11am-10pm* €€

Venus of Dolní Věstonice

space, designed by German-born architect Ludwig Mies van der Rohe, was completed in 1930 for the Jewish industrialist family of Greta and Fritz Tugendhat, though they had to flee eight years later. Entry is by a 60- or 90-minute **guided tour** (tugendhat.eu; adult/child 400/250Kč), ideally booked at least a month in advance. However, free garden access is without reservation, linking to the art nouveau **Villa Löw-Beer** that belonged to Greta's parents.

Admire the world's oldest ceramic figurine

The **Moravian Museum** (mzm.cz; adult/child 170/110Kč) has a repository of six million natural history, archaeology and ethnography artefacts housed in the reconstructed 1616 Dietrichstein Palace. Collections span the Palaeolithic era to the Middle Ages, and despite the lack of English text, come here for the museum's prized exhibit: the 30,000-year-old **Venus of Dolní Věstonice** – considered to be oldest ceramic figurine in the world, found during an excavation in the South Moravian village in 1925.

Discover the origins of genetic science

In the mid-19th century, Augustinian monk Gregor Mendel began experimenting with pea plant breeding in a monastic

BRNO'S BEST COFFEE

Adam Neubauer, three-time Barista of the Year from Brno's top coffee shop, MONOGRAM Espresso Bar, shares his favourite spots. monogramespresso-bar.cz

Take 5 If you want to feel like a local, head to this place in the eastern Židenice neighbourhood. There's great coffee, excellent pastries, and friendly owners behind the bar. **Kafe Fridrich** Head north of the centre to this cosy cafe. They serve tasty coffee and incredible vegan sweet treats – the banana bread is possibly the best in the city. **Typika** Brno's recently opened hangout has a coffee garden in the courtyard of the Moravian Gallery. Spacious and comfortable; you might end up staying a few hours. **Kimono** This small and hip espresso bar has a stylish wood-panelled interior and serves top brew classics and speciality coffees.

DRINKING IN BRNO: OUR PICKS

Super Panda Circus: Find the door behind the circus curtain, ring the buzzer and indulge in this unique, hidden cocktail world. *7pm-2am Mon & Tue, 6pm-2am Wed-Sat*	**Bar, Který Neexistuje:** The 'bar that doesn't exist' is the city's trendy-decked cocktail bar behemoth. *5pm-2am Sun-Tue, to 2.30am Wed & Thu, to 3.30am Fri & Sat*	**4pokoje:** This neon-lit, exposed-brick hipster hangout turns buzzing early-hours bar after its daytime bistro persona. *5pm-1am Mon & Tue, to 3am Wed, to 4am Thu-Sat*	**Schrott:** Brewery and bar with courtyard garden in an old industrial building with unique upcycled scrap decor. *3pm-1am Mon-Sat, 3pm-midnight Sun*

WHY I LOVE OLOMOUC

Becki Enright, Lonely Planet writer

There's Prague's showy magnificence and Brno's alternativeness, but what is it about Olomouc that makes it unmatched by any other Czech city? Its cobblestone core is a cultural evolution – you can walk through the riverside gardens below the old walls, have coffee in an old Jesuit commune, step inside baroque, Renaissance and art nouveau houses, dine in part of the old fortress and admire modern murals. I love Olomouc because it has nothing to prove; it's grand without being flashy. Like its Holy Trinity Column construction, the city's admiration comes from its own people; for us visitors, its modesty is its majesty.

Hercules' Fountain, Olomouc

garden in a suburb of Brno; humble observations that unknowingly founded genetic science. Only after his death was Mendel revered as the 'Father of Genetics' for his discovery. The **Mendel Museum** (*mendelmuseum.muni.cz; adult/child 130/100Kč*), an institution of the Masaryk University, is in the precinct of the abbey where Mendel lived and details his life's work and the story of his revolutionary findings through audiovisual exhibits and personal objects.

Olomouc

TIME FROM BRNO: **1HR**

Somehow, Olomouc has evaded discovery; Czechia's prettiest city outside Prague flies entirely under the radar. Once the seat of the Czech monarchy and Moravia's first capital before it moved to Brno, the town is plump with grandeur. Its well-preserved urban core is a municipal conservation area, protecting its main squares ringed with baroque buildings, fountains and the centrepiece UNESCO World Heritage monument the Holy Trinity Column. Olomouc was a barricaded city and Habsburg military centre until the end of the 19th century, and is now fringed by remnants of the medieval and crown fortresses.

Admire squares, fountains & UNESCO monuments

The star of Olomouc's main **Upper Square** (Horní náměstí) is the 32m-high **Holy Trinity Column** (Sloup Nejsvětější

EATING & DRINKING IN OLOMOUC: OUR PICKS

Hanácká hospoda:
Modern-twist beer hall in an old Renaissance palace, with contemporary-traditional Czech classics and share platters. *hours vary* €€

Long Story Short:
From fortress bastion and military bakery to contemporary cuisine eatery, with small bites, grill plates and veggie dishes. *8am-10pm Mon-Sun* €€

Konvikt Bistro & Bar:
Trendy hangout in a former 17th-century Jesuit house with ecclesiastical trims. Come here for the veggie-laden lunch menu. *8.30am-10pm Mon-Fri* €

Café na cucky: Have breakfast and brunch in this arty lounge cafe that's also a gallery and theatre space. *1-9pm Mon, 8am-9pm Tue-Sat, 9am-7pm Sun* €

Trojice), an 18th-century devotional masterpiece carved by local artists with depictions of 18 saints, 12 light bearers, 12 apostles, and the Assumption of Mary and the Holy Trinity. It took 37 years to build. The largest and tallest baroque sculpture in Europe, it was inscribed on the UNESCO World Heritage list in 2000.

The Gothic-towered, 15th-century **Town Hall** (Radnice) is known for its **Astronomical Clock,** renovated in the 1950s communist era in the style of socialist realism. The mosaic is topped by the folk tradition *Ride of the Kings* and worker murals at its base. Its moving procession of proletariat workers can be seen at noon. South of the action, **Lower Square** (Dolní náměstí) is an alfresco square of cafes punctuated with the 1715 Marian Plague Column.

Around these landmarks are six mythological baroque fountains built between 1683 and 1735. On Upper Square: the **Hercules' Fountain** (Herkulova kašna) and **Caesar's Fountain** (Caesarova kašna), and **Mercury's Fountain** (Merkurova kašna) north of it. On Lower Square: **Neptune's Fountain** (Neptunova kašna) and **Jupiter's Fountain** (Jupiterova kašna). The Rome-inspired **Tritons' Fountain** (Kašna Tritonů) is on the road to the cathedral.

Visit palaces, cathedrals & churches

The city's origins trace back to **Ostrava Castle** on **Wenceslas Square** (Václavské náměstí). Little remains of the medieval site where the Přemyslid dynasty ended with the assassination of King Wenceslas III in 1306. Some ruins are visible in the **Archdiocesan Museum**, packing 1000 years of Olomouc Archdiocese culture into art collections and the Romanesque **Bishop's Palace** *(muo.cz; adult/child from 250/150Kč).*

The bastion is the 100m-high **St Wenceslas Cathedral** *(Katedrála sv Václava; katedralaolomouc.cz),* a 12th-century Romanesque basilica rebuilt in Gothic style, with a crypt entombing Olomouc bishops. The adjacent **Archbishop's Palace** *(arcibiskupskypalac.cz; tours 180/120Kč)* has been the headquarters for Olomouc archbishops since 1685 and was where Franz Joseph I was declared Emperor of Austria in 1848.

The Olomouc Archdiocese's significance is reflected in its mass of Roman Catholic churches. The 15th-century Gothic **St Maurice** (Chrám sv Mořice) houses Central Europe's largest organ with 10,000 booming pipes. The tri-domed 17th-century **Church of St Michael** (Kostel sv Michala) glimmers with neo-baroque interiors, while the 18th-century **Church of the Virgin Mary of the Snow** (Kostel Panny Marie Sněžné) pops with colourful stucco. The tiny **Chapel of St Jan Sarkander** (Kaple sv Jana Sarkandra) was built in 1909 upon the prison site where priest John Sarkander was tortured to death in 1620 for refusing to divulge confessions. His canonisation as Moravia's patron saint occurred in 1995 in Olomouc with Pope John Paul II.

OLOMOUC'S PRESTIGIOUS PUNGENT CHEESE

Love it or hate it, you haven't been to Olomouc until you've tasted its culinary speciality. *Olomoucké tvarůžky* is a distinctive Czech delicacy, a matured cheese with a pungent aroma and piquant flavour. This tiny yellow dairy disk is a Haná region tradition dating back to the 15th century; it is considered Czechia's oldest cheese and an integral part of Moravian heritage. You'll find it on menus around the city, served fresh, fried, spread and garnished. The cheese is so important that it is celebrated annually at the Olomouc Cheese Festival in April: a mix of folk pageantry, chef presentations and musical revelry, with cheese and its best accompaniment, beer.

Places We Love to Stay

€ Budget €€ Midrange €€€ Top End

Prague
MAP p152

Malá Strana (Lesser Town)

Little Quarter Hostel €
Gleamingly clean and perched halfway between Charles Bridge and Prague Castle. Book early.

Dům U Velké Boty €€ The quaint 'House at the Big Boot' is set on a quiet square, five minutes' walk from the castle and Charles Bridge.

Golden Well Hotel €€€ A secluded, elegant Renaissance house that is a popular choice for honeymooners in Prague.

Staré Město (Old Town)

Ahoy! Hostel € A pleasant, welcoming and peaceful hostel (definitely not for the pub-crawl crowd).

Design Hotel Josef €€ The work of London-based Czech architect Eva Jiřičná; the minimalist theme is evident in the stark white lobby with glass staircase.

Dominican €€€ Housed in the former monastery of St Giles, this luxury hotel is bursting with character and is full of delightful period details.

Nové Město (New Town)

Sophie's Hostel € Chic step up from a typical hostel; contemporary style, with oak-veneer floors and stark, minimalist decor. Book way in advance.

Icon Hotel €€ Pretty much everything in this gorgeous boutique hotel on a hidden street behind Wenceslas Square has a designer stamp on it.

Mosaic House €€ Modern, clean and eye-catching, fully in keeping with the hotel's 1930s functionalist design ethos.

Bohemia

Karlovy Vary

Villa Basileia €€ Long-established guesthouse by the Teplá River, with very cosy rooms and a restaurant within walking distance of the city's sights.

Hotel Romance Puškin €€ Superb spa-area location, with very comfortable rooms and a cooked breakfast.

Pension Villa Rosa €€ Perched high above the river, the family-run Villa Rosa combines traditionally furnished rooms with a spectacular location.

Plzeň (Pilsen)

Hotel Astory € The most convenient hotel for the main train station and the Prazdroj Brewery, with clean and well-kept 21st-century rooms.

Hotel Rango €€ Plzeň's most character-packed boutique hotel, with sumptuous rooms, a great restaurant and a convenient location.

Český Krumlov

Hotel Myší Díra €€ This hotel has a superb location overlooking the river, and bright, spacious rooms with lots of blonde wood and quirky handmade furniture.

Hotel Konvice €€ An attractive, old-fashioned hotel with romantic rooms and period furnishings. Many rooms have impressive old wood-beamed ceilings.

Moravia

Brno

10-Z Bunker € An extraordinary stay in a former nuclear fallout shelter, foregoing comforts for a more authentic experience, even if just for one night.

Hotel Avion €€ Reconstructed functionalist-style hotel designed by Czech architect Bohuslav Fuchs. A National Cultural Monument with colour block rooms and a design museum.

Barceló Brno Palace €€€ Prestigious heritage building from the 1850s turned luxury hotel with 199 rooms, a courtyard lobby bar and fine-dining restaurant.

Olomouc

Miss Sophie's Olomouc €€ Restored 14th-century listed monument building with eight boutique-antique rooms. The in-house cafe serves a local coffee roast and homemade food.

Long Story Short €€ Sophisticated hostel with dorms and private rooms. The on-site cafe, bistro and bakery nods to the site's former use as a military bakery.

Practicalities

LGBTIQ+ Travellers
Czechs are generally tolerant of same-sex couples. Prague is the most open-minded city; the industrial areas of north Bohemia and north Moravia have the most conservative views. Rarely will openly gay couples experience any kind of negative reaction. Same-sex registered partnerships have been possible since 2006.

Health
Tap water is safe to drink and there are no serious threats to health. Watch for ticks, though, when hiking or camping in forests and grasslands. Ticks can carry two serious diseases: tick-borne encephalitis and Lyme disease. Use repellents, cover exposed legs and periodically check your skin for bites.

Insurance
Insurance is not compulsory to travel to Czechia but it's good to have. Consider a policy that covers flight cancellation and medical care. Alternatively, or additionally, EU travellers can apply for the European Health Insurance Card (EHIC) that covers emergency medical treatment free of charge.

Public Toilets
Public toilets are more plentiful in Prague than elsewhere in the country. Nearly all Prague metro stations have a public toilet. Most public toilets charge either 10Kč or 20Kč. Have small change ready.

EGOTRIPONE/SHUTTERSTOCK

Charles Bridge (p155), Prague

Opening Hours
Banks 8am–5pm Monday to Friday
Bars noon–2am
Clubs 11pm–4am Thursday to Saturday
Restaurants 11am–10pm
Supermarkets 7am–10pm
Shops 9am–5pm Monday to Friday, 9am–1pm Saturday

Accessible Travel
Authorities have made steady progress in making Czechia accessible to all, though challenges remain. Prague's airport is mainly barrier-free and has 20 contact points from which passengers with disabilities can call for assistance. As for getting around Prague, many (but not all) metro stations have lifts. Choose accommodation carefully, as only the most modern hotels have fully accessible facilities.

Public Holidays
New Year's Day 1 January
Easter Monday March/April
Labour Day 1 May
Liberation Day 8 May
Sts Cyril & Methodius Day 5 July
Jan Hus Day 6 July
Czech Statehood Day 28 September
Republic Day 28 October
Struggle for Freedom & Democracy Day 17 November
Christmas Eve/Day 24/25 December
St Stephen's Day 26 December

Language

An accent mark over a vowel in written Czech indicates it's pronounced as a long sound. Note that air is pronounced as in 'hair', aw as in 'law', oh as the 'o' in 'note', ow as in 'how', uh as the 'a' in 'ago', kh as the 'ch' in the Scottish loch, and zh as the 's' in 'pleasure'. Also, r is rolled in Czech and the apostrophe (') indicates a slight y sound.

Basics

Hello. Ahoj. *uh·hoy*
Goodbye. Na shledanou. *nuh·skhle·duh·noh*
Excuse me. Promiňte. *pro·min'·te*
Sorry. Promiňte. *pro·min'·te*
Please. Prosím. *pro·seem*
Thank you. Děkuji. *dye·ku·yi*
Yes. Ano. *uh·no*
No. Ne. *ne*
What's your name? Jak se jmenujete *yuhk se yme·nu·ye·te*
My name is ... Jmenuji se ... *yme·nu·yi se ...*
Do you speak English? Mluvíte anglicky? *mlu·vee·te uhn·glits·ki*
I don't understand. Nerozumím. *ne·ro·zu·meem*

Transport

bus	autobus	*ow·to·bus*
plane	letadlo	*le·tuhd·lo*
train	vlak	*vluhk*

One ... ticket jízdenku ... *yeez·den·ku*
to (Telč), do (Telče), *do (tel·che)*
please. prosím. *pro·seem*
one-way. jedno-směrnou. *yed·no·smyer·noh*
return. zpáteční. *zpa·tech·nyee*

Emergencies

Help! Pomoc! *po·mots*
Go away! Běžte pryč! *byezh·te prich*

Call the doctor/police! Zavolejte lékaře/policii! *zuh·vo·ley·te lair·kuh·rzhe/po·li·tsi·yi*
I'm lost. Zabloudil. *zuh·bloh·dyil*
I'm ill. Jsem nemocný. *ysem ne·mots·nee*
Where are the toilets? Kde jsou toalety? *gde ysoh to·uh·le·ti*

Eating & Drinking

What would you recommend? Co byste doporučil/doporučila? (m/f) *tso bis·te do·po·ru·chil/do·po·ru·chi·luh*
Do you have vegetarian food? Máte vegetariánskájídla? *ma·te ve·ge·tuh·ri·ans·ka yeed·luh*
I'd like the bill/menu, please. Chtěl/Chtěla bych účet/jídelníček prosím. (m/f) *khtyel/khtye·luh bikh oo·chet/yee·del·nyee·chek ... pro·seem*
I'll have ... Dám si ... *dam si ...*
Cheers! Na zdraví! *nuh zdruh·vee*

Shopping & Services

I'm looking for ... Hledám ... *hle·dam ...*
How much is it? Kolik to stojí? *ko·lik to sto·yee*
That's too expensive. To je moc drahé. *to ye mots druh·hair*
bank. banka. *buhn·kuh*
post office. pošta. *posh·tuh*
tourist office. turistická informační kancelář. *tu·ris·tits·ka in·for·muhch·nyee kuhn·tse·larzh*

NUMBERS

1	**jedan**	*ye·dan*
2	**dva**	*dva*
3	**tři**	*trzhi*
4	**čtyři**	*chti·rzhi*
5	**pět**	*pyet*
6	**šest**	*shest*
7	**sedam**	*se·dam*
8	**osm**	*o·sm*
9	**devět**	*de·vyet*
10	**deset**	*de·set*

SERGII FIGURNYI/SHUTTERSTOCK

Tram, Prague (p150)

Arriving & Getting Around

Václav Havel Airport Prague is the main air gateway. From the airport, taxis and public transport quickly bring you to the centre. Prague's main train and bus stations are connected to major European cities and the gateways for onward travel within Czechia.

Public Transport in Prague
The public transport network of metros, trams and buses is comprehensive and relatively cheap. Buy tickets at ticketing machines in metro stations or on tram cars, and validate tickets in special yellow stamping machines.

Prague Ticket Costs
Tickets for Prague's buses, trams, metro and trolleybuses are timed with 30-minute (30Kč) and 90-minute (40Kč) validity. One-day (120Kč) and three-day (330Kč) passes are also available and can make for good value.

Driving Essentials
Hire cars at Prague airport or points around the country, and drive on the right. The speed limit is 50km/h in urban areas, 90km/h on secondary roads and 130km/h on motorways. The blood alcohol limit is 0g/L.

Long-Haul Train & Bus Travel
Train and bus routes cover the entire country and are practical for moving around. Trains are best for covering large distances, such as from Prague to Brno or Olomouc. Buses are more practical for shorter distances and select routes, as from Prague to Karlovy Vary or Český Krumlov. Most trains depart from **Praha Hlavní Nádraží** (main station). Most buses use Prague's **Florenc Bus Station**.

MONEY
Currency: Czech crown (Koruna česká; Kč)

CHANGING MONEY
Avoid private exchange booths at Prague airport or around heavily touristed areas, as these places invariably charge high commissions. Instead, withdraw cash from bank ATMs using your own debit or credit card. Czech ATMs require a four-digit PIN.

CARD PAYMENTS
Paying with credit or debit cards is common around the country and often preferable to cash. The only exceptions might be smaller shops in outlying areas. Ticket machines at Prague metro stations and on trams also allow for card payments.

TIPPING
Tipping is not widespread in Czechia but very much appreciated in restaurants and cafes. Tip 10% to reward good service or round up to the nearest 10Kč or 100Kč increment (depending on the amount).

For places to stay
in Estonia, see
p192

MATT MUNRO/LONELY PLANET

Above: Tallinn (p178); Right: Festival, Setomaa (p187)

Curated by
Angelo Zinna

Estonia

A CULTURAL CROSSROADS

Ruled and influenced by different empires throughout its history, Estonia has developed a distinct character all its own.

Estonia has long been defined by its strategic position at the crossroads of Northern Europe's sea routes. It was part of the Hanseatic League trading bloc during the Middle Ages and later absorbed into the Swedish kingdom, and its identity grew increasingly tangled as the Russian Empire conquered its territory in the early 18th century. Independence followed the Russian Empire's collapse in 1917, but Estonia's larger neighbours never ceased to view this tiny nation as an essential pawn on their geopolitical chessboard. Estonians would have their nationhood removed by both Nazi and Soviet forces during WWII, a conflict followed by nearly five decades of USSR rule. Today, most Estonians tend to resent the 'post-Soviet' label, although a large portion of the population – over 20% – is composed of ethnic Russians who either moved in Soviet times or are descended from migrants.

Despite its convoluted past, Estonia is a nation looking forward. In cities, folk music festivals go hand in hand with a thriving contemporary art scene, and former industrial districts live a second life as design-centric creative hubs filled with galleries and international restaurants. Outside urban areas, nature maintains a central role in the local way of life. Half the country is covered by forests and 2000 islands spill from the coastline. Whether you're visiting to escape the crowds or to decipher its layered culture, Estonia awaits discovery.

ALEXANDER GAFARRO/SHUTTERSTOCK

THE MAIN AREAS

TALLINN
Modern capital with a medieval heart. **p178**

TARTU & THE SOUTH
Cradle of culture. **p184**

PÄRNU & THE WEST
The summer capital. **p188**

Find Your Way

Over half of Estonia is covered by forests and a third of the population is concentrated in the capital, leaving the majority of the country dotted with small settlements surrounded by nature.

Tallinn, p178

Dynamic, tech-driven capital with a UNESCO-listed Old Town. Discover medieval roots, some of the Baltics' best museums and art-filled parks.

Tartu & the South, p184

Home of Estonia's first university, Tartu is a friendly place, kept vibrant by its seasonally changing student population.

Pärnu & the West, p188

Estonia's summer capital is the country's prime beach destination, a wellness-centred, family-friendly town with resorts and 19th-century villas.

BUS & TRAIN

With patience, all of Estonia can be visited using public transport. Cheap, reliable buses run regularly. The northern train line links Tallinn to Narva and Paldiski, while two lines travel south to Pärnu and Tartu (book via elron.ee).

CAR

Your own vehicle is the fastest way to move around the country, which can be crossed from north to south in three hours. Major rental companies operate in Tallinn and Tartu.

Gulf of Finland

Loksa

Kehra

TALLINN Maardu

Keila Tallinn Great Town Guild Hall Hall

Paldiski

Haapsalu

Lihula

Virtsu

Vormsi

Muhu

Orissaare

Kärdla

Hiiumaa

Käina

Saaremaa

Kuressaare

Kuressaare Episcopal Castle

Sääre

Kolka

Rakvere

Tamsalu

Paide

Türi

Vändra

Sindi

Pärnu

Jõhvi

Iisaku

Lake Peipsi

Mustvee

Kallaste

Põltsamaa

Võhma

Suure-Jaani

Soomaa National Park

Viljandi Teutonic Order Castle

Viljandi

Lake Võrtsjärv

Karksi-Nuia

Tartu Estonian National Museum University of Tartu Museum

Elva

Otepää

Torva

Rujiena

LATVIA

Valga

Valka

Strenči

Smiltene

Vastse-Kuuste

Võru

Rõuge

Valmiera

Lake Pihkva

Pskov

RUSSIA

Alūksne

40 km

20 miles

MO WU/SHUTTERSTOCK

Town Hall Square (p178), Tallinn

Plan Your Time

Tallinn tends to grab all the attention with its cultural attractions, but save some time to explore the islands and rural towns of the south.

A Day in the Capital

● Spend your morning exploring Tallinn's Old Town, from **Town Hall Square** (p178) to elevated **Toompea** (p180). Seek traces left behind by the Hanseatic League in the **Great Guild Hall** (p179), then enter the stunning **Alexander Nevsky Cathedral** (p180), before lunch in **Telliskivi** (p180).

● In the afternoon, stroll Kadriorg Park and visit the art museum **Kumu** (p182). Conclude at the **Estonian Maritime Museum** (p183) and its extension at **Seaplane Harbour** (p183).

Three Days to Explore

● Dedicate a few days to discovering southern Estonia's fascinating culture. Walk through Tartu's Old Town and climb up Toomemägi to the remains of **Tartu Cathedral** (p185). Head to **Aparaaditehas** (p186) for a tour of this refurbished industrial area's galleries.

● Spend day two touring the **Setomaa** (p187), home of the musical Seto minority, starting in the village of Värska and continuing to Obinitsa. On day three head to charming **Viljandi** (p187).

SEASONAL HIGHLIGHTS

SPRING
Soomaa National Park experiences a 'fifth season' as floods transform it into a kayaking playground.

SUMMER
Estonia celebrates Jaanipäev (Midsummer's Day) on 24 June with huge bonfires and folk music festivals.

AUTUMN
The weather is typically moody in autumn. Prices tend to decrease together with tourism numbers.

WINTER
Winters are famously harsh in Estonia, but Christmas markets light up the squares of Tallinn and Tartu.

Tallinn

MEDIEVAL CAPITAL | MUSEUMS | HARBOUR CITY

GETTING AROUND

Tallinn's Old Town is best explored on foot, but to reach many of the sights in the suburbs you'll need to get on a bus or rely on the electric scooters that seem to have taken over the city. Bus tickets can be purchased with contactless cards directly on the bus (cash is not accepted) or online at tallinn. pilet.ee. Timetables are available at *transport.tallinn.ee.*

☑ TOP TIP

Tallinn's train station sits northwest of Old Town. Buses depart from the station 2km southeast of the centre. The compact inner city is walkable, while trams and intercity buses link the suburbs. You can purchase one-hour public transport tickets by tapping your contactless card on the vehicle, or via tallinn.pilet.ee.

Soon after Tallinn entered the Hanseatic League mercantile alliance in the late 13th century, it became the most important port of the Gulf of Finland and a crucial junction on the Baltic Sea's trade routes. The resulting wealth led to the construction of the best-preserved medieval city of Nordic Europe, still contained within its original walls and guarded by 26 red-roofed watchtowers. Old Town (Vanalinn) is divided into two equally attractive sections – Toompea, on the hill, and the Lower Town – but the historic heart of the city once known as Reval is only part of the allure.

When the centre starts feeling a bit too much like a medieval theme park, exit the walls to find neighbourhoods of traditional wooden houses, modernist structures built for the 1980 Moscow Olympics and glass office towers housing an ever-growing tech sector. From the creative district of Telliskivi to the imperial art park of Kadriorg, getting to know Tallinn rewards a few days of any visitor's time.

The Heart of Old Town

Under the eye of Old Thomas

The oldest cobbled alleys of Tallinn's historic core all seem to converge in **Town Hall Square** (Raekoja Plats), the epicentre of the Lower Town expanding under the shadow of the Town Hall's spire. Functioning as a marketplace until the end of the 19th century, Raekoja Plats is now the ideal starting point to explore the UNESCO-listed Old Town, the open-air museum tributing the Hanseatic roots of Estonia's capital.

Tallinn's Gothic **Town Hall** *(raekoda.tallinn.ee; entry adult/child €7/5),* rising tall on the square's southern side, is one of the oldest municipal buildings in Northern Europe. Originally erected in the 15th century, it continues to dominate Old Town's skyline with its 64m spire, topped by a statue of Old Thomas (Vana Toomas), Tallinn's most notable icon and guardian of the city since 1530. You can visit the building's

TALLINN

HIGHLIGHTS
1 Great Guild Hall
2 Tallinn Town Hall

SIGHTS
3 Alexander Nevsky
   Cathedral
4 Estonian Maritime
   Museum
5 Town Hall Square

SLEEPING
6 ibis Styles Tallinn
7 Imaginary Hostel
8 Schlössle Hotel
9 St Olav Hotel
10 von Stackelberg
   Hotel

EATING
11 III Draakon
12 Katusekohvik Maru
13 Peet Ruut
14 Pegasus

DRINKING & NIGHTLIFE
15 Botaanik
16 Sessel
17 Valli Bar
18 Whisper Sister

SHOPPING
19 Telliskivi Flea Market

interior between 25 June and 31 August, or on a private visit with a certified guide during the rest of the year (book ahead).

Hanseatic Wall St

Inside the Great Guild Hall

The **Great Guild Hall** (*ajaloomuuseum.ee/great-guild-hall; entry adult/child €14/9*) stands as one of Pikk St's most prominent buildings, its imposing size reflecting the wealth and power of the merchant guilds that once met here. Completed in 1410, its design reflects the real-estate tax system of 15th-century Northern Europe – the wider the facade, the higher the tax bill. Behind its entry doors, adorned with two lion head knockers, a vaulted hall was designed for public celebrations and meetings of major international traders. The Guild Hall served as Tallinn's main business centre until the 19th century, with stock-market negotiations eventually moving into the palace. Much of what is known about the Hanseatic League today comes from documents such as the ancient ledgers on display in the museum, used for record-keeping by merchants. While the main hall is devoid of decorations, the small guild hall features lunette paintings from 1869 by

⚒ EATING IN TALLINN'S OLD TOWN: OUR PICKS

Peet Ruut: Organic cuisine at its best, Peet Ruut cares as much about flavours as the origins of each ingredient. *6-10pm Mon-Sat* €€

Pegasus: This restaurant has been serving fine food for half a century, but you can't tell from its modern cuisine. *noon-11pm Mon-Thu, noon-midnight Fri & Sat, 1-10pm Sun* €€

III Draakon: Eel soup and sausages in a playful, medieval-inspired Town Hall Square tourist restaurant. *11am-10pm* €€

Katusekohvik Maru: Access the 'Fat Margaret' rooftop by booking a table in Maru's outdoor terrace overlooking the city walls. *10am-10pm* €€

Leopold Dietrich Ernst von Pezold and Theodor Albert Sprengel, members of the Baltic German community that formed the majority of the upper class in 19th-century Estonia.

Toompea's Orthodox Cathedral

Step into Alexander Nevsky Cathedral

Sitting some 30m above the lower part of Tallinn's Old Town, Toompea, or Cathedral Hill, has long functioned as the city's centre of power, continuing to do so to this day. Home of Estonia's parliament, the fortified citadel presents itself as a collection of stately palaces and towering churches, offering a much quieter atmosphere than its lower counterpart. Brimming with sacred icons enclosed in golden frames and candles lit by Orthodox devotees, the onion-domed **Alexander Nevsky Cathedral** sits right in front of the Toompea Castle and the neoclassical post office, well preserved despite its historically unpalatable presence. Named after the Prince of Novgorod, the cathedral was completed in 1900 during the final stage of the Russian Empire's dominion over Estonia and risked demolition as the country gained its independence two decades later. The Soviets initially planned to convert the church into a planetarium – it didn't happen, and the Alexander Nevsky Cathedral was shut for 50 years, reopening to the public in 1991.

Telliskivi Creative City

Eat, drink and thrift in Tallinn's former industrial district

'Craft', 'artisanal', 'organic' and other trendy buzzwords recur often in graffiti-decorated Telliskivi, the area that resulted from the 2009 regeneration project of this industrial corner of Tallinn north of the railway station. Rundown warehouses and former factories located in the once-dodgy Kalamaja district are now home to an eclectic mix of cafes, bars, shops and galleries – plus a **weekly flea market**. It's lively both day and night.

Kadriorg's Art, Classical & Contemporary

Imperial gardens turned museum hub

Removed from the bustle of Tallinn's Old Town, Kadriorg Park is the unchallenged art centre of Estonia's capital, housing museums brimming with classical and contemporary

A BRIEF HISTORY OF THE HANSEATIC LEAGUE

Much of what you see today in Tallinn's Old Town is the result of the city's role as a commercial hub on the Baltic coast. While the Hanseatic League had a major impact on the development of Baltic cities, its history remains largely obscure. Emerging in the 12th century and flourishing from the 13th to the 17th centuries, its primary purpose was to protect the economic interests and trading privileges of an emerging merchant class, ensuring safe passage for goods across the Baltic and North Seas. Tallinn, then known as Reval, became a crucial member of the Hanseatic League in 1285. Its strategic location brought immense prosperity to Reval, resulting in the construction of Tallinn's fortified walls, merchant houses and grand churches.

DRINKING IN TALLINN: OUR PICKS

Whisper Sister: A tiny plaque on Pärnu St (no 12) marks this speakeasy-style cocktail bar – blink and you'll miss it. *6pm-12.30am Sun-Thu, to 2.30am Fri & Sat*

Valli Bar: Historic bar in front of the Sõprus cinema, attracting a local crowd with its cheap beer. *noon-1am Mon-Fri, to 2am Fri & Sat, to midnight Sun*

Sessel: Walk through a souvenir shop to get to Sessel, a cocktail bar overlooking Viru St that also offers sushi. *noon-1am Sun-Thu, to 3am Fri & Sat*

Botaanik: An intimate, welcoming corner cocktail bar serving some of the best cocktails in town. Book ahead to secure a table. *6pm-midnight Thu, to 1am Fri & Sat*

TOP EXPERIENCE

Lahemaa National Park

Covering 725 sq km, Lahemaa National Park is Estonia's largest national park. Hiking, cycling, camping, kayaking and other activities are all great ways to explore the bogs, bays, lakes and forests of this rural landscape, easily reached from Tallinn. A number of villages and glamping facilities dot the area, allowing you to stay close to the action and away from the crowds.

Viru Bog Trail

Bog Walking on the Viru Trail

The **Viru Bog Trail** extends above the bogs formed in prehistoric times, considered the oldest landscapes in Estonia. The boardwalk runs between the lakes before connecting to a hiking path that runs through the pine forest. The full loop is 5.5km.

Manors & Palaces

The Baltic German nobility built opulent villas in Lahemaa, some of which still stand today. **Palmse Manor**, first built in 1720 and later reconstructed, is Lahemaa's prime historic building, housing the park's visitor centre, a museum with period furniture and clothing, and a restaurant. South of the beach town of Võsu is **Sagadi Manor**, a late baroque complex built by the von Fock family in the mid-18th century. Besides a hotel, the complex is also home to a Forest Museum run by Estonia's State Forest Management Centre.

Village Hopping

In Viinistu, a fish processing plant has been converted into the **Viinistu Art Museum**, housing the private artwork collection of Jaan Manitski, the Viinistu-born businessman and former Minister of Foreign Affairs of Estonia. In charming Käsmu, the **Käsmu Sea Museum**, housed inside a Russian-era border-guard station, displays hundreds of sea-related objects that offer a glimpse into the settlement's long-standing relationship with the Gulf of Finland.

TOP TIPS

● The Lahemaa Visitor Centre is found at Palmse Manor, in one of the former stables of the complex.

● Loksa is the main town within the park's borders, followed by Võsu. Both are small, but are connected to Tallinn via public transport.

PRACTICALITIES

● Hiking-trail info is available at rmk.ee or via the RMK app.

● For bus schedules see transport.tallinn.ee.

ESTONIA'S SONG FESTIVAL

The UNESCO-inscribed Estonian Song Festival is the country's most important music event, held in the Song Festival Grounds near Kadriorg Park every five years. The event, first held in Tartu in 1869, is more than just a concert. Gathering up to 70,000 spectators, it's a powerful expression of Estonian identity.

During Soviet rule it served as a covert form of protest and a way to preserve national culture – the event's immense scale and its role in keeping the Estonian language and traditions alive make it the single most important gathering in the country. A parade running through Tallin's central streets, where choirs wear the traditional clothing of their regions, inaugurates the start of the event.

works on the lush grounds first commissioned by Russian Tsar Peter the Great in the early 18th century. Manicured gardens, mirror-like ponds and oak-shaded paths blend in this 70-hectare park on the outskirts of the city centre. The architectural centrepiece of Kadriorg Park is its homonymous palace, a baroque construction backed by a symmetrical French garden Peter the Great had built as a gift to his wife, Empress Catherine I, between 1718 and 1725.

Today, the palace is home to a branch of the Art Museum of Estonia. The main hall of **Kadriorg Art Museum** is one of Northern Europe's most impressive pieces of baroque architecture, with intricate stucco decorations symbolising the tsar's power and the initials of Peter and Catherine nestled above the opposing fireplaces. The Estonian Art Museum, or **Kumu**, is contained inside a futuristic, semicircular building designed by Finnish architect Pekka Vapaavuori and showcases the evolution of Estonian art from the 18th century to the present day. Begin with the heritage Baltic German painters such as Oskar Georg Adolf Hoffmann and Carl Timoleon von Neff, moving forward to the early-20th-century constructivist movement known as the Group of Estonian Artists, which depicts society's entrance into tech-driven modernity.

PANDORA PICTURES/SHUTTERSTOCK

Estonian Maritime Museum

Tallinn & the Baltic Sea

Visit the Estonian Maritime Museum and Seaplane Harbour

Much of Tallinn's history took place on the water. Two kid-friendly museums retrace the evolution of seafaring from the Middle Ages to modern times – from epic battles to marine archaeology and Cold War spy games. Set inside an artillery tower known as 'Fat Margaret' is the **Estonian Maritime Museum**. Here a collection of over 700 exhibits, including the 20m *Koge* shipwreck dating to the 14th century, traces the history of navigation in the Baltic Sea. Of the 17 model ships exhibited around the archaeological remains, eight come to life thanks to augmented reality.

Under the three concrete domes of the 1917 hangar known as **Seaplane Harbour**, you'll find one of Europe's most intriguing maritime museums, opened in 2012 after a long restoration process and updated in 2024. Occupying a large section of the hangar is the 59.5m *Lembit* submarine, built in the UK between 1935 and 1937 for the Estonian navy. You can enter its claustrophobia-inducing interiors to get a feel of life underwater and walk through the vessel's eight sections, from the engine rooms to the sleeping quarters.

FESTIVALS IN TALLINN

Besides the Song Festival, Tallinn hosts many events, especially during the summer months.

Old Town Days: Old Town's largest cultural festival celebrates ancient traditions in early June.

Tallinn Street Food Festival: In early June, the Song Festival Grounds turn into a huge, open-air restaurant filled with food trucks.

PÖFF Black Nights Film Festival: One of the Baltics' most important film festivals takes place in November.

Tallinn Craft Beer Weekend: Tallinn's Craft Beer Weekend celebrates the local beer scene by gathering breweries small and large in the city's Creative Hub in May.

Tallinn Music Week: International acts are hosted all around the city during the capital's loudest week, in April.

Tartu & the South

CULTURE HUB | HISTORIC UNIVERSITY | OLD TOWN

Places

Tartu p184
Viljandi p187
Setomaa p187

 TOP TIP

The Tartu Smart Bike Share has made 750 regular and e-bikes available to the public at 69 stations around the city. You can rent a bike *(starting at €2 per hour)* via the Tartu Smart Bike mobile app and drop it off at any station in town.

Fresh off a year as European Capital of Culture, Estonia's second city has long been defined by its role as a cradle of ideas. The Livonian Brothers of the Sword made Dorpat, as the city was then known, their regional power centre in the 1220s and within decades the city joined the Hanseatic League and became the third-most-important Livonian city, after Riga and Tallinn. Since 1632, when the Kingdom of Sweden founded the Academia Gustaviana, the city has attracted bright minds and innovators in the arts and the sciences. A calm city of less than 100,000, Tartu remains vibrant thanks to its population of international students. Around Tartu, religious and linguistic minorities keep ancient traditions alive in the picturesque countryside. On the shores of Lake Peipsi, Europe's largest transboundary lake, Russian-speaking descendants of Old Believers keep ancient rituals alive in their onion-domed churches. Further south, the musically gifted Setos perform hypnotic chants.

Tartu

Musical Town Hall Square

The *Kissing Students* statue – a city symbol recently renovated as part of the 2024 Capital of Culture programme – stands in

---

GETTING AROUND

Although Tartu is Estonia's second-largest city, its centre is small and best visited on foot. Public transport runs frequently to sights outside of Old Town – take bus 7 to get to the Estonian National Museum and Raadi Park, and bus 1 or 2 to reach Aparaaditehas. Both sides of the Emajõgi River are lined with cycling paths, allowing you to easily explore the city on two wheels. Exiting the city is best done by car, but many places are reachable by public transport. **Go Bus** *(gobus.ee)* runs services from Tartu's bus station to most towns in the region. Buses are efficient and on time, but not frequent – check the schedule on peatus.ee, as some areas are only covered once or twice a day.

SVETLANA MAHOVSKAYA/SHUTTERSTOCK

Tartu Cathedral

Tartu's **Town Hall Square**. This open space is framed by restaurant terraces that converge towards the 18th-century **Town Hall** (Raekoja plats), built by German architect Johann Heinrich Bartholomäus Walter following a fire that destroyed much of the city in 1775. The Town Hall still serves as the local government's seat – only the Tartu Visitor Centre and the historic pharmacy found on the ground floor can be accessed. The baroque tower topping the Town Hall houses Estonia's biggest carillon, a system of 34 bells that play five times a day at 9am, noon, 3pm, 6pm and 9pm.

Ruins of the cathedral

The Gothic skeleton of **Tartu Cathedral**, the largest in the country, has stood on top of Toomemägi since the 13th century, when the knights of the Livonian Order conquered the city. The cathedral took two centuries to complete before being largely destroyed during the Livonian War (1558–83) and ceasing to function as a place of worship, leaving Toomemägi with just its ruins ever since. In the early 19th century, the University of Tartu rebuilt parts of the cathedral and turned its main hall into a library. Today, the cathedral houses the **University of Tartu Museum** (*muuseum.ut.ee; entry adult/child €9/6*). You can visit the elegant White Hall; on its balcony are all the gifts given to

EATING & DRINKING IN TARTU: OUR PICKS

Gunpowder Cellar: Former military storehouse serving heartwarming dishes and a long list of local beers and ciders. *noon-10pm Sun-Tue, to 1am Wed-Sat* €€

Kampus: With a show kitchen facing pedestrian Rüütli, Kampus offers a Spanish-influenced menu of light lunch meals and hearty mains. *noon-9pm Tue-Thu, to 1am Fri-Sun* €€

Ihamaru Pizza & Käbliku Brewery Taproom: Pair excellent wood-fired pizza with one of the craft beers from the Käbliku. *4-11pm Mon-Thu, noon-11pm Fri-Sun* €

Kolm Tilli: Serving international cuisine from brunch to dinner, with a street-food menu if you're just looking for something light. *9am-11pm Mon-Fri, to 1am Sat, 10am-10pm Sun* €

SETO LEELO

The ancient polyphonic singing tradition known as *leelo* has long been one of the defining features of the Seto people, and continues to be performed during festivals, and events such as funerals and weddings. It's typically performed by a group of women led by a 'song mother'. While many songs are passed down through generations, 'song mothers' are praised for their ability to improvise, creating verses on the spot to form a hypnotic rhythm, somewhere between a lament and a lullaby. Recently, the Estonian Literature Museum has created a digital platform to collect historic recordings of Seto music – on the website of **Seto Singing Heritage** (*laul.setomaa.ee*) you can now listen to original songs dating as far back as the 1920s and learn about the structure of melodies.

TRABANTOS/SHUTTERSTOCK

the university by prominent guests. The core of the exhibition is found in the Morgenstern Hall, spanning the 5th and 6th floors, where besides the historic library you'll find some of the oldest models of the cathedral and the university's founding act.

Estonia's cutting-edge national museum

The **Estonian National Museum** (*erm.ee; entry adult/child €15/10*) was designed to reflect Raadi Park's history as a military airport – the impressive glass-clad building was created as an extension of the asphalt airstrip – and has over 140,000 objects covering the history of Estonian customs and traditions. While this may seem like an unusual location for such an important institution – Raadi Park is 2.7km from Tartu's city centre – it is worth the trip. Most of the space is used for the 'Encounters' permanent exhibition, a massive showcase of everyday objects tracing the transformation of everyday life in Estonia, from the Stone Age to independence.

From 'everything factory' to creative hub

Bombed in 1941, the Aparaaditehas quarter was reborn in the Soviet era as a multifunctional industrial site where boots, refrigerators, umbrellas and car parts were produced to be shipped all over the USSR. In the 1970s, during Aparaaditehas' peak, more than 1500 people were employed here. Today, **Aparaaditehas** follows in the footsteps of Tallinn's Telliskivi (p180) and other European 'creative districts', with its buildings repurposed as a culture hub. A large abstract mural is the focal point of the courtyard, where art galleries and artisanal bakeries share the industrial architecture with coworking spaces, record stores and tattoo studios.

Viljandi Teutonic Order Castle

Viljandi

TIME FROM TARTU: 1¼HR

Viljandi's medieval fortress

Charming Viljandi is celebrated for its cultural scene, which comes to life during summer through major open-air events such as the Viljandi Folk Music Festival. Set on a hill overlooking **Lake Viljandi**, the crumbling remains of the **Viljandi Teutonic Order Castle** stand as the region's most treasured landmark. German Knights of the Catholic Teutonic Order settled in Viljandi in the early 13th century, erecting the fortress in 1224. The Polish-Swedish wars of the 1600s brought the castle to its ruinous state. Reach the leafy hill where the archaeological site is found via the 1879 suspension bridge running for 50m across the ditch on the southern side of the park.

Setomaa

TIME FROM TARTU: 1¼HR

Home of the Setos

Setomaa is home to the Seto minority, a group of Orthodox Christians whose Finno-Ugric language finds its best expression in the *leelo* polyphonic singing tradition. To get a glimpse of rural life in Setomaa visit Värska's **Seto Farm Museum**, a complex of wooden houses and stables depicting the living and working conditions of families in the pre-industrial era. The **Obinitsa Seto Museum** offers a window into the region's history, with an emphasis on the role of women in Seto society. Women have been historically leading the preservation of the *leelo* singing tradition and 'song mothers' continue to be respected figures in the community. An important piece of living culture is the **Obinitsa Kunstisaal** (Obinitsa Art Gallery), run by writer Kauksi Ülle and her husband, painter and silversmith Evar Riitsaar.

Pärnu & the West

18TH-CENTURY GRANDEUR | THE BEACH | SPA LIFE

Places

Pärnu p188

Soomaa National Park p191

Haapsalu p191

Kuressaare p191

 TOP TIP

During summer months many concerts are held in Pärnu, both in old-school venues such as the Kuursaal, a former casino turned restaurant, and in parks such as Vallikäär and Munamäe.

As spring ends and the weather warms up, Pärnu comes to life with Estonians, Finns and Latvians heading to the Baltic Sea. Doubling as a relaxing, wellness-oriented resort and party town, Pärnu attempts to cater to both families and hedonists. Its historic core boasts a collection of colourful palatial residences dating back centuries as well as a vibrant restaurant scene, while the shallow water lapping its sandy beach favours slow strolls over long swims. With so much to detain visitors in Pärnu itself, the resort's hinterland is often neglected, despite offering plenty of its own charm. Haapsalu provides for visitors in search of coastal relaxation, while boggy Soomaa National Park offers canoeing, kayaking, bog walking, or simply observing the scenery from a hammock. The wild, windswept West Estonian Archipelago is worth a detour, starting from Saaremaa, the largest island in the region.

Pärnu

Mapping the Old Town's magnificence

The 15th-century **Red Tower**, once part of Pärnu's medieval fortress, is the only piece of architecture from the Hanseatic era to survive (reconstructed) and houses a small **museum** (*parnumuuseum.ee/tower; entry adult/child €7/5*) tracing the

---

GETTING AROUND

Pärnu centre's pedestrian streets make for pleasant walks, but, with cycle paths crisscrossing the city and its surroundings, greater Pärnu is best explored by bicycle. The Baltreisen Bicycle Rental shop rents bikes for €11 per day from under the giant mural on Pühavaimu St. For a relaxing cruise with **Pärnu**

Cruises (*parnucruises.ee*), hop on the 1963 MS *Kuha*, departing four times a day from Tallinn Gate. The coast and countryside is best explored with your own vehicle. Organised tours to Soomaa National Park usually include transport, and a bicycle can get you far, given the low traffic on the flat roads of western Estonia.

A DRIVE AROUND HIIUMAA

This road trip around the West Estonian Archipelago's second island can be done in one (long) day, or broken into two with a night's stop in Kärdla.

START	END	LENGTH
Sõru Harbour	Heltermaa	160km; 7hr+

From the tiny **1 Sõru Harbour** make your way north to the Kõpu Peninsula along the island's western flank. Near the imposing **2 Kõpu Lighthouse**, originally built by Hanseatic League merchants in the 16th century, find the red **3 Ristna Lighthouse** and the surfing beach at **4 Surf Paradiis**. A 31m **5 wooden copy of the Eiffel Tower** awaits in a small amusement park of quirky structures built by local craftsman Jaan Alliksoo in Reigi, followed by the **6 Hiiumaa Military Museum** and the **7 Tahkuna Lighthouse** on the Tahkuna Peninsula. Following the 80 road, you'll reach the **8 Hill of Crosses**, a collection of hundreds of wooden crucifixes built by 18th-century Swedes, then Kärdla, Hiiumaa's

capital. Stop for lunch at the **9 Hiiumaa Pruulikoja Resto** and after a stroll through the town, drive south toward Kassari. Make a brief stop at the **10 Lavendlitalu** (lavender field). Continue south to Käina, Hiiumaa's second town, where the modern **11 Windtower Experience** (Elamuskeskus Tuuletorn) houses a five-floor, family-friendly museum dedicated to nature's role in shaping Hiiumaa's identity, plus a 20m climbing wall, the highest in all the Baltics. South of Käina is the Kassari Reserve, extending to the promontory **12 Sääre Tirp**, a wild, hikable strip of land emerging from the sea. **13 Heltermaa** is Hiiumaa's port town, connecting the island with the outside world.

Surf Paradiis The Paradise Beach Bar is an isolated bar and cafe overlooking the waves. It opens in summer in Ristna's Surf Paradiis.

Lavendlitalu The lavender of Lavendlitalu only blooms in late spring; stop by any time at the shop to pick up locally made lavender products.

Heltermaa While waiting for the ferry, you can stop at Heltermaa's Handicraft House, filled with quirky mementos and souvenirs.

FLAVOURS OF ESTONIA

Simple and hearty, Estonian cuisine reflects the country's climate and connection to nature. Here are some key dishes to look for:

Baltic herring *(räim)* **and sprats** *(kilu):* A recurring presence in Estonian cuisine – try a *kiluvõileib* (sprat sandwich; sprat served on dark rye bread with butter and a hard-boiled egg).

Mulgipuder: Some consider it the national dish – a filling porridge made from mashed potatoes and barley, often served with bacon. It even made it onto UNESCO's Intangible Cultural Heritage list in 2024.

Sült: A savoury meat jelly, often made with pork, popular for festive occasions. If it sounds unappealing, just wait until you see it.

Verivorst: Estonia's blood sausage is a traditional winter and Christmas dish, typically served with lingonberry jam and sauerkraut.

ALEXANDRE.ROSA/SHUTTERSTOCK

history of the structure and the surrounding city. Inside the nearby **Pärnu Museum** *(parnumuuseum.ee; entry adult/ child €12/9)* you are met with the skeleton of the Pärnu cog, a 7.9m, 14th-century shipwreck found accidentally in 1990 on the banks of the Pärnu River. As you continue through the museum's rooms, you'll learn how, from a Stone Age settlement known as Pulli, Pärnu grew to become an important Hanseatic node on the Baltic and later a resort town with the – perhaps misplaced – desire to compete with the French Riviera.

Estonia's favourite stretch of sand

Lying behind the neoclassical building of the **Pärnu Mud Baths**, built in 1926 and now managed by the Hedon Hotel, the city's broad, sandy beach is the reason most people visit in the summer. On the southern edge of the beach, you'll find the **Pärnu Surf Centre**, where you can rent kayaks and SUP boards or join a windsurfing course. Next to it, a short boardwalk forms the 'meadow trail', leading to the **Pärnu Grasslands Nature Reserve**, which runs for 3km along the coast to the **Raeküla Watchtower**.

 EATING IN PÄRNU: OUR PICKS

Wrapimaja: Between a swim and a spa session stop by for tasty wraps and refreshing rhubarb lemonades. *noon-midnight Sun-Thu, to 2am Fri & Sat* €

Vehverments Bar & Tostadas: Like eating at grandma's, if your grandma had Mexican tostadas and a selfie-suited house. *noon-11pm Mon-Thu, to midnight Fri & Sat, to 10pm Sun* €

VoVa: A creative and comforting menu of tapas and full meals, along with an extensive beer and cocktail list. *noon-10pm Sun-Thu, to midnight Fri & Sat* €€

Villa Wesset: Heritage building between the beach and the city centre that houses one of Pärnu's best restaurants. Veg options available. *noon-midnight Sun-Thu, to 1am Fri & Sat* €€€

Pärnu Mud Baths

Soomaa National Park

TIME FROM PÄRNU: **40MIN**

Experience the 'fifth season'

Covering an area of some 360 sq km, **Soomaa National Park** is well known for turning hikers into kayakers during the 'fifth season' in spring, when the rain and snow melt causing the rivers to overflow. The park's **visitor centre** is in the middle of the park, 12km from Jõesuu. The easy Riisa study trail is a popular walking path, running for 4.8km on a boardwalk.

Haapsalu

TIME FROM PÄRNU: **2HR**

Spa-town heritage

Stretching around the crumbling remains of **Haapsalu Episcopal Castle**, the city's **Promenade** is ideally positioned for summer evenings strolls along the bay. Haapsalu has been welcoming wellness tourists to its spas for over a century and the relaxed atmosphere is still part of the allure. From the onion-domed **Church of Mary Magdalene**, reach the dreamy **Haapsalu Kuursaal**, a green and white wooden villa on the seaside promenade that used to be a favourite holidaying destination for the 19th-century Russian aristocracy.

Kuressaare

TIME FROM PÄRNU: **3HR**

Inside Kuressaare's Episcopal Castle

With a population of just over 13,000 people, Kuressaare, the capital of Saaremaa, is the obvious starting point to explore the West Estonian Archipelago. At its core sits the **Kuressaare Episcopal Castle**, one of the best-preserved fortifications in Estonia. Inside, the **Saaremaa Museum** *(samu.ee; entry adult/ child €12/9)* covers the country's history from medieval times.

Places We Love to Stay

€ Budget €€ Midrange €€€ Top End

Tallinn

MAP p179

Imaginary Hostel € One of Old Town's long-standing hostels (and often the cheapest), with mixed dorms only and beehive-like beds that offer a little more privacy than usual.

St Olav Hotel €€ Excellent location and price, but to get to your room you'll need to find your way through a labyrinth at this historic hotel. Rooms are more spacious than other basic Old Town hotels and a buffet breakfast is included.

ibis Styles Tallinn €€ A safe bet right outside Old Town's walls by Lindamägi. Modern, bright clean rooms, 24-hour reception and comfy beds at a budget friendly price, close to the railway station and Kalamaja.

von Stackelberg Hotel €€ Access this elegant property from the courtyard surrounding a fountain and stay in tastefully furnished rooms away from the crowds but near all the sights.

Schlössle Hotel €€€ The colourful exterior of this Old Town palatial hotel contrasts with the elegant stonework and plush decor of the interior.

Lahemaa National Park

Viinistu Art Hotel €€ A former fish-processing plant in front of the local art museum has been converted into a simple waterfront hotel filled with paintings. Great breakfast and restaurant.

Palmse Distillery Guesthouse €€ Nestled behind the manor house and the greenhouse, this converted 19th-century distillery makes you feel at home on the historic Palmse property.

Vihula Manor €€€ The most luxurious of the Baltic German manor houses converted into hotels, with sophisticated rooms designed for relaxation and on-site spa treatments available.

Tartu

Hektor Design Hostel € Matching the vibe of the surrounding Aparaaditehas, this 'smart' hostel comes with a sauna and a gym, plus many modern touches and a laundry room.

Villa Margaretha €€ An elegant art nouveau villa in the picturesque Karlova district, with an excellent restaurant.

Hotel Tartu €€ A midrange choice in an updated 1960s building that offers straightforward rooms near the bus station, the river and Old Town.

Antonius Hotel €€€ An Old Town boutique hotel with elegant, antique furniture and top-notch service.

Pärnu

Tiia Guesthouse € The cheapest rooms in town are in this basic but clean wooden

home, close to the action. Shared bathrooms.

Tervise Paradiis €€ A large family-oriented hotel, with an adjoining waterpark and beach views from the balconies.

Villa Andropoff €€ In the secluded beachside forest of Valgeranna, this modernist hotel once used by the Soviet political elite is now an architectural monument.

Villa Ammende €€€ This art nouveau villa has been successfully restored to become one of Pärnu's most refined boutique hotels.

Haapsalu

Päeva Villa €€ Pastel rooms, each with their own theme, in a family-run guesthouse with a peaceful atmosphere.

Hestia Hotel & Spa €€€ This contemporary hotel is all about relaxation. Spa treatments are the main draw, but the views aren't bad either.

Kuressaare

Hotel NOSPA €€ Modern (although a little anonymous) rooms by St Nicholas Church, with balconies, powerful showers and a shared kitchen. Automated check-in and little to no staff around.

Ekesparre €€€ A refined 10-room historic boutique hotel right in front of the Episcopal Castle. Originally built in 1908, it's now Kuressaare's top hotel.

Practicalities

LGBTIQ+ Travellers
Estonia is generally considered a safe and welcoming destination for LGBTIQ+ travellers. While attitudes can be more conservative in rural areas, major cities like Tallinn have a visible LGBTIQ+ scene. In 2024, Estonia legalised same-sex marriage.

Health
Apart from tick-borne diseases, which can be a danger in grassy and forested areas, and slippery streets during icy winters, there are no major health concerns specific to Estonia. The main thing to keep in mind is that you may find yourself far from a doctor or a hospital when visiting remote areas.

Russian Travellers
Following Russia's invasion of Ukraine in 2022, Estonia closed its border to most Russian citizens. Russian citizens with a short-term Schengen visa are not allowed to enter Estonia for tourism, regardless of the visa-issuing country. Also, as of 2025, Estonia no longer recognises non-biometric passports issued by Russia.

Ice Roads
In winter, Estonia has official ice roads linking the islands to the mainland. These seasonal routes form across the frozen Baltic Sea in the coldest months and are regulated by special rules, including recommended speeds and distances between vehicles.

MNSTUDIO/SHUTTERSTOCK

Tallinn (p178)

The RMK App
The 'RMK Loodusega koos' app, developed by the State Forest Management Centre (RMK) provides information and tools for hiking and camping in Estonia's forests and natural areas. Find hundreds of trails and maps, with details on where you can stop for the night if you're going to be out for consecutive multiple days.

Tap Water
Tap water is generally considered good to drink in Estonia; you can always fill up your water bottle in public restrooms without any concerns.

Public Holidays
New Year's Day 1 January
Independence Day (Iseseisvuspäev) 24 February
Easter March/April
Spring Day (Kevadpüha) 1 May
Whit Sunday May/June
Victory Day (Võidupüha) 23 June
St John's Day/Midsummer's Day (Jaanipäev) 24 June
Independence Restoration Day (Taasiseseisvumispäev) 20 August
Christmas Eve 24 December
Christmas Day 25 December
Second Day of Christmas 26 December

Language

Double vowels in written Estonian indicate they are pronounced as long sounds. Note that air is pronounced as in 'hair', aw as in 'law', ea as in 'ear', eu as the 'u' in 'nurse', ew as 'ee' with rounded lips, oh as the 'o' in 'note', ow as in 'how', uh as the 'a' in 'ago', kh as in the Scottish loch, and zh as the 's' in 'pleasure'.

Basics

Hello. Tere. *te·re*

Goodbye. Nägemist. *nair·ge·mist*

Excuse me. Vabandage/Vabanda. (pol/inf) *va·ban·da·ge/va·ban·da*

Sorry. Vabandust. *va·ban·dust*

Please. Palun. *pa·lun*

Thank you. Tänan. *tair·nan*

Yes. Jaa. *yaa*

No. Ei. *ay*

What's your name? Mis on teie nimi? *mis on tay·e ni·mi*

My name is ... Minu nimi on ... *mi·nu ni·mi on ...*

Do you speak English? Kas te räägite inglise keelt? *kas te rair·git·te ing·kli·se keylt*

I don't understand. Ma ei saa aru. *ma ay saa a·ru*

Transport

boat laev *laiv*

bus buss *bus*

plane lennuk *len·nuk*

train rong *rongk*

One ... ticket (to Pärnu), Üks ... pilet (Pärnusse), *ewks ... pi·let (pair·nus·se)*

please. palun. *pa·lun*

one-way ühe otsa *ew·he o·tsa*

return edasi-tagasi *e·da·si·ta·ga·si*

Emergencies

Help! Appi! *ap·pi*

Go away! Minge ära! *ming·ke air·ra*

Call the doctor/police! Kutsuge arst/politsei! *ku·tsu·ge arst/ o·li·tsay*

I'm lost. Ma olen ära eksinud. *ma o·len air·ra ek·si·nud*

Where are the toilets? Kus on WC? *kus on ve·se*

Eating & Drinking

What would you recommend? Mida te soovitate? *i·da te saw·vit·tat·te*

Do you have vegetarian food? Kas teil on taimetoitu? *kas tayl on tai·met·toyt·tu*

I'd like the bill/menu, please. Ma sooviksin arvet/menüüd, palun. *ma saw·vik·sin ar·vet/me·newt pa·lun*

I'll have a ... Ma tahaksin ... *ma ta·hak·sin ...*

Cheers! Terviseks! *tair·vi·seks*

Shopping & Services

I'm looking for ... Ma otsin ... *ma o·tsin*

How much is it? Kui palju see maksab? *ku·i pal·yu sey mak·sab*

That's too expensive. See on liiga kallis. *sey on lee·ga kal·lis*

bank pank *pank*

market turg *turg*

post office postkontor *post·kont·tor*

NUMBERS

1	üks *ewks*
2	kaks *kaks*
3	kolm *kolm*
4	neli *ne·li*
5	viis *vees*
6	kuus *koos*
7	seitse *say·tse*
8	kaheksa *ka·hek·sa*
9	üheksa *ew·hek·sa*
10	kümme *kewm·me*

Tallinn Baltic Station

Arriving & Getting Around

Tallinn is the main point of entry for those who reach Estonia by sea or air. Overland travellers can easily reach Estonia from Latvia – Riga is just a couple of hours away from the border.

By Ferry from Helsinki
A dozen ships a day arrive from Helsinki, on the opposite side of the Gulf of Finland, docking at the Estonian capital's harbour. From Tallinn's port, Old Town can be reached on foot in under 20 minutes.

Arriving by Air
Tallinn Airport is the main gateway, offering frequent connections to major European cities. Frequent buses provide easy access to the city centre. Tartu has Estonia's second international airport.

Driving Essentials
Car-rental prices start at around €40 per day. Given the short distances between cities, a small car is usually enough. The speed limit is 50km/h in urban areas, 90km/h outside of cities. The blood alcohol limit is 0.2g/L.

Public Transport
Buses serve rural areas only once or twice per day, so make sure to check schedules if you're planning a day trip. Intercity buses such as those with Lux Express or Flixbus are generally comfortable. Train tickets are slightly cheaper when bought online at elron.ee. The railway system is small and very efficient. As of 2025, the three Baltic capitals can be reached within a single day by train.

MONEY
Currency: Euro (€)

CASH
Cash seems to be disappearing from Estonian cities, although it's still commonly used for smaller transactions in markets. It's a good idea to keep some euros in your pocket, but it's likely that you won't end up using them. Currency exchange points are easy to find in cities, but ATMs generally offer better rates.

CREDIT & DEBIT CARDS
Credit and debit cards are accepted almost everywhere in Estonia, especially Visa and MasterCard. You won't have trouble using them in hotels, restaurants, larger shops and for online bookings. Occasionally, smaller establishments or shops in remote areas might only accept cash.

DIGITAL PAYMENTS
Digital payments, including mobile payment apps and contactless payments, are popular in Estonia, a country known for its advanced digital infrastructure.

Curated by
Kata Fári

Hungary

STUNNING ARCHITECTURE AND THERMAL SPAS

Hungary is home to one of Europe's most stunning capitals, thermal waters galore and people whose language you'll probably never speak, but who you'll definitely want to meet.

Hungary might be small, but it packs quite a punch. The country is steeped in history and tradition, its bounty of Art Nouveau architecture is astonishing, its thermal waters are restorative and its cuisine is as delicious as it is hearty. Budapest lays claim to the crown of most stunning capital in Europe, but it's so much more than a pretty face. With parks brimming with activity, museums filled with treasures, pleasure boats on the Danube and Turkish-era thermal baths belching steam, the Hungarian capital is a delight both by day and night.

In a country as flat as a *palacsinta* (pancake), Northern Hungary is as hilly as it gets, with towns rich in culture, vineyards renowned the world over and villages that cherish their traditions. Northwest of Budapest, the Danube Bend is a region of low peaks and attractive river towns steeped in history and the cultures of those who settled here. Southwest is Central Europe's largest lake, Lake Balaton (aka the Hungarian Sea), the favourite summer destination of locals, where sailing, soaking and stand-up paddleboarding is a way of life.

To the south and east is Hungary's heartland, the Great Plain, an intoxicating cocktail of countryside imbued with moody romance, splendid architecture and national parks.

BUDAPEST SPAS

THE MAIN AREAS

BUDAPEST	DANUBE BEND	LAKE BALATON	NORTHERN HUNGARY
Scenic beauty, high culture, hot nightlife. **p200**	Historical river towns vie for visitors' attention. **p212**	Warm days at Central Europe's largest lake. **p215**	Wine, baroque architecture, folklore and forests. **p216**

For places to stay in Hungary, see p218

MARAKO85/SHUTTERSTOCK

Left: Lukács Baths (p200), Budapest; Above: Széchenyi Chain Bridge (p205), Budapest

Find Your Way

Hungary has no domestic flights as the country is small enough to get around by train, bus or boat. The public transport system is reliable and the roads are good. A car is only needed for rural Hungary.

TRAINS & BUSES

MÁV (*mavcsoport.hu*) operates reliable services to Hungary's major towns. Volánbusz runs an extensive bus network. The **Hungary Pass** (*18,900Ft*) provides unlimited travel throughout Hungary (available via the BudapestGO and MÁV apps or BKK, MÁV and Volánbusz ticket offices).

BOAT

Mahart PassNave (*mahartpassnave. hu*) runs excursion boats and hydrofoils on the Danube River from Budapest to places like Szentendre, Visegrád and Esztergom from April to September. **Balaton Shipping Company** (*bahart.hu*) passenger ferries serve about 20 ports on Lake Balaton.

Danube Bend, p212

Flanked by attractive towns, the Danube makes its bend 50km north of Budapest, flowing west towards Western Transdanubia.

Northern Hungary, p216

Comparatively hilly, with main attractions that can be found around Eger and, 130km to the east, Tokaj.

Budapest, p200

The Queen of the Danube awaits with astonishing architecture, healing thermal baths and an unforgettable nightlife scene.

Lake Balaton, p215

Hungary's largest body of water. The 235km shoreline is dotted with villages a few minutes' drive from one another.

AUSTRIA

SLOVAKIA

BRATISLAVA

Eisenstadt • Mosonmagyaróvár

Fertő-Hanság National Park

Győr Tatabánya

Kisbér

Szombathely

Jánosháza

Székesfehérvár

Veszprém

Balatonfüred

Balaton Uplands National Park

Tihany

Hévíz

Lake Balaton

Nagykanizsa

Kaposvár

Zselic Region

Ormánság Region

Dunaújváros

Dunaföldvár

Tamási

Szekszárd

Pécs

Dráva River

Duna-Dráva National Park

CROATIA

Osijek

Esztergom

Danube River

Szentendre

Visegrád

Dunántúl

Dunaújváros

Baja

SERBIA

Salgótarján

Duna-Ipoly National Park

Gödöllő

Parliament

Liberty Monument

BUDAPEST

Open-Air Ethnographical Museum

Valley of the Beautiful Women

Gyömrő

Kiskunlacháza

Kiskunság National Park

Bugac

Kiskunfélegyháza

Kecskemét

Szolnok

Great Plain

Lake Tisza

Hortobágy National Park

Sárköz Region

Szeged

Békéscsaba

Kunszentmárton

Miskolc

Bükk National Park

Eger

Füzesabony

Szerencs

Tokaj

Rakamaz

Polgár

Nyíregyháza

Kisvárda

Satu Mare

ROMANIA

Oradea

Berettyóújfalu

Püspökladány

Körös-Maros National Park

Debrecen

100 km

50 miles

CLAR MASSIMILIANO/SHUTTERSTOCK

Royal Palace (p204), Budapest

Plan Your Time

Hungary holds so much to see and do that you could easily fill a fortnight, but if you have less time, follow your interests to create your own curated trip.

Pressed for Time

● If you only have a day or two, focus on beautiful Budapest and explore both sides. Head up to the historic Castle District on the **funicular** (p204) and take in the views from the **Royal Palace** (p204) and **Fisherman's Bastion** (p204). Spend the afternoon soaking at **Széchenyi** (p200) or **Gellért Baths** (p200); in the evening take a river cruise offered byone of the various boat companies downtown.

A Week-Long Stay

● A week is enough to balance culture, nature and relaxation. After exploring **Budapest** (p200), you can day-trip to the **Danube Bend** (p212) to see charming local towns. In summer, **Lake Balaton** (p215), Central Europe's largest lake, is a must for sailing, stand-up paddleboarding and soaking. In autumn, **Northern Hungary** (p216) is best for hikes and discovering Hungary's world-renowned wine culture.

SEASONAL HIGHLIGHTS

SPRING

From March to June, Hungary is in full bloom, and Easter traditions are in full swing in historic Hollókő.

SUMMER

Scorching summer begins with Tihany's **Lavender Festival** (p215) in late June. The perfect time to relax at scenic Lake Balaton.

AUTUMN

Hungary's forests turn a riot of red and brown; it's a great time for hiking and touring the wine regions, particularly Tokaj-Hegyalja.

WINTER

Winter may be mighty cold, but it's the perfect time to relax in thermal baths and enjoy marvellous Christmas markets.

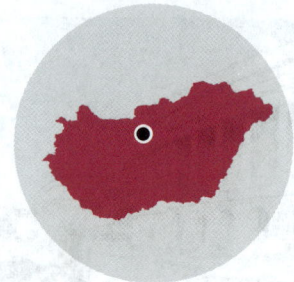

Budapest

SCENIC BEAUTY | HISTORIC SPAS | NIGHTLIFE

GETTING AROUND

Budapest is easy to navigate. The Danube clearly defines west and east: Buda and Pest. The public transport system is safe, efficient and inexpensive, and taxis are reasonably priced. You can also get around by bicycle, electric scooter or on foot. The BudapestGO app for public transport in the city offers several key features, including ticket and pass purchases, real-time route planning, a map, timetables and service updates. The city's official bike-sharing scheme is with the green MOL Bubi bikes.

☑ **TOP TIP**

Public transport tickets not only have to be purchased but also validated. Digital tickets come with a QR code scanner that you can use on machines at stations or the side of buses and trams before boarding, and passes have a QR code for inspection.

Budapest is a dazzling gem of a city, but its beauty is not all God-given: humankind has also played a role in shaping its pretty face. The city is an architectural treasure trove, with enough baroque, neoclassical, eclectic and Art Nouveau buildings to satisfy everyone. Overall, Budapest has a fin-de-siècle feel, for it was in the late 19th century, during the capital's golden age, that much of what you see today was built.

With parks brimming with activity, museums filled with treasures, pleasure boats on the Danube and Turkish-era thermal baths belching steam, the Hungarian capital is a delight both by day and night. Stroll along the Duna korzó, Pest's riverside embankment walkway, or cross any of the Danube bridges, and you'll pass young couples embracing passionately. It's then that you'll feel the romance of a place that, despite all the attempts from both within and without to destroy it, has never died.

Soak Away Your Worries

Take the plunge in a thermal bath

Hardly anything feels more relaxing in Budapest than plunging into a thermal pool and soaking away your stress in muscle-melting mineral-rich waters. Taking the waters is a way of life here, and the country – especially its capital – is a paradise for those seeking relaxation, healing and a bit of quirky local culture. Budapest lies on a geological fault line separating the Buda Hills from the Great Plain, and some 40,000 cubic metres of warm, mineral-rich water spurt forth each day. Hence the sobriquet, the 'City of Spas' – find the perfect combination of relaxation and restoration at one of several bathhouses in town. The most notable are Gellért Baths (unfortunately closed for renovations until 2028), the most beautiful bathhouse of all; **Széchenyi Baths** (*szechenyibath.hu; 10,000-17,000Ft*), Europe's largest spa complex in a wedding-cake-like building; **Lukács Baths** (*lukacsfurdo.hu; 3600-8300Ft*), a more local, health-oriented

Széchenyi Baths

WINE WITH A VIEW

Every September, the Royal Palace becomes a magnificent backdrop for the **Budapest Wine Festival**, when wooden kiosks are set up side-by-side at this historic venue to serve the country's finest red, white and sparkling wines from various regions, as well as a plethora of foreign bottles. A wide range of gastronomic delights is also available – many are prepared especially for the occasion and pair perfectly with the wines on offer. Various events, wine-focused workshops and concerts also take place in the gorgeous setting. This is one of the most elegant wine festivals in the country, and a perfect place to get familiar with lesser known but highly praised wines from all over the country. Tasting is by the glass, but bottles are also available.

destination; **Rudas Baths** *(rudasfurdo.hu; 9800-15,800Ft),* an original Turkish baths with a contemporary touch and a rooftop hot tub; and **Veli Bej Baths** *(irgalmasrend.hu/ site/velibej/home; 4500-6000Ft),* a traditional Turkish bath with a modern twist.

Walk Down Memory Lane

Explore the Castle District on foot

The World Heritage–listed Castle District is home to historic sights, charming cobblestone streets, fascinating museums and stunning viewpoints that set the stage for a journey back in time. With a majestic monument on practically every corner, it's unparalleled when it comes to sightseeing. There's hardly another neighbourhood in the city with so many heavyweight sights crammed into such a compact space: the Royal Palace (p204), Fisherman's Bastion (p204) and neo-Gothic Matthias Church (p204) are all steps away from one another. Wear comfortable shoes for the cobblestone streets.

EATING & DRINKING IN THE CASTLE DISTRICT: OUR PICKS

White Raven Skybar & Lounge: Atop the Hilton Budapest, the city's highest sky bar offers jaw-dropping views and delicious drinks and finger food. *noon-10pm* €€€

Royal Guard Restaurant & Cafe: With a facade adorned with intriguing statues and weaponry, the Royal Guard houses a lovely cafe-restaurant. *11.30am-9.30pm* €€

Savoyai Terasz: Delicious coffee and dazzling views right at the foot of the Royal Palace. Plenty of musical events in the warmer months. *10.30am-8pm* €€

4 perc és kávé: This bite-sized cafe is fully vegan, making java mostly from oat milk. *8.30am-6pm Mon-Fri, from 9am Sat & Sun* €

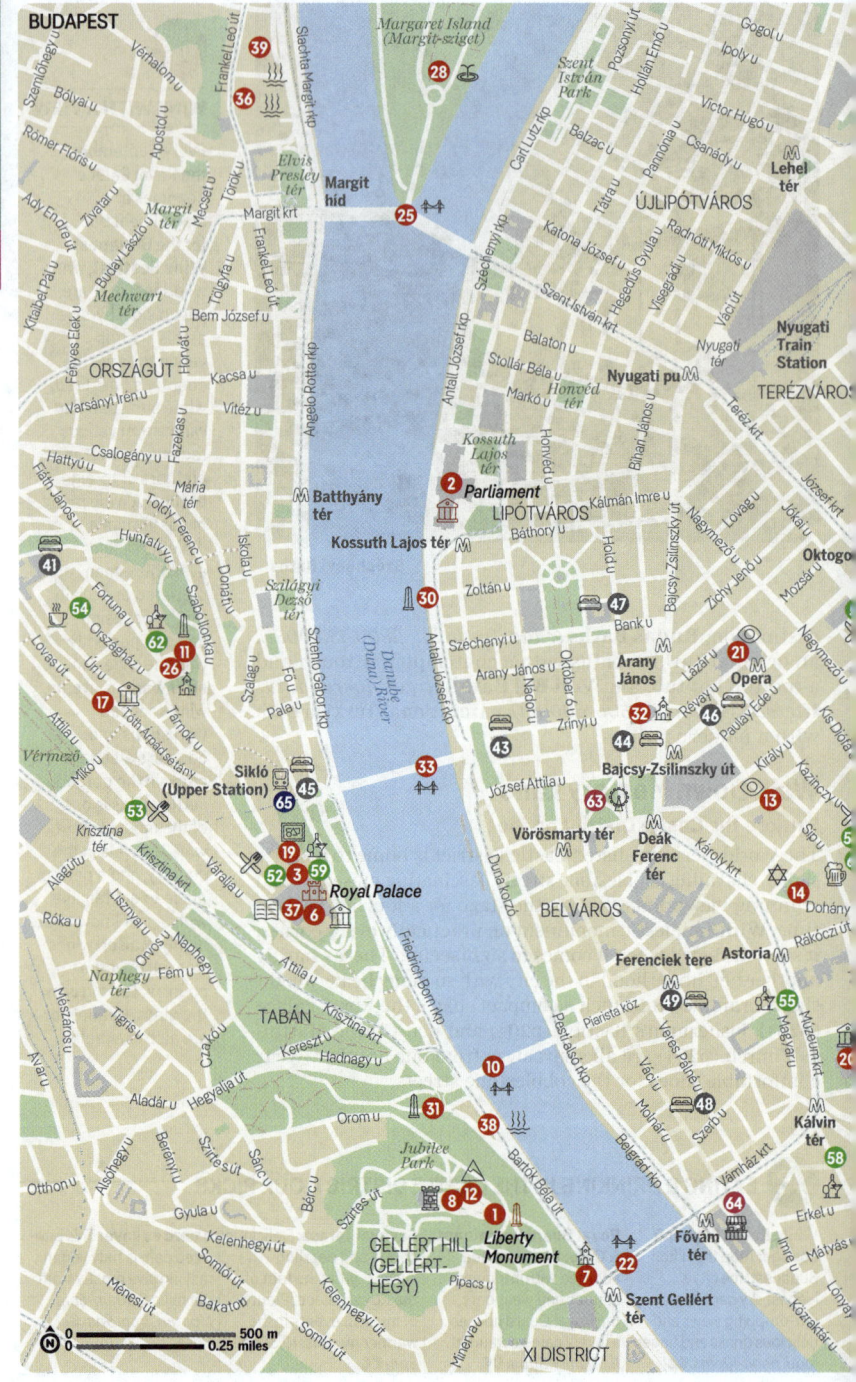

BUDAPEST

Margaret Island
(Margit-sziget)

Szent
István
Park

ÚJLIPÓTVÁROS

Lehel
tér

Margit
híd

Nyugati
Train
Station

TERÉZVÁROS

ORSZÁGÚT

Nyugati pu

Meehwart
tér

Kossuth
Lajos
tér

Parliament

LIPÓTVÁROS

Oktogo

Batthyány
tér

Kossuth Lajos tér

Szilágyi
Dezső
tér

Arany
János

Opera

Danube
(Duna/
River)

Siklo
(Upper Station)

Bajcsy-Zsilinszky út

Royal Palace

Vörösmarty tér

Deák
Ferenc
tér

BELVÁROS

Dohány

TABÁN

Ferenciek tere Astoria

Kálvin
tér

Jubilee
Park

GELLÉRT
HILL
(GELLÉRT-
HEGY)

Liberty
Monument

Főväm
tér

Szent Gellért
tér

0   500 m
0   0.25 miles

XI DISTRICT

HIGHLIGHTS
1 Liberty Monument
2 Parliament
3 Royal Palace
4 Széchenyi Baths

SIGHTS
5 Budapest Zoo
6 Castle Museum
7 Cave Church
8 Citadel
9 City Park
10 Elizabeth Bridge
11 Fisherman's Bastion
12 Gellért Hill
13 Gozsdu udvar
14 Great Synagogue
15 Heroes' Square
16 Holocaust Memorial Centre
17 Hospital in the Rock Nuclear Bunker Museum
18 House of Terror
19 Hungarian National Gallery
20 Hungarian National Museum
21 Hungarian State Opera House
22 Liberty Bridge
23 Liszt Ferenc Academy of Music
24 Liszt Ferenc Memorial Museum
25 Margaret Bridge
26 Matthias Church
27 Museum of Fine Arts
28 Musical Fountain
29 Palace of Art
30 Shoes on the Danube
31 St Gellért Monument
32 St Stephen's Basilica
33 Széchenyi Chain Bridge
34 Vajdahunyad Castle

ACTIVITIES
35 BalloonFly

36 Lukács Baths
37 National Széchenyi Library
38 Rudas Baths
39 Veli Bej Baths

SLEEPING
40 Anantara New York Palace Hotel
41 Baltazár
42 Corinthia Hotel Budapest
43 Four Seasons Gresham Palace Hotel
44 Hotel Central Basilica
45 Hotel Clark Budapest
46 Hotel Moments Budapest
47 Hotel President Budapest
48 Loft Hostel
49 Párisi Udvar Hotel

EATING
50 Gettó Gulyás
51 Menza
52 Royal Guard Restaurant & Cafe
53 Stand25

DRINKING & NIGHTLIFE
54 4 perc és kávé
55 Csendes Létterem
56 Instant-Fogas
57 New York Café
58 Púder Bárszínház
59 Savoyai Terasz
60 Szimpla Kert
61 Városliget Café
62 White Raven Skybar & Lounge

ENTERTAINMENT
63 Ferris Wheel of Budapest

SHOPPING
64 Nagycsarnok

TRANSPORT
65 Funicular
66 Keleti (Eastern) Train Station

203

Castle on the Hill
Visit the enormous Royal Palace

Crowning Castle Hill, the **Royal Palace** towers over Budapest with a commanding presence. This immediately recognisable, emblematic attraction houses the **Hungarian National Gallery** *(mng.hu; entry adult/child 5400/2700Ft)* in buildings A to D, containing an overwhelming collection of thousands of artefacts presenting the development and rise of the fine arts in Hungary from the 11th century onwards; the **Castle Museum** *(varmuzeum.hu; entry adult/child 3800/1900Ft)* in building E tells the story of Budapest from prehistoric times to the present day; and the **National Széchenyi Library** *(oszk.hu; day pass 1200Ft)* is in building F. Don't miss out on the view from the Royal Palace's dome, accessible with your ticket to the Hungarian National Gallery.

Mesmerising Views
Marvel at Fisherman's Bastion

The bone-white, 140m-long neo-Gothic **Fisherman's Bastion** offers one of the prettiest panoramas over the Pest skyline. Its name comes from the medieval guild of fishermen responsible for defending this stretch of the old castle wall. Only the upstairs **viewing platform** *(adult/child 1500/750Ft)* requires a ticket.

Fun on the Funicular
Ascend Castle Hill in style

If you want to sneak some fun into reaching the Royal Palace, hop on the **funicular** *(adult/child 5000/2000Ft)*. Its steep 95m-long track, climbing at a speed of 1.5m per second, is a quick and convenient way up Castle Hill from the banks of the Danube, providing splendid views en route.

An Eerie World Underground
Venture below Castle Hill

The **Hospital in the Rock** *(sziklakorhaz.eu; entry adult/child 9500/4800Ft)* is a real underground hospital that was turned into a nuclear bunker and kept secret for decades – the government only declassified its existence in 2002. There are some 200 lifelike wax figures, original furniture, medical equipment and even a whole helicopter underground. Visit on one of the one-hour guided tours that depart hourly from 10am to 6pm.

Frescoes & Organ Music
Admire the Matthias Church

Perched high above Szentháromság tér, the **Matthias Church** *(matyas-templom.hu; entry adult/child 3100/2500Ft)* is a neo-Gothic confection. The interior features a beautiful combination of wooden statuary, colourful frescoes and gold-leaf detail. One of the best ways to enjoy the cathedral's interior is to attend one of the many classical concerts held here.

RAZAK.R/SHUTTERSTOCK

Fisherman's Bastion

All Aboard the Cutest Ride

Take a trip on the Children's Railway

One of the best ways to explore the Buda Hills, a favourite hiking spot of locals, is by riding the **Children's Railway** *(gyermekvasut.hu; entry adult/ child 1000/500Ft),* which is operated almost entirely by kids. The staff, aged 10 to 14 and dressed in smart uniforms, hold all the positions on the railway, from conductors to signallers, while a little adult supervision keeps things on track (the engineers, thankfully, are grown-ups). The Children's Railway operates year-round, giving you a different view of the Buda Hills each season.

An Island in the Middle of the City?

Walk around Margaret Island

Neither Buda nor Pest, Margaret Island (Margit-sziget) sits in the middle of the Danube. Just 2.5km long, it's not graced with many significant sights, but you can easily spend half a day exploring its swimming complexes, thermal spa, gardens and centuries-old ruins; on a hot summer afternoon, it makes for a lovely escape. The main attraction is the **Musical Fountain** that puts on a dramatic display five times a day, with jets 'dancing' to music and shooting up to 10m in the air. Catch the last show at 9pm, when the fountain is illuminated by hundreds of coloured lights.

Strenuous Climb for Splendid Views

Climb Gellért Hill

You can climb one of Budapest's most iconic landmarks, the 235m-high, tree-dotted **Gellért Hill**, surmounted by the **Cita-del** and the **Liberty Monument**, a proud lady watching over Budapest with the symbol of peace, a palm branch, in her hands.

KNOW YOUR BRIDGES

While there are over a dozen bridges in Budapest, you'll spend most of your time photographing or crossing only a handful of them. One of the most striking and the star of many a photograph is the **Széchenyi Chain Bridge**, which was the first permanent bridge connecting Buda and Pest when it was inaugurated in 1849. The second was **Margaret Bridge**, which doglegs in the middle allowing it to stand at right angles to the Danube where it converges at the southern tip of Margaret Island. Sage-green **Liberty Bridge** is the locals' favourite, while slender and elegant gleaming-white **Elizabeth Bridge** connects the city centre with Gellért Hill. In WWII all of Budapest's bridges were blown up, though later rebuilt.

205

FRANK WAGNER/SHUTTERSTOCK

Parliament

From the top, the views of Buda, the Pest skyline and the gently curving Danube River are unbeatable. On the way, expect peaceful rest stops, a playground and slide park, and even the **Cave Church** *(sziklatemplom.hu; entry adult/child 1200/1000Ft)*, a functioning church set inside a cave – a real sight to behold.

Ghosts of Communism Past

Explore this huge open-air park

Memento Park *(mementopark.hu; entry adult/child 3000/1200Ft)* provides a sneak peek behind the Iron Curtain, guarding the gigantic statues of Lenin, Marx, Engels, homegrown heroes and other types of communist propaganda that were removed from the streets of Budapest after the fall of the Berlin Wall in 1989. You can opt for a guided tour or wander around on your own, but don't miss the park's top attraction, a pair of gigantic boots. It's a replica of the original 8m-high bronze statue of Stalin that was pulled down from its plinth on Dózsa György út in City Park during the 1956 Uprising and sawed apart until only the boots remained.

 EATING IN BUDAPEST: HUNGARIAN FOOD

Városliget Café: A long-standing restaurant serving tasty local fare, from traditional bean soup to schnitzel, along with lake views. *noon-10pm* €€

Menza: Retro-chic place with a modern take on Hungarian cuisine plus international favourites; try the red-wine beef stew. *11am-11pm* €€

Gettó Gulyás: The best place to try *pörkölt* (traditional beef stew) and *gulyás*, Hungary's favourite soup. *noon-11pm* €€

Stand25: Hungarian classics like goulash and *somlói* cake by Bocuse d'Or Europe winner Tamás Széll. *noon-4pm & 6pm-midnight Mon-Sat* €€

Hungary's Largest Building
Tour the Parliament

The **Parliament** (*parlament.hu; entry adult/child from 4500Ft*) stretches for 268m along the left bank of the Danube in Pest. It's a vast, stately building and repository of national treasures, a symbolic counterweight to the Royal Palace on Castle Hill across the river. The building is a blend of many architectural styles (neo-Romanesque, neo-baroque). You can take a 45-minute tour by audio guide of the North Wing; be sure to see one of the country's most important national symbols, the Holy Crown of Hungary.

History's Dark Side
A moving Holocaust memorial

On the Danube embankment south of the Parliament is a monument to Hungarian Jews shot and thrown into the river by members of the fascist Arrow Cross Party in 1944. Called **Shoes on the Danube**, it's a simple but poignant display of 60 pairs of old-style boots and shoes in cast iron along the riverbank.

The Country's Most Sacred Catholic Church
Visit the Basilica of St Stephen

The neoclassical cathedral, the largest in Budapest, is in the form of a Greek cross and can accommodate 8000 worshippers. The interior of **St Stephen's Basilica** glimmers in low-lit splendour, with Károly Lotz' golden mosaics on the inside of the dome seeming to produce a light all of their own. Its major drawcard is the Holy Dexter (or Holy Right), the mummified right hand of St Stephen, first king of Hungary, who was credited with establishing the Kingdom of Hungary and introducing Christianity as the state religion. The top of the dome, which offers fantastic views, can be reached on foot or via lifts. There are three ticket types: for the basilica, the treasury and the dome.

A Quick Spin
Short but sweet Ferris wheel flight

Dominating Erzsébet tér, the **Ferris Wheel of Budapest** (*oriaskerek.com; entry adult/child from 4300/2300Ft*) offers stunning panoramic views of Pest and across the Danube to Buda, and it's an easy way to get a view of the capital. Board after dark; the flight is particularly impressive at night.

A Night at the Opera
Music, laughter and a beautiful building

The neo-Renaissance **Hungarian State Opera House** (*opera.hu*) was completed in 1884 and is among the most beautiful buildings in Budapest. It's worth a visit as much to admire the incredibly rich decoration inside as to view a performance and hear the perfect acoustics. Tickets range from affordable to astronomical, but standing room costs next to nothing – or join one of the three one-hour daily **tours** (*9000Ft*) in English, which include a 10-minute performance at the end.

WHO WAS ST GELLÉRT?

A hill, a bath, a hotel, a city square and a metro station are all named after one man: St Gellért. But who was this guy? St Gellért was an Italian missionary who ended up in Hungary around 1020, after a storm disrupted his pilgrimage. King Stephen convinced him to stay, tutor his son and convert the masses to Christianity. After being named a bishop, he went on to live the life of a hermit. Unfortunately, legend has it that after the king died in 1038, the pagan Magyars hurled the bishop to his death in a spiked barrel. His **statue** now stands on the spot of his martyrdom, gazing peacefully down over the city.

In the Footsteps of Franz Liszt
Music academy and museum

Opened in 1875, the **Liszt Ferenc Academy of Music** *(zeneakademia.hu)* is today housed in a newer Art Nouveau building built in 1907 and is both a university and Budapest's top classical-music venue. The renovated interior is worth visiting on a **guided tour** *(5300Ft)* if you're not attending a performance. The wonderful little **Liszt Ferenc Memorial Museum** *(lisztmuseum.hu; entry adult/child 3000/1500Ft),* housed in the Old Music Academy, is where the great composer lived in a 1st-floor apartment for five years until his death in 1886. The rooms are filled with his instruments, furniture, books, portraits and personal effects.

The Continent's First Metro
Take a ride on the historic underground

One of Budapest's four metro lines, the **Millennium Underground Railway** is by far the oldest. Indeed, it was the first underground railway to open in continental Europe, preceding the Paris metro by 14 years. Today it runs for 4.4km below Andrássy út, serving 11 stations; to change direction, you must exit and cross the street.

Descend into Darkness
See the House of Terror

The **House of Terror** *(terrorhaza.hu; entry adult/child 4000-2000Ft)* is a moving museum focusing on the atrocities of Hungary's fascist and Stalinist regimes and commemorates their victims. It's set up in the former headquarters of both the Arrow Cross Party (Hungarian Nazis) and, later, the Communist Secret Police, used for interrogating and torturing 'enemies of the state'. The walls were allegedly extra thick to muffle the screams.

A Trip Back to the Belle Époque
The most beautiful cafe in the world

An ever-present queue outside the **New York Café** *(newyorkcafe. hu),* once voted the most beautiful coffee house in the world, will certainly catch your eye in Erzsébetváros. Inside, you can immerse yourself in authentic 19th-century coffee-house culture amid gilded and marble surfaces, etched glass and frescoes, and live Hungarian music. During Hungary's belle époque, renowned writers were often seen putting pen to paper here.

Europe's Largest Synagogue
Explore the Great Synagogue

With its crenellated red-and-yellow glazed-brick facade and two enormous Moorish-style towers, Budapest's stunning **Great Synagogue** *(jewishtourhungary.com; entry adult/ child 13,000/10,500Ft),* also called the 'Dohány utca Synagogue', is the largest Jewish house of worship in Europe, seating 3000 people. Visit for its majestic architecture, the Hungarian Jewish Museum and Archives, and the Holocaust Tree of

PFEIFFER/SHUTTERSTOCK

Gozsdu udvar

THE SPIRITS OF HUNGARY

Hungary's two most famous spirits are *pálinka* and Unicum. *Pálinka* is distilled from a variety of fruits and is akin to a strong brandy or eau de vie. It kicks like a mule and is served in most bars, some of which carry an enormous range – and almost all Hungarian households have suspicious mineral water bottles filled with homemade *pálinka*. Unicum's medicinal-looking bottle is instantly recognisable. The bitter aperitif has been around since 1790 – prepared according to a secret formula and aged in oak casks, it's available in four different tastes. The liqueur was apparently baptised by Austro-Hungarian Emperor Joseph II; when tasting it for the first time, he exclaimed, *'Das ist ein Unikum!'* (This is unique!).

Life Memorial. Admission includes an informative 45-minute tour in eight languages – tours start every 30 to 60 minutes.

Let the Party Begin

One long courtyard, lots of fun

Erzsébetváros has Budapest's most exciting nightlife, and **Gozsdu udvar** is its heart. It's a continuous 'courtyard' running a few hundred metres between Király utca 13 and Dob utca 16. A residential complex of seven blocks and six interconnecting courtyards when it was built in 1901, and part of the Jewish Ghetto during WWII, it's now lined with bars, clubs, cafes and restaurants, and pulses with music from dusk to dawn.

Harrowing History

Reminisce at the Holocaust Memorial Centre

The **Holocaust Memorial Centre** *(hdke.hu; entry adult/child 3600/1600Ft)* is the only public collection in the country that deals exclusively with the history of the Holocaust. Housed in a striking modern building that opened in 2002, the thematic permanent exhibition traces the rise of anti-Semitism in Hungary and follows the path to the genocide of the country's Jewish and Roma communities. A sublimely restored synagogue in the central courtyard, designed by Leopold Baumhorn and completed in 1924, hosts temporary exhibitions on the mezzanine level.

Romkocsma Is Where It's At

Boozing at ruin bars

Throwing back drinks at a ruin bar *(romkocsma)* filled with the most random knick-knacks is a real Budapest experience. The granddaddy of them all is **Szimpla Kert** *(szimpla.hu)*

Nagycsarnok

HUNGARIKUMS

The culinary heritage of Károly Gundel (founder of City Park's famed Gundel Restaurant) is a Hungaricum, alongside many other wonderful things such as *lángos* (deep-fried dough with toppings), *pálinka* (fruit brandy), Herend porcelain, *teqball* and PICK salami. But what is a Hungarikum? The term refers to a collection of unique, culturally significant and nationally recognised products, practices or values from Hungary that embody the essence of the country's heritage. These can include food and beverages, agricultural practices, folk art, traditions, inventions and even natural phenomena. Being recognised as a Hungarikum is a mark of prestige and a point of national pride, signifying the importance of these products or practices to Hungarian identity and heritage.

in Erzsébetváros, and some say it's still the best. **Instant-Fogas** *(instant-fogas.com)* is where two ruin bars merged to form the biggest in town. The quirkiest one is **Csendes Létterem** *(facebook.com/csendesvintagebar)* in Belváros and a slightly more upscale one is **Púder Bárszínház** *(puderbar.hu)* in Southern Pest.

The History of Hungary
Visit the Hungarian National Museum

The **Hungarian National Museum** *(mnm.hu; entry adult/child 3500/1750Ft)* houses the nation's most important collection of historical relics. It traces the history of the Carpathian Basin from the Stone Age and that of the Magyar people and Hungary from the 9th-century conquest to the fall of communism. If you visit just one museum in Budapest, make it this treasure trove.

The Biggest Deal in Town
Shop and eat at Nagycsarnok

Nagycsarnok *(piaconline.hu)* or the 'Great Market Hall', opened in 1897 and is the city's biggest market. Gourmets will appreciate the variety of treats available here for less than you'd pay in the shops on nearby Váci utca. Head up to the 1st floor for Hungarian folk costumes, dolls, painted eggs, embroidered tablecloths, leather goods, carved hunting knives and other souvenirs, as well as cooked foods like *kolbász* (sausage), *pörkölt* (stew) and *lángos* (deep-fried dough with toppings).

Diamonds & Rust on Sale
Flea-market finds

One of the biggest flea markets in Central Europe, **Ecseri Piac** *(piaconline.hu)* sells everything from antique jewellery and Soviet army watches to top hats (and a fair amount of stolen antique goods too, it's said). Early Saturday is the best time to go for treasures. To get here, take bus 54 from Pest's Boráros tér, or for a quicker journey, express bus 84E, 89E or 94E from the Határ út stop on the M3 metro line.

A Park with Pizzazz

Spend an afternoon in City Park

Serene **City Park** (Városliget) is the Pest side's green lung and Budapest's favourite recreational space. But don't just think plentiful picnic spots and groomed gardens; City Park is home to major landmarks such as the world-renowned Széchenyi Baths (p200); the city's most famous plaza, Heroes' Square; the faux-historic but fairy-tale **Vajdahunyad Castle**; the enormous **Budapest Zoo and Botanical Garden**; a lovely lake (and ice-skating rink in winter), and a handful of outstanding museums. And all of this within just 15 minutes of the city centre.

Meet Hungary's Heroes

Awe at Heroes' Square

This picture-perfect plaza concluding tree-lined Andrássy út is Budapest's largest and most symbolic square, serving as an elegant gateway to City Park. Framed by monumental statues narrating the tale of Hungary's formation and resilience and flanked by two major museums, the **Museum of Fine Arts** and the **Palace of Art** (Kunsthalle), **Heroes' Square** offers a blend of culture, striking architecture and history. It's especially majestic at night.

Take Flight in a Hot-Air Balloon

Have a go at BalloonFly

If you observe Budapest's cityscape, you'll likely spot a hot-air balloon adding a dash of red and white to the Pest skyline. This is **BalloonFly** *(balloonfly.hu; entry adult/child 10,000/5000Ft),* which takes visitors for a flight up to 150m above City Park, providing a stunning bird's-eye view, with landmarks like Széchenyi Baths, Vajdahunyad Castle and Heroes' Square en route.

WHY I LOVE BUDAPEST

Kata Fári, Lonely Planet writer
You know that sudden gush of love you get when you look at somebody you've known forever but for a split second realise again just how beautiful they are? For me, this happens every time I cross a bridge in Budapest. My love story with the city has seen splashes at stunning spas, nights lost at random ruin bars, hikes through the Buda Hills, laps around Margaret Island, books read at century-old coffee houses, romantic boat trips on the Danube, and daily dog walks in a park centred by a castle. I love Budapest because it's elegant, historic, romantic, bohemian and random all at once, and even though I know it like the back of my hand, it still manages to surprise me time and again.

Beyond
Budapest

WINE | LAKES | THE DANUBE

Places

Danube Bend p212
Lake Balaton p215
The Great Plain p215
Northern Hungary p216

☑ TOP TIP

The best time to visit Hungary is during the shoulder seasons of spring (March–May) and autumn (September–November), which have pleasant weather and generally fewer crowds. Lake Balaton is at its best but busiest in summer, while the country is a winter wonderland during the Christmas holidays.

Though Budapest is a superstar city and the main reason why most travellers visit Hungary, the country has much more to offer, from vineyards to tranquil countryside. Central Europe's largest lake, Lake Balaton, is the favourite summer destination of locals, where beaching and boating is a way of life. The wine regions in Northern Hungary grow grape varieties you may have never heard of but will end up gushing about. The Danube Bend's romantic towns are perfect for a quick spring getaway, while in the colder months, the hiking trails and the Great Plain's rural romance are ready to steal your heart.

Danube Bend

TIME FROM BUDAPEST: 1HR

The Danube Bend is lined with romantic riverside towns that vie for visitors' attention. Travelling upriver from Budapest, the Danube draws you deeper into its spell as you leave the day-trippers behind in the arts-focused town of Szentendre (St Andrew), round the eponymous bend and pass the impressive citadel of Visegrád. Beyond that, the Danube swirls past Esztergom, which, like Visegrád, was once a royal seat of sorts but in contrast, Esztergom is a religious centre dominated by a vast hilltop basilica, which is Hungary's largest church. Due to its close proximity and easy accessibility, the Danube Bend makes a perfect getaway from Budapest.

Szentendre's open-air ethnographical museum

Situated 5km from **Szentendre** (take bus 878), this **ethnographical museum** *(skanzen.hu; entry adult/child 4000/2000Ft)* is an unusual plunge into a fascinating 'alternative village reality'. As you wander or ride on a hire bike through the grounds, you'll find yourself transported into a picturesque setting of immaculately reconstructed Hungarian rural architecture and

---

GETTING AROUND

Travelling around the country is easy and affordable, and Hungary is also a manageable size, with most inland journeys from Budapest only taking a couple of hours. Trains take you most places, while buses take care of the rest.

Sailing up the Danube Bend or cycling are fun alternatives. Driving is only necessary if you're planning to see the country's remote corners. For those travelling extensively, the Hungary Pass provides unlimited public transport.

ROMANIA

Tokaj

Nyíregyháza

Hajdúnánás

Debrecen

Miskolc

Hajdúböszörmény

Berettyóújfalu

Bükk
National
Park

Mezőkövesd

Great
Plain

Lake
Tisza

Eger

Salgótarján

Szolnok

Hódmezővásárhely

Cegléd

Nagykőrös

Kiskunfélegyháza

Szeged

Hollókő

Szentendre

Gödöllő

Gyömrő

BUDAPEST

Kecskemét

Bugacpuszta

Visegrád

Pilis Park
Forest

Érd

Dunaújváros

SLOVAKIA

Esztergom

Tatabánya

Székesfehérvár

Baja

Veszprém

Lake Balaton

Szekszárd

Győr

Tihany

Pécs

Mosonmagyaróvár

Balatonfüred

Balaton Uplands
National Park

Kaposvár

BRATISLAVA

VIENNA

AUSTRIA

Eisenstadt

Szombathely

Zalaegerszeg

Őrség National
Park

Hévíz

Nagykanizsa

CROATIA

100 km

50 miles

0

0

PERFECTION IS SHALLOW

What makes Lake Balaton so beloved for outdoor recreation? According to the Balaton Limnological Research Institute, the shallowness and high water quality create possibilities for so many activities.

Central Europe's largest freshwater body (594 sq km) is incredibly shallow, with an average depth of about 3m. This promises delightful summer temperatures since waters don't take long to warm up; it also creates calm tides for enjoying water sports and plentiful recreation.

Shallowness does, however, make Lake Balaton sensitive to environmental disturbances, especially heat waves and algae blooms. That's why local conservation efforts are so important – particularly in recent years, with increasingly unpredictable conditions due to climate change.

MIKHAIL MARKOVSKIY/SHUTTERSTOCK

Esztergom Basilica

villages and lured into a sense of actually being there. As you move through the different sections, you encounter hired extras in costume going about village life: artisans, craftspeople and peasants sitting on church steps, picking flowers or simply acting in character. A highlight is crossing the remote border post into 'Romania' and reaching a reconstructed town square in Transylvania with a pharmacy, working cafe and more. The museum is open from April to October.

Visegrád's magnificent hilltop castle

In **Visegrád**, it's an invigorating hike to the **Citadel** (wear decent shoes), and once you reach the top you'll have some of the region's finest views over the Danube. The exhibits inside the citadel are unlikely to knock your sweaty socks off, but they include a bit of armoury and a large waxwork of the Congress of Visegrád in 1335. Enjoy the view and the walk around the walls, and feel the wind whistling around you from the crown of this 330m hilltop. A spectacular 180-degree panorama opens up over the Danube and the hills beyond. The scene becomes a 360-degree view as you walk along the walls.

See Hungary's largest church

Perched on top of Castle Hill, **Esztergom Basilica** is Hungary's largest church and is famous for its distinctive 72m-high central dome (100m from the crypt to the top), making this basilica visible in all its monumental glory for kilometres around. By far the most strenuous but attractive approach to Castle Hill is via the so-called Cat's Stairs (Macskalépcső). These well-hidden and unmarked stone steps off Berényi Zsigmond utca zigzag relentlessly to the top of the hill. Benches to rest on become more plentiful the higher you climb, with a spectacular view over the Danube River making the effort worthwhile. Entry to the basilica is through a side door. While the church itself is free, there are admission fees for the treasury, the crypt and to climb the dome.

Lake Balaton

TIME FROM BUDAPEST: 2½HR

Historical wonders, impressive food and wine, and an unparalleled spa scene: Lake Balaton is where Hungarians relish the good life. During the dog days, resorts and guesthouses are packed with holidaymakers beaching and boating in opaque, turquoise-hued waters. Beyond the postcard-perfect marinas and famously shallow swimming waters, Central Europe's biggest lake has a wealth of attractions that may be surprising – Balaton is equal parts quaint and chic. Thermal spas, wellness centres and campsites reel visitors in, but it's Balaton's hearty 'everything stew' of outdoorsy experiences that makes the destination highly memorable: sipping wines overlooking handsome vineyards, cycling adventures passing dreamy coasts and lavender fields, and tiny towns packed with historical treasures.

Catch lavender fever in Tihany

No visit to Lake Balaton is complete without seeing **Tihany**. The town's famous lavender fields traditionally blossom from mid-June to early July. During this time, aromatic purple fields explode around the peninsula and coincide with activities and events for the annual **Lavender Festival**. Lavender picking is only allowed in public areas, for example on the so-called **Lavender Trail**.

Swimming and shoreside fun in Balatonfüred

There's no better spot to wade into Lake Balaton's famously comfortable waters than from the two main beaches at **Balatonfüred**, **Esterházy Strand** (*balatonfuredistrandok.hu*) and **Kisfaludy Strand**. Unfolding along the row of bars and restaurants of the **Tagore Sétány** (the lake-hugging promenade), both beaches (walking from the marina, Esterházy comes first, followed by Kisfaludy) are known for their lively atmosphere. Lots of water activities are on offer at both, from paddleboating to SUP rentals, as well as shady spots for relaxing between dips and good toilet and changing facilities.

Soak in miracle waters in Hévíz

Just under 9km from Keszthely at the western tip of Lake Balaton, the village of **Hévíz** lays claim to the world's largest swimmable thermal lake, which is fed by 80 million L of thermal water daily. **Hévízi-tó** (*heviz.hu/en/lake-heviz*) is an incredible sight. The temperature averages 33°C and never drops below 22°C, even in winter, allowing you to bathe when the surrounding fir trees have turned icy.

The Great Plain

TIME FROM BUDAPEST: 2HR

What the Outback is for Australians or the Wild West for Americans, the Great Plain is for Hungarians. The Hortobágy region is the home of Hungarian cowboys and amazing horse shows, while Kecskemét and Szeged are cities to explore for culture, architecture and that charming countryside feel.

VISEGRÁD GROUP

The centrepiece of the citadel is a waxwork that graphically depicts how the Visegrád Group began. The year was 1335 and the kings of Bohemia, Hungary and Poland came together in Visegrád to make deals, form an anti-Habsburg alliance, resolve disputes and eat well, judging by this waxy portrayal. This was the first diplomatic cooperation between the so-called 'Visegrád countries'. In 1991, the Visegrád Group was formed between Hungary, Czechoslovakia and Poland to promote cooperation and mutual interests. It later became the Visegrád 4 when Slovakia became an independent country. Friction over approaches to the war in Ukraine have tested the glue holding the group together, but so far their shared interests have prevailed over their differences.

ASZÚ, THE KING OF WINES

Volcanic soil, a sunny climate, two rivers and mountains have helped make Tokaj-Hegyalja Hungary's most renowned wine region. It is most famous for Tokaji Aszú, a sweet golden nectar made with ripe grapes infected with 'noble rot': *Botrytis cinerea* mould that almost turns them into raisins on the vine, but grows only in years with the right climatic conditions (not too rainy, not too dry). Aszú can be blended from any of the six grape varieties grown in the Tokaj region but the most important is the indigenous Furmint. Aszú wines are rated according to the number (five or six) of *puttony* (25L carriers of individually picked grapes) of Aszú paste added to each barrel of base wine to increase sweetness.

Paintings, peacocks and majolica in Kecskemét

Lying halfway between the Danube and Tisza Rivers in the southern Great Plain, **Kecskemét** boasts some of the finest architecture of any small city in Hungary. Along with colourful Art Nouveau and Secessionist buildings, its museums and the region's excellent *barackpálinka* (apricot brandy) are major draws as well. An Art Nouveau masterpiece, **Cifrapalota** *(kkjm.hu; entry adult/child 1800/900Ft)* was built in 1902–03 by Géza Márkus. The grand townhouse is a visual feast with a whimsical majolica facade, a grand hall flaunting peacock motifs and a courtyard with fairy-tale flair. Exhibits inside include 19th- and early-20th-century Hungarian art as well as artefacts from Avar graves – mystical remnants from 6th-century Central Asian warriors.

Horse tricks and sand steppes

About 35km south of Kecskemét, **Bugacpuszta** *(bugacpuszta. hu)* is the easiest gateway to the rambling and disjointed Kiskunság National Park. Steer straight to the **Karikás Csárda**, a traditional inn, to buy tickets to the park and the popular Horse Show offered on Wednesdays, Fridays, Saturdays and Sundays between May and September. During this tightly choreographed 40-minute spectacle, horse herders crack their bullwhips and ride five horses at full tilt while standing on the rear two.

Flowers, leaves and waves in Szeged

The cultural capital of the Great Plain and Hungary's third-largest city, **Szeged** is an embracing town that's easy to love. A romantic symphony of lily-and-ivy motifs dancing across an undulating facade that juts out like a ship's bow, **Reök Palace** (1907) is an architectural showstopper and the crown jewel of Szeged's rich Art Nouveau scene. Step inside and you'll be just as wowed by the interior, especially the frilly wrought-iron staircase. Afterwards, pop into the street-level cafe **Reök Kézműves Cukrászda** for artisanal French pastries crafted by a two-time national cake champion.

Northern Hungary

TIME FROM BUDAPEST: 3HR

Northern Hungary is as hilly as the country gets. Hike on forested trails amid lovely rolling hills and scout castle ruins. Towns rich in culture, world-famous vineyards and villages that cherish their traditions make Northern Hungary an excellent place to connect with the country's spirit and history.

Eger's valley of the wine cellars

Cradled by vineyards and brimming with ornate baroque buildings, **Eger** (pronounced 'egg-air') is a jewellery box of a town with loads to see and do. A wine lover's fantasy come true, the famed **Valley of the Beautiful Women** *(Szépasszony-völgy; szepasszonyvolgy.info),* about 2km southeast of Eger's city centre, is home to several dozen wine cellars that welcome visitors who'd like to sample local vintages. Most open from 10am or noon to 6pm, until 8pm or later June to September,

Hollókő Castle

THE BETYÁRS: BANDITS OF THE PUSZTA

The Great Plain highwaymen were infamous outlaws who ruled the vast, wild spaces of the *puszta* (Great Plain) in the 19th century. Many were landless farmers, seasonal workers, former soldiers or unemployed herders who turned to ambushing travellers and horse carriages to make ends meet. Operating in small, tight-knit gangs, these bandits struck fear into the hearts of travellers and traders passing through the unpatrolled, remote areas. Their daring heists and narrow escapes became the stuff of legend, with tales spreading far and wide. While they were definitely criminals, some saw them as Robin Hood–like folk heroes rebelling against social injustice. Eventually the law caught up with them, leading to their decline by the late 1800s.

and some close on Mondays. Carved into volcanic rock, they're arrayed along a horseshoe-shaped road with a park in the middle, with a row of restaurants on the side.

Quick trip to centuries past

Long the home of the minority Palóc people, **Hollókő** *(holloko.hu)* is famous for the folk architecture of its **Old Village** (Ófalu), a UNESCO World Heritage Site since 1987. Unchanged for well over a century, its whitewashed wattle-and-daub houses – with carved balconies and overhanging porch roofs, bedecked with flowers in summer – are arrayed along a single main street, Kossuth utca. Although geared towards tourists (almost all domestic), Hollókő still manages to feel like a living, breathing village. The Old Village can be visited year-round but not much is open from November to March. Many visitors begin by walking from the tourist office through the woods to the hilltop **Hollókő Castle** *(Hollókői Vár; 3000Ft),* a distance of 1km. Built in the 13th century, the imposing stone structure looks like the setting for a fairy tale.

Taste Tokaj's liquid gold

At the confluence of the Bodrog and Tisza Rivers, the town of **Tokaj** is the commercial and touristic hub of the 27-village Tokaj-Hegyalja wine region. To sample the Tokaj region's extraordinary wines, head to a wine cellar *(pince),* cafe or restaurant that offers wine by the glass – they're dotted around the town centre.

Places We Love to Stay

€ Budget €€ Midrange €€€ Top End

Budget

Budapest
MAP p202

Shantee House € Share a yurt with your friends or that special someone in the Zen-like garden of Budapest's first hostel.

Loft Hostel € Friendly backpacker magnet with great kitchen, TV room with skylight, funny artwork and super-helpful staff.

Hotel President Budapest €€ Welcoming 150-room hotel on a beautiful street, with a stunning rooftop bar and a huge jadeite *turul* (falcon-like totem of the ancient Magyars and now a national symbol) in the lobby.

Baltazár €€ Family-owned boutique hotel offering individually decorated rooms with vintage furniture.

Hotel Central Basilica €€ The name says it all at this very central hotel opposite the basilica with 47 rooms, 10 of which face it.

Four Seasons Gresham Palace Hotel €€€ This one-of-a-kind luxury 179-room hotel was created out of the stunning Art Nouveau Gresham Palace (1906).

Párisi Udvar Hotel €€€ This stunner of a 110-room hotel is in the heart of one of the most beautiful buildings in Pest.

Anantara New York Palace Hotel €€€ Blends grandeur and comfort with luxurious rooms, an excellent spa and the historic New York Café next door.

Hotel Clark Budapest €€€ Stay at adults-only Hotel Clark for relaxation by the foot of the Chain Bridge and head up to the rooftop bar for lovely views.

Hotel Moments Budapest €€€ Stunning Art Deco hotel with 99 large rooms, an impressive lobby and an enviable location on UNESCO-listed Andrássy út.

Corinthia Hotel Budapest €€€ The hotel's lobby – a double atrium with a massive marble staircase – is among the most impressive in the city.

Szentendre

Bükkös Hotel & Spa €€€ Adults-only hotel pitching especially to couples on romantic breaks, with spa and massages. Central location, contemporary atmosphere and good breakfasts.

Visegrád

Hotel Silvanus €€€ On a forested hillside near the citadel, this large hotel has great views, an outdoor pool and spa. It was given a makeover in 2024.

Esztergom

Alabárdos Panzió és Apartmanház €€ Immaculate, quiet and very professionally run pension at the foot of the basilica and close to the museums. It also has apartments.

Tihany

Houses of History €€€ Charming B&B rooms set in 19th-century thatched-roof buildings formerly belonging to an abbey. Boasts a pool and also public beach access.

Balatonfüred

Füred Camping € Bungalows and caravans, plus a pool and direct lake access, offer relaxation on a budget. One of the largest camping grounds on the lake.

Anna Grand Hotel €€€ Once a sanatorium, today it's Balatonfüred's most historic grand hotel. Period antiques alongside modern furnishings abound; views of the hotel's courtyard and Gyógy tér square.

Kecskemét

Boutique Hotel Center €€ Slicked up in 2020, this pet-friendly outpost in the heart of town sports modern designer rooms accented with abstract art. Rates include a breakfast buffet.

Szeged

Noir Hotel €€ Superb, central pad marries high style with affordability and has spacious studios with sleek black-surface kitchens, ultra-comfy beds and terraces or balconies.

Eger

Hotel Estella €€ Half a block south of the Old Town, on the upper floors of a late-communist-era university building. Rooms are modern and well kept. Excellent value.

Hollókő

Tugári Vendégház €€ Old cottage in Hollókő with four charmingly furnished rooms and a communal kitchen for making food and friends.

Tokaj

Toldi Fogadó €€ Eclectic art adds a contemporary touch to this town-centre inn with good-sized rooms, a 15m pool, Jacuzzi and sauna.

Practicalities

LGBTIQ+ Travellers
While Budapest has a solid gay scene and gay visitors generally have a good time in Hungary, the country's stance on LGBTIQ+ issues is out of step with many other parts of Europe. The Hungarian government strongly promotes a conservative Christian agenda and still imposes laws against the local LGBTIQ+ community. While travellers aren't generally affected, be aware that PDA may attract unwanted attention.

Health
Hungary doesn't have any serious health risks, but it's still wise to make predeparture preparations. The European Health Insurance Card (EHIC) allows EU citizens to receive emergency state-provided healthcare.

Scams to Avoid
Dodgy restaurants and clubs in Budapest's party district (inner District VII) may overcharge foreigners, so check prices before you order. Don't hail taxis off the street and avoid the seemingly friendly touts waiting outside popular places – call a reputable company instead.

Bottled Drinks
When buying bottled or canned drinks in Hungary, you'll pay an additional 50Ft deposit per bottle, refundable when you return your empty bottles to any of the designated redemption machines inside bigger supermarkets.

ALLA SIMACHEVA/SHUTTERSTOCK

Funicular (p204), Budapest

Solo Travel
Hungary is a popular and generally safe destination for solo travellers. Budapest has a massive array of budget-friendly and social accommodation options, including hostels that organise pub crawls and other outings. Women travelling alone should not encounter any particular problems besides some mild local machismo.

Public Holidays
New Year's Day 1 January
Memorial Day of the 1848 Revolution 15 March
Easter March/April
Labour Day 1 May
Whit Monday May/June
Foundation of the State 20 August
Memorial Day of the 1956 Revolution 23 October
All Saints' Day 1 November
Christmas Day 25 December

Language

A symbol over a vowel in written Hungarian indicates it's pronounced as a long sound. Double consonants should be drawn out a little longer than in English. Note also that aw is pronounced as in 'law', eu as the 'u' in 'nurse', ew as 'ee' with rounded lips, and zh as the 's' in 'pleasure'. Finally, keep in mind that r is rolled in Hungarian and that the apostrophe (') indicates a slight y sound.

Basics

Hello. Szervusz/Szervusztok. (sg/pl) *ser·vus/ser·vus·tawk*

Goodbye. Viszlát. *vis·lat*

Excuse me. Elnézést kérek. *el·ney·zeysht key·rek*

Sorry. Sajnálom. *shoy·na·lawm*

Please. Kérem/Kérlek (inf/pol) *key·rem/keyr·lek*

Thank you. Köszönöm. *keu·seu·neum*

Yes. Igen. *i·gen*

No. Nem. *nem*

What's your name? Mi a neve/neved? (pol/inf) *mi o ne·ve/ne·ved*

My name is ... A nevem ... *o ne·vem ...*

Do you speak English? Beszél/Beszélsz angolul? (pol/inf) *be·seyl/be·seyls on·gaw·lul*

I don't understand. Nem értem. *nem eyr·tem*

Transport

bus busz *bus*

plane repülőgép *re·pew·lēū·geyp*

train vonat *vaw·not*

One ... ticket Egy ... jegy *ej ... yej*
to (Eger), (Eger)be. *(e·ger)·be*

one-way csak oda *chok aw·do*

return oda-vissza *aw·do·vis·so*

Emergencies

Help! Segítség! *she·geet·sheyg*

Go away! Menjen innen! *men·yen in·nen*

Call the doctor! Hívjon orvost! *heev·yawn awr·vawsht*

Call the police! Hívja a rendőrséget! *heev·yo o rend·ēūr·shey·get*

I'm lost. Eltévedtem. *el·tey·ved·tem*

I'm ill. Rosszul vagyok. *raws·sul vo·dyawk*

Where are the toilets? Hol a vécé? *hawl o vey·tsey*

Eating & Drinking

What would you recommend? Mit ajánlana? *mit o·yan·lo·no*

Do you have vegetarian food? Vannak Önöknél vegetáriánus ételek? *von·nok eu·neuk·neyl ve·ge·ta·ri·a·nush ey·te·lek*

I'll have ... ... kérek. *... key·rek*

Cheers! Egészségetekre! *e·geys·shey·ge·tek·re*

I'd like the ... ... szeretném. *... se·ret·neym*

bill A számlát *o sam·lat*

menu Az étlapot *oz eyt·lo·pawt*

Shopping & Services

I'm looking for ... Keresem a ... *ke·re·shem o ...*

How much is it? Mennyibe kerül? *men'·nyi·be ke·rewl*

That's too expensive. Ez túl drága. *ez tül dra·go*

market piac *pi·ots*

post office postahivatal *paw·sh·to·hi·vo·tol*

NUMBERS

1	**egy** *ej*
2	**kettő** *ket·tēū*
3	**három** *ha·rawm*
4	**négy** *neyj*
5	**öt** *eut*
6	**hat** *hot*
7	**hét** *heyt*
8	**nyolc** *nyawlts*
9	**kilenc** *ki·lents*
10	**tíz** *teeze*

Tram, Budapest (p200)

MONEY
Currency: Hungarian Forint (Ft)

CASHLESS PAYMENTS
Most restaurants, hotels, shops, car-hire companies and petrol stations across Hungary accept credit cards, especially Visa and MasterCard. American Express isn't always accepted.

CASH
When travelling outside Budapest, it's wise to carry cash in case it's not possible to pay by card. Smaller shops and ice-cream parlours appreciate coins and might struggle to break larger banknotes.

TIPPING
Add at least 10% for table service at restaurants. Instead of leaving money on the table, tell the server how much you want to pay in total, including the tip. Many restaurants already add a service fee of about 12% to 15% – check the receipt or ask before paying.

Arriving & Getting Around

For most travellers visiting Hungary, Budapest is the main point of entry. Ferenc Liszt International Airport is about 16km southeast of the city centre. The main international train station in Budapest is Keleti railway station.

From the Airport
Shuttle bus 100E to/from central Pest (stop: Deák Ferenc tér) runs daily round the clock. A combination bus (200E) and metro is a bit cheaper but slower. Taxis are the fastest way to get to/from the airport.

Hungary Pass
If you're planning on travelling around the country, consider buying a Hungary Pass, good for unlimited travel throughout Hungary. It's valid for almost all services with **Budapest Public Transport** *(BKK; bkk.hu),* suburban and regional buses, HÉV suburban railways and regional trains.

Validating Tickets
Budapest public transport tickets have to be validated after purchase. Digital tickets have a QR-code scanner (codes are on the sides of buses, trams and on ticket machines) and passes have their own QR codes that controllers check.

BudapestGO
The BudapestGO mobile app for public transport has several key features. You can buy and store digital tickets and passes directly on the app (don't forget to validate tickets with QR codes and show passes to inspectors). It also provides route planning and a map, timetables, and information on routes, connections and travel times, as well as updates on potential delays and other relevant information.

For places to stay in Kosovo, see p230

JESS KRAFT/SHUTTERSTOCK

Above: Sinan Pasha Mosque (p228), Prizren; Right: Prizren Fortress (p228)

Curated by
Anthony Ham

Kosovo

A YOUNG AND BEAUTIFUL NATION

Witness history being written in this excited new nation filled with Ottoman history, marvellous medieval monasteries, breathtaking hiking trails and spirited locals.

Many who've never been to Kosovo will warn you not to visit. That's their loss. Europe's newest country has the energy of an excited teenager, both curious and aspirational, and (aside from some parts of the north) it's perfectly safe to visit. Walk the capital Pristina's pedestrian boulevards with young locals who have a glimmer in their eye when talking about their new nation. See an ancient fortress, mosques and churches in Prizren's charming Old Town. Visit fresco-filled Serbian Orthodox monasteries and hike the Peaks of the Balkans, one of Europe's most buzzworthy trails.

Kosovo declared independence from Serbia in 2008, and while it has been diplomatically recognised by the majority of countries, there are still many – notably Serbia, Russia and Spain – that see its borders as a dotted line. Memories of the 1998–99 war that killed more than 13,000 and displaced hundreds of thousands remains top of mind, and, close to the northern border, ethnic Serbs and NATO forces – which intervened to protect Kosovo's Albanian majority during the war and maintain a peacekeeping force – eye each other warily. Yet Kosovo is ready to grow into adulthood. See in real time how this once traditional society is modernising, learn about its heart-wrenching history and wander its serene mountains. And go now before this off-the-beaten-track destination sees the same crowds as its neighbours.

THE MAIN AREAS

PRISTINA	**PRIZREN**	**GJAKOVA**	**PEJA**
Maturing capital city. **p226**	Historic cultural core. **p228**	Balkan bazaars and mosques. **p229**	Spectacular monasteries. **p229**

Find Your Way

Kosovo is small at under 11,000 sq km. If you're not on a tight schedule and don't mind some walking, taking the bus is a no-brainer. A car, as always, will give you more control.

Gjakova, p229

Between Prizren and Peja, this fascinating provincial town has one of the oldest, longest bazaars in the Balkans, as well as mosques and nearby wine country.

Pristina, p226

Spend a day or two wandering around and people-watching from the bars, cafes and restaurants in this young capital city.

Peja, p229

Popular as a gateway for hikes into the nearby mountains, Peja also grants access to Orthodox monasteries from the Middle Ages.

BUS

Buses in Kosovo are frequent and most sites are centralised around the three main cities, so you can easily save money and avoid chaotic traffic by taking public transport.

CAR

A vehicle lets you go off the beaten track and provides more mobility if doing day hikes in the mountains. Just do yourself a favour and park your car in the cities, as urban driving can be a nightmare.

Prizren, p228

There's so much history packed into this little Old Town, including a fortress, mosques, churches and artisanal shops.

Gračanica Monastery (p227)

Plan Your Time

Kosovo is small and contains few attractions. It's easy enough to get around, and certainly worth spending a week to explore before crossing into nearby Western Balkans countries.

Three Days to Travel Around

● Spend a day enjoying Kosovo's capital, **Pristina** (p226) and getting a taste for traditional cooking. Visit the Serbian Orthodox **Visoki Dečani Monastery** (p229) for superb medieval frescoes, then head to cultural capital **Prizren** (p228) to explore and watch the sunset from its fortress. Return to Pristina via 14th-century **Gračanica Monastery** (p227).

An Active Week

● Enjoy **Pristina** (p226)), then visit **Gračanica Monastery** (p227). Next, head for historic **Prizren** (p228): sacred buildings, a mountaintop fortress with exceptional views and fine filigree jewellery. **Gjakova** (p229) has a fabulous bazaar and one of Kosovo's most beautiful mosques. To round out your trip, visit **Visoki Dečani Monastery** (p229) and **Patriarchate of Peć** (p229) in Peja.

SEASONAL HIGHLIGHTS

SPRING

Cash in on lower prices and avoid the summer heat and crowds. With mild weather, it's a fine time to visit.

SUMMER

Explore Kosovo and attend Prizren Fest (p226) or DokuFest (p226)) in Prizren. Potentially Europe's quietest high season.

AUTUMN

Great weather for hiking the Accursed Mountains along the transnational Peaks of the Balkans Trail. Autumn colours.

WINTER

Snowshoe or ski Kosovo's untouched slopes (especially the Shar Mountains). Warm up with a red from the Rahovec wine region.

Pristina & Around

KOSOVAR CUISINE | HISTORIC ARCHITECTURE | MEDIEVAL MONASTERIES

Places

 TOP TIP

Summer is a good time to be in Prizren, with events like **Prizren Fest** *(prizrenfest. com)* in July. In early August, the city hosts Kosovo's biggest film festival: the **DokuFest International Documentary and Short Film Festival** *(dokufest.com).*

Most Kosovo journeys begin in Europe's newest capital, which is full of optimism and potential. Pristina doesn't have many attractions, but has an appealing and unpretentious charm. Prizren, Kosovo's second city, is more noticeably historic. Where else can you photograph a fortress, a mosque and an Orthodox church all in the same frame? Climb to the fortress and take in the views, shop for fine filigree jewellery and join locals for a meal along the river or at a cafe near the old-town fountain. Gjakova (Đakovica in Serbian) is an appealing small city about halfway between Prizren and Peja. It's a relaxed place in the Kosovar heartland and is famous for the Ottoman Čaršija e Madhe, one of the longest bazaars in the Balkans. Save time to visit the remarkable monasteries around Peja.

Pristina

Get a taste of local culture

Pristina, Europe's newest capital, is like the Balkans 20 years ago and it holds fast to its culinary traditions more than most Balkan cities. For a great local *qebabtore* (kebab place)*,* try family-run **Gjakova e Vjetër** *(facebook.com/gjakovaevjeter);* it's been around longer than most locals can remember. Tucked behind shops off Rr Johan V Hahn, **Babaghanoush** has pretty *meze* platters of Mediterranean dips along with lentil patties

---

GETTING AROUND

Up to three buses hourly run between Prizren and Pristina (two hours), with less frequent but still regular services to/from Peja (1½ to two hours), Skopje in North Macedonia (three hours) and Tirana in Albania (three hours). From Gjakova's small bus station, there are regular buses to Pristina (1½ hours), Prizren (one hour) and Peja (one hour).

Each of these places has an old town at its core and is best explored on foot. If you rent a car, parking can cost as little as €12 for 24 hours.

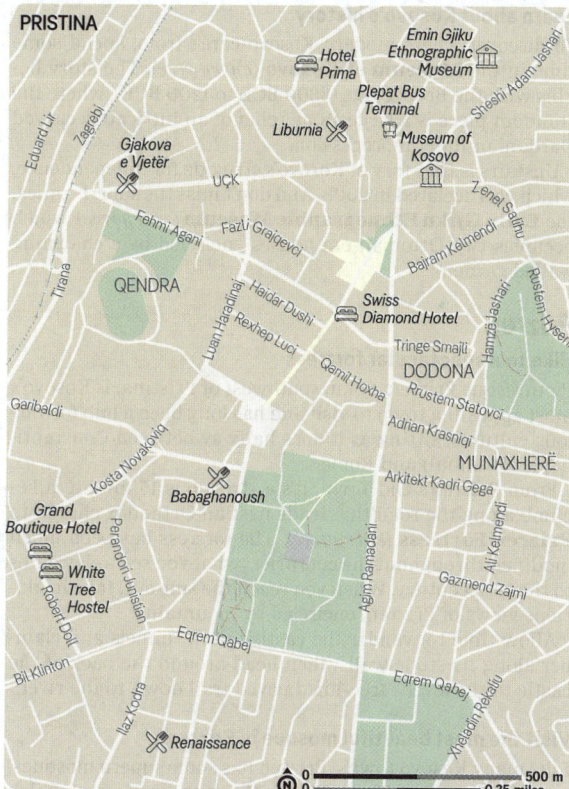

PRISTINA

Eduard Lir
Zagrebi
Hotel Prima
Emin Gjiku Ethnographic Museum
Sheshi Adam Jashari
Plepat Bus Terminal
Gjakova e Vjetër
Liburnia
Museum of Kosovo
UÇK
Fehmi Agani
Fazli Grajqevci
Zenel Salihu
Bajram Kelmendi
Tirana
QENDRA
Luan Haradinaj
Haidar Dushi
Rexhep Luci
Qemil Hoxha
Swiss Diamond Hotel
Tringe Smajli
DODONA
Rrustem Statovci
Hamza Jashari
Rustem Hyseni
Garibaldi
Kosta Novakovic
Adrian Krasniqi
Arkitekt Kadri Gega
MUNAXHERË
Grand Boutique Hotel
Babaghanoush
Perandori Dioklian
Ali Kelmendi
White Tree Hostel
Robert Dolli
Agim Ramadani
Gazmend Zajmi
Iliaz Kodra
Eqrem Qabej
Bil Klinton
Eqrem Qabej
Xheladin Rekaliu
Renaissance

N   0   500 m
     0   0.25 miles

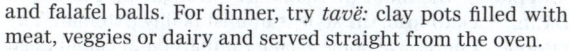

and falafel balls. For dinner, try *tavë*: clay pots filled with meat, veggies or dairy and served straight from the oven.

Liburnia *(facebook.com/Liburnia)* is a great dinner option, with homemade bread to die for, folk music, and tangled vines and flowers cascading from the roof beams. Expect traditional Albanian mountain cooking with staples such as slow-cooked goat and steaming casseroles.

Also excellent, **Renaissance**, a seasonal organic restaurant south of Pristina's centre, has no menu – just a delicious three-course meal, including local wine and *rakija* (fruit brandy).

See Serbian Orthodox frescoes

Around 10km southeast of downtown Pristina, the Serbian enclave community of **Gračanica** is home to the Serbian Orthodox **Gračanica Monastery** *(entry €3)*. Built in 1321 by King Stefan Milutin, the UNESCO World Heritage five-dome church is filled with gorgeous frescoes depicting biblical scenes. There are 4000 faces in the church, which, as local legend has it, were painted by Greek artists in under 20 seconds each.

To get here, take the regional bus towards Gjilan from Pristina's **Plepat Bus Terminal** and get off near Gračanica Park.

KOSOVO FOOD

In Kosovo, most culinary traditions are often indistinguishable from those of Albania. Most prominent is stewed and grilled meat or fish. *Kos* (goat's-cheese yoghurt) is eaten alone or with almost anything. Other highlights include Turkish kebabs, *gjuveç* (baked meat and vegetables), *fli* (flaky pastry pie served with honey) and *tavë* (meat baked with cheese and egg). Turkish influences are also strong, with *byrek* (pastry with cheese or meat). The local beer is Peja (from the town of the same name), a *boza* (fermented drink) is a local speciality, and Vranac is red wine from the Rahovec (Orahovac) region of Kosovo. Pristina has the greatest variety, and the possibility of finding vegetarians dishes is growing, though still largely restricted to the capital.

THE KOSOVO WAR IN A NUTSHELL

In 1989, Kosovo's autonomy within Yugoslavia was suspended by Slobodan Milošević. Ethnic Albanian leaders declared independence from Serbia in 1990. Ethnic conflict heightened and the Kosovo Liberation Army (KLA) formed in 1996. In March 1999, a US-backed plan to return Kosovo's autonomy was rejected by Serbia, which moved to empty the province of its non-Serbian population. After Serbia refused to desist, NATO unleashed a bombing campaign on 24 March 1999. Nearly 850,000 Kosovo Albanians fled to Albania and Macedonia, telling of mass killings and forced expulsions. In June Milošević agreed to withdraw troops, air strikes ceased, the KLA disarmed and the NATO-led Kosovo Force (KFOR) took over. Independence followed in 2008.

Learn about Kosovo's history

To discover where modern Kosovo came from, spend some time in the **Museum of Kosovo** (*entry free*). The story begins with the Bronze Age (3300 BCE to 1200 BCE), where the standout piece is a large stone relief of an intricately carved Dardanian funeral procession.

Upstairs is the story of Kosovo's struggle for independence, which was declared in 2008. And don't miss the superb annex, the **Emin Gjiku Ethnographic Museum** (*entry free*), which occupies two Ottoman-era houses encircled by a charming walled garden.

Prizren

Hike to a spectacular fortress

Picturesque Prizren, 86km southwest of Pristina, is Kosovo's most appealing town to visit and has long been a hub for various cultures, sitting as it does halfway between Constantinople (Istanbul) and Rome.

From Prizren's Old Town, it's a strenuous 15-minute hike-climb along the road that leads past an Orthodox church to **Prizren Fortress** (*entry free*). The fortress has been much modified throughout the centuries; what you see today dates to the 18th century. When you reach the summit, take in glorious views of Prizren, encircled by mountains.

Allow time to wander the castle's dark tunnels and clamber along its stone walls, then head around the back of the castle to the lovely, tree-lined paved trail down to the river.

Visit the most beautiful mosque in Prizren

Like many Kosovo towns, Prizren has some superb mosques, none more so than **Sinan Pasha Mosque** (*entry free*), which towers over the main thoroughfare through the Old Town. Dating back to 1615, the style is unmistakably Ottoman. The mosque's impressive dome, slender minaret and colonnaded facade form a fabulous sight from the street. Venture inside (except during prayer times) to admire the detailed frescoes.

Remove your shoes before entering; women should wear a headscarf.

Shop for traditional jewellery

In the 15th and 18th centuries, Prizren was known throughout the Ottoman Empire for filigree – the delicate art of silver threading. Back then, filigree techniques were used to

EATING IN PRIZREN & GJAKOVA: OUR PICKS

Te Syla 'Al Hambra': Around since the 1960s, unpretentious Te Syla in Prizren does some of Kosovo's best kebabs. It's that simple. *7am-11pm* €

Restaurant Marashi: Riverside, beside a majestic old sycamore tree in Prizren. Traditional Albanian dishes share the menu with steaks cooked on hot stones. *8am-11pm* €€

Čaršija e Jupave: Hotel restaurant serves cold cuts, *tavë Elbasan* (lamb in yogurt and garlic) and *tavë Gjakova* (veal with tomatoes and vegetables). *11am-11pm* €€

Hani i Haraçisë: This former *caravanserai* (inn) in Gjakova is great for traditional dishes like veal *tavë* (hotpot). *8am-midnight* €€

decorate the handles of curved pistols and rifles, quite apart from traditional costume jewellery for locals. Today, the art form continues in jewellery shops found near the fountain in the historic centre and across the bridge on **Rr Adem Jashari**.

By providing an outlet for the work of a new generation of young artisans, tourism is helping to revive a centuries-old tradition that was in danger of disappearing.

Gjakova

Explore markets & the mosque bazaar

Around 89km southwest of the capital, Gjakova's Great or Grand Bazaar, the **Čaršija e Madhe**, was first laid out in the 15th century, when Kosovo lived under the rule of the Ottoman Empire. This makes it Kosovo's oldest surviving bazaar by quite a margin. And although it has been much modified through subsequent centuries, it's not difficult to imagine the bazaar during Ottoman times, particularly when the melodic Islamic call to prayer echoes through it.

The utterly superb **Hadum Mosque** *(entry free)* is one of the most beautiful in the Balkans. It is widely considered to be a classic example of early Islamic architecture in the region. The slender stone minaret suggests great antiquity, but it is a faithful replica of the original structure that was felled during the Kosovo War: the original mosque was built late in the 16th century. Inside, exquisite tile work and stone features encircle the prayer hall beneath the 13.5m-diameter dome with an extraordinarily intricate collection of floral motifs, geometric patterns, sweeping arabesques, and inscriptions or verses from the Quran.

Peja

Marvellous medieval monasteries

On the outskirts of Peja, 85km west of Pristina, the **Patriarchate of Peć** *(entry free, audio guide €2)* a UNESCO World Heritage medieval monastery, was historically used to crown kings. The Serbian Orthodox monastery dates back to the 1230s and includes a captivating cavernous church covered in vivid frescoes. Try to visit around 5pm to hear the sung prayers and chants of the elderly, black-clad nuns. With the last shafts of sunlight catching some of the frescoes, it's a haunting experience that evokes the Middle Ages.

South of Peja, don't miss the **Visoki Dečani Monastery** *(decani.org; entry free)*, which was built by Serbian King Stefan Dečanski in the early 14th century. On the outskirts of the town of Desan, the onyx-and-breccia-stone building features 10,000 painted figures, including the only medieval fresco of Jesus carrying a sword (meant to chop sins, not enemies in battle). The frescoes here are in the best condition of any frescoes that adorn Kosovo's monasteries. Before leaving, stop by the shop to grab a bottle of wine and cheese produced by the monastery's 25 resident monks.

You will need to bring your passport or ID card to gain entry to both monasteries.

KOSOVO'S HUMAN MOSAIC

According to the 2024 census, the population of Kosovo was 1.59 million; 92% are Albanian. Although the census put the number of Serbs at 1.5% of the population, the census excluded Serbian enclaves in the country's north, while many Serbs elsewhere in the country boycotted the census. Most estimates suggest that between 6% and 8% of people in Kosovo are Serbian, and most of these live in 10 protected enclaves (or exclaves, depending who you ask). Other ethnic minorities include Bosniak, Gorani, Roma, Turkish, Ashkali and Egyptian. The main religious groups are Muslim (mostly Albanians), Serbian Orthodox and Roman Catholic.

Places We Love to Stay

€ Budget €€ Midrange €€€ Top End

Pristina
MAP p227

White Tree Hostel € Cool backpacker hostel run by well-travelled owners; it feels more like an Albanian beach resort than a downtown Pristina bolthole.

Grand Boutique Hotel €€ Family home turned 10-room hotel with a walnut-tree-shaded garden, farm-fresh breakfasts and free bottle of wine.

Hotel Prima €€ Intimate, family-run and quiet, this is one of the best sleeps in Pristina. Count on high-standard rooms and friendly service.

Swiss Diamond Hotel €€€ This five-star international hotel has opulent rooms with classic luxury decor and facilities.

Prizren

Driza's House € This excellent budget place has well-equipped dorms, is quieter than many hostels, and breakfast is a great place to meet travellers.

Ura Hostel € Clean, modern hostel with air-con, a big hangout area and terrific location in the historic centre.

Hotel Prizreni €€ A pleasant combination of traditional and modern, with 12 small-but-stylish rooms and a perfect location.

Guri i Kuq Hotel & Vila €€€ With the ambience of a mountain lodge, this place has a fab restaurant, cosy wood-walled rooms and stunning views from its high perch.

Tiffany €€€ Cosy six-room boutique place with modern rooms, excellent bathrooms and flowerpots everywhere. There's an on-site restaurant.

Gjakova

Happy Hotel €€ Newish hotel rooms in a restored 300-year-old building. Some rooms have balconies overlooking the bazaar and there's a patisserie downstairs.

Hotel Čaršija e Jupave €€ Wooden beams, artworks on the walls, colourful decor, massage showers and great service. There's a memorable in-house restaurant as well, and free underground parking.

Peja

Stone Bridge Hotel € Modern hotel with 10 white-and-grey rooms and plush mattresses, smack in the heart of Peja.

Dukagjini Hotel €€ Peja buzzes around this 1951 stone-built hotel with small but grandly decorated rooms, a pool and a hot tub; 1st-floor rooms have huge terraces overlooking the square.

Hotel Kulla e Zenel Beut €€ An Ottoman-era stone-and-wood building with modern rooms and a fantastic restaurant.

Doa Boutique Hotel €€€ North of the Old Town and occupying a handsome villa, the Doa has rooms with wooden floors and Persian carpets, great bathrooms and a lovely vine-shaded garden.

Dukagjini Hotel

Practicalities

Time Zone
Kosovo runs on Central European Time (GMT/UTC plus one hour). The 24-hour clock is used, as is Daylight Saving Time, with clocks going forward the last Sunday in October, and back the last Sunday in March.

Tourist Information
Despite its growing tourism industry, Kosovo has few tourist centres, and nothing in Pristina. Tour operators and hotels often take up the slack, with extensive local information on everything from transport to attractions.

Smoking
One-third of the adult population (and half of adult men) smoke in Kosovo. While cafe terraces are filled with chain-smoking locals, there's a smoking ban for enclosed public spaces, so most venues are smoke-free inside.

Mobile Phones
Coverage is excellent throughout the country, and it's easy to obtain a SIM card with data for as little as €10; simply bring your passport to one of the offices of the mobile-phone providers. At the time of writing, Kosovo was still rolling out its 5G network; MTS Ipko and Vala are the local carriers.

COLORMAKER/SHUTTERSTOCK

Prizren (p228)

Opening Hours
Banks 8am–5pm Monday to Friday, to 2pm Saturday
Bars 8am–11pm
Clubs 8pm–3am Thursday to Saturday
Shops 8am–6pm Monday to Friday, to 3pm Saturday
Restaurants 8am–midnight

Etiquette
Kosovo is a generally conservative country, with complex rules of etiquette; however, these rarely affect travellers. Eat and drink plentifully of whatever is given to you whenever it is given. In rural areas, local women don't normally shake hands with strangers. And always dress modestly and generally cover up when visiting mosques or Serbian monasteries.

Public Holidays
Note that traditional Islamic and Orthodox Christian holidays are also observed, including Ramadan and Orthodox Easter.
New Year's Day 1 January
Independence Day 17 February
Kosovo Constitution Day 9 April
Labour Day 1 May
Europe Day 9 May

231

Language

In Albanian – also understood in Kosovo and North Macedonia – *ew* is pronounced as 'ee' with rounded lips, *uh* as the 'a' in 'ago', *dh* as the 'th' in 'that', *dz* as the 'ds' in 'adds', and *zh* as the 's' in 'pleasure'. Also, *ll* and *rr* are pronounced stronger than when they are written as single letters.

Basics

Hello. Tungjatjeta. *toon·dya·tye·ta*
Goodbye. Mirupafshim. *mee·roo·paf·sheem*
Yes. Po. *po*
No. Jo. *yo*
Please. Ju lutem. *yoo loo·tem*
Thank you. Faleminderit. *fa·le·meen·de·reet*
What's your name? Si quheni? *see choo·he·nee*
My name is ... Unë quhem ... *oo·nuh choo·hem ...*
Do you speak English? A flisni anglisht? *a flees·nee ang·leesht*
I don't understand. Unë nuk kuptoj. *oo·nuh nook koop·toy*

Emergencies

Help! Ndihmë! *ndeeh·muh*
Go away! Ik! *eek*
I'm ill. Jam i/e sëmurë. (m/f) *yam ee/e suh·moo·ruh*

Call the doctor/police! Thirrni doktorin/policinë! *theerr·nee dok·to·reen/po·lee·tsee·nuh*

Eating & Drinking

What would you recommend? Çfarë më rekomandoni? *chfa·ruh muh re·ko·man·do·nee*
I'll have... Dua... *doo·a*
Cheers! Gëzuar! *guh·zoo·ar*
I'd like the bill/menu, please. Më sillni faturën/menunë, ju lutem. *muh seell·nee fa·too·ruhn/ me·noo·nuh yoo loo·tem*

Shopping & Services

I'm looking for ... Po kërkoj për ... *po kuhr·koy puhr ...*
How much is it? Sa kushton? *sa koosh·ton*
Cheers! Gëzuar! *guh·zoo·ar*
That's too expensive. Është shumë shtrenjtë. *uhsh·tuh shoo·muh shtreny·tuh*

NUMBERS

1
një *nyuh*

2
dy *dew*

3
tre *tre*

4
katër *ka·tuhr*

5
pesë *pe·suh*

6
gjashtë *dyash·tuh*

7
shtatë *shta·tuh*

8
tetë *te·tuh*

9
nëntë *nuhn·tuh*

10
dhjetë *dhye·tuh*

English & Other Tourist Languages

While most people dealing with tourists on a daily basis speak English extremely well, that's not true of the entire population. English is taught in schools, but the older generations are more likely to know some German, Russian or, along the coast, Italian.

FROM LEFT: YU XICHAO/SHUTTERSTOCK, JOHNER IMAGES/GETTY IMAGES

Pristina International Airport

MONEY

Currency: Euro (€)

CASH

Kosovo has been allowed to use the euro as legal tender since 2002, despite not being a member of the EU or eurozone. Virtually everyone prefers cash, with cards rarely (if increasingly) accepted. Bring an emergency supply of euros.

ATMS

You'll receive euros at ATMs. Some ATMs will ask you whether you accept or decline the ATM's conversion rate – always decline (and/or choose euros) for a lower fee/better rate.

CREDIT CARDS

Paying with credit cards is still rare at restaurants or accommodation, although it's becoming more widespread.

TIPPING

Tipping isn't expected in Kosovo, though you can round up or give up to 10% if you appreciated the service.

Arriving & Getting Around

Entering Kosovo is generally a breeze, with welcoming and bureaucracy-free immigration and customs. Visitors from many countries do not need a visa to stay in Kosovo for fewer than 90 days.

By Air

Pristina International Airport is 18km from the centre of Pristina. At the time of writing, flights could not enter through Serbian airspace. Airlines include Wizz, Austrian and Swiss.

By Land

Kosovo has open land borders with Montenegro, Albania, North Macedonia and Serbia (open only inbound to Kosovo). Be sure to forewarn police and obtain a cross-border permit if hiking across borders.

Entering from Serbia

To travel between Serbia and Kosovo, you'll need to enter Kosovo from Serbia first. If you arrived here via Albania or North Macedonia and want to visit Serbia, you will need to go via a third country.

Car Hire

Driving here can be erratic, though roads are generally good. Never drive after dark, when headlights seem to be optional. High speed is also a concern. Pristina has car-hire options from the main companies (Europcar and Avis), as well as less expensive local companies. Not all car-rental companies elsewhere in Europe will allow you to take your vehicle into Kosovo. Always ask when booking.

233

Curated by
Leonid Ragozin

Latvia

DUNES AND BALTIC FORESTS

Where a stunning coastline meets an elegant capital city and clear lakes sparkle amid mysterious forests.

Latvia is a country of blues and greens: its blues reflect the changing hues of the sea and inland lakes, while its greens come in the soothing shades of the forest canopy that covers the hinterland. That's from afar. A closer look reveals ever more colours: the golden radiance of sand dunes and luxuriant beaches; the brownish hue of peat bogs sprinkled with cranberry red. The pastel tones of its capital's art nouveau district; the hardened black timber and grey boulders that form the walls of the old barns dotting the countryside.

Latvia is defined by the juxtaposition of its capital, Rīga, with the rest of the country. Latvia's only large city, Rīga is where a whopping 52% of the country's population lives. This is one of the highest ratios of city-to-countryside dwellers in Europe. It's a fantastically cosy and welcoming place that doesn't fall over itself in order to please, but displays many quiet, understated charms.

The country beyond Rīga is surprisingly diverse, with four historical regions presenting an intriguing interplay of distinct landscapes and idiosyncratic towns: agricultural Kurzeme in the west, hilly and forested Vidzeme in the north, history-rich Zemgale in the south and the lakelands of Latgale in the east.

But the real treasure is the coastline – 500km of stunning beaches and pine-covered dunes that line the Gulf of Rīga and beyond, stretching all the way to the open sea in the west.

KAVALENKAVAVOLHA/GETTY IMAGES

THE MAIN AREAS

For places to stay
in Latvia, see
p249

VIESTURS JUGS/SHUTTERSTOCK

Left: Rīga (p238); Above: Gauja National Park (p245)

236

Find Your Way

No matter what direction you're headed, Latvia can be crossed in a few hours. This is an easy country to get around.

Gauja National Park, p245
Latvia's outdoor playground, where a quiet river meanders through forested hills.

BUS & TRAIN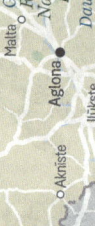
Latvia has an extensive network of bus routes designed to reach most small villages and even standalone farmsteads. The train network is limited to suburban destinations near Rīga and select destinations around the country.

CAR
A car provides travellers with more flexibility. The road network is generally good, although there are almost no real motorways.

BELARUS

ESTONIA

Tartu

Viljandi

Pōlva

Tōrva

Valga

LITHUANIA

Kupiškis

Zarasai

Ludza

Gauja
Rāzna
National
Park

Daugava
River

Krāslava

Daugavpils

Ilūkste

Aknīste

Aglona

Malta

Rēzekne

Varakļāni

Teiči
Nature
Reserve

Lubāna

Balvi

Gulbene

Alūksne

Ape

Valka

Smiltene

Jaunpiebalga

Madona

Koknese

Jēkabpils

Bauska

Lielvārde

Jelgava

Salaspils

Rīgas
Doms

RĪGA

Baltā
Kāpa

Sigulda
Turaida Museum
Reserve

Cēsis
Castle

Valmiera

Gauja
National
Park

Limbaži

Rūjiena

Saulkrasti

Salacgrīva

Vidzeme
Coast

Gulf of Rīga

Jūrmala

Rīga Central
Market

St Peter's
Church

Saldus

Jaunpils

Mažeikiai

Dobele

Kandava

Kuldīga

Ventas
Rumba

Naval Church
of St Nicholas

Liepāja

Jūrkalne

Ventspils

Ugāle

Ovīši

Dundaga

Roja

Kolka

Mērsrags

*Lake
Engure*

Baltic Sea

**Gulf of
Rīga, p242**
Almost 300km of mostly uninterrupted beaches lined with pine-covered dunes.

Rīga, p238
The Latvian capital is an elegant cosmopolitan city with a medieval Old Town and beautiful beaches close at hand.

Kurzeme & Zemgale, p247
A beautiful baroque palace, rolling hills, maritime forests, vibrant port cities and Baltic German legacy.

0   100 km
0   50 miles

BORIS STROUJKO/SHUTTERSTOCK

Rīga's Old Town (p238)

Plan Your Time

Latvia is a compact country with a lot to offer, so it's possible to pack plenty of activities into a limited amount of time.

Pressed for Time

● If you only have a few days, base yourself in the capital, **Rīga** (p238), and take in as much of it as you can, from the Old Town with its spired churches and museums to the art nouveau buildings of the Jugendstil quarter. Make sure you allocate at least half a day for a trip to the seaside in **Jūrmala** (p242) or **Saulkrasti** (p244).

Five Days or More

● With more time, start with **Rīga** (p238), then venture to **Kuldīga** (p248)to admire the famous waterfall. Proceed to the lively port city of **Liepāja** (p248) for a healthy dose of seaside fun. Back in Rīga, make a dash for **Rundāle Palace** (p247) near Bauska, from where you can continue on to Lithuania.

SEASONAL HIGHLIGHTS

SPRING
Days get longer and the whole country is in bloom. Storks begin to return from their African holiday.

SUMMER
The entire nation repairs to the coastal dunes, forested lakes or the countryside.

AUTUMN
It's getting dark again, but the national holiday season is in full swing and Rīga is decked out with light installations.

WINTER
There's finally enough snow for cross-country skiing in Rīga or downhill skiing in Sigulda.

Rīga

HISTORY | JUGENDSTIL | LAID-BACK AMBIENCE

GETTING AROUND

Rīga's airport is served by bus 22. To avoid taxi scams, it's safer to use Bolt and wait for your ride in the 2nd-floor arrivals hall. Trams, buses and trolleybuses *(rigassatiksme.lv)* are essential if venturing beyond the city centre. Buses and trolleybuses may have the same number but run on different routes. Fares are paid with e-talons. Buy and refill them at Narvesen convenience stores or vending machines aboard newer trams. A single 90-minute journey costs €1.50 including transfers, but you need to validate your ticket again if changing transport.

☑ **TOP TIP**

There are no must-sees in Rīga – just go with the flow and do your thing. Sip coffee, visit Gothic churches and museums, shop for fresh produce at the markets and amble from one friendly bar to another when night falls.

Rīga is an independent and slightly mysterious place. It's always elegantly dressed despite its modest income and it keeps its house in good order. Riga has seen a lot, but won't tell you everything.

The city's architectural styles are what remains of her former overlords. The tall spires and cobbled streets of the Old Town (Vecrīga) are the legacy of Baltic German and Swedish rulers. The art nouveau facades in the centre hark back to the Russian Empire. Gloomy apartment blocks on the outskirts are the remnants of the Soviet footprint.

Having re-emerged as the capital of independent Latvia three decades ago, Rīga continues to add tasteful, history-conscious modern architecture, yet maintains a homey look. The border with the countryside, coastal dunes and pristine woods is blurred, with furry visitors occasionally venturing into town and wild mushrooms on sale at farmers markets.

Rīga's Cradle

See the city's beginnings

In 1201, the crusading bishop Albert von Buxhoeveden resolved to build a city on the site of an old marketplace at the mouth of the Daugava River. The spot he chose is now called **Jāņa sēta** (St John's courtyard). This is where the chronicled history of Rīga begins, which makes this enclosure, guarded by a partly reconstructed 13th-century wall, the best point to begin your exploration of Rīga's Old Town, also known as Vecrīga.

Once inside, note the curving lines above the red-brick gates – they are said to depict the back of the donkey that carried Jesus into Jerusalem. The gist of it is, 'follow Christ'. The courtyard bears the name of the adjacent **St John's Church** *(janabaznica.lv),* a 13th- to 19th-century amalgam of Gothic and baroque styles. It was first mentioned when the citizens installed catapults on the roof and successfully drove back attacking Livonian knights. Walk through Jāņa sēta into a square dominated by the needle-shaped **St Peter's Church** *(svpetera.lv; entry adult/student/child €9/7/3).*

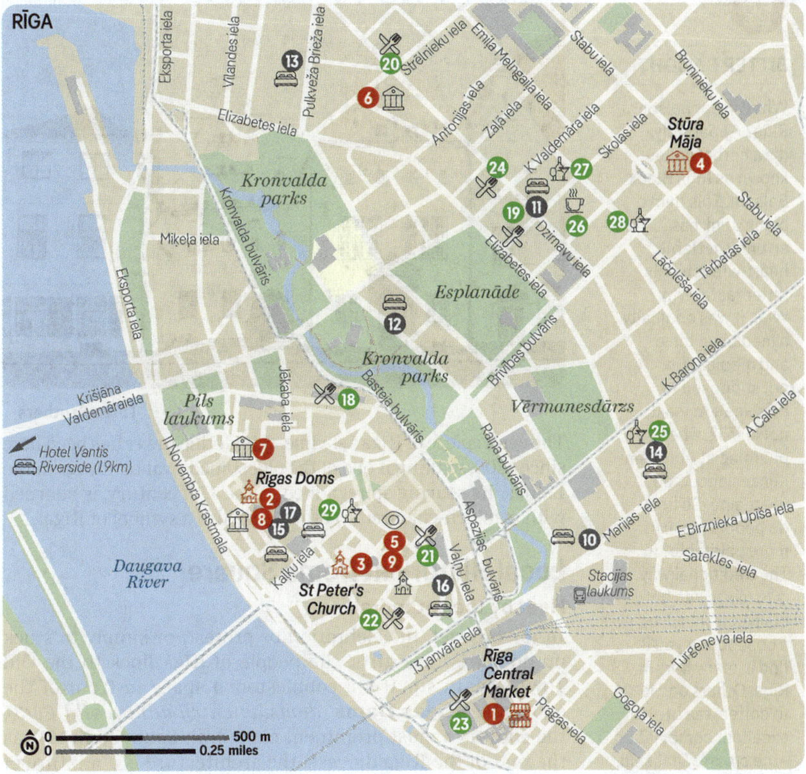

RĪGA

Kronvalda parks

Esplanāde

Kronvalda parks

Vērmanesdārzs

Pils laukums

Hotel Vantis Riverside (1.9km)

Rīgas Doms

Daugava River

St Peter's Church

Rīga Central Market

0 — 500 m
0 — 0.25 miles

⭐ **HIGHLIGHTS**

1 Rīga Central Market
2 Rīgas Doms
3 St Peter's Church
4 Stūra Māja

🔴 **SIGHTS**

5 Jāņa sēta
6 Janis Rozentāls & Rūdolfs Blaumanis Museum

7 Latvian Architecture Museum
see 6 Rīga Art Nouveau Centre
8 Rīga History & Navigation Museum
9 St John's Church
see 7 Three Brothers

⚫ **SLEEPING**

10 Cinnamon Sally
11 Edvards

12 Grand Poet
13 Hestia Hotel Jugend
14 Hotel Bergs
15 Hotel Justus
16 Naughty Squirrel
17 Neiburgs

🟢 **EATING**

18 3 Pavaru
19 Babo
20 Buberts
21 BURZMA

22 Milda
23 Siļķītes un Dillītes
24 Zivju Lete

🟢 **DRINKING & NIGHTLIFE**

25 Čē
26 Kalve
27 Kaņepes Kultūras Centrs
28 Miit
29 Piana Vyshnia

🍴 WHERE TO EAT IN CENTRAL RĪGA: OUR PICKS

Buberts: Away from the crowds, Buberts serves meat and fish dishes of variable provenance accompanied by craft beer. Good for breakfast. *8am–10pm* €

Zivju Lete: Contemporary cafe with bare-brick walls, wooden floors and date-friendly tables. Think fish and chips and towering seafood platters. *noon–10pm* €€

Siļķītes un Dillītes: By the fish hall at the Central Market, this scallop-sized cafe combines superb seafood with draft beer. Try the herring with cottage cheese. *9am–5pm* €

Babo: Sleek Georgian place serving all you'd expect – *khachapuri* (cheese pastries), *khinkali* (dumplings) – but with a touch of chic. Great wines. *noon–11pm* €€

239

BITTER DELIGHT

What's your poison, Rīga? Apparently, it's a herbal liqueur known as Rīga Black Balsam. This thick black drink has an unforgettable, heart-wrenchingly bitter taste. Why? Well, it was originally a medicinal tonic and medicine is not supposed to be sweet. At least, not in 1752, when pharmacist Abraham Kunze concocted the recipe. So how do people make it more palatable? The traditional way is to mix it with hot blackcurrant juice, a concoction you'll find in many bars in Rīga. Others add it to coffee, tea or – an excellent combination – ice cream. That said, some people drink it on the rocks. Care to join them?

SERGEJ25/SHUTTERSTOCK

Three Brothers

The centrepiece of Rīga's skyline, this Gothic tower has been here since 1209, making it one of the oldest medieval buildings in the Baltics. Its soaring spire, added in the 17th century, is adorned with a golden-coloured weathercock, also a symbol of Rīga.

Local History at Dome Square

Meet by the cathedral

In joy or grief, in celebration or protest, or simply to stock up on Christmas gifts, the people of Rīga flock to the Old Town's main square: a cobblestoned space in front of the enormous **Rīgas Doms** (doms.lv; entry adult/child €5/3), the country's most prominent cathedral. Founded in 1211 as the seat of the Rīga diocese, the architecture is a mixture of styles spanning the 13th to the 18th centuries: Romanesque, Gothic and baroque, with the trademark Hanseatic feature of glazed black bricks. At the back of the cathedral, the **Rīga History & Navigation Museum** (rigamuz.lv; entry adult/student/child €10/6/3), founded in 1773, presents the sweep of local history from the Bronze Age all the way up to WWII.

Nearby, three old stone houses, dubbed the **Three Brothers**, form a photogenic row and exemplify Old Rīga's diverse collection of architectural styles. No 17 is over 600 years old, making it the oldest dwelling in town. The middle one (17th century) houses the **Latvian Architecture Museum** (archmuseum.lv; free).

WHERE TO EAT AND DRINK IN THE OLD TOWN: OUR PICKS

3 Pavaru: Stellar chefs run this jazzy culinary show, with improvisation and seasonal freshness at the heart of the menu. *5-11pm* €€€

Milda: Deep dive into Baltic gastronomy: creatively reinvented Latvian and Lithuanian staples and a chatty chef who won a nod from Michelin. *noon-11pm* €€

BURZMA: The food court at the top of the Galerija Centrs shopping mall combines stylish eateries and sweeping views of the Old Town. *10am-11pm* €

Piana Vyshnia: A transplant from Lviv in Ukraine, this perpetually heaving place celebrates *vyshnevka* – a sweet cherry liquor ubiquitous in Eastern Europe. *11am-3am*

Game of Fancy

Explore the Jugendstil quarter

Rīga entered the 20th century as the sixth-largest city in the Russian Empire, and was also rapidly expanding under ambitious mayor George Armitstead, a native Rigan of British origin. In 1901 the city celebrated its 700th anniversary by inaugurating a new street, Alberta iela, built in the revolutionary Jugendstil (art nouveau) style. Today, this street runs through the heart of the Jugendstil quarter, erected during a period of rapid development and social optimism. The architect responsible for many of the buildings was Mikhail Eisenstein, who happened to be the father of filmmaker Sergei Eisenstein (of *Battleship Potemkin* fame). See the full range of his talents in five adjoining buildings, from Nos 2a to 8. **Rīga Art Nouveau Centre** *(jugendstilsriga.lv)* is inside the house architect Konstantīns Pēkšēns built for himself, incorporating images of plants and animals characteristic of Latvia into ornamental reliefs. In the same entrance, surmount the wonderfully lavish stairwell to the 5th floor to find the **Janis Rozentāls & Rūdolfs Blaumanis Museum** *(memorialiemuzeji. lv; entry adult/concession €2/1)*, the former dwelling of a famous painter and his equally famous writer friend.

The KGB's Shadow

Notorious HQ of the secret police

Ominously located on a 17th-century execution site, the fin-de-siècle building known as **Stūra Māja** *(Corner House; okupacias muzejs.lv; guided tour adult/concession €15/9)* is remembered by generations of Latvians as the headquarters of the Soviet secret police. Arbitrary arrests, torture, executions – it all happened here. The museum can only be visited on a guided tour. There are five English-language tours daily, between 11am and 4pm.

Make Trade not War

The city's main market

In what might be the world's most large-scale act of 'beating swords into ploughshares', several German-built WWI zeppelin hangars were brought into the city in the 1920s and converted into pavilions for **Riga Central Market** *(centraltirgus.lv)*. Today, it's a landmark and a place where friends bump into each other while shopping for smoked fish, forest mushrooms, fruit, homemade bread... you name it. Most of the action happens outside; the hangars are now mostly food courts.

AN ARCHITECT'S PICKS IN JUGENDSTIL

Aleksejs Birjukovs is a co-founder of the MARK Arhitekti bureau in Rīga. Here are his favourite buildings in Jugendstil.

School Nr 40, Tērbatas iela 15-17 (Konstantīns Pēkšēns and Eižens Laube; 1905): Wonderful example of national romanticism, based on ethnic mythology.

Vilandes iela 11 (Rudolf Heinrich Zirkwitz): Massive, ornate house renovated by an altruistic investor.

Brīvības iela 85 (Eižens Laube; 1912): Jugendstil with neo-Gothic flavour; Laube is the architect I admire most in Rīga.

Kalēju iela 23 (Pauls Mandelštams; 1903): This rental apartment in Old Rīga is a shiny example of early Jugendstil. The architect died in the Holocaust.

WHERE TO DRINK IN CENTRAL RĪGA: OUR PICKS

Čē: Scruffy and cavernous, with anarchic outdoor seating – the ultimate bohemian haunt with a good choice of draft and bottled beer. *4pm-1am*	**Kaņepes Kultūras Centrs:** Old music school converted into a beer garden, presided over by a giant green lion on the roof. Essential concert venue. *4pm-late*	**Kalve:** For local connoisseurs, this tiny joint in Baznīcas iela is the place for a morning cup. The filter coffee 'day's brew' is especially good. *8am-6pm*	**Miit:** A sociable place that serves a mean coffee as well as vegetarian lunches and desserts. *8am-8pm*

Gulf of Rīga

PERFECT BEACHES | DUNE WALKS | JET-SET VIBES

Gulf of Rīga

Ragaciems · Ādaži
· Lapmežciems
Ķemeru National Park · Jūrmala · **Rīga**
· Kalnciems · Salaspils

Places

Jūrmala p242
Northern Coast p243

☑ TOP TIP

In any season, you can get off at Bulduri, walk towards the beach and join the promenading crowds headed in the direction of Majori.

On the map, Latvia's gulf resembles a pair of open jaws. The water in this inner sea is even less salty than the Baltic, while Estonia's islands shelter it from serious storms. The coast on both sides of Rīga is an almost uninterrupted stretch of exquisite sand and romantic pine-covered dunes. Sitting on a massive sandbar formed by the Lielupe River, Jūrmala is Rīga's backyard beach and what passes for Latvia's golden mile, a playground for jet-setters and minigarchs from the east (the Russian language still prevails here). This strip of wealthy suburbia squeezed between the river, the railway line and the sea stretches for 32km. North of Rīga, the dune-dominated terrain is less developed and even more beautiful. Suburban trains run in both directions, making beach hopping easy. The Jūrtaka hiking trail runs along the coast; cycling is also a great way to get around.

Jūrmala

Stroll the strand

The **beach** in Jūrmala doubles as Latvia's longest and flashiest promenade. The white sand is hard-packed and ideal for walking or making sand castles. Come here in any season and you'll see strolling urbanites, cyclists or even skiers gliding along the seafront when there's enough snow. In winter,

---

GETTING AROUND

From Rīga, hop on a frequent train to head in either direction along the gulf. Trains with the destinations Dubulti, Sloka or Tukums serve stations in Jūrmala. Trains heading to Skulte, Saulkrasti or Carnikava serve the northern coast.

In addition to the railway line that runs through Jūrmala, there's a local bus network that connects railway stations and villages beyond Jūrmala. Saulkrasti municipality runs a similar, albeit smaller, network.

Jūrmala is convenient for bicycles, which you can rent at Velopark *(velopark.lv)* in Bulduri, or you can cycle all the way from Rīga.

TRABANTOS/SHUTTERSTOCK

Jomas iela

JŪRMALA TRAIN STATIONS

When arriving in Jūrmala by train, where to alight is a matter of taste. Here are some tips to help you decide.

Bulduri: A quieter part of Jūrmala, with restaurants and a short promenade leading to the sea.

Dzintari: Somewhat set back from the sea, but close to a park and convenient for its namesake concert hall.

Majori: This station has a picture-perfect setting and is in the centre of the action.

Dubulti: Has an art gallery inside the station and glimpses of old Jūrmala nearby.

Asari: Another beautiful station and a 10-minute walk from an unspoilt stretch of beach.

you'll still spot the occasional desperado dipping into the icy water. Few developments have encroached on the bluffs behind the sand, leaving the beach largely unspoiled with only the odd cafe here and there. Jūrmala's oldest area near the Dzintari, Majori and Dubulti stations resembles Prussian resorts on the German Baltic coast, its skyline dominated by elegant timber-framed villas, some of which have intricate wood-carved decor. The heart of the action is the 1km-long pedestrian street, **Jomas iela**, which runs between Majori and Dzintari stations.

Northern Coast

Pick your beach

While most visitors flock to Jūrmala, the beaches north of Rīga are markedly quieter, wilder and more visually attractive – with pristine white sand and a faint whiff of resin carried by the wind from the pine-covered dunes. The train line runs just beyond the resort area of Saulkrasti, with stops every couple of kilometres, which makes it convenient not just for lazing by the sea but also for walking chosen stretches of the **Jūrtaka coastal trail** *(baltictrails.eu)*.

WHERE TO EAT IN THE GULF OF RĪGA: OUR PICKS

36.Line: Relocated to Dubulti, this is Jūrmala's prime dining location with seafood and a grill. You might spot the occasional ex-Soviet celebrity. *1-10pm* €€€

Kinza House: Jūrmala is full of Caucasian restaurants; this is the best for Georgian cuisine. Gorge on *khachapuri* and *khinkali* if you can get a seat. *noon-10pm* €€

Bitīte: Good for a quick coffee or hearty breakfast. The elevated terrace is a prime vantage point overlooking Jūrmala's pedestrian Jomas St. *8.30am-9pm* €

Abra: A family cafe by the dunes in Saulkrasti, serving Latvian *karbonādes* (pork chops) and standard East European fare. *11am-4pm Fri, 24hr Sat & Sun* €

JOYGAYM/SHUTTERSTOCK

Baltā Kāpa

Vecāķi is the first train station by the beach north of the Daugava River. It feels like a low-key Jūrmala with large old villas and a few cafes along the main promenade. At **Kalngale** station, an atmospheric promenade runs through a darkly beautiful coniferous forest to a white-sand beach. In **Garciems**, a boardwalk follows a beautiful little river seasonally dammed by beavers.

Saulkrasti's dune of perfection

Get off at Pabaži station and walk 1.3km to **Baltā Kāpa** (White Dune), a viewpoint on top of a high cliff, where a fertile, forest river streams through the white sands on its last stretch before reaching the sea. This is one of the most enchanting places along the entire Latvian coast, and the wooden walkway along the 18m-high cliffs affords sweeping views of the Gulf of Rīga. The **Sunset Trail** (Saulrieta taka) runs to the centre of **Saulkrasti**, where you'll find an artfully designed beach with a cluster of restaurants. An additional perk is the deep water near the seafront, which makes for better swimming than elsewhere.

Gauja National Park

HIKING | RAFTING | CASTLES

Gauja National Park encompasses an enchanting landscape of forested hills that guard the meandering white ribbon of the Gauja River. Providing vertical dimension to a lowland country, these hills – unironically referred to as 'Latvian Switzerland' – draw hikers, rafters (it's not quite white water) and downhill skiers. There's even a bobsled track and a facility imitating zero gravity that's accessible to the public. But the main pull is the quiet, unpretentious beauty of this area – especially in autumn, when the hills are ablaze in yellow and bright red. Gauja Valley is Latvia's top outdoors destination, with Sigulda serving as its hub, but it also comprises medieval castles and charming little towns, as well as various historical monuments, entertainment parks and old mansions, known as *muižas*, which have been converted into hotels. Most of these attractions are located along the Mežtaka (Forest Trail) route.

Places

Sigulda p245
Cēsis p246
Līgatne p246

☑ TOP TIP

Start your exploration of Gauja National Park at the excellent Tourist Information Office at the train and bus station. It's stocked with walking maps and is the place to find out about daily events and tours.

Sigulda

A scenic river valley

Sigulda is a manifestation of what Latvians regard as an ideal life and aesthetic perfection. The town is a sprawling area of

---

GETTING AROUND

The most memorable way to traverse Gauja National Park is by hiking or cycling the Mežtaka trail. But to reach the trailhead, you'll need to take a combination of train and buses. Cēsis lies on the same train line as Sigulda and is also served by buses from Rīga, via Sigulda. Līgatne's train station is located by the main road leading to Estonia and Russia, 8km from the town centre. There are a few direct daily buses to Cēsis. Otherwise, catch a local bus to Augšlīgatne on the main highway and proceed from there.

Sigulda's attractions are spread out. The place is a cyclist's paradise, with several rental shops around town, including Veloriba by the train station. Bus 3112 connects Sigulda and Turaida, with eight to nine services a day. Bolt is widely available.

Many local attractions are deep in the woods, accessible only by car, bicycle or a long hike.

FOREST TREKS

The trans-Baltic Forest Trail, known as **Mežtaka** *(baltictrails. eu)* in Latvia, follows the course of the Gauja River through the national park. The trail leaves from a key road junction near Gauja village and runs all the way to Valmiera. This is one of the most beautiful legs of the entire route. Stages tend to be fairly long, ranging from 19km to 26km, with limited options for bailing mid-route. If you only want to hike one section, choose between the Sigulda–Līgatne or Līgatne–Cēsis stages. Factor in extra time for the Līgatne nature trails if you choose the former.

large private homes surrounded by manicured grass and apple orchards, with plenty of space for lonely walks and bicycle rides through the magnificent valley of the Gauja River. A quintessential Sigulda experience is to cross the Gauja Valley, enjoying terrific views in all directions, in a cute **cable car** *(siguldaadventures.com; €19 return)* that departs from a precipice in the centre of town. This takes you to the **Krimulda Manor** *(krimuldamuiza.lv)* on the other side of the valley.

Explore the Turaida castle

Turaida *(turaida-muzejs.lv; entry adult/concession €8/from €2)* means 'God's Garden' in ancient Livonian and this green knoll capped with a castle is indeed an enchanting place. The red-brick edifice with its tall cylindrical tower was built in 1214 on the site of a Liv stronghold and reconstructed in the 1980s. A museum inside the castle's 15th-century granary offers an interesting account of the Livonian state from 1319 to 1561; additional exhibitions can be viewed in the 42m-high Donjon Tower and the castle's western and southern towers. Turaida is across the river from Sigulda and served by frequent buses from the railway station.

Cēsis

A stunning Livonian town

The Livonian knights who were responsible for founding Wenden (which became Cēsis seven centuries later) must have had a romantic side. The remarkable **Cēsis Castle** *(cesupils.lv; entry adult/concession €12/8)* is actually two castles in one, forming a single museum. The moody dark-stone towers belong to the restored old castle. You're handed a candle lamp at the start of your visit, making your exploration of the dark ruins suitably atmospheric. Back in town, make sure you visit the 13th-century **St John's Church** *(cesusirds.lv)*, where armour-clad Livonian knights prayed and buried their dead.

Līgatne

A chef's shack

Many of us dream of owning a little countryside house with a garden, and celebrity chefs are no exception. But only the latter would turn their home into a Michelin restaurant. Ēriks Dreibants based his brainchild, **Pavāru Māja** *(pavarumaja.lv)*, in an old maternity home that's surrounded by a garden where most of his ingredients are grown. Opt for a four-course lunch (€59) or an eight-course dinner (€99); book online.

 WHERE TO EAT IN GAUJA NATIONAL PARK: OUR PICKS

Jāņa Tirgus: This modern market hall is mostly a food court with a quality pizzeria in the middle. But you can also shop for produce here. *10am-8pm* €€

Doma Kafejnīca: Enjoy wraps, burgers, stir-fries and heavenly fruit-filled desserts in an enchanted garden. *11am-8pm Tue-Sun* €

Cēsu Maize: This artisanal bakery is always warm and redolent with the aroma of freshly baked bread. Owners can talk you through old recipes. *10am-6pm* €

HE Vanadziņš: High-end Nordic cuisine in a charming courtyard in the heart of Cēsis. *5-10pm Thu-Fri, noon-8pm Sat & Sun* €€€

Kurzeme & Zemgale

OPULENT PALACE | WATERFALLS | BEACHES

Western Latvia, known as Kurzeme, is surrounded by the sea on two sides. The milder climate here is more conducive to agriculture, unlike the forested north and east. It's a land of rolling hills, rapeseed fields that bloom in spring and storks' nests that preside over every village. This area was under Baltic German influence for almost 700 years – a story that culminated in the 17th century when the Duchy of Courland briefly turned itself into a mini-empire with overseas possessions in Africa and the Caribbean. What remains today are quaint Prussian-style towns and the castles and palaces of the Baltic German nobility. This ambience spills into the more forested southern part of Latvia, known as Zemgale. Typically lumped together with Kurzeme, these two regions share much of the same history.

☑ TOP TIP

For a full Karosta prison experience in Lijepāja, you can 'get arrested' and spend the night in prison. Conditions vary from semi-authentic to prison chic. For an additional donation, you can also arrange your escape.

Rundāle Palace

The abode of an adventurist

Built as a grand residence for the duke of Courland, Ernst Johann Biron, the magnificent **Rundāle Palace** *(rundale.net; entry including gardens adult/student/child €17/10.50/5.50)* is a monument to 18th-century aristocratic ostentatiousness and rural Latvia's architectural highlight. It was designed by Italian baroque genius Bartolomeo Rastrelli, who is best known for the Winter Palace in St Petersburg. About 40 of the

---

 GETTING AROUND

Kuldīga, Liepāja and Bauska (for Rundāle Palace) are all served by frequent buses from Rīga's central station. Additionally, there's at least one train a day between Rīga and Llepāja. Four buses a day run between Kuldīga and Liepāja, making it easy to visit both on the same trip.

Local buses connect Bauska's bus station to Rundāle Palace roughly hourly. You don't need local transport in Kuldīga. In Liepāja, the adjacent train and bus stations are connected to the centre by the tram line. Tickets can be bought from the driver, but only with a card.

palace's 138 rooms are open to visitors, as are the wonderful formal gardens, inspired by those at Versailles. Biron was the lover of Anna Ioanovna, the empress of Russia from 1730 to 1740, and a notorious adventurist in Russia. Rundāle Palace is 12km east of Bauska in Zemgale.

Kuldīga

A humble Niagara Falls

A newcomer to the UNESCO heritage list, charming Kuldīga – formerly known as Goldingen – has a Grimm Brothers' vibe and a striking setting above what is allegedly the widest waterfall in Europe, **Ventas Rumba**. This description might be a truth-stretcher – not in terms of width (249m), but in calling a human-sized drop in the riverbed a waterfall. Still, it's a truly awe-inspiring sight when seen from above. A zigzagging ribbon of white water runs across the Venta River, the banks overflowing with lush greenery. A stunning 19th-century red-brick bridge is a few hundred metres away. The deep lagoon is a favourite place for swimming and the location of the city beach.

Liepāja

Harbour fun and ghosts of the past

Liepāja is the type of city where you'll want to hum an uplifting tune as you stroll around the harbour and Old Town. The stunning white-sand **Blue Flag Beach** plays no small part in achieving this effect, as does the colourful harbour that serves as the city's prime nightlife spot. Old trees, manicured flower beds, water features, elegant walkways and cycling trails make the 3km-long **Seaside Park** the very definition of an urban oasis.

But this is also a place ridden with the ghosts of the past. The former navy garrison district of Karosta is located across the canal from central Liepāja. Its most striking landmark is the magnificent Russian Orthodox **Naval Church of St Nicholas**, whose massive golden cupola rises above drab Soviet-era *khruschevka* apartment blocks.

Also spooky is the beating heart of Karosta's tourism industry: the **Karosta Prison** *(karosta.lv; entry adult/student €8/5)*. Not exactly a Gulag, it was used by all political regimes throughout history as a detention centre for disobedient sailors. Conditions were torturous, as you'll be able to attest following a guided tour of the dark prison cells covered in Russian-language graffiti.

HISTORY OF KURZEME

The historical region in Latvia's west takes its name from the Curonians, a medieval Baltic group who also lent their name to the Curonian spit in Lithuania. The German crusaders of the Livonian Order subjugated them in the 13th century and continued to rule the region up until the Russian Revolution of 1917. When the Livonian Order collapsed in the 16th century, its last master Gotthard von Kettler set up the Duchy of Courland. The duchy was a disobedient vassal of the Polish-Lithuanian Commonwealth, and as the latter was increasingly consumed by the Russians, it drifted in that direction as well. It played an outsized role in St Petersburg politics for a few decades before being formally annexed by Russia in 1795.

WHERE TO EAT AND DRINK IN KULDĪGA & LIEPĀJA: OUR PICKS

Bārs Didro: Fantastic food and cocktails in a Kuldīga bar run by professional philosophers who also hold occasional intellectual discussions. *6-9pm Wed-Sat* €€

Celms maize: This artisanal bakery in Kuldīga serves fantastic breakfast sets and omelettes, all accompanied by freshly baked bread. *8am-4pm* €

MO Liepāja: Hard to define in culinary or geographic terms, this place is all about fresh, diverse ingredients. Great value for a Michelin spot. *noon-11pm Tue-Sun* €€

Spīķeris 53: Imaginative Baltic fish meals and craft beer inside an old warehouse. Outdoor tables face Liepāja's harbour. *4-10pm* €€

Places We Love to Stay

€ Budget €€ Midrange €€€ Top End

Rīga
MAP p239

Cinnamon Sally € This hostel is relentless in its efforts to create a homey and sociable atmosphere. By the train station.

Naughty Squirrel € Backpacker Old Town star with homey dorms and a ritual shot of booze at check-in.

Hotel Justus €€ A tidy upper-floor hotel, with angled ceilings in the rooms following the roofline. In the Old Town.

Edvards €€ Room design matches the laconic no-nonsense elegance of this house, built in 1890, in the heart of things in central Rīga.

Hestia Hotel Jugend €€ Convenient for the Jugendstil quarter, this hotel is artfully designed with brightly coloured rooms and comfy beds.

Hotel Vantis Riverside €€ On rustic Ķīpsala Island facing the passenger port terminal, come here for another perspective on Rīga. Airy rooms with lots of sun and modern amenities.

Neiburgs €€€ Occupying one of Rīga's finest art nouveau buildings, Neiburgs blends historic details with contemporary touches.

Hotel Bergs €€€ A refurbished 19th-century building embellished with a Scandi-sleek extension, the 37 spacious rooms at the Hotel Bergs embody the term 'luxury'.

Grand Poet €€€ It doesn't get any plusher than these park-facing rooms with fine retro touches. The location couldn't be more central.

Gulf of Rīga

Parus Boutique Hotel €€ One of the Prussian-style villas that defines Jūrmala. Has 12 traditionally decorated rooms.

Pine Resort €€ Located on a quiet plot well off Rīgas iela, this small hotel is close to the best beach in Saulkrasti.

Hotel Jūrmala Spa €€€ The rooms in this towering black behemoth are on the small side, but they look brand new. Some come with sweeping sea views.

Sigulda

Mazais Līvkalns €€ No place is more romantically rustic than this idyllic retreat at the forest's edge.

Hotel Sigulda €€ The oldest hotel in Sigulda, built by Kropotkin. Charming facade, but rooms are fairly bland.

Spa Hotel Ezeri €€€ A luxurious spa complex that has fairly simple rooms with contemporary decor.

Cēsis

Glūdas Grava €€ Five studios with glassy front walls and individual entrances in a renovated brick garage.

Kārlamuiža €€ In the village of Kārļi, this former aristocratic manor has been reborn as a gentrified country hotel.

Villa Santa Hotel €€ Three 19th-century wooden buildings have been transformed into a lovely hotel deep in the woods.

Kuldīga

Jēkaba Sēta € This typical Latvian inn, complete with a pub, has standard-looking rooms with wooden furniture.

2 Baloži € Perched above a stream, this wooden house has Scandinavian-style rooms.

Hotel Metropole €€ Kuldīga's main hotel features a modern pale-colour palette and spacious rooms overlooking the Town Hall Square.

Noliktava No 5 €€ An astonishingly stylish place that fuses post-industrial and modern Nordic with elements of Soviet nostalgia. The name refers to Kuldīga's Soviet-era petrol station.

Virkas Muiža €€ This beautiful manor house with an ornate wooden front terrace has plush rustic-styled rooms with wood-dominated interiors.

Liepāja

Fontaine Valhalla Hotel € Inexpensive, brightly decorated rooms with shared bathrooms in a cosy wooden building near the harbour.

Hotel Roze €€ Stylish and comfortable, this pale-blue wooden villa has spacious rooms, each uniquely decorated.

Seven Sisters €€ Comfy self-check-in rooms in a quiet, village-like part of central Liepāja. Common kitchen, garden and plenty of parking spaces.

Promenade Hotel €€€ The poshest hotel in Kurzeme occupies an enormous grain warehouse facing the harbour.

Practicalities

LGBTIQ+ Travellers
Latvia is generally quite tolerant. At the time of writing, its president, Edgars Rinkēvičs, was the first openly gay national leader in Europe. Same-sex civil unions were recognised in 2024. But conservative anti-LGBTIQ+ forces are strong and casual homophobia is not uncommon.

Health
If you spend time in Latvia's dunes or forests in between May and July, getting bit by a tick is not a question of if but when. Consider getting an encephalitis jab (done long in advance) and watch out for Lyme disease.

Smoking
Smoking is widespread, but it is forbidden in restaurants (except terraces), parks, public transport stops and most other public places, as well as in the presence of a child or pregnant woman. House committees often ban smoking inside flats. Rental apartments are normally non-smoking zones.

Visas
Latvia is part of the EU and the Schengen zone, which means the vast majority of Western travellers don't need visas for visits up to 90 days. There was a virtual ban on visas for Russian and Belarusian citizens at the time of writing.

LN TEAM/SHUTTERSTOCK

Turaida castle (p246), Sigulda

Opening Hours
Banks 9am–6pm Monday to Friday
Government offices 8am–4pm Monday to Friday
Shops Supermarkets are typically open from 8am until 10pm or 11pm. Other shops close earlier, especially in the countryside.

Language
Latvian is one of two living Baltic languages and one of the most ancient Indo-European language groups.
Hello. Sveiks. *svayks*
Goodbye. Atā. *a·taa*
Thank you. Paldies. *pal·deas*
Yes. Jā. *yaa*
No. Nē. *nair*

Public Holidays
New Year's Day 1 January
Easter Sunday March/April
Labour and Convocation of the Constituent Assembly of Latvia Day 1 May
Declaration of Latvian Independence Day 4 May
Midsummer Day 23 June
St John's Day 24 June
Proclamation of the Republic of Latvia 18 November
Christmas 24–26 December
New Year's Eve 31 December

Bus, Rīga (p238)

MONEY

Currency: Euro (€)

CREDIT CARDS & CASH

You'll rarely need to pay in cash in Latvia, except at the market or when leaving a tip. ATMs are ubiquitous. Visa and MasterCard are universally accepted, American Express and UnionPay less so.

DIGITAL PAYMENTS

Most terminals around the country accept digital payments either through your phone or watch. The Mobilly app is great for buying all kinds of transportation tickets.

TIPPING

Tipping isn't really expected, but it's customary to leave a 10% tip if you're happy with restaurant service or to drop some coins into the tip jar at bars and coffee shops.

Arriving & Getting Around

The majority of visitors enter Latvia either via Rīga International Airport or by bus from Estonia or Lithuania. Intercity buses are the dominant mode of domestic transportation; trains also serve some crucial routes.

Arriving by Air

Rīga International Airport is a well-run operation. Car hire and a cash machine are located in the arrivals hall. Taxis wait at the entrance, but it's better to use Bolt to avoid scams.

Getting Around by Bus

The bus network in the countryside is organised in such a way that you're never far from the nearest stop. Check schedules and fares at *autoosta.lv* or *1188.lv*, or use the Mobilly app.

Arriving by Bus

Buses from Tallinn, Vilnius and Kaunas arrive at Rīga International Bus Station in the heart of the city. The main streets can be reached by buses 3 and 21.

Other Transport

Trains are particularly useful for Jūrmala and the northern beaches. Other lines connect to destinations in Gauja National Park and Latgale. There are also daily trains to Liepāja. Car hire is available, but most locals use rideshare services like Bolt and CityBee. Latvia is criss-crossed by bicycle and hiking paths like the Baltic Coastal Trail (Jūrtaka) and Forest Trail (Mežtaka).

For places to stay in Lithuania, see p269

SUN CLOCK – © KLAUDIJUS PUDYMAS, SCULPTOR. ASTA.SABONYTE/SHUTTERSTOCK

Above: Parnidis Dune (p265), Nida; Right: Hill of Crosses (p263), Šiauliai

Curated by
Anna Kaminski

Lithuania

UNSPOILED NATURE MEETS MILLENNIAL HISTORY

Traverse coastal dunes, lake-dotted forests and vibrant cities, and admire intricate woodcarvings in the Baltics' most creative country.

A sliver of land flanked by pine forest and covered with giant sand dunes jutting into the Baltic Sea, the largest of the three Baltic states is also the most beguiling. It has ancient forests teeming with wildlife, hundreds of lakes and a coastline strung with white-sand beaches, all of which make it irresistibly appealing to fresh-air fiends. Tranquil roads bisect the rolling countryside and its timeless villages, providing ideal terrain for touring cyclists and unhurried road-trippers.

Though Lithuania traded paganism for Catholicism long ago, pagan-style wooden grave markers still dot its cemeteries, while other traces of its past shine through in Lithuania's age-old craft of woodcarving and folk-metal music. More agrarian than its neighbours, Lithuania is also more homogeneous, and became even more so when the majority of its Jewish population was wiped out during the Holocaust.

Its two main cities are distinct in character: Vilnius beckons with baroque finery, cobbled streets and a multitude of churches, while creative Kaunas bristles with gorgeous interwar architecture and pays homage to basketball – the nation's passion. Lithuania's charms are many and varied: where else can you visit a nuclear power plant, explore genteel country manors, dine on exceptional seasonal cuisine and – above all – immerse yourself in the unspoilt nature of this land, to which the national identity is so deeply tied?

GORSH13/GETTY IMAGES

THE MAIN AREAS

Find Your Way

Lithuania is easy to navigate on public transport, though cars are useful for reaching remote attractions. The country's flatness encourages cycling, and the seasonal boats connect the Curonian Spit to the Curonian Lagoon.

CAR

Driving is best for remote destinations. Parking in labyrinthine Old Town is tricky. In major cities Bolt and Spark offer car rentals by the minute or hour. Winter tyres are compulsory mid-November through March.

BUS & TRAIN

An extensive bus network links major cities and smaller towns. Trains are useful for travel between Vilnius and Kaunas or Vilnius and Klaipėda. Download the Autobusų Bilietai and LTG Link apps.

Vilnius & Eastern Lithuania, p256

Lithuania's capital is also the gateway to Trakai Island Castle and Aukštaitija National Park.

Kaunas, Central & Southern Lithuania, p261

Kaunas beckons with quirky museums while Šiauliai's Hill of Crosses, Druskininkai's spas and Panevėžys' art are all within easy reach.

Curonian Spit & Western Lithuania, p265

Hike up giant sand dunes, cycle forest trails, sun yourself on Baltic beaches and explore a centuries-old castle.

LATVIA

BELARUS

RUSSIA (KALININGRAD REGION)

Baltic Sea

0 — 100 miles
0 — 200 km

Skuodas
Mažeikiai
Seda
Naujoji Akmenė
Joniškis
Gruzdžiai
Linkuva
Pasvalys
Biržai
Skaistkalne

Palanga
Kretinga
Salantai
Lake Plateliai
Amber Museum
Plungė
Rietavas
Laukuva
Varniai
Lake Lūkstas
Telšiai
Šiauliai
Hill of Crosses
Radviliškis
Kuršenai
Smilgiai
Panevėžys

Klaipėda
Klaipėda Castle Museum
Priekule
Švėkšna
Okediena
Šilutė
Skaudvilė
Tauragė
Jurbarkas
Ožkabaliai
Kelmė
Raseiniai
Kėdainiai
Ukmergė

Juodkrantė
Nida
Parnidis Dune

Sovetsk
Pagėgiai
Šakiai
Vilkija
Nemunas
Vilkaviškis
Kybartai
Pilviškiai
Marijampolė
MK Čiurlionis Museum of Art
KAUNAS
Museum of Occupations and Freedom Fights
Jonava
Vievis
VILNIUS
Vilnius Cathedral
Palace of the Grand Dukes of Lithuania

Rokiškis
Zarasai
Lake Sartai
Lake Sartai
Dusetos
Lake Antalieptė
Utena
Aukštaitija National Park
Ignalina
Visaginas
Švenčionys
Pabradė
Nemenčine
Maišiagala
Trakai
Juozapinė
Grūtas Park
Čepkeliai Strict Nature Reserve

Vabalninkas
Kupiškis
Anykščiai
Molėtai
 Širvintos
Širvintos
Giedraičiai
Gelvonai

Seirijai
Merkinė
Varėna
Rūdiškės
Šalčininkai

MINSK

Lazdijai
Leipalingis
Alytus
Druskininkai
Lida

Oligaviškės

Venta
Venta
Mūša
Nevėžis
Nemunas
Neris (Vilija)
Neris (Vilija)
Merkys

Palace of the Grand Dukes of Lithuania (p258), Vilnius

Plan Your Time

Hit Vilnius and Kaunas, then spend several days hiking and cycling the Curonian Spit and/or Aukštaitija. Palanga's beaches, Druskininkai's spas and Šiauliai's pilgrimage site are nice extras.

If You Only Do One Thing

● Focus your energy on **Vilnius** (p256) and the cobbled Old Town. Then visit **Gediminas Castle** (p258), the **Palace of the Grand Dukes of Lithuania** (p258) and the **Museum of Occupations and Freedom Fights** (p258). Other museums include the **National Art Gallery** (p259) and **Museum of Culture and Identity of Lithuanian Jews** (p259).

If You Have More Time

● Visit the **Curonian Spit** (p265), walk or cycle its long-distance trails and hike up giant sand dunes. Visit **Trakai Island Castle** (p260), and day-trip to **Aukštaitija National Park** (p260). Or haunt **Kaunas** (p261) and its UNESCO-recognised modernist architecture, **Art Deco Museum** (p262), **Amsterdam School Museum** (p262), **KGB Atomic Bunker** (p263) and **MK Čiurlionis Museum of Art** (p263).

SEASONAL HIGHLIGHTS

SPRING
Late spring is excellent for hiking in national parks. Temperatures are mild and days are long.

SUMMER
Lithuania is loveliest in summer when days are long and the Baltic Sea beaches beckon.

AUTUMN
Autumn colours and fewer visitors make this an ideal time for the long-distance Baltic Coastal Trail or Forest Trail.

WINTER
Wintry cities blanketed in snow can be magic. Don't miss the Christmas markets in Vilnius and Kaunas.

Vilnius & Eastern Lithuania

HISTORY | DINING | NATURE

Places

Vilnius p256
Trakai p260
Aukštaitija National Park p260

 TOP TIP

Planning on intensive sightseeing? Download the **Vilnius Pass** (govilnius. lt; €37/47/56 per 24/48/72 hours), which grants free/discounted access to numerous museums. To arrange an English-language guided hike or kayak trip in Aukštaitija National Park, contact Visaginas-based **LitWild** (litwildtravel.com).

Lithuania's dreamy, compact capital celebrated its 700th birthday in 2023 and has a marvellously intact Old Town. It's rare in that locals actually live here, and its cobbled streets lined with weather-worn buildings testify to centuries of turbulent history. Today, these same buildings burst forth with independent boutiques, restaurants and lively cafes and bars.

Vilnius doesn't hide its scars and imperfections. The former 'Jerusalem of the north' lost 150,000 of its Jewish community in WWII. The baroque, Gothic and Renaissance churches of the city's historic heart sit alongside Holocaust museums, former ghetto remnants, preserved KGB torture chambers and buildings left derelict by decades of neglect. Yet optimism perseveres.

An easy day trip from Vilnius, tiny Trakai beguiles with its castle in the middle of a lake. East of Vilnius, Aukštaitija National Park beckons with its dense forest, plentiful lakes, small villages, and hiking and cycling trails.

Vilnius

Vilnius' mighty cathedral

Occupying a spot originally dedicated to the worship of Perkūnas, the Lithuanian thunder god, the neoclassical **Vilnius Cathedral** (katedra.lt) with its freestanding **belfry**

⊕ GETTING AROUND

Much of the compact Old Town is pedestrian. Hire bicycles at CycloCity stations or from Velotakas (velotakas.lt). Download the Bolt app for electric scooters and rideshares.

Buses and trolleybuses run from 5am to midnight. Download the Trafi app to purchase bus tickets (€1). The train and bus stations serve all major destinations around Lithuania, including Trakai (20 minutes). Aukštaitija National Park's main town, Ignalina, is well connected to Vilnius by daily buses (two hours) and trains (eight daily, 1½ to 1¾ hours); trains have cycle racks.

VILNIUS

Lukiškių aikštė

National Art Gallery (1.3km)

Museum of Occupations and Freedom Fights

Jakšto gatvė

Vienuolio gatvė

Gedimino prospektas

Tilto gatvė

Vilniaus gatvė

Žygimantų gatvė

Nerís River

Radvilų gatvė

Žvejų gatvė

Rinktinės gatvė

Vrublevskio gatvė

Savivaldybės aikštė

TAURAKALNIS

Pamėnkalnio gatvė

Jogailos gatvė

Palace of the Grand Dukes of Lithuania

Vilnius Cathedral

Cathedral Square

Gediminas Hill

Tauro gatvė

Kalinausko gatvė

Liejyklos gatvė

Šv. Ignoto gatvė

Daukanto aikštė

Vilnius University

Šv. Mykolo

Maironio gatvė

13

Basanavičiaus gatvė

Pylimo gatvė

Vilniaus gatvė

19

12

23
18

15

Didžioji gatvė

Bokšto gatvė

UŽUPIS

Trakų gatvė

24

NEW TOWN (NAUJAMIESTIS)

Ševčenkos gatvė

Pylimo gatvė

Lydos gatvė

Vingrių gatvė

Ligoninės gatvė

Mėsinių

21

22

16

TYMO

Subačiaus gatvė

Naugarduko gatvė

Aguonų gatvė

Raugyklos gatvė

Pylimo gatvė

Šaltinių gatvė

Arklių gatvė

25

Mindaugo gatvė

Algirdo gatvė

20

Daukšos gatvė

0   400 m
0   0.2 miles

11

BEST TOURS IN VILNIUS

Velotakas Bike & Tours: Small-group cycle tours of Vilnius' top landmarks, plus bicycles for hire. *(velotakas.lt)*

Vilnius With Locals: Highly recommended Soviet Vilnius and Jewish Vilnius walking tours, as well the Vilnius Old Town tour with snacks. *(vilni-uswithlocals.com)*

Oreivystės Centras: Soar above the Gothic spires of Old Town or over Trakai Castle in a hot air balloon at dawn or sunset. *(ballooning.lt)*

Feel Z City: Electric scooter and cycling tours, artsy Vilnius walks, craft beer tastings and more, either as a group tour or private venture. *(feelzcity.com)*

Baidares Vilniuje: Book in advance for kayaking tours along the Neris River, including an atmospheric dusk/ night venture. *(baidaresvilniuje.lt)*

(bell tower) is a national symbol and the city's most instantly recognisable building. It has pride of place on **Cathedral Square**. Tour the crypt *(bpmuziejus.lt; entry adult/child €12/6),* the final resting place of many prominent Lithuanians, including Vytautas the Great (1350–1430).

Summit Castle Hill

The birthplace of the city, 48m-high **Gediminas Hill** stands sentinel over Vilnius, its red-brick tower offering fantastic views over Old Town. Its strategic location has been the site of fortified buildings since Neolithic times. Ascend to **Gediminas Castle** via **funicular** *(single/return €2/3)*. Inside, the museum *(lnm.lt/en/museums; entry adult/child €8/4)* elaborates on centuries of warfare and the castle's history as a nobles' prison.

The seat of Lithuanian royalty

On a site settled since the 4th century stands the 17th-century **Palace of the Grand Dukes of Lithuania** *(valdovurumai.lt/en; entry adult/child €16/8),* revamped and transformed into an excellent museum of Lithuanian history, with over 300,000 archaeological findings. Highlights include a comprehensive history of the country, peppered with larger-than-life characters; the reconstructed private apartments of Lithuania's grand dukes and the treasury; and vivid depictions of life in the Middle Ages, from warfare to epic feasts.

Eastern Europe's oldest university

In the heart of Old Town is **Vilnius University** *(muziejus. vu.lt; entry adult/child €8/4),* founded by the Jesuits in 1579 and comprising a red-roofed labyrinth of Gothic, baroque, Renaissance, classicist and eclectic-style buildings joined by 13 courtyards. Join a thematic tour – a good option to avoid getting lost in the maze-like layout and for in-depth overviews of women in academia and the Observatory of Ideas. It's closed on Sundays.

Anti-Soviet resistance

This former headquarters of the KGB is now home to the **Museum of Occupations and Freedom Fights** *(olkm.lt/en; entry adult/child €6/3),* closed on Mondays and Tuesdays and dedicated to thousands of Lithuanian partisans and intelligentsia who were murdered, imprisoned or deported by the Soviet Union from WWII until the 1960s. Backlit photographs,

EATING IN VILNIUS: OUR PICKS

Lokys: Game roasts are the main event at this 'hunter's restaurant' inside vaulted 16th-century merchant's cellars. *noon-midnight* €€	**Ertlio Namas:** Tasting menus of re-created centuries-old recipes (roe-deer sausage with pumpkin pudding) come with elaborate backstories. *5-11pm Mon-Sat* €€€	**Halès Turgus:** Traditional produce stalls mingle with en vogue eateries at the pungent 1906 food market. *7am-6pm Mon-Fri, to 3pm Sat* €	**Maurizio's Italian Food:** Chequered tablecloths, bonhomie and excellent Neapolitan-style pizza baked in a wood-fired oven. *noon-10pm Sun-Thu, to 11pm Fri & Sat* €€

Gediminas Castle

wooden annexes and a disorienting layout sharpen the impact of past horrors outlined in graphic detail. The basement prison cells are particularly unsettling, from the padded one to the cell once partially filled with icy water.

A window into the Litvak world

The excellent **Museum of Culture and Identity of Lithuanian Jews** *(jmuseum.lt; entry adult/child €6/3)* lets you explore Litvak (Lithuanian Jewish) history, culture, traditions and daily life through a mixture of written sources, films, interactive displays, photography and evocative Vilnius cityscapes by Lithuania's most prominent 20th-century Jewish painter, Rafael Chwoles. Learn about the achievements of world-famous Litvaks and delve into Litvak literature, music and visual arts. It's closed on Mondays.

The biggest repository of Lithuanian modern art

The vast **National Art Gallery** *(ndg.lt/en.aspx; entry adult/ child €8/4),* closed on Mondays, is the country's most comprehensive collection of Lithuanian art from the 20th and 21st centuries. Arranged chronologically across 12 halls according to specific themes such as 'Crisis and rebellion', 'Women artists from interwar Vilnius' and 'At the crossroads of the epochs', it charts the story of a country striving towards its own artistic identity – under foreign occupation and as an independent country.

 EATING & DRINKING IN VILNIUS: OUR PICKS

14Horses: Use your hands to tackle beef tartare with fermented strawberries and pancakes with smoked eel on the four-course tasting menus. *5-11pm Tue-Sat* €€

Nineteen18: Industrial-style decor and a 10-course menu that may include chicken caramel, mushroom dumplings and desserts involving ants. *6-11pm Tue-Sat* €€€

Alaus Biblioteka: Sip your Lithuanian seasonal brew, surrounded by books, at this friendly bar with rotating craft beers on tap and by the bottle. *5pm-midnight*

Apoteka Bar: Reimagined mixology classics and autumn-in-a-glass originals, served beneath heavy wooden beams. *6pm-midnight Sun, Wed & Thu, to 2am Fri & Sat*

ASTA SABONYTE/SHUTTERSTOCK

Trakai Island Castle

A Brief History of Vilnius' Jews

For centuries, Vilnius flourished as a centre for Jewish culture, with 60,000 Litvaks (Lithuanian Jews) making up almost half of the population. When the Germans invaded the Soviet Union in 1941, Vilnius fell within days. The Small Ghetto was established north of Vokiečių gatvė and destroyed 46 days later, its 11,000 inhabitants killed between 6 September and 20 October 1941 at Paneriai. The Large Ghetto was created in September 1941 south of Vokiečių gatvė to hold workers valuable to the German war effort. It was liquidated in September 1943, with 26,000 Jews perishing at Paneriai, and 10,000 shipped to concentration camps. Only 6000 Vilnius Jews survived the war.

Trakai

Visit Trakai Island Castle

Sitting on a 2km-long peninsula, attractive Trakai was appointed by Grand Duke Gediminas as Lithuania's capital in the early 14th century. Take the bridge to the **Trakai Island Castle** (*trakaimuziejus.lt; entry adult/child €12/6*) – Lithuania's most photogenic redoubt. Its labyrinthine museum covers the history of the town and the castle, and the setting is worth the day trip from Vilnius.

Aukštaitija National Park

Lithuania's oldest national park

Encompassing dense forest, lakes and wildlife, **Aukštaitija National Park** is the perfect place to enjoy hiking, cycling, swimming, canoeing and paddleboarding. In Palūšė, 8km west of the main town of Ignalina, rent canoes, paddleboards and bikes from **Tiki Tours** (*info.tikitours.lt*). Several of the hiking trails (3.5 to 22km) and cycle loops (25 to 110km) start in Palūšė, taking in the park's tiny settlements and attractions, including Ginučiai's 19th-century watermill and the Ancient Beekeeping Museum near Stripeikiai.

Kaunas, Central & Southern Lithuania

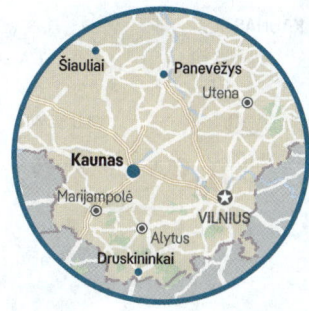

ARCHITECTURE | MUSEUMS | QUIRKY SIGHTS

Sitting at the confluence of the Nemunas and Neris Rivers, Lithuania's second city Kaunas served a two-decade stint as the country's capital after Poland annexed Vilnius in the interwar period. It then became the centre of anti-Soviet dissent when Lithuania was forcibly incorporated into the USSR. Brimming with innovations in art, design and AI, the former European Capital of Culture (2022) is also the home of Lithuanian basketball, and its clutch of excellent museums rivals those in Vilnius.

Kaunas is divided into two halves. The cobbled Old Town has a medieval castle, handsome square and numerous restaurants and churches, while New Town, bisected by the tree- and restaurant-lined Laisvės alėja, features the lion's share of museums, as well as attractive art deco architecture.

North of Kaunas, Šiauliai draws visitors from afar with its unique pilgrimage site; Panevėžys features a superb contemporary art museum. South of Kaunas, Druskininkai entices with its spas and Soviet statuary.

Places

☑ TOP TIP

If you're interested in modernist architecture, book tours of the **Amsterdam School Museum** and/or **Art Deco Museum** in advance. Ditto the **KGB Atomic Bunker** if you're into Soviet memorabilia. Basketball fans: catch a **BC Žalgiris** game in season (Oct–Apr).

🧭 GETTING AROUND

Old Town and New Town are walkable and a 10-minute stroll from one another. Hire a bicycle or Bolt e-scooter from multiple pickup points.

Buses and trolleybuses (*kvt.lt*) run from 5am to 11pm and are handy for reaching outlying attractions. Bus 29G runs hourly to the airport 10km north of the city centre; bus tickets from the driver cost €1.

There are numerous daily trains to Vilnius (one to 1½ hours), plus frequent buses to many destinations.

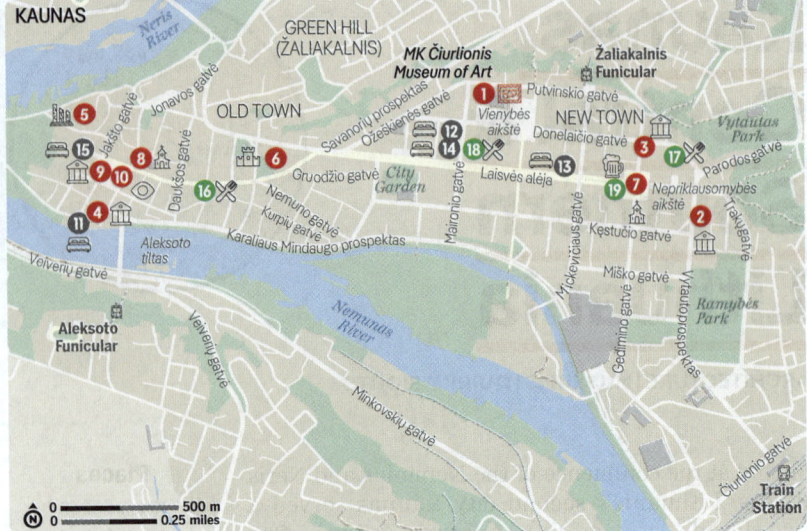

Kaunas

Two re-created apartment museums

Between 2016 and 2021, two young businessmen acquired two apartments from the interwar era, painstakingly restored them and opened them up to private tours. At the **Art Deco Museum** *(artdecomuziejus.lt/en; tours €25),* the 'experiential' small-group excursion feels like an intimate, time-travelling visit to a friend's home. Find out how the Lithuanian well-to-do lived in the interwar period, sit on satin chairs, sip sparkling wine, learn the purposes of unusual furnishings and cutlery, and gain an appreciation for a world that vanished with Soviet occupation.

A few blocks away, at the **Amsterdam School Museum** *(amsterdamomokyklosmuziejus.lt/en; tours €25),* the guide demonstrates clever compartments in cabinets, a hidden side-board in the bedroom and other secret features. You then return to the lounge to learn of the fates of the bon vivant Jewish owner and the other Jewish occupants of the building during the war.

A stroll through Kaunas

Take a stroll around Kaunas' cobbled Old Town, beginning with the **Town Hall Square**, lined with 15th- and 16th-century German merchants' houses and centred on the 17th-century former **Town Hall**. Detour to the magnificent **House of Perkūnas**, a 15th-century merchant's residence, then walk north to the remains of the 14th-century **Kaunas Castle**, a bastion against Teutonic attacks around which the town originally grew. Pass by the red-brick 16th-century **Sts Peter & Paul Cathedral**, then follow the pedestrianised Vilniaus gatvė to the 1826 neo-baroque, interwar **Presidential Palace of Lithuania**. Finally, take New Town's pedestrianised Laisvės alėja to neo-Byzantine **St Michael's Cathedral** (1895) at its eastern end.

The art of MK Čiurlionis

One of Lithuania's oldest and grandest galleries, the **MK Čiurlionis Museum of Art** *(ciurlionis.lt; entry adult/child €10/5)* is the place to acquaint yourself with the paintings of Mikalojus Konstantinas Čiurlionis (1875–1911), arguably the country's greatest modernist artist and composer. Besides the permanent collection of his dreamlike landscapes, themed temporary exhibitions juxtapose his works against contemporary art, while conceptual VR journeys take you deep inside Čiurlionis' paintings. It's closed on Mondays.

Back in the USSR

Enter this former 1960s factory in western Kaunas to find yourself surrounded by busts of Lenin and communist banners. Your guide then ushers you into a Soviet-era atomic shelter designed to protect factory workers from radiation in case of nuclear war. **KGB Atomic Bunker Museum** *(atominis bunkeris.lt, tours by prior arrangement €15)* is a labour of love: an ever-growing private collection of objects from the USSR and beyond. Highlights include the re-created KGB interrogation office with its torture chair, ingenious KGB murder weapons and the gas mask room.

Šiauliai

An unusual pilgrimage site

Some 10km north of Šiauliai is the **Hill of Crosses**, covered in thousands of crosses that symbolise defiance, hope and compassion. Take your time wandering past the rows, taking in fine examples of ironwork, traditional Lithuanian *koplyt-stulpis* (wooden carvings topped with a roof) and magnificent sculptures of the Sorrowful Christ (Rūpintojėlis) – planted in tribute to 9/11 or Covid-19 victims, Ukrainian civilians killed by Russian missiles and a number of other personal reasons.

Panevėžys

Icon-O-Stasys

In central Panevėžys, the minimalist four-storey **Stasys Museum** *(stasysmuseum.com/en; entry adult/child €8/4)* is a fitting tribute to the celebrated local artist Stasys Eidrigevičius. The inaugural Icon-O-Stasys exhibition is an engrossing retrospective of Stasys' artistic endeavours, from his minimalist one-line drawings and the dreamlike world of his *Ex Libris* sketches to surreal photography and the wonderful mask series, *Sorrows*. It's closed on Mondays.

HISTORY OF THE HILL OF CROSSES

Some claim that the Hill of Crosses was created by the bereaved families of warriors killed in battle. Pagan traditions tell of sacred fires being lit here, long before the first crosses appeared (allegedly in the 14th century), multiplying after every uprising against the Russian tsars. Although planting a cross during Soviet times was an arrestable offence, pilgrims continued to commemorate those killed or deported to Siberia. In 1961, the Red Army destroyed the 2000-odd crosses and dug ditches at the hill's base, but overnight more crosses appeared. In 1972, they were destroyed after the immolation of a Kaunas student. Upon Lithuania's independence in 1991, the hill comprised over 40,000 crosses, which have multiplied tenfold since.

 EATING & DRINKING IN KAUNAS: OUR PICKS

Bernelių Užeiga: Munch on herring, meaty stews, beetroot soup and dumplings amid stuffed animal heads and rustic decor. *11am-10pm Sun-Thu, to 11pm Fri & Sat* €

Avilys: Wash down Lithuanian standards or beer snacks with pints of mead or unfiltered house beer in an atmospheric stone cellar. *noon-midnight* €€

Uoksas: Chef Artūras Naidenko crafts tasting menus from sustainable, seasonal ingredients from around the Baltic. *6-10pm Tue-Fri, 3-11pm Sat* €€

Genys Taproom: A heavy-rock soundtrack, outdoor terrace and 10 Kaunas-brewed beers on tap. *5pm-2am Mon-Fri, noon-2am Sat & Sun*

THE ARCHITECTURE OF OPTIMISM

Between 1919 and 1939, when the Polish annexation of Vilnius made Kaunas Lithuania's capital, the city underwent rapid urbanisation. This resulted in the construction of over 1500 buildings in modernist styles, from art deco, neoclassicism and traditionalism to functionalism and the Amsterdam School. Standout examples include the historicist Romuva Cinema with a glass turret (1940) at Laisvės alėja 54; the monumental Church of the Resurrection (1934); the art deco Jewish Bank (1925) at Laisvės alėja 106; and the Fire Station (1932) at Kanto gatvė 1 – a curved building with a concave facade and twin towers. In 2023, 44 buildings in Kaunas' New Town and Žaliakalnis (Green Hill) were granted European Heritage status.

TARTEZY/SHUTTERSTOCK

Grūtas Park

Druskininkai

A Baltic spa day

Experience the genteel spa town of Druskininkai, renowned for centuries for the healing properties of its mineral-rich waters, by drinking said waters at the riverside **Biuvetė**. Then opt for healing mud and mineral-water soaks at the **Medical SPA Eglės Sanatorija**, herbal and vertical baths at **Mana Sleep & Spa**, or mud baths, volcanic stone treatments, salt-room sessions and Charcot's showers at the **Grand Spa Lietuva**.

Graveyard of Soviet statuary

Some 8km east of the spa town of Druskininkai, **Grūtas Park** (*grutoparkas.lt; entry adult/child €15/9*) pays black-humoured homage to a dark period of Lithuania's history. Wander along forested trails flanked by barbed wire, watchtowers and a moat past multiple Lenins, Stalins, prominent Lithuanian communists and freedom fighters.

 EATING IN IN ŠIAULIAI, PANEVĖŽYS & DRUSKININKAI: OUR PICKS

Bleu de Frenkel: Chanterelle soup, Manhattan pizza and cheesecake presented in a dining room in Šiauliai. *11am-10pm Sun-Thu, to 11pm Fri & Sat* €€

Galerija XX: Updated takes on Lithuanian classics, an appealing outdoor terrace and good cheesecake make this a firm Panevėžys favourite. *10am-11pm* €€

Sicilia: Druskininkai's top spot delivers wood-fired pizza and vaguely Italian-style fish and seafood with aplomb. *10am-11pm Sun-Thu, to 11pm Fri & Sat* €€

Bukhara: *Plov* and *shashlik* (grilled meat skewers) are standouts at this carpet-clad Uzbek restaurant in Druskininkai. *noon-10pm Sun-Thu, to 11pm Fri & Sat* €€

Curonian Spit & Western Lithuania

OUTDOOR ADVENTURE | BEACHES | CASTLE

According to legend, the sea goddess Neringa created the long sliver of land that juts out into the Baltic Sea, forming a protected harbour for local fishers. Its natural origins are no less enchanting. The Curonian Spit (Kuršių Nerija) was formed around 5000 years ago and today it's the youngest part of Lithuania: a mile across, 98km long and split almost evenly between Lithuania and Russia. Its dense birch and pine forests, crisscrossed by cycling trails and home to part of the long-distance Baltic Coastal Trail, shelter elks, wild boars and roe deer, while its extraordinary, wind-sculpted giant sand dunes have earned it the nickname 'Lithuania's Sahara'. Stay in one of four picturesque fishing villages – Nida, Juodkrantė, Pervalka or Preila – to explore.

Back on the mainland, Klaipėda (formerly Prussia's Memel) is the gateway to the Spit with a fantastic castle museum. Further north, Palanga is a quintessential Baltic beach resort; both have excellent dining scenes.

☑ **TOP TIP**

The Spit is particularly busy during the summer season (mid-June to end of August) and accommodation prices are high, particularly in Nida; book weeks in advance. Outside of peak season, many restaurants and bars shut down.

Nida
Lithuania's Sahara

Towering over the Curonian village of Nida, the 52m-high **Parnidis Dune** is simultaneously mighty and fragile – a

---

 GETTING AROUND

A passenger ferry connects Klaipėda's Old Ferry Port and the Spit. Car ferries run from Klaipėda's New Ferry Port.

A 50km bicycle trail runs between Nida and Smiltynė; rent bikes in Nida and Juodkrantė. Buses travelling to Nida via Juodkrantė stop in Preila and Pervalka in summer. Buses from

Nida to Kaunas and Vilnius stop in all four villages year-round.

From Klaipėda, trains run to Vilnius (4¼ hours, four daily) via Šiauliai (1¾ hours). Intercity bus destinations include Kaunas, Vilnius, Nida and Šiauliai. Half-hourly buses (25 minutes) connect Klaipėda and Palanga.

NERINGA'S SHIFTING SANDS

Neringa's distinctive landscapes and unique marine, archaeological and cultural heritage are under threat both from human impact and natural forces (the wind and tides). Intensive logging and the resulting deforestation in the 17th and 18th centuries destabilised the sand dunes, which began to move towards the Curonian Lagoon, burying the oldest villages – some relocated several times, trying to outpace the shifting sands.

In 1768, an international commission set about replanting the forests in a bid to anchor the dunes, and there are constant efforts to prevent erosion today using brushwood hedges. But the sands are still moving, at least 1m a year, so it's more important than ever to stick to designated trails.

delicate landscape of mountain pines, meadows and fine blonde sand speckled with purple searocket flowers. A 1700m-long path winds its way along Nida's waterfront through pine forest and then up a steep flight of stairs to a series of boardwalks and viewpoints. At the summit, 'Lithuania's Sahara' – a grand panorama of sand dunes, scrubland and forest – unfolds all the way to the Russian border, a mere 4km away.

Amber creations through the ages

At Nida's state-of-the-art, subtly lit **Mizgiris Amber Museum** (*ambergallery.lt; entry adult/child €12/6*), a dramatic documentary reconstruction plays out on the undulating screen, explaining how amber is created, extracted and processed. Peer at insects suspended within golden depths and peruse chunks of unprocessed amber, millennia-old anthropomorphic figurines, amulets from ancient graves and the Perkūnas (Thunder) Stone – the world's largest piece of amber, weighing 3.8kg. Then venture upstairs to view amber transformed into unusual jewellery and off-the-wall creations by Lithuania's amber masters.

Hike the Baltic Coastal Trail

One of the most scenic stretches of the long-distance **Baltic Coastal Trail** (*baltictrails.eu/en/coastal*), which runs for 1322km from Lithuania's Nida to Tallinn, Estonia, is the 18km-long day hike from Nida to Pervalka. Follow it around Bulvikis Cape, through pine forest, past coastal reeds and birdlife, and around Preilos Bay and its small sandy beach. In Preila, ascend Preilos Hill (57m) for spectacular views of the Curonian Lagoon. Passing another small sandy beach in Karvaiciu Bay, skirt Pervalkos Cape before finding yourself in one-street Pervalka. Press on through pine woods to Zirgu ragas (Horse Cape) for fantastic vistas of the huge Dead Dunes in the distance.

Adrenaline adventures

In summer, take to the waters of the Curonian Lagoon on an SUP or canoe, rented from Nida operator **Irklakojis** (*irklakojis.lt; €10 per hour*). Alternatively, join one of their paddleboarding tours or a 'blokarting' safari (windsurfing on land) along the beach that stretches along the Baltic side of the Curonian Spit. Alternatively, head for **Neringos Sporto Mokykla** to learn flyboarding (*€20 per hour*) or wingfoiling (*€60 per hour*). Winter adrenaline thrills include ice-blokarting.

 EATING ON THE CURONIAN SPIT: OUR PICKS

Tik Pas Joną: Select mackerel, carp or eel from the smoking rack, then wash it down with *gira* or beer on tap in Nida. Takeaway available. *11am-10pm* €€

Sena Sodyba: Cold beetroot soup, dumplings and platefuls of grilled meat with all the trimmings, served in a garden setting in Nida. *noon-9pm* €

Juodkrantės Šašlykinė: The wonderfully marinated grilled pork and chicken *shashlik* hit your palate just right at this casual spot in Juodkrantė. *noon-10pm* €

Žvejonė: Chow down on grilled halibut, eel soup and other fish specialities at this waterfront Juodkrantė restaurant. *noon-10pm* €€

Witches' Hill

Juodkrantė

Among the witches

Follow the Raganų Kalnas sign into the old-growth forest in Juodkrantė to a coven of wooden sculptures that's taken shape along a woodland trail up **Witches' Hill** since 1979. The figures represent various characters from regional folklore, from knights, devils and dwarves to Neringa the sea goddess, a witch with a lopsided bosom and an intricately carved Lucifer peering through the Gates of Hell.

Klaipėda

City defences, Prussian-style

Founded by the Teutonic Order in the 13th century, the moat-protected **Klaipėda Castle** *(mlimuziejus.lt; entry adult/ child €7/3.50)* was revamped in 2021. The high-tech museum inside its restored curtainwalls and tunnels tells the story of Klaipėda from its origins to post-Soviet independence, with presentations enhanced by clever interactive elements. In a separate tunnel, the bunker-like **Museum 39/45** captures Lithuania's suffering during WWII with its tense background music, wartime paraphernalia and digital displays. The castle is closed on Mondays.

 EATING IN KLAIPĖDA & PALANGA: OUR PICKS

Stora Antis: This atmospheric 19th-century cellar elevates classic Lithuanian fare (baked duck, bean soup, pan-fried plaice) to haute-cuisine heights. *6-11pm Fri & Sat* €€

Etno Dvaras: Rustic Lithuanian mini-chain serves potato pancakes, roast meat with horseradish, soups and homemade *gira*. *11.30am-11pm Sun-Thu, noon-1am Fri & Sat* €

Žuvinė: Dine on zander with beetroot cream, smoked eel or halibut with black lentils in an interior straight out of *Architects' Digest*. *11am-10pm Sun-Thu, to midnight Fri & Sat* €€

Restoranas 1925: Committed to dairy fats and filling dumplings, this handsome timbered tavern has been catering to hungry crowds since 1925. *11am-11pm Thu-Sun* €

LIFE'S A BEACH IN NERINGA

A 50km-broad sweep of white sand that's so fine it squeaks underfoot, the Neringa beach spans the length of the Baltic side of the Spit. Dune-backed and pine-scented, it's divided into sections. The beach sections nearest to Nida, Juodkrantė, Preila and Pervalka are separated into mixed, women only (clothing is optional on women-only and nudist stretches) and pet-friendly sections and marked accordingly. Changing booths, steps down to the beach and volleyball courts are de rigueur. The Blue Flag beaches in Nida and Juodkrantė come with lifeguard stations, Nida's beach is wheelchair-accessible and the waters are shallow and hugely popular with families. Outside the designated beaches, you have vast stretches of sand entirely to yourself.

Palanga beach

Palanga

A beach holiday, Lithuanian style

Stroll Palanga's pedestrianised, pine-fringed **Basanavičiaus gatvė** for a full-on sensory assault of beeping arcade machines, bungee trampolines, merry-go-rounds, bumper cars, portrait artists, restaurants and beer gardens. The smells of pine, candy floss and popcorn fill the air as buskers serenade passers-by and beachgoers queue up for ice cream. At the western end you'll find Palanga's 18km-long, white-sand **beach**, reachable via wooden boardwalks that lead through the forest and over the dunes and are punctuated with beach bars. The atmosphere is relaxed and welcoming, and lazy days of sunbathing and swimming beckon.

Discover the Amber Museum

Housed inside a 19th-century neoclassical palace, built by Count Feliksas Tyszkiewicz in 1897 at the heart of Palanga's Botanical Park, Palanga's fantastic **Amber Museum** (*lndm.lt/pgm; entry adult/child €8/4*) is home to 30,000 pieces of 'Baltic gold'. The exhibits take visitors through all aspects of amber, from its formation and collection to its use in human adornment, from Neolithic times to the present day. Don't miss terrific temporary exhibitions of leading Lithuanian jewellery designers. It's closed on Mondays.

Places We Love to Stay

€ Budget €€ Midrange €€€ Top End

Vilnius
MAP p257

Jimmy Jumps House € Movie nights, pub crawls, tank-driving tours and free waffles at this centrally located party hostel.

25 Hours Hostel € Arty loft dorms, snug doubles, women-only digs, guest kitchen and fantastic Gates of Dawn location.

Bernardinų B&B €€ Baroque flourishes and original frescoes make each room unique at this family-owned B&B within an 18th-century townhouse.

Domus Maria €€ This austere guesthouse inside a former 17th-century monastery features spacious rooms, some with Gates of Dawn views.

The Joseph €€ Original brick walls and heavy wooden beams highlight contemporary art in seven individually styled rooms in this 19th-century building.

Artagonist €€€ Stylish art-filled rooms, a giant wall mural and glass dome await at this 19th-century merchant house.

Hotel Pacai €€€ Slumber beneath timber beams amid centuries-old statuary at this restored 17th-century palace with gourmet restaurants.

Aukštaitija National Park

Tiki Inn € Polynesia-themed lakeside inn in Palūšė, with a terrace for sunset watching, hot tubs, sauna, free water-sports equipment and spartan rooms.

Lake & Library Hotel €€ Ignalina's lovely boutique hotel, with individually curated rooms overlooking Gavys Lake, a beach and volleyball court. Excellent breakfast.

Kaunas
MAP p262

Monk's Bunk Kaunas € Backpackers trade travel stories at Kaunas' well-equipped original hostel; spacious dorms and a knowledgeable host.

Villa Kaunensis € Spartan rooms with high ceilings overlooking Old Town square; the guest kitchen is a boon.

Moxy €€ Instagrammable bar and sleek, minimalist rooms await at this trendy New Town spot.

Daugirdas Hotel €€ At this handsome Old Town boutique hotel, 16th-century stonework and timber beams come with heated floors and jacuzzis.

HOF Hotel €€ Super-central yet quiet New Town location, helpful staff, business-style rooms and apartments with balconies.

Šiauliai

Juro Guest House € Spotless guesthouse located a short stroll away from most museums; super-helpful owner.

Šaulys Hotel €€ Šiauliai's swankiest choice has plush rooms in understated greys, a 1950s-style restaurant and English-speaking staff.

Panevėžys

Conviva Hotel €€ Tall ceilings, crimson carpets, sizeable rooms and a central location off the main square.

Hotel Romantic €€€ A converted old mill with Panevėžys' plushest rooms and an excellent restaurant terrace overlooking the park.

Druskininkai

Art Hotel €€ Wooden mansion comprising spacious studios in soothing blues and whites, with bold contemporary art and high-beamed family apartments.

Aqua Hotel €€ Perfect for a family stay, this three-star hotel is part of the vast Aqua Park complex; good breakfast buffet.

Curonian Spit

Sodyba Nidoje € Five spotless ensuite rooms in a central traditional wooden house in Nida, with kitchen access and picnic tables in the garden.

Miško Namas €€ Nab a room with a balcony or kitchenette at this immaculate Nida guesthouse with a library and garden.

Vila Flora €€ Central 19th-century timber villa in Juodkrantė, with split-level rooms.

Klaipėda

Preliudija € Minimalist, modern rooms await at this handsome mid-19th-century guesthouse in the heart of Old Town.

Michaelson Boutique Hotel €€ Atmospheric 18th-century warehouse comes with updated wood-beamed rooms in sleek greys and creams overlooking the Danė River.

Palanga

Vila Ramybė € Individually styled pastel-hued rooms (some with terraces) on a quiet street.

Life Balance Spa Hotel €€€ A spa and floor-to-ceiling windows are the perks at this glass-and-chrome stunner in a pine grove.

Practicalities

LGBTIQ+ Travellers

Lithuania is one of EU's lowest-ranked countries for LGBTIQ+ rights: homosexuality is decriminalised but same-sex marriage is banned and social attitudes are conservative. Vilnius, Kaunas and Klaipėda have small gay scenes. The National LGBT Rights Organization (*lgl.lt*) is a useful resource for travellers.

Electricity

Lithuania's electricity supply is 230V and plugs are mostly of the European two-round-pin variety. Travelers from outside Europe usually need an adapter.

Smoking

It's prohibited to smoke in restaurants and other enclosed public spaces (including bus stops) in Lithuania, as well as outdoor cafe and bar terraces. The same rules apply to vaping.

Visas

Visas are not required for citizens of the EU, USA, Canada, Japan, New Zealand, Australia or the UK for visits up to 90 days. From late 2025 onwards, non-EU visitors may need to apply for an ETIAS visa waiver in advance in order to be allowed to enter the Schengen area. Visit migracija.lt for further information.

LUKAS JUOCAS/SHUTTERSTOCK

Kaunas (p262)

Opening Hours

Banks 9am–5pm Monday to Friday
Government offices 8am–5pm Monday to Friday
Post offices 9am–7pm Monday to Friday, 9am to 2pm Saturday
Restaurants noon–11pm
Shops 9am–7pm Monday to Saturday; some open Sunday

Language

Symbols on vowels in written Lithuanian indicate they are pronounced as long sounds.
Hello. Sveiki. svay·ki
Goodbye. Viso gero. vi·so ge·ro
Excuse me. Atleiskite. at·lays·ki·te
Please. Prašau. pra·show
Thank you. Ačiū. aa·choo
Yes. Taip. taip
No. Ne. ne
I don't understand. Aš nesuprantu. ash ne·su·pran·tu
Cheers! Į sveikatą! ee svay·kaa·taa

Public Holidays

New Year's Day 1 January
Independence Day 16 February
Lithuanian Independence Restoration Day 11 March
Easter Sunday & Monday March/April
International Labour Day 1 May
Feast of St John (Midsummer) 24 June
Statehood Day 6 July
Assumption of Blessed Virgin 15 August
All Saints' Day 1 November
Christmas (Kalėdos) 25 and 26 December

MONEY

Currency: Euro (€)

CASH & CARD
Multilingual ATMs are ubiquitous in cities and towns; even villages are likely to have one. Carry cash for small purchases (museums, bus tickets, market produce).

DIGITAL PAYMENTS
Digital payments are the norm at most businesses, particularly in bigger towns and cities. In rural destinations it's a good idea to carry cash.

TIPPING
Tipping 10% in restaurants is the norm; even if paying by card, tip with cash. In hotels, tipping is restricted to top-end establishments. Taxi drivers don't expect a tip; round up the fare for assistance with baggage.

Arriving & Getting Around

There are a variety of ways to get to Lithuania, including flights to its two main airports (Vilnius and Kaunas), two international ferry services, and train and bus services from across Europe.

Arriving by Air
Lithuania's two main airports are in Vilnius and Kaunas. Palanga Airport receives seasonal summer flights. Vilnius Airport is connected to central Vilnius by train and bus. Ryanair hub Kaunas is served by buses.

Arriving by Bus, Train & Boat
Eurolines and Lux Express buses connect Vilnius and Kaunas to Europe. A daily train links Kraków and Warsaw with Tallinn and Riga via Kaunas and Vilnius. Ferries from Kiel (Germany) and Karlshamn (Sweden) dock in Klaipėda.

Driving Essentials
Lithuanian roads are in good condition; car hire is offered in all major cities. Spark *(spark.lt)* is the electric carshare service. Winter tyres are compulsory from mid-November through March. Blood alcohol limit is 0.4g/L.

Getting Around
Lithuania's national bus network links all major cities and smaller towns. Buy tickets using the Autobusų Bilietai *(autobusubilietai.lt)* website or app. Larger cities and towns are well covered by public transport. LTG trains *(ltglink.lt)* are comfortable and cheap; handy routes include Vilnius to Kaunas, Vilnius to Klaipėda via Šiauliai, and Vilnius to Ignalina.

Curated by
Owen Morton

Moldova

UNDERGROUND WINE LABYRINTHS AND SOVIET MEMORABILIA

Visitors to Moldova love its cosmopolitan capital and excellent wine, as well as its quirky, Soviet-tinged breakaway state.

Wedged between Romania and Ukraine, Moldova is for the most part culturally Romanian but spent the latter half of the 20th century as part of the Soviet Union. Its road to independence was rocky, with a short civil war eventually leading to the establishment of the breakaway state of Transnistria, and political crises and corruption defining the 1990s and early 2000s. Since 2009, however, the country has begun to steer a path towards EU membership. And now, thanks to the expansion of budget airlines, it's seen an increase in travellers looking to discover a less-heralded destination.

It's easy to see the country's appeal: the capital, Chișinău, is a lively city and convenient base for trips to the further-flung areas. And anyone with a passing interest in wine should pay a visit to one of Moldova's wine cellars: the most impressive are Milestii Mici and Cricova, both of which comprise hundreds of kilometres of limestone tunnels. Further north, Soroca offers insight into small-town Moldova. To the south, Căușeni's colourful frescoes delight admirers of Byzantine-style church art.

But it's fair to say that Moldova is most famed for Transnistria, a breakaway state where the Soviet Union lives on. Blocky architecture, concrete monuments, extensive use of the hammer-and-sickle motif and statues of Lenin standing proudly in front of brutalist government offices provide the rare opportunity to travel back in time to the USSR.

MAZUR TRAVEL/SHUTTERSTOCK

THE MAIN AREAS

CHIȘINĂU	**ORHEIUL VECHI**	**SOROCA**	**TRANSNISTRIA**
Cosmopolitan capital city. **p276**	Cave monasteries in a river valley. **p281**	Low-key riverside town. **p283**	USSR-flavoured breakaway state. **p284**

For places to stay in Moldova, see p287

TRABANTOS/SHUTTERSTOCK

Left: Wine cellar, Cricova (p281); **Above:** St Mary's Church (p282), Orheiul Vechi

Find Your Way

Moldova is a relatively small country. The capital Chişinău is centrally located; it makes sense to base yourself here and explore the outlying sights on day trips.

BUS

There are good bus and minibus connections throughout Moldova, starting at the three bus stations in Chişinău. The tourist office can provide up-to-date information on which bus station serves which destination.

CAR

Driving in Moldova is easy, and offers the opportunity to see the country at your own pace. Roads are well maintained, driving standards are relatively high, parking is easy and there's rarely much traffic.

Transnistria, p284

A breakaway self-declared country, Transnistria evokes the long-gone days of the USSR.

Soroca, p283

The northern riverside town of Soroca is centred around a medieval castle.

Orheiul Vechi, p281

The country's top archaeological site contains ruins from every era of Moldovan history.

Chişinău, p276

Moldova's friendly capital is home to several diverting museums, as well as attractive parks and the finest restaurants and bars in the country.

UKRAINE

ROMANIA

Black Sea

0   40 km
0   20 miles

Odesa
Palanaca
Tiraspol
Bendery
Căuşeni
Basarabeasca
Grigoriopol
CHIŞINĂU
Dubăsari
Orheiul Vechi
Orhei
Criuleni
Cricova
Călăraşi
Rîbniţa
Hânceşti
Cimişlia
Comrat
Cahul
Vulcăneşti
Ungheni
Bârlad
Vaslui
Tecuci
Iaşi
Făleşti
Bălţi
Floreşti
Soroca
Camenca
Stânca Costeşti
Briceni
Ocniţa
Mogyliv-Podilsky
Yampil
Dniester
Nistru (Dniestr)
Prut

LEONID ANDRONOV/SHUTTERSTOCK

Arc de Triomphe (p276), Chişinău

Plan Your Time

Moldova's relatively small size means you can get a good sense of the country over a long weekend, but giving yourself extra time will allow you to dig deeper.

A Weekend in Chişinău

● Spend day one exploring **Chişinău** (p276): wander its parks and grand avenues, visit the museums and enjoy a stop in a cafe. On day two, take a day trip: either head to **Bender** (p284) for a surreal sense of return to the USSR or join a tour at **Milestii Mici** (p280) to enjoy a subterranean trip through Moldova's wine industry.

A Week to Explore

● With a week, you can take in most of Moldova's highlights. After visiting **Chişinău** (p276), **Bender** (p284)) and **Milestii Mici** (p280), head north to the country's foremost archaeological site, **Orheiul Vechi** (p281), and continue on to the riverside town of **Soroca** (p283) for an overnight stay. Or visit the gorgeous Byzantine-style frescoes in Căuşeni's **Church of the Assumption** (p286).

SEASONAL HIGHLIGHTS

SPRING
Milder temperatures make this a great time to spend a weekend in the city.

SUMMER
The country comes alive with bustling pavement cafes in towns and colourful countryside wildflowers.

AUTUMN
Early September is the grape harvest season: this is the perfect time to enjoy a wine-focused visit.

WINTER
It's dark and cold in winter, but if you catch a sunny day, the country is gorgeous under a blanket of snow.

Chișinău

SOVIET ARCHITECTURE | PAVEMENT CAFES | GREEN PARKS

GETTING AROUND

Although Chișinău is a reasonably large city, travellers will probably want to stick to the central area, which is very walkable: it's mostly flat, and the streets are laid out in a grid pattern that makes it easy to navigate. Minibuses and trolleybuses ply the route along the central Ștefan cel Mare Boulevard, and you may also need them to reach the north or south bus stations (route 9 goes to both). Taxis are easy to flag down and inexpensive. If you're driving, parking is free almost everywhere except around Cathedral Park.

☑ TOP TIP

Chișinău's friendly and helpful tourist office, just southeast of Cathedral Park, has plenty of information on things to do around the entire country. Their bus timetables tell you which of the three bus stations you need to reach your destination.

From its origins as a small medieval village, Chișinău grew into a city after Moldova became part of the Russian Empire in the 19th century. Largely flattened in WWII, it was rebuilt in classic Soviet style, with wide avenues, concrete apartment blocks and socialist-realist monuments. It went through a rough patch after independence, but has now emerged as a welcoming, cosmopolitan city with a lively pavement cafe culture (in summer, at least), diverting museums and excellent restaurants, bars and hotels. Although there may not be any traditional must-see attractions here, Chișinău is an extremely pleasant place and you could find yourself spending more time here than you expected.

Enjoy Chișinău's Central Green Space

Explore Cathedral Park

Any exploration of Chișinău should begin in **Cathedral Park**, which is centred around the city's cathedral, a vast, white domed beast with a separate bell tower. Southwest of the cathedral is Chișinău's very own **Arc de Triomphe**, erected in 1870 to celebrate Russia's victory over the Ottoman Empire. In summer, the park is a popular gathering spot.

Delve into Moldova's Past

Tread the palatial halls of the National History Museum

To get an introduction to Moldova's past, head to the **National History Museum** (*nationalmuseum.md; entry 50MDL; closed Mon*). Don't miss the remarkable hoard of ancient Greek armour found at Olănești – the bronze Attican helmet with carved panthers on the sides is especially fine – after which there's a wealth of exhibits from the 19th and 20th centuries. Finally, in the basement, there's an unflinching exhibition exploring the Gulag system and the crimes of the Soviet regime.

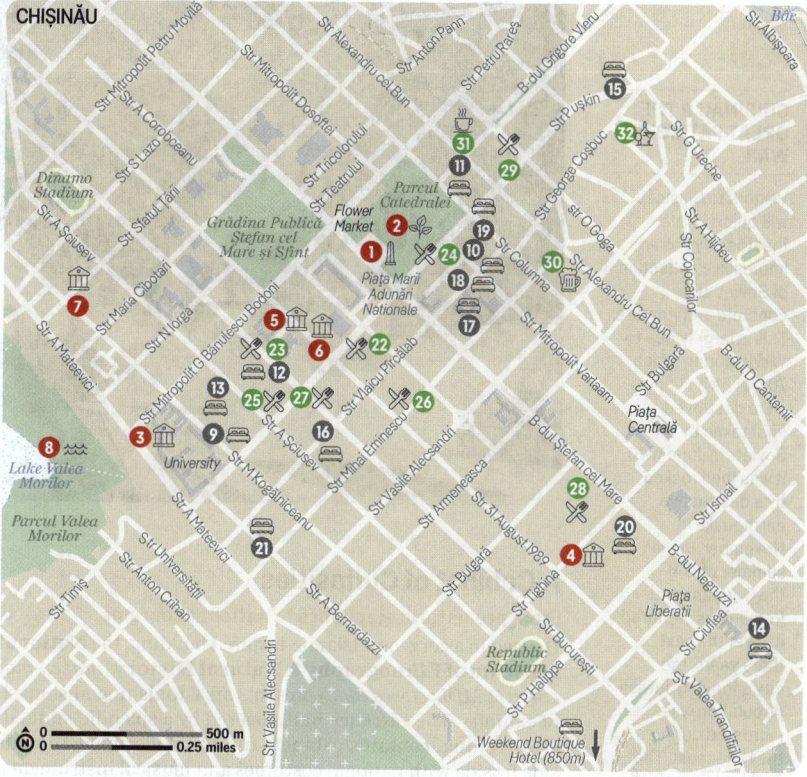

CHIȘINĂU

An Introduction to Moldovan Art

Explore the grandiose Fine Arts Museum

Art lovers should head straight to the **National Museum of Art** (mnam.md; entry 50MDL; closed Mon). The ground floor is home to contemporary sculpture, early-20th-century portraiture, and religious icons, while upstairs you'll find more recent works. Mihau Grecu and Valentina Rusu-Ciobani – Moldova's most celebrated 20th-century artists – are well represented here. Rusu-Ciobani's *Friendship* is particularly fun, depicting a crowd of people sporting delightful 1970s clothing and hairstyles.

CHIȘINĂU & THE GREAT PATRIOTIC WAR

Visitors to Chișinău will quickly note that the city has an impressive collection of Soviet-style concrete architecture. This is largely due to WWII, during which 70% of its buildings were destroyed. First taken by the Soviets in June 1940, it was then rocked by a destructive earthquake in November. In the summer of 1941 the Germans and Romanians captured it. Over the next three years, the city's thriving Jewish population was murdered during the Holocaust. The Red Army eventually retook the city in August 1944. The city's **Military History Museum** *(entry 50MDL)* offers an engaging look at these events, though note that the exhibits do not shy away from the horrors of war.

A Cabinet of Curiosities

From prehistoric elephants to national costume

Housed in a gorgeous, Islamic-inspired building, the **National Museum of Ethnography & Natural History** (*muzeu.md; entry 50MDL; closed Mon*) presents an astonishing mishmash of exhibits. The entrance hall, covered by a splendid stained-glass ceiling, contains cabinets full of taxidermied animals side by side with national costumes and musical instruments. Other impressive displays include a detailed topographic model of Moldova and an enormous fossil skeleton of a deinotherium (a type of prehistoric elephant).

Lenin at the Lake

Take a stroll in Valea Morilor Park

Another of Chișinău's attractive green spaces, the **Valea Morilor Park** is centred around a large lake. You'll likely enter the park near the Graeco-Roman rotunda, from which you can descend the Cascades, an ornate staircase that passes pleasant fountains and colourful flower beds. At the bottom, head to your right to circumnavigate the lake – keep your eyes

DRINKING IN CHIȘINĂU: OUR PICKS

Alt Ceva: Popular craft-beer pub with an industrial vibe and old-school cartoons playing on a big screen. *4pm-2am Mon-Thu, to 4am Fri & Sat, to midnight Sun*

Crème de la Crème: Chișinău's best people-watching spot, on the corner of the pedestrian Str Eugen Doga. *7.30am-9.30pm Mon-Fri, 8am-10pm Sat & Sun*

Marlène: Fabulously decadent cocktail bar that evokes the 1920s. Settle into the velvet chairs and enjoy the jazzy soundtrack. *4-11pm Mon-Fri, to midnight Sat & Sun*

Via Wine Bar: This wine bar is a short walk from Cathedral Park, with a well-selected list of Moldovan wines. *10am-10pm Mon-Fri, from noon Sat & Sun*

TRABANTOS/SHUTTERSTOCK

Valea Morilor Park

FROM MEDIEVAL VILLAGE TO MODERN CITY

Chișinău isn't a particularly old place: the first known mention dates from 1436, when it was an insignificant village in the Principality of Moldavia. Its growth into a city took place in the 19th century, after it became a part of the Russian Empire in 1812.

Following the Russian Revolution, it became the capital of the short-lived Moldavian Democratic Republic; 20 years later, the city was almost entirely destroyed in World War II. During the Soviet years, Chișinău became the capital of the Moldavian SSR and subsequently the capital of independent Moldova in 1991.

open for the tiny golden sculpture of the Little Prince, which sits atop one of the fence posts. At the west end of the park, Lenin hunters can veer to the right to reach the Madison Park events venue, outside which stands a statue of old Vladimir.

Close to the park is the defiantly old-school **City History Museum** (*facebook.com/muzeul.chisinaului; entry 50MDL; closed Mon),* housed in a gorgeous 19th-century water tower. Its cabinets full of dusty artefacts and photographs tell the story of Chișinău's history from its origins through to 1991, at which point history abruptly stops. The room covering the later Soviet period, with its delightfully retro tape players and DJ decks, is particularly diverting.

 ## EATING IN CHIȘINĂU: OUR PICKS

Black Rabbit Gastro Burrow: Smart restaurant with a stylish industrial feel, serving modern European dishes and decent veggie options. *10am–midnight* €€

Fuior: Upmarket, central restaurant with a contemporary Moldovan menu: try the carp fillet with polenta or the braised lamb with carrot cream. *11am–11pm* €€€

Taifas: Atmospheric restaurant serving traditional Romanian dishes, often accompanied by folk-music performances. *11am–10pm Mon–Sat, to 9pm Sun* €€

Wine Gogh: Stylish basement restaurant with a meaty menu and Van Gogh–inspired decor. *11am–10pm Mon, 11am–11pm Tue–Fri, noon–11pm Sat & Sun* €€

Eli-Pili: Eclectically decorated place with an extensive menu of light meals such as pancakes and dumplings. It's also a lively bar by night. *9am–2am* €

Little Napoli: Chișinău's best pizza restaurant has a wood-fired oven, cosy dining room and pavement seating for summer evenings. *11am–10pm* €€

Sincer: Popular modern cafe offering healthy breakfast and lunch choices, including soups, salads and sandwiches. *8am–9pm* €

Tbilisi: This garden restaurant has a menu of Georgian cuisine: *khachapuri* cheese breads, hearty stews and *khinkali* dumplings. *11am–11pm Mon–Sat, 11am–10pm Sun* €€

Beyond
Chișinău

UNDERGROUND WINERIES | PAINTED CHURCHES | SOVIET TIME CAPSULE

GETTING AROUND

The majority of destinations throughout the country can be reached by bus from one of Chișinău's three bus stations; if in doubt, the tourist office can tell you which station you need. If you're self-driving, the country is easy to navigate, with well-maintained roads originating in the capital and plenty of helpful signposting.

A number of Moldova's highlights can be found outside Chișinău, where the sights take in the full span of the country's history. The Orheiul Vechi archaeological site is one of Moldova's top outings, its ruins spread along an attractive river valley. In the northern town of Soroca, you'll find a splendid fortress. To the east, meanwhile, is the breakaway republic of Transnistria, in which the spirit of the USSR lingers on. Closer to Chișinău, meanwhile, are the wineries of Milestii Mici and Cricova, which produce some of the country's best wines and occupy remarkable underground labyrinths of limestone tunnels. These two destinations are perfect for a day of wine tasting.

Milestii Mici

TIME FROM CHIȘINĂU: **30MIN** 🚗 / 🚌

Marvel at the world's largest wine collection

Just 14km south of Chișinău is the massive **Milestii Mici** wine producer and cellar *(milestii-mici.md; tours from 350MDL)*. Buggies convey visitors from the beautiful gardens – complete with fountains dispensing wine-coloured water (red and white) – into chilly subterranean tunnels. Originally a limestone mine, the 200km of tunnels here are a consistent 12°C to 14°C year-round – ideal for wine storage, for which the passages have been used since 1968.

The tour's highlight is a visit to the remarkable labyrinth that is the bottle-storage chamber, which is listed in the Guinness World Records as the world's largest wine collection, comprising 1.5 million bottles. You'll also see the hidden room where 50,000 of the winery's most valuable bottles were stashed to escape destruction under Gorbachev's 1985 prohibition law, before emerging through some enjoyably Indiana Jones-esque secret doors into the tasting room. Inevitably, there's also a wine bar in the garden. It's the perfect spot for a cheap glass or two.

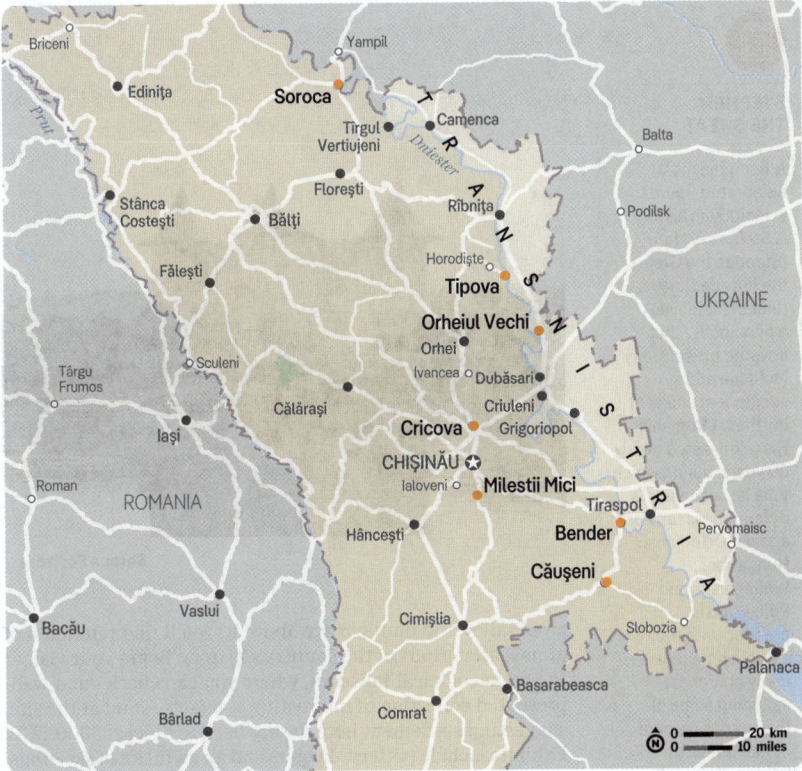

Cricova

TIME FROM CHIŞINĂU: **30MIN** /

Limestone tunnels and celebrity wine storage

The **Cricova Wine Cellars** *(cricova.md; tours from 600MDL)* are an easy 15km north of Chişinău and offer a similar cellar tour in another former limestone mine. Stop first in an underground cinema for a somewhat excitable film about the history of wine in general and at Cricova in particular. Afterward, you'll visit the sparkling wine–production plant and have a look around the wine-storage chamber where famous personalities ranging from Angela Merkel to Michelle Yeoh keep their wines. Not on display is the sizeable portion of Herman Göring's wine collection, seized by the USSR at the end of WWII and now stored here. The final stop is in the grandiose complex of tasting rooms. The nautically themed one is the most impressive, if a little inexplicable.

Orheiul Vechi

TIME FROM CHIŞINĂU: **1HR** /

Moldova's most important archaeological site

Spread around the village of **Butuceni** (and not, confusingly, the namesake town of Orhei) is the archaeological site of **Orheiul Vechi** *(orheiulvechi.com; entry free).* In this striking

---

☑ TOP TIP

Most places can be reached as a day trip from Chişinău, though Soroca is far enough away that an overnight stay is advisable, unless you're on a very tight timeframe.

281

STEPHEN THE GREAT

Among the most celebrated figures in Moldovan history is Ștefan cel Mare (Stephen the Great), the 15th-century ruler of Moldavia, a principality that covered present-day Moldova and a substantial chunk of northeast Romania. His reign lasted nearly 50 years, during which time he successfully defended his territory against Ottomans, Hungarians, Wallachians and Poles, and is credited with the establishment of many churches, including some of the famous painted monasteries in Romania's Suceava County. After his death he became a national hero, inspiring Romanian and Moldovan nationalism throughout the 19th and 20th centuries. Look for him on every denomination of the lei banknote.

OKSANA2010/SHUTTERSTOCK

Soroca Fortress

river valley and on the ridge above it, you'll find remnants of almost all periods of the country's history. Begin your visit at the archaeological museum, where you can check out a well-presented collection of interesting artefacts found at the site, suggesting settlement here dating back to at least 3500 BCE. Exhibits include pottery, daggers and an awful lot of skeletons.

Walk up the road into the village of Butuceni where the main sites are located. Call in at the **ethnographic museum** – a small dwelling done up as a 19th-century homestead – then head uphill via the stairs, aiming for the gold-domed roof of **St Mary's Church**. The church stands at the centre of what was once an ancient fortress that occupied this strategic spot, commanding fine views of the river valley on either side. It's worth taking a walk beyond the church along the ridge to enjoy those views. About five minutes on, the surefooted can descend a rough but marked path on the ridge's north side to reach the **Bosie cave monastery**, an extensive collection of cells and chambers hewn into the cliff. Don't miss the medieval Slavonic inscription adorning the doorway of the easternmost cave.

 EATING AROUND ORHEIUL VECHI

Eco-Resort Butuceni: Attractively rustic place neaer the Ethnographic Museum, with a slightly touristy menu of traditional cuisine. *10am-10pm* €€

Inspir: Small snack hut ideal for relaxing in a deckchair or hammock with a coffee or ice cream. On the opposite side of the valley from Butuceni. *10am-8pm* €

Moara Veche: For a light lunch, this hole-in-the-wall in the village is perfect: the menu includes paninis and pastries, and the coffee is good. *10am-6pm Wed-Sun* €

Villa Etníca: In the centre of the village is this hotel-restaurant, with a good menu of decent Moldovan meals. *noon-10pm* €€

Returning the other way along the ridge, the bell tower marks the entrance to tiny **Pestera cave monastery**, less extensive than Bosie but considerably easier to access. It's also of interest as it's still in use as an active church filled with icons, candles and incense.

Elsewhere in the valley lie scattered ruins from various eras, including the remains of a mosque and a church, and the fairly sizeable Turkish bathhouse down by the river. A reasonably well-marked walking trail links all the spots of interest. You can pick up a map at the museum or car park booth. Expect to spend from several hours to a full day here.

Tipova
TIME FROM CHIȘINĂU: 1½HR 🚗/🚌

Clerics in the caves

One of Moldova's more unusual religious establishments, the **Tipova Monastery** *(entry 10MDL)* is hollowed into the limestone cliffs on the west bank of the Dnister River, about 100km north of Chișinău. From the parking area, walk to the right of the modern yellow church, following a track towards the cliff edge, where you'll find rough stone steps leading down to the ticket booth. From here you can enter the monastery to the right, which dates back at least as far as 1700. Some chambers are just bare rock, some remain in use as a church or simple shrines, and others have been converted into an informative museum. If you take the path to the left from the ticket booth, you'll find older and simpler cave monastery complexes, including one in which legend claims King Stephen the Great married one of his wives.

Soroca
TIME FROM CHIȘINĂU: 2¼HRS 🚗/🚌

Views from castle ramparts

For an enjoyable day trip to one of Moldova's smaller cities, head to Soroca, which has a pair of distinctive attractions. The principal draw is the splendid **Soroca Fortress** *(facebook .com/cetatesoroca; entry 30MDL; closed Mon & Tue)*, which sits down by the Dnister River and is marvellously picturesque, with five witch-hat turrets. Inside, the doors off the central courtyard lead to rooms with museum displays of limited interest; more enticing is the chance to climb onto the ramparts and enjoy views over the town and river.

Elsewhere, from a small car park just south of town, you can ascend the 647 steps to the somewhat phallic **Candle of Gratitude** *(entry free),* an immense finger of concrete

MOLDOVA & THE VINE

Moldova's winemaking tradition may extend as far back as 2800 BCE, though it seems the region first became known for its wine in the late medieval period under the reign of Stephen the Great. By 1914, it was the principal winemaking region of the Russian Empire, a position it retained while part of the USSR. The vineyards suffered a setback during the 1980s following Gorbachev's campaign against alcohol, but since independence the industry has flourished anew, exporting its wine primarily to the EU. The country produces both red and white varieties, though the reds are arguably better. Those from the Purcari Winery are particularly celebrated.

 EATING IN SOROCA

Coffee In: Just next to the fortress, this simple little place is handy for a pick-me-up coffee and pastry. *7.30am-11.30pm* €

Dulcinella: Have a sweet tooth? Make a beeline for Dulcinella. There's a delightful selection of cakes and pastries, washed down by good strong coffee. *8am-8pm* €

La Faleza: Soroca's best restaurant has a delicious menu that's primarily Asian, but also stretches to steak, pizza and pasta. *10am-10pm Tue-Sun, from noon Mon* €€

Salat: On Soroca's central square, Salat offers an extensive budget menu, with options ranging from soups and salads to steaks and sushi. *10am-10pm* €

standing atop a hill. It houses an uninteresting chapel, and is primarily worth a visit for the splendid views over town and the Dnister River, with western Ukraine on the other side.

Transnistria

TIME FROM CHIȘINĂU: 1¼HR 🚗 / 🚌

Moldova is perhaps best known for being home to the breakaway state of **Transnistria**, a self-governing, self-declared independent country that occupies the territory east of the Dnister River. Infamous for its apparent refusal to accept the fall of the Soviet Union, Transnistria retains a unique vibe, with statues of Lenin, eternal flames and blocky monuments galore.

With the exception of the town of **Bender**, the UK FCDO advises against travelling to the territory of Transnistria, owing to the region being outside the control of the Moldovan government. That said, many travellers visit the area trouble-free: there are numerous tour operators – including **PMR Tours** *(pmr-tours.com)* and **Young Pioneers** *(young pioneertours.com)* – who can arrange trips. It's also easy to visit independently by taking the frequent buses from Chişinău. Even self-driving into the territory presents no problems. The main pitfall to be wary of is the territory's name: it prefers the Russian-language Pridnestrovie, even to the extent of declaring that using the term Transnistria is illegal.

There are entry points to Transnistria on all the main roads into Bender. You'll need your passport, and though entry is technically free, be prepared to pay a fee of between €5 and €10. If you're driving, you'll also need to wait while forms are filled out authorising your entry. The process rarely takes longer than half an hour. Once you're in, you'll need some money: Transnistria has its own currency, the **Transnistrian ruble**. You can exchange dollars or euros at all banks. Payment by card is sometimes possible, but don't rely on it.

Most visitors to Transnistria head straight to the capital, Tiraspol. Here, on the main Pokrovskaya St is Transnistria's most iconic sight: a vast statue of Lenin, his coat billowing in the revolutionary breeze, standing in front of the parliament building. Opposite is the town's historical museum (closed for renovation at the time of writing) adjacent to an avenue of remembrance for the Great Patriotic War and the 1990s separatist conflict. A gold-domed chapel, an eternal flame and a tank on a pedestal complete the ensemble.

Bender

TIME FROM CHIȘINĂU: 1HR 🚗 / 🚌

From castles to communism

Bender is the gateway to the breakaway republic of Transnistria, but its principal attraction is its 15th-century **fortress** *(bendery-fortress. com, 25 rubles)*, which sits in the centre of a slightly Disneyish park and has been given a sympathetic restoration and is crowned with turrets. There are two small museums inside: the Historical Museum presents the story of Bender alongside some interesting artefacts and enjoyable models and dioramas, while the Museum of Torture is distastefully lurid. The real joy of the fortress is walking the ramparts and taking in the views from the observation tower over the main entrance.

THE STRUVE GEODETIC ARC

In 1816, the Russian scientist Friedrich von Struve began a series of triangulations to calculate the exact size and shape of the Earth, a project that took him nearly 40 years to complete. His 34 calculations were made at various points across Norway, Sweden and what was then the Russian Empire, stretching from Hammerfest to Stara Nekrasivka on the Ukrainian–Romanian border. His work was of enough significance that the sites were inscribed on the UNESCO World Heritage list in 2005. One of the calculations was taken in Rudi, 40km west of Soroca. Marked by an obelisk, it's Moldova's only UNESCO site.

MOLDOVA'S BEST SOVIET MEMORABILIA

Mosaics, Chișinău: There are numerous Soviet mosaics dotted around the city; the best takes up an entire wall in the central bus station.

The Circus, Chișinău: This vast circular arena features a pair of juggling figures cast in bronze above the entrance.

Palatul Municipal de Cultură, Bălți: On the side of this building is a splendid Soviet bas-relief depicting arts and culture.

Bender: Central Bender is a Soviet open-air museum, with statues of Lenin, bas-reliefs and grandiose monuments galore.

Comrat: Down in the autonomous region of Gagauzia, Lenin is still live and kicking. Head to the central government building to find the statue.

Lenin statue, Comrat

285

FROM TAJIKISTAN TO THE MOON

To learn more about Moldova's experience before and during WWII, read Robert Frimtzis' memoir *From Tajikistan to the Moon*. Born to Jewish parents in Bălți in 1930, Frimtzis and his family were forced to flee the Nazi occupation when he was just 11 – a journey that took them from Moldova all the way to Central Asia. From there, Frimtzis was able to immigrate to America where he earned a master's degree from Columbia University and then worked on the developing space programme. The early chapters of his book tell the story of his childhood in Bălți and the terrifying reality of the advance of the German army.

Bender fortress (p284)

The fortress is about a kilometre north of the centre, which itself is worth exploring for its Soviet time-capsule vibe. Start by walking south down the river through **October Park**, past the blocky concrete *Monument to Soviet Power*, until you reach the derelict port building – note its golden ship bas-relief. Head west from here to the **Palace of Culture** and check out its impressive mosaics, before wandering into the town centre along Lenin St. It won't be long before you find **Komsomol Park**, which has the requisite Lenin statue opposite the monumental Gorky cinema: pop your head inside for a glimpse of its ornate lobby.

Căușeni

TIME FROM CHIȘINĂU: 1¼HR

Admire Byzantine-style frescoes

The straggly southern town of Căușeni is worth visiting for its **Church of the Assumption** *(entry 4 MDL),* which dates to around the 17th century. A squat building, it looks unimpressive from outside, but the interior is a riot of colour: every surface, including the ceiling, is bedecked with Byzantine-style frescoes depicting stories from the New Testament. Although there are similar churches in northern Romania, this one is unique for Moldova. The frescoes date from about 1760, and have been restored by a team of Moldovan and Romanian experts.

EATING IN BENDER: OUR PICKS

Canteen CCCP: Get back in the USSR in this splendid self-service canteen, adorned with Soviet memorabilia aplenty. *8am-8pm* €

Georgia: Serves all the Caucasian classics: *khinkali* dumplings, *khachapuri* cheese bread and delicious grilled meats. *10am-midnight* €€€

La Vida: Central and popular restaurant with an extensive menu of international choices, ranging from pizza and pasta to sushi. *10am-1am* €€

Slavny Pekar: Pleasant bakery outside the Palace of Culture, with great pastries and desserts, and good strong coffee. *8am-8pm* €

Places We Love to Stay

€ Budget €€ Midrange €€€ Top End

Chişinău
MAP p277

Amazing Ionika Hostel € This chilled place is Chişinău's best hostel, with mixed dorms and private rooms available. It also arranges tours of the city and the rest of the country. Book ahead – it's popular.

Hotel Chişinău € For an authentic Soviet experience, try the Hotel Chişinău, a splendid (if slightly decaying) enormity on United Nations Sq.

City Park Hotel € Smart and modern rooms in one of the best locations in town, just north of Cathedral Park. Nab a room on the seventh floor for excellent views. Breakfast not included.

TA Collection Hotel € Smart and modern hotel with 45 clean, quiet rooms in a convenient central courtyard just off the Bulevardul Ştefan cel Mare.

Tapok Hostel € If Ionika Hostel is full, Tapok makes a worthy second choice. It's clean and friendly, and has a reasonably handy location.

Weekend Boutique Hotel € A little out of the centre, this quirky hotel (with artworks on the exterior of the building) has over-the-top decor and the unusual opportunity to rent a goldfish for the night.

Bristol Central Park €€ With an enviable position just down from Cathedral Park, the rooms at the Bristol have slightly faded glamour exuding early 20th-century charm. Book in advance: walk-in rates are just silly.

Glass Cube €€ Modern and attractively priced place with the eponymous glass-cube architectural feature helping it stand out from the crowd. Coffee and tea, but no breakfast available.

Komilfo Hotel €€ 1970s retro-kitsch is the name of the game here: brown carpets, gold-yellow wallpaper and green-tiled bathrooms. Style aside, it's spotless and comfortable.

Lion's Hotel €€ Stylish rooms in a handy spot on a quiet street, a short walk from the central parks. Breakfast, served on the top-floor terrace, is good.

Gregory Hotel €€€ Attractive boutique hotel with plush rooms equipped with stylish wooden furniture and balconies with city views. Good buffet breakfast and smooth service make it worth the splurge.

Nobil Boutique Luxury Hotel €€€ In a shiny glass tower with a delightfully bling lobby, Nobil's rooms are actually reasonably restrained and tasteful. The 7th-floor restaurant and bar offers decent city views, and there's also a good spa.

Radisson Blu Leogrand Hotel €€€ Chişinău's well-located Radisson has a gorgeous lobby with stained-glass ceiling and wine-themed murals. The rooms are predictably swish and comfy, and there's the requisite spa, gym, casino and wine shop.

Richmond €€€ Modern hotel near the central parks, with stylish rooms and a pleasant covered-terrace wine bar.

Cricova

Curtea Domneasca € Attractively rustic hotel on the east edge of Cricova; it's an easy walk to the winery. Beds are comfy, the welcome is warm and the breakfast is good.

Giowine €€ The most upmarket place to stay in Cricova, Giowine has smart rooms, a swimming pool, a sauna and a good restaurant.

Soroca

Central Hotel € True to its name, the Central Hotel is just off Soroca's main square. It won't be winning many awards, but it's cheap, clean and a perfectly decent place to lay your head.

Hotel Europa 1928 € Hotel complex 10 minute's walk south of the main square, with simple but clean rooms, a swimming pool and an unexpected pirate ship–themed decking area on the river bank.

Bender

Stary Bastion €€ Bender's smartest hotel by far, this hotel-restaurant-spa complex in the castle park is decorated in a ridiculously opulent style. It can be noisy, though, with parties and karaoke overnight.

Practicalities

LGBTIQ+ Travellers
Although same-sex activity is not illegal, LGBTIQ+ travellers may encounter intolerant attitudes. Same-sex partners are not legally recognised. In Transnistria, same-sex activity is legal, but in 2024 the government announced laws banning 'propaganda for non-traditional sexual relations'.

Crime
Moldova is a generally safe destination, though you should watch out for pickpocketing and bag snatching in Chișinău. Possession, use and smuggling of illegal drugs will likely result in lengthy jail sentences.

Natural Disasters
Minor tremors are not uncommon in Moldova, though earthquakes are rare. The last significant earthquake affecting the country was in 1986, measuring 7.1 on the Richter scale; similar quakes occurred in 1977 and 1940.

Visas
Citizens of the UK, EU, US, Canada, Australia, New Zealand and others can enter Moldova without a visa. South Africa is a notable exception. If you need a visa, you can apply for one online at mfa.gov.md/en. If you're visiting Transnistria you'll need to get an entry permit; this is most easily arranged at the border upon arrival.

DAN MORAR/SHUTTERSTOCK

Orthodox Easter celebration, Chișinău (p276)

Opening Hours
Cafes and restaurants in Moldova tend to open in the late morning and stay open until the late evening, while bars usually open from mid-afternoon. Standard shop hours are 9am to 6pm. Museums and tourist attractions are sometimes closed on Monday.

Language
Romanian is the official language of Moldova.
Hello. Bună ziua. boo-nuh zee-wa
Goodbye. La revedere. la re-ve-de-re
Excuse me. Scuzați-mă. skoo-za-tsee-muh
Please. Vă rog. vuh rog
Thank you. Mulțumesc. mool-tsoo-mesk
Yes. Da. da
No. Nu. noo
Do you speak English? Vorbiți engleza? vor-bee-tsee-gle-za

Public Holidays
New Year's Day 1 January
Orthodox Christmas 7–8 January
Orthodox Easter April/May
Victory Day 9 May
Children's Day 1 June
Independence Day 27 August
Romanian Language Day 31 August
Christmas Day 25 December
Although not a public holiday, the celebrations for **National Wine Day** (first weekend in October) are worth attending.

Bus, Chișinău (p276)

MONEY

Currency: Moldovan Lei (MDL)

CASH

While most places in Moldova take cards, you may need cash for smaller payments in museums and historic sites, especially outside Chișinău. ATMs are common and there's rarely any problem getting change, even if you pay with large notes.

CARD & DIGITAL PAYMENTS

An increasing number of places in Moldova take card and digital payments, in particular hotels and restaurants. Both Visa and Mastercard are commonly accepted.

TRANSNISTRIAN RUBLES

If you plan on visiting Transnistria, know that you'll need a different currency. The Transnistrian ruble is the only accepted legal tender inside the breakaway republic, and the only place to get it is in a Transnistrian bank. Bring dollars, euros or lei to exchange.

Arriving & Getting Around

Most travellers arrive in Moldova by air. Chișinău's Eugen Doga Airport is 13km southeast of the city centre, with frequent bus connections into town. Taxis are easy to flag and cost around 150 MDL.

Overland Arrivals & Departures

Daily trains run from Bucharest and Iași in Romania to Chișinău. International bus links (eg FlixBus) run direct to Bucharest, Budapest, Bratislava, Brno and even a few places that don't begin with B.

Buses

The best way to get around Moldova is by bus. You can go everywhere from Chișinău, though you need to know which of the three bus stations to use. Ask at the tourist office.

Transnistria

If you're travelling to Transnistria by bus, you'll need to head to Chișinău's slightly chaotic central bus station. There's a small kiosk outside next to Croissant & Coffee that can sell you a ticket.

Car Hire

Driving in Moldova is easy: the roads are in good condition, signs are clear and there's rarely much traffic outside of Chișinău. Parking is generally free, even in Chișinău. Car-hire companies can be found at the airport. Police stops are infrequent and easy: show your documents and they'll wave you on. If an oncoming car flashes its headlights, it's most likely a warning that there are police ahead.

For places to stay
in Montenegro,
see p300

© DIDIER MARTI/GETTY IMAGES

Above: Kotor (p295); Right: Lake Skadar National Park (p298)

Curated by
Peter Dragicevich

Montenegro

MOUNTAINS, COAST AND ANCIENT TOWNS

With so much natural beauty squeezed into such a small area, Montenegro is a miniature marvel.

Montenegro may be one of Europe's newest and smallest nations, but it pushes well above its weight in the desired destinations stakes. A large reason for this is the extravagant beauty of its compact coastline. Nowhere is this more pronounced than in the extraordinarily picturesque Bay of Kotor, where the enclosing mountains dip their feet directly into crystalline waters.

Every summer tens of thousands descend on Montenegro's tiny Adriatic Coast, cramming the beaches and packing into the walled towns scattered along its length. When the crowds get to be too much, it's easy to escape to the mountains. In less than an hour you can be hiking along wild trails, tasting wine in remote villages or kayaking through the water lilies on vast Lake Skadar. Push a little further and there's rafting, canyoning and skiing, and even wilder corners to explore.

Montenegro's often painful position on the dividing lines of civilisations has bequeathed it a diverse and fascinating set of historic remnants. You'll find Illyrian ruins, Greek cemeteries, Roman mosaics, Byzantine frescoes, Serbian monasteries, Venetian palaces, Ottoman mosques, Austrian forts and lots of zany Yugoslav-era hotels and monuments.

Combine that with a Mediterranean climate and lots of delicious things to eat and drink, and you'll begin to see why this wee nation has such an outsized reputation.

CHRISTOPHER MOSWITZER/SHUTTERSTOCK

THE MAIN AREAS

COASTAL MONTENEGRO
Walled towns set alongside clear waters. **p294**

INLAND MONTENEGRO
Mountains, lakes and monasteries. **p297**

Find Your Way

Less than 300km from tip to toe, Montenegro is as compact as they come. A wall of mountains separates the coast from the interior, but the regions are well connected by highways.

Inland Montenegro, p297

The mountainous interior encloses Montenegro's historic capital, Orthodox monasteries and the biggest lake in the Balkans.

BUS

Buses are the major form of public transport here. They connect all towns and cities, and are generally comfortable and reliable. Each major town has a bus station with timetables that are prominently displayed.

Coastal Montenegro, p294

Ancient walled towns jut out over crystalline waters on the Bay of Kotor and along the Adriatic Coast.

CAR

Having a private vehicle at your disposal will give you the most flexibility and access to some spectacular routes. Driving can be stressful, however, with heavy summertime traffic, parking problems, narrow roads and daredevil drivers.

0   50 km
N
0   25 miles

TRIFF/SHUTTERSTOCK

River Gate (p296), Kotor

Plan Your Time

Don't be fooled by its size: you could easily spend weeks exploring Montenegro and not be bored – especially if you factor in time for hiking and lying on the beach.

Just One Day

● Make the walled town of **Kotor** (p295) your priority. Get lost in the maze of lanes, call into whichever churches you stumble across and stop to pat the cats. In the late afternoon, head to **Perast** (p294) and take the five-minute boat ride to **Gospa od Škrpjela** (p294). Afterwards, stroll along the waterfront to watch the sunset before sitting down to a seafood feast.

Five Day Full Monty

● Split your first day between **Perast** (p294) and **Kotor** (p295). On day two take the serpentine road up through **Lovćen National Park** (p298) to **Cetinje** (p297), stopping at the **Njegoš Mausoleum** (p298) along the way. Visit **Ostrog Monastery** (p299) on day three, then backtrack to **Lake Skadar** (p298). Spend the following morning on the lake, then drop down to **Budva** (p296).

SEASONAL HIGHLIGHTS

SPRING

Coastal tourism bursts back to life at Easter. April is a lovely time to visit, although the water will still be chilly.

SUMMER

Peak season, with high temperatures and large crowds. On the plus side there's lots going on, including festivals in Perast and Kotor.

AUTUMN

A wonderful time to visit. The waters are still warm but the crowds have thinned out. Great weather for hiking.

WINTER

Snow falls on the mountains; the coast shuts down. Kotor celebrates Carnival in the lead up to Lent (usually late winter).

Coastal Montenegro

WALLED TOWNS | BEACHES | MEDIEVAL BUILDINGS

Places

GETTING AROUND

Regular buses connect the major towns of the coast, all of which have centrally located stations with timetables displayed prominently. In busy times, be prepared for traffic snarls. Vehicle ferries head across the narrow strait at the centre of the Bay of Kotor every 20 minutes (half-hourly after midnight). The journey only takes about five minutes; expect queues in summer.

☑ TOP TIP

While you're driving along the coast, keep an eye out for the various monasteries. All of them welcome visitors, as long as you're respectful and demurely dressed (no bare shoulders or above-the-knee shorts or skirts).

It's hard to avoid superlatives when talking about Montenegro's coast. Simply put, this is one of the world's great beauty spots. To the north is the fjord-like Bay of Kotor (Boka Kotorska), where majestic mountains rise precipitously from slate-grey waters. Driving around the bay, the views are never short of gorgeous.

Next up is the Budva Riviera, the part of the Adriatic Coast that roughly coincides with the area that remained under Venetian rule when the Ottoman Empire pushed north in the 16th century. Despite mammoth hotel developments marring prime spots, it remains strikingly beautiful.

As you head south you'll start to see the minarets of mosques rising from ethnic Albanian villages, culminating in the Muslim-majority town of Ulcinj. South of Ulcinj, a near-constant stretch of beach extends from the Milena Canal all the way to the Albanian border, broken only by the two arms of the Bojana River.

Perast

TIME FROM KOTOR: **20MIN** 🚗

Once a rich and powerful Venetian maritime hub – churning out ships and sea captains in quantities completely disproportionate to its diminutive size – petite Perast has learned to be content with merely being gorgeous. Despite having just one main street, this small town boasts 16 churches and 17 formerly grand palazzi.

Take a boat to Gospa od Škrpjela

Capped by a 17th-century stone church with a sky-blue dome, **Gospa od Škrpjela** *(Our Lady of the Rocks; church & museum €3)* is one of a pair of picturesque islets sitting just off Perast. It was artificially created around a crag where, on 22 July 1452, an icon of the Madonna and Child was found. Every year on that date, locals row over with stones to continue the task of the island's creation in a festival known as Fašinada.

Try to visit the island early or late in the day, as the church and adjoining museum (full of nautical knick-knacks and votive

Perast

paintings) can get uncomfortably crowded. In summer, boats line up on the Perast waterfront to ferry people there and back; off season, you may need to ask around. The larger boats operated by **Dado** *(shiptravel-dado.me; return €5)* are a good option as they depart roughly every 10 minutes, allowing you to stay on the island as long as you like. The smaller boats wait on the island for a predetermined time. Be sure to shop around as prices can range from €5 to €10 per person for the return voyage.

Kotor

TIME FROM BUDVA: **35MIN**

Wedged between brooding mountains and a moody corner of the bay, achingly atmospheric Kotor (pronounced '*koh-tor*') is perfectly at one with its setting. Hemmed in by walls snaking improbably up the surrounding slopes, the town is a medieval maze of churches, cafe-strewn squares and Venetian palaces. It's a place where the past coexists with the present, where lines of laundry flutter from wrought-iron balconies and hundreds of cats loll in marble laneways. Come nightfall, the illuminated city walls glow as serenely as a halo. Behind the bulwarks, the streets buzz with bars and live music.

Climb Kotor's city walls

The **Kotor City Walls** *(entry €15)* are the town's defining feature; a system of defensive ramparts and fortifications that arc up the mountain to a height of 260m above sea level. It's a hard,

KOTOR THROUGH TIME

It's thought that an ancient Illyrian fortress once stood where St John's Castle is now. However, Kotor first entered the historical record in 168 BCE as the Roman town Acruvium, which survived until the 5th-century Ostrogoth invasion. After the Slavs arrived, Kotor developed as a city-state. During the Middle Ages, it passed through periods of Byzantine, Bulgarian, Serbian, Hungarian and Bosnian suzerainty before the Venetians eventually got the upper hand in 1420. The city owes much of its present look to nearly 400 years of Venetian rule, when it was known as Cattaro. In 1813 it joined briefly with Montenegro for the first time, but the Great Powers handed it to Austria, who held it until WWI.

EATING IN KOTOR: OUR PICKS

Taraca Resto Bar: Tucked alongside the river, with an international menu, vegetarian and vegan options, and Yugoslav memorabilia on the walls. *8am-11pm* €€

Platanus: Popular cafe and pizzeria in Dobrota, with excellent service and a good breakfast selection, including eggs, croissants and porridge. *7am-1am* €€

Marenda Grill House: Aged steaks and traditional grills, including massive mixed platters for sharing, near the roundabout in Škaljari. *7am-11pm* €€€

Galion: Kotor's fanciest restaurant serves upmarket modern cuisine (especially seafood) in a romantic waterfront setting by the marina. *noon-11pm* €€€

BUDVA'S BEST BEACHES

Slovenska Plaža: Budva's heaving main beach stretches out for 1.6km. In summer, the promenade morphs into a bustling strip of fast-food outlets, bars and market stalls.

Pizana Beach: A marginally less chaotic small beach just to the north of the Old Town.

Ričardova Glava: 'Richard's Head' is a pretty little beach with the town walls as its backdrop, immediately south of the Old Town.

Mogren Beach: Beautiful, double-bayed Mogren is Budva's best beach. You can hardly see any buildings when you're lying on the fine pebbles here – a rare treat for the Budva Riviera.

Jaz Beach: The blue waters and broad sands of Jaz lie just off the highway, west of Budva.

RUSLAN HARUTYUNOV/SHUTTERSTOCK

Budva beach

shadeless slog to the top, and there's a hefty admission charge, but the views are glorious. When tackling the walls in summer, avoid the heat of the day and bring plenty of water with you.

The main entry point is near the **River Gate**. From here, there are 1350 steps and 1200m of path ahead of you. At a solid pace, it takes around 45 minutes to reach **St John's Castle** at the very top, built in the 15th century on the site of an ancient fortress.

Budva

TIME FROM CETINJE: **30MIN** 🚌

Budva is a place where history and beach culture collide. It's a photogenic walled town with ancient provenance, anchored on one end by a long sweep of beach that's jam-packed with thousands of holidaymakers in summer. Spreading back from the beach and gradually making its way up the surrounding slopes is a chaotic jumble of hotels and apartment blocks, with bigger, flashier ones being built all the time.

Explore the Old Town

Budva's Old Town has been settled for at least 2500 years, with the Venetians ruling the roost for nearly 400 of them. Within its 15th-century walls, it's as if time stopped in the Renaissance, and overdevelopment is but a troubling rumour. Hidden within the marbled lanes is the **Budva Museum** *(entry €3)*, which does a great job of condensing the town's story into a concise narrative.

 EATING IN BUDVA: OUR PICKS

Konoba Bocun: Friendly little locals' tavern tucked away in a residential street, serving breakfast, sandwiches and traditional grills. *noon-8pm Mon-Sat* €€

Coco Bar, Food & Sea: Local-centric beach restaurant, and for good reason. Epic people watching, gorgeous views, beach playground for kids. *8am-11pm* €€

Konoba Portun: Charismatic Mićko doesn't believe in freezers – dishes at this stone-walled Stari Grad seafooder are determined by the daily catch. *2-11pm* €€€

Piano Nobile: Upmarket steak and burger bar in a beautiful Venetian building, spilling onto a little square. *1pm-1am* €€€

Inland Montenegro

MOUNTAINS | NATIONAL PARKS | HISTORIC CITIES

Away from the coast, nearly all of Montenegro is mountains, punctuated only by the occasional mirror-like lake and deep river canyon. The main exceptions to this are the plains around the nation's capital, Podgorica, spreading south to vast Lake Skadar.

Montenegro's statehood and cultural identity sprang from the slopes of Mt Lovćen, the mighty massif rising up above Kotor and Budva. It's here that the nation's origin story was formed – that of an indomitable warrior people holding strong while all around others fell to the Ottomans. The mountain's slopes of black beech trees give it a moody complexion, which bequeathed the nation its name: Crna Gora or 'Black Mountain' ('Monte Negro' in Italian).

The region's mountainous terrain lends itself to a large variety of outdoor pursuits, especially in its five national parks. But arguably the biggest thrill of all is to be found by simply driving around and enjoying the views.

Cetinje

TIME FROM BUDVA: **30MIN**

The capital of Montenegro until it was subsumed into the first incarnation of Yugoslavia in 1918, Cetinje (pronounced '*tse-tee-njeh*') is a refined, low-rise, pedestrian-friendly city filled with parks and elegant early-20th-century buildings. It sits in an idyllic green basin within the Lovćen massif, with craggy karstic peaks visible on every horizon.

With a population of 14,500, Cetinje is more like a large town than a city, but has more than its fair share of museums and galleries. Podgorica may be the nation's administrative capital, but Cetinje is the cultural capital.

Visit the royal palace

If you prefer to learn about history and culture by osmosis while poking around royal palaces and other heritage buildings, the **National Museum of Montenegro** (*Narodni muzej*

Places

Cetinje p297

Lovćen National Park p298

Lake Skadar National Park p298

Ostrog Monastery p299

GETTING AROUND

Podgorica is Montenegro's main transport hub, with good bus connections to all of its cities and major towns. A train line between Serbia and the coast stops at both Podgorica and Lake Skadar. Having a car will give you far more flexibility to explore the mountainous north, but be aware that some routes become snowbound in winter.

☑ TOP TIP

If you're planning to visit a few national parks, buy the annual pass *(€14; nparkovi. me/sections/1/online-tickets)*. Aside from Lovćen and Lake Skadar there are three parks in the north and east of the country.

WHO WAS NJEGOŠ?

One name that keeps coming up in these parts is Petar II Petrović Njegoš. At 2m tall, he was a towering figure in every sense of the word. But why is he so highly regarded?

Njegoš was born in the village of Njeguši in 1813. While still a teenager, he was appointed *vladika* (prince-bishop), the last to hold that title. His rule saw Montenegro increase diplomatic ties with Russia and evolve into a modern state with a functioning secular government, which required the unification of Montenegro's fractious tribes. On top of that, he was also a poet and philosopher, considered one of the greats of Montenegrin and Serbian literature. He died of tuberculosis in Cetinje in 1851, aged 37.

Crne Gore; narodnimuzej.me; combined ticket adult/child €20/10) is for you.

The main attraction is the **Museum of King Nikola** *(adult/child €8/4)*. This maroon-coloured palace on the main square was built in 1871 and, while grand, it still manages to feel like the kind of place that a family could live in.

Lovćen National Park

TIME FROM CETINJE: **10MIN**

Nature, views and architecture

Lovćen National Park *(nparkovi.me; entry €3)* is a 62-sq-km expanse taking in the peak of Mt Lovćen (1749m) and large tracts of forest crisscrossed with hiking paths and mountain-biking trails.

The park's cultural and architectural highlight is the **Njegoš Mausoleum** *(Njegošev mauzolej; narodnimuzej.me; entry adult/child €8/4),* which sits atop the massif's second-highest peak (1657m). Inside, under a golden mosaic canopy, a 28-tonne statue of national hero Petar II Petrović Njegoš rests in the wings of an eagle, carved from a single block of black granite by Ivan Meštrović.

Lovćen is more easily reached from Cetinje, but there's also an extraordinary 7km serpentine road connecting it to Kotor via 25 hairpin turns. The drive is thrilling and unsettling in equal measure, especially if you meet a large vehicle coming in the opposite direction.

Lake Skadar National Park

TIME FROM CETINJE: **30MIN**

Birds, islands and water lilies

Shared between Montenegro and Albania, Lake Skadar is the largest lake in the Balkans. On the Montenegrin side, an area of 400 sq km was declared a national park in 1983, protecting one of the richest habitats for birdlife in Europe.

There's no better way to experience the lake than aboard a boat or kayak. The options are many and varied, depending on which kind of craft you prefer, your interests (birdwatching, island monasteries, ruined fortresses), where you launch from and the season. Whichever trip you choose, the scenery is guaranteed to be gorgeous.

It's easy to arrange a tour or hire a kayak from stalls in Virpazar, Vranjina and Rijeka Crnojevića. All of these are in the upper reaches of the lake, which is where you'll see the most water lilies. Recommended operators include **Golden Frog**

EATING IN CETINJE: OUR PICKS

Polastičara Tara kod Sulja: Diner serving delicious *burek* (savoury pies) and sweet pastries. *7am-6pm Mon-Sat, to noon Sun, reduced hrs Nov-Apr* €

Verige: Food is prepared the traditional way, over wood and charcoal, in this hospitable roadside *pečenjara* (roastery). Cash only. *8am-11pm* €€

Kole: It serves omelettes and pasta, but the artery-clogging local specialities, served in giant portions, are the thing to try here. *7am-11pm* €€

Nacionalni Restoran Belveder: Traditional restaurant near Lipa Cave serving *ispod sača*–style meats (cooked under a dome covered with embers). *10am-10pm Easter-Nov* €€

Lake Skadar National Park

(skadarlakecruise.com), **Boat Milica** *(boatmilica.com)* and **Kingfisher** *(skadarlakeboatcruise.com).*

Undiscovered Montenegro *(undiscoveredmontenegro. com)* specialises in multi-day active itineraries, including kayaking and birdwatching cruises.

Ostrog Monastery

TIME FROM CETINJE: 1½HR

Montenegro's most revered religious site

There's something strangely affecting about **Ostrog Monastery** *(Manastir Ostrog; manastirostrog.com).* The setting is certainly part of it, positioned 900m above the verdant Zeta Valley and visible for miles around. Founded in 1665 within caves in a cliff face, the gleaming white **Upper Monastery** *(Gornji manastir)* gives the impression that it has grown out of the very rock.

Pilgrims queue to visit a tiny fresco-covered cave church that houses the fabric-wrapped remains of St Basil of Ostrog (Sv Vasilije Ostroški), the Serbian Orthodox bishop from Hercegovina who founded the monastery. Respectful tourists are welcome to join them.

PANORAMIC ROADS

You could argue that most of Montenegro's roads qualify for the title of 'panoramic route', but the National Tourist Organisation has officially designated four such routes and supported them with road signs, brochures and, for two of them (Durmitor and Korita), on-the-road audio guides. The 76km **Durmitorski prsten** (Durmitor Ring; route 2) circles through the mountains from Žabljak, visiting villages that are completely cut off by snow for months on end. It's well worth taking the suggested detour to Curevac (1625m) for exceptional Tara Canyon views. The other routes are the 800km **Kruna Crne Gore** (Crown of Montenegro; route 1), the 283km **More i visine** (Sea and Heights; route 3) and the 65km **Krug oko Korita** (Circuit around Korita; route 4).

 EATING AROUND LAKE SKADAR: OUR PICKS

Poslednja Luka Fr:iendly spot above the Crnojević River offering a short but delicious menu of lake fish and other local produce. *11am-8pm Tue-Sun* €

Stari Most: Freshwater fish experts (especially eel, trout and carp), located on Rijeka Crnojevića's riverside promenade. *11am-7pm* €€

Konoba Demidžana: Upmarket restaurant by the water in Virpazar showcasing traditional fish dishes and grilled meat. *8am-11pm* €€

Restoran Jezero: By the park office in Vranjina, serving tasty freshwater fish dishes and meaty grills on a lovely lakeside terrace. *8am-10pm* €€

Places We Love to Stay

€ Budget €€ Midrange €€€ Top End

Perast

Apartments Gudco €€
Two spacious, stone-walled apartments above a centuries-old family house. They're not flash but they have laundry facilities, dishwashers and million-dollar views.

Hotel Conte €€€
Not so much a regular hotel as a series of deluxe apartments in neighbouring heritage buildings.

Kotor

Montenegro Hostel 4U €
Buzzy party hostel in Dobrota with fun-loving staff who somehow manage to keep the place clean.

Old Town Hostel €€
Sympathetic renovations have converted this 13th-century palazzo into one of the best hostels in the country. Private rooms available.

Apartments Wine House €€
Cosy stone-walled apartments (three studios, one two-bedroom) offering a warm welcome in the heart of the Old Town.

Vila Panonija €€
Old stone house in Dobrota converted into a pleasant little hotel – or is it a large guesthouse?

Palazzo Radomiri €€€
A honey-coloured early-18th-century palazzo on the Dobrota waterfront transformed into a first-rate boutique hotel.

Hotel Astoria €€€
The decor straddles the line between fantastic and fantastical, but the rooms are luxurious and the Old Town location can't be beaten.

Hotel Vardar €€€
This lovely Old Town hotel is elegantly furnished with modern decor, offering glamour without the kitschy glitz.

Budva

Freedom Hostel €
Beloved, sociable hostel with a small courtyard and tidy little rooms scattered between three buildings.

Sailor House €€
Centuries-old Stari Grad house with welcoming hosts, nicely decorated bedrooms and a guest kitchen.

Stella di Mare €€
Friendly staff, tidy rooms with balconies, and far more reasonable rates (doubles from €85) than neighbouring Bečići resorts.

Hotel Kadmo €€€
Hotel in a quieter block near the bus station, with spacious rooms, roof terrace and pool.

Hotel Budva €€€
Elegant hotel with a spa centre, a swimming pool and a waterfront location that's tough to beat.

Villa M Palace €€€
There's a seductive glamour to this modern block of luxurious apartments near the Stari Grad.

Cetinje

Hotel Dapčević €
This unpretentious, family-run hotel is a short stroll from all of the sights. Rooms are spacious, clean and comfortable.

Casa Calda €
A cluster of attractive and thoughtfully equipped apartments set behind a family home with a large lawn.

La Vecchia Casa €
This period house captures the essence of old Cetinje. There's a tranquil rear garden and the rooms are full of antiques.

Gradska Cetinje €€€
The fanciest option in Cetinje is this new hotel occupying a converted mansion next to King Nikola's Palace.

Lake Skadar National Park

Villa Miela Lake Retreat €€
A beautifully restored and stylishly furnished traditional house near Virpazar, with a pool, a communal kitchen and tranquil views.

Hotel De'Andros €€€
Right in the heart of Virpazar, this recent remodelling of a Yugoslav-era hotel has sacrificed period features for comfort and contemporary style.

Ostrog Monastery

Ostrog Monastery Guesthouse €
This simple guesthouse near Ostrog's Lower Monastery offers tidy single-sex dorm rooms. It's designed for pilgrims; expect to be woken early.

Hotel Sokoline €€€
Perched near Ostrog Monastery, this roadside hotel has upmarket rooms, extraordinary views and a rooftop restaurant.

Practicalities

LGBTIQ+ Travellers
Montenegrin society is conservative, and life for local LGBTIQ+ people can be extremely difficult. That said, travellers are unlikely to encounter problems, but only if they're willing and able to be reasonably discreet.

Accessible Travel
There are few provisions for travellers with disabilities in Montenegro. The mobility-impaired will find the cobbled lanes and steps challenging. It's common in Montenegro for cars to park on footpaths (presuming there is a footpath), making things exceptionally difficult for wheelchair users.

Smoking
Smoking is banned in most indoor public spaces, although not everyone follows the rule. The ban includes public transport, hotel lobbies, restaurants, bars and clubs, but not casinos. Smoking on the terraces of bars and restaurants is allowed, and smoke inevitably wafts inside.

Health
Travel insurance isn't legally required to visit Montenegro, but it is strongly advised. Tap water is generally drinkable, but there can sometimes be problems in summer. If you're unsure, ask.

KIRK FISHER/SHUTTERSTOCK

Clock tower, Kotor (p295)

Opening Hours
You'll soon realise that most Montenegrins have an extremely flexible approach to opening hours, and these can vary throughout the year, especially in tourist areas. Most shops close on Sunday. Some museums close on Monday, or for the whole weekend in winter.

Safe Travel
Safety standards can be lax in Montenegro, and tourists have died in avoidable rafting, ziplining and jet-ski accidents. Be wary when booking activities – cheapest isn't always best. When choosing an operator, ask around and check online reviews. When rafting, make sure you're given a functioning helmet and life jacket. Don't go canyoning in bad weather.

Bars, Cafes & Restaurants
In cafes and bars, take a seat and wait to be served. Whether you're in a restaurant or a bar, keep note of your waiter, as they're responsible for taking all your orders and settling the bill. When the waiter delivers your order, they'll drop the *račun* (bill) into a little glass on the table.

Language

The official language of Montenegro is Montenegrin, but other languages used in the country include Albanian, Bosnian, Croatian and Serbian.

Basics

Hello. Zdravo. *zdra*-vo
Goodbye. Doviđenja. do-vi-*je*-nya
Yes. Da. da
No. Ne. ne
Please. Molim. *mo*-leem
Thank you. Hvala. *hva*-la
Excuse me. Oprostite. o-*pro*-stee-te
Sorry. Žao mi je. *zha*-o mee ye
What's your name?
Kako se zovete /zoveš? (pol/inf)
ka-ko se zo-ve-te/zo-vesh
My name is ... Zovem se ...
zo-vem se...
Do you speak English? Govorite
li engleski? *go*-vo-ree-te lee
en-gle-skee
I don't understand. Ne razumijem.
ne ra-*zoo*-mee-yem

Directions

Where's...? Gdje je...? gdye ye...
What's the address?
Koja je adresa? *ko*-ya ye a-*dre*-sa
Can you show me (on the map)?
Možete li da mi pokažete (na mapi)?
mo-zhe-te lee da mee *po*-ka-zhe-te
(na *ma*-pee)

Signs

Ulaz Entrance
Izlaz Exit
Toaleti/WC Toilets
Muški Men
Ženski Women
Otvoreno Open
Zatvoreno Closed
Zabranjeno Prohibited

Time

What time is it? Koliko je sati?
ko-*lee*-ko ye *sa*-tee
It's (10) o'clock. (Deset) je sati.
(*de*-set) ye *sa*-tee
Half past (10). (Deset) i po.
(*de*-set) ee po
morning jutro *yoo*-tro
afternoon poslijepodne
po-slee-ye-*pod*-ne
evening veče ve-che
yesterday juče *yoo*-che
today danas *da*-nas
tomorrow sutra *soo*-tra

Emergencies

Help! Upomoć! oo-po-moch
Leave me alone! Ostavite me na
miru! o-sta-vee-te me na *mee*-roo
I'm ill. Ja sam bolestan/bolesna.
(m/f) ya sam *bo*-le-stan/*bo*-le-sna
Call a doctor! Zovite ljekara!
zo-vee-te lye-*ka*-ra
Call the police! Zovite policiju!
zo-vee-te po-*lee*-tsee-yoo

Eating & Drinking

What would you recommend?
Šta biste preporučili? shta *bee*-ste
pre-po-*roo*-chee-lee
That was delicious.
To je bilo izvrsno. to ye *bee*-lo
eez-vr-sno
Please bring the menu/bill.
Molim vas donesite jelovnik/
račun. *mo*-leem vas do-*ne*-see-te
ye-lov-neek/*ra*-choon

NUMBERS

1
jedan
ye-dan

2
dva *dva*

3
tri *tree*

4
četiri
che-tee-ree

5
pet *pet*

6
šest *shest*

7
sedam
se-dam

8
osam *o*-sam

9
devet *de*-vet

10
deset *de*-set

Road above Bay of Kotor (p295)

MONEY

Currency: Euro (€)

CREDIT CARDS & DIGITAL PAYMENTS

Credit cards are widely accepted, but not always at cafes, bars, kiosks and museums. Places that accept credit cards are also likely to accept digital payments. Don't rely on either as your only option.

CASH

It pays to have coins and small notes when paying for coffee and small purchases. ATMs dispense large notes.

TIPPING

Tipping isn't expected but is appreciated. In cafes, bars and taxis, round up to the nearest euro. For guides and waiters, leave up to 10% (in cash), but only if you're completely satisfied with the service. If not, don't feel obliged to leave anything. Tipping in hotels is unusual.

Arriving & Getting Around

Montenegro has two international airports – Tivat and Podgorica – and a de facto third in Croatia (Dubrovnik Airport), just 17km from the border. Ferries arrive from Italy and Croatia in summer.

Buses

The local bus network is extensive and reliable. Intercity buses are usually comfortable and air-conditioned. Stations display the bus timetables prominently, and staff are on hand to help out. Visit *busticket4. me* for timetables and tickets.

Parking

Many municipalities have replaced meters with app-based payment, which makes things tricky if you don't have a phone with internet connection. However, most towns also have designated parking lots where you can pay in cash.

Car Hire

Cars can be hired from airports and larger towns. Cowboy operators are rife. If the online price seems cheap, expect to be hit with a hefty insurance surcharge. Take photos of any pre-existing damage.

Entry Points

Montenegro has land borders with Croatia, Bosnia and Hercegovina, Serbia, Kosovo and Albania. At the crossing you'll need to present your vehicle registration documents and a locally valid insurance policy such as a European Green Card. Check that your policy covers Montenegro. Tivat and Podgorica airports are small and facilities are limited, but both have free wi-fi, ATMs, taxi stands and rental-car desks.

Curated by
Anthony Ham

North Macedonia

WILD NATURE, ANCIENT HISTORY

North Macedonia is a Balkan treasure, a little-known world of medieval monasteries, historic towns and stirring natural beauty.

North Macedonia may be small but it's rich in glorious scenery and cultural heritage. This is a realm that has always stood at the crossroads of history and in the path of invading armies. The result is part Balkan and part Mediterranean, with strong traces of Greek, Roman and Ottoman legacies.

Glittering Lake Ohrid and its historic namesake town have etched out a place for North Macedonia on the tourist map, but travel further and you'll find dramatic mountains with blissfully quiet walking trails, lakes and riding opportunities. The national parks of Mavrovo, Galičica and Pelister are cultivating some excellent cultural and culinary tourism initiatives; these gorgeous regions are little explored, so if you want to get off the beaten track in Europe, this is the place.

Although North Macedonia has a small core of excellent places to stay, traditional restaurants serving fresh food, and professional local tour operators, tourism infrastructure isn't always what it could be. But therein, too, lies part of the country's charm: at times, exploring North Macedonia can feel like a magical DIY adventure.

Throw in some enchanted Ottoman old towns, superb Orthodox monasteries, stunning hiking trails, some Roman ruins and one of Europe's least-known wine regions, and North Macedonia may just be the finest Balkan sensation waiting to be discovered.

COLORMAKER/SHUTTERSTOCK

THE MAIN AREAS

SKOPJE & AROUND
Historic bazaar and modernist architecture. **p308**

LAKE OHRID
Ancient lake, ancient villages. **p308**

MAVROVO NATIONAL PARK
Magnificent monasteries, pretty villages, blissful hikes. **p311**

BITOLA
Medieval town and gateway to the wild. **p311**

For places to stay in North Macedonia, see p312

Left: Skopje Old Town (p309); Above: Church of Sveti Jovan (p310) and Lake Ohrid

Find Your Way

Take the time to discover compact North Macedonia's cities, towns, traditional villages and, especially, its beautiful national parks, mountains and lakes. Outdoors lovers will find plenty to keep them occupied.

CAR

You don't need a car to get around Skopje and Ohrid Town, but renting one is best for discovering the rest of North Macedonia, especially if you want to reach villages and outdoor-activities spots.

BUS

If you're not in a hurry, buses can get you between most cities and towns. Skopje serves the majority of domestic destinations. During summer and on Sundays (when most locals travel), prebook for Ohrid.

Skopje & Around, p308

Dive into the capital's historic Čaršija (old Ottoman bazaar), then seek out modernist architecture and riverside monuments.

Bitola, p311

Immerse yourself in a North Macedonian provincial town, with a Čaršija and the country's premier Roman ruins.

Mavrovo National Park, p311

Meet the monks at grand Sveti Jovan Bigorski Monastery in the hills of the national park.

Lake Ohrid, p308

Discover the vastness and mystery of this seductive lake and explore Ohrid's distinctive old quarter up to clifftop Church of Sveti Jovan.

SERBIA

KOSOVO

Delcevo

Kocani

Radoviš

Štip

Sveti Nikole

Rzrancani

Belec

Ropotovo

Prilep

Kruševo

Demir Hisar

Bitola

Resen

Negotino

Kavadarci

Konopište

Strumica

Valandovo

Vardar

GREECE

Tikveš Lake

Lakavica

Bregalnica

SKOPJE

Dracevo

Gorna Belica

Sopotnica

Dlhovo

Nizhepole

Ohrid

Lake Ohrid

Struga

Vevčani

Debar

Galičnik

Mavrovo

Mavrovi Anovi

Mavrovo Lake

Mavrovo National Park

Gostivar

Stence

Pirok

Tetovo

Šhurr Mountain National Park

Galičica National Park

Trpejca

Radožda

Sveti Naum Monastery

Lake Prespa

Drin

Treska

Vardar

ALBANIA

Kicevo

0   50 km
0   25 miles

N

Mavrovo National Park (p311)

Plan Your Time

North Macedonia has plenty of possibilities if you like alfresco fun mixed in with historical towns. You'll need a few days to really savour the activities and dig into the history of the country.

One Week to Explore

● Spend a couple of days in **Skopje** (p308), then head straight to **Ohrid Town** (p308) to swim in the lake, stroll waterside villages and explore frescoed medieval churches at **Sveti Naum Monastery** (p310). Don't miss **Mavrovo National Park** (p311) for mountain hiking and local food. Finish at **Lake Prespa** (p311) and the ruins on the island of **Golem Grad** (p311).

More Than a Week

● Having enjoyed **Skopje** (p308), **Ohrid Town** (p308), **Lake Ohrid** (p308) and **Lake Prespa** (p311), stop in **Bitola** (p311), with its Ottoman quarter and ancient ruins, and discover North Macedonia at its historic and least touristy best. Next, visit **Mavrovo National Park** (p311) and stay in historic villages while you hike, ride and (in winter) ski your way through the park.

SEASONAL HIGHLIGHTS

SPRING
March can be cold and Orthodox Easter sees lots of local travellers. Temperatures warm up in May; attractions remain quiet.

SUMMER
Summers are for swimming in Lake Ohrid and mountain hiking. July and August have lots of festivals, but are overcrowded.

AUTUMN
September has fewer crowds and festivals. Hiking trails close in October. November is really cold.

WINTER
Mini high season in December and January. Carnival (Vevčani) and skiing (Mavrovo) are popular. It's bitterly cold at altitude.

Skopje & Around

HISTORIC TOWNS | MAGICAL LAKE | SCENIC LANDSCAPES

☑️ **TOP TIP**

For the best views of Skopje, take the cable car to **Mt Vodno** – a 10-minute journey during which you'll get to see the entire sprawl of the city. Take the 'Millennium Cross' special bus or a taxi from Skopje's **bus station** to the cable-car station.

Skopje is one of the most intriguing capitals in the Balkans. It combines an easygoing atmosphere, plenty of charm and tasty local cuisine with stirring architecture and rich history. Its Ottoman- and Byzantine-era sights are focused around the city's delightful Čaršija, bordered by the 15th-century Kameni Most (Stone Bridge) and Tvrdina Kale Fortress. Beyond the capital, the mysterious Lake Ohrid is a wonderfully seductive sight and among the most magical places in the Balkans. Mirror-like and dazzling on sunny days, it's a beautiful place, especially in and around the ancient town of Ohrid, with its cobbled streets, distinctive architecture and lakefront bars. East of Ohrid, Galičica National Park has mountain villages and Magaro Peak, which can be climbed. The gorges, pine forests, karst fields and waterfalls of Mavrovo National Park, North Macedonia's largest, offer a wonderful change of pace for visitors, while Bitola could just be North Macedonia's most enchanting old town.

Lake Ohrid

Explore the old quarter

Alongside its serene lake, **Ohrid Town's old quarter** cascades down steep streets, dotted with beautiful churches and offering sweeping views from the heights. Car Samoil St is lined

---

 GETTING AROUND

Skopje International Airport (21km east of the city centre) is a minor hub with direct air services to regional cities and beyond. Shuttle buses with **Vardar Express** (vardarexpress. com) run between it and the city. Driving is generally hassle-free; the main worries are

poor signage and finding somewhere to park. You'll need a car to reach small villages like Vevčani. Otherwise, buses connect Skopje with Ohrid Town (from where buses run along the lakeshore), Mavrovo and Bitola.

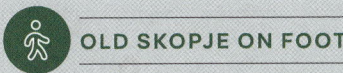

OLD SKOPJE ON FOOT

Walk from the river, through the Old Town and up to the fortress, passing museums and architectural gems; allow a day if you visit every museum.

START	END	LENGTH
Ploštad Makedonija	Tvrdina Kale Fortress	2km; 2hr

Begin south of the river, in ❶ **Ploštad Makedonija** (Macedonia Sq), the centrepiece of Skopje's audacious nation-building-through-architecture project. From the square, cross the ❷ **Stone Bridge**, then turn right (southeast) to the ❸ **Archaeological Museum of Macedonia**, a huge pile of Italianate-styled marble. Returning northwest, the ❹ **Museum of the Macedonian Struggle for Statehood & Independence** is fascinating for its subtlety-free propaganda. Much better is the mirrored-glass ❺ **Holocaust Memorial Center for the Jews of Macedonia**, commemorating North Macedonia's all-but-lost Sephardic Jewish culture. A short walk northeast brings you to the 19th-century Macedonian Orthodox ❻ **Sveti Dimitrija Church**. Across the

road, the ❼ **National Gallery of Macedonia** occupies the Daut Pasha Amam (1473), once the largest Turkish baths beyond İstanbul and a magical setting for the mainly modern art from across the country. The Old Town, the Čaršija, begins north across Bul Goce Delčev. Make for the ❽ **Čifte Amam**, which houses temporary exhibitions, and then the partially submerged ❾ **Sveti Spas Church**. Above the Old Town, the ❿ **Museum of North Macedonia** inhabits a concrete brutalist structure. Almost across the street, the ⓫ **Mustafa Pasha Mosque** dates back to 1492 and has a delightful rose garden. Continue the climb to the walk's literal high point, the 6th-century ⓬ **Tvrdina Kale Fortress**, for great views over the city.

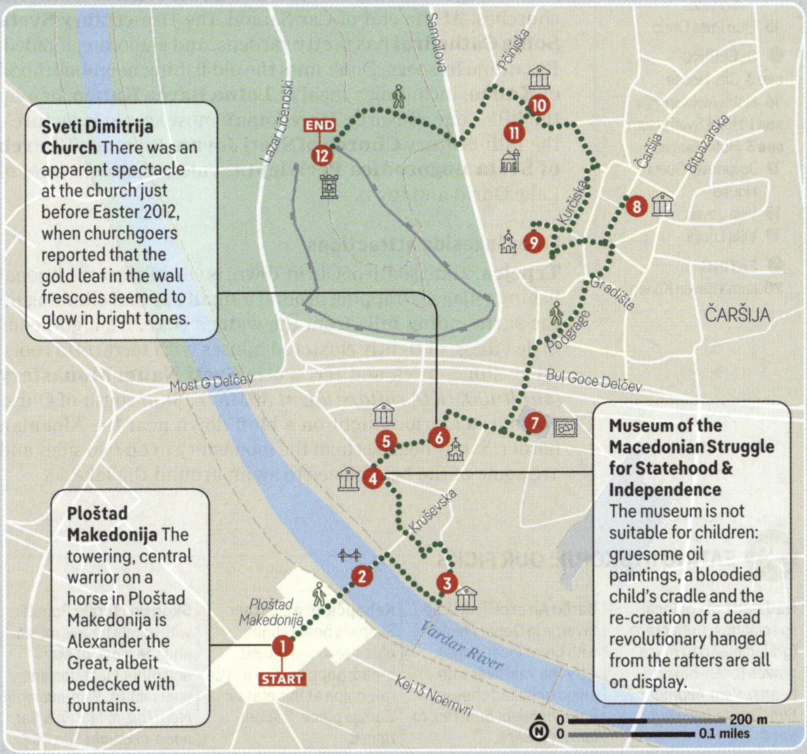

Sveti Dimitrija Church There was an apparent spectacle at the church just before Easter 2012, when churchgoers reported that the gold leaf in the wall frescoes seemed to glow in bright tones.

Museum of the Macedonian Struggle for Statehood & Independence The museum is not suitable for children: gruesome oil paintings, a bloodied child's cradle and the re-creation of a dead revolutionary hanged from the rafters are all on display.

Ploštad Makedonija The towering, central warrior on a horse in Ploštad Makedonija is Alexander the Great, albeit bedecked with fountains.

START

END

Samoilova · Pčinjska · Lazar Ličenoski · Čaršija · Bitpazarska · Kurišište · Gradište · Poŭenije · Kruševska · ČARŠIJA · Bul Goce Delčev · Most G Delčev · Ploštad Makedonija · Vardar River · Kej 13 Noemvri

0 — 200 m
0 — 0.1 miles

⭐ **HIGHLIGHTS**
1 Sveti Naum Monastery
2 Trpejca

🔴 **SIGHTS**
3 Bitola
4 Church of Sveta Bogorodica Perivlepta
5 Church of Sveti Jovan
6 Galičica National Park
7 Golem Grad
8 Kaneo
9 Lake Prespa
10 Magaro Peak
see 3 Stara Čaršija
11 Sveta Bogorodica Bolnička & Sveti Nikola Bolnički
12 Sveta Sofija Cathedral
13 Vevčani
14 Vevčani Springs

🔴 **ACTIVITIES**
see 3 Balojani Tourist Services
15 Free Pass Ohrid

⚫ **SLEEPING**
see 3 City House
16 Hotel Aleksandrija
see 1 Hotel Sveti Naum
see 3 Hotel Teatar
17 Jovanovic Guest House
18 Villa Jovan
19 Villa Lucija

🟢 **EATING**
20 Letna Bavča Kaneo

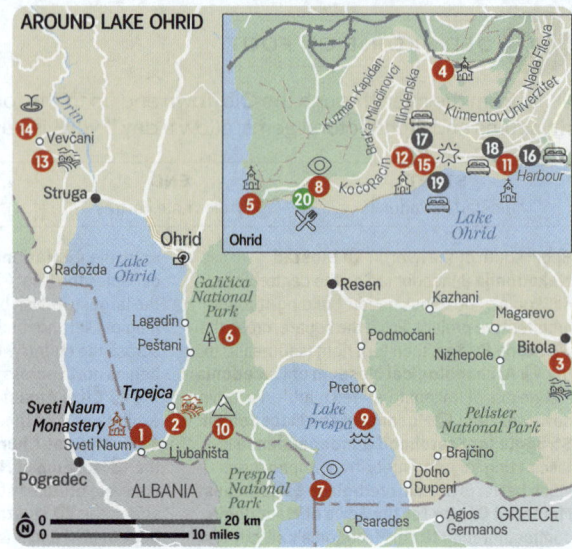

with beautiful traditional architecture, as well as frescoed **Sveta Bogorodica Bolnička** and **Sveti Nikola Bolnički** churches. At the end of Car Samoil, the 11th-century **Sveta Sofija Cathedral** has pretty gardens, and elaborate, if faded, Byzantine frescoes. Don't miss the old fishing neighbourhood of **Kaneo**, including a meal at **Letna Bavča Kaneo**, or – up the hill – one of North Macedonia's most scenic structures, the 13th-century **Church of Sveti Jovan**. From the **Church of Sveta Bogorodica Perivlepta**, enjoy magical views of Lake Ohrid and town.

Enjoy lakeside attractions

Trpejca, 21km south of Ohrid Town, is Ohrid's last traditional fishing village. Wrapping around a small bay and climbing up the surrounding hills from the water's edge, it's a gorgeous little village of tightly clustered houses with terracotta roofs.

The stone, brick and terracotta **Sveti Naum Monastery** *(adult 100MKD, child/student 30MKD),* 8km south of Ohrid Town, is a glorious sight on a bluff down near the Albanian border. Sandy beaches hem the monastery in on two sides and are some of the best places to swim around the lake.

 EATING IN SKOPJE: OUR PICKS

Nadžak: Lots of local specialities, from *skara* (grilled meat) to *tavče gravče* (oven-baked beans). *9am–midnight Sun–Thu, to 1am Fri & Sat* €

Barik: An excellent little taverna in Debar Maalo, with great local dishes – try the veal liver with onion or baked cheese. *8am–midnight Sun–Thu, to 1am Fri & Sat* €

Kebapčilnica Destan: Skopje's best kebabs, plus seasoned grilled bread, peppers and a little raw onion at this classic Čaršija place. *9.30am–11pm* €

Skopski Merak: Popular with locals for live music and the menu of *skara* and other Macedonian specialities. *9am–midnight Mon–Thu, to 1am Fri & Sat, noon–midnight Sun* €€€

High above the northwestern corner of Lake Ohrid is one of the loveliest villages anywhere in North Macedonia. Ninth-century **Vevčani**, 28km from Ohrid Town, is one of the oldest villages in the country. Locals love it for its cool mountain air in summer, its traditional restaurants and **Vevčani Springs** *(adult/child 30/15MKD)* that writhe and burble through the forest at the top of the village.

Galičica National Park

A wild lake and magical island

The rippling, rock-crested massif of **Galičica National Park** *(galicica.org.mk/en)* separates Lakes Ohrid and Prespa and is home to **Magaro Peak** (2254m). You can dedicate half a day to hiking Magaro, a moderate, 8km loop hike (around four hours in total). From the top you'll get spectacular views of both lakes.

After your descent, cool off by swimming at **Lake Prespa**, and spend a day visiting the island of **Golem Grad**, Lake Prespa's star attraction, with ruins dating back as far as the 4th century. The only way to book a trip to Golem Grad is through **Villa Prespa Hotel** *(villaprespa.com)*. Visits take place from June to October, and start at around €80 per person.

Mavrovo National Park

Hike, ski or ride the trails

The largest of North Macedonia's four national parks, **Mavrovo National Park** *(npmavrovo.org.mk/en; free)* is rich in lakes, forests and vertiginous canyons. You can stay at the **Sveti Jovan Bigorski Monastery** (p312), and choose from 20 different hiking trails, which range from 1.7km (45 minutes) to 27km (five to eight hours). The excellent national park website has a brief description and elevation chart for each hike. Our favourite path is the 5.5km trail that connects Galičnik and Janče. **Shar Outdoors** *(sharoutdoors.com)* can arrange a guide.

Zare Lazarevski Ski Centre *(skimavrovo.com; day ticket 1300MKD)*, North Macedonia's top ski resort, is hugely popular with locals and with skiers from across the Balkans.

Sherpa Horse Riding *(horseriding.com.mk; per person from €40)* arranges lovely excursions around Mavrovo. Rides range from 2½ hours to seven days through mountain valleys and traditional villages.

Bitola

Visit the bazaar

Crumbling and colourful 18th- and 19th-century townhouses, coupled with an authentic, workaday Čaršija, make **Bitola** worth a few days of your time. In its 19th-century Ottoman heyday, Bitola's **Stara Čaršija** was one of the finest in the Balkans. More than just a market, it was a regional centre of artisan traditions, with more 3000 shops and workshops crammed into Bitola's bazaar. That number may have fallen to closer to 70, but the same spirit lingers.

TOURS IN NORTH MACEDONIA

Free Pass Ohrid: Tailored tours to Galičica National Park, wine touring around Tikveš, boat trips and paragliding around Lake Ohrid. *(freepassohrid.mk)*

Bicycle MK: Guided day tours in Skopje, plus North Macedonia–wide adventures. All equipment is provided. *(bicycle.mk)*

Macedonia Experience: Horse riding, bike riding, community tourism forays into Mavrovo National Park, wine tasting and Ohrid excursions, all from a Skopje base. *(macedonia experience.com)*

Macedonia Travel: Large Skopje agency. Day trips to Canyon Matka and Ohrid, and off-the-beaten-track destinations. *(macedoniatravel. com)*

Balojani Tourist Services: Bitola-based operator: guided hiking, biking, gastronomy, wildlife-watching tours countrywide.

Places We Love to Stay

€ Budget €€ Midrange €€€ Top End

Skopje

Urban Hostel & Apartments €
A converted residential house with a sociable front garden, close to the main train station.

Hotel Senigallia €€ Once a boat, now a hotel with rooms that evoke classic semi-luxurious cabins, Hotel Senigallia has a great location and lots of character.

Hotel Solun €€€ Just off the main square, this stylish, beautifully designed place has modern and elegantly decorated rooms.

Hotel City Park €€€ Fresh rooms, modern and bright, some with balconies; the location is excellent, opposite the City Park.

Lake Ohrid   MAP p310

Villa Jovan € This utterly charming restoration of an 1856 mansion has nine rooms in the heart of the Old Town, with suitably creaky floors and wooden beams, and a cosy atmosphere.

Villa Lucija € Deep in the Old Town, and right on the lakefront with a riverside terrace, Lucija has warmly decorated, breezy rooms with lake-view balconies.

Hotel Sveti Naum € On the grounds of the Sveti Naum Monastery, some of this hotel's rooms have lovely lake views.

Jovanovic Guest House €€ This Old Town property has two studio apartments; the top-floor apartment's balcony has one of the best views in town, over the lake and Sveta Sofija Cathedral.

Hotel Aleksandrija €€ Rooms here vary from old-fashioned retro to slick designer; many of the latter have lake views from their big balconies.

Mavrovo National Park

Baba i Dede € Charming Galičnik guesthouse with a restaurant serving traditional homemade food.

Sveti Jovan Bigorski Monastery € For a unique experience, bed down in this famous monastery. It's more comfortable than you might expect, and while you might share a room, it's a soulful experience.

Hotel Tutto €€ This eco-hotel with a great restaurant has supremely comfortable rooms; the ones at the front have fine views from their balconies.

Bitola

Hotel Teatar € One of the loveliest hotels in the country; the sensitive design keeps true to the image of a traditional Ottoman house.

City House € This family-run mini-hotel has terrific rooms and a couple of apartments just off Širok Sokak; excellent breakfasts and an atrium cafe are further highlights.

IGOR PANEVSKI/SHUTTERSTOCK

Sveti Jovan Bigorski Monastery

Practicalities

Mobile Phones

If using a mobile (cell) phone, buying a local SIM card (from as little as €10, including data) is good for longer stays. Coverage is generally excellent throughout the country. North Macedonia uses the GSM phone system, which means that American CDMA phones won't work here.

Time Zone

North Macedonia runs on Central European Time: one hour ahead of GMT. For Daylight Saving Time, clocks go forward on the last Sunday in October, and back on the last Sunday in March.

Smoking

North Macedonia generally follows EU regulations banning smoking inside public places, but the rules are casually broken in many restaurants, bars and hotels. Around half (48.4%) of adult North Macedonians smoke.

Etiquette

North Macedonians are usually warm and welcoming, but socially conservative. Most are either Orthodox Christian or Muslim and neither religion deems it appropriate for women to bare much flesh; be aware that if you're a woman and wearing skimpy clothing you will get stared at. In churches and mosques, both men and women should cover their knees and shoulders.

FILIP P/SHUTTERSTOCK

Trpejca (p310)

Opening Hours

Banks 7am–5pm Monday to Friday
Cafes & Restaurants 8am–midnight
Museums Many close on Mondays
Shops 9am–6pm

Public Holidays

New Year's Day 1 January
Orthodox Christmas 7 January
Orthodox Easter Week March/April/May
Labour Day 1 May
Saints Cyril and Methodius Day 24 May
Ilinden Day 2 August
Independence Day 8 September
Revolution Day 11 October
St Clement of Ohrid Day 8 December

Language

Macedonian is written using the Cyrillic alphabet. Note that *dz* is pronounced as the 'ds' in 'adds', *zh* as the 's' in 'pleasure', and *r* is rolled.

Basics

Hello. Здраво. *zdra·vo*
Goodbye. До гледање. *do gle·da·nye*
Yes. Да. *da*
No. Не. *ne*
Please. Молам. *mo·lam*
Thank you. Благодарам. *bla·go·da·ram*
Excuse me. Извините. *iz·vee·nee·te*
Sorry. Простете. *pros·te·te*
What's your name?
Како се викате/викаш?
ka·ko se vi·ka·te/vi·kash
My name is ... Јас се викам ... *yas se vi·kam ...*
Do you speak English?
Зборувате ли англиски? *zbo·ru·va·te li an·glis·ki*
I don't understand.
Јас не разбирам. *yas ne raz·bi·ram*

Emergencies

Help! Помош! *po·mosh*
Go away! Одете си! *o·de·te si*
I'm lost. Се загубив. *se za·gu·biv*
I'm ill. Јас сум болен/болна. (m/f)
yas sum bo·len/bol·na

Eating & Drinking

What would you recommend?
Што препорачувате вие?
shto pre·po·ra·chu·va·te vi·e
Cheers! На здравје! *na zdrav·ye*
I'd like the bill/menu please.
Ве молам сметката/мени.
ve mo·lam smet·ka·ta/me·ni

Waxing Cyrillical

The following list shows the letters of the Macedonian and Serbian/Montenegrin Cyrillic alphabets. The letters are common to all languages unless otherwise specified.

Cyrillic	Sound	Pronunciation	Cyrillic	Sound	Pronunciation
А а	a	short as the 'u' in 'cut'	Љ љ	ly	as the 'lli' in 'million'
		long as in 'father'	М м	m	as in 'mat'
Б б	b	as in 'but'	Н н	n	as in 'not'
В в	v	as in 'van'	Њ њ	ny	as the 'ny' in 'canyon'
Г г	g	as in 'go'	О о	o	short as in 'hot'
Д д	d	as in 'dog'			long as in 'for'
Ѓ ѓ	j	as in 'judge' (Macedonian only)	П п	p	as in 'pick'
			Р р	r	as in 'rub' (but rolled)
Ђ ђ	j	as in 'judge' (Serbian/Montenegrin only)	С с	s	as in 'sing'
			Т т	t	as in 'ten'
			Ќ ќ	ch	as in 'check' (Macedonian only)
Е е	e	short as in 'bet'			
		long as in 'there'	Ћ ћ	ch	as in 'check' (Serbian/Montenegrin only)
Ж ж	zh	as the 's' in 'measure'			
З з	z	as in 'zoo'			
Ѕ ѕ	dz	as the 'ds' in 'suds' (Macedonian only)	У у	u	as in 'rule'
			Ф ф	f	as in 'fan'
И и	i	short as in 'bit'	Х х	h	as in 'hot'
		long as in 'marine'	Ц ц	ts	as in 'tsar'
Ј ј	y	as in 'young'	Ч ч	ch	as in 'check'
К к	k	as in 'kind'	Џ џ	j	as in 'judge'
Л л	l	as in 'lamp'	Ш ш	sh	as in 'shop'

FROM LEFT: MARIUS KARP/SHUTTERSTOCK, PHOTOLOHI/SHUTTERSTOCK

Skopje airport

MONEY
Currency: Denar (MKD)

CASH & ATMS
Most tourist businesses, including lower to midrange hotels, only accept cash. North Macedonia's national currency may be the denar, but many tourist-related costs (eg tours and hotels) are quoted in euros. It usually works out better if you pay for smaller expenses in denars. ATMs are widespread in major towns, but surprisingly hard to find around Lake Ohrid, except in Ohrid Town itself.

CREDIT CARDS
Credit cards can often be used in larger cities (especially in hotels and restaurants), but don't rely on them outside Skopje.

TIPPING
North Macedonia doesn't have a tipping culture except at upmarket restaurants, where 10% is the norm.

Arriving & Getting Around

Skopje and Ohrid are well connected to other Balkan tourist hubs as well as wider international destinations. See the website Airports of Macedonia *(airports.com.mk)* for information about flights to/from North Macedonia.

By Air
Skopje is the only international airport in North Macedonia for flights from the rest of Europe. Budget airlines have improved its modest number of connections, and it's now linked pretty well to major European cities.

By Land
Buses connect Skopje or Ohrid with Pristina, Tirana, Sofia, Belgrade, Thessaloniki and other cities in neighbouring countries. From Skopje it's also possible to get to Ljubljana, İstanbul and Zagreb.

Driving Essentials
Drive on the right side of the road. The speed limits are 120km/h on motorways, 80km/h on open roads, and 50–60km/h in towns. Seatbelt and headlight use (even during the day) is compulsory, if not universally observed.

Visas
Entering North Macedonia is usually hassle-free. Citizens of any of the former Yugoslav republics, Australia, Canada, the EU, Iceland, Israel, New Zealand, Norway, Switzerland, Türkiye and the USA, and many other countries, can stay for three months without needing a visa. Check the website of the **Ministry of Foreign Affairs** *(mfa.gov.mk)* if unsure of your status. Your passport must have at least six months' validity when entering the country.

For places to stay in Poland, see p342

CINEMATOGRAPHER/SHUTTERSTOCK

Above: Old Town Market Square , Warsaw (p323); Right:Złota Brama, Gdańsk (p338)

Curated by
Marc Di Duca

Poland

A WARM, WELCOMING AND RESILIENT NATION

Poland is all about history: its millennium-long tale is set against centuries of European power struggles and features a cast of millions.

If you were to put together a list of countries with 'most eventful pasts', Poland would be high up in the rankings. The Slavic nation has spent centuries at the pointy end of history, grappling with war, invasion and meddling neighbours. 'Poland has not yet perished' goes the rather pessimistic first line of the national anthem, and indeed, no Russian tsar or German dictator ever managed to suppress the Poles' strong sense of nationhood and cultural identity.

In fact, Poland is thriving. The country's economic revival from one of the world's poorest nations, where petrol and food were once rationed, to a modern, vibrant economy has been remarkable. Its cities are modernising, its infrastructure is expanding and it occupies a strategic, central location within the EU and NATO. As a result, bustling Warsaw and Kraków exude a sophisticated energy that's a heady mix of old and new.

Away from the cities, Poland is geographically diverse, from its northern beaches to the long chain of mountains on its southern border. In between, towns and cities are dotted with ruined castles, market squares and medieval churches.

Although prices have skyrocketed in recent years, Poland is still good value. And as the Poles continue to reconcile their distinctive national identity with their location at the heart of a troubled Europe, it's become a fascinating time to visit.

LIYA, BLUMESSER/SHUTTERSTOCK

THE MAIN AREAS

WARSAW
Nation's capital with bags of history. **p320**

KRAKÓW
Poland's best-preserved city. **p326**

WESTERN POLAND
Vibrant, off-the-beaten-path destination. **p333**

POMERANIA
Beaches, castles and 20th-century history. **p337**

Find Your Way

Poland is big: it's the ninth-largest country in Europe. Journey times can be longer than you expected, but infrastructure is improving. Apart from the southern mountains, the country is largely flat.

TRAIN

Rail is the most convenient way to travel. The network is relatively cheap and there are some high-speed rail services. Some of the old tracks and rolling stock remain in service, however.

AIR

Domestic flights are operated by LOT with a hub in Warsaw. There are few direct flights between other cities. Flying can save you hours on the trains.

Pomerania, p337

The capital of the north is Gdańsk, where you'll find great museums, the country's best beaches and the story of the Solidarity movement.

Warsaw, p320

An intriguing mix of royal palaces, communist-era architecture and compelling museums. Low-key and refreshingly few tourists.

Kraków, p326

Explore museums that unravel the city's complicated history and enjoy Poland's most sophisticated dining and entertainment.

Western Poland, p333

Two of Poland's most happening cities are Poznań and Wrocław. The first is a confident business centre; the second is a student town.

---

0 ——— 200 km
0 ——— 100 miles

Rostock

Schwerin

GERMANY

BERLIN

Baltic Sea

Słowiński National Park

Hel

Łeba

Słupsk

Koszalin

Kołobrzeg

Szczecin

Stargard

Szczeciński

Gorzów

Wielkopolski

Zielona Góra

Głogów

Jelenia Góra

Karpacz

Legnica

Wrocław

Opole

Racibórz

Panorama

Ostrava

CZECHIA

Brno

Gdańsk

European

Solidarity Centre

Museum of WWII

Malbork

Malbork Castle

Grudziądz

Bydgoszcz

Toruń

Piła

Poznań

Poznań Cathedral

Porta Posnania

Interactive

Heritage Centre

Leszno

Łódź

Piotrków

Trybunalski

Częstochowa

Katowice

Oświęcim

LITHUANIA

Suwałki

Ełk

Lake Mamry

Olsztyn Lake

Śniardwy National Park

Ostróda

Ostrołęka

Łomża

Biebrza

National Park

Białystok

BELARUS

WARSAW

Wilanów Palace

Warsaw Rising Museum

POLIN Museum of the History of Polish Jews

Radom

Kielce

Schindler's Factory

St Mary's Basilica

Kraków

Wieliczka Salt Mine

Tamobrzeg

Teespol

Biała Podlaska

Lublin

Zamość

Roztocze National Park

Chełm

Rzeszów

Lviv

UKRAINE

Bieszczadzki National Park

SLOVAKIA

Vistula

Odra

SEQOYA/SHUTTERSTOCK

Market square, Kraków (p326)

Plan Your Time

Poland could easily fill up a month of travels, so choose your destinations carefully to create an itinerary that's best suited to your availability.

Pressed for Time

● If you can only visit one place in Poland, then it should be **Kraków** (p326), Poland's tourist epicentre – it's a bit like Prague but with a more authentically Eastern European feel. There are museums galore as well as lots of Jewish and WWII heritage; when the sightseeing is over, there are many excellent, cosy taverns to retreat to.

A Week in Poland

● Start in **Kraków** (p326) with its royal sights, Jewish culture and WWII heritage, before taking a train to **Warsaw** (p320) to climb the PKiN Tower, feast in milk bars and ramble through royal gardens and palaces. From there, hop aboard a short flight to **Gdańsk** (p337), where beaches and museums dedicated to amber, WWII and the Solidarity trade union await.

SEASONAL HIGHLIGHTS

SPRING
The first flowers appear on the plains, but in April the sleet is still falling by the Baltic.

SUMMER
Poland can surprise with sweltering temperatures and high humidity. Ideal for Baltic beach days.

AUTUMN
The forests of southern and eastern Poland put on a fiery show and the cities are at their busiest.

WINTER
Snow can fall everywhere in Poland, but it's heaviest in the mountains. Sub-zero temps prevail for months.

Warsaw

MUSEUMS | ARCHITECTURE | HISTORY

☑ **TOP TIP**

On the right bank of the Vistula, the Praga neighbourhood has two beaches: Rusałka is near the zoo and has views of the Old Town skyline; Poniatówka is near the National Stadium and Saska Kępa. Borrow deck chairs, towels and other beach gear for free in summer.

By the end of 1945, the Polish capital of Warsaw lay in ruins. Rebuilding began almost immediately and it's a process that continues to this day. You'll encounter restored baroque, Gothic, neoclassical and Renaissance buildings in the Old and New Towns; gems of the post-WWII socialist-realist period, such as the grandiose Palace of Culture & Science; and innovative 21st-century revamps of old factories and other industrial sites.

Original fragments and treasures from Poland's turbulent past are preserved in a superb selection of museums. The exhibitions at the huge Warsaw Rising Museum, the even bigger POLIN Museum of the History of Polish Jews and the intriguingly curated Museum of Warsaw leave no stone unturned.

This is also a city blessed with plenty of greenery. Enjoy the parklands at Wilanów, aptly described as Poland's Versailles, and stroll the shady paths of Łazienki Park to encounter petite royal palaces and an ornamental lake.

Take a Tour of the Royal Castle

History rebuilt

Warsaw's **Royal Castle** *(zamek-krolewski.pl; entry adult/ concession 60/45zł)* began life in the 14th century as a wooden stronghold and evolved into one of Europe's most splendid

---

GETTING AROUND

Warsaw Chopin Airport *(lotnisko-chopina. pl)*, 9km south of the city centre, has frequent buses and less-frequent trains to central Warsaw (30 minutes). From **Warsaw Modlin Airport** *(modlinairport.pl)* 39km north of the city, there's a bus connection to central Warsaw (one hour). Two efficient train lines provide access across much of Warsaw, but the distance between stations can be long. Local trains can also be used for crossing the city, most handily between the two sides of the Vistula River. Warsaw's extensive network of buses and trams is the fastest way to get around. Bolt and Uber are best for taxis.

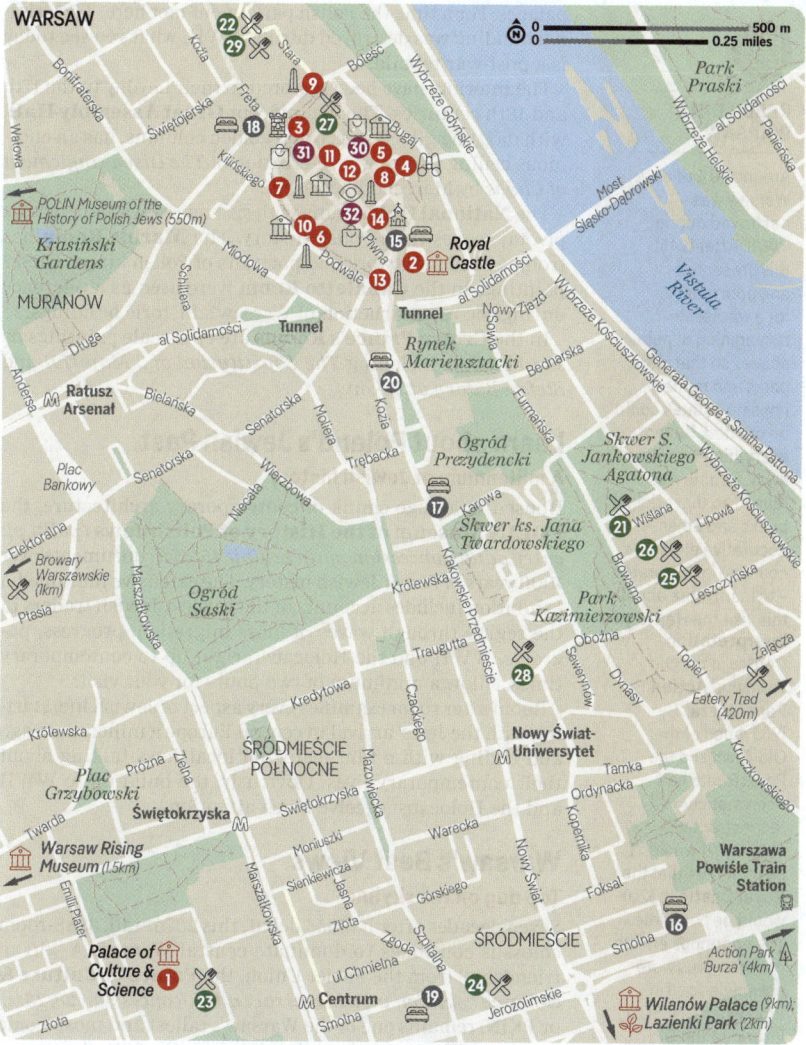

WARSAW

⭐ **HIGHLIGHTS**

1 Palace of Culture &
   Science
2 Royal Castle

🔴 **SIGHTS**

3 Barbican
4 Dung Hill Terrace
5 Heritage Interpretation
   Centre
6 Jan Kiliński Monument
7 Little Insurgent
   Monument

8 Mazovia
9 Mosaic House
10 Museum of Artistic and
   Precision Crafts
11 Museum of Warsaw
12 Old Town Market
   Square
13 Sigismund's Column
14 St John the Baptist
   Cathedral

⚫ **SLEEPING**

15 Castle Inn
16 Chopin Boutique B&B
17 Hotel Bristol
18 Oki Doki Hostel Old
   Town
19 PURO Warsaw
   Downtown
20 Safestay Warsaw Old
   Town

🟢 **EATING**

21 Bez Gwiazdek

22 Enoteca
23 Kulturalna
24 Między Nami
see 18 Mon Nom
25 Oma
26 SAM Powiśle
27 Sambal
28 Syrena Irena
29 Żyto

🔴 **SHOPPING**

30 Dom Sztuki Lodowej
31 Lapidarium
32 Polish Poster Gallery

321

REBUILDING WARSAW

Around 70% of Warsaw was destroyed during WWII. After 1945, this presented an opportunity for a wholesale reimagining of public spaces so that more parks and modern housing estates could be created. But not everything was swept away. Rubble was reused so that original bricks and other decorative elements could be incorporated – to learn more about this visit the **Heritage Interpretation Centre** in the Old Town and **Action Park 'Burza'**. By 1953 much of the Old Town and the Royal Route had been meticulously reconstructed, although it wouldn't be until 1984 that the **Royal Castle** (p320) would be complete. The enormous efforts of Varsovians were acknowledged in 1980 when UNESCO inscribed the Old Town on its World Heritage list.

palaces. For a time the Polish parliament met here. The original building was destroyed during WWII; what you see today is a post-war rebuild.

The interiors have been restored to their heyday in the 17th and 18th centuries. The magnificent **Great Assembly Hall**, with dazzling gilded stucco and golden columns, has an enormous ceiling painting, a re-creation of *The Disentanglement of Chaos* by Marcello Bacciarelli.

The **National Hall** is hung with six huge canvases depicting pivotal scenes from Polish history. The **Marble Room** has trompe l'oeil paintwork and portraits of Polish kings. The 22 paintings in the **Canaletto Room** were used as a reference during the reconstruction of Warsaw's historic buildings.

In the **Crown Prince's Rooms** are epic-scale paintings by Jan Matekjo, including *The Constitution of 3 May 1791* and *Stefan Batory at Pskov*.

Learn about Poland's Jewish Past

A millennium of Jewish history

Housed in a huge chunk of contemporary architecture, the **POLIN Museum of the History of Polish Jews** *(polin.pl; entry adult/concession main exhibit 45/35zł)* documents over 1000 years of Polish Jewish history. The extensive multimedia exhibition includes accounts of the earliest Jewish traders in the region through waves of mass migration, progress, pogroms, WWII and the Holocaust, right up to contemporary times. Allow a minimum of two hours for your visit.

Room after room examines every aspect of Jewish life, starting with the Jews' arrival in central Europe a millennium ago and ending with a film featuring local Jews talking about their contemporary lives. Obviously, the build-up to WWII and the Holocaust receive much attention.

Warsaw's Best Views

Top dog on the skyline

Seven decades after its 1955 debut, this 237m-tall, 3288-room colossus continues to dominate central Warsaw. A 'gift of friendship' from the Soviet Union, the **Palace of Culture & Science** *(pkin.pl; viewing terrace adult/concession 28/23zł)*, or PKiN, remains one of the Warsaw's tallest and most iconic buildings. The highlight is the view from the 30th-floor viewing terrace, accessed via a superfast lift.

 EATING IN OLD TOWN & NEW TOWN: OUR PICKS

Mon Nom: Lovely bistro, with potted plants and quirky art on the walls; a great breakfast or lunch spot. *9am-10pm Mon-Fri, to 11pm Sat & Sun* €€	**Sambal:** Indonesian restaurant serving authentic dishes such as *rendang padang*, a beef and coconut milk stew. *noon-9pm Tue-Fri & Sun, to 10pm Sat* €€	**Żyto:** Facing New Town Square, this Ukrainian restaurant serves hearty bowls of borscht and other regional dishes. *noon-10pm* €€	**Enoteca** Classy choice overlooking attractive New Town Square; good for Polish and Italian food or a simple glass of wine. *noon-10pm* €€€

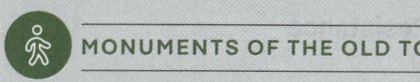

MONUMENTS OF THE OLD TOWN

If you know where to look, you'll find fascinating historical and artistic monuments dotted around the Old Town.

START	END	LENGTH
Castle Square	Museum of Artistic and Precision Crafts	1.5km; 1-2hr

Spend a moment in Castle Sq, overlooked by the 22m **1** **Sigismund's Column**, and consider that in 1945 all around you would have been rubble. Walk along ul Świętojańska to **2** **St John the Baptist Cathedral**, Warsaw's mother church. Continue ahead to the **3** **Old Town Market Square**. The picturesque square's central statue is the symbol of the city: Syrenka, the fierce mermaid brandishing a sword. Head inside the **4** **Museum of Warsaw** to see the original statue.

Exit the square along ul Celna – look through a gate to see the bas relief **5** **Mazovia** created in 1966 by sculptor Edmund Majkowski. Nearby, in **6** **Dung Hill Terrace** overlooking the Vistula,

is the *Strong Man* statue. Continue along ul Brzozowa to the stout fortress walls that partly encircle the Old Town. Look out to the New Town beyond, where you can see a striking socialist-realist **7** **mosaic** covering the side of one building.

Check out the stalls of craftspeople and artists in the **8** **Barbican** before continuing around the fortress to find the poignant **9** **Little Insurgent Monument**. Further along the walls is the **10** **Jan Kiliński Monument** and a clock with copper and gold-leaf zodiac signs on the side of the **11** **Museum of Artistic and Precision Crafts**.

The **Little Insurgent Monument** commemorates the child soldiers who died during the 1944 Warsaw Uprising.

Atop **Sigismund's Column** is a statue of Sigismund III Vasa (1566–1632), the Swedish-born king of Poland.

Jan Kiliński was a colonel during the failed 1794 Kościuszko Uprising against Russian and Prussian influences in Poland.

MURANÓW

Old Town Market Sq

MARIENSZTAT

Skwer Aliny Scholtz

0 — 200 m
0 — 0.1 miles

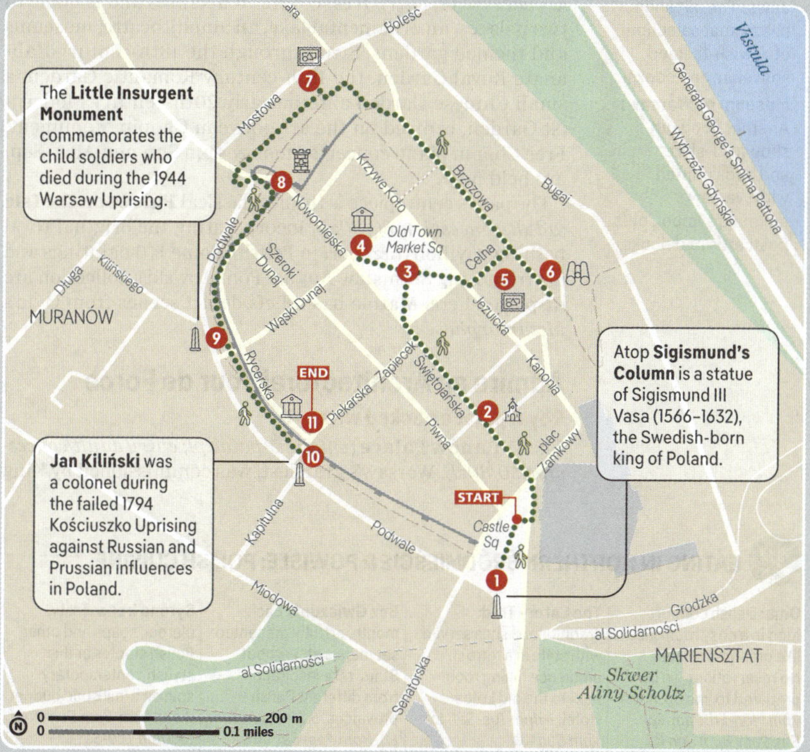

A Doomed Resistance

Warsaw in WWII

A former tram power station houses the **Warsaw Rising Museum** *(1944.pl; entry adult/concession 35/30zł)*, which covers in forensic detail Warsaw's heroic, doomed uprising against the German occupation in 1944. It's an immersive, dark and at times claustrophobic experience that evokes the horror of the times and the courage of the fighters.

The ground-floor exhibition begins with the division of Poland between Nazi Germany and the Soviet Union in 1939 and moves through the major events of WWII. An elevator then takes you to the mezzanine (2nd floor) and the start of the uprising in 1944 with day-by-day displays.

A life-size reproduction of the B-24J Liberator heavy bomber, used to drop supplies for insurgents, fills much of the ground-floor Liberator Hall. Here you can also watch newsreel films shot during the uprising, as well as a six-minute 3D film that re-creates the view from a flight over the devastated city in 1945.

Leafy Royal Grounds

Take a walk in Łazienki Park

Once a royal hunting ground, **Łazienki Park** *(lazienki-krolewskie.pl; entry free)* covers 76 hectares and is home to two palaces, an ornamental lake, an amphitheatre, museums and themed gardens. Stroll through the 18th-century Italianate Royal Garden, the 19th-century Romantic Garden, a small Chinese Garden and the early 20th-century Modernist Garden, centred on the art nouveau Chopin Monument. Free Chopin piano concerts (noon & 4pm Sun mid-May–Sep) are held here.

The park's centrepiece is the neoclassical **Palace on the Isle** *(adult/concession 60/30zł)*, incorporating the original royal bathing pavilion *(łazienki* in Polish). Some 140 paintings and art from King Stanisław August Poniatowski's collection are displayed here. Marble bas-reliefs depict scenes from Ovid's *Metamorphoses.*

Admire an Architectural Tour de Force

Royal palace packed with art

The **Wilanów Palace** *(wilanow-palac.pl; entry adult/concession 50/30zł)*, Warsaw's grandest, was commissioned by King

 EATING IN NORTHERN ŚRÓDMIEŚCIE & POWIŚLE: POLISH CUISINE

Oma: Delish comfort food in a cosy room just like grandma's house. No reservations, so be prepared to line up. *noon-9pm Mon-Fri, 9am-9pm Sat, 9am-8pm Sun* €€

The Eatery Trad: Traditional dishes served with style in a retro ambience dining room next to the old Lotos Hotel. *1-11pm Tue-Sat, to 9pm Sun* €€

Bez Gwiazdek: Each month, artfully presented set menus at 'Without Stars' take inspiration from different Polish provinces. *5.30-10pm Tue-Fri, from 4pm Sat* €€€

Syrena Irena: Tasty pierogi, soups and other Polish staples at this stylish contemporary spin on a 'milk bar' budget diner. *11am-8pm Sun-Wed, to 10pm Thu-Sat* €

CINEMATOGRAPHER/SHUTTERSTOCK

Łazienki Park

Jan III Sobieski in 1677. It changed hands several times over the centuries, with each new owner adding a bit of baroque here and a touch of neoclassical there. Miraculously, Wilanów survived WWII almost unscathed, and many of its furnishings and art were retrieved and reinstalled after the war.

The route through the palace involves some doubling back, but there are attendants to show the way. The tour starts with the **Princess Marshall Lubomirska's Apartments**, an immaculately restored salon dating from the late 18th century and including the magnificent Chinese and Hunting Rooms.

The **White Hall**, the palace's largest room, is hung with portraits of successive owners of Wilanów; the stairs here lead to the **Potocki Art Gallery**, displaying works of art gathered by the Potocki family, owners of Wilanów from 1799 to 1821.

Enveloping the palace is a splendid 45-hectare **park** *(adult/concession 10/5zł)*, where the landscaping ranges from a fragrant lily and rose garden to the Orangery, dotted with contemporary sculptures.

WARSAW FIGHTS BACK

Every year on 19 April at noon and 1 August at 5pm sirens sound across Warsaw and people fall silent. This is in remembrance of the beginning, respectively, of the **Ghetto Uprising** (lasting 29 days) and **Warsaw Uprising** (lasting 63 days) in 1943 and 1944, and of those who fought bravely against the city's Nazi German occupiers.

In 1944, insurgents took control of large parts of Warsaw by creating barricades from ripped-up paving slabs and using the sewers as underground communication lines. Sadly, the hoped-for support from the Allies and the Soviets failed to arrive, even though the Red Army was camped just outside Warsaw. In both uprisings, well over 250,000 Poles lost their lives.

 EATING IN NORTHERN ŚRÓDMIEŚCIE & POWIŚLE: CASUAL SPOTS

SAM Powiśle: Relaxed bakery, cafe and deli with dishes made from organic produce. *8am-8pm* €€

Między Nami: Vibey cafe-bar serves delicious open sandwiches for breakfast. *4pm-midnight Mon, 10am-midnight Tue-Thu, 10am-1am Fri & Sat, 10am-8pm Sun* €€

Kulturalna: Great spot for something tasty in a spacious hall off the main lobby of the Teatr Dramatyczny in PKiN. *noon-midnight Sun-Thu, to 2am Fri & Sat* €€

Browary Warszawskie: Drink craft beer brewed on site and dig into culinary treats either from the brewery or the food hall. *noon-10pm Sun-Thu, to midnight Fri & Sat* €€

Kraków

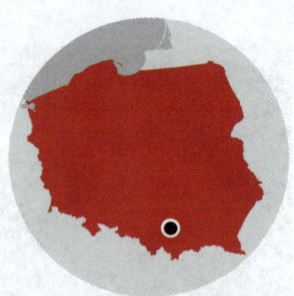

HISTORY | ARCHITECTURE | CULTURE

☑ **TOP TIP**

Head to one of Kraków's communist-era bars *mleczny* (milk bars) for a trip down nostalgia lane to the 1980s and a wallet-friendly canteen meal of omelettes, pierogi, soup, mashed potatoes and other belly-fillers. Due to the increasing cost of living, they've seen a resurgence recently.

The southern metropolis of Kraków is the former capital of Poland and one of the finest medieval cities in all of Europe. The most quintessentially Polish destination, it's a place steeped in legends of dragons and kings. Its thousand years of history kicked off with plundering Tatar hordes and continued on through multiple royal dynasties, the waxing and waning of empires, the unfurling of Europe-wide trade routes in the Middle Ages, the decline that followed after the Polish capital was moved to Warsaw in the 16th century, the terror of the Nazi regime during WWII and decades of communist repression – all followed by its rejuvenation as a tourist magnet. Kraków's turbulent history bequeathed it layers of architecture, which survived WWII largely intact. And while the Holocaust casts a long shadow, Jewish culture is enjoying a renaissance in the rejuvenated Kazimierz district.

A Medieval Marketplace Unveiled

Explore an interactive subterranean museum

When Kraków's market square was undergoing renovations around two decades ago, the remains of the original millennium-old marketplace were found beneath the Cloth Hall. They have since been transformed into **Rynek Underground** (*muzeumkrakowa.pl; entry adult/child 25/17zł*), a subterranean 'Middle Ages meets the 21st century' experience.

 GETTING AROUND

Trains and buses run from the airport to the central Kraków Główny train station and the adjacent bus station every 30 minutes (20 minutes, 4am to midnight). Thirty-minute taxi rides to the city centre cost 80 to 100zł with Kraków Airport Taxis and 40 to 75zł with Uber or Bolt.

The best way to explore the grid-like neighbourhoods is on foot. Kraków's integrated tram and bus system runs from 5am to 11pm, with less frequent night services after 11pm. Purchase tickets via the Jakdojade app or at the machines at tram stops and validate them on board.

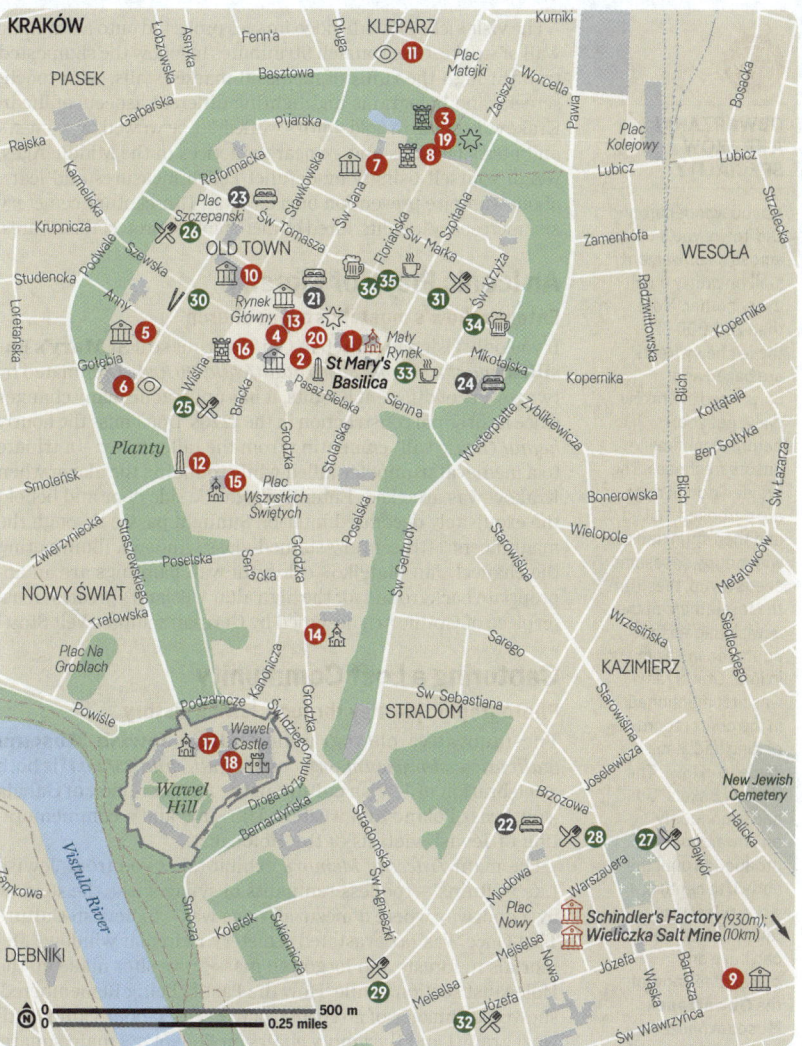

KRAKÓW

⭐ **HIGHLIGHTS**

1 St Mary's Basilica

🔴 **SIGHTS**

2 Adam Mickiewicz
3 Barbican
4 Cloth Hall
5 Collegium Maius
6 Collegium Novum
7 Czartoryski Museum
8 Florian Gate
9 Galicia Jewish Museum
10 Historical Museum of Kraków
11 Obwarzanek Museum
12 Papal Window
13 Rynek Underground
14 St Andrew's Church
15 St Francis' Basilica
16 Town Hall Tower
17 Wawel Cathedral
18 Wawel Royal Castle

🔴 **ACTIVITIES**

19 Free Walking Tour
20 Kraków Pub Crawl

⚫ **SLEEPING**

21 Bonerowski Palace
22 Dream Hostel
23 Globetrotter Guest House
24 Hotel Gródek

🟢 **EATING**

25 Antler Poutine & Burger
26 Charlotte Chleb i Wino
27 Dawno Temu Na Kazimierzu
28 Karakter
29 Kropka Krákow
30 Kuku Taiwanese
31 Milkbar Tomasza
32 Pierwszy Stopień

🟢 **DRINKING & NIGHTLIFE**

33 Bonobo
34 House of Beer
35 Pożegnanie z Afryką Cafe
36 Viva la Pinta

OBWARZANKI: A KRAKÓW SPECIALITY

As you wander around Old Town, you'll come across an *obwarzanki* stall on pretty much every corner. More than 200,000 of these chewy treats are baked and consumed in Kraków daily; get yours before lunchtime to ensure freshness. The braided dough rings are parboiled, baked and then sprinkled with poppy or sesame seeds – yup, these are the forefathers of the Jewish bagels that appeared in Kazimierz in 1610. *Obwarzanki* was first mentioned in the court records of King Ladislaus II Jagiello in 1394. The Kraków Bakers' Guild had a monopoly on *obwarzanek* production until the early 17th century, when rules were relaxed. Anyone can bake an *obwarzanek* now at the **Obwarzanek Museum** (*muzeumobwarzanka.com*), including you.

The visit kicks off with video images projected onto a dramatic wall of smoke. Give yourself 90 minutes to follow the signposted trail through the ruins of medieval market stalls, with touch-screens and holograms highlighting different aspects of life in Kraków. Peer into a goldsmith's workshop, be wowed by women's and men's fashions and skincare practices in the Middle Ages, weigh yourself using long-defunct Polish measures and learn about 'vampire prevention burials' at an 11th-century cemetery and mercenary knights, hired by merchants to protect their wares.

An Iconic Place of Worship

Enter Kraków's most illustrious church

If you only visit one church in Old Town, make it **St Mary's Basilica** (*mariacki.com; entry adult/child 18/10zł*). Dominated by two towers of different heights, it has undergone many changes since its original construction in the 1220s. Don't miss the hourly *hejnał* (bugle call) emanating from the taller tower – a tribute to a medieval trumpeter killed while sounding the alarm when Kraków was attacked. Enter through the side door and behold the exquisitely decorated interior. Sunlight passes through the magnificent 14th-century stained-glass windows, illuminating the chancel. Jan Matejko's colourful wall paintings are an appropriate background for the high altar – Poland's greatest masterpiece of Gothic art, designed by German sculptor Veit Stoss.

Capturing a Lost Community

Photographic journey through Jewish history

The innovative photographic **Galicia Jewish Museum** (*galiciajewishmuseum.org; entry adult/child 35/25zł*) is both a celebration of Jewish culture in the former region of Galicia (southeast Poland and western Ukraine) and a commemoration of Jewish victims of the Holocaust.

The main *Traces of Memory* exhibit takes you from 'Jewish Life in Ruins' – roofless remnants of synagogues, the shadow by a doorway where a mezuzah once was – to 'Jewish Culture That Once Was' (a devastated cemetery, a circular window). Memorials in forests and forgotten mass grave sites make up the Holocaust section, while 'How the Past Is Being Remembered' showcases images of a reconstructed slave labour camp, anti-Nazi graffiti and the empty chairs on Podgórze's main square. At the end, there's a hopeful note in the form of 'Revival of Jewish Life': images of Festival of Jewish Culture concerts and young Jews partaking in the March of the Living.

EATING IN OLD TOWN: BUDGET BITES

Antler Poutine & Burger: This tongue-in-cheek Canadian burger joint also dishes up poutine (fries smothered in gravy and melted cheese). *noon-10pm* €

Milkbar Tomasza: A modern take on a traditional Polish *bar mleczny*, where panini sit proudly beside pierogi. *8am-6pm Mon-Sat, from 9am Sun* €

Kuku Taiwanese: Bowls of Taiwanese curry, dumplings with chilli sauce and sesame soup noodles are served with maximum efficiency. *11.30am-9.30pm* €

Charlotte Chleb i Wino: Warsaw restaurant outpost, known for croissants, croque monsieurs and sandwiches, along with French wine and coffee. *7am-midnight* €

Wawel Royal Castle

On any given day, Wawel Royal Castle – Poland's answer to Buckingham Palace and Westminster Abbey – teems with visitors. Its glorious mishmash of Romanesque, Renaissance and Gothic architecture – the product of conquests, fashion and multiple royal dynasties – plus glittering treasures, looming towers and verdant grounds demonstrates why Kraków is a world-class city.

Wawel Cathedral

The Royal Castle

In centuries past, the ground-floor **State Rooms** were where royals received guests, held court and entertained. Pass through the vast, individually styled halls, liberally sprinkled with oil paintings and 16th-century Flemish tapestries, including the ostentatious Throne Room.

The **Royal Private Apartments** are the 1st-floor bedchambers, with modestly proportioned beds that feature carved four-poster frames. The Renaissance furnishings of King Sigismund the Old, the painted ceiling beams of the royal guest room and the tiny bejewelled 'Hen's Foot' (Queen Jadwiga's chapel) in the 14th-century Belvedere Tower stand out.

Below, vaulted Gothic rooms hold the **Treasury's** sceptres and orbs, gold goblets, royal banners, textiles and exotic objects acquired by King Sigismund III.

Wawel Cathedral

Built on the orders of Władysław the Short (1306–33), the first king to be crowned here, the current incarnation of **Wawel Cathedral** (1364) is actually the third, with the 1020 CE original and its successor having burned down. Arguably the most important building in Poland, the cathedral has hosted the coronation of virtually every Polish king and queen. Poland's monarchs occupy tombs in the cathedral and the royal crypt.

TOP TIPS

- Book your visit to Wawel Royal Castle in advance.

- You can visit the castle grounds free of charge.

- You can either book tickets to Wawel Royal Castle's separate attractions or get a day pass that covers everything.

- Entry to Wawel Cathedral must be purchased separately.

PRACTICALITIES
- wawel.krakow.pl/en
- adult/child from 49/37zł
- 10am-4pm Mon, 9am-5pm Tue-Sun

PODGÓRZE'S UNLIKELY HERO

Podgórze was home to at least two prominent Gentiles who risked their lives to save Jews during the Holocaust. The best known is Oskar Schindler, the heavy-drinking profiteer and anti-hero, whose story was told to millions through Thomas Keneally's book *Schindler's Ark* (1982) and Steven Spielberg's *Schindler's List* (1993).

Schindler originally saved the lives of Jews because he needed their cheap labour at his enamelware factory, and he used his connections and paid bribes in order to keep his employees from being shipped off to concentration camps. As is movingly quoted at the end of Spielberg's film, in reference to a passage in the Talmud, 'Whoever saves one life, saves the world entire'.

KANUMAN/GETTY IMAGES

Wieliczka Salt Mine

Learn about Schindler & the Polish Resistance

Museum of German occupation

Covering the German occupation of Kraków during WWII, the interactive **Schindler's Factory** (*muzeumkrakowa.pl/en; entry adult/child 40/35zł*) – one of Kraków's most popular museums – is housed in the former enamel factory of Oskar Schindler, the Nazi industrialist immortalised in Steven Spielberg's 1993 film *Schindler's List*.

The 30-minute introductory film showcases ordinary Cracovians telling their (often horrific) stories of life under German occupation. You then pass through labyrinthine rooms, each revolving around a specific theme. Sepia photographs, original radio and video footage, period objects, multimedia installations and individual stories of the city's residents immerse you in the unsettling prewar years and the first days of the war. Move on to the German repression of the city's Jewish residents and members of the Polish resistance, and the outright horror of the deportations to the death camps.

Though abandoned after WWII, Oskar Schindler's former office survived intact. The room's centrepiece is a symbolic Survivors' Ark – a giant translucent cube filled made of thousands of enamel pots, similar to the ones made by Schindler's employees.

EATING IN KAZIMIERZ: OUR PICKS

Karakter: Whole-animal dishes like tripe and sweetbreads, plus conventional offerings for the offal-averse. Three-course lunch (63zł) is a steal. *1-11pm* €€

Pierwszy Stopień: While the dishes at this plant-bedecked spot lean carnivore, the pearl barley kashotto with white asparagus is a thing of beauty. *1-10pm* €€

Kropka Kraków: Modern Polish joint with globally-tinged dishes (pierogi with Korean-style sauce) and natural wines. *4-10pm Tue-Fri, from 1pm Sat & Sun* €€

Dawno Temu Na Kazimierzu: Atmospheric Jewish-themed restaurant shows off hearty variations of lamb and duck in a tiny candlelit space. *10am-11pm* €€

Delve Deep into the Wieliczka Salt Mine

Three hundred kilometres of salt

Some 14km southeast of Kraków, the UNESCO-listed **Wieliczka Salt Mine** *(wieliczka-saltmine.com; entry adult/child 156/124zł)* has been welcoming tourists since 1722 and today is one of the area's most popular attractions. It's a subterranean labyrinth of tunnels and chambers – a whopping 300km distributed over nine levels, the deepest being 327m underground – dug out by miners over the centuries right up until 1996. A small part is open to the public via two guided tours: the **Tourist Route** and the **Miners' Route**. Highlights of the Tourist Route include the 17th-century Chapel of St Kinga, a subterranean church measuring 54m by 18m by 12m, and the enormous Stanisław Staszic Chamber, which measures 36m in height and has hosted a subterranean bungee jump and even an underground balloon flight.

The immersive three-hour Miners' Route gives you a deep appreciation for the demanding and perilous profession. Visitors dress in grey miners' coveralls and hard hats and are given a headlamp and emergency respirator. You then make your way through narrow workmanlike passages.

It is cool in the tunnels so bring a sweater. Buy tickets online in advance, particularly for the English-language tours, which sell out.

The Horror of Auschwitz-Birkenau

The Nazis' most infamous concentration camp

Many visitors combine a stay in Kraków with a visit to the **Auschwitz-Birkenau Memorial & Museum** *(auschwitz.org)*. Some 1.1 million people – mostly Jews – died at Auschwitz-Birkenau between 1941 and 1945: they were gassed, worked to death and mistreated. The scale of the place and the scope of the horror can be overwhelming. It is not a place to bring children.

Both sections of the camp – Auschwitz I and the much larger outlying Birkenau (Auschwitz II) – have been preserved and are open to visitors free of charge. It's essential to visit both to appreciate the extent and the inhumanity of the place.

Oświęcim (the Polish name for Auschwitz) has frequent train services from Kraków (65 to 100 minutes). Local buses run constantly between the station and the Auschwitz I entrance. Or you can walk the 1.5km in about 20 minutes. Frequent buses also link Auschwitz I with Birkenau; the walk is 3km.

KRAKÓW'S BEST TOURS

Free Walking Tour: Old Town tours depart four times daily from March to October (less frequently November to February). *(freewalkingtour.com)*

Kraków Pub Crawl: Classic drinking tour visits four venues and starts out from the Main Market Square. *(krawlthroughkrakow.com)*

Delicious Poland: Superb foodie tours of Kazimierz that involve sampling typical Polish food and drink until you're fit to burst. *(deliciouspoland.com)*

Jarden Tourist Agency: Personalised Jewish-themed tours, including two- and three-hour walking tours of Kraków's Kazimierz and Podgórze. *(jarden.pl)*

Cracow City Tours: Decent range of walking and bus tours, including a popular four-hour coach tour and excursions to the Wieliczka Salt Mine and Auschwitz-Birkenau. *(cracowcitytours.pl)*

 DRINKING IN OLD TOWN: OUR PICKS

Pożegnanie z Afryką: Burlap sacks full of coffee, earth-coloured decor and nicely brewed espresso define this *Out of Africa*–themed coffee shop. *10am-8pm*

Bonobo: Linger over an espresso, cake or a glass of red wine at this well-stocked travel bookshop. *noon-11pm Mon-Fri, from 3pm Sat & Sun*

House of Beer: Sink into a leather sofa and choose from 21 draught beers and over 200 bottles from Poland, Germany, Lithuania and Belgium. *2pm-midnight*

Viva La Pinta: Award-winning microbrewery pouring a range of craft beers in a courtyard garden. Popular in summer. *4pm-midnight Sun-Thu, to 2am Fri & Sat*

THE ROUTE OF KINGS & QUEENS

This walk through the Old Town's cobbled streets follows the 400-year-old coronation route of Poland's kings and queens.

START	END	LENGTH
Florian Gate	Wawel Royal Castle	1.6km; 2½hr

Start at ❶ **Florian Gate**, the most important of Kraków's eight medieval gates. Together with the 15th-century ❷ **Barbican** – an impenetrable defence tower that withstood several sieges – the gate forms the City Defence Walls museum. Detour along ul Pijarska to ❸ **Czartoryski Palace**, then continue down ul Florianska to ❹ **St Mary's Basilica** (p328). Try to be here on the hour to hear the bugle call. Walk past the ❺ **monument to Adam Mickiewicz** (Poland's greatest literary hero) before cutting through the bustling ❻ **Cloth Hall**, a medieval shopping arcade in the middle of Rynek Główny, Europe's largest medieval town square. Head to its northwest corner to visit the ❼ **Historical**

Museum of Kraków inside the 17th-century Krzysztofory Palace. Proceed to the 14th-century ❽ **Town Hall Tower** for lofty Old Town views. Head to ul Jagiellonska and pass by ❾ **Collegium Maius**, followed by the neo-Gothic ❿ **Collegium Novum** (1873–87), then cut through the park that encircles Old Town to pass the ⓫ **Bishop's Palace** where former Pope John Paul II made appearances at the 'Papal Window'. Walk past ⓬ **St Francis' Basilica** and turn right onto busy ul Grodzka. You'll pass ⓭ **St Andrew's Church** – an 11th-century Romanesque fortress church – before turning down the cobbled ul Kanonicza that leads to ⓮ **Wawel Royal Castle** (p329).

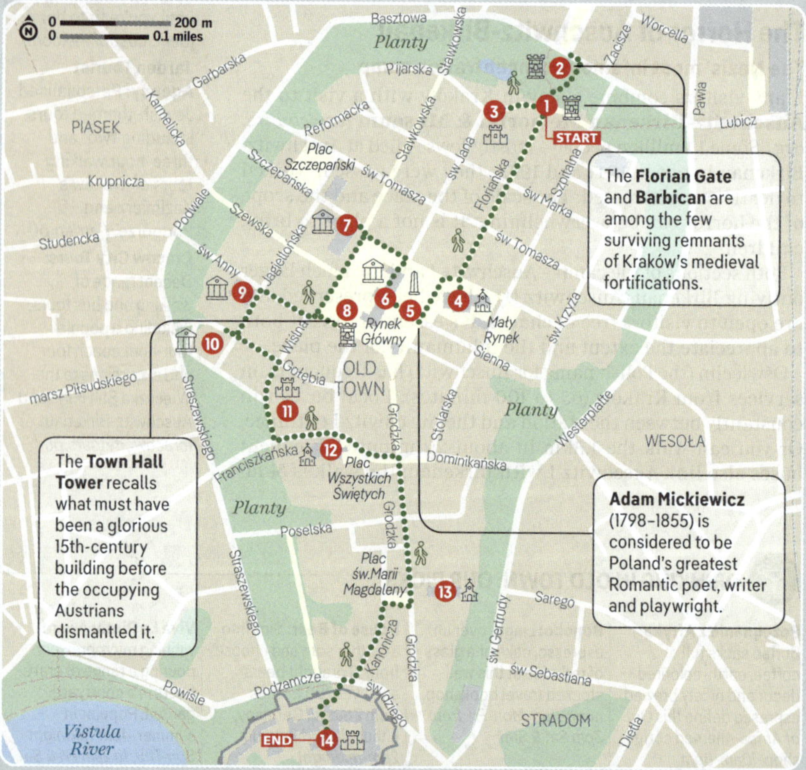

The **Florian Gate** and **Barbican** are among the few surviving remnants of Kraków's medieval fortifications.

The **Town Hall Tower** recalls what must have been a glorious 15th-century building before the occupying Austrians dismantled it.

Adam Mickiewicz (1798–1855) is considered to be Poland's greatest Romantic poet, writer and playwright.

Western Poland

ARCHITECTURE | HISTORY | NIGHTLIFE

The western Polish cities of Wrocław and Poznań are worthwhile stop-offs on a wider Poland tour. Slightly off the trodden path from Poland's main attractions, these two cities have a lot to offer travellers who make the effort to reach them.

Wrocław is the capital of Silesia and Poland's fourth-largest city, and its 12 islands, 130 bridges and verdant riverside parks on the Odra River are idyllic. The beautifully preserved ecclesiastic district on Cathedral Island is a treat for lovers of Gothic architecture.

Poznań's city centre buzzes and hums as locals head to its many restaurants, pubs and clubs. The city has bags of heritage, from medieval times to the mid-20th century, when Poznań rebelled in a big way against communist rule.

Wrocław

Everyone loves Wrocław (vrots-wahf) and it's easy to see why. The capital of Lower Silesia is a more manageable version of Kraków, with similar culture and entertainment offerings, plus an appealing character all its own.

Visit the old Town Hall

Poznań's Renaissance town hall, topped with a 61m-high tower, instantly attracts attention. Its graceful form replaced a 13th-century Gothic structure, which burned down in the early 16th century. Every day at noon two metal goats appear through a pair of small doors above the clock and butt their horns together 12 times, in deference to an old legend. These days, the town hall is home to the city's Historical Museum.

Wrocław's toughest climb and best view

Of the many towers you can climb in Wrocław, the most difficult – but most rewarding – is the 91m-high tower of the

Places

Wrocław p333

Poznań p334

GETTING AROUND

Wrocław is 3½ hours from Warsaw and three hours from Kraków by train. The city has an efficient network of trams and buses *(MPK; mpk. wroc.pl)* covering the city centre and suburbs; however, almost everything is within easy walking distance of the Rynek.

Poznań is relatively compact and the major museums are centrally located. The tram network is useful, but not all stops sell tickets.

☑ TOP TIP

Wrocław's helpful tourist office is centrally located at Rynek 14 and is open daily.

HERE COME THE DWARFS

Across Wrocław, you may (literally!) stumble upon **tiny bronze dwarfs** horse-riding, bellringing, singing, sleeping and much more. Measuring up to 30cm, the dwarfs pop up everywhere. Indeed, by 2025, there were more than 1100 and more continue to appear. The tourist office distributes a popular 'Find the Dwarf' map. There are also apps and a Dwarfs Festival in September, with a big weekend of games, culture and fun.

Wrocław's dwarf obsession began with Orange Alternative, a 1980s dissident group that used ridicule as a weapon during the humour-free days of communism. It painted pictures of orange-capped *krasnale* (dwarfs) on places where the authorities had painted over anti-government graffiti – cleverly drawing attention to the critical messages.

14th-century **Church of St Elizabeth** *(Kościół Św Elżbiety; elzbieta.archidiecezja.wroc.pl; tower adult/child 17/11zł)*, reached via a narrow set of 304 steps. What awaits is arguably the most expansive panorama in the city. Back on the ground, the 14th-century Gothic basilica has a triple nave reaching 30m and is lined by medieval chapels.

Wander the most evocative quarter

Cathedral Island (Ostrów Tumski) – which actually became connected to the mainland in the 19th century – was the cradle of Wrocław. It was here that the Ślężanie, a tribe of West Slavs, constructed their stronghold in the 7th or 8th century. In 1000, Wrocław's first church was built here.

The centrepiece of Cathedral Island, the **Cathedral of St John the Baptist** *(Archikatedra Św Jana Chrzciciela; katedra.wroclaw.pl; chapels & tower adult/child 35/25zł)* is a three-aisled Gothic basilica built between the 13th and 16th centuries with three beautiful **baroque chapels**. For views, climb 40 steps and a lift will then whisk you to the top of the 91m-high **tower**.

A wonder all around

A grand spectacle in its day, the **Racławice Panorama** *(Panorama Racławicka; mnwr.pl; entry adult/child 50/35zł)* still impresses. A giant cyclorama wrapped around the internal walls of a rotunda depicts the battle for Polish independence. It took place at Racławice, 40km northeast of Kraków, on 4 April 1794 between the Polish army and Russian troops. The Poles won, but it was all for nought: months later, the nationwide insurrection was crushed by the tsarist army and Poland ceased to exist as a nation until WWI.

Savouring the art of old

The **National Museum** *(Muzeum Narodowe; mnwr.pl; entry adult/child 20/15zł)* is a trove of fine art from across the ages, including medieval sculpture, Silesian paintings, ceramics, silverware and furnishings from the 16th to 19th centuries. The collection covers most of Poland's big names; be prepared for moody portraits and massive battle scenes.

Poznań

Poznań was founded in the 9th century on Ostrów Tumski (Cathedral Island) during the reign of Duke Mieszko I, Poland's first ruler, and became the seat of power along with Gniezno.

 EATING IN WROCŁAW: TOP CHOICES

Restauracja Lwia Brama: Top-flight restaurant serves modern Polish fare in an inviting medieval cellar on Cathedral Island. Refined service. *noon-10pm* €€€

Baba: Much lauded upscale yet homestyle Polish bistro helmed by top chef Beata Śniechowska. Always buzzy, with a surprising local wine list. *4-8pm* €€€

Le Gosse Restauracja: Popular neighbourhood bistro with refined air aided by white tablecloths; it does a smashing breakfast. *9am-11pm* €€

Restauracja Wrocławska: Specialises in Silesian fare and great beer. Hearty dishes include seasoned pork, beef, mushroom and potato dishes. *noon-10pm* €€

Poznań Cathedral

In the Second Partition of Poland in 1793, the city fell under Prussian occupation and was later renamed Posen, a period that ended with the Wielkopolska Uprising in 1918. But the city is also famous for another rebellion: the massive June 1956 Uprising that led to calls for political change.

Explore Cathedral Island and Śródka

Located east of the Old Town across the Warta River, **Ostrów Tumski** (Cathedral Island) is where Poznań was founded. The original 9th-century settlement was gradually transformed into an oval stronghold surrounded by wood-and-earth ramparts, with an early stone palace. Mieszko I added a cathedral and further fortifications, and by the end of the 10th century, Poznań was the most powerful stronghold in the country. The best way to appreciate the double-towered Gothic **Poznań Cathedral** (Katedra Poznańska; katedra.archpoznan.pl; entry free), its architecture and its historical background is by picking up an audio guide from the nearby **Porta Posnania Interactive Heritage Centre** (Porta Poznania ICHOT; bramapoznania.pl; entry adult/child 28/22zł).

POZNAŃ'S FESTIVAL CALENDAR

Blues Express: Summer odyssey of blues concerts at train stations, starting in Poznań. (bluesexpress.pl)

Old Jazz Festival: Mid-September, with local and international jazz performers. (oldjazzfestival.pl)

Malta Festival Poznań: Late June, with alternative theatre and other arts. (malta-festival.pl)

St Martin's Day: On 11 November, with a parade from the Church of St Martin (Kościół św Marcina) to the Imperial Palace (Zamek).

Enter Enea Music Festival: Open-air jazz concerts in late May/June at Jezioro Strzeszyńskie, a lake 12km north of town. (entereneafestival.pl)

BitterSweet Festival: Top international music acts, held in Citadel Park in September. (bittersweetfestival.pl)

DRINKING IN POZNAŃ'S CENTRE: OUR PICKS

SARP Social Club: Wednesday night jam sessions are a highlight at this bar, often with a jazz-funk flavour. 11-1am Tue-Thu & Sun, from 4pm Mon, 11-3am Fri & Sat

Dragon Social Club: Eclectic pub and music venue with a relaxed vibe for a diverse, alternative crowd. noon-1am Mon-Wed & Sun, to 3am Thu-Sat

Blue Note Jazz Club: Opens for gigs; not all of them are jazz. Check the website at bluenote. poznan.pl. hours vary

Brovaria: Microbrewery serving its own Pilsner, honey, dark, wheat and seasonal beers. Also has a restaurant and hotel. noon-11pm Mon-Sat, 11am-8pm Sun

LONGFIN MEDIA/SHUTTERSTOCK

Monument to the Victims of June 1956

The June 1956 Uprising in Poznań

The June 1956 industrial strike in Poznań was the first mass protest in the Soviet Bloc, erupting just three years after Stalin's death. It originated in the city's largest industrial plant, the Cegielski Metalworks (then named after Stalin), when workers demanded a refund on an unfairly charged tax. A strike ensued, escalating into a full-scale protest when 100,000 people – one-quarter of Poznań's population at the time – gathered on Plac Mickiewicza, demanding 'bread and freedom' and improved working conditions. Ignored by city officials, an angry crowd stormed police headquarters and the Communist Party building, releasing 257 prisoners from jail. The uprising deteriorated into bloodshed after tanks and troops were brought in. Seventy-six people died and many more were wounded or arrested in this little-known struggle. Today, it is depicted at the **Museum of Poznań June 1956** (*Muzeum Poznańskiego Czerwca 1956; wmn.poznan.pl; entry adult/child 15/10zł*). The small museum is located downstairs in a neo-Romanesque castle, where you can take a fascinating step back into the events. English descriptions are limited. Across the road is the evocative **Monument to the Victims of June 1956**.

 EATING IN POZNAŃ'S CENTRE: OUR PICKS

Pyra Bar: Lots of potato dishes, some of which are vegetarian and gluten-free. Or just hang out with a drink. *11am-9pm Sun-Thu, to 11pm Fri & Sat* €

Republika Róż by Andrzej Gołąbek: Menu of hearty, well-prepared Polish mains. Excellent soups, salads and burgers, too. *noon-10pm Tue-Sat, to 8pm Sun* €€

Fromażeria: Acclaimed restaurant with a cheese-tasting menu, combining Polish and French traditions. *5-10.30pm Mon-Thu, to midnight Fri & Sat, 2-10pm Sun* €€€

MUGA: Seasonal international dishes in this long-standing gourmet favourite, with an affiliated Casa de Vinos wine bar. *5-10pm Tue-Sat* €€€

Pomerania

CASTLES | HISTORY | BEACHES

History, amber, beaches and red bricks have shaped Poland's breezy northern province, one of Poland's most engaging regions.

Cream-hued beaches shelving into the nippy Baltic Sea, wind-crafted dunes vivid against leaden skies, stern red-brick churches and castles erected by a medieval order of pious knights and silenced shipyards that once seethed with anti-communist tumult – this is Pomerania, Poland's north, a land of many faces.

The epicentre of Pomerania is Gdańsk, northern Poland's metropolis, a rapidly modernising city with a photogenic historic centre. Like most of the region, Gdańsk has changed hands many times over the centuries, each invader bequeathing a layer of architecture and culture for today's visitors to enjoy.

South of Gdańsk, top billing goes to Malbork Castle, once the mothership of the Teutonic knights and still the world's largest brick building.

Places

Gdańsk p337
Malbork p340

☑ TOP TIP

Buy amber at Gdańsk's Amber Museum, Mariacka St and the amber market in the Foregate at the western end of Długa St.

Gdańsk

Follow the Royal Way

Lined by the city's grandest facades, Gdańsk's **Royal Way** was the route Polish kings traditionally paraded down during their periodic visits. Of Poland's three Royal Ways (Warsaw, Kraków and Gdańsk), Gdańsk's is the shortest at just 500m long.

🧭 GETTING AROUND

Gdańsk has a comprehensive public transport network that's cheap and easy to use. Buses, trams and the SKM train service run to every corner of the city and beyond. Single tickets cost just 4.80zł, and a 24-hour pass is 22zł. The website of the public transport company *(ztm.gda.pl)* has a useful journey planner. This flat city can also be seen by bike and shared scooters. That said, the best way to see the old historical centre is on foot. Trains run regularly from Gdańsk to Malbork.

Starting at the western end, turn your back on rumbling Okopowa to face the **Upland Gate** (Brama Wyżynna), the traditional entry point for kings dating from 1574. It now houses the Pomerania Regional Tourist Office. A few steps east rises the **Foregate**, a large 15th-century construction that has served as an execution site, a jail, the city's amber museum and now an amber market. Just beyond the Foregate's hefty doors stands the 17th-century **Złota Brama** (Golden Gate), a triumphal arch. On the other side extends **ul Długa** (Long St) with its many rebuilt townhouse gables.

After 325m, ul Długa suddenly widens out into **Długi Targ**, Gdańsk's showpiece square. On your left gurgles the famous **Neptune Fountain**, behind which lurks the **Artus Court Museum**, part of the Historical Museum of Gdańsk. Also on the right, near the western end of the square, is the city's modest tourist office. Blocking the way to the riverfront is the Royal Way's exit, the 16th-century **Green Gate** (Brama Zielona). Meant as a residence for the king (who never stayed there), it once housed the office of Lech Wałęsa, leader of Poland's first independent trade union and Nobel Peace Prize winner, when he was president. It is now home to the National Museum's photographic exhibition.

Tour Gdańsk's must-see museum

Opened in 2016, the **Museum of WWII** *(muzeum1939.pl; entry adult/concession 32/22zł)* is a bold addition to the northern end of Gdańsk's waterfront. A must-visit attraction, it traces the fate of Poland during the world's greatest conflict, focusing on human suffering. Few leave unmoved. The museum covers 5000 sq m, so a minimum of three hours is needed to do the main exhibit justice.

Opened by local lad and Polish prime minister Donald Tusk in 2017, the museum occupies one of Gdańsk's most striking buildings. Outside, all you can see is a wedge of glass and steel, like a missile that has wedged itself into the earth without exploding. Most of the structure that houses the main exhibition is a bunkerish, brutalist grey concrete block, 14m underground.

The museum is divided chronologically into three sections with 18 individual spaces. The first section examines the causes of the war, tracing the rise of Hitler, the Nazis and other totalitarian regimes after WWI. Section two largely deals with the human suffering caused during WWII, from concentration camp prisoners and the persecuted Polish intelligentsia to soldiers on the front line and those subjected to forced labour. The third and final section looks at how WWII ended and its impact on Europe after 1945. The museum is free on Tuesdays.

A glimpse into prehistory at the Amber Museum

Gdańsk's **Amber Museum** *(muzeumgdansk.pl; entry adult/child 37/26zł)* has become an unmissable attraction since it opened in 2020. It's housed in dramatic style within the massive red-brick hulk of the Great Mill, a medieval structure that has long since ground its last grains.

The interior of the Great Mill has been blacked out to enhance the glow of the nuggets, blobs and small boulders of prehistoric tree sap that seem to be illuminated from within. The lower floor looks at amber in its natural form, with slabs containing insects and plants (inclusions) and lumps in all shapes, sizes and colours, as well as lots of information on how amber is formed and why there is so much of the stuff in the Baltic. The upper floor explores what people have used amber for over the millennia: from medicine to tools to crucifixes, chess sets and furniture. For those in the market for Baltic gold, the best is saved for last in the shape of a large amber jewellery shop.

TOP SOUVENIRS

Amber: Milky white, treacle gold and liver red hunks of fossilised resin wash up on Baltic beaches after winter storms.

Goldwasser: Spice-infused liqueur with flakes of 22-karat gold has been distilled in Gdańsk since 1598. Yes, you can drink it!

Kashubian handicrafts: The region south of Gdańsk produces some distinctively Slavic handicrafts, such as ceramics and linen.

Solidarność memorabilia: A Lech Wałęsa moustache, a 1980s pin badge or just about anything bearing the famous Solidarność logo: memorabilia celebrating the famous trade union makes for a unique souvenir.

Jopenbier: Made by the PG4 microbrewey near the train station, this is Gdańsk's traditional beer.

 ## EATING IN GDAŃSK: BEST LOCAL FOOD

Pomelo Bistro Bar: Using ingredients from mostly local suppliers, the menu at this eclectic, colourful place features Kashubian dishes. *9am-10pm €€*

Restauracja Motlava: Almost gourmet versions of Polish and Kashubian dishes in an understated dining environment. *noon-10pm €€*

TYGLE: Finely crafted local dishes populate the refreshingly brief menu at this well-run restaurant with an upmarket feel. *9am-9pm Mon-Sun €€*

Stacja Food Hall: In the Galeria Metropolitana mall, this food hall has hard-to-find Kashubian options. *noon-10pm Mon-Thu, to midnight Fri & Sat, to 9pm Sun €*

GDAŃSK TOURIST CARD

The Gdańsk Tourist Card *(kartaturysty. visitgdansk.com)* grants free entry to many of the city's attractions, including the Amber Museum, the National Maritime Museum and the Historical Museum of Gdańsk, as well as discounts to other attractions and restaurants. The slightly over-complicated card comes in two versions: Explorer and Premium Explorer, the difference being that Premium gives you access to more attractions while the simple Explorer card is more focused on families. You also have the option of adding public transport tickets to your package. Cards are valid for 24/48/72 hours (65/75/85zł) and are available from the city's municipal tourist offices or online. Download the card to your phone to save 5zł.

Solidarity at the shipyard

North of the city centre, Gdańsk's former shipyard played a major role in bringing an end to communism in Eastern Europe. Led by shipyard electrician Lech Wałęsa, it was here that dockers punched a hole in the communist monolith, the resulting cracks spreading to the Berlin Wall and the Iron Curtain.

The first structure you'll see at the shipyard is the striking **Monument to the Fallen Shipyard Workers**, which commemorates those killed in the riots of 1970. This was the first monument in a communist country to commemorate the ideology's own victims.

Though the vast majority of production facilities have been cleared away, the original Lenin shipyard gates have been left untouched, the huge 'STOCZNIA GDAŃSKA' sign a great selfie spot.

The main attraction in the shipyard area is the excellent **European Solidarity Centre** *(ecs.gda.pl; entry adult/child 35/30zł)*, housed in a purposefully ugly example of 21st-century architecture. Its rusty steel plates were designed to evoke ships under construction. The extensive permanent exhibition examines Poland's post-war fight for freedom, from the Gdańsk shipyard strikes of the 1970s to the round-table negotiations of the late 1980s and beyond. The displays blend state-of-the-art multimedia with actual artefacts. Don't miss it.

A short stroll through the now-landscaped former shipyard brings you to the **Sala BHP**, the shipyard's former Health and Safety Building. This is where the dock workers' 21 demands were famously signed off; it has been left exactly as it was then.

Malbork

Visit the world's largest red-brick castle

Malbork Castle *(zamek.malbork.pl; entry adult/concession 80/60zł)* is the largest in Poland – and indeed in Europe. This massive, UNESCO-listed, red-brick complex on the banks of the Nogat River was begun by the Teutonic Knights in the 13th century and served as the order's headquarters for almost 150 years.

Visits are by a self-guided audio tour that ushers you through the complex at a resonable pace. First up is the **Middle Castle** where the Grand Masters' Palace sports grand interiors, including the kitchen with its 6m-wide fireplace and the Great Refectory, the largest chamber in the castle. Opposite is an excellent amber museum, a highlight of the tour. The prescribed route then continues to **St Anne's Chapel**, where 12 of the Grand Masters are buried.

 ### EATING IN GDAŃSK: BEST TRADITIONAL RESTAURANTS

Restauracja Gdańska: Hearty traditional dishes amid antiques and model ships at Gdańsk's most famous restaurant. *noon-10pm* €€€

Restauracja Pod Łososiem: Founded in 1598 and famous for its fish dishes, this is one of Gdańsk's most highly regarded restaurants. *9am-9pm* €€€

Kubicki: Top Gdańsk restaurant dating from more than a century ago. It serves 100% local dishes. *1-10pm* €€€

Tawerna Dominikańska: Popular with tourists and locals, this contemporary restaurant by the river serves well-presented local favourites. *10am-1am* €€

EWG3D/GETTY IMAGES

Malbork Castle

Next comes the **High Castle** with its spectacular arcaded courtyard. This was the monastic part of the castle, where monks would sit in session in the Chapter House before heading for the refectory. The mock-up of the monks' medieval kitchen is an aromatic affair with nary a potato or tomato in sight.

One of the most striking interiors is **St Mary's Church**, accessed through a beautiful Gothic doorway known as the Golden Gate. Damaged during the bombardment of 1945, renovation ended in 2016 with the walls left as bare brick – a powerful reminder of the Red Army shells.

History of Malbork Castle

This immense castle took shape in stages. First came the so-called High Castle, the formidable central bastion begun around 1276. When Malbork became the Teutonic Knights' capital in 1309, the fortress expanded. The Middle Castle was built to the side of the high one, followed by the Lower Castle. The whole complex was encircled by three rings of defensive walls. The Polish army seized Malbork in 1457 during the Thirteen Years' War when the military power of the knights started to erode. Malbork then became the residence of Polish kings visiting Pomerania. After the First Partition in 1772, the Prussians turned it into barracks. Despite sustaining serious damage during WWII, the entire complex has been rebuilt.

Places We Love to Stay

€ Budget €€ Midrange €€€ Top End

Warsaw
MAP p321

Oki Doki Hostel Old Town
€ Prime-location hostel with pleasant dorms and private rooms, a well-equipped kitchen and inviting social spaces.

Safestay Warsaw Old Town
€ Large and lively hostel with comfy beds, clean bathrooms, well-equipped kitchens, a choice of dorms (some women only) and private rooms, and a friendly on-site bar.

Castle Inn €€ Overlooking Castle Sq, this creatively designed 'art hotel' has quirkily themed rooms, including Jungle, Orient Express and Comic Book.

Chopin Boutique B&B €€
Vintage furniture lends each room a unique vibe. Superb breakfast buffet, free bicycles and nightly Chopin recitals. Also pet friendly.

PURO Warsaw Center €€
Polish brand of Scandi-style design hotels has a winner with its brand-new, perfectly located property. The Loreta bar has great skyline views.

Hotel Bristol €€€ Warsaw's most historic address where VIPs and celebs have stayed throughout the decades. Its neoclassical facade conceals original art nouveau features.

Kraków
MAP p327

Globetrotter Guest House
€ Spacious, wallet-friendly private rooms (singles, doubles and quads) in a quiet Old Town corner. Has tea/coffee facilities,

laundry service and guest fridge.

Dream Hostel € A mixture of 5-bed dorms and private en-suites with lime-green accents in a handy central location. A sound Kazimierz choice; the guest kitchen is a bonus.

PURO Kráków Kazimierz
€€ Stylish rooms, spot-on technology, a well-equipped gym and all-day brasserie attract millennial professionals.

Hotel Gródek €€ A tranquil cul-de-sac location, rooftop terrace overlooking the Old Town and a library with a cosy bar are perks at this intimate boutique hotel with individually-designed rooms.

Bonerowski Palace €€€ Luxe 14th-century palace featuring Europe's largest Swarovski chandelier, medieval portals and restored polychrome decor; the 16 antique-furnished rooms and suites come with marble bathrooms.

Wrocław

Babel Hostel € Close to the train station, pleasant budget accommodation, dorms and private rooms in renovated apartment rooms with pretty decor. Funky common room.

Wrocław Patio €€ Spread behind the Victorian facades of two adjoining tenements overlooking the Church of St Elizabeth and connected by a sunny courtyard. Has comfortable rooms in many styles.

Hotel Monopol €€€ Top hotel holds 120 luxurious rooms behind an elaborately sculpted facade. Bonuses include a panoramic rooftop restaurant and bar, pool, sauna and a breakfast buffet.

Poznań

Hotel Stare Miasto €€ Good value choice featuring a tastefully chandeliered foyer and spacious breakfast room. Bright, decent-sized rooms with some cheaper smaller singles.

Hotel Altus Poznań €€ Old Town high-rise hotel on Święty Marcin with stylish rooms and great views from the upper floors.

Puro Poznań Stare Miasto
€€€ Central location, underground car park, designer decor, comfortable lobby, helpful staff and sharply styled bedrooms flooded with light.

Gdańsk
MAP p338

Camping Nr 218 Stogi €
Gdańsk's best-known campsite at Stogi Beach. Good facilities, but it gets overcrowded in July and August.

Hotel Podewils €€€ Vintage guestrooms, elegant period furniture, carpet bags of old-world charm and an unrivalled view of the Old Town across the Motława River.

Gotyk House €€€ Gothic-themed guesthouse squeezed into Gdańsk's oldest building. Has a wonderful location next to St Mary's Church.

Practicalities

LGBTIQ+ Travellers
Poland isn't a place that welcomes overt displays of LGBTIQ+ sexual orientation. Since 1990, this deeply religious country has found LGBTIQ+ rights tough to handle. The populist Law and Justice Party openly encourages anti-gay sentiments.

Health
Poland has a good healthcare system. Urban hospitals are on par with Western Europe, but in rural areas this may not be the case. You'll need an EHIC (European Health Insurance Card) to access care for free. A UK GHIC (Global Health Insurance Card) will get you free emergency treatment.

Electricity
Polish current works on 230V/50Hz. Almost all sockets in Poland are the modern European two-prong type. If travelling from outside Europe you'll need an adapter.

Smoking
Poland has had a comprehensive smoking ban since 2010, and lighting up is prohibited in all public places. However, because of the relatively high number of smokers in the country, many ignore this rule, especially at public transport stations. Cheaper hotel rooms in Poland can still have a bit of a stale cigarette smell.

BBA PHOTOGRAPHY/SHUTTERSTOCK

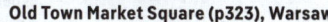

Old Town Market Square (p323), Warsaw

Opening Hours
Banks 9am–5pm Monday to Friday, to 1pm Saturday
Offices 8am–4pm Monday to Friday
Post Offices 8am–8pm Monday to Friday, to 1pm Saturday
Restaurants 11am–11pm
Shops 8am–6pm Monday to Friday, 10am–8pm Saturday
Supermarkets 7am–10pm Monday to Saturday

Visas
Poland is part of the Schengen Area. Visitors from the UK, USA, Australia, New Zealand, Canada, Japan and many other countries do not need visas. Most visa-free nations outside the EU can stay for a maximum of 90 days out of 180.

Public Holidays
New Year's Day 1 January
Epiphany 6 January
Easter Sunday & Monday March/April
Labour Day 1 May
Constitution Day 3 May
Pentecost Sunday 7th Sunday after Easter
Corpus Christi 9th Thursday after Easter
Assumption Day 15 August
All Saints' Day 1 November
Independence Day 11 November
Christmas 25 and 26 December

Language

Polish vowels are generally pronounced short. Nasal vowels are pronounced as though you're trying to force the air through your nose, and are indicated with n or m following the vowel. Note that ow is pronounced as in 'how', kh as the 'ch' in the Scottish loch, and zh as the 's' in 'pleasure'. Also, r is rolled in Polish and the apostrophe (') indicates a slight y sound.

Basics

Hello. Cześć. *cheshch*
Goodbye. Do widzenia. *do vee·dze·nya*
Excuse me. Przepraszam. *ps·he·pra·sham*
Sorry. Przepraszam. *pshe·pra·sham*
Please. Proszę. *pro·she*
Thank you. Dziękuję. *jyen·koo·ye*
Yes. Tak. *tak*
No. Nie. *nye*
What's your name?
Jak się pan/paninazywa? (m/f pol)*yak shye pan/pa·nee na·zi·va*
My name is ...
Nazywam się ... *na·zi·vam shye ...*
Do you speak English? Czy pan/pani mówi *chi pan/pa·nee moo·vee* po angielsku? (m/f) *po an·gyel·skoo*
I don't understand.
Nie rozumiem. *nye ro·zoo·myem*

Transport

boat łódź *wooj*
bus autobus *ow·to·boos*
plane samolot *sa·mo·lot*
train pociąg *po·chonk*
One ... ticket Proszę bilet *pro·she bee·let* **(to Katowice),** ... (do Katowic) ... *(do ka·to·veets)* **please.**
one-way w jedną stronę *v yed·nom stro·ne*
return powrotny *po·vro·tni*

Emergencies

Help! Na pomoc! *na po·mots*

Go away! Odejdź! *o·deyj*
Call the doctor/police!
Zadzwoń po lekarza/policję!*zad·zvon' po le·ka·zha/po·lee·tsye*
I'm lost. Zgubiłem/Zgubiłam się. (m/f) *zgoo·bee·wem/zgoo·bee·wam shye*
I'm ill. Jestem chory/a. (m/f) *yes·tem kho·ri/a*
Where are the toilets?
Gdzie są toalety? *gjye som to·a·le·ti*

Eating & Drinking

What would you recommend? Co by pan polecił? (m)/Co by pani poleciła? (f) *tso bi pan po·le·cheew/tso bi pa·nee po·le·chee·wa*
Do you have vegetarian food? Czy jest żywność wegetariańska? *chi yest zhiv·noshch ve·ge·tar·yan'·ska*
I'd like the ..., please. Proszę o rachunek/jadłospis *pro·she o ra·k·hoo·nek/. ya·dwo·spees*
I'll have ... Proszę ... *pro·she ...*
Cheers! Na zdrowie! *na zdro·vye*

Shopping & Services

I'm looking for ... Szukam ... *shoo·kam*
How much is it? Ile to kosztuje? *ee·le to kosh·too·ye*
That's too expensive. To jest za drogie. *to yest za dro·gye*
market targ *tark*
post office urządpocztowy*oo·zhond poch·to·vi*
tourist office biuroturystyczne*by·oo·ro too·ris·tich·ne*

NUMBERS

1
jeden *ye·den*

2
dwa *dva*

3
trzy *tshi*

4
cztery *chte·ri*

5
pięć *pyench*

6
sześć *sheshch*

7
siedem *shye·dem*

8
osiem *o·shyem*

9
dziewięć *jye·vyench*

10
dziesięć *jye·shence*

Tram, Kraków (p326)

MONEY

Currency: Złoty (zł)

CASH VERSUS CARDS

Even a mobile coffee machine on the back of a bike might take a credit or debit card. However, always carry some cash just in case.

EUROS

The common currency is not likely to make an appearance any time soon, but you can still pay with euros at major tourist sights and most city hotels, and even some restaurants.

ATMS

ATMs are ubiquitous in cities and towns, but villages rarely have one. Stick to banks and avoid free-standing Euronet ATMs in shops, which give a much poorer rate of exchange than other ATMs and charge a fee.

Arriving & Getting Around

Poland may be Eastern Europe's best served country by air, with flights from across the continent and overseas. Improving transport infrastructure means getting around is not the trial it once was.

City Transport
All Polish cities and large towns have bus, tram and even metro services that are cheap and efficient. Download the relevant transport app on your smartphone to avoid hassling with tickets.

Polish Trains
PKP (*Polskie Koleje Państwowe; pkp.pl*) is the main train operator. The system is undergoing extensive modernisation with new tracks and stations coming online every week. PKP also runs trains to other European cities.

Driving Essentials
Drive on the right and have headlights switched on day and night, year-round. The blood alcohol limit is 0.2g/L. Road conditions are improving, but watch out for bad surfaces and potholes in rural areas.

Arriving by Air
With over 20 million passengers annually, Warsaw's Chopin Airport (WAW) is the busiest in the country. Ryanair has its own airport: Modlin (WMI), 40km north of the capital. Kraków (KRK) and Gdańsk (GDN) also have busy airports with domestic and international connections. There are flights to Poland from around the world, including North America, the Middle East and Asia.

Curated by
Mark Baker

Romania

RURAL CHARM, UNSPOILT NATURE, ENERGETIC CITIES

One of Europe's last undiscovered bastions, Romania has an appealing blend of modern cities and timeless villages, pitched amid forests and soaring mountains.

Beautiful and beguiling, Romania's rural landscape remains relatively untouched by the country's urban evolution. It's a land of aesthetically stirring hand-ploughed fields, sheep-instigated traffic jams and lots of homemade plum brandy – or *țuică* as it's known locally.

Many visitors focus their attention on Transylvania, with its eye-catching natural beauty and medieval legacy of fortified Saxon towns like Brașov and Sighișoara. Bram Stoker's fictional *Dracula* added a darker, more mystical cast to the forests and mountain passes, and towering Bran Castle appears straight out of central casting as an imaginary setting for this Victorian melodrama. Across the Carpathian chain, the UNESCO-listed painted monasteries dot the northern province of Bucovina. The country's fiery, 16th-century origin story – forged in conflict with the then-expanding Ottoman Empire – is colourfully illustrated on the facades of the churches here.

Further east, the Danube Delta, where the mighty Danube River empties into the Black Sea, remains a pristine nature reserve that's home to more than 300 species of birds, including many rare varieties. It's an ideal spot for birders, of course, but with miles of marshland and empty beaches, the delta appeals to nature lovers of all stripes. Energetic cities, including Brașov, Sibiu and especially Bucharest, have excellent hotels and restaurants as well as loads of culture – both the highbrow and lowbrow variety. Together, they showcase Romania as a rapidly evolving European country.

NATALIA SOKOLOVSKA/SHUTTERSTOCK

THE MAIN AREAS

BUCHAREST
Romania's bustling capital never sleeps.
p350

TRANSYLVANIA
Saxon folkways and gorgeous scenery.
p356

BUCOVINA MONASTERIES
Riveting history told through colourful frescoes. **p362**

THE DANUBE DELTA
Coastal wildlife and pristine nature. **p365**

For places to stay in Romania, see p368

Left: Bucharest Old Town (p355); Above: Bran Castle (p357), Transylvania

Find Your Way

Romania is a deceptively large country, divided by the Carpathian Mountains. Trains and buses are viable modes for getting around, but travel can be slow. Hiring a car gives you options, but highways can be crowded.

TRAIN

Trains are handy for travel from Bucharest north to Braşov and Sighişoara, but less practical for Transylvania's smaller towns and villages. Trains also link Bucharest with Suceava, a handy jumping-off spot for the Bucovina monasteries.

BUSES & FERRIES

Buses run between nearly every Romanian town and city, though navigating timetables can be tricky. Much of the Danube Delta is closed to car traffic; travel by passenger ferry or water taxi from Tulcea instead.

Bucovina Monasteries, p362

Rugged mountains and forests form an epic backdrop to magnificent monasteries and churches.

The Danube Delta, p365

Natural serenity of delta waterways, plus age-old cultural histories and hidden beaches.

Bucharest, p350

Romania's capital has left communism behind and is charging ahead with urban regeneration and culinary and cultural offerings.

Transylvania, p356

Picturesque peaks, brawny castles and fortified churches stand watch over timeless towns and rustic hideaways.

UKRAINE

MOLDOVA

Chernivtsi

Rădăuți
Voroneț
Suceava
Piatra-Neamț
Bacău
Iași
Vaslui

Bistrița
Citadel
Târgu Mureş
St Mary's
Sighişoara
Evangelical Church
Sibiu
Sebeş

Cluj-Napoca
Deva
Sebeş
Caransebeş
Moravița

Oradea

Arad

Timişoara

Szeged

HUNGARY

SERBIA

Mureş

Danube

Orşova

Târgu Jiu

Craiova

Făgăraş Mountains

Carpathian Mountains

Olt

Bran Castle
Braşov
Sinaia
Piteşti
Ploieşti

Buzău

Brăila

Galați

Siret

Prut

Ialomița

Danube

BULGARIA

Giurgiu

Romanian Athenaeum
Palace of Parliament
Spring Palace
BUCHAREST

Călăraşi

Hârşova

Babadag

Tulcea
Sulina

Histria

Constanța

Negru Vodă
Mangalia

Black Sea

100 km
50 miles

DRAGOS ASAFTEI/SHUTTERSTOCK

Calea Victoriei (p350), Bucharest

Plan Your Time

Distances are large, particularly in Transylvania. Organise your time according to your interests and plan transport carefully.

Bucharest City Break

● Tour the vast **Palace of Parliament** (p351). Pair this with a stop at the **Spring Palace** (p351), the opulent former-Ceaușescu residence. Stroll on **Calea Victoriei** (p350) for a look at 'Little Paris'. Enjoy a drink in idyllic **Sera Eden** (p355) and a promenade in **Cișmigiu Garden** (p355). Sip coffee in the **Old Town** (p355) and sample new Romanian cuisine at a spot like **KAIAMO** (p351).

A Week to Spare

● Spend a day ambling around **Bucharest** (p350), then take a train to **Brașov** (p356) – Transylvania's main event – for castles, activities and beer at street-side cafes. Spend a day in the medieval citadel of **Sighișoara** (p358). Carry on to **Sibiu** (p359) or switch it up with a tour of the painted monasteries in **Bucovina** (p362), before returning to the capital.

SEASONAL HIGHLIGHTS

SPRING
Budding trees mark spring's arrival, especially in the capital city. May is particularly busy in Bucharest, with multiple festivals.

SUMMER
July and August are hot and crowded everywhere. Beat the heat by heading into the mountains.

AUTUMN
The cultural calendar is rolling in Bucharest with the biannual **George Enescu International Festival** of classical music.

WINTER
Ski season is in full swing in Transylvania; Christmas holidays add cheer. Sibiu and the surrounding villages are particularly festive.

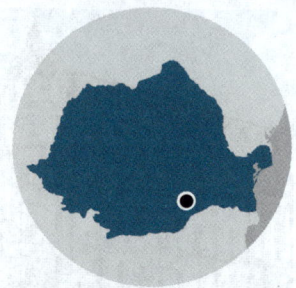

Bucharest

URBAN ENERGY | HISTORY | MUSEUMS

GETTING AROUND

Bucharest is a big city, and you'll quickly hit your 10,000 steps. The metro reaches most places visitors want to go, but you'll still find yourself walking quite a bit from the stations to your destination. Rideshares like Uber and Bolt are plentiful and reasonably priced; this is the preferred way to get around for residents. The public transport network includes buses and trams, but these are more for daily commuters and less practical for visitors.

☑ TOP TIP

Bucharest truly shines when it comes to outdoor garden bars and cafes. After a long day of hitting the pavement, repair to one of these hidden oases to relax over a glass of wine or fresh-made lemonade. We've listed some of our favourites (p355).

Bucharest has changed considerably since communism fell in 1989, bringing an end to 40 years of darkness and isolation. Centuries-old Byzantine churches stand alongside French-built belle-époque palaces (which once prompted the nickname 'Little Paris'), accompanied by a buzzing cafe culture. The Palace of Parliament that former dictator Nicolae Ceaușescu defiantly imposed on the city still looms large. It's certainly worth a visit, but look past this controversial building and instead get lost in historic side streets where late 19th- and early 20th-century manors abound, with garden bars often tucked behind. The museum scene is excellent and new Romanian cuisine is worthy of the Michelin-star limelight.

Amble through Little Paris

Neoclassical and beaux-arts buildings

Any visit to Bucharest begins with a walk along elegant **Calea Victoriei**, the capital's main thoroughfare. The early 20th century was Bucharest's most prosperous era, and during the reign of Carol I, the first king of Romania, large neoclassical buildings and beaux-arts palaces sprang up; by the end of the 1930s, the city had acquired the moniker Little Paris.

The **Equestrian Statue of Carol I** propped up in front of the Central University Library makes for a nice introduction to the capital's past, sitting right next to the site of events from the 1989 Revolution that ended the communist regime. Facing it is the former Royal Palace, today housing the **National Museum of Art** (*Muzeul Național de Artă; mnar.ro; entry adult/senior/student 32/16/8 lei*).

Nearby is the emblematic **Romanian Athenaeum** (*Ateneul Român; filarmonicaenescu.ro/en; entry 15 lei*), a classical music venue that can be visited outside rehearsals and performances. From May to early October, the street has a festival-like atmosphere on weekends and is pedestrian-only during 'Open Streets'., a new initiative when major roads are closed to traffic, turning the city centre into a pedestrian-only space

ANNA KUZKINA/SHUTTERSTOCK

Palace of Parliament

Follow the Dictator's Trail

Visit a traumatic mega-palace

A must-see highlight for many, the gigantic and exorbitant **Palace of Parliament** (*cic.cdep.ro; entry adult/student tour 60/30 lei*) was commissioned by dictator Nicolae Ceauşescu in 1984, during a period of economic hardship. It's the world's second-largest administrative building after the Pentagon. For locals, it's also a painful reminder of Ceauşescu's traumatic ambitions. Today, the eclectic-style building houses the Romanian Parliament and the **National Museum of Contemporary Art** (*mnac.ro; entry adult/senior/student 32/16/8 lei*). Even so, much of it remains unused. Of the 1100 rooms, only 400 are finished. Visits are by guided tour only, reserved in advance by telephone (*+0733-558-102*). Don't forget your passport.

Follow up with a visit to the **Spring Palace** (*Palatul Primăverii; casaceausescu.ro; entry adult/concession 75/65 lei*), the former residence of Ceauşescu, his wife Elena and their three kids. At a time when the population was facing daily power cuts, food rationing and limited heating during long winters, this gilded mansion with a private cinema, decadent spa and peacocks roaming about in the garden stands in glaring contrast. Book online for guided tours.

BUCHAREST'S ORIGINS

Originally certified as a royal residence in 1459 during Vlad Ţepeş' rule of Wallachia, the ruins of Bucharest's **Old Princely Court** date from the 15th century. Directly across from the ruins is **Hanu' lui Manuc**, the oldest inn in town and known for its restaurant serving Romanian food. **Old Princely Court Church** is Bucharest's oldest church (16th century); it's a revered place of worship where hundreds of pilgrims arrive on Tuesdays to pray to the relics of St Anthony the Great. Street names such as Covaci (blacksmiths), Şelari (saddle makers) and Blănari (furriers) tell the story of occupations practiced centuries ago. Str Lipscani is the biggest, named after the city of Leipzig (many of the traders at the time brought their wares from there).

EATING IN BUCHAREST: BEST FOR NEW ROMANIAN CUISINE

KAIAMO: Theatrically set, experimental Romanian cuisine by chef Radu Ionescu-Fehér. A 50 Best Discovery restaurant close to Herăstrău. *6pm-11pm Tue-Sat* €€€

NOUA. Bucătărie Românească: Chef Alex Petricean's signature tasting menu 'Romania on a plate' is served in seven acts. *6pm-9pm Wed-Sat* €€€

Noua B.A.R: More casual, equally fascinating universe of Romanian dishes with a twist, and brunch-like tantalising treats. *hours vary* €€

KANÉ: Farm-to-table at its best with contemporary Romanian creativity in a historic building brought back to life. *6.30pm-11pm Wed-Sat* €€€

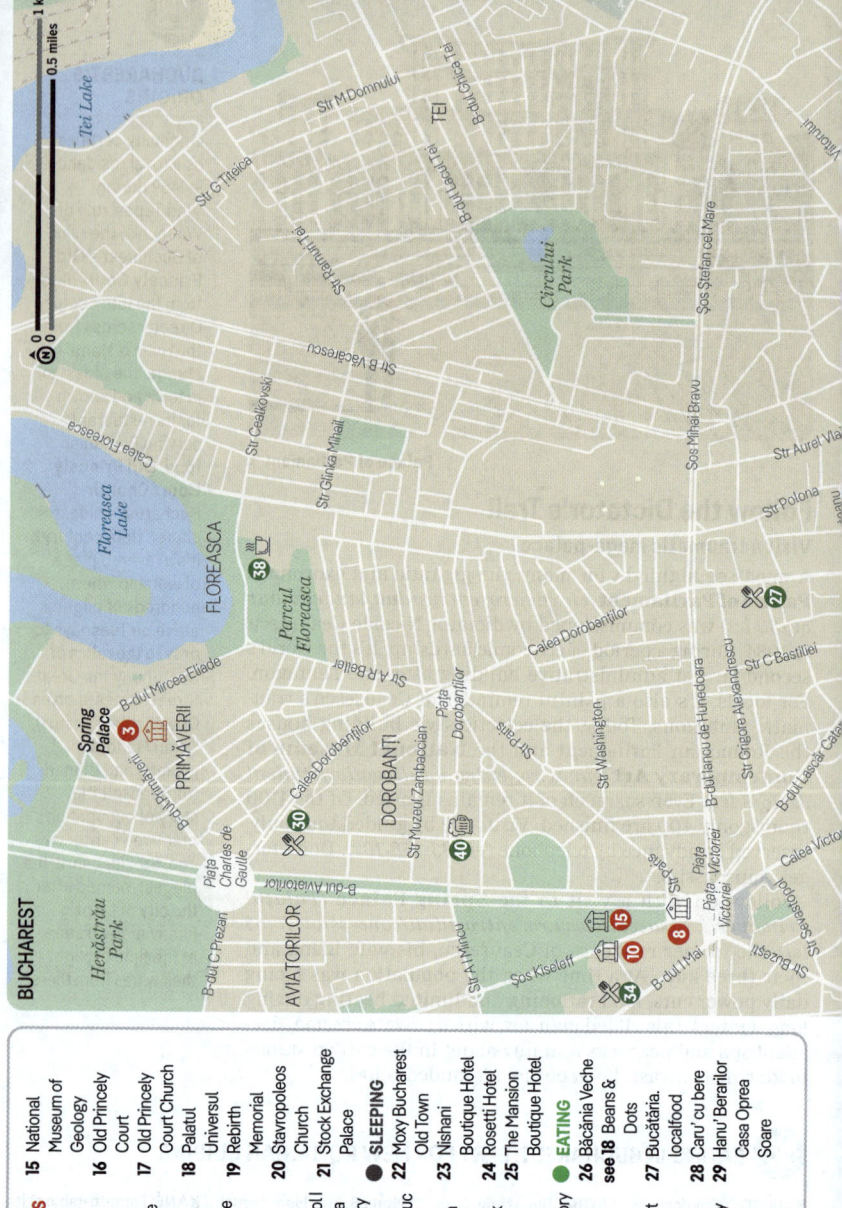

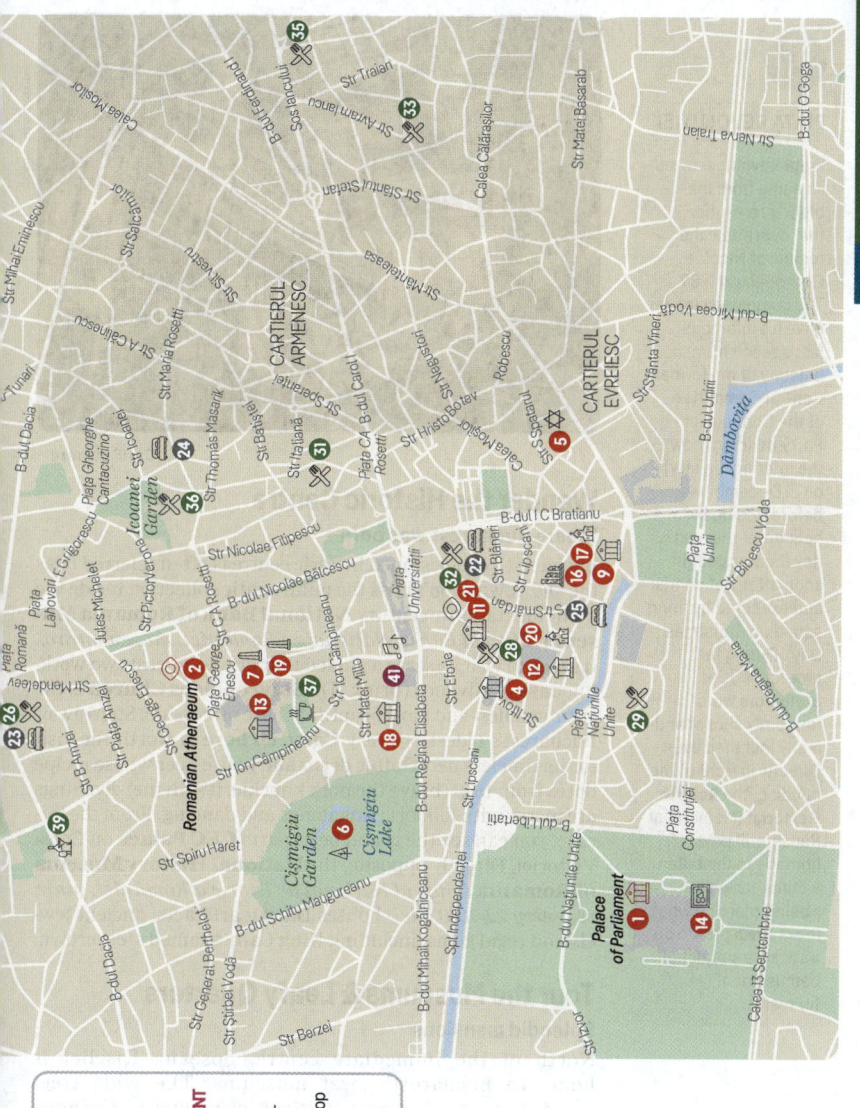

PIAȚA REVOLUȚIEI

Piața Revoluției takes its name from the bloody revolution that overthrew the regime of Nicolae Ceaușescu in 1989. The communist leader gave his infamous last speech from the balcony of the former Central Committee of the Communist Party building (now the Interior Ministry) on 21 December before fleeing by helicopter the next day (he was caught soon after, put on trial and executed by firing squad on Christmas Day). During that time, crowds of protestors were randomly shot at and many lost their lives. Directly in front of the building, the **Rebirth Memorial** (Memorialul Renașterii) pays homage to the fallen victims, its white obelisk piercing what looks like a potato on a stick – a subject of bemusement for many.

Caru' cu bere

Wander the Historic Centre

Where Bucharest was born

Bucharest's cobblestoned historic centre is often referred to as the Old Town. Don't miss the numismatic collection inside the monumental 19th-century **National Bank of Romania Museum** *(Muzeul Băncii Naționale a României; muzeu.bnr.ro)*. It's free to visit; reserve a guided tour online at least two working days in advance (bring ID). **Stavropoleos Church** is the city's smallest and most beautiful house of worship. Steps away, Bucharest's oldest brewery **Caru' cu bere** is worth the visit for its timeless neo-Gothic decor and house beer whose recipe dates from 1879 (brave the pork knuckle, it's divine). Evenings are merry with folkloric singalongs and dancing. From the terrace, you can see the grand beaux-arts **CEC Palace** on Calea Victoriei. Directly opposite, the **National History Museum of Romania** *(Muzeul Național de Istorie a României; mnir. ro; entry 22/10/0.5 lei)* houses Dacian artefacts, ancient jewels and regal gems, including King Carol's famed steel crown.

Tour the Museums & Leafy Quarters

Splendid mansions

North of the immediate centre, Șoseaua Kiselef is home to Bucharest's best museums. The wide tree-lined boulevard starts with kid-favourite **Grigore**

EATING IN BUCHAREST: BEST FOR ROMANIAN FOOD

Băcănia Veche: The go-to place for authentic meals in Piața Romană. Artisanal delicacies and a cosy, dim-lit garden. *noon-10pm Mon-Sun* €€

Hanu' Berarilor Casa Oprea Soare: Interwar-inspired menu and historic brewery in a splendid neo-Romanian manor near Piața Unirii. *8am-midnight Mon-Sun* €€

Bucătăria.localfood: Where Millennials go for comfort food. Unfussy menu and playful locale, just off Piața Romană. Reserve. *1-10pm Wed, noon-10pm Thu-Sun* €€

Mosafir: Charming bistro in a heritage building, combining bistronomy with Romanian cuisine, focusing on local, seasonal ingredients. *1-10pm Wed-Sun* €€

Antipa Natural History Museum *(Muzeul de Istorie Naturală Grigore Antipa; antipa.ro; entry adult/senior/student 32/16/8 lei).* The **Museum of the Romanian Peasant** *(Muzeul Țăranului Român; muzeultaranuluiroman.ro; entry adult/senior/student 20/10/5 lei)* is a classic for its collection of peasant costumes, religious icons and folkloric bits and bobs, with a gift shop and restaurant on-site. In an extraordinary early 20th-century building, the **National Museum of Geology** *(Muzeul Național de Geologie; geology.ro; entry adult/student/senior 15/10/5 lei)* is less visited, but highly worthwhile.

Hang Out in Cișmigiu
Energetic quarter and beautiful city park

With its cluster of bars, shops and galleries, the Cișmigiu district has become a designated 'Creative Quarter'. It's also home to **Cișmigiu Garden**, the oldest public park in town. Walking past the Art Nouveau Hotel Cișmigiu, you soon find yourself by **Palatul Universul**, a former printing house brought back to life as a culture hub. Inside, **FIX Me a drink** serves botanical cocktails, while **Apollo111** runs a great bar and hosts disco nights. Also worth checking out is the buzzing **Beans & Dots** speciality coffee store.

Down the block, **Control Club** is an undisputed favourite for live indie and electronic music concerts. The leafy garden terrace is open all year long. For a chilled spot to mingle, sip a craft beer or coffee, head to artsy **Artichoke Social House**.

Bucharest's Emerging Old Town
Perfect spot for people-watching

The Old Town made a dramatic U-turn a decade ago and turned into a party hotspot. Amid heritage sites and Byzantine-like churches, a mismatch of mass tourism and shops coexists. Certain streets are paving their own way. For example, at the intersection of Doamnei with Str Ion Ghica, presided over by the imposing **Stock Exchange Palace**, a design/coffee hub is shaping new grounds. Local architects have joined forces in a manifesto of sorts, converting the area into a vibrant, here-to-stay community.

Start by people-watching on the buzzing sidewalk of **La Vita e Velo**, a bike shop and cafe that is as enticing as its good looks suggest. Across the street in Ghica House is **ESHTE Shop & Café**, a creative space fostering Romanian artisans and contemporary designers, with exclusive items found only here. Entering the courtyard next door, long-enduring **Circa 1703-3071** is a vintage-seeker's dream; an eclectic shop opened by an architect who's passionate about antiques.

JEWISH BUCHAREST

Bucharest's Jewish quarter was once home to a vibrant community during the interwar period of the 20th century – some 70,000 people, representing 11% of the city's population, lived here. The majority of the neighbourhood was destroyed during the 1980s to make room for the enormous Palace of Parliament. A handful of monuments survived. A replica of Leopoldstädter Tempel (Vienna's largest synagogue, destroyed in 1938), the red-brick **Choral Temple** *(entry 10 lei)* is a stunning example. In the area, several residential buildings remain. The most remarkable is the legacy of Marcel Iancu, a Romanian-Israeli architect who was the brain behind Bucharest's modernist architecture. One example is the Solly Gold building, found at B-dul Hristo Botev 34.

DRINKING IN BUCHAREST: BEST GARDEN BARS

Sera Eden: Part greenhouse, part botanical sanctuary, this posh garden cafe lies behind a historical villa. *noon-11pm Mon-Fri, 10-11pm Sat & Sun*	**Grădina Monteoru:** Urban garden turned party hotspot on the site of Casa Monteoru, one of Netflix's *Wednesday* locations. *5pm-2am Mon-Fri, noon-2am Sat & Sun*	**Mercato Comunale:** Food trucks and local craft beer in a hip, relaxed garden with a playground and stage for live events. *hours vary*	**Grădina Floreasca:** Stylish alfresco cafe by the pool, set in Floreasca Park. Hosts occasional jazz evenings. *10am-midnight Mon-Sun*

Sighişoara
Mediaş
Făgăraş
Sibiu
Codlea
Mt Moldoveanu
Braşov
Sinaia

Transylvania

MOUNTAINS | MYSTERY | HISTORY

Places

GETTING AROUND

Slow-moving but reliable train services connect Bucharest with major towns and cities in Transylvania. The national rail service, CFR *(cfr.ro)*, has a passenger timetable on its website. That said, a car is essential for getting to smaller towns and villages, monasteries and trailheads. Note that in summer, the region's highways, particularly the stretch over the Carpathians from Bucharest to Braşov, get very crowded.

☑ TOP TIP

Transylvania covers a big area. Cities are linked by crowded highways and trains. If time is limited, it's best to focus on one or two cities or regions rather than trying to take in the entire province.

After a century of being name-checked in literature and cinema, the word 'Transylvania' now enjoys worldwide recognition. The mere mention conjures a vivid landscape of mountains, castles, spooky moonlight and at least one well-known count with a wicked overbite. Unexplained puncture wounds notwithstanding, Transylvania is all those things and more. A melange of architecture and chic sidewalk cafes enliven the towns of Braşov, Sighişoara and Sibiu.

Braşov & Around

TIME FROM BUCHAREST: **3HR** 🚆

Gothic spires, medieval gateways, Soviet blocks and a huge Hollywood-style sign: Brasov's skyline is instantly compelling. A number of medieval watchtowers still glower over the town. Between them sparkle baroque buildings and churches, while easy-going cafes line main square Piaţa Sfatului. Visible from here is forested Mt Tâmpa, sporting 'Brasov' in huge white letters.

Find your bearings on the main square

Any visit must begin with the city's beautiful, sweeping main square, **Piaţa Sfatului**, the envy of many Romanian towns and cities. At the centre of the square (actually an overgrown triangle) stands the **Council's House** (Casa Sfatului), from 1420, topped by the Trumpeter's Tower, in which the town councillors would meet. These days, the building is home to the small local history museum; you can still hear the trumpeters play from the tower every day at 6pm, or at noon on weekends. Pedestrianised Str Republicii trails off from here and is stuffed with more bars, cafes and ice cream joints.

Visit the Black Church

The **Black Church** *(Biserica Neagră; bisericaneagra.ro; entry adult/concession 25/20 lei)* may be Braşov's only true 'must see'. The church dates from the late 14th century and is the country's largest Gothic church (the bell tower stands 65m high). It got its name from its charred appearance following the Great Fire of 1689. Despite the crowds, the interior feels hushed and peaceful. The acoustics are helped by the 16th- to

Piaţa Sfatului, Braşov

19th-century Anatolian rugs that are draped across the interior; these were once placed on pews reserved for church donors.

Climb the medieval town walls

Large parts of Braşov's fortification system from the Middle Ages are still standing. Raised in stages between 1400 and 1650, the walls and towers were built in anticipation of attacks by the Turks. Seven bastions were built at the most exposed points, each one defended by a guild whose members tolled their bastion bell. The most popular spot to see the old walls is along the fortification's western section, which parallels a stream and pedestrianised Str După Ziduri. A good access point is 200m south of the Black Church. Above here, on the hillside, are two watchtowers – the **Black Tower** (Turnul Negru) and **White Tower** (Turnul Alb) Despite the names, both are brownish in colour. It's possible to climb to the towers for dramatic views, but be forewarned: the going is steep. Two impressive gates into the walled city, the 19th-century **Schei Gate** (Poarta Schei) and the 16th-century **Catherine's Gate** (Poarta Ecaterinei), were part of the old fortification system.

Venture out to Bran Castle and Râşnov Fortress

Thanks to Bram Stoker's novel *Dracula*, **Bran Castle** *(Castelul Bran; bran-castle.com; entry adult/senior/student 90/60/50 lei)*

A REAL FAIRY-TALE CITY

Incredibly, Braşov does a star turn in the Brothers Grimm classic *The Pied Piper of Hamelin*. After the piper leads the children away, they somehow dig a hole to Transylvania and wind up here. Indeed, this playful place has many tales as colourful as its pastel-hued streets, but the city's real history is a bit more prosaic. Braşov was established on an ancient Dacian site in 1211 by the crusading order of Teutonic Knights. Braşov grew into a Saxon-controlled mercantile colony named Kronstadt (Brassó in Hungarian). The Saxons built ornate churches and townhouses, all protected by a massive wall that still stands. The Romanians were required by law to live outside the walls, at Schei.

WHERE TO EAT IN BRAŞOV: OUR PICKS

La Ceaun Michael Weiss: Focused on Romanian food. There's a section of cauldron and slow-cooked dishes, including *bulz* (roasted polenta). *noon-10pm* €€

Am Rosenanger: A German-flavoured restaurant that serves Saxon and other Transylvanian specialities, such as spätzle noodles with paprika. *noon-10pm* €€

Bistro de l'Arte: This two-decades-old bistro still turns out some of the city's most inventive cooking. *noon-11pm* €€

La Birou: Elaborate and delicious breakfasts with plenty of fresh vegetables and other healthy ingredients. *8am-4pm* €

FROM BRAŞOV WITH LOVE

Between 1950 and 1960, when Romania still considered itself Moscow's buddy, Braşov was officially named 'Stalin City'. Stalin's rule tampered with much more than the town's name: forced industrialisation yanked thousands of rural workers from the countryside and plonked them down in the city in an attempt to crank the totalitarian motor of industry. One of the first displays of public opposition to the Nicolae Ceauşescu government flared up here in 1987. Thousands of disgruntled workers took to the streets demanding basic foodstuffs. Ceauşescu called in the troops and quashed the uprising, though it paved the way for protests across Romania that would topple the regime two years later.

EUGENE LOZOVSKI/SHUTTERSTOCK

Viscri fortified church

is arguably Romania's best-known tourist attraction – though connections to Stoker's fictional vampire or the historical Wallachian prince, Vlad Ţepeş, are thin. That said, your first glimpse of this spectacular fortress-castle, rising above the town on a rocky promontory, will take your breath away. Teutonic knights first built a wooden fortress at this strategic location between Wallachia and Transylvania in the 13th century. For centuries the castle was controlled by Braşov's Saxons, and then fell into the hands of Romania's ruling monarchy after WWI. Commonly paired with Bran Castle on day trips from Braşov, nearby **Râşnov Fortress** *(Cetatea Râşnov; celatea-rasnov.ro)* roosts precariously on a rocky hilltop. It was built by Teutonic knights to guard against Tatar and Turkish invasions. Walk up to the fortress from the village or take a lift *(round trip adult/child 30/20 lei)*.

Sighişoara & Around   TIME FROM BRAŞOV: 2HR 🚌

Saxon settlers first started coming to Sighişoara (Schässburg in German) as early as the 12th century, by invitation of the then-ruling Hungarian kings. The magnificent fortress town they built welcomes visitors to the present day. Indeed, so resplendent are Sighişoara's pastel-coloured buildings, stony lanes and medieval towers, you'll rub your eyes in disbelief. During the Middle Ages, the booming commercial centre supported

WHERE TO EAT IN SIGHIŞOARA: OUR PICKS

Mimoza: In a lovely setting on a cobbled street, Mimoza has an eclectic menu that includes Romanian and Thai dishes as well as pizza. *9am-midnight* €€

Joseph T: Arguably Sighişoara's best restaurant. Romanian and international dishes, plus very good steaks. *7.30am-10.30am, 5pm-midnight* €€

Geurgius Krauss: A fancy establishment in a beautiful citadel setting with Art Deco interiors. Romanian and pan-European dishes. *7.30am-midnight* €€€

Alex Bakery: A little bakery selling delicious *plăcintă* (fried pastries) with all kinds of fillings, both fruity and meaty. We loved the plum-filled ones. *7.30am-10pm* €

more than a dozen traditional guilds, and towers still honour trades like 'Tinsmiths' and 'Tailors'. If Sighişoara doesn't sate your thirst for medieval splendour, it'll make a great jumping-off point to explore Saxon villages such as Viscri and Biertan.

Visit Sighişoara's citadel

From the moment you arrive, you'll want to scramble up to Sighişoara's towering medieval **citadel**. There are several ways to access the citadel; the main stairway starts north of the main square, Piaţa Hermann Oberth. The highlight is the glorious **Clock Tower**, whose multicoloured-tiled roof glitters like the scales of a dragon. The tower was built in the 14th century and expanded 200 years later. It contains Sighişoara's wonderfully old-school history **museum** *(muzet.ro; entry adult/student 20/5 lei)*, looking like a curio shop filled with centuries-old furniture and household items filling up cramped rooms at different levels. Climb to the top of the tower where you can have a close look at the clock mechanism and wooden figurine. Above it all is an observation platform providing a 360-degree panorama of red-tiled roofs and surrounding mountains.

Find idyllic Transylvanian towns

About 40km southeast of Sighişoara, the village of **Viscri,** with a medieval fortification system and flanked by bucolic meadows, epitomises the romance of rural Transylvania. Britain's King Charles, in his days as Prince Charles, put the town on the tourism map decades ago, and it's fair to say the place has never looked better. The only sounds you'll hear (aside from other visitors) are the rattle of horse-drawn carts and the clank of a blacksmith's workshop. The highlight is the medieval **fortified church** *(adult/concession 20/10 lei)*. Its splendidly restored whitewashed walls and tiled roof, in their day, represented a feat of medieval engineering. Rising sharply above a huddle of Saxon-style buildings, the **fortified church** *(entry 20 lei)* at **Biertan**, 30km southwest of Sighişoara, is a poetic sight. Its late Gothic church, ringed by concentric walls and flanked by soaring buttresses, is among the most impressive in Transylvania.

Sibiu

TIME FROM BRAŞOV: 2½HR

Sibiu is awash in aristocratic elegance. Noble Saxon history emanates from every Art Nouveau facade and gold-embossed church, all parked elegantly around graceful squares. Renowned composers Strauss, Brahms and Liszt all played here during the 19th century, and Sibiu has stayed at the forefront of Romania's cultural scene. Houses with distinctive eyelid-shaped windows (imagine a benign Amityville Horror House) watch a cast of artists and buskers on the street below. Cafes and bars inhabit brick-walled cellars and luminously decorated attics.

Stroll expansive Piaţa Mare

Strolling is the best way to take in Sibiu's highlights. Start out at **Piaţa Mare** (Large Square). This enormous square was laid out in the 14th century as a market and later used for public executions. It's dominated by the **Roman Catholic Cathedral**

DUBIOUS DRACULA LINKS

Bram Stoker poached the name for his fictional character Dracula from the annals of medieval Wallachian history. But it was the Romanian-born American historian Radu Florescu who linked Dracula to Vlad Ţepeş, a real historical figure. His father, Vlad II, was the first to call himself 'Dracul' (dragon), thus founding the Drăculeşti dynasty. Florescu made his assertions not in a scientific paper, but in a series of pop-history books that were propelled to fame by US TV networks. He was the one who claimed that Vlad Ţepeş was born in Sighişoara, even pointing at a specific house in the fortress that now contains one of several Dracula-themed funhouses. There is no historical evidence to back this up.

THE 'VIA TRANSILVANICA' HIKING TRAIL

An amazing feat of cooperative efforts, the Via Transilvanica hiking trail *(viatransilvanica.com)* traverses Romania from Bucovina to Banat via the whole of Transylvania. It's divided into eight large sections, all with Latin names pointing to the history of corresponding regions. In Transylvania's northeast, the Terra Siculorum section runs through the mainly Hungarian Székely Land via Praid and Sovata. The Terra Saxonum section goes through Viscri, Saschiz, Sighişoara, Criş, Malancrav, Biertan and onwards to Mediaş. Beyond the latter it connects to Terra Dacica which passes through Alba Iulia. A separate branch, Terra Borza Tectonica, branches off south towards Braşov. The entire route is well-marked and complemented with a dedicated smartphone app with guides in several languages.

(Biserica Romano-Catolică Sfânta Treime), built in baroque style between 1726 and 1738. The interior gleams with gold decoration and bright frescoes. The **Brukenthal Palace** *(Palatul Brukenthal; brukenthalmuseum.ro; entry adult/senior/student 50/25/12.5 lei)*, at Piaţa Mare 5, is the most important building. It once served as the residence of Transylvanian governor Samuel von Brukenthal (1721–1803) and now exhibits European art from the 15th to 18th centuries. The most valuable works include a 16th-century painting by the German Renaissance master Lucas Cranach the Elder and one of the Flemish painter Pieter Brueghel's busy winter landscapes – but the interior is the main attraction. Not far from Piaţa Mare, the **History Museum** *(Muzeul de Istorie; brukenthalmuseum.ro; entry adult/senior/student 36/18/9 lei)* goes deep into the town's origins, with illuminating exhibitions about the Saxon guilds and local handicrafts.

Move on to Piaţa Mică

After sprawling Piaţa Mare, **Piaţa Mică** (Small Square) immediately feels homier and more manageable. The square is lined with decent restaurants and cafes. Make a note to return at night, when the lighting gives the place a fairy-tale feel. The **Bridge of Lies** (Podul Minciunilor), an innocent-looking 19th-century iron bridge at the square's northern end, is filled with legend. Depending on whom you ask, the name stems either from the dishonest merchants who once did business here or young lovers swearing their undying affection (or virginity). If you tell a lie while standing on it, it's supposed to creak.

Don't miss Piaţa Huet

Tiny **Piaţa Huet**, to the west of Piaţa Mică, is dominated by the city's pride and joy: **St Mary's Evangelical Church** (Catedrala Evanghelică Sfânta Maria). Sibiu's Gothic centrepiece rises more than 73m over the Old Town. Don't miss climbing the tower (200 steps) for the city's best panorama. While inside, marvel at ghoulish stone skeletons, 17th-century tombs and the largest organ in Romania, all framed by a magnificent arched ceiling. Built in stages from the mid-1300s to 1520, the church was planted atop the site of an older 12th-century sanctuary.

See the ASTRA ethnographic museum

The **ASTRA National Museum Complex** *(muzeulastra.ro; entry adult/student 35/9 lei)*, 5km south of Sibiu, claims to be both Romania's and Europe's largest outdoor ethnographic

WHERE TO EAT IN SAXON LAND: OUR PICKS

Taverna Antika: A quaint garden under the castle wall in Biertan. Aptly for a Saxon village, the food is mostly sausages and pork knuckles. *noon-10pm* €€

Unglerus Medieval Restaurant: In Biertan, Unglerus has satisfying goulash, fried trout and a standout wine cellar. *9am-10pm* €€

Cafe & Artizanat: Shady courtyard cafe in Viscri that's an ideal lunch spot, with daily local specials. *noon-7.30pm Tue-Sun* €€

Hanul Greweln: A welcoming inn in the town of Mediaş, with a crowd-pleasing selection of pasta and meat dishes. *10am-10pm* €€

FABIANIRWIN/SHUTTERSTOCK

ASTRA National Museum Complex

museum: it covers a whopping 96 hectares. Even if ethnography or folkways are not your thing, it's worth spending a few hours here to marvel at the diversity of people who have lived and thrived in the territory of modern-day Romania. The heart of the museum is the immense open-air exhibition space, where churches, water mills, inns, forges, wineries, farmhouses and traditional homes have been lovingly reconstructed to show off the ingenuity of traditional cultures.

From Roman village to Saxon centre

Sibiu traces its roots to Roman times, when it was known as Cibinium. The city rose to its peak influence during the Saxon period, when its 19 guilds were protected by sturdy city walls with 39 towers and four bastions. The Habsburgs ruled Transylvania from here between 1692 and 1791 and again from 1849 to 1867, when Sibiu served as the seat of the Austrian governors. In the late years (1987–89) of the Nicolae Ceaușescu dictatorship, Sibiu was home to Ceaușescu's son and heir-apparent, Nicu. The city is also the birthplace of former Romanian president Klaus Iohannis, who served as city mayor until 2014, when he succeeded Traian Băsescu as president.

 WHERE TO EAT IN SIBIU: OUR PICKS

Crama Sibiul Vechi: Sibiu's most evocative restaurant, with Romanian fare such as cheese croquettes, meatballs and peasant's stew with polenta. *noon-10pm* €€

Weinkeller: Romantic alleyway behind St Mary's Evangelical Cathedral, featuring traditional Romanian mains and Transylvania wines. *6pm-11pm* €€

Kulinarium: The best of several restaurants lining Piața Mică, serving smoky Austrian sausages, spinach soup with quail eggs, trout with wild rice and more. *noon-11pm* €€

Pardon Cafe & Bistro: Delightful hideaway by the city walls that's happily cluttered with antiques. Outdoor seating looks towards the watchtowers. *9am-11pm* €€

Bucovina Monasteries

HISTORY | ARCHITECTURE | NATURAL BEAUTY

GETTING AROUND

Public transport is thin on the ground in Bucovina and this is one place where it really pays off to have a car. The monasteries are located roughly 20km to 30km from one another, and guesthouses and restaurants are spread throughout the region. An alternative to driving would be to book a guided day tour, with transport included (p364). The nearby city of Suceava makes a good base for exploring the monasteries. It's home to some decent hotels and it's also where many of the regional tour operators are based.

North and west of the city of Suceava, in the northern province of Bucovina, a half-dozen beautifully frescoed monasteries *(romaniatourism.com/painted -monasteries.html; admission per monastery 10 lei)* number among Romania's leading attractions. These UNESCO-protected monasteries are not simply works of art in their own right, but are deeply tied to the rule of 15th-century Moldavian leader Ştefan cel Mare and the region's cultural and religious struggle against the Ottoman Empire – indeed, to the origins of Romania itself. The setting, amid forested hills and tiny villages, couldn't be lovelier.

Arbore Monastery

A tiny but lovely church

Arbore Monastery (Mănăstirea Arbore), in the village of Arbore, receives a fraction of the visitors and hence feels more private and special. The small scale allows you to study the paintings up close to appreciate the skill and techniques involved. The monastery dates from 1503 and was the brainchild of local nobleman Luca Arbore. It took just five months to build but four decades to paint. The tiny interior consists of just three chambers: the chamber nearest the altar has a well-preserved votive painting (on the facing wall) of Arbore and his family offering the church to God. The tombs of Arbore and his family sit in another chamber. The interior is in the process of long-term restoration and may be closed during your visit.

Humor Monastery

A fortress surrounded by ramparts

Founded by Chancellor Theodor Bubuiog under Moldavian Prince Petru Rareş, **Humor Monastery** (Mănăstirea Humor), built in 1530, is surrounded by ramparts, with a three-level brick-and-wood lookout tower. The narrow walls enclosing the last stretch of stairway were designed so that defending soldiers could kill attacking Turks one by one. Humor's

BUCOVINA MONASTERIES

predominantly red-and-brown exterior frescoes (1535) are divided topically. On the southern wall's left-hand side the Virgin Mary is commemorated; on the right, St Nicholas' life and miracles are captured. Other features to look for include a badly faded depiction of the 1453 siege of Constantinople, with a parable depicting the prodigal son's return.

Moldoviţa Monastery

See Prince Rareş' surviving throne

Built in 1532, **Moldoviţa Monastery** (Mănăstirea Moldoviţa) occupies a fortified quadrangular enclosure with tower, gates and well-tended lawns. The central painted church has been partly restored and features impressive frescoes from 1537. The southern exterior wall depicts the 626 CE siege of Constantinople under a combined Persian-Avar attack. The besiegers are depicted in Turkish dress – keeping parishioners concentrated on the then-contemporary foe. Inside the sanctuary, on a wall facing the carved iconostasis, a pious Prince Petru Rareş offers the church to Christ. The monastery's museum displays Rareş' original throne.

☑ **TOP TIP**

Visitors are expected to act and dress respectfully. In practice, this means you should cover your legs and shoulders. These rules are often waived on hot days. If you turn up in shorts, cover yourself with one of the capes hanging near the entrance.

 EATING NEAR THE PAINTED MONASTERIES: OUR PICKS

Antique: Unexpectedly elegant restaurant in Rădăuţi. It's worth a special trip – the chefs aim for something higher than traditional cooking. *11am-11pm* €€€

Popasul Domnesc: This beautiful, modern resort in Voroneţ has an excellent restaurant with a terrace overlooking the monastery. Reserve. *11am-10pm* €€

Casa Humor: West of Gura Humorului, offering delicious traditional food, local cheese and a memorable version of the classic dessert *papanaşi* (pastry). *noon-10pm* €€

Popas Turistic Bucovina: Perfect spot to grab a well-prepared lunch of traditional Bucovinian cooking near the Suceviţa Monastery. *10am-9.30pm* €€

BEST TOURS FOR SEEING THE MONASTERIES

The monasteries are scattered over a wide area, which entails a lot of driving. Instead of driving yourself, join a guided tour for both convenience and added historical context. Here are some of our favourite tours:

Explore Bucovina: Group tours of the Painted Monasteries as well as customised trips.
(explorebucovina.com)

Hello Bucovina: Wide variety of tours, including day trips to the Painted Monasteries and other regional sights.
(hellobucovina.com)

Painted Monasteries of Bucovina: Knowledgeable guided tours led by local Sorin Fodor.
(paintedmonasteries.ro)

DENNY VAN DER VAART/SHUTTERSTOCK

Sucevița Monastery

Sucevița Monastery
Bucovina's largest painted monastery

Sucevița Monastery (Mănăstirea Sucevița), built from 1582 to 1601, is the largest Bucovina monastery. It's perhaps best known for its exterior fresco *The Ladder of Virtues*, with its 32 steps to heaven, near the main entry. It exhorts priests to righteous behaviour and to avoid the unfortunate fate of the clerics depicted tumbling from the ladder due to their sins. The church's tomb room contains the coffins of monastery founders Simion and Ieremia Movilă. The continuity of the Old and New Testaments is emphasised on the southern exterior wall, where a tree grows from the reclining figure of Jesse, flanked by ancient Greek philosophers. The Virgin, depicted as a Byzantine princess, stands nearby, with angels holding a red veil over her head.

Voroneț Monastery
Church with a famous blue hue

Built in just three months and three weeks by Ștefan cel Mare following a key 1488 victory over the Turks, **Voroneț Monastery** (Mănăstirea Voroneț) is widely considered the masterpiece of the bunch. It's the only painted monastery that has an internationally recognised colour associated with it. 'Voroneț Blue', a vibrant cerulean hue created from lapis lazuli and other ingredients, is prominent in its frescoes. A 2011 fresco restoration in the entryway revealed the incredible quality of these paintings even more clearly. The wondrous size, scope and detail of *The Last Judgement*, which fills the entire exterior western wall, has earned near-universal accolades as being the most marvellous of the Bucovina frescoes.

The Danube Delta

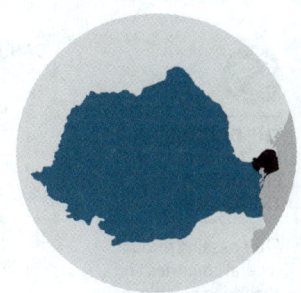

NATURE | WILDLIFE | BEACHES

The sprawling Danube Delta features a fantastic, tangled network of ever-eroding canals, riverbeds and wetlands. Come here to discover remote fishing villages, miles of reed-lined water channels, stretches of deserted coast and one of the world's great sanctuaries for migrating birds. The region's main port, Tulcea, is a natural jumping-off point for moving deeper into the delta. The city has a pleasant riverside promenade with pretty views out over the Danube. In warm weather, the promenade is lined with private boat operators offering a variety of excursions on slow boats and speedboats. Two Black Sea coastal towns, Sulina and Sfântu Gheorghe, have excellent pensions, restaurants and beaches, yet retain a remote, cut-off feel. Both make good bases for exploring the delta's hidden channels and quaint fishing villages.

> ☑ **TOP TIP**
>
> Tulcea's **Tourism Information Centre** (*romaniatourism.com/ danube-delta.html*) has maps and can also help plan boat trips.

Hire a Boat to Explore the Delta

Ride the waves through the wetlands

From May to September, Tulcea's riverside promenade is lined with private boat operators, all offering a similar mix of guided excursions (from two to eight hours) into the delta. Highlights include **Mila 23**, a sleepy fishing village north of the delta's Sulina channel. Longer tours carry on to the wonderfully preserved village of **Letea**, known for its wild horses, and then on to **Sulina**, along the delta's central channel. Prices

---

 GETTING AROUND

Tulcea is easy to reach by bus. The bus station is located at the western end of the promenade near the passenger-ferry terminal and within walking distance of hotels and restaurants. To access destinations within the delta, the state-run ferry operator **Navrom** (*navromdelta.ro*) operates year-round passenger ferries that depart from the port at the western end of the promenade. Buy tickets on the Navrom website or in person at the Navrom Terminal. Alternatively, more expensive water taxis run from the promenade to popular spots within the delta, like Sulina and Sfântu Gheorghe.

THE DANUBE DELTA: A EUROPEAN TREASURE

After passing through several countries and absorbing countless lesser waterways, the Danube River empties into the Black Sea south of the Ukrainian border. The Danube Delta is one of the country's leading attractions. At Tulcea, the river splits into three separate channels: the Chilia, Sulina and Sfântu Gheorghe, creating a constantly evolving 4187-sq-km wetland of marshes, floating reed islets and sandbars. The region provides sanctuary for 300 species of bird and 160 species of fish. Reed marshes cover 1563 sq km, constituting one of the largest single expanses of reed beds in the world. The delta is a haven for wildlife lovers, birdwatchers, fishers and anyone wanting to get away from it all for a few days.

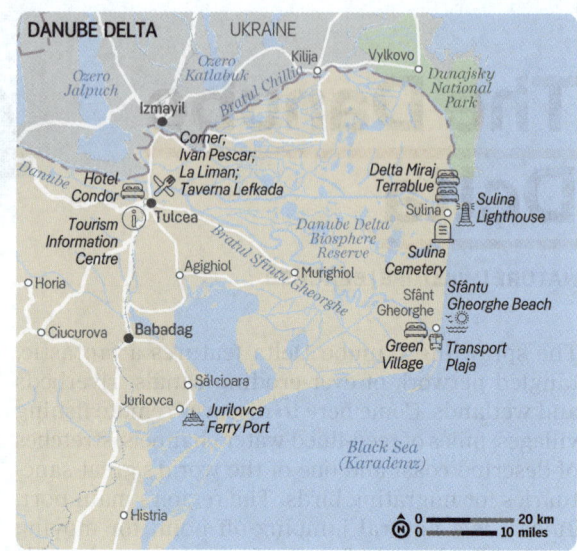

are standard across operators. Shorter trips start at around 120 lei per person, with longer journeys costing up to 200 or 300 lei per person. Excursions typically leave between 8am and 11am. Wear a hat and pack plenty of sunscreen.

Discover Sulina's Fascinating History

Coastal town and former HQ

The tiny Black Sea coastal town of Sulina, on the eastern end of the central Sulina channel and about 65km east of Tulcea by ferry, has the same beautiful beaches and opportunities for exploring the delta as other villages, but has a richer history than most. In the mid-19th century, tiny Sulina served as the headquarters of one of the world's earliest multinational organisations: the European Commission of the Danube. Learn about Sulina's rich cultural diversity at the **Sulina Lighthouse** (*icemtl.ro; entry adult/child 20/10 lei*), the headquarters of the commission. Maybe the best place to get a feel for the seaport in its heyday is the remarkable **Sulina Cemetery** (*discover-sulina.com; entry free*), where the various faiths and nationalities still rub shoulders, so to speak, in a tiny, harmonious setting. Don't miss the row of

 EATING IN TULCEA: OUR PICKS

Ivan Pescar: Excellent traditional fish soup, as well as grilled fish and various stews and seafood concoctions. *noon-10pm* €€

La Liman: The best option close to Tulcea's passenger ferry port. Decent local specialities, plus plenty of fish offerings. *8am-11pm* €€

The Corner: Convenient location across from the Central Eco-Tourism Museum of the Danube Delta makes it a lifesaver for a drink or pizza. *8am-11pm* €

Taverna Lefkada: Family-run and more intimate than most restaurants along Tulcea's port. Greek slant, with nice yogurt-based desserts. *Tue-Sun noon-9pm* €€

fallen British sailors from the 19th century, laid to rest just in front of the cemetery's small chapel. Not far from here, find the grave of a pirate, identified by the trademark skull and crossbones. Sulina Beach, just beyond the cemetery, is a clean, tranquil spot to swim in the Black Sea.

Relax at Sleepy Sfântu Gheorghe

Beautiful, isolated delta town

There's not much to do in tiny Sfântu Gheorghe, at the eastern edge of the southern Sfântu Gheorghe channel, and that's precisely the point. The only way to get here is by boat (100km east of Tulcea by ferry), which keeps the crowds away. Take your pick between lazing on the beautifully pristine **Sfântu Gheorghe Beach** or exploring the waterways on a private boat trip, negotiated with a local fisherman. The beach is 4km east of the town centre. Walk 40 minutes or take the **Transport Plaja** *(5 lei)*, a tractor-hauled transport wagon that leaves the village every 20 minutes from June to September.

Find an Isolated Beach at Gura Portiței

Arguably Romania's best Black Sea beach

The low-key resort at **Gura Portiței**, 50km south of Tulcea, occupies a perilously thin strip of sand that separates the coastal lakes of Golovița and Razim from the wider Black Sea. The main attraction is the long beach and clean water for swimming. Many visitors opt to bed down at a quaint fisherman's house in the coastal village of Jurilovca and head to the **Jurilovca Ferry Port** for the 30-minute ride *(one-way 50 lei)* or private boat *(one-way 40 lei)* across the lake.

Places We Love to Stay

€ Budget €€ Midrange €€€ Top End

Bucharest
MAP p352

Rosetti Hotel €€ Boutique aparthotel grafts contemporary design onto a historic, early 20th-century villa. A block south of Grădina Icoanei.

Nishani Boutique Hotel €€ This newly appointed boutique hotel near Piața Romană has a great mix of modern design and traditional elements. Serves Aromanian cuisine.

Moxy Bucharest Old Town €€ Hip hotel with playful design and a state-of-the-art video wall. Comfortable rooms, great breakfast and communal workspace.

The Mansion Boutique Hotel €€ Stylish hotel right in the middle of the action on pedestrian Str Franceză. Each room has a unique theme.

Transylvania

Braşov

Secret Boutique Hostel € Newish hostel that's close to the action yet quiet, with spotless, well-appointed six- and eight-bed dorms.

Belfort €€ Clean, bright midrange hotel above the city and just below Mt Tâmpa. Some rooms have mountain views.

Schuster Boarding House €€€ Luxuriously reconstructed townhouse with a glorious rooftop terrace. Easy walking distance from the central square.

Sighişoara

Central Park €€ Unexpectedly opulent hotel with artwork, European antiques and chandeliers sparkling above a grand stairway.

Joseph Hayn Apartments €€ If you had a Transylvanian Saxon grandma, this would be her apartment. Filled with mid-20th-century ambience, complete with a vinyl player in some of the rooms.

Casa Savri €€ Outstanding citadel guesthouse with an ideal mix of modern amenities and traditional Saxon decor and furnishings.

Sibiu

B13 € Popular, well-run hostel with a great central location on the main pedestrian street.

Art Hotel €€ Handsome boutique, perfectly situated in the trendy Lower Town just minutes from the main sights.

Rosen Villa Sibiu €€ High-end guesthouse in a quiet residential neighbourhood, within walking distance of the train and bus stations.

Bucovina Monasteries
MAP p363

Acasă în Bucovina €€ Upscale farmhouse lodging southeast of the town of Gura Humorului. Horse-and-buggy rides will be a treat for kids. Excellent restaurant.

Casa Verde €€ Traditional Voroneț guesthouse with friendly owners; the setting is a five-minute walk from the monastery.

La Roată €€ Collection of detached guesthouses 500m west of the Gura Humorului town centre. Has spacious rooms, beautiful views and kid-friendly attractions like a playground and table tennis.

MyContinental €€ Ideal three-star option in central Suceava, offering excellent value, an outdoor terrace for breakfast and a central location within walking distance of the main square.

Hotel Sonnenhof €€€ Fancy four-star place in Suceava, located 3km outside of town along the Târgu Neamț road. Has an excellent in-house restaurant and relaxing, high-end breakfasts.

Danube Delta
MAP p366

Hotel Condor €€ Modern high-rise in Tulcea. Opened in 2023 and still has that clean 'new car' smell. Good central location, 200m from the promenade.

Terrablue €€ Spotless modern pension in Sulina, with two outdoor pools and a small terrace on the river. Located in a rural area 2km west of the port area. Arrange transport directly with the pension.

Delta Miraj €€ Homey hotel/pension located 3km west of Sulina's port. Has a lovely riverside terrace for relaxing and a popular outdoor pool. Arrange transport in advance from Sulina port.

Green Village €€€ Four-star resort has the best facilities in Sfântu Gheorghe. Accommodation is in bungalows with thatched roofs designed to harmonise with the delta setting.

Practicalities

LGBTIQ+ Travellers
Romania is a conservative society and LGBTIQ+ attitudes are generally negative. Progress has been made in protecting the rights of LGBTIQ+ individuals, but same-sex partnerships are not recognised. Bucharest has a large gay community and attitudes tend to be more tolerant in larger cities.

Safe Travel
Romania is a safe country and travellers needn't worry about taking any special precautions. That said, small-scale theft, scams and pickpockets can still be a problem. Always lock car doors and watch wallets and purses in crowded areas. Never change money on the black market; this is always a scam.

Accessible Travel
Romania is not yet well-equipped for people with disabilities, though there has been noticeable improvement in recent years. Stairs and uneven footpaths will pose challenges, and ramps and accessible toilets are few and far between. Newer hotels and international chains should be equipped to handle guests with special needs. Always ask when booking.

Toilets
There are few public toilets and those that do exist are often not clean. Use better facilities at restaurants and fast-food chains, hotels or highway petrol stations when you have the chance.

MO WU/SHUTTERSTOCK

Sighişoara (p358)

Opening Hours
Banks 9am–5pm Monday to Friday
Museums 10am–5pm
Offices 8am–5pm Monday to Friday
Post Offices 8am–7pm Monday to Friday
Restaurants 9am–11pm
Shops 9am–6pm Monday to Friday, to 2pm Saturday

Insurance
Insurance is not required when travelling to Romania, but it is recommended. Consider purchasing comprehensive insurance that covers both medical care and flight cancellations. EU residents can get a free European Health Insurance Card (EHIC), which covers emergency medical treatments without charge.

Public Holidays
Many public holidays correspond with important events on the Orthodox calendar.
New Year 1 and 2 January
Orthodox Easter Monday April/May
Labour Day 1 May
Pentecost May/June, 50 days after Easter Sunday
Assumption of Mary 15 August
Feast of St Andrew 30 November
Romanian National Day 1 December
Christmas Day 25 December
Boxing Day 26 December

Language

Note that ew is pronounced as 'ee' with rounded lips, oh as the 'o' in 'note', ow as in 'how', uh as the 'a' in 'ago', and zh as the 's' in 'pleasure'. The apostrophe (') indicates a very short, unstressed i (almost silent).

Basics

Hello. Bună ziua. *boo·nuh zee·wa*

Goodbye. La revedere. *la re·ve·de·re*

Excuse me. Scuzaţi-mă. *skoo·za·tsee·muh*

Sorry. Îmi pare rău. *ewm' pa·re ruh·oo*

Please. Vă rog. *vuh rog*

Thank you. Mulţumesc. *mool·t-soo·mesk*

Yes. Da. *da*

No. Nu. *noo*

What's your name? Cum vă numiţi? *koom vuh noo·meets'*

My name is ... Numele meu este ... *noo·me·le me·oo yes·te ...*

Do you speak English? Vorbiţi engleza? *vor·beets' en·gle·za*

I don't understand. Eu nu înţeleg. *ye·oo noo ewn·tse·leg*

Transport

boat vapor *va·por*

bus autobuz *ow·to·booz*

plane avion *a·vyon*

train tren *tren*

One ... ticket (to Cluj), please. Un bilet (până la Cluj), vă rog *oon bee·let ... (pew·nuh la kloozh) vuh rog*

one-way dus *doos*

return dus-întors *doos ewn·tors*

Emergencies

Help! Ajutor! *a·zhoo·tor*

Go away! Pleacă! *ple·a·kuh*

Call the ...! Chemaţi ...! *ke·mats' ...*

 doctor un doctor *oon dok·tor*

 police poliţia *po·lee·tsya*

I'm lost. M-am rătăcit. *mam ruh·tuh·cheet*

I'm ill. Mă simt rău. *muh seemt ruh·oo*

Where are the toilets? Unde este o toaletă? *oon·de yes·te o to·a·le·tuh*

Eating & Drinking

What would you recommend? Ce recomandaţi? *che re·ko·man·dats'*

Do you have vegetarian food? Aveţi mâncare vegetariană? *a·ve·tsi mewn·ka·re ve·je·ta·rya·nuh*

I'll have ... Aş dori ... *ash do·ree ...*

Cheers! Noroc! *no·rok*

I'd like the Vă rog, aş dori..., *vuh rog ash ... do·ree ...* **please.**

 bill nota de plată *no·ta de pla·tuh*

 menu meniul *me·nee·ool*

Shopping & Services

I'm looking for ... Caut ... *kowt ...*

How much is it? Cât costă? *kewt kos·tuh*

That's too expensive. E prea scump. *ye pre·a skoomp*

market piaţă *pya·tsuh*

post office poşta *posh·ta*

tourist office biroul de informaţii turistice *bee·ro·ool de een·for·ma·tsee too·rees·tee·che*

Accommodation

campsite teren de camping *te·ren de kem·peeng*

guesthouse pensiune *pen·syoo·ne*

hotel hotel *ho·tel*

youth hostel hostel *hos·tel*

Do you have a ... room? Aveţi o cameră ...? *a·vets' o ka·me·ruh ...*

 single de o persoană *de o per·so·a·nuh*

 double dublă *doo·bluh*

NUMBERS

1
unu *oo·noo*

2
doi *doy*

3
trei *trey*

4
patru *pa·troo*

5
cinci *cheemcj'*

6
şase *sha·se*

7
şapte *shap·te*

8
opt *opt*

9
nouă *no·wuh*

10
zece *ze·che*

Subway train, Bucharest (p350)

Arriving & Getting Around

Bucharest's **Henri Coandă International Airport**, 16km north of the capital, is the primary point of entry for most travellers. Other cities with major airports include Cluj, Sibiu, Iaşi and Timişoara.

MONEY

Currency: Romanian Leu (Lei)

CHANGING MONEY

The best place to exchange money is an ATM. You can also change money at private exchange booths *(casa de schimb)*, but be wary of commission charges and ask how many lei you will receive before handing over your bills. You may need to show a passport to change money.

CARD PAYMENTS

International credit and debit cards, as well as contactless payment options, are widely accepted at hotels, restaurants and shops. In rural or isolated areas, where ATMs are limited, you'll need to carry some cash.

TIPPING

Tip 10% for good service in restaurants. Round up taxi fare to the nearest lei. Tip the cleaning staff 5 to 10 lei per night in hotels.

Trains & Buses

Trains are slow but reliable for travelling between large cities. Most services are run by the national rail company Căile Ferate Române *(CFR; cfrcalatori. ro)*. Buses and smaller maxi-taxis go nearly everywhere, but the system can be confusing.

Road Conditions

Romanian roads are crowded and often in poor condition. The country has limited stretches of four-lane motorway; most travel will be along two-lane national highways. When calculating journey times, figure on 50km per hour.

Visas

Romania is part of the EU's common border Schengen zone. EU nationals don't need a visa. Those from the US, Canada, UK, Australia and New Zealand can stay for up to 90 days in any six months.

Parking

Cars offer more flexibility than trains or buses and are essential for visiting out-of-the-way attractions, like monasteries and trailheads. Note that parking can be tight to non-existent in cities. When booking accommodation always ask about parking facilities; it's usually best to pay extra for parking rather than search for a spot on your own.

Russia is currently considered **unsafe to visit**

Above: Statue of Tsar Alexander II and Cathedral of Christ the Saviour; Right: Red Square and St Basil's Cathedral

Curated by
Leonid Ragazin

Russia

THE WORLD'S LARGEST COUNTRY AT WAR

Russia's all-out attack on Ukraine creates serious risks for Western travellers.

In 2014, Russia annexed Crimea, beginning what was initially a low-intensity conflict with Ukraine. At the time, it was still safe to visit this massive, diverse and fascinating country. But that all changed in February 2022, when a full-scale invasion of Ukraine turned Russia into a no-go zone – at least for the nationals of major Western countries. In the wake of the invasion, hundreds of thousands fled Russia: this included most of the political opposition, independent journalists and regular citizens. People left partly for moral reasons, and partly out of fear of harsh and arbitrary new laws that criminalise any criticism of the war and the Russian military, which could lead to lengthy prison sentences.

Russia spans 11 time zones, and a flight from Moscow to Vladivostok in the far east takes over eight hours. Unsurprisingly, this enormous territory, occupying one-third of the Eurasian landmass, encompasses a plethora of climatic zones and landscapes, from the Arctic tundra and taiga boreal forest in Siberia to hot steppes, semideserts and lush subtropics in the Caucasus. It has its share of iconic travel destinations: St Petersburg, Moscow's Kremlin and Red Square, the gorgeous Baikal – the planet's oldest and deepest lake – as well as the volcanic Kamchatka Peninsula, filled with bears and geysers.

That said, the Asian part of Russian beyond the Ural Mountains – larger and more resource-rich – is mostly uninhabitable due to its severe climate. This explains why nearly 80% of Russians live in the country's European part, which is referred to as 'Central Russia' despite it being in the west. East of the Urals, meanwhile, is an archipelago of population centres stretching along the Trans-Siberian railway, which runs along the southern edge of Siberia towards Vladivostok – an epic journey that was once a major drawcard for travellers.

Russia Today

On the face of it, life in Russia feels largely unchanged by the war with Ukraine. Even as the West imposed harsh sanctions, increased defence production spurred a mini economic boom. Moscow, St Petersburg and other large cities are flourishing. For many people the war seems far away from their daily life, despite the occasional Ukrainian drone strike. As for frontline casualties, the people who have suffered the most are those from the most destitute classes and the peripheral regions. The middle-class majority in large population centres has been largely unaffected.

The government excels in pinpoint repression by targeting only a few while instilling fear in millions. Posting a Ukrainian flag on social media, openly criticising the war or expressing support for the opposition (branded as 'extremists' under the Russian law) are all actions that may result in a harsh prison sentence. But the goal of such policies is not imprisonment: it is to drive dissidents out of the country. The number of political prisoners was under 1700 at the time of writing.

At press time, the conflict in Ukraine was at a crossroads. US President Donald Trump was pushing for peace, but a failure to achieve a ceasefire could result in a greater escalation.

History

Russia only emerged in its current nation-state form, with ethnically defined borders and an 80% ethnic Russian population, in 1991. The country's previous incarnations, all encompassing different geographical realms, have become highly politicised in the wake of the Russo-Ukrainian conflict.

The Kyivan Rus and the Tatar-Mongol Yoke

The semi-legendary 9th-century Viking warrior Rurik, a leader of the Rus tribe, established a dynasty that was initially based in Novgorod. The Rus would dominate the emerging Russian state for the next 600 years. Rurik's successor Prince Oleg moved the capital to Kyiv, starting a polity that became known as Kyivan Rus.

Kyivan princes imported Orthodox Christianity and the Cyrillic alphabet from the Byzantines. They also began colonising Finno-Ugric and Baltic tribal lands to the northeast, founding a trading post called Moscow, first mentioned in 1147.

Kyiv's dominance ended when Batu Khaan of the Golden Horde sacked the city in 1240 and conquered most other Russian principalities, ushering in a period known as the Tatar-Mongol Yoke. The Horde didn't meddle in local affairs, ruling instead via vassal Russian princes. In a political context requiring shrewd diplomatic skills, Moscow gradually emerged as the centre of power. The Grand Prince Dmitry defeated the Mongols in the battle of Kulikovo Pole in 1380, although the vassalage formally lasted for another hundred years.

Moscow tsardom

Ivan III, the first Moscow ruler to be called tsar (from Caesar), became known as 'the collector of Russian lands' following his

WHY IS VISITING RUSSIA DANGEROUS?

In 2025, entering Russia was not difficult for most passport holders, but there are good reasons why Western governments warn against visiting in unequivocal terms.

Western visitors have occasionally been arrested on dubious charges and then wind up languishing in prison, often for years, before eventually being swapped for Russian prisoners. Foreigners can also be prosecuted under Russia's harsh legislation, which punishes any criticism of the war in Ukraine or support of the opposition on social media. Russia also maintains a long list of 'undesirable organisations', which includes major Western NGOs like Amnesty International. An affiliation with any of these undesirables is considered a crime. Finally, there is the war itself. Ukraine has demonstrated a capacity to carry out strikes on Russian territory. In 2024, its kamikaze drones hit targets deep inside Russia.At the moment, one needs a pressing reason to travel to Russia and a clear-eyed view of the potential risks. Your government will have little leverage if you wind up in jail.

Barents Sea
Murmansk
Naryan Mar
Salekhard
SWEDEN
Pechora
Ob
White Sea
Kem
Arkhangelsk
FINLAND
Petrozavodsk
Lake Onega
Khanty Mansiysk
Baltic Sea
TALLINN
Syktyvkar
Irtysh
St Petersburg
ESTONIA
Sukhona
Vologda
LATVIA
Pskov
RĪGA
Veliky Novgorod
Yaroslavl
Kostroma
Kirov
Perm
Tyumen
Kaliningrad
Tver
Ivanovo
Yekaterinburg
LITHUANIA
Yoshkar Ola
Kurgan
VILNIUS
MOSCOW
Chelyabinsk
WARSAW
Smolensk
Vladimir
Nizhny Novgorod
Kazan
MINSK
Kaluga
Ufa
BELARUS
Ulyanovsk
Ural
Tobol
POLAND
Bryansk
Tula
Ryazan
Saransk
Oryol
Penza
Samara
Lipetsk
Tambov
Orenburg
KYIV
Kursk
Voronezh
Saratov
Belgorod
Ural
UKRAINE
Don
Volgograd
KAZAKHSTAN
ROMANIA
CHIŞINĂU
Aral Sea
Rostov-on-Don
Volga
BUCHAREST
Elista
Astrakhan
Crimea
Krasnodar
Black Sea
Stavropol
UZBEKISTAN
BULGARIA
Cherkessk
Grozny
Caspian Sea
0 1000 km
0 500 miles
Nalchik
Makhachkala

subjugation of rival city-states. Moscow's consolidation of power morphed into imperial expansion under Ivan IV (known as Ivan the Terrible in the West), who sacked the remnants of the Golden Horde on the Volga and turned it into Russia's main river.

The end of the Rurik dynasty in 1598 precipitated a period known as the Smuta (Troubles). The Poles seized Moscow in 1610, but the invasion united Russia and a popular militia ousted them in 1612. The following year, the enthronement of 16-year-old Mikhail Romanov began a dynasty that would rule until 1917.

The Russian Empire

At the beginning of the 18th century, the young tsar Peter the Great undertook sweeping Western reforms that transformed Russia into a major European power. He defeated Sweden in the Great Northern War and built a new imperial capital, St Petersburg. In the late 18th century, the German-born Catherine the Great conquered swathes of land in what is now Ukraine; the enslavement of peasants reached its peak during the same period.

Napoleon invaded Russia in 1812 – the French imperator's biggest blunder. Despite capturing Moscow, he was driven out of the country and the Russian army marched all the way to

FAST FACTS

Capital Moscow
Population 143 million
Area 17,098,246 sq km
Official language Russian
Time zone GMT+2 through GMT+12
Currency Ruble

MOSCOW: AN INSIDER'S VIEW

Moscow resident **Yekaterina** reflects on life in the city during the war.

In the summer of 2025, Moscow feels excessively gorgeous and mellow. Gardens and flowerbeds are in bloom everywhere. Electric buses run on time and are extremely quiet. Roughly six new metro stations are opened every year. Food couriers in the streets mingle with hip-looking youngsters. There has been a never-ending succession of public events: a corgi parade, a triathlon, a flea market, a cinema festival. Also padel – everyone is playing padel this year. After a game of padel, we go to an open-air terrace for brunch or a glass of wine, despite the chilly weather. We talk about the interminable renovations in the Moscow streets, which annoys everyone. This is one subject that's okay to discuss openly – unlike the war, drone attacks and the increasingly absurd bans on saying or doing all sorts of things. The noise from asphalt pavers disrupts the conversation, but people say: 'We can put up with it'. Whatever they mean by that.

GARY LATHAM/LONELY PLANET

Lenin bust

Paris. Returning officers brought back new subversive social ideas and the failed 1825 uprising of idealistic aristocrats, known as the Decembrists, inspired revolutionary movement.

Tsar Alexander II abolished serfdom in 1861 and launched progressive reforms of the courts and local government. But revolutionaries assassinated him in 1881, ushering in a reactionary period.

The Soviet period

The last of the Romanovs, Nicholas II, lost a war with Japan and suppressed a nationwide uprising in 1905. By dragging Russia into WWI, he precipitated a democratic revolution and the abolition of the monarchy in February 1917. In October of the same year, the Bolsheviks, under Marxist Vladimir Lenin, seized power in a coup and defeated other political factions in the ensuing civil war. A new multinational state, the Soviet Union, was created in 1922, with a Russian republic, the RSFSR, as its largest constituent part.

Communist rule brought about rapid industrialisation and urbanisation as well as a reign of terror under Joseph Stalin in the 1930s. Hundreds of thousands were executed, millions languished in Gulag labour camps or died in artificial famines and forced deportations.

This was followed by an even greater catastrophe when Nazi Germany invaded the USSR in June 1941. Soviet losses in WWII were an estimated 25 to 27 million people, of which around half were from the RSFSR. The war's most decisive battles – Stalingrad, Kursk and the siege of Leningrad – took place in the territory of today's Russia, and Soviet troops seized Berlin in May 1945.

Stalin's death in 1953 brought about a transition from mass terror to a period of liberalisation under Nikita Khrushchev. Prone to bewildering eccentricity, he was deposed in 1966. His successor Leonid Brezhnev oversaw a detente in relations with the US, but the Soviet economy was becoming increasingly dysfunctional and uncompetitive.

Brezhnev's politburo made the fateful mistake of invading Afghanistan in 1979 – a move that drained the USSR's already scarce economic resources. Brezhnev died in 1982 as a much-ridiculed gerontocrat. The reform-minded Mikhail Gorbachev came to power in 1984, opening the final chapter in Soviet history.

Gorbachev launched political and economic reforms collectively branded as *perestroika* (reconstruction), which soon spun out of control. Mass rallies in Moscow demanded democratic change while the mishandled economy rapidly deteriorated.

In 1989, the Soviet Bloc in Eastern Europe collapsed, while Boris Yeltsin emerged as the pro-democracy leader of the RSFSR and Gorbachev's nemesis. The climax came in August 1991, when party hardliners staged a military coup and arrested Gorbachev at his dacha in Crimea. Yeltsin led a successful resistance and rallied millions to defend democracy, thus sidelining Gorbachev for good. At the end of 1991, together with the leaders of Ukraine and Belarus, Yeltsin abolished the USSR and sent the newly emerged Russian national state on its own precarious journey.

Post-Soviet period

Yeltsin also launched 'shock therapy' reforms that caused hyperinflation and instantly drove millions into abject poverty. The period of democratic rule in the 1990s is remembered by Russians as a time of institutional degradation, a bloody war in Chechnya, uncontrolled crime, rampant corruption and national humiliation.

As the 20th century drew to a close, what people wanted most of all was a semblance of stability. And this came through Yeltsin's chosen successor, Vladimir Putin. The former KGB officer began his rule in late 1999 by subjugating Chechnya. He also appointed a technocratic government that implemented prudent fiscal policies and undertook long-delayed institutional reforms. Simultaneously, he tightened the state's grip on the media and the political system at large.

Putin was still flirting with democracy when he stepped down in favour of his faithful ally Dmitry Medvedev in 2008. But he ran for presidency again in 2012, a decision that precipitated the Bolotnaya protests in Moscow. These protests saw rising star Alexey Navalny emerge as the leader of the opposition.

Meanwhile, relations with the US-led West were deteriorating following NATO's 2008 decision to expand to Ukraine and Georgia. A short-lived war with the latter flared up a few months later. In 2014, Putin responded to Ukraine's Maidan revolution by annexing Crimea and launching an armed conflict in the east of Ukraine.

This low-intensity conflict changed in 2022, when Putin order an all-out invasion of Ukraine in a dramatic move that changed European history. With all eyes on the invasion, he also managed to get rid of Navalny, who survived a near-lethal poisoning in 2020 but died in prison the following year.

RUSSIA OUTSIDE RUSSIA

Visits to Russia might be problematic for both moral and security reasons, but obtaining firsthand knowledge from Russians about their culture has never been easier. The lion's share of educated Russian elite fled the country in the wake of the all-out invasion in Ukraine. Estimates put the scope of emigration between 500,000 and 1 million people. This mass flight went in many directions, with numerous opposition activists, journalists and cultural figures ending up in the EU, especially in cities such as Berlin, Rīga and Vilnius. Major diasporas were also formed in Georgia, Armenia, Serbia and Montenegro. Some went as far as Buenos Aires. The result is that some of the most prominent Russian performers or writers can only be seen in the West. Celebrities like Boris Grebenshchikov ('Russia's Bob Dylan'), famous rock bands like DDT and B2, and Gen Z stars like Monetochka tour the world without ever returning to Russia. If you happen to be interested in Russian culture, keep an eye out for them in your hometown.

Curated by
Brana Vladisavljević

Serbia

DIVERSITY OFF THE BEATEN PATH

History galore, festive spirit and a medley of landscapes and cultures all define this little-visited country in the heart of the Balkans.

BRANKO JOVANOVIC/SHUTTERSTOCK

A sense of history permeates Serbia. The nation's fate has been shaped by its position on Europe's crossroads ever since the Slavs' arrival in the Balkans. Some would say sheer *inat* – a trait of proud defiance – steered it through epic tribulations and triumphs alike, from the centuries of Turkish and Habsburg dominance to victories in two world wars and the boom and bust of Yugoslavia.

Byzantine, Ottoman, Austro-Hungarian and socialist modernist architectural styles compete across Serbia in a visual timeline of its turbulent past. The 20th century left swathes of communist-era concrete atop a multicultural urban mosaic: between the art nouveau of Subotica and minaret-studded Novi Pazar, medieval Orthodox monasteries and Belgrade's brutalist showpieces, the contrasts couldn't be more pronounced. The diversity is equally apparent in Serbia's great outdoors. Vojvodina's sunflower-covered lowlands rise through the forested hills of Šumadija towards the edges of the Dinaric and Carpathian mountain ranges, while enormous river gorges, ancient karst caves and peculiar rock formations punctuate the country's remote corners. These distinctive landscapes remain the habitats of endangered wildlife species including brown bears and griffon vultures.

Still, it's the social dynamism that stays with you. Trumpet-blasting festivals and *rakija* (fruit brandy)-making prowess are vital manifestations of Serbian élan, as much as the country's sporting successes and acclaimed arts inherited from Yugoslav days.

THE MAIN AREAS

BELGRADE
Spirited metropolis in constant transition. **p382**

NOVI SAD
Multicultural hub on the Danube. **p387**

TARA NATIONAL PARK
Mountain scenery, outdoor action, wildlife. **p389**

ĐERDAP NATIONAL PARK
Iron Gates gorge and medieval fortresses. **p391**

For places to stay in Serbia, see p392

TRABANTOS SHUTTERSTOCK

Right: Kalemegdan Fortress (p382), Belgrade; Above: Golubac Fortress (p391)

Find Your Way

Serbia's main places of interest to travellers are fairly spread out in all directions from the capital, but extensive public transport and good motorways make exploring the country pretty straightforward.

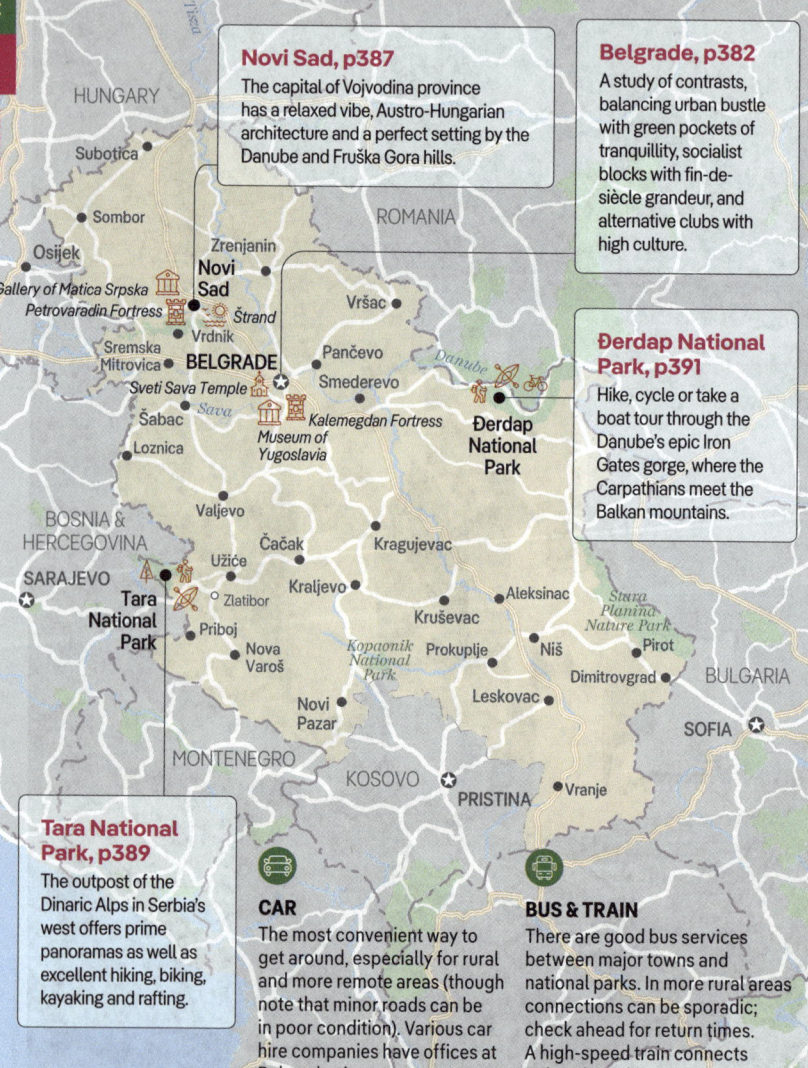

Novi Sad, p387
The capital of Vojvodina province has a relaxed vibe, Austro-Hungarian architecture and a perfect setting by the Danube and Fruška Gora hills.

Belgrade, p382
A study of contrasts, balancing urban bustle with green pockets of tranquillity, socialist blocks with fin-de-siècle grandeur, and alternative clubs with high culture.

Đerdap National Park, p391
Hike, cycle or take a boat tour through the Danube's epic Iron Gates gorge, where the Carpathians meet the Balkan mountains.

Tara National Park, p389
The outpost of the Dinaric Alps in Serbia's west offers prime panoramas as well as excellent hiking, biking, kayaking and rafting.

CAR
The most convenient way to get around, especially for rural and more remote areas (though note that minor roads can be in poor condition). Various car hire companies have offices at Belgrade airport.

BUS & TRAIN
There are good bus services between major towns and national parks. In more rural areas connections can be sporadic; check ahead for return times. A high-speed train connects Belgrade and Novi Sad.

HUNGARY
Subotica
Sombor
Osijek
Gallery of Matica Srpska
Petrovaradin Fortress
Sremska Mitrovica
Šabac
Loznica
BOSNIA & HERCEGOVINA
SARAJEVO
Užiće
Priboj
Nova Varoš
Novi Pazar
MONTENEGRO
Tisa
Zrenjanin
Novi Sad
Štrand
Vrdnik
BELGRADE
Sveti Sava Temple
Sava
Museum of Yugoslavia
Kalemegdan Fortress
Valjevo
Čačak
Kraljevo
Zlatibor
Kopaonik National Park
Vršac
Pančevo
Smederevo
ROMANIA
Danube
Đerdap National Park
Kragujevac
Kruševac
Prokuplje
Leskovac
KOSOVO
PRISTINA
Aleksinac
Niš
Stara Planina Nature Park
Pirot
Dimitrovgrad
BULGARIA
SOFIA
Vranje
Adriatic Sea
Tara National Park

0   100 km
0   50 miles

Petrovaradin Fortress (p388), Novi Sad

Plan Your Time

There's more than big-city Belgrade to keep travellers engaged. Novi Sad has a relaxed vibe and cultural sights while national parks provide plenty of opportunity for outdoor adventures.

A Long Weekend

● Devote your stay in **Belgrade** (p382) to exploring its historical, epicurean and outdoor highlights. Learn about its past at **Kalemegdan Fortress** (p382) and the **Museum of Yugoslavia** (p383), sample new Balkan cuisine and traditional *kafana* (cafe or tavern) fare, and enjoy the city's **clubbing** (p386) scene. In summer, have a swim on **Ada Ciganlija** (p384) or take in the views over Belgrade from **Mt Avala** (p384).

A Week to Explore

● From Belgrade, catch the train to **Novi Sad** (p387) for a day in this Habsburg-flavoured town, touring its galleries and the **Petrovaradin Fortress** (p388) or chilling out on **Štrand** (p389) beach. Outdoor adventures await south of Belgrade. Two national parks, **Tara** (p389) in the west and **Đerdap** (p391) in the east, offer hikes, bike rides and boat trips on the Drina and Danube Rivers.

SEASONAL HIGHLIGHTS

SPRING

The pleasant weather is ideal for hiking or biking in the national parks. Belgrade's cultural and sports calendar is packed.

SUMMER

Summers are scorching; river kayaking or rafting is a great way to cool off. Major music festivals take place countrywide.

AUTUMN

The wine harvest brings festivals – the perfect time for wine tasting, ideally along with farmstead dining in Vojvodina province.

WINTER

Hit the slopes in Serbia's ski resorts. Snowshoeing along the mountain trails is a great way to escape the après-ski crowds.

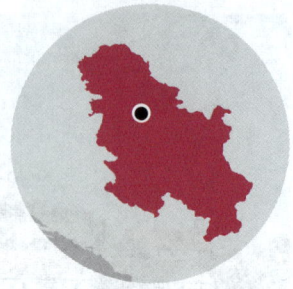

Belgrade

YUGO-NOSTALGIA | CREATIVITY | NIGHTLIFE

GETTING AROUND

From the airport, bus 72 goes to the central Zeleni Venac stop, A1 minibus runs to the main bus station and Slavija Sq, and bus 600 goes to the train station. If catching a taxi, head to the ticket machines in the arrivals hall to get a receipt (the fare is fixed according to zones). Belgrade's public transport (free since 2025) includes buses, trolleybuses and trams; tram 2 is a circular route around Stari Grad. Local ridesharing apps include CarGo and Yandex.

☑ TOP TIP

Stari Grad (Old Town) is loosely defined by pedestrian Knez Mihailova, central Republic Sq and Terazije thoroughfare. Other key areas include Dorćol (to the east from Kalemegdan Fortress), Vračar (around the Sveti Sava Temple) and Zemun (across the rivers from Stari Grad).

Belgrade is full of contradictions. Seemingly its only constant is the urban bustle – with a controversial waterfront development the latest addition to an ever-evolving skyline – but the sunsets on Kalemegdan's ramparts remain as serene as they would have been when the Celts first settled on the promontory above the Sava and Danube Rivers. Its Ottoman conquerors, battling over the city with Austria-Hungary, called it Dar-ul-Jihad (House of Wars); yet it arose from the ashes countless times over two millennia and came to be a cradle of progress during its Yugoslav heyday. Its Serbian name, Beograd, translates as 'White City', although its fin-de-siècle mansions and communist-era monoliths sport many shades of grey.

Belgrade is both a microcosm of Serbia (just stroll any of its green markets) and a world apart. Its history is bewildering, its nightlife enviable and its spirit – from theatre stages to basketball courts, from street art to cocktail bars – is the reason to keep coming back.

A Crash Course in Belgrade's History

Tracing the White City's past

Although repeatedly destroyed and rebuilt over the centuries, Belgrade has significant relics of its tumultuous past.

The White City's ground zero is **Kalemegdan Fortress** (*beogradskatvrdjava.co.rs; fortress grounds free, audio guide with map 300RSD*), first settled by the Celts and expanded by the Romans; much of what stands today is the product of 18th-century Austro-Hungarian and Ottoman reconstructions. Get an audio guide at the souvenir shop and look for attractions including the **Big Gunpowder Magazine** (housing Roman sarcophagi and tombstones), lonesome **Nebojša Tower** (a Turkish-era dungeon), the spooky **Roman Well** (actually built by the Austrians), ivy-swathed **Ružica Church** (a former garrison chapel) and the symbol of Belgrade, the **Victor Monument** by Ivan Meštrović.

One of the world's largest Orthodox basilicas, the neo-Byzantine **Sveti Sava Temple** (*hramsvetogsave.rs*) in Vračar

BELGRADE

Gardoš Tower, Saran (2.4km)

Veliko Ratno Ostrvo

Great War Island

Dunav (Danube River)

Kalemegdan Park

Kalemegdan Fortress

DORĆOL

Dunavska Drugstore (700m)

Ušće Park

NEW BELGRADE

Brankova

Hilandarska

VRAČAR

Sava River

Ada Ciganlija

Ada Ciganlija

Ada Bridge

Beograd Centar (Prokop Station)

Hajd Park

Hipodrom

Topčiderska Zvezda

Sveti Sava Temple

Museum of Yugoslavia

Topčider Park

Košutnjak Hill

0   1 km
0   0.5 miles

⭐ HIGHLIGHTS
1 Ada Ciganlija
2 Kalemegdan Fortress
3 Museum of Yugoslavia
4 Sveti Sava Temple

🔴 SIGHTS
5 Big Gunpowder Magazine
6 Museum of Contemporary Art
7 National Museum
8 Nikola Tesla Museum

⚫ SLEEPING
9 Arka Barka
10 El Diablo Hostel
11 Hostel Bongo
12 Hotel Moskva
13 Mama Shelter
14 Savamala Bed & Breakfast
15 Smokvica B&B
16 Square Nine

🟢 EATING
17 Ambar
18 Dva Jelena
19 Iva New Balkan Cuisine

🟢 DRINKING & NIGHTLIFE
20 Cetinjska 15
21 Druid Bar
22 Klub 20/44
23 Krafter
24 Lenja Buba
25 Wine Art Bar

🔴 ENTERTAINMENT
26 Silosi

🔴 SHOPPING
27 Belgrade Design District
28 Bombondžija Bosiljčić
29 Ivko
30 Parfimerija Sava
31 Rakia Shop
see 20 Yugovinyl

---

holds special historical significance. On this spot the Ottomans burnt the relics of St Sava, the founder of the Serbian Orthodox Church. Ponder the scale of the project, completed after almost a century. Inside, the glittering mosaics (including the 1248-sq-metre mosaic adorning the cupola) are astonishing. Over in Zemun, **Gardoš Tower** (*adult/child 300/200RSD*) was erected in 1896 to mark the millennium of Hungarian statehood and has wonderful Danube views. Mosey around this baroque neighbourhood – Austria-Hungary's border town for nearly two centuries – to appreciate its quaint atmosphere.

Serbia's capital has a particular Yugo-nostalgic appeal. The **Museum of Yugoslavia** (*muzej-jugoslavije.org; entry adult/*

Yugotour: Mini road trip through the Yugoslav era in the iconic Zastava car, taking in the socialist modernist architecture of New Belgrade. *(yugotour. com)*

Food & Culture Tour Belgrade: Get introduced to Serbian cuisine and customs with passionate local foodies. *(foodtour belgrade.com)*

Belgrade Art Tours: Explore independent art galleries and the White City's subculture, including its thriving street art. *(belgradearttours. com)*

iBikeBelgrade: A great way to enjoy the city: these cycling tours go everywhere, from Ada Ciganlija to Zemun. *(ibikebelgrade.com)*

No Fat No Stress: Kayaking tours that take you out on the Danube to secluded Beljarica wetlands, aka 'Belgrade's Amazonia'. *(facebook .com/nofatnostress)*

child 600/300RSD) is ex-Yu history HQ and it's attached to the 'House of Flowers' mausoleum of Marshal Tito, the former socialist federation's lifelong president; free guided tours in English take place on Saturdays. Among many fascinating exhibits are the Relay of Youth batons carried across Yugoslavia for Tito's birthdays and unique gifts from foreign dignitaries.

The Culture Map of Belgrade

Tour the capital's top museums

The stately home of the **National Museum** *(narodnimuzej.rs; entry adult/child 300/150RSD, Sun free)* has archaeological treasures – with a special focus on the prehistoric cultures of Vinča and Lepenski Vir plus the Roman era – and galleries filled with Serbian masterpieces. Observe the development of the nation's artistic expression from Romanticist Đura Jakšić to surrealist Milena Pavlović-Barili.

The beehive-like modernist building of the **Museum of Contemporary Art** *(msub.org.rs; entry adult/child 600/300RSD)*, surrounded by a sculpture garden, stages exhibitions from its trove of 20th-century art such as video performances by Belgrade native Marina Abramović and graphic production by the Yugoslav avant-garde Zenitism movement. Release your inner nerd with some sci-fi-ish interactive elements at the **Nikola Tesla Museum** *(tesla-museum.org; Serbian/English tours 400/800RSD, cash only)*. On display are some of the great scientist's inventions and tools, as well as personal items and the sphere-shaped urn containing Tesla's ashes. Guided tours (on the hour) last 45 minutes.

Green Belgrade

Find oases in the Big Smoke

While Kalemegdan Park is Belgrade's central outdoor sprawl, there are plenty of nature havens around the city.

An easy escape from the urban buzz (16km from central Belgrade), **Mt Avala** is a favourite with cyclists. Take in the panoramic vista over Belgrade, the plains of Vojvodina and Šumadija's hills from the observation platform of the tallest **tower** in the Balkans (204.5m) *(avalskitoranj.rs; entry adult/child 400/200RSD)*.

Come summertime, Belgraders flock to the pebbly lakeside beach on **Ada Ciganlija** *(adaciganlija.rs)*, a verdant island – now attached to the riverbank – on the Sava River. The beach has carried the Blue Flag designation since 2012. There are two main bicycle rental locations: near the roundabout after you cross the embankment and by the big car park on the southern side of the lake.

EATING IN BELGRADE: OUR PICKS

Dva Jelena: Renowned old-school *kafana* (tavern), established in 1832; sample national classics like *Karađorđeva šnicla* (kajmak-stuffed escalope). *10am-1am* €€

Iva New Balkan Cuisine: Head chef Vanja Puškar reinvents local gastronomy in a fusion of flavours and organic ingredients. *9am-midnight Mon-Sat, to 11pm Sun* €€

Ambar: Set in trendy Beton Hala, Ambar is popular for its small-plate takes on Balkan staples and a long craft *rakija* (fruit brandy) list. *hours vary* €€€

Šaran: Sample the daily catch turned into delicacies like the 'Smederevo-style' pike at Zemun's best fish restaurant. *4pm-1am Tue & Wed, 1pm-1am Thu-Sun* €€€

BELGRADE'S TOP FESTIVALS

Belgrade Dance Festival: See the world's major dance troupes – from Akram Khan Company to Compañía Nacional de Danza – in March and April.

Mikser Festival: Belgrade's creative side is in the spotlight in May, with a programme of music, design, sustainable development and quirky innovation.

Belgrade Summer Festival: Sample innovative music, dance, theatre and visual arts around the city in July and August.

Bitef: Week-long showcase of experimental and traditional European theatre in September, launched in 1967.

October Salon: Prestigious biennial exhibition of contemporary visual arts, featuring local and international artists, in September and October.

BEST SHOPPING IN BELGRADE

Belgrade Design District: Small boutiques showcase emerging local fashion designers, jewellers, artists and designers.

Bombondžija Bosiljčić: Handmade sweets – a tradition handed down for three generations – including *ratluk* (Turkish delight).

Parfimerija Sava: Old-world perfumery (established in 1954), with unique hand-mixed scents and vintage bottles.

Yugovinyl: Fantastic record store, with about 20,000 albums in all possible genres and a big focus on Yugo-era new wave.

Ivko: Famous women's fashion label with colourful knitwear inspired by Serbian folk motifs.

Rakia Shop: *Rakija* in a range of flavours, plus delicacies like *ajvar* (red-pepper spread) and *slatko* (fruit preserve).

BADAI/SHUTTERSTOCK

Silosi, Belgrade Marina

The Night Is Young
Go clubbing in the White City

Belgrade has a reputation as one of the global party cities – indeed, its clubs stay thumping till the early hours.

Dorćol's repurposed industrial spaces are now hubs of alternative culture and nightlife. The clubs and bars sharing the address of **Cetinjska 15** – the ramshackle grounds of a former brewery – are the go-to destination for indie music, craft beer, vegan bites, LGBTIQ+ parties and lots more. Over at Belgrade Marina, **Silosi** (*silosi.rs*) is a brutalist complex of four giant silos covered with striking murals, hosting festivals, art exhibitions, DJs and other happenings; it has stunning sunsets, too.

A number of venues have firmly positioned Belgrade on Europe's clubbing map. **Barutana** (*facebook.com/barutanabeograd)* is a summer club in the former **gunpowder magazine** on Kalemegdan Fortress, hosting legendary open-air raves. **Klub 20/44** (*facebook.com/klub2044*) draws an alternative crowd and top electronica DJs; until recently a cult *splav* (river barge) on the Sava, it has started a new chapter on land. At **Drugstore** (*drugstorebeograd.com),* another stalwart of Belgrade's underground scene, you can party to techno sounds in a former slaughterhouse.

DRINKING IN BELGRADE: OUR PICKS

Druid Bar: Speakeasy-evoking nook with vinyl music, impeccably dressed bartenders and skilfully mixed cocktails. *5pm-midnight Sun-Thu, to 1am Fri & Sat*

Lenja Buba: The small cocktail bar at Belgrade Urban Distillery serves top concoctions – including *rakija*-based ones, naturally. Cash only. *5pm-midnight*

Krafter: Sample rotating Serbian craft-beer choices on draught at this industrial-chic venue on a leafy pavement. *9am-midnight Sun-Thu, to 1am Fri & Sat*

Wine Art Bar: Enjoy a glass of Serbian vino at the wonderful rooftop terrace on an atmospheric Dorćol corner. *noon-midnight Sun-Thu, to 1am Fri & Sat*

Beyond Belgrade

OUTDOOR ADVENTURE | HISTORY | RURAL LIFE

North of the capital is Novi Sad, a Habsburg-flavoured cultural hub. To the south, two scenic national parks provide outdoor adventures galore.

While much younger than Belgrade, Novi Sad is no ordinary second city. The capital of Vojvodina province was a stronghold of national culture in the Habsburg-ruled north; in recent times, its formidable fortress played host to the legendary EXIT music festival. Other draws are its venerable museums and galleries, one of Serbia's best beaches and a thriving bicycle culture.

Rich legacies of times past abound in southern Serbia – from brooding Ottoman-era forts along the Danube to sacred Orthodox monasteries cradled in green valleys. Out west, Tara National Park makes a scenic stage for hiking, biking, kayaking and rafting. In the east, the mighty Danube substitutes Serbia's lack of coastline with its widest and deepest stretches in Đerdap National Park.

Novi Sad

TIME FROM BELGRADE: **36MIN**

The capital of culture

It's no accident that in 2022 Novi Sad became the first non-EU city to carry the prestigious title of European Capital of Culture. To appreciate the significance of this creative hub, tour its esteemed museums and galleries.

Trace the province's past from the earliest days at the **Museum of Vojvodina** *(muzejvojvodine.org.rs; entry adult/child 300/200RSD)* to understand its multi-ethnic character, and stroll through an early 20th-century urban landscape for a glimpse into the trades of the epoch.

The **Gallery of Matica Srpska** *(galerijamaticesrpske.rs; entry adult/child 400/200RSD, Fri free)* displays centuries of masterpieces, from Byzantine icons to modernist paintings by the likes of Vojvodina's own Sava Šumanović. Curator-led themed tours on weekends cost 1200RSD.

Places

Novi Sad p387
Tara National Park p389
Đerdap National Park p391

GETTING AROUND

The high-speed train between Belgrade and Novi Sad runs frequently and takes 36 minutes.

The gateway to Tara National Park is Bajina Bašta, which has good bus connections with Belgrade; from Bajina Bašta, buses go to Mitrovac, Kaluđerske Bare and Perućac within the park.

The scenic Đerdap Hwy (State Rd 34) winds its way along the Danube through Đerdap National Park; sporadic buses connect Kladovo, Donji Milanovac and Golubac with Belgrade.

NOVI SAD

Fish i Zeleniš
Project 72
Café Veliki
Hotel Veliki
Miloša Bajića
Masarikova
Museum of Vojvodina
Laze Telečkog
Pavla Papa
Varadin Bridge
NS Bike
Varad Inn
Bulevar Mihajla Pupina
Petrovaradin Fortress
Trg Modene Slobode
Platona
Leopold I
Gallery of Matica Srpska
City Museum of Novi Sad
Maksima Gorkog
Bulevar Cara Lazara
Dunav (Danube River)
Bulevar Oslobodenja
Gogoljeva
Jirečekova
Sunčani Kej
Bulevar Cara Lazara
Jasmin A Maslina
Limanski Park
Kineska Četvrt
Štrand
Bulevar Despota Stefana
Sunčani Kej
Fisherman's Island
Dunavski Rafting
Liberty Bridge

0 ___ 400 m
0 ___ 0.2 miles

The Habsburgs' bastion

Towering over the river on a 40m-high volcanic slab, **Petrovaradin Fortress** is one of Europe's biggest fortresses and one of its best preserved. Constructed using slave labour between 1692 and 1780, its dungeons have held notable prisoners including Karađorđe (founder of Serbia's royal dynasty) and Yugoslav president Tito. Check out the iconic 'drunken' clock tower: the size of the minute and hour hands are reversed so far-flung fisherfolk can tell the time.

For a unique perspective on Petrovaradin, the **City Museum of Novi Sad** *(museumns.rs; entry adult/child 400/200RSD)* has insight into the citadel's history and organises tours in

☑ **TOP TIP**

Novi Sad's go-to nightlife spot is **Laze Telečkog** street, lined with bars to suit every whim. In summer, check out the bars along **Štrand** (p389) beach. The **Kineska Četvrt** creative district is a jumble of rehearsal garages and alternative clubs.

 EATING IN NOVI SAD: OUR PICKS

Café Veliki: A must for its foodie overview of Vojvodina, from goulash to *gomboce* (plum-stuffed dumplings). *8am-11pm Sun-Thu, to midnight Fri & Sat* €€

Project 72: Smart bistro with inventive small plates (like oxtail with celery puree) based on organic produce and a strong Serbian wine list. *noon-11pm* €€

Fish i Zeleniš: Charming Mediterranean-inspired nook serving vegetarian and pescatarian meals from locally sourced ingredients. *noon-11pm* €€

Jasmin A Maslina: In a refined setting bathed in light, the focus is on seasonal produce; the creative menu changes quarterly. *noon-11pm Tue-Sun* €€€

English (1300RSD) of a fraction of its 16km and four levels of creepy-but-cool *katakombe* (underground tunnels).

For 25 years, the fortress has been filled with thousands of revellers each July during **EXIT Festival** (*exitfest.org*).

A day by the Danube

Novi Sad's **Štrand** (*entry 70RSD*) is a 700m-long sandy beach that is thronged with bars and stalls come summertime. When the tide is low, you can cross over from its western end to the small **Fisherman's Island**. Technically a peninsula, it's a wonderful spot for a picnic or lazy stroll.

Dunavski Rafting (*dunavskirafting.com; 2 people per hr 300RSD*) rents out canoes and kayaks for paddling around Fisherman's Island. Novi Sad's stretch of the Danube Cycling Path, along **Sunčani Kej** (Sunny Quay), makes for pleasant pedalling. **NS Bike** (*per day 170RSD*) rents out bicycles.

Tara National Park

TIME FROM BELGRADE: **3HR**

Go wild in the Dinaric Alps

Some of Serbia's most impressive scenery is found within the 250-sq-km **Tara National Park** (*nptara.rs*), set along the Bosnian border. With densely forested slopes and the dramatic Drina River canyon, this easternmost outpost of the Dinaric Alps is a true outdoor playground. A wide range of adventures is organised by **Republik Tours** (*republiktours.com*), and if you prefer to go solo, the visitor centres at Perućac and Mitrovac have maps and rent out kayaks and bikes.

Cutting through steep limestone cliffs, the emerald Drina creates a stunning background for water-based activities. **Tara Tours** (*taratours.rs; entry adult/child rafting 1000/500RSD, cruise 3000/1500RSD*) has rafting for beginners and full-day boat cruises. Contact **Green Bear** (*greenbear.rs; three-hour tours per person €40*) for stand-up paddleboarding from Vrelo waterfall to the remarkable 'Little House on the Drina'. The placid **Perućac** and **Zaovine** Lakes are popular kayaking spots.

Hikers are in for a treat along Tara's 30 marked trails; see the park website for maps. For easy treks, nine official lookouts provide stupendous views – **Banjska Stena** (1065m), 6km from Mitrovac, overlooks Perućac Lake, while **Crnjeskovo** (980m), 3km from Kaluđerske Bare, rises above Rača Gorge. Also crisscrossing the park are major mountain-biking routes. **Visoka Tara** is a 26km loop along forest and gravel paths, starting and ending at Šljivovica village. **Carska Tara** is a 42km trail from Kaluđerske Bare to Perućac, on a combination of macadam and asphalt.

VILLAGE LIFE

Bački Monoštor: Watch horseshoe and fishing-net makers at work in the heart of Gornje Podunavlje nature reserve, aka 'the Amazon of Europe'.

Kovačica: Village in Vojvodina famous for its naïve art; **Kovačica Naïve Art Gallery** has rotating exhibitions and paintings for sale.

Guča: Home of the boisterous **Guča Festival**, featuring a competition of *trubači* (trumpeters) from across Serbia since 1961.

Sirogojno: On the slopes of Zlatibor mountain, this **open-air museum** with wooden cottages is a snapshot of 19th-century rural life.

Gostuša: Remote 'stone village' on Stara Planina (Old Mountain); its houses are covered from base to roof with plates made of local stone.

 EATING AROUND TARA: OUR PICKS

Tarsko Jezero: At Zaovine Lake, classic local dishes come with stunning views; get the *duvan čvarci* (shredded pork cracklings) appetiser. *9am-8pm* €€

Tarvil: A novelty for Tara, this modern Zaovine spot with panoramic views adds Cuban cusine and vegetarian choices to the Balkan staples. *9am-10pm* €€

Viskonti: Mećavnik resort's stylish restaurant, with books and wine bottles lining a long wall, serves pastas and pizzas plus national cuisine. *7am-11pm* €€

Studenac: Terrace views of the 'Little House on the Drina' in Bajina Bašta; go for the trout or *pljeskavica* (spicy hamburger). *7am-11pm Mon-Sat, from 8am Sun* €€

389

SPAS & WINERIES

Vrnjačka Banja: Serbia's premier spa destination, with landscaped parkland, heritage villas and plenty of wellness treatments on offer.

Sokobanja: Framed by mountains, this spa town has a working Ottoman-era **hammam** (with men's and women's pools).

Negotin region: Negotin's **Rajac** and **Rogljevo** villages feature bucolic 19th-century *pimnice* (wine cellars) made of stone.

Župa wine region: Rustic 19th-century *poljane* (winegrowers' lodges) are preserved across Župa. **Ivanović Winery** is the region's most famous.

Fruška Gora wineries: Just outside Novi Sad, Fruška Gora hills are home to small, family-owned vineyards. **Kovačević Winery** is one of the oldest.

Wine celler, Rogljevo

DMZ001/SHUTTERSTOCK

Đerdap National Park

Adventure along the Danube

Serbia's largest national park and its first UNESCO Global Geopark, the 637-sq-km **Đerdap** (*npdjerdap.rs; entry to protected areas 290RSD*) is where the Carpathian and Balkan mountain ranges meet; it's increasingly a contender for outdoor adventures with Tara in the west. **Nature Travel Office** (*naturetraveloffice.com*) runs multi-activity group tours around the park.

The limestone cliffs of the Iron Gates gorge soar for 100km along the Danube, which reaches its narrowest and deepest points here – a fantastic setting for activities on the water. **Wild Serbia** (*wildserbia.com; tours €69*) organises full-day Đerdap kayaking tours with transport from Belgrade. Alternatively, see the Iron Gates highlights by speedboat from Tekija (one hour) with **Đerdap Boat Tours** (*djerdapboat tours.com; 1500RSD*) or take a two-hour trip through the gorge with **Golubac from a Boat** (*golubacizbrodica.rs; adult/child 1500/750RSD*).

With signposted paths and lookouts, the park provides rewarding hikes; register with the visitor centre in Donji Milanovac (*office@npdjerdap.rs*) before setting off. There are nine marked trails, of which two 7km paths lead from Đerdap Hwy to the peaks of Mt Miroč: **Veliki Štrbac** (768m), overlooking the narrowest part of the Iron Gates, and **Mali Štrbac** (626m), with views of the gigantic Decebalus rock sculpture across the Danube.

The international **EuroVelo 6** cycling path hugs the Danube for 110km through the park. For those without their own wheels, **ACE Adventure** (*ace-adventurecentre.com; tours €270*) has two-day cycling tours along the river between Ram and Golubac fortresses.

MEDIEVAL MONASTERIES & FORTRESSES

Studenica: UNESCO-listed monastery established in 1196, Studenica has the acclaimed *Life of Virgin Mary* fresco cycle.

Sopoćani: Romanesque monastery built by King Stefan Uroš I in 1265. Its frescoes are prime examples of medieval art.

Manasija: Protected by massive walls with 11 towers, this 15th-century monastery is known for the *Holy Warriors* fresco.

Golubac: Fourteenth-century fortress with nine towers, set on a rocky promontory at the entrance to the Danube's Iron Gates gorge.

Maglič: Guardian of the Ibar valley since the 13th century, Maglič fortress has fantastic views over central Serbia's green hills.

 ## EATING AROUND ĐERDAP: OUR PICKS

Nana: Modern place in Golubac offering Mediterranean-inspired pastas, risottos, burgers and salads in addition to standard local fare. *8am-10pm* €€

Jezero: Try delicacies like grilled Miroč cheese at this Kladovo tavern with a timber-framed interior. *8am-midnight Mon-Fri, from 10am Sat & Sun* €€

Lepenska Ribica: Typical checkered-tablecloths *kafana* in Donji Milanovac serving hearty grub from fish soup to *roštilj* (grilled meats). *9am-10pm* €€

Restoran Dinčić: At Silver Lake, settle in on the rounded terrace facing a lush garden for a leisurely meal of freshwater fish specialities. *8am-11pm* €€

Places We Love to Stay

€ Budget €€ Midrange €€€ Top End

Belgrade

MAP p382

El Diablo Hostel € Lovely small hostel set in a townhouse right next to Skadarlija, with dorms plus two private rooms, and super-welcoming staff.

Hostel Bongo € Unbeatable location in a passage off Terazije. Scandi minimalist style with bright colours, sweet garden terrace and experienced staff.

Arka Barka € Bobbing off Ušće Park, this 'floating house' has dorms and rooms with hand-painted walls, plus free bike and scooter use and fresh river breezes.

Smokvica B&B €€ Rustic-chic B&B in a whitewashed 19th-century mansion in Dorćol; rooms have vaulted ceilings, hardwood floors and supersonic showers.

Savamala Bed & Breakfast €€ Cool B&B located in a 1908 building in Savamala quarter, offering 11 rooms furnished in mid-century modern style.

Dominic Smart Luxury Suites €€ With four equally convenient locations across Stari Grad, these elegant and spacious suites are an excellent midrange option.

Hotel Moskva €€€ A Secession-style icon on Terazije, the 123-room Moskva is laden with old-world glamour; past guests include Albert Einstein and Indira Gandhi.

Mama Shelter €€€ The whimsical design hotel, a skip from Kalemegdan Park, attracts millennials with fun rooms and fab sunset views from its large rooftop restaurant.

Square Nine €€€ The work of Brazilian architect Isay Weinfeld, just off Knez Mihailova; luxury rooms have limestone bathrooms and there's a rooftop Japanese restaurant.

Novi Sad

MAP p388

Varad Inn € Hostel with a lovely garden cafe, set in a baroque-style building from 1714 in Petrovaradin's Lower Town; rooms with private bathrooms.

Hotel Veliki €€ Convenient central location just off pedestrian Zmaj Jovina, huge comfortable rooms and a hip restaurant representing Vojvodinian cuisine.

Leopold I €€€ Luxury hotel set atop Petrovaradin Fortress, with both baroque-style and modern rooms; the two restaurant terraces have great Danube views.

Tara National Park

Hotel Tara €€ A great option at Kaluđerske Bare, this hotel built of stone and wood has a warm atmosphere, 18 spacious rooms and a restaurant.

Vila Drina €€ Convenient for activities around Perućac Lake, with 15 rooms in pleasing pastel tones; the stately building is next to a small waterfall.

Mećavnik Resort €€€ A cluster of small rural houses in Drvengrad movie-set village, featuring smart units with wood details and folk-design touches.

Đerdap National Park

Zeleni Zaliv €€ Unwind in wood-and-clay cabins in Poreč Bay, just outside Donji Milanovac; slow-food dining on demand, plus kayaks and paddleboards for rent.

Vila Dunavski Raj €€ Family-owned B&B secluded in a pine forest near Golubac, serving tasty organic breakfasts. Large balconies for chilling out on.

Eko Farma Kladovo €€ These tidy bungalows on the outskirts of Kladovo are great for families; optional buffet-style meals, bike rental and on-site animal farm.

DR IGI/SHUTTERSTOCK

Leopold I

Practicalities

LGBTIQ+ Travellers

As evidenced by the furore over
Belgrade's early Pride parades
(chronicled in the 2011 comedy
Parada), life is not all rainbows for
the LGBTIQ+ community in Serbia.
Discretion is advised. Check out
prajd.rs for the latest news.

Health

Serbia has a reciprocal healthcare
agreement with many EU states;
this covers most emergency
medical care except for emergency
repatriation. Excellent, affordable
healthcare is readily available in the
cities – Serbia is a dental-tourism
destination for those in the know. For
minor illnesses, chemists can give
advice and sell over-the-counter
medication.

Etiquette

Greetings usually involve three
kisses on the cheeks.
Dress conservatively if visiting
monasteries, and walk backwards
out of a church.
Make eye contact during toasts. The
person who initiated the drinks will
insist on paying.

Smoking

Smoking is banned in enclosed areas
such as offices, shops, hotels and
public transport. However, it's still
largely permitted in restaurants and
bars, where enforced nonsmoking
sections are a rarity. It's usually
pointless asking someone to
put out their cigarette in these
establishments.

MARK PELF/SHUTTERSTOCK

Ada Ciganlija beach (p384)

Opening Hours

Banks 9am–5pm Monday to Friday
Bars 11am–midnight (later on weekends)
Restaurants 8am–midnight
Shops 8am–7pm Monday to Saturday

Visas

Tourist visas for stays of up to 90 days aren't required for
citizens of the EU, UK, USA, Australia, New Zealand and Canada.
Officially, visitors must register with the police. Hotels will do
this for you, but if you're staying in private accommodation, you
should register within 24 hours of arrival. This is rarely enforced,
but a lack of registration confirmation upon leaving Serbia could
result in a fine.

Public Holidays

New Year 1 and 2 January
Orthodox Christmas 7 January
Statehood Day 15 and 16 February
Orthodox Easter April/May
Labour Day 1 and 2 May
Armistice Day 11 November

Language

The official language is Serbian and the official writing system uses both the Roman and Cyrillic alphabets.

Basics

Hello. Zdravo/Здраво *zdra·vo*

Goodbye. Doviđenja/Довиђења *do·vee·dje·nya*

Yes. Da/Да *da*

No. Ne/Не *ne*

Please. Molim/Молим *mo·lim*

Thank you. Hvala/Хвала *hva·la*

Excuse me. Izvinite/Извините *iz·vee·nee·te*

Sorry. Žao mi je/Жао ми је *zha·o mi ye*

What's your name?
Kako se zovete/zoveš? (pol/inf)
Како се зовете/зовеш?
ka·ko se zo·ve·te/zo·vesh

My name is …
Zovem se …/Зовем се … *zo·vem se*

Do you speak English?
Govorite/Govoriš li engleski? (pol/inf)
Говорите/Говориш ли енглески?
go·vo·ri·te/go·vo·rish li en·gle·ski

I don't understand.
Ne razumem./Не разумем.
ne ra·zu·mem

Shopping & Services

I'm looking for...
Tražim …/Тражим…
tra·zhim

How much is it?
Koliko košta …?/Колико кошта …? *ko·li·ko kosh·ta*

That's too expensive.
To je preskupo./То је прескупо.
to ye pre·sku·po

Emergencies

Help! Upomoć!/Упомоћ!
u·po·moch

Go away! Idite!/Идите! *i·di·te*

Call …! Zovite …!/Зовите … !
zo·vi·te

    a doctor lekara/лекара *le·ka·ra*

    the police policiju/полицију.
po·li·tsi·yu

I'm lost.
Izgubljen/Izgubljena sam. (m/f)
Изгубљен/Изгубљена сам. (m/f)
iz·gub·lyen/iz·gub·lyena sam

I'm ill.
Ja sam bolestan/bolesna. (m/f)
Ја сам болестан/болесна. (m/f)
ya sam bo·le·stan/bo·le·sna

Eating & Drinking

What would you recommend?
Šta biste preporučili?
Шта бисте препоручили?
shta bi·ste pre·po·ru·chi·li

Do you have vegetarian food?
Da li imate vegetarijanski obrok?
Да ли имате вегетаријански оброк?
da li i·ma·te ve·ge·ta·ri·yan·ski o·brok

Cheers! Živeli!/Живели! *zhi·ve·li*

I'd like the bill/menu please.
Mogu li dobiti račun/jelovnik, molim?
Могу ли добити рачун/јеловник, молим?
mo·gu li do·bi·ti ra·chun/ye·lov·nik mo·lim

NUMBERS

1
jedan/један
ye·dan

2
dva/два
dva

3
tri/три *tri*

4
četiri четири
che·ti·ri

5
pet/пет *pet*

6
šest/шест
shest

7
sedam/ седам
se·dam

8
osam/осам
o·sam

9
devet/девет
de·vet

10
deset/десет
de·set

Nikola Tesla Airport, Belgrade

MONEY

Currency: Serbian Dinar (RSD)

CASH

ATMs and exchange offices are easy to find in towns and cities; cash is still indispensable in villages and remote areas. Have some cash on hand for markets, newsstands, taxi rides and public transport, as well as for admission fees.

CREDIT CARDS

Major debit and credit cards, particularly Visa and MasterCard, are accepted by hotels, restaurants, shops, petrol stations and when booking tours. Not many taxis accept card payments; specify when booking if you need to pay by card.

TIPPING

Tips in restaurants or for tour guides are not obligatory, but 10% is a good idea for satisfactory service and always appreciated; it's also customary to round up the taxi fare.

Arriving & Getting Around

Belgrade airport receives most international flights. With extensive bus services countrywide and good main roads, it's easy to get around. For flexibility and convenience to reach remote and rural destinations, it's best to hire a car.

Arriving by Air
Belgrade's **Nikola Tesla Airport** is the country's main entry point. The national carrier is Air Serbia. **Niš Constantine the Great Airport** is small and serviced by Wizz Air, Ryanair, Turkish Airways and Air Serbia.

Buses
There are good long-distance bus connections. Major cities have public bus systems. In Belgrade, public transport (including buses, trolleybuses and trams) is free since 2025. In Novi Sad, buy single-ride tickets from the driver.

Taxi/Rideshare
Taxis can be flagged down or ordered; make sure the meter is turned on. Not many taxis accept credit card payments. Belgrade's rideshare app is CarGo; there's also Yandex but no Uber. For long-distance carpooling, use the BlaBlaCar app.

Driving Essentials
Belgrade airport has major car rental offices. Petrol stations are easy to find around the country. Street parking in all bigger towns is regulated by zones/hours; tickets can often be paid only via SMS (in Serbian). The speed limit is 50km/h in towns, 80km/h outside towns, 100km/h on expressways and 130km/h on motorways. You must drive with short headlights on, even in the daytime.

For places to stay in Slovakia, see p413

BEATRICAB/SHUTTERSTOCK

Above: Lomnický štít (p410), Tatranská Lomnica; Right: Blue Church (p404), Bratislava

Curated by
Luke Waterson

Slovakia

MAJESTIC MOUNTAINS, CASTLES AND MEDIEVAL MARVELS

Close to tourist hotspots Vienna and Budapest, Slovakia will always be beautifully off-piste. This is its allure: ornate historic architecture and astounding mountainous terrain that remains perennially crowd free.

Nature defines Slovakia. The capital Bratislava has an Old Town full of arresting medieval and baroque buildings, but the forest-swaddled hills looming just behind it dominate the proceedings. These soon swoop into the serrated summits of the High Tatras, Europe's smallest alpine mountain range, yet still home to many of Eastern Europe's loftiest peaks and the Carpathians' very highest. Then there's the east's gorge-gouged national park Slovenský Raj; UNESCO-listed, cave-riddled Slovenský kras; and another UNESCO spectacle, the primeval beech forests of the Carpathians. In the south, the Danube River frames the landscape.

Consequently, the culture here is of a back-to-nature, down-to-earth sort: hiking, cross-country skiing, alfresco fire-pit grill-ups, overnight sojourns in middle-of-nowhere mountain houses, traditional costumed dances and brightly hued wooden architecture all showcase the countryside's extraordinarily vivid folklore.

Tradition is not lost here, as it can be in more urbanised nations. Surrounded by busier destinations like Austria (west), Czechia (northwest) and Hungary (south), this under-the-radar country may not receive the attention it deserves. But if you dig entire districts, villages and towns of seamlessly preserved medieval buildings, if you're entranced by the world's densest concentration of castles, if you yearn for thick forests and jagged mountains and prefer these places to be untrammeled and peaceful, Slovakia should be your next adventure.

KAYO/SHUTTERSTOCK

THE MAIN AREAS

BRATISLAVA
Slovakia's capital and castle-dotted surroundings. **p400**

WESTERN SLOVAKIA
More castles and national parks. **p406**

HIGH TATRAS & EASTERN SLOVAKIA
Mountains and medieval townscapes. **p409**

Find Your Way

Slovakia's centre-of-Europe location extends from Austria and Czechia in the west, Hungary in the south, Poland in the north and Ukraine in the east.

POLAND

UKRAINE

HUNGARY

CZECHIA

AUSTRIA

Vistula

Tisza

Danube

Bardejov
Prešov
Michalovce
Spiš Castle
Levoča
Košice
Kežmarok
Ždiar
Slovenský Raj National Park
Poprad
Zakopane
Popradské pleso
Liptovský Mikuláš
Ružomberok
Jasná
Banská Bystrica
Banská Štiavnica
Vrátna Valley
Martin
Vlkolínec
Prievidza
Žilina
Čičmany
Trenčín
Trenčín Castle
Piešťany
Nitra
Trnava
Bratislava Forest Park
Hlavné námestie
St Martin's Cathedral
BRATISLAVA

0   50 miles
0   100 km

Western Slovakia, p406

Steep forests and hidden fortresses enchant throughout the countrified Malé Karpaty (Small Carpathians).

High Tatras & Eastern Slovakia, p409

Come here for hiking, skiing and *chata* (mountain house) stays. Continue east for medieval towns and stunning landscapes.

Bratislava, p400

The medieval centre delights. Connoisseurs relish the museums while nature-lovers embrace the proximity of the river and tree-cloaked hills.

CAR

It's 4½ hours' drive (437km) from Bratislava to Košice via Nitra and Poprad. This journey runs almost the entire west-to-east length of Slovakia. Cars help in remote rural areas and poorly connected destinations like Banská Štiavnica.

TRAIN

From Bratislava, the main cross-country line has hourly links to Trenčín (1¼ hours), Žilina (two hours; for Malá Fatra national park), Poprad (four hours; for the High Tatras) and Košice (5½ hours). Trains serve Vienna and Budapest, too.

Hlavné námestie (p400), Bratislava

Plan Your Time

One week is sufficient for Slovakia's highlights. Use Bratislava or Košice as your base: the former for culture, the latter for mountain scenery.

A Weekend Break

● Begin in **Bratislava's** comely medieval Old Town, discovering knockout square **Hlavné námestie** (p400) and **Bratislava Castle** (p403) for city views. Visit some cafes: Bratislava's are special. Take an afternoon picnic to hilly **Bratislava Forest Park** (p404). On day two, head to icons like the **Blue Church** (p404), **City History Museum** (p401) or a half-day exploration of castle **Hrad Devín** (p406).

A Week or More

● Spend two to three days in Bratislava, and don't miss the **Danubiana Meulensteen Art Museum** (p404) and the fortress **Červený Kameň** (p407). Tour **Trenčin Castle** (p407), then proceed to Poprad to explore the **High Tatras** (p409) for two days. Wander medieval gems **Levoča** (p412) and **Bardejov** (p412), and finish in dignified Košice, arranged around **St Elizabeth's Cathedral** (p412).

SEASONAL HIGHLIGHTS

SPRING
Bratislava City Days enlivens the capital with street performances and openings of normally off-limits city spaces.

SUMMER
Bratislava Cultural Summer delivers two months of music. In July, check music fest Pohoda (Trenčin) or Východná Folk Festival (High Tatras).

AUTUMN
Western Slovak towns and the Tokaj wine region near Košice celebrate grape harvest; Pezinok has the biggest wine festival.

WINTER
Bratislava's **Christmas Markets** (p402), which begin in late November, brighten the city centre.

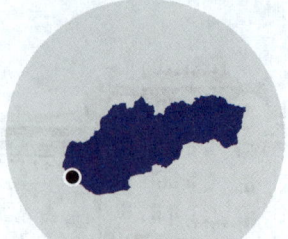

Bratislava

ARCHITECTURE | CAFES | COUNTRYSIDE EXCURSIONS

GETTING AROUND

Walking around the Old Town is best, though wheelchairs and prams may struggle with the cobbled streets. Trolleybuses run from Hlavná stanica train station to the Old Town and Koliba for Bratislava Forest Park. Take buses from Most SNP bus station to Hrad Devín or Danubiana Meulensteen Art Museum. Trains (from Hlavná stanica) or buses (from main bus station Mlynské nivy) link the capital with Western Slovakia. Seasonal boats connect Bratislava and Devín.

☑ **TOP TIP**

Bratislava's Old Town invites you to linger, but don't limit your time to just this area: Bratislava Forest Park, Danubiana Meulensteen Art Museum and stupendous castles like those at Devín are all a part of Bratislava's rich tapestry.

Bratislava is an ideal mid-sized city, big enough to have a swag bag of internationally significant sights yet sporting a centre small enough to stroll. Abutting dramatic nature – its suburbs ascend into the lonely foothills of the Malé Karpaty (Small Carpathians) and its Old Town brushes the Danube – it's also well-connected to major cities like Vienna, Budapest and Prague.

At the centre of Europe, Bratislava has always been prone to invasions. It fell to Roman, Hungarian and Austrian invaders, was briefly incorporated in early Slavic states, and spent time as a socialist country following WWII. This historical hotchpotch explains a cityscape that interweaves a stone castle built by the Slavic Great Moravian people, medieval Hungarian burghers' houses and baroque palaces, and some startling Soviet brutalism.

Yet, as you unwind in an elegant cafe-bar in the lively Old Town, with live music reverberating nearby, you'll likely opine that Bratislava – upheaval aside – has had the last laugh.

Meander the Old Town
Bratislava's iconic medieval heart

No matter how often you visit Bratislava, acquainting yourself with the city on foot always works wonders. Enter the Staré mesto (Old Town) through the only surviving city gate from Bratislava's 13th-century walls, **Michael's Gate** *(Michalská brána; muzeumbratislava.sk; adult/child €6/4)*. Buy tickets in nearby **Red Crayfish Pharmacy** and climb the small baroque tower for stunning panoramas. Afterwards, walk cobbled Michalská, Biela and Františkánske námestie to **Hlavné námestie**, the city's main square and the showcase for some of its most beloved historic buildings.

Among the architectural set-pieces, the standout is **Stará radnica** (Old Town Hall), a 14th-century clocktower-crested

BRATISLAVA

HIGHLIGHTS
1 Blue Church
2 City History Museum
3 Hlavné námestie
4 St Martin's Cathedral

SIGHTS
5 Bratislava Castle
6 Bratislava City Gallery
7 Hviezdoslavovo námestie
8 Michael's Gate
9 Most SNP
10 Museum of Jewish Culture
11 Nedbalka Gallery
12 Red Crayfish Pharmacy
13 Roland's Fountain
14 Slovak National Gallery
15 Stará radnica
16 Watcher

SLEEPING
17 CHORS Like a Hotel
18 Marrol's Boutique Hotel
19 Roset Boutique Hotel

EATING
20 Black.
21 Bratislava Flagship
22 Bratislavský Meštiansky Pivovar
23 Cafe Verne
24 Emil
25 Gatto Matto
26 Modrá Hviezda
27 Sky Bar & Restaurant
28 Soupa

ENTERTAINMENT
29 KC Dunaj
30 Slovak National Theatre
31 Slovak Philharmonic

INFORMATION
32 Tourist Information Centre

TRANSPORT
33 LOD
34 Twin City Liner

complex that's among Slovakia's oldest standing structures. This encompasses the excellent **City History Museum** (*Múzeum mesta Bratislavy; muzeumbratislava.sk; adult/child €8/4*) charting Bratislava's importance down the ages, from its role as monarchical crowning place to its guilds and crafts. Tickets include entry to the Apponyiho Palace, prime Bratislava views from the tower and a ground-floor exhibition on local viticulture (tastings cost extra).

SLOVAKIAN WINE

The vineyards carpeting Western Slovakia's Malé Karpaty are a somewhat surprising landscape feature. But winemaking traditions run deep: viticulture here predates Roman occupation. Southeast Slovakia's honey-like Tokaj wines, which King Louis XIV called 'the king of wines, wine of kings', are Slovakia's most distinctive; the Malé Karpaty region, meanwhile, produces wonderful whites. Pezinok, with its wine cellars, winemaking museum and mid-September wine festival, makes an atmospheric spot to sample the local wines. Malá Tŕňa, southeast of Košice, is the Tokaj region hub. Several Bratislava bars and the City History Museum – which has an expert-selected collection featuring any year's 100 best wines – are the capital's best places to partake.

SAIKO3P/SHUTTERSTOCK

Bratislava Castle

In the square's centre, **Roland's Fountain** supposedly dates to 1572. It's topped by a knight who bears a likeness to ex-Hungarian king Maximilian II. According to local legend, he bows every New Year's Eve. Bratislava's fabled **Christmas Markets** present the square Hlavné námestie at its loveliest.

Marvel at St Martin's Cathedral
The crowning place of Hungarian monarchs

St Martin's Cathedral (*Dóm svätého Martina, dom.fara.sk; entry free*), with its terracotta roof and white walls sheering to an 85m-high spire, has a colourful history: it was the coronation place for 19 Hungarian kings and queens between 1563 and 1830, a time when Ottoman invasions made the previous monarch-making spot (Székesfehérvár) too dangerous. The interior of this 14th- and 15th-century Gothic sanctuary also has four chapels, a horseback statue of St Martin, extensive crypts and stained-glass windows to hold you in thrall.

Boat Trips along the Danube
Bratislava by water

Bratislava is the fourth-biggest city on the EU's longest river and Danube boat trips, conveniently departing from the Staré

 EATING IN BRATISLAVA: CAFES AND SNACKS

Black.: Coffee roasters concentrate on the exquisite coffee here, also tempting with cakes and vegan sandwiches. *9am-6pm* €

Emil: In the Mirbach Palace, Emil serves coffee and light bites in its vaulted interior and courtyard. *10am-10pm Tue-Sat, to 8pm Sun, to 6pm Mon* €

Bistro St Germain: This chic eatery concocts breakfasts, three-tier sandwiches, burgers and wraps. *11am-11pm Mon & Tue, from 8am Wed-Sat, 8am-9pm Sun* €

Soupa: Friendly to wallets, dietary restrictions and the environment, veggie- and vegan-friendly Soupa is a stalwart choice. *8am-6pm Mon-Fri* €

mesto's southern edge east of Most SNP, are a fun way to appreciate the city and its fetching surrounds. Trips with **LOD** *(lod.sk)* head upriver to Hrad Devín (p406), a crag-top castle on the Slovakia–Austria border *(€24 return; daily Apr-Sep, weekends Oct & Nov)*, and along Bratislava's stretch of the Danube *(€15 return; daily Apr-Sep)* to catch optimal Old Town vistas. **Twin City Liner** *(twincityliner.com; from €25 one-way; 1½ hours)* runs boats upriver to Vienna, also passing Hrad Devín and Donau-Auen National Park's tranquil forested riverbanks.

Climb to Bratislava Castle

A fortified settlement from the beginning

The capital's dominant landmark is the huge four-turreted **Bratislava Castle** *(snm.sk; grounds free, museum adult/child €14/7)*, standing on its own hilltop across the ring road west of the Staré mesto. The 9th-century remnants of the original Great Moravian castle are still on display and the 13th-century **Crown Tower** can be climbed for bird's-eye views. The current castle's white walls and terracotta roofs were mostly achieved in the 1760s under renowned Habsburg monarch Maria Theresa. Today, the Renaissance- and rococo-styled fortress can be explored through its **Museum of History**, which provides an overview of Slovakia from medieval times onward and serves as an access point to the castle's interior, including the Crown Tower. But the free-of-charge **grounds** are the highlight: the **baroque gardens** and zigzagging pathways afford beautiful views of the Danube-wrapped Staré mesto.

Stroll along the Hviezdoslavovo námestie

Home to performing arts and quirky statues

Long tree-lined **Hviezdoslavovo námestie** *(free)* is probably the most appealing city square for lingering. At the eastern end are the historic building of the 1886-built **Slovak National Theatre** (closed for repairs, with shows currently at the **New SND**, just southeast of the Staré mesto) and Reduta Palace housing the **Slovak Philharmonic** *(filharmonia.sk; tickets from €16)*. Prefer quirky to queen-like? Check much-loved statue **Watcher** *(Čumil; visitbratislava.com; free)*, a statue of a worker emerging from a manhole. It's north of the square along Rybárska brana.

INDEPENDENCE STRUGGLES

Short-lived Slavic kingdoms Samo's Empire (c 631–c 658 CE) and Great Moravia (c 833–c 927 CE) both encompassed parts of Slovakia. But Slovak history has largely taken place under the jurisdiction of foreign powers, in particular the Hungarians, who controlled Slovakia between 895 CE and 1918. After WWI, a temporary Slovak Socialist Republic was created in the southeast before Slovakia was incorporated into Czechoslovakia. Then came German (WWII) and Soviet (1947–91) control. Only in 1993, after the Velvet Divorce brought separation from Czechia, did Slovakia become permanently independent. Bratislava's Námestie SNP is the cradle of Slovak independence: this was where crowds gathered during the run-up to the fall of communism.

EATING IN BRATISLAVA: BEST RESTAURANTS

| Modrá Hviezda: The 'Blue Star' specialises in glamorous Slovak dishes, like venison with caramel-cognac sauce. *5.30-10pm Wed-Fri, noon-10pm Sat & Sun* €€€ | Bratislava Flagship: Popular intro to Slovak cuisine in a vault-roofed former theatre. *11am-10pm Mon-Thu, 11am-11pm Fri, noon-11pm Sat, noon-10pm Sun* €€ | Gatto Matto: Out-of-this-world pizza is the driving force of this Italian restaurant within a smart townhouse near St Martin's Cathedral. *11am-10pm* €€ | Roxor: The journey to this standout near Račianske mýto park 2km north of the Staré mesto is repaid by Bratislava's best burger experience. *11am-9pm* €€ |

BUDGET-FRIENDLY TIPS

Slovakia is among Europe's cheapest countries to travel in. These tips will help you save even more. The Bratislava Card *(card.visitbratislava. com)*, starting at €30 for 24 hours, secures free entry or discounts to a number of the capital's attractions and eating and drinking spots. Many city experiences are free anyway, like the Bratislava Castle grounds and stellar viewpoints, including the Slavín War Memorial and Bratislava Forest Park.

Meanwhile, a restaurant's set menu *(denné menu)* often gets you a substantial one- or two-course meal for a few euros. Heading across Slovakia, train travel is cheap, with a Bratislava–Košice fare costing under €20. Public transport, be it the train or bus, is affordable, reliable and reaches most key places.

Hike Around Bratislava Forest Park
Explore the Small Carpathians

The **Malé Karpaty** (Small Carpathians) forested massif sweeps northeast across Western Slovakia to Slovakia's best national parks in the Carpathians proper. Bratislava's northern suburbs rise into the foothills through **Bratislava Forest Park** *(visitbratislava.com; free)*. Amid these hilly, thickly wooded footpaths and biking trails is the **Kamzík TV mast** *(veza.sk; observation deck €7)*, its revolving restaurant and viewpoint marking the park's high point. From Hlavná stanica, take bus 145 or trolleybus 44 to final stop Koliba: Kamzík is then a 1.75km walk.

Bratislava's Blue Church
The city's prettiest building

Dedicated to St Elisabeth of Hungary, the early 20th-century **Blue Church** *(modrykostol.fara.sk; free)* is a powder-blue-and-cream vision. The edifice is an art nouveau masterpiece, from its undulating arches to cupola-crested clocktower tip (36.8m). See the website for its limited opening hours.

From Contemporary Art to White-Water Rafting
Danube-based delights in Čunovo

Countrified suburb Čunovo has two top-tier Bratislava attractions right on the Danube – although each is likely to attract a different type of person. The main draw is Slovakia's most spectacular art gallery. Atop a gorgeous river promontory, the **Danubiana Meulensteen Art Museum** *(danubiana. sk; adult/child €12/6)* impresses with its waterside location and outdoor sculpture garden. Inside, floor-to-ceiling gallery windows overlooking the Danube are the eye-catching accompaniment to contemporary art displays, including works by groundbreaking Slovak artists like Rudolf Sikora and Miroslav Cipár.

Practically adjacent to the museum is the world-class watersports complex **Divoka Voda** *(divokavoda.sk)*, its two churning channels offering Class II to IV rapids for instructor-guided white-water rafting *(from €35 per 1½ hours)* and kayaking *(from €10 per hour)*.

To get here, take bus 91 from Most SNP bus station to end-of-the-line Čunovo and walk (3km). Alternatively, hire bikes from **Bike Bratislava** *(bikebratislava.sk; €25 per day)* and cycle from the Staré mesto (19km via riverside cycleways).

Oddball Tours of the Soviet Era
Take in the city's brutalist landmarks

Slovakia was where the Eastern Bloc once met the West, and Soviet-era builders consequently made bold brutalist statements along the frontier in Bratislava. Most striking in the Staré mesto is **Most SNP** *(u-f-o.sk; adult €9.90)*, a

Slavín War Memorial

bridge outlandishly crowned by a 95m-high bar-restaurant and flying saucer-shaped observation deck. It rises above the ring road where it crosses the Danube. Across the bridge to the south is the super suburb **Petržalka**, Europe's largest Soviet-era housing estate.

Another exceptional viewpoint is the **Slavín War Memorial** (*visitbratislava.com; free*), northwest of the Staré mesto on Slavín Hill. The monument, topped by a swastika-crushing soldier, honours the Soviet soldiers who died liberating Bratislava from German forces in 1945; it was built between 1957 and 1960.

Visit these and many other Soviet-era landmarks with the fun offbeat tours run by **Authentic Slovakia** (*authentic slovakia.com; per person in normal/Soviet-era vehicle €35/55*).

BEST MUSEUMS & GALLERIES

Bratislava City Gallery: The best bit about this nationally important art collection, spread across the Mirbach and Pálffy Palaces, is Pálffy Palace's 'Passage' exhibit featuring 15,000 books, arranged around mirrors, which creates the illusion of peering into a never-ending library.

Slovak National Gallery: Engaging riverside art space hosting the city centre's best contemporary art exhibits.

Museum of Jewish Culture: Compelling museum located in the city's former Jewish quarter, which was largely destroyed during the construction of the Bratislava ring road.

Nedbalka Gallery: Focuses on displays of 20th-century Slovak art and sculpture, impressively arranged around an atrium.

DRINKING IN BRATISLAVA: BEST BARS

KC Dunaj: Alternative cultural centre with a rooftop bar and eclectic performances from live music to comedy. *4pm-1am Thu-Sat, to midnight Sun-Wed*

Bratislavský Meštiansky Pivovar: This brewery serves its own beers along with traditional Slovak dishes. *11am-11pm Tue-Sat, to 10pm Sun & Mon*

Cafe Verne: Mingle with locals to sample buzzing Bratislava nightlife in this boho spot. *9am-midnight Mon-Thu, 9am-1am Fri, 10am-1am Sat, 10am-midnight Sun*

Sky Bar & Restaurant: Drinks, especially cocktails, and Spanish-influenced cuisine with stunning Staré mesto views. *5pm-midnight Tue-Sat*

Western Slovakia

CASTLES | ANCIENT MINING TOWN | NATIONAL PARK

Places

 TOP TIP

A great way to explore Western Slovakia is on foot in the Malé Karpaty hills. The beautiful 102km Štefánikova Magistrála trail runs across the region from Hrad Devín at the Slovakia–Austria border to Bradlo. The path is named after Slovak WWI hero Milan Štefánik.

Western Slovakia is an outdoor playground of bedazzling, forest-cloaked and castle-flanked mountains that increase in magnitude as they approach the peaks of the High Tatras to the east. And best of all? It's easily visited on day trips from Bratislava. In addition to splendid strongholds, like those at Devín, Čcrvený Kameň and Trenčín, there's also the enchanting UNESCO-listed medieval mining settlement of Banská Štiavnica in the south and an explosion of greenery in the folklore-rich Malá Fatra National Park further east. The latter was once the stomping ground of Slovakia's real-life Robin Hood: Juraj Jánošík, a 17th-century bandit-turned-hero, and the topography befits that of an outlaw's lair, with bulky mountains tumbling into concealed forested ravines. Meanwhile, the Malé Karpaty (Small Carpathians) range of hills ramparts the region's north, presiding over the homonymous wine region that yield much of the country's best vino.

Devín

TIME FROM BRATISLAVA: **25MIN** 🚋

Embattled borderland bastions

Bratislava's suburbs stretch to the Austrian border, where clifftop castle **Hrad Devín** (*hraddevin.mmb.sk; €8*) guards the Danube's confluence with the Morava. First built in stone in the 13th century, it contains an archaeological exhibition

---

🧭 **GETTING AROUND**

Regular trains head northeast from Bratislava to Trenčín (1¼ hours) and Žilina (two hours), the jumping-off point for Malá Fatra National Park. Buses connect Bratislava to the important castles of Devín, Červený Kameň and Bojnice. Buses are also best from Bratislava to Banská Štiavnica, though there are fewer services. And don't discount walking. Picturesque pathways, including the long-distance Štefánikova Magistrála, thread the entire region through its lovely forested hills.

Trenčín Castle

CASTLES AND CRACKING VIEWPOINTS

Hrad Bojnice: This spellbinding, still-furnished turreted affair is the most fairy-tale-like fortress. It's 60km southeast of Trenčín and 177km northeast of Bratislava.

Hrad Beckov: A whopping fortress presiding over the Váh River valley from a 60m-high crag; 20km southwest of Trenčín.

Hrad Červený Kameň: Above Častá, 37km northeast of Bratislava, this furnished 16th-century castle stands out amid the green Malé Karpaty slopes.

Vrátna Valley: Climb by cable car through Malá Fatra National Park to access ridge hikes at 1500m.

Čičmany: This village, a 1¼-hour bus ride southwest of Žilina, is a cherished vestige of Slovak folklore.

Kalvaria: The best panoramas of Banská Štiavnica come from the baroque chapel complex.

showcasing site finds from Neolithic times onwards and stages summertime events from kid-friendly medieval games to DJ sessions. Bus 29 links Devín to Bratislava's Most SNP bus station. Boats (p403) run here too.

Trenčín

TIME FROM BRATISLAVA: 1¼HR

Castle-topped medieval treasure

Trenčín, the 2026 European Capital of Culture, is a dashing, richly historic city built around a beguiling square. The cityscape's climax is cragtop **Trenčín Castle** *(muzeumtn.sk; adult/child €9/4, with tour €12/5)*, its storied walls dating to the 11th century. A famous Roman inscription from 179 CE on the cliff beneath the castle can be glimpsed from the Hotel Elizabeth.

Banská Štiavnica

TIME FROM BRATISLAVA: 3½HR

Magical mining tour

Sparkling like the silver once found in its hills, this UNESCO-listed 13th-century mining town is a trove of riches. Top sights include burghers' houses from the 16th to 18th century, the

 EATING BEYOND BRATISLAVA: OUR PICKS

La Piazetta: Suave space in castle-crowned Trenčín for some of Slovakia's finest Italian cuisine. *11am-10pm Mon-Thu, to 11pm Fri, noon-10pm Sat* €€

Gurmánsky Grob: Brilliant spot with an inviting garden 20km northeast of Bratislava. Sample traditional Slovak oven-roasted goose. *11am-10pm* €€

Terchovská Koliba Diery: Scenic restaurant near Terchová's Horné Diery gorge evokes a romanticised shepherd's hut, with traditional Slovak fare. *10am-9.30pm* €€

Elizabeth Cukráreň & Kaviareň: Pamper yourself in Piešťany, then enjoy coffee, cake or local wine at this elegant spa complex. *9am-9pm* €

JAROMOND/SHUTTERSTOCK

Malá Fatra National Park

astounding hillside chapel complex **Kalvária** *(kalvaria.org; free)* and the dignified centrepiece **Old Castle** *(muzeumbs. sk; adult/child €8/4)*. Delve into the centuries-old mining heritage at the **Open-Air Mining Museum** *(muzeumbs.sk; adult/child €14/7)* 2km west of town, where 90-minute guided tours explore old mine passageways. Buses from Bratislava change at Zvolen; trains take longer.

Malá Fatra National Park

TIME FROM BRATISLAVA: 3HR 🚆 + 🚌

Folklore, gorges and mountain magic

This tantalising 226-sq-km mountainous swathe is greener and less visited than the High Tatras. Yet it contains some serious summits, including high point **Velký Kriváň** (1708m), plus extensive hiking trails and a beautiful ski area.

Northern village Terchová makes the best base. It's crested by the **Juraj Jánošík Statue**, which honours the local folk hero and outlaw, whose birth and exploits in these parts imbue the peaks with added mystique. The must-do hike is **Horné Diery** *(slovakia.com; free)* a precipitous waterfall-splashed gorge reached via a three-hour out-and-back trail with ladder-and-chain sections. Access it from Hotel Diery, 2km east of Terchová. A photogenic road south of Terchová rises to Vrátna Výťah and the **Vratna Valley ski area** *(vratna.sk; day pass €25)*. Take **Vrátna Cable Car** *(€21 return)* for a spectacular 15-minute ascent to the Snilovské saddle (1524m) below Chleb Peak. Ski slopes (Dec-Mar) and more hiking trails beckon up top.

Buses connect Terchová to Žilina (45 minutes) and Vrátna Výťah (15 minutes).

High Tatras & Eastern Slovakia

MOUNTAINS | OUTDOOR ADVENTURE | MEDIEVAL TOWNS

Welcome to the 1.5-mile-high club: the jagged peaks of the High Tatras (Vysoké Tatry) have some 25 summits that surpass 2400m. These are Slovakia's highest mountains and some of the highest in Eastern Europe as well. The encompassing Tatras National Park (Tatranský národný park), accessed from Poprad by mountain railway, cable car and hiking trails, is Slovakia's top outdoor destination. It's home to skiing, phenomenal hiking – including the famous 72km-long Tatranská Magistrála, a rugged hike that traverses the whole range – and more eclectic activities such as dogsledding, river trips, bear-spotting and overnighting in high-altitude huts.

But don't forget to lower your gaze from the snowy summits and turn further east. Slovakia's second city Košice and a surfeit of UNESCO World Heritage Sites – from medieval towns Levoča and Bardejov to ornate wooden churches and cave-ridden karst – will make your moments in Eastern Slovakia as eye-catching as they are esoteric.

High Tatras
Head to the mountain resorts

If you crave proximity to the raw power of the mountains without sacrificing a cent of comfort, the High Tatras resorts are for you. **Tatranská Lomnica** is on the eastern side, the

Places

Poprad p409
Tatranská Lomnica p409
Starý Smokovec p410
Štrbské Pleso p410
Košice p412

☑ TOP TIP

There is a great deal to see in this relatively small region. Love mountain scenery? Stick to the High Tatras for drama, Slovenský Raj for beauty or Slovenský kras for off-piste karst. Culture? Košice. History? Košice with journeys out to Levoča, Bardejov and around.

⊙ GETTING AROUND

The dependable Bratislava–Košice train line serves Poprad, Spišská Nová Ves (change for buses to Levoča and Slovenský Raj National Park), Presov (change for trains to Bardejov) and Košice, where you can get buses to the likes of caving hotspot Slovenský kras and the Tokaj wine region. The Tatras Electric Railway links Poprad to outdoor activity bases in the High Tatras, with cable cars ascending further into the mountains.

HIGH TATRAS DAY HIKES

These are our favourite High Tatras day hikes, easily accessed via public transport.

Ždiar to Veľké Biele Pleso (4½hr): Climb from winsome Ždiar to the mountain tarn where the Tatranská Magistrala multi-day trail begins.

Štrbské Pleso to Popradské Pleso (1½hr): Link two alpine lakes, then replenish calories at Horské Hotel Popradské Pleso at trail's end.

Hrebienok & Studeny Potok Circuit (1½hr): Forest loop from the funicular top station passes by delightful waterfalls.

Štrbské Pleso to Kriváň (7hr): Out-and-back trek from Slovakia's prettiest mountain lake to its prettiest peak Kriváň (2494m).

Smokovec resorts of Starý (Old), Novy (New), Horný (High) and Dolný (Low) Smokovec are in the middle, and Štrbské pleso is to the west.

From **Tatranská Lomnica**, Slovakia's most hair-raising cable car ascends to **Lomnický štít** *(vt.sk; adult/child return to Skalnaté pleso €32/24, return Skalnaté pleso–Lomnický štít €59/51)*, the nation's second-highest summit at 2634m. Take a six-seat chairlift to Štart, then the gondola to **Skalnaté Pleso** *(vt.sk; free)*, a winter sports area and hiking trailhead beside a lake, which is poised infinity pool–style on the mountainside. A vertigo-inducing cable car then soars an additional 855m in under nine minutes to the mountaintop. Timeslots can sell out quickly; you get 50 minutes on the summit to take pictures and enjoy refreshments in the cafe. **Ski Resort Tatranská Lomnica** *(vt.sk; day pass €55/41)* has some dramatic pistes: the black run from Lomnické sedlo is Slovakia's steepest.

In the Smokovec area, the 19th-century resort **Starý Smokovec** makes the most atmospheric base. Learn how to climb the toughest summits and other extreme activities with the **Mountain Guide Society** *(tatraguide.sk; tours €400-500)*. You can also climb to **Hrebienok**, complete with restaurant, gallery and trailheads, for some thrilling and demanding hikes. Access is via the **Hrebienok Funicular** *(vt.sk; return adult/child €15/12)*.

The most dazzling resort, however, is **Štrbské Pleso**, set around a divine forest lake. Lakeside lodges here provide the High Tatras' best places to stay. Take out a **row boat** *(strbskepleso.sk; €23 per 40 minutes)*, walk around the lake, or dine along its shores. The best hike is the 1½-hour climb through forest to wild-feeling **Popradské pleso** lake, from where bigger peaks rise up.

All resort areas are connected by mountain railway to Poprad.

Off-piste thrills

Ready for some outdoor adventure? Sign up for an excursion run by **Adventoura** *(adventoura.eu; per person from €130)*. Search the High Tatras for brown bears on a bear-watching tour (Jun-Oct), try dog-sledding in winter or go rafting down the Dunajec River gorge in summer. Both white-water rafts and traditional wooden rafts are available.

Hut-to-hut hikes

If you've ever trekked in the Alps, then you're likely familiar with the hut-to-hut system that enables hikers to spend multiple nights in the backcountry without having to pitch a tent. Slovakia's mountain

 EATING IN THE HIGH TATRAS: OUR PICKS

Vino & Tapas: In Poprad, this brick-walled place creates food art with great wine pairings. *11am-2.30pm & 6-9.30pm Tue-Fri, 6-9.30pm Sat* €€€

Felka Café & Brew Bar: Probably the High Tatras' best barista coffee, bagels and cakes, on the road to Poprad Airport. *8am-6pm Mon-Fri, from 9am Sat & Sun* €

Koliba Patria: On the Strbské pleso lakeshore, Slovak mountain dishes, like deer goulash or sheep's cheese dumplings, are exemplary. *11.30am-9pm* €€

Humno Tatry: Lively chalet-style restaurant, cocktail bar and club, by the Tatranská Lomnica cable-car base station. *11am-10pm Sun-Thu, to 3am Fri & Sat* €€

Štrbské pleso

MACIEJ PAVLIK/SHUTTERSTOCK

ranges, including the High Tatras, have a similar network of mountain huts: this is the best way to experience the country's mountainous terrain. For a small fee, you can stay in the beautiful *chaty* (mountain huts) situated strategically across the range. The four-day traverse on the well-signposted **Tatranská Magistrala** trail, from Vel'ke biele pleso (east) to Podbanské (west), is a phenomenal hut-to-hut experience. Our favourite overnight huts? Lakeside **Chata pri zelenom plese** (p413) *(chataprizelenomplese.sk)* is a 30-minute hike from the trailhead, and wood-ensconced **Zamkovského chata** *(zamka.sk)* is perfect for night two. Accommodation is basic but dinner and breakfast are usually available and the mountain panoramas are unbeatable. Figure on €50 for a bed, breakfast and dinner, or €18 for just a bed.

Eastern Slovakia

Central Europe's greatest fortress

UNESCO-listed masterwork **Spiš Castle** *(Spišský hrad; spisskyhrad.com; adult/child €8/4)* is one of Europe's largest fortifications. The 12th-century stronghold sprawls for four hectares through bulwarks and bulky defensive walls over a hilltop 1km east of village Spišské Podhradie. Views from the fortifications are fantastic and far-reaching. In summer, **night tours** *(adult/child €10/8)* are atmospheric, crowd-beating ways to explore this prodigious ruin. From Poprad, it's an hour-long bus ride east to Spišské Podhradie's main square; the entrance to the castle, clearly visible from here, is 850m southeast.

Gorgeous hikes in Slovenský Raj

Discerning outdoor-lovers routinely cite **Slovenský Raj National Park** *(Slovak Paradise; npsr.sk; free)* and its forests, cliffs, ravines and waterfalls as harbouring the country's finest hiking. The standout stretch departs from **Podlesok**: it's a two-hour ascent up a precipitous ladder- and technical-assist

411

UNMISSABLE UNESCO SITES

Levoča: This town, 40 minutes by bus from Poprad, is festooned with Gothic-Renaissance buildings like the Church of St Jacob, which has a wondrous altar.

Bardejov: Dazzlingly intact Middle Ages trading hub of bewitching, steep-roofed buildings. It's 1¾ hours north of Košice by train.

Hervartov Church: Finest of the nine wooden churches of the Slovak Carpathians, representing the crossroads between Roman Catholic and Greek Orthodox faiths. It's 19km southwest of Bardejov.

Poloniny National Park: Forested expanse that's part of UNESCO's Ancient and Primeval Beech Forests of the Carpathians. Access from Runina, 122km northeast of Košice.

trail through **Suchá Belá Gorge**. Return via Kláštorisko, and descend to the Hornád River and riverbank paths to return to Podlesok. Altogether, it's a five-hour loop. From Hrabušice, 2km northeast of Podlesok, buses (or a 5km walk) reach Spišský Štvrtok and mainline trains.

Visit Košice, Slovakia's second city

Košice is Eastern Slovakia's biggest city, with a nexus of culture and historic architecture along **Hlavné námestie**. This long plaza of flower-bedecked gardens and cafes is in the running for the hotly contested title of 'Slovakia's prettiest town square'. The main feature is Slovakia's largest church, **St Elizabeth's Cathedral** (*domsvalzbety.sk; free, tower adult/ child €3/2*), with gaudily elaborate roof decorations: climb the north tower's 160 stone steps for the city centre's finest views. Also on the square is Slovakia's first musical water feature, the **Singing Fountain** (*visitkosice.org; free*) and, two blocks east, the quaint thoroughfare of workshops known as **Hrnčiarska** (*visitkosice.org; free*), which showcase centuries-old trades such as blacksmithing and herbal medicine.

Go underground in Slovenský kras

Rožnava, 50 minutes by train from Košice, is the stop-off for delving into **Slovenský Kras National Park**, which comprises the Slovakian part of one of Europe's greatest cave systems. Of the many cavernous marvels, **Domica Cave** (*ssj. sk; tour adult/child €10/5*), one hour southwest of Rožnava by train and bus, is the largest, with tours that include an underground boat ride. The extraordinary **Dobšinská Ice Cave** (*ssj.sk; tour adult/child €12/6*), packed with ice and enthralling speleothems (mineral deposits), is one hour north by bus.

 EATING IN KOŠICE: OUR PICKS

San Domenico Caffe: Trailblazer for vegan food in Košice, with first-rate cakes a block off the main square. *7.30am-7.30pm Mon-Sat, from 9am Sun* €

Republika Východu: Superb bistro offering everything from fruit-and-granola bowls to succulent beef cheeks. *8am-10pm Mon-Thu, to 11pm Fri & Sat, to 8pm Sun* €

Pub u Kohúta: Atmospheric pub serving hearty Slovak fare alongside Hrnčiarska's traditional crafts workshops. *11am-2pm & 4-11pm Mon-Fri, noon-midnight Sat* €

Slávia: Art nouveau diamond with a glass-roofed restaurant on the main square and a Slovak-international menu. *8am-11pm Mon-Fri, 9am-11pm Sat, 9am-10pm Sun* €€€

# Places We Love to Stay

€ Budget €€ Midrange €€€ Top End

Bratislava

MAP p401

CHORS Like a Hotel € Hostel or hotel? The small-but-smart 'capsule rooms' at this well-appointed place start cheap. Even the dorms are comprised of separate private cabins. Round-the-clock bar and all-you-can-eat breakfasts (€8).

Loft Hotel Bratislava €€ Retro industrial chic is the theme in the Loft's sleek 111 rooms, perfectly complementing the cool on-site brewery-restaurant Fabrika.

Hotel Arcus €€ Outside of the centre, near gorgeous Medická záhrada, these relaxed middleweight digs have high-ceilinged rooms either with balcony or overlooking the serene garden.

Marrol's Boutique Hotel €€€ The capital's most sophisticated accommodation is this neo-baroque boutique choice with an elegant restaurant, spa and fitness centre.

Roset Boutique Hotel €€€ With an art nouveau exterior, these generous, minimalist apartments on the Staré mesto's edge are both practical (safes; kitchenettes) and luxurious (towelling robes; turn-down service).

Hotel pri Mlyne €€€ Take the bus from Bratislava's Lamač train station to Lozorno (25 minutes) to reach this romantic oasis with a spa and landscaped grounds. Countryside peace and city proximity.

Pezinok

Palace Art Hotel €€€ Elegant, park-enfolded 800-year-old chateau in the wine town of Pezinok, with two beautiful restaurants.

Piešťany

Ensana Thermia Palace €€€ Flanked by gardens and resplendent with art nouveau design, this palatial complex is *the* place to experience Piešťany's fabled spa culture.

Trenčín

Hotel Elizabeth €€ Yellow-and-cream art nouveau beauty below Trenčín Castle crag that's a visitor attraction itself. Trenčín's Roman inscription, carved in 179 CE, can be seen from its terrace.

Banská Štiavnica

Divná Pani Luxury Gallery Rooms €€€ Plush, idiosyncratic central Banská Štiavnica burgher house. Each room is an art gallery; the cafe is a statue-dotted library.

Malá Fatra National Park

Hotel Diery €€ Whitewashed apartments and rooms have a wellness area, *koliba* (rustic Slovak restaurant) and, right outside, the trailhead for Malá Fatra's breathtaking Horné Diery gorge.

High Tatras

Chata pri zelenom plese € Our pick for a *chata* (mountain hut) stay: superlative High Tatras ridge views from the cosy bar-restaurant alongside Zelené pleso lake, a tough two-hour hike from the Skalnaté pleso cable-car station.

Horský Hotel Popradské Pleso € Epitomises Slovakia's 'Horský Hotel' tradition: basic but beautifully located hotels in remote mountain locales. This lake-fronting place has a restaurant and outdoor sauna/hot tub. It's a 90-minute hike up from Štrbské pleso.

Ginger Monkey Hostel € The High Tatras' eastern flanks, the Belá Tatras, have charming Ždiar as their base, and this brightly painted, wood-built hostel is the village's most atmospheric lodging.

Grand Hotel Kempinski €€€ The best address at the best High Tatras resort: lovely lakeside Štrbské pleso. Outstanding mountain luxury from the bathtubs and minibars in the rooms to the chandelier-hung pool. Exquisite peak-dotted panoramas.

Košice

Penzión Slovakia €€ The 11 rooms above the Rosta steakhouse, a stone's throw from Košice's main square, each represent a different Slovak city.

Ecohotel Dália €€ Excellent 37-room, lower-middle-range choice several blocks from the main square. Among Slovakia's first ecohotels.

Levoča

Hotel U Leva €€ Fronting Slovakia's most magnificent medieval townscape: Levoča's lovely main square. Rooms exude warm-hued colours and substantial polished wood. There's a prepossessing vaulted restaurant.

Practicalities

Tourist Information
Slovak Tourist Board *(slovakia. travel/en)* Slovakia's official tourist resource online.
Tourist Information Centre *(visitbratislava.com)* Bratislava's helpful main tourist office, near Hlavné námestie.
Visit Košice Infopoint *(visitkosice. org/en)* Košice's tourist office, on the main square Hlavné námestie.

Health & Safe Travel
The biggest risks in Slovakia come in the great outdoors. Bears reside in mountainous areas: stick to marked paths. Mountain exploration comes with other dangers: avalanches, rapidly changing weather and, of course, tumbling over sheer rock faces. Seek advice before attempting mountain hikes.

Etiquette
Greetings Start conversations politely: Slovaks are initially quite formal, but soon open up.
Privacy Respect personal space and don't ask intrusive questions until you get to know someone better.
Clothing Never wear revealing clothing in a church; always take off your shoes when entering someone's home.

Electricity
Type E sockets are most common here: two round holes plus the earth pin.

Tatranská Lomnica (p410)

Opening Hours
Banks 8am–5pm Monday to Friday
Restaurants 11am–10pm
Museums 9am–4pm Tuesday to Sunday
Cable cars 9am–4pm

Entry & Exit Formalities
Slovakia is in the Schengen area, an EU territory that allows Schengen citizens, and many others, free movement across internal borders without checks. Non-EU passports should still have an expiry date of ideally six months or longer after the visitor's intended departure date. Most visitors don't need visas for stays of under 90 days.

Language
Hello. Ahoj.
Good morning. Dobré ráno.
Good day. Dobrý deň.
Good evening. Dobré večer.
Goodnight. Dobrú noc.
How are you? Ako sa maté (formal), Ako sa maš (informal)
Cheers! Na zdravie!
Bon apetit. Dobru chut.'
Do you understand? Rozumiete? (formal), Rozumieš? (informal)
I understand/don't understand. Rozumiem/Nerozumiem.
Do you speak English? Hovorité po anglicky?
Excuse me! Prepáčte!

Bratislava–Košice train (p409)

Arriving & Getting Around

The main visitor entry point is Bratislava's MR Štefánik Airport, which serves many European destinations. Getting around Slovakia is a breeze via its superb, regular and punctual train and bus network.

Arriving by Air
Besides Bratislava airport, there's a well-connected airport in Košice. Vienna (one hours' drive from Bratislava) has more flight options, especially for destinations outside Europe.

Arriving by Train
Bratislava makes a handy cross-Europe rail stop, with trains throughout the day regularly arriving from Vienna (one hour), Budapest (2¼ hours) and Prague (4¼ hours).

Arriving by Boat
The most stylish way to arrive is via boat along the Danube. Boats ply the Vienna–Bratislava route at least once daily from March to November, and less frequently in winter.

Getting Around
Within Slovakia, trains are best. From Bratislava, major destinations include Trenčín (change for some of Western Slovakia's best castles), Žilina (for Malá Fatra National Park), Poprad (for connections to the High Tatras, plus other places like Levoča), Prešov (for Bardejov) and Košice. Buses will get you to all other places.

MONEY
Currency: Euro (€)

CASH OR CARD?
There are ATMs that accept international cards in nearly all towns and cities, and even many villages. Most hotels, restaurants and attractions countrywide take card payments. Nevertheless, carry cash as a back-up for purchases at markets, museum tickets and even accommodation in remoter locations – scenarios in which paying with a card may be impossible.

TIPPING
Slovaks don't tip consistently. However, tipping of up to 10% for main restaurant meals is becoming increasingly common in tourist hubs like Bratislava. Rounding up restaurant bills and taxi fares at least one or two euros as a minimum is common practice.

Curated by
Mark Baker

Slovenia

RELAXING TOWNS AND PRISTINE NATURE

Living proof that the best things really do come in small packages.

From the soaring peaks of the Julian Alps and the subterranean magic of the Postojna and Škocjan caves, to the sparkling emerald-green lakes and rivers and the short but sweet coastline along the Adriatic Sea, tiny Slovenia – with a surface area of just 20,000 sq km and a population of two million people – really does have it all. A welcoming mix of climates brings warm Mediterranean breezes up to the foothills of the Alps, where it can snow even in summer. And with more than half of its total surface still covered in forest, Slovenia does more than simply claim it's 'green', it really is one of the greenest countries on earth.

The country is first and foremost an outdoor destination. The list of activities on offer is endless, with the most popular pursuits being skiing, hiking and, increasingly, cycling. Fast rivers like the Soča cry out to be rafted and there are ample chances to try out more niche activities like horse riding, ballooning, caving and canyoning.

But don't sleep on Ljubljana. Slovenia's capital is a culturally rich city that values sustainability over unfettered growth. Enlivened by native-son Jože Plečnik's buildings and beautification projects and a pretty riverside location, Ljubljana is worth a couple of days of pleasant rambling. See the castle, museum-hop and enjoy Slovenia's best cafes and restaurants.

UNAPHOTO.COM/SHUTTERSTOCK

THE MAIN AREAS

LJUBLJANA
Slovenia's green, livable – and fun – capital city. **p420**

LAKE BLED & JULIAN ALPS
Mountain peaks, perfect lakes and blue-green rivers. **p426**

SLOVENIAN KARST & COAST
Stunning caves and a romantic Adriatic port city. **p428**

For places to stay in Slovenia, see p430

NOSOVA ELIZAVETA/SHUTTERSTOCK

Left: Franciscan Church of the Annunciation (p424), Ljubljana; Above: Bled Island (p426), Lake Bled

SLOVENIA

Find Your Way

The best of Slovenia includes sightseeing in Ljubljana, the highlights of the lakes and peaks of the Julian Alps, and the country's unique karst and coast region.

TRAINS & BUSES

Public transport is good and you won't necessarily need a car to get around. Trains and buses can take you to all the places coveted here. We've noted, where appropriate, whether train or bus is the better option.

CAR

Cars are practical for moving around the country quickly. That said, don't use your own vehicle to get around Ljubljana. The centre is largely closed to car traffic, and walking and cycling are much more practical.

Ljubljana, p420

Enjoy low-stress strolling around Slovenia's immediately charming capital city.

Slovenian Karst & Coast, p428

Mix in credible caving with the sea breezes, sunsets and seafood along the Adriatic Coast.

Lake Bled & Julian Alps, p426

Take in the beauty of Lake Bled and then swim or paddle at Lake Bohinj and Bovec.

HUNGARY

AUSTRIA

ITALY

CROATIA

Hodoš
Murska Sobota
Beltinci

Maribor

Dravograd
Sloveni Gradec
Celje
Žalec
Hrastnik
Trbovlje
Zagorje ob Savi
Litija

Krško

Ravne na Koroškem
Velenje

Kranj
Kamnik
Domžale

Škofja Loka

LJUBLJANA

Grosuplje
Ivančna Gorica
Trebnje
Novo Mesto
Ribnica
Kočevje

Vrhnika
Cerknica
Postojna
Ilirska Bistrica

Logatec
Postojna Cave
Pivka

Idrija
Divača
Škocjan Caves
Lokev

Nova Gorica
Ajdovščina
Lipica

Jesenice
Krajnska Gora
Mt Triglav
Bled Castle
Bled
Lake Bled
Bled Island
Lake Bohinj
Most na Soči

Klagenfurt

Trieste
Tartinijev Trg
Piran
Koper
Izola

Adriatic Sea

Sava
Soča

0   40 km
0   20 miles

MATEJ KASTELIC/SHUTTERSTOCK

Triple Bridge (p424), Ljubljana

Plan Your Time

Two to three days is sufficient for the major sights in Ljubljana. You can cover the country's highlights in a week.

A Weekend in Ljubljana

● Explore **Ljubljana Castle** (p420), then wind through the tiny squares of the **Old Town** (p422). Admire **Prešernov trg** (p424) and take in the perplexing geometry of Jože Plečnik's **Triple Bridge** (p424). Wander through the **Central Market** (p422) or float down the Ljubljanica River in a **historic boat** (p425). Spend day two touring Plečnik's **National & University Library** (p425) or the **City Museum of Ljubljana** (p425).

A Week's Sightseeing

● Begin in Ljubljana before heading up to Bled to see one of the world's prettiest **lakes** (p426). Check out the equally beautiful **Lake Bohinj** (p427) and then raft the rapids of the **Soča River** (p427). Head south to see two of Europe's most impressive caves: **Postojna** (p428) and **Škocjan** (p429). Finish up at the breathtaking port of **Piran** (p429).

SEASONAL HIGHLIGHTS

SPRING
Expect sunshine, warm temps and wildflowers in Alpine valleys. It's still too cold to swim in the Adriatic.

SUMMER
Coastal resorts like Piran fill to the brim. Lakes Bohinj and Bled are warm enough to swim in.

AUTUMN
Mountain air grows cooler and swimming winds down. Resorts like Bled and Bohinj hold their last big shindigs.

WINTER
It's ski season in the Julian Alps. Carnival celebrations are held around the country in February or early March.

Ljubljana

CITY FUN | MUSEUMS | ARCHITECTURE

GETTING AROUND

Central Ljubljana is closed to motor-vehicle traffic, so take public transport or walk, which is a delight. The main promenade follows the Ljubljanica River and is lined by restaurants and cafes. Ljubljana is also ideal for cyclists, and there are bike lanes and special traffic lights everywhere. Hire bikes from the popular **BicikeLJ** *(bicikelj. si)* bicycle-sharing system for a nominal fee. From April through October, the Slovenian Tourist Information Centre rents bikes and hands out bike maps.

☑ TOP TIP

Start at the **Ljubljana Tourist Information Centre**, where the enthusiastic staff dispense information, maps and useful literature. They can help book accommodation and also offer a range of interesting city tours.

Throughout history, Ljubljana (loo-BLI-ah-nuh) has always retained the relaxed ambience of a small town, rather than a sprawling metropolis. This is a feeling that continues to this day: Slovenia's capital is one of Europe's greenest and most liveable urban spaces. Car traffic is restricted in the centre, leaving the leafy banks of the emerald-green Ljubljanica River, which flows through the city's heart, free for pedestrians and cyclists to enjoy. In summer, cafes set up terrace seating along the river. Slovenia's master of minimalist design, Jože Plečnik, graced the capital with beautiful bridges and buildings, as well as dozens of classical design elements such as pillars, pyramids and obelisks, which exist solely to make the city even prettier. Attractive cities are often described as 'jewel boxes', but here the name really fits.

Castle Hill

Ljubljana's stately castle has stood guard over the town since medieval times (12th century) and grew in importance in the 15th century under the Habsburg monarchy as a bulwark against Ottoman encroachment. These days, it's the first port of call for visitors wanting to know more about the origins of the city or simply to have some fun.

Explore Ljubljana Castle

Hike or ride a **funicular** up to lofty **Ljubljana Castle** *(ljubljanskigrad.si)*. There's tons of fun things to do up here, including many activities designed for families and small children. If you don't have much time or don't want to spend much money, the grounds are free to enter. Note, however, you'll have to pay to see the historic chambers, including the castle **Watchtower** and the **Chapel of St George**, and to visit the **Virtual Castle**, **Slovenian History Exhibition** and **Museum of Puppetry**. See the various options and admissions packages in the sidebar (p422).

LJUBLJANA

CASTLE TICKET OPTIONS

The castle grounds are free to roam, but the various attractions require paid admission. Several combined-ticket options are available, depending on what you want to do. **Basic admission** *(adult/child €15/10.50)* covers entry to the viewing towers, puppet museum, exhibition on Slovenian history and the Virtual Castle. For tickets with a multilingual audioguide add €4 to the adult admission and €3 per child. The **Time Machine** *(adult/child €19/13.50)* ticket includes the basic sights plus a costumed guided tour. The **Escape Castle** *(per person €19)* option includes the basic sights plus participation in a castle escape room. **Friderik and the hunt for a prison number** *(per family €24)* is a scavenger hunt designed for families with young children.

KIRK FISHER/SHUTTERSTOCK

Old Town & Central Market

Sandwiched between the slopes leading up to the castle and the Ljubljanica River, Ljubljana's narrow Old Town (Staro Mesto) is the city's oldest quarter. It's comprised of three contiguous, evocative squares – more like one long, lovely alleyway – that run from Mestni trg to Stari trg and Gornji trg as you move south and east. The adjoining **Central Market** follows the Ljubljanica River as it bends eastwards. The market's dominant feature is Plečnik's dramatic neo-Renaissance Plečnik Colonnade.

Gawk and shop at Plečnik Colonnade

At first glance, the massive **Plečnik Colonnade** *(free)* looks like something from classical Greece or Rome, and that was Plečnik's intention in working out his neo-Rennaisance plan for the complex. The colonnade and surrounding farmers market are not just aesthetic pleasures but gourmet ones, too. Shops and stands around the square sell everything from meats and cheeses to fresh fruit and veg – this is a great place to stock up on provisions. Most vendors open from 6am to 6pm on weekdays, with shorter hours on Saturday. Pogačarjev trg serves as

BEST FOR EATING IN LJUBLJANA: OUR PICKS

Gostilna Na Gradu: Treat yourself to Slovenian specialities at Ljubljana Castle at this Michelin Bib Gourmand winner. *noon-10pm Mon-Sat, to 5pm Sun* €€

Pop's Place: Centrally located craft beer and burger bar that's become a must-visit. Avoid traditional meal times: it gets busy. *noon-midnight* €€

JAZ by Ana Roš: Michelin-starred chef Ana Roš brings her inventive dishes using locally sourced ingredients to Ljubljana at prices that won't break the bank. *noon-midnight Mon-Sat* €€€

Vino & Ribe: This unassuming spot in the Old Town has a small but excellent menu of grilled fish, fried fish, sardines and carafes of house wine. *noon-10pm* €€

Dragon Bridge

DRAGON OBSESSIONS

With those scary-looking dragons on Dragon Bridge and a dragon prominent on the city's coat of arms, many visitors assume Ljubljana's dragon obsession goes back centuries. While dragon symbols have been floating around since medieval times, the city's fling with dragons is a relatively modern affair. Just before the turn of the 20th century, a wily mayor named Ivan Hribar apparently persuaded the authorities in Vienna that Ljubljana needed a new crossing over the Ljubljanica and submitted plans for a 'Jubilee Bridge' to mark 50 years of Franz Joseph's reign. The early designs for what's today Dragon Bridge envisaged winged lions, but these were swapped out at the last minute for dragons. The rest is history.

the setting for the weekly popular food fair **Odprta Kuhna** ('Open Kitchen') held on Fridays from March to October.

Look inside Ljubljana's Town Hall

Walk inside the city's striking Gothic **Town Hall** *(visit ljubljana.com; free)*, the seat of the city's government since the late 15th century, to find a late Renaissance courtyard, arcaded on three levels, where theatrical performances once took place. Look above the south portal leading to a second courtyard to see a unique relief map of medieval Ljubljana as the city appeared in the second half of the 17th century.

Snap a photo of Dragon Bridge

The much-loved **Dragon Bridge**, topped with four scary-looking dragons, one on each corner, and adorned with 16 smaller dragons, is prime Instagram territory. Indeed, it's fair to say if you don't take a shot of one of those dragons, well, then you haven't actually been to Slovenia. Aside from dragon imagery, the bridge, built in Viennese Secession (art nouveau) style in 1901, is regarded as one of the most beautiful bridges of this particular style ever built.

BEST COFFEE IN LJUBLJANA: OUR PICKS

Cafe Čokl: This fair-trade place near the foot of the castle's funicular station roasts its java in-house; see the chalkboard for daily specials. *7am-6pm*

Kavarna Zvezda: Possibly the best cakes in Ljubljana, with pride of place going to the *gibanica* (layer cake of poppy seeds, walnut and curd cheese). *8am-9pm Mon-Sat, 10am-8pm Sun*

Stow Cafe: Fresh-roasted speciality coffee in the Ljubljana City Museum. Tell the museum ticket office you're going to the cafe to avoid the admission fee. *10am-6pm Tue-Sun*

Črno Zrno Specialty Coffee: In the Old Town, light-roasted coffee from Colombia as well as special 45-minute guided tastings (per person from €25). *11am-3.30pm Mon-Sat*

STEPH COUVRETTE/SHUTTERSTOCK

Prešernov Trg & Center

Tiny **Prešernov trg** serves as the centrepiece of Ljubljana's wonderful architectural aesthetic. The square, a public space of understated elegance, serves not only as the link between Center (the modern part of the city) and the historic Old Town but also as a favourite meet-up point. Taking pride of place is the **Prešeren Monument**, erected in honour of Slovenia's greatest poet, France Prešeren (1800–49).

Contemplate the Triple Bridge

The **Triple Bridge** *(free)* runs south from Prešernov trg to the Old Town. When it was built as a single span in 1842 it was nothing spectacular, but between 1929 and 1932 super-star architect Jože Plečnik added the two pedestrian side bridges and furnished all three with stone balustrades and lamps. The name was changed and, almost a century later, the bridge was added to the UNESCO World Heritage list, along with several sites recognised as 'Plečnik's Ljubljana'.

Explore the Franciscan Church

The 17th-century salmon-pink **Franciscan Church of the Annunciation** *(marijino-oznanjenje.si; entry €3),* could well

BEST FOR DRINKS IN LJUBLJANA: OUR PICKS

Kolibri: Sip exquisitely crafted cocktails in a cosy nook on a hidden corner in Center. *7pm-midnight*

Ferdinand: Great cocktails, craft beers and cosy outdoor seating on a quiet stretch of the Old Town. *9am-midnight*

Wine Bar Šuklje: Welcoming wine bar for sampling highly rated wines from Bela Krajina in southeastern Slovenia. *9am-11pm*

Pritličje: By day, a popular cafe with convenient sidewalk terrace. By night, a lively bar and cultural centre. *9am-1am Sun-Wed, to 3am Thu-Sat*

Ljubljanica River

CITY PLANNER EXTRAORDINAIRE

Few architects have had as great an impact on their hometown as Jože Plečnik. Born in Ljubljana in 1872, Plečnik was educated in Graz and studied under architect Otto Wagner in Vienna. From 1911 he spent a decade in Prague teaching and helping renovate Prague Castle. Plečnik's list of Ljubljana creations is endless: from the National and University Library and colonnaded Central Market to the cemetery at Žale, where you can see his own simple headstone. He was also a city planner, and redesigned the banks of the Ljubljanica River, including the Triple Bridge, and Tivoli Park. His eclecticism alienated him from mainstream modern architecture during his lifetime, and he was relatively unknown outside his home country when he died in 1957.

be the unofficial symbol of the city, and is just as striking inside as it on the outside. Enter through a small door to the left of the main entrance to find a riot of baroque design inside.

Learn about Roman-era Ljubljana

The excellent **City Museum of Ljubljana** *(mgml.si; adult/child €8/6)* is strong on Ljubljana's Roman origins as the colony of 'Emona'. The museum highlights a reconstructed street that once linked the eastern gates of Emona to the Ljubljanica as well as a collection of well-preserved classical artefacts.

Tour Plečnik's masterpiece library

Among all the buildings the architect and urban planner Jože Plečnik designed for Ljubljana, the working **National & University Library** *(nuk.uni-lj.si; adult/child €5/free)* is widely considered his masterpiece. Art historians contend this is where the great man aligned his designs and materials with the larger purpose of the building itself: the acquisition of knowledge. The **Main Reading Room** sports huge glass walls and stunning lamps, which were also designed by Plečnik. The library is open to visitors from 10am to 6pm Monday to Friday and 2.30pm to 6pm on Saturday.

Sail the Ljubljanica River

Sailing along the Ljubljanica River is a relaxing and fun way to take in the city. Several companies run tours, but only the creatively named **Barka Ljubljanica** *(Ljubljanica Boat; barka-ljubljanica.si; tours adult/child €15/7)* operates a wooden vessel. It's 10m long and carries up to 48 people on a 50-minute tour. Boats depart hourly from the Breg embankment, just below **Novi trg**.

Lake Bled & Julian Alps

OUTDOOR ADVENTURE | BLISSFUL VIEWS | HISTORIC CASTLES

Places

☑ TOP TIP

Time your visit to avoid the summer high season (July and August) when tour buses descend upon the lake and camper vans clog the narrow streets. Winter snow can make roads impassable in these parts. Vršič Pass closes most years from November to April.

The Julian Alps region is the Slovenia of tourist posters: mountain peaks, mirror-like lakes and blue-green rivers. Prepare to be charmed by Lake Bled (with an island and a castle!) and surprised by Lake Bohinj (how does Bled score all that attention when down the road is Bohinj?). The lofty peak of Mt Triglav, at the centre of a national park of the same name, may dazzle you enough to prompt an ascent.

Lake Bled

TIME FROM LJUBLJANA: 1HR 🚌

With its bluish-green lake, handsome church on an islet, a medieval castle clinging to a rocky cliff and some of the highest peaks of the Julian Alps as a backdrop, Bled has become Slovenia's most popular resort. It attracts everyone from honeymooners to backpackers, who come for the romantic setting, hiking, biking, water sports and canyoning.

Take in the castle, lake and island

Lake Bled is best explored on foot and by boat. Three footpaths signposted 'Grad' lead to **Bled Castle** *(blejski-grad. si; entry to castle & museum €17)* and if you start around the **Blejsko Srce** (Heart of Bled) it should take you between 15 and 25 minutes. Magical, tiny **Bled Island** sits in the middle of the lake and is just as picturesque up close. Board one of the *pletna* (a wooden boat that resembles a Venetian gondola) at **Gondolas Mlino** *(round trip €18)* for a short ride that feels like a time machine. Once you arrive, climb the 99 stairs into the **Church of the Assumption** *(blejskiotok.si; €12).*

 GETTING AROUND

Bus connections from Ljubljana to Bled and Bohinj are frequent and cheap. Buses are also good for moving between places within the region. Both lake areas are compact and walkable. The area is committed to sustainable travel so drivers can stow their cars and hit the foot or bike paths to move around. The Soča Valley is spread out and easiest to explore by car.

Lake Bohinj

Lake Bohinj may lack Bled's glamour, but it's less crowded and in many ways more authentic. It's an ideal summer holiday destination. People come primarily to swim in the crystal-clear water, and to enjoy leisurely cycling and walking trails as well as outdoor pursuits like kayaking and horse riding. It's 26km southwest of Bled.

Go swimming, boating and paddleboarding

Lake Bohinj's chilly waters warm to a swimmable 22°C in July and August. You can enter the water from any point on shore, though the decent small beaches on both the northern and southern shores are most convenient. Some beaches on the northern shore are reserved for naturists. Adventure outfitters around the lake rent kayaks, canoes and SUP boards and provide guides for hiking and mountaineering. In winter you can go skiing, snowshoeing and ice climbing. We've listed our favourite excursions in the sidebar.

Soča Valley

The Soča Valley, particularly the arresting blue-green colour of the Soča River, is just as stunning as you've heard, and neither photos nor written descriptions do it justice. It's worth exploring slowly, from the frothy rapids to the placid streams. Thrill-seekers flock to the town of Bovec for outdoor fun.

Whitewater rafting on the Soča

Whitewater rafting on the Soča River is one of the most thrilling adventures Slovenia offers. Several outfitters run trips down the river from bases around Bovec. **Nature's Ways** (*econaturesways.com*) runs guided white-water rafting and canyoning adventures for small groups, with an emphasis on minimal environmental impact. And lots of screaming, of course. **Soča Rafting** (*socarafting.si*) was the first rafting company in Slovenia and is still at the top of its game, offering novelties such as hydrospeed, where you glide along the river and might get mistaken for a fish. For something different, **Adrenalin Park Bovec** (*ziplineslovenia.si*) features more than 3km of ziplines over the Julian Alps. They also rent e-bikes, scooters and kayaks.

BEST OF BOHINJ OUTDOORS

Savica Waterfall: An easy(ish) stroll through lush forest leads to one of Slovenia's most magnificent waterfalls.

Mostnica Gorge: Spend the day listening to the sounds of the forest as you follow wooded paths towards a heavenly valley.

Hike & Bike: Organises nighttime walks by lantern around the lake and guided forest therapy meditation sessions.

Electric Boat Tours: Operates throughout the year between Ribčev Laz and Ukanc; there's no better way to take in the lake.

Vogel Ski Centre: The 22km of runs make this a top skiing destination. It's 1540m above the lake's southwestern corner and accessible by cable car from Ukanc.

BEST FOR EATING IN BLED & BOHINJ: OUR PICKS

Park Restaurant & Cafe: The creator of Bled's trademark *kremšnita* (cream cake) recipe is still the best, according to almost everyone. *11am-10pm* €€

Bled Castle Restaurant: Recognised as one of the top sustainable restaurants in Europe, this elegant dining room overlooks Lake Bled. *noon-10pm* €€

Hotel Bohinj: The chic hotel restaurant near Lake Bohinj is open for lunch, snacks and dinner, with a wide range of main courses and desserts. *noon-10pm* €€

Majer'ca: Modern Alpine cuisine near Lake Bohinj, with multi-course tasting menus you can design yourself. *4-10pm Mon-Fri, 1-9pm Sat & Sun* €€

Slovenian Karst & Coast

CAVES | ADRIATIC SUNSETS | SEAFOOD

Places

Postojna Cave p428
Piran p429

☑ **TOP TIP**

Parking is tight along Slovenia's coast, particularly in Piran. Work out parking in advance with your hotel. For Piran, parking is only available at Garage Fornače, outside the Old Town. Shuttle buses (5am to 1am) connect the parking area and town centre.

The Karst region is a limestone plateau stretching from the Gulf of Trieste to the Vipava Valley. Rivers, ponds and lakes can disappear and then resurface in the Karst's porous limestone, often resulting in underground caverns like the fabulous caves at Postojna and Škocjan. To the southwest, Slovenia's short Adriatic Sea coastline (just 47km) features clean beaches, boats for rent and delicious seafood, with the highlight being the port of Piran.

Postojna Cave

TIME FROM LJUBLJANA: **1HR** 🚌

The jaw-dropping Postojna Cave system, a series of caverns, halls and passages, extends underground for some 24km and is two million years old. Visits are by 1½-hour guided tours, with much of the distance covered by electric train. Note the cave has a constant temperature of 8°C to 10°C, so a warm jacket and decent shoes are advised.

Tour a subterranean wonderland

Stepping through the entrance of **Postojna Cave** *(postojnskajama.eu; adult/student/child in high season €32.90/25.90/19.50; tours hourly 9am-6pm, daily Jul & Aug, fewer departures rest of year)* takes you from the clear light of the Mediterranean hinterland and into the darkness and then, as your eyes adjust, into another world. Few places in Slovenia have the power to dazzle quite like this. Guided tours unveil 5km of the expansive cave. Entering the **Great Mountain** cavern feels like stepping into the secret den of a James Bond villain or some kind of Hollywood special effects scene. From there, you pass through dry galleries adorned with delicate stalactites, needle-shaped formations and even translucent 'curtains'.

 GETTING AROUND

Postojna lies 53km southwest of Ljubljana and is connected to the capital by regular buses and trains. Buses running between Ljubljana and the coast stop at Divača, from where a bus continues on to the Škocjan Caves. That said, a car is more practical for reaching these caves. Regular buses travel between Ljubljana and Piran. Once in town, the port area is small and walkable. Note that cars are restricted in Piran's Old Town.

See more jaw-dropping beauty at Škocjan Caves

The immense complex of **Škocjan Caves** (*park-skocjanske-jame.si; guided tour adult/concession/child €18/14/9*), just 20km southwest of Postojna, is – for many travellers – a rival to Postojna Cave for the title of Slovenia's best cave experience. The Škocjan cave system was formed by the Reka River, which carves its way through a gorge beneath Škocjan village and then vanishes into the Dead Lake. Two-hour guided tours begin at 500m-long **Silent Cave**, which is filled with beautiful stalactites, stalagmites and flowstones that resemble snowdrifts. Silent Cave ends at the **Great Hall**, 120m wide and 30m high – it's a fantasy world of exotic dripstones, deposits and mighty stalagmites.

Piran

TIME FROM LJUBLJANA: **2HR**

Clustered in a tight huddle of stone and terracotta on a narrowing peninsula in the northern Adriatic, Piran (Pirano in Italian) sparkles as the crown jewel of Slovenia's 47km coastline. Wander the twisty alleyways of the impeccably preserved Old Town with its Venetian Gothic architecture, climb to the summit for a gorgeous church, medieval walls and incredible views, or just chill in the elegant main square, Tartinijev trg.

Stroll the centre of a lovely port

Most explorations of Piran begin in the graceful, oval-shaped, pastel-hued **Tartinijev trg**. The 'square' is named after Giuseppe Tartini (1692–1770), an 18th-century composer, violinist and Piran's favourite native son. A **statue** honours the great man in the centre of the square; his birthplace, **Tartini House** (*facebook.com/casatartini; entry free*), hosts cultural events and exhibitions. Next door is the cute 1818 **Church of St Peter** with its twin Doric columns. Other highlights to enjoy from the outside include the grand **Court House** and the porticoed 19th-century **Municipal Hall**, home to the helpful **tourist information centre** at the western end of the square.

BEST SUNSET SPOTS IN PIRAN

Piran Town Walls: Soak in the amazing views from the preserved medieval walls high up above town.

Boat Harbour: Pick any vantage point along the coastal boardwalk, but this one is glorious in the late afternoon.

Hotel Piran Rooftop: The rooftop bar of Piran's iconic hotel is the classiest place in town for a sundowner.

Bell Tower: It may close just before sunset, but there are great views here; watch the spectacle over town from just outside the door.

Strunjan Landscape Park: About an hour's walk along the coast from Piran, this trail takes you up on 80m-high cliffs with amazing views.

BEST FOR EATING IN PIRAN: OUR PICKS

Fritolin Pri Cantini: First choice of the places on Trg 1 Maja and a classic Old Town experience: order calamari under a cosy grape-wine canopy. *11am-9pm* €

Sarajevo 84: Order a plate of beans and some *čevapčiči* (spicy meatballs of beef or pork) with Bosnian bread and you'll be set for the day. *10am-10pm* €

Restaurant Neptune: Try delicious dondoli clams (sea truffles) and other top-notch seafood and pasta at this old-school joint. *noon-3pm & 6-10pm Wed-Mon* €€

Stara Gostilna: The home kitchen of young Michelin-starred chef Kristian Zule features lobster ravioli, perfect seafood and a huge wine list. *6am-midnight Mon-Sat* €€€

429

Places We Love to Stay

€ Budget €€ Midrange €€€ Top End

Ljubljana

MAP p421

Prešernov Trg

City Hotel Ljubljana €€ Good-value, central high-rise with clean rooms. It's a short walk from the train and bus stations and has an excellent breakfast buffet and a welcoming reception. Book ahead as it's popular in season.

AS Boutique Hotel €€€ Step inside a hidden courtyard just steps from Prešernov trg to find this upscale boutique, tastefully decorated with stunning contemporary art and a fashionable mid-century feel. Some rooms offer castle views.

Old Town

AdHoc Hostel € Well-situated, efficiently run hostel right on the Ljubljanica River has brightly painted, airy dorms and several private doubles. Good choice for hitting the coffee bars and restaurants along the riverbank.

Hotel Bloom €€ Lovely boutique below Gornji trg features eye-catching art deco styling and 10 newly refurbished rooms, with lovely hardwood floors and tasteful furnishings. Enjoy your breakfast or an evening drink in the hidden back garden.

Center

Urban Boutique Hotel €€ Great-value, upscale three-star with quiet, high-standard rooms

and an excellent breakfast that features lots of locally sourced items and made-to-order eggs. The Center location is close to the sights, yet removed from the noise of busy Slovenska cesta.

Hotel Mrak €€ Cosy, family-run hotel with 35 refurbished rooms set in an older building. Almost opposite the Križanke on Trg Francoske Revolucije, it's ideally located for culture vultures. The back courtyard is lovely for breakfast in nice weather.

Bled

Old Parish House €€ The former property of the Parish Church of St Martin has been transformed into a welcoming guesthouse with timber beams, hardwood floors and chic finishes.

Hotel Triglav Bled €€€ An historic facade hides modern touches and lakeside views, plus a fine restaurant that makes coming home after a day on the water a true pleasure.

Lake Bohinj

Boutique Hotel Majer'ca €€ Scandi cool rooms in Stara Fuzina with views of the mountains and private saunas for the lucky few who snag the suites.

Hotel Bohinj €€ Equal parts sumptuous and wacky, this restored lodge spares no

expense spoiling its guests while maintaining a true soul. Ask about the nightclub.

Postojna

Lipizzaner Lodge €€ Pleasant rural guesthouse run by a Welsh-Finnish couple with brilliant local expertise. You'll feel enveloped in the local countryside, but still close to everything.

Hotel Jama €€€ Literally atop Postojna Cave, this huge socialist-era hotel was renovated and turned into luxury lodging with great views; pay extra for a front-facing room.

Piran

Hostel Adriatic Piran € Offering dorms and rooms of varying sizes, this is one of the only budget options in Piran. Rooms are plain but nicely looked after. Shared bathrooms.

Guesthouse Rosemary €€ Tucked away in the back streets but within walking distance of everything, Rosemary has polished wooden floorboards, wrought-iron furnishings and great reviews from travellers.

PachaMama €€€ Built by travellers for travellers, this excellent guesthouse sits just off Tartinijev trg and has 12 fresh rooms, decorated with timber and lots of travel photography.

Practicalities

LGBTIQ+ Travellers
Slovenia is a largely tolerant destination and members of the LGBTIQ+ community are unlikely to face any overt forms of discrimination. Ljubljana is especially welcoming and same-sex couples holding hands on the street, for example, are unlikely to attract even a passing glance.

Health
Slovenia is a safe country, and travellers needn't worry about taking any special precautions. Tap water is safe to drink and of very good quality. Like much of Central Europe, Slovenia's forests and grasslands are filled with ticks. On hikes or treks, use repellent and cover up exposed skin.

Toilets
Public toilets, especially in Ljubljana, are plentiful and relatively easy to find. Unlike in many European countries, toilets are often free of charge. Authorities are working to make toilets accessible for travellers with disabilities.

Insurance
Consider a policy that covers flight cancellations and medical care. Alternatively, or additionally, EU travellers can apply for the European Health Insurance Card (EHIC) that covers emergency medical treatment outside their home country free of charge.

ALESSANDRO ZAPPALORTO/SHUTTERSTOCK

Tartinijev trg (p429), Piran

Opening Hours
Banks 8.30am–12.30pm & 2pm–5pm Monday to Friday
Pubs 11am–midnight Sunday to Thursday, to 2am Friday & Saturday
Restaurants 11am–10pm
Shops 8am–7pm Monday to Friday, to 1pm Saturday

Accessible Travel
Slovenia is reasonably accessible for travellers with disabilities. Facilities include public telephones with amplifiers, pedestrian crossings with beepers, Braille on maps at bus stops, sloped pavements, ramps in government buildings and reserved parking spaces.

Ljubljana is largely wheelchair-accessible. The centre is mostly flat; pavements have kerb cuts. Most buses are equipped with lifts. Old Town's cobblestone streets are a challenge.

Public Holidays
New Year's 1 and 2 January
Prešeren Day (Culture Day) 8 February
Easter & Easter Monday March/April
Insurrection Day 27 April
Labour Day 1 and 2 May
National Day 25 June
Assumption Day 15 August
Reformation Day 31 October
All Saints' Day 1 November
Christmas Day 25 December
Independence Day 26 December

Language

Slovene belongs to the South Slavic language family, along with Croatian and Serbian (although it is much closer to Croatia's northwestern and coastal dialects). It also shares some features with the more distant West Slavic languages through contact with a dialect of Slovak. Although most Slovene adults speak at least one foreign language, often English, German or Italian, any effort on your part to speak the local tongue will be rewarded.

Basics

Hello. Zdravo. *zdra·vo*
Goodbye. Na svidenje. *na svee·den·ye*
Excuse me. Dovolite. *do·vo·lee·te*
Sorry. Oprostite. *op·ros·tee·te*
Please. Prosim. *pro·seem*
Thank you. Hvala. *hva·la*
You're welcome. Ni za kaj. *nee za kai*
Yes. Da. *da*
No. Ne. *ne*
What's your name? Kako vam/ti je ime? (pol/inf) *ka·ko vam/tee ye ee·me*
My name is … Ime mi je … *ee·me mee ye …*
Do you speak English? Ali govorite angleško? *a·lee go·vo·ree·te ang·lesh·ko*
I don't understand. Ne razumem. *ne ra·zoo·mem*

Directions

Where's the …? Kje je …? *kye ye …*
What's the address? Na katerem naslovu je? *na ka·te·rem nas·lo·voo ye*
Can you show me (on the map)? Mi lahko pokažete (na zemljevidu)? *mee lah·ko po·ka·zhe·te (na zem·lye·vee·doo)*
How do I get to …? Kako pridem do …? *ka·ko pree·dem do …*
Is it near/far? Ali je blizu/daleč? *a·lee ye blee·zoo/da·lech*
(Go) Straight ahead. (Pojdite) Naravnost naprej. *(poy·dee·te) na·rav·nost na·prey*

Time

What time is it? Koliko je ura? *ko·lee·ko ye oo·ra*
It's (one) o'clock. Ura je (ena). *oo·ra ye (e·na)*
half past seven pol osem *pol o·sem* (literally 'half eight')
in the morning zjutraj *zyoot·rai*
in the evening zvečer *zve·cher*
yesterday včeraj *vche·rai*
today danes *da·nes*
tomorrow jutri *yoo·tree*

Emergencies

Help! Na pomoč! *na po·moch*
Go away! Pojdite stran! *poy·dee·te stran*
I'm lost. Izgubil/Izgubila sem se. (m/f) *eez·goo·beew/ eez·goo·bee·la sem se*
Where are the toilets? Kje je stranišče? *kye ye stra·neesh·che*
I'm ill. Bolan/Bolna sem. (m/f) *bo·lan/boh·na sem*
Call … Pokličite …! *pok·lee·chee·te*
  a doctor zdravnika *zdrav·nee·ka*
  the police policijo *po·lee·tsee·yo*

Eating & Drinking

What would you recommend? Kaj priporočate? *kai pree·po·ro·cha·te*
Cheers! Na zdravje! *na zdrav·ye*
I'd like the …, Želim …, *zhe·leem …*
please. prosim. *pro·seem*
  bill račun *ra·choon*
  menu jedilni list *ye·deel·nee leest*

NUMBERS

1
en *en*

2
dva *dva*

3
trije *tree·ye*

4
štirje *shtee·rye*

5
pet *pet*

6
šest *shest*

7
sedem *se·dem*

8
osem *o·sem*

9
devet *de·vet*

10
deset *de·set*

Ljubljana Airport

MONEY
Currency: Euro (€)

CHANGING MONEY
ATMs are ubiquitous and offer better rates for changing money than private exchange booths. That said, many banks, post offices, tourist offices and exchange bureaus do change money. Banks usually charge a commission of 1%. Other agencies charge 3%.

CARD & DIGITAL PAYMENTS
Paying with credit or debit cards is common around the country and often preferable to cash. The only exceptions might be smaller shops in outlying areas. Ticket machines in Ljubljana's buses now also accept card payments.

TIPPING
Hotels Gratuity for cleaning at your discretion.**Pubs** Not expected unless table service provided. **Restaurants** 10% for decent service.**Taxis** Round up fare to nearest euro.

Arriving & Getting Around

Ljubljana Airport is the country's only international airport. The airport is 27km north of the city and well connected by taxi or shuttle bus. Slovenia is thoroughly integrated into European rail and bus networks.

Public Transport in Ljubljana
Central Ljubljana is walkable but use buses to reach outlying neighbourhoods. Buses operate from 5am to 10.30pm (fare €1.30). Pay fares with a contactless debit card or purchase a magnetic 'Urbana' card.

Driving
Before driving in Slovenia, purchase an **e-vignette** online (*evinjeta.dars.si*), required to drive on major highways. Vignettes can also be purchased at petrol stations near the border. The price is €16/32 per week/month.

Driving Essentials
Drive on the right.
The speed limit is 50km/h in urban areas, 90km/h on secondary roads and 130km/h on motorways.
Blood-alcohol limit is 0.05%.

Long-Haul Train & Bus Travel
Train and bus routes cover the entire country. Trains are generally more useful for covering longer distances, such as from Ljubljana to Maribor. Buses are more useful for shorter distances and on select routes, such as from Ljubljana to Lake Bled or to Piran. Trains and buses depart from the **Ljubljana Train Station**.

Ukraine is currently considered **unsafe to visit**

SODEL VLADYSLAV/SHUTTERSTOCK

Above: Kyiv; Right: Banksy graffiti, Kyiv

Curated by
Leonid Ragazin

Ukraine

A COUNTRY UNDER BRUTAL ATTACK

If you travel to any part of Ukraine, you will be risking your life.

All of Ukraine was an active war zone at the time of writing, following Russia's all-out invasion that began in February 2022. Artillery fire has flattened entire cities and towns along the frontlines in the east, while other parts of Ukraine – especially Kyiv and Odesa – are subject to constant drone and missile attacks. As of August 2025, almost 7 million people had left Ukraine due to the war. This is the equivalent of 17% of the country's pre-war population; most of those who have fled are women and children.

No matter how the war ultimately ends, it is already clear that Ukraine will emerge from the conflict as a vastly different country. At the time of writing, about one-fifth of Ukrainian territory was occupied by Russia, with tiny chunks of land being added every day as the Russian army slowly progresses

Crimea was one of Ukraine's main tourist destinations prior to its annexation in 2014. Following Russian annexation, visits to Crimea were technically still possible and even encouraged by Russia, but those who dared to go were considered to be in direct violation of Ukrainian laws.

The country's other attractions remain under Ukrainian control. These includes Kyiv, Ukraine's beautiful and ancient capital, the marvellously flamboyant port city of Odesa and elegant Lviv. Although visiting the country is not impossible, you need a legitimate work- or family-related reason to go. While many foreigners travel to Ukraine as aid workers and advisors, war tourism is unethical and a bad idea, as is any self-styled political activism, however well-intentioned. Peace talks initiated by US President Donald Trump had produced some hope for a ceasefire at the time for writing.

OLEKSANDR POPENKO/SHUTTERSTOCK

THE SCALE OF DESTRUCTION

Since the start of Russia's invasion, parts of Ukraine have experienced destruction on a massive scale. Even if the war ends soon, the mining region of Donbas and other frontline areas will be too dangerous to travel in for years because of the cluster ammunition and land mines that both sides have used. At the time of writing, the most devastated areas in Donbas – once a densely populated and urbanised industrial region – were on the Russian side of the frontline. Some cities, like Bakhmut, have been almost completely erased from the face of earth by heavy artillery. On the Ukrainian-controlled side, Kharkiv, the country's second-largest city, suffered most due to its proximity to the Russian border. Kyiv, Odesa and Dnipro have also been hit hard multiple times. Russian strikes have extended as far as Lviv and Mukachevo in the country's far west. Although civilian casualties have been comparatively low, key infrastructure will take years to rebuild.

Ukraine Today

At the time of writing, war defined every aspect of life in Ukraine. The invasion began with air raids and missile attacks on major Ukrainian cities in the wee hours of 24 February 2022. But the 'shock and awe' attack didn't lead to Ukraine's capitulation. Instead, over three and a half years later, the war is still ongoing.

Kyiv, Lviv, Odesa and other major Ukrainian cities have retained some semblance of normal life throughout the conflict, although night-time attacks have forced people to sleep in bomb shelters and upended their lives in multiple other ways, including blackouts and interruptions in the water supply.

Forced enlistment, often carried out using brutal or outright criminal methods, has compelled many men to stay at home for days on end. Others have risked their lives in order to escape, whether by traversing the Carpathian Mountains or swimming across the rivers on the border of the EU. While millions of women and children have gone on to start new lives in the West, most men remain in Ukraine as a result of the ban on travel for all men eligible for the draft (aged 25 to 55): the result is millions of separated or broken families. The brutal demographic and social realities of wartime Ukraine defy imagination.

The conflict had reached a crossroads at the time of writing, with the Trump-led US trying to bring both sides to the negotiating table. The potential success of these efforts remains an open question.

History

Kyiv is the cradle of Ukrainian, Russian and Belarusian nationhood. This has created a range of highly politicised interpretations, especially during times of armed conflict involving all three countries.

Kyivan Rus

In the 9th century, a Viking tribe known as the Rus founded the original East Slavic state. Tracing their roots to the semi-legendary Prince Rurik, the Vikings moved their capital from Novgorod, in today's Russia, to Kyiv in 879, establishing the polity known as Kyivan Rus and claiming control of the lucrative trade route between Constantinople and Northern Europe.

Kyivan Rus reached its pinnacle under the rule of Volodymyr the Great (978–1015), when it stretched from the Volga to the Danube and the Baltic. Volodymyr also established Orthodox Christianity as the pre-eminent religion. Internal feuds between rival princes and nomadic attacks from the east eventually led to the disintegration of the first state in East Slavic lands.

The Mongol Invasion

After the Mongol Golden Horde sacked Kyiv, the city was largely abandoned and the centre of power shifted to the northeastern Rostov-Suzdal principality, where Moscow would eventually come into being.

Map labels

Bryansk
Voronezh
MINSK
Kursk
BELARUS
RUSSIA
Chornobyl Exclusion Zone
Chernihiv
Seym
Pripyat
Desna
Occupied by Russia
Chornobyl
Kharkiv
Luhansk
KYIV
Poltava
Rivne
Cherkasy
Lutsk
Dnipro River
Donetsk
POLAND
Zhytomyr
Kremenchuk
Dnipropetrovsk
Lviv
Ternopil
Vinnytsya
Uman
Kirovohrad
Zaporizhzhya
Mariupol
Khmelnytsky
Pivdenny Buh
Ivano-Frankivsk
Kakhovske Reservoir
Berdyansk
Melitopol
Mt Hoverla
Chernivtsi
Mykolaiv
Sea of Azov
Uzhhorod
MOLDOVA
Askaniya-Nova National Park
Carpathian National Nature Park
Kherson
Crimea (Occupied by Russia)
CHIŞINĂU
Odesa
Simferopol
ROMANIA
Dunaysky National Park
Sevastopol
Danube
Black Sea
BUCHAREST
0   200 km
0   100 miles

As the Golden Horde disintegrated in the 15th century, much of today's Ukraine turned into a zone permanently contested by the Crimean Khanate, one of the Horde's fragments, the fledgling Moscow tsardom and the emerging Polish-Lithuanian union. By the 1340s, the latter had taken control of the Galicia-Volynia principalities in the west of today's Ukraine, sending Lviv and the surrounding lands on a different trajectory than the rest of the Kyivan Rus.

The Cossacks

The power vacuum in the steppe on both sides of the Dnipro River was gradually filled by runaway serfs and outlaws who mixed with the remaining nomadic populations. These people became known as the Cossacks. The most famous group of Cossacks lived on the lower Dnipro, in a fortified island community called the Zaporizhya Sich.

Although they were officially under Polish-Lithuanian rule from 1569, the Cossacks often rebelled and remained staunchly Orthodox. In 1654 they formed their own so-called Hetmanate to assert the concept of Ukrainian self-determination. But the ensuing conflict only led to a change of overlords, from Polish to Russian, and attempts to rebel against Moscow failed miserably. In 1775 Catherine the Great ordered the destruction of the last Cossack stronghold.

FAST FACTS

Capital Kyiv
Population 41 million (pre-war estimate)
Area 603,628 sq km
Official language Ukrainian
Time zone GMT+3
Currency Hryvna (UAH)

KYIV AT WAR

Kyiv resident **Yury** reflects on life in the city during the war.

The war has lasted so long that it's hard to remember life without it. Many friends and relatives are at the front, some for more than three years now. Kyiv and Kharkiv, where my father and two shattered apartments remain, were hit especially hard. Nighttime missile and drone strikes are part of the routine. In the first years, there were blackouts and water cuts, but it's less common now. My wife and I got a corgi who we named Orlyk, after the author of the first Ukrainian constitution. But the dog refuses to go for evening walks: a couple of times there were explosions nearby and now he digs his paws in. Many people in Kyiv still go to bomb shelters. We don't. Life goes on: traffic jams in the downtown, small hopes, cognitive dissonance. Everyone wants peace, but no one wants to give away what is ours. I believe Ukraine will still surprise the world.

ANDREAS WOLOCHOW/SHUTTERSTOCK

Independence Monument, Kyiv

The Russian Empire

Under Russian rule, Ukraine saw an unprecedented economic boom as the empire expanded into the sparsely populated steppe east and south of Kyiv. Cossacks and Ukrainian and Russian peasants were the largest groups of colonists, followed by Jews, Germans, Greeks and Bulgarians, all of whom were invited by the crown to cultivate the phenomenally productive land, which soon became known as the 'breadbasket of Europe'.

In 1772, Prussia, Austria and Russia decided to carve up Poland. Under the resulting Partitions of Poland (1772–95), most of western Ukraine was handed to Russia, but the far west around Lviv went to the Habsburg Empire. The Ukrainian nationalist movement was born in Kyiv in the 1840s, but when the tsarist authorities there banned the Ukrainian language from official use in 1876, the movement's focus shifted to Austrian-controlled Lviv.

Soviet Rule

Following WWI and the collapse of the tsarist monarchy, Ukraine had a shot at independence, but the international community was unsupportive. In the aftermath of the Russian Civil War, most of today's Ukraine wound up as the Ukrainian Soviet Socialist Republic, founded in 1922. Swathes of today's western Ukraine, however, became part of the newly independent Poland.

In the first decades of the Soviet rule, the initial policy of 'Ukrainization', encouraging the expansion of Ukrainian language into political and cultural spheres, soon gave way to Stalin's terror and a man-made famine, known in Ukraine as the Holodomor, which today is sometimes described as a deliberate genocidal policy.

Ukraine's entire territory became one the main battlefields of WWII. Entire cities were levelled and some 6 to 8 million Ukrainians, at least 1.6 million of them Jews, were killed. In the post-war arrangement, western Ukraine remained firmly under Soviet control, with both the USSR and Poland conducting population swaps and suppressing Ukrainian nationalist resistance.

After the death of Stalin, Nikita Khrushchev, a self-styled Ukrainian, took the reins of the USSR and once again expanded Ukraine's territory by placing Crimea under its control. He was succeeded by the Ukrainian-born Leonid Brezhnev, but his rule was associated with Ukraine's increasing Russification.

The catastrophe at the Chornobyl nuclear power station in 1986 spurred the rise of Ukrainian nationalism. Ukraine proclaimed independence in the wake of the failed August 1991 coup in Moscow and sealed the decision in a referendum in December that same year.

Independence

The three and a half decades of Ukrainian independence were a roller-coaster that began with a deep economic crisis. Leonid Kuchma, a Soviet-style rocket-factory manager, came to power in July 1994 and stayed in place for 10 years. But growing discontent led to the peaceful Orange Revolution of 2004, which was triggered by accusations of electoral fraud in favour of Kuchma's perceived appointee, Viktor Yanukovych.

In the following years, the pro-Western Orange coalition failed miserably to eliminate corruption or improve the economy, and Yanukovych was elected president in 2010. While exacerbating corruption, Yanukovych tried to appease both the West and Moscow by simultaneously pursuing integration with EU and maintaining strong links with Russia. Ultimately, he had to make a choice and at the end of 2013 he made the fateful decision to embrace Russia. This precipitated the drama of the second Maidan revolution, which culminated in brutal fighting in the centre of Kyiv. Dozens of people were killed and Yanukovych eventually fled to Russia.

As pro-Maidan forces in Kyiv celebrated victory, Moscow responded by annexing Crimea and launching a stealthy annexation of the Donbas mining region with the help of local separatists. The new Ukrainian government sent in troops and an armed conflict ensued, with Moscow effectively commanding separatist forces and backing them up with regular troops. The first phase of the conflict was partially defused by the Minsk agreements of 2015, which left parts of the Donetsk and Luhansk regions under Russia's de facto control.

In the 2019 election, the first post-Maidan president Petro Poroshenko lost heavily to comedian Volodymyr Zelensky, who ran on the platform of mending relations with Russia. His talks with Putin in Paris resulted in a ceasefire, but Zelensky then changed tack at the beginning of 2021 by clamping down on Putin's key Ukrainian ally Viktor Medvedchuk and launching a campaign for NATO membership.

Putin responded by positioning Russian troops on the Ukrainian border in March 2021. This started a period of dangerous brinkmanship and mishandled diplomacy between Moscow, Kyiv and the West. Failing to change the Ukrainian stance, Putin ordered an all-out invasion 11 months later.

UKRAINIAN REFUGEES

Maybe a Ukrainian restaurant popped up in your neighbourhood in recent years. The reason for that is the war. In the wake of Russian aggression, about 7 million Ukrainians fled the country. Most went to the EU, although a sizeable share preferred Russia for reasons pertaining to family or politics. Since Ukraine has banned draft-eligible men from leaving the country, the vast majority of refugees are women and children. This has created a demographic time bomb and is additionally a massive resilience test for families. The longer the war goes on, the more rooted the refugees become in their adopted countries and the less chance there is that they will ever return. Ukrainian refugees are proverbially industrious. In countries that have been smart about licensing and language classes, like Czechia, they are giving back more to local economies than they are taking. They also tend to be proud ambassadors of Ukrainian culture and cuisine. Be sure to visit your nearest *borsch* station when you get a chance.

TOOLKIT

The chapters in this section cover the most important topics you'll need to know about in Eastern Europe. They're full of nuts-and-bolts information and valuable insights to help you understand and navigate Eastern Europe and get the most out of your trip.

Getting Around the Region
p442

Accommodation
p444

Family Travel
p446

Health & Safe Travel
p448

Nuts & Bolts
p450

Food, Drink & Nightlife
p452

Responsible Travel
p454

LGBTIQ+ Travellers
p456

Accessible Travel
p457

Quirky Ways to Get Around
p458

Bridge over Soča River (p427), Slovenia

Getting Around the Region

Travelling around Eastern Europe is a wonderful experience. The region is less touristy and more undiscovered than Western Europe, which gives it a unique charm. Getting around by air is a breeze, the trains are scenic and the buses affordable.

TRAVEL COSTS

Train from Prague to Budapest
from €20

10-day Eurail/ Interrail pass
approx €447

Flight from London to Budapest
from €20

Petrol
€0.69 to €1.70 per litre

Air

There are many budget airlines operating in Eastern Europe; if you want to travel longer distances quickly, flying can be a good option. Major cities like Prague, Budapest, Kraków and Belgrade are connected by a full schedule of regular flights within the region, while other routes are seasonal and come to life only in summer or for the ski season. Bigger countries also have domestic flights, although unless you need to cover ground quickly, there's rarely a need to fly internally.

Train

Eastern Europe has a solid railway network, though the quality and punctuality can vary by country. Major railway hubs include Prague (Czechia), Budapest (Hungary), Bucharest (Romania) and Belgrade (Serbia). Albania has no international train services and trains aren't the best way to get around in countries like Montenegro, Moldova and North Macedonia.

Bus

Often the most affordable option for getting around, buses are a viable alternative to the railway network in many Eastern European countries. They're generally a better option for getting around in countries across the Balkans, including Albania, Bulgaria, Bosnia & Hercegovina, Croatia, Kosovo, Montenegro, North Macedonia and Serbia. Buses generally complement the rail system rather than duplicate it, though in some countries – notably Hungary, Czechia and Slovakia – you'll often have a choice between the two options.

Eurail/Interrail Pass

The Interrail (interrail.eu; for European residents) and Eurail (eurail.com; for non-European residents) passes offer unlimited train travel in many European countries. Prices vary, so do the maths to see if you'll end up saving money or not, as train travel in Eastern Europe is inexpensive.

DRIVING ESSENTIALS

Drive on the right, overtake on the left

Seatbelts are mandatory

.00

Blood-alcohol limit ranges from 0.0% to 0.3%

Tip

If you're covering long distances, consider overnight trains (eg Prague to Budapest). They're a good way to save on accommodation costs, but be sure to book your bunk in advance.

THE WAR IN UKRAINE

At the time of writing, Russia and Ukraine were still at war with each other, and though entering these countries is technically possible, travel is not recommended unless it is considered absolutely essential. If entering Ukraine, a valid passport and visa (if required) are mandatory, along with proof of the trip's purpose, financial solvency and comprehensive medical insurance covering potential military risks. All crossing points on the borders with Russia and Belarus are closed to foreigners. For more details on the associated risks, see our Russia coverage (p373), Ukraine coverage (p435) and Belarus coverage (p72).

Border Crossings

A key advantage of travelling within Europe, the Schengen Agreement – the world's biggest visa-free area – allows free movement of people within a large chunk of the continent, including Bulgaria, Croatia, Czechia, Estonia, Hungary, Latvia, Lithuania, Poland, Romania, Slovakia and Slovenia. Countries that aren't part of the agreement like Albania, Belarus, Bosnia & Hercegovina, Kosovo, Macedonia, Moldova, Montenegro, Serbia, Russia and Ukraine still require border checks. For up-to-date details, see schengenvisainfo.com. Once you enter a Schengen Area country, you can travel between all of the member states without border checks. You must still carry a valid passport or ID card and you may still be subject to occasional passport or identity document checks at airports or bus stations, especially in high-security periods.

Visas

Visas are generally not required for most Eastern European countries for stays of up to 90 days, but a few countries such as Russia (including Kaliningrad) and Belarus do require them for many nationalities. Do note, however, that at the time of writing, Lonely Planet did not recommend travel to either Russia or Belarus.

Digital Entry & Exit

In October 2025, the EU began the gradual rollout of a new Entry/Exit System (EES), with full implementation expected by April 2026. The new system will register all non-EU nationals travelling into and out of the Schengen Area. Upon your first entry into the Schengen Area, non-EU nationals will be fingerprinted and have their photo taken. This system will replace passport stamps.

LOCAL TRANSPORT

Eastern Europe's major cities generally have good public transport. The metro networks are excellent in Warsaw (Poland), Prague (Czechia), Budapest (Hungary), Bucharest (Romania) and Sofia (Bulgaria). Eastern European shared vans or cars (eg *furgon* in Albania) don't leave on a fixed schedule and serve as both inter- and intra-city transport. Trolleybuses powered by electricity and trams are also popular, though they vary greatly in speed and modernity.

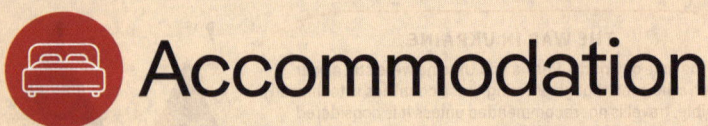

Accommodation

Hotels, hostels and Airbnbs are found all over Eastern Europe, but it's in the privately-owned pensions and guesthouses that you get a real feel for what life is like in this part of the world.

Hostels

You'll find a huge number of hostels in Eastern Europe, though they vary widely in character and quality. Generally, you get a bed for the night plus use of communal facilities, like a kitchen where you can prepare your own meals. Private hostels may also have amenities like lounges, laundry facilities and games rooms, while some in Prague, Bucharest and Budapest are serious party venues offering theme nights and pub crawls. Hostels in Eastern Europe are not only for the young.

Camping

Eastern Europe's numerous camping grounds are generally inexpensive and family friendly. They are best suited to beach holidays or travellers with cars, as they tend to be far from city attractions, though some are accessible by public transport. Many camping grounds in Eastern Europe rent small on-site cabins, bungalows or caravans for double or triple the camping fee. The standard varies from country to country: they're unreliable in Romania, crowded in Slovenia and Hungary (especially on Lake Balaton) and variable in Czechia, Poland, Slovakia and Bulgaria. Some countries, including Moldova and Belarus, have few official camping grounds, but you can usually find somewhere to pitch a tent. Croatia's coast has nudist camping grounds galore (signposted FKK, the German acronym for naturist), which enjoy secluded locations. Wild camping is legal in the Baltics and parts of Poland and the Balkans; ask local people about the situation before you pitch your tent on a beach or an open field.

Seasons

High season is usually in July and August, with a winter peak season around Christmas. Hostels and cheap hotels fill up quickly, especially in popular backpacker destinations such as Prague and Budapest.

European Tourist Tax

Also called a city tax, the European Tourist Tax usually consists of a fee that applies per person, per night, payable locally. Eastern EU countries have lower rates than Western and Southeastern EU countries.

STAY AT A REAL MANSION

If you're a romantic at heart, a fan of architecture or you're just after some *Downton Abbey* vibes, you're in for a treat with Eastern Europe's so-called castle hotels.

Set in elegant, historic mansions that are reminiscent of castles or palaces, these hotels offer an unforgettable experience, where you can feel like a king or queen for a day or two.

Hungary, Slovakia, Czechia, Slovenia and Poland all operate hotels in breathtaking buildings; just search for 'castle hotel' in your destination country to find them – in Hungary, the Association of Hungarian Castle Hotels runs an informative website (*kastelyszallodak.hu/en/hotels*).

Though they're normally pricier than an average hotel, castle hotels are not as expensive as a luxury five-star option.

Airbnb & Hotels

When travelling with your family or group of friends, renting an apartment on Airbnb could be an excellent option. They are often better value than a hotel room and you can self-cater, but the quality varies greatly.

All major capitals have beautiful boutique hotels and big-name five-star resorts with price tags to match, as well as cheaper but decent hotels galore. Breakfast is often included in the price of the room.

Guesthouses & Pensions

Private guesthouses or pensions are common throughout Eastern Europe. Often family-run, they offer a much more personal service than a hotel, though there's less privacy and it's generally a less polished operation – don't expect speedy wi-fi or a 24-hour reception desk. Guesthouses are priced somewhere between hotels and homestays, they typically have fewer than a dozen rooms and there may be a small restaurant or bar on the premises. The staff are often lovely and welcoming locals, but their English may be limited.

Homestays

Homestays are a wonderful way of getting a glimpse into local life – something you won't be able to do at a hotel or hostel. In many Eastern European countries like Czechia, Hungary or Slovenia, travel or tourist agencies can arrange accommodation in private rooms in local homes, or you can find options yourself on Airbnb or by searching online.

HOW MUCH FOR A NIGHT IN A...

Hostel
€10–20

Cheap hotel
€20–40

5-star hotel
€100–300

Castle hotel
€80–300

Glamping

Luxury tents, bungalows and pods featuring amenities like spas, hot tubs and gourmet dining...the glamping phenomenon has now reached Eastern Europe. The diverse nature experiences vary, from the Adriatic Coast of Croatia to the mountain regions of Romania to the natural beauty of Slovenia. Check out dedicated glamping platforms like Glamping Hub (glampinghub.com).

Rental Accommodation

If you're planning a longer stay, renting an apartment from a local could be exceptionally good value, and you can get a real feel for the city you're staying in. They're generally advertised in social media groups and through local agencies. Be vigilant: make sure there is an official contract and never send money in advance unless you're sure the deal is genuine.

SUSTAINABLE CHOICES

Farm lodgings and eco-minded homestays are a well-developed concept in several Eastern European countries, including Estonia, Hungary, Latvia, Lithuania, Slovenia and Serbia. It's like staying in a private room or pension, except that the participating farms are in picturesque rural areas and may have nearby activities such as horse riding, kayaking, skiing and cycling – though they may be far away from main cities. See World Wide Opportunities on Organic Farms (wwoof.net) for information about volunteering on organic farms in exchange for room and board. They're a great way to connect with locals and immerse yourself in a country's culture.

Family Travel

Eastern Europeans are family orientated and travelling here with your kids is generally hassle-free. Family discounts and reduced prices are common, and there are plenty of kid-friendly attractions.

Accommodation

While hotels can be a good option – many cater to families with larger rooms and play areas – privately-owned guesthouses can offer a more comfortable, home-like environment, and they may end up being much cheaper. In countries like Poland, Hungary, Romania, Croatia, Albania and Bulgaria, you can find clean, comfortable guesthouses with homely vibes. Private apartments booked through services like Airbnb or Booking.com may also offer all the mod cons and serve as a temporary home.

Family Facilities

Breastfeeding in public isn't that common in Eastern Europe, so discretion is advised. Outside hotels and the major capitals, nappy-changing facilities aren't always easy to find, nor are they reliably clean. Eastern Europe has tons of green spaces and playgrounds where children can let off some steam. Prams are widely used, so in bigger cities many restaurants and major sights are accessible.

Neccessities

Find items like baby food, infant formula, milk (soy and cow), disposable nappies and other essentials at supermarkets or pharmacies.

BEST ATTRACTIONS FOR FAMILIES

Lake Balaton, Hungary (p215) Central Europe's largest lake has famously shallow waters with slides and paddleboats.

Ljubljana Castle, Slovenia There are lots of activities designed especially for families and small children.

Postojna Cave, Sloveni Ride an underground mini train and spot stalagmite and stalactite formations.

Museum of Illusions, Zagreb Hologram pictures, puzzles and educational games offer a fun mental workout.

Kravica Waterfall, Bosnia & Hercegovina Make unforgettable memories of swimming beneath a waterfall.

FAMILY TRAVEL ON A BUDGET

Many museums, attractions and public-transport networks offer discounts for families, such as free or discounted entry for children up to a certain age or discounted tickets for larger families. If you have teens or older children, student ID cards often provide significant discounts for attractions, trains and buses. Some cities offer passes (eg Prague Card, Budapest Card) that provide access to multiple attractions at a reduced price, which may be worth it if you're planning to see multiple attractions in one city. At some breakfast cafes and restaurants, children can eat for half-price.

MULIGENERATIONAL LIVING

Multigenerational living, where three or more generations of a family live together, is more common in Eastern Europe than in the West, particularly in countries like Romania, Latvia and Bulgaria. Younger people, especially in the 25 to 35 age group, are more likely to live with their parents, due to economic constraints, job insecurity and cultural norms that emphasise strong family bonds. Eastern Europeans are highly family oriented.

Dining Out

Dining out is much cheaper than in Western Europe, and traditional Polish milk bars and Hungarian bistros offer hearty meals at a fraction of the price of a Western European equivalent. Most restaurants have highchairs – though the number may be limited – and a menu for kids that includes crowd-pleasers like chicken nuggets, chips and spaghetti. If you don't see a kids' menu, you can ask for a half-portion serving of something or a simple dish made especially for the little ones. If you'd like to save money, opt for self-catering meals by visiting local grocery stores or markets. Fresh produce is inexpensive in Eastern Europe.

Tip

Carry some coins for treats, especially for ice-cream, vending machines or purchases in small shops.

Driving

In many Eastern European countries, children under 12 are not permitted to sit in the front seat of a car and must instead sit in the back in a car seat, booster seat or booster cushion that's appropriate for their age and weight. Most car rental companies will have car seats.

Best Time to Visit

For pleasant weather and fewer crowds, consider travelling to major towns during spring (March to May) or autumn (September to November). These shoulder seasons may not be warm enough, however, for a proper family beach holiday in Croatia, Albania, Montenegro or Bulgaria, which are best in summer.

CHILDCARE

Childcare is considered more of a high-end service than in Western Europe, but may be available at some of the swankier hotels.

SANTA CLAUS IS COMING TO TOWN...EARLY

In some Eastern European countries, Santa Claus – Svatý Mikuláš in Czech, Mikulás in Hungarian, Sveti Nikola in Croatian, Święty Mikołaj in Polish – traditionally comes to town on the eve of 6 December, the feast day of St Nicholas, bringing gifts to well-behaved children. He is often accompanied by two helpers: a good angel and the mean, hairy, horned creature called Krampus who helps discipline the naughty ones. In countries like Hungary, Croatia, Slovakia, Ukraine and Romania, children typically leave their clean, shiny boots on the windowsill at night, which are filled with goodies by the next morning. On Christmas Eve, it's generally Baby Jesus who decorates the tree and leaves gifts for children. This means that various kid-friendly events start taking place in early December in most parts of Eastern Europe.

Health & Safe Travel

While Eastern Europe is generally safe for travellers, it's important to take certain precautions and consider health and safety factors to ensure your trip goes smoothly.

TRAVEL INSURANCE

For peace of mind, a travel-insurance policy to cover theft, loss and medical problems is always a good idea. Some insurance policies will specifically exclude 'dangerous activities', such as scuba diving, motorcycling and even hiking, while winter sports and car-rental coverage are sometimes limited. Always check the fine print. Check to see if your policy covers ambulances and an emergency flight home as well.

The European Health Insurance Card (EHIC)

With the European Health Insurance Card (EHIC), residents of EU countries and Switzerland, Iceland, Norway and Liechtenstein are entitled to free or reduced-cost emergency healthcare in EU countries under the same conditions as local residents. In the UK, the GHIC (Global Health Insurance Card) has replaced the EHIC. Every EU individual needs their own card, which covers urgent, temporary needs like emergency treatment and the management of chronic conditions, but does not cover planned medical treatment or private care. Healthcare systems and costs vary by country, so check the rules for your destination before you travel.

Alcohol

In many Eastern European countries, alcohol consumption plays a significant cultural role, and social drinking is deeply ingrained. Countries like Moldova, Belarus, Russia and Ukraine often rank among the highest in the world in terms of alcohol consumption. The region has a long history of alcohol production, particularly spirits, and each country has its own eau de vie, such as vodka in Poland and Russia, *pálinka* in Hungary and *raki* in the Balkans. Alcohol plays an important role in socialising – binge drinking is often normalised in some societies, and people may consume large quantities of alcohol in one sitting, especially in social settings or celebrations. And it may also lead to public health issues, including accidents – drink driving is a major problem – violence and overall well-being. For travellers, it's important to understand the local drinking culture. If invited to drink, it's polite to partake in a toast or share a drink, but you can always refuse if you don't wish to participate.

Basic Healthcare

In most of Eastern Europe, good basic healthcare is readily available and pharmacists can give valuable advice and sell over-the-counter medication for minor illnesses. If more specialised help is needed, they'll point you in the right direction. Capital cities all have major hospitals with English-speaking staff, but large hospitals can be found in numerous towns as well. By Western European or North American standards, healthcare is often cheap – though pricier in EU member states than in non-EU countries.

TAP WATER

In major cities in Eastern Europe, tap water is generally safe to drink. If you're unsure, especially in rural areas, check with locals.

Vaccinations

There are no mandatory vaccinations for entering Eastern Europe, but some are recommended. Routine vaccinations to consider are: MMR (measles, mumps and rubella), DTP (diphtheria, tetanus, pertussis), Hepatitis A and B, and rabies pre-exposure vaccine if you plan on spending a lot of time in remote places or in the company of animals. No matter what, you should always go to a hospital immediately if there is a chance you have been exposed to rabies. Note that most vaccines don't produce immunity until two weeks after the shot, so visit your doctor at least a month before departure to ensure you are up to date.

Drugs

Drugs are illegal in every country in Eastern Europe, and the region generally has a zero-tolerance policy toward drug use. The laws are strict and penalties can be severe. In the case of harder drugs, it's imprisonment. Avoid people trying to sell you questionable substances on the street at night.

Beach Safety

The Black Sea and Baltic Sea have varying levels of safety based on your specific location and potential hazards. While there are many areas that are safe for swimming and recreation, always use dedicated beaches and pay attention to local warnings.

WILDLIFE & INSECTS

Eastern Europe isn't home to many dangerous animals – bears and wolves live in remote mountainous regions of countries like Romania and Slovakia, but they tend to avoid humans. In forested areas, ticks can be a concern, as they can carry diseases like encephalitis and Lyme disease. Wear long sleeves and trousers when hiking, use insect repellent and check your body after hikes. In summer, mosquitoes can be abundant in swampy areas and near lakes.

Petty Crime & Scams

Eastern Europe is generally safe, but petty crime and scams can happen anywhere, so it's best to be vigilant. Be mindful of your belongings in crowded areas, especially on public transport, and avoid people aggressively selling stuff on the street. Don't leave anything of value, including luggage, on car seats. In big cities like Bucharest, Prague or Budapest, taxi drivers may try to overcharge tourists, so always use a reputable company or book through a reliable app like Uber or Bolt. Check the price of drinks at dodgy pubs and bars to avoid getting ripped off. Some people may pretend to be collecting donations for a charity – it's safer to avoid giving money to individuals and donate directly to an organisation.

Nuts & Bolts

Emergency number

The EU emergency number (112) is used widely in Eastern Europe. It works for urgent services including the police, fire and medical emergencies.

Internet Access

In all decent-sized towns in Eastern Europe, wi-fi is commonly available in cafes, hotels, restaurants, malls, hostels, libraries and other public spaces. In rural areas, especially mountainous ones, connections may be slow or even drop.

Major telecoms operators like T-Mobile, Vodafone or local carriers will have coverage throughout major cities and towns. SIM cards are often inexpensive and can be bought at the airport or online, and should include prepaid data.

Public Toilets

In most of Eastern Europe, public toilets are few and far between and often unclean. When present, they're often staffed and require a small fee. Locals generally prefer facilities in cafes, fast-food chains, museums or malls; you usually need to be a customer.

Time Zones

Eastern Europe spans three time zones: Central European Time (GMT+1), Eastern European Time (GMT+2) and Further-Eastern European Time or 'Moscow Time' (GMT+3). When it's noon in New York, it's 6pm in Warsaw, 7pm in Sofia and 8pm in Moscow. All countries, except Russia and Belarus, employ daylight savings. Clocks go forward an hour at the start of daylight savings, which is usually on the last Sunday in March. They are set back one hour on the last Sunday in October.

OPENING HOURS

Opening hours vary by country; we've listed the most common hours here. Saturday and Sunday are official days off, though most shops and cafes are open daily.

Banks 9am–4pm

Bars and clubs 6pm–late

Breakfast cafes 8am–6pm

General working hours 9am–6pm

Restaurants 11am–11pm

Shops and stores 9am–7pm, reduced hours or closed on Sundays

Supermarkets 7am–9pm, reduced hours or closed on Sundays

Smoking

While smoking rules in the region vary by country, they are generally moving towards more comprehensive bans in public spaces, aligning with EU directives. Smoking indoors is largely banned across enclosed public spaces, including restaurants, bars, workplaces, hospitals, public transport terminals and educational institutions. Many countries, like Lithuania, Latvia, Hungary and Croatia, prohibit smoking within a few metres of school entrances, playgrounds, and bus and train stops. In Lithuania, smoking is even prohibited on apartment balconies if at least one neighbour objects. In Hungary, smoking-related products can only be purchased in state-licenced tobacco shops.

Electricity
Types C & F
220-240V

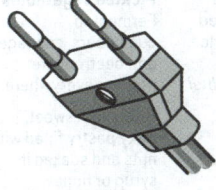 

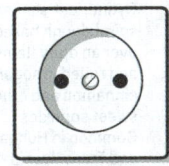 

Type C
220V/50Hz

Type F
230V/50Hz

ETIQUETTE

Greetings A firm but friendly handshake is a common greeting, especially when meeting somebody for the first time. Women generally give each other air kisses, but it depends on familiarity and personal preference.

Gifts If you're invited to a local household, it's polite to bring something small and thoughtful as a gift. For men, it's generally a bottle of alcohol. For women, a bouquet of flowers will do – make sure you give an odd number of flowers, as even numbers are generally reserved for funerals.

Manners Eastern Europeans may be more direct and personal than you are used to. It's part of the culture and isn't meant to be rude or intrusive. To some travellers, Eastern Europeans' dour expressions come off as serious or unfriendly, but it's just a cultural norm. Under the surface, people are warm and hospitable.

PUBLIC HOLIDAYS

The following list is not exhaustive. Public holidays also comprise national days, saints' days, International Women's Day and other celebrations depending on the country. Some countries celebrate Orthodox Christmas Eve (6 January) and Christmas Day (7 January). Here's an overview of some significant public holidays across Eastern Europe.

New Year's Day
1 January

Orthodox Christmas (Julian calendar)
7 January

Easter dates vary according to Eastern and Western Christian traditions

Labour Day 1 May

Christmas Day (Gregorian calendar)
25 December

Food, Drink & Nightlife

TOOLKIT

FOOD, DRINK & NIGHTLIFE

When to Eat

Breakfast 7am–10am. A simple meal of bread, cold cuts, cheese, yoghurt and coffee or tea.

Lunch noon–2pm. The biggest meal of the day, generally consisting of soup, meat, potatoes and dessert. Set meal deals are common.

Dinner 6pm–9pm. A lighter meal than lunch; often consists of leftovers.

Where to Eat

Bistros Many countries have casual eateries that serve traditional food like chicken paprikash, pierogi and schnitzel with local beer and wine. Look for bistros or *étkezde* in Hungary and *bar mleczny* in Poland.

Kafanas Traditional taverns or inns found across the Balkans, often with live folk music. Hearty stews, grilled meats *(ćevapi)* and local spirits feature.

Ruin bars Budapest is the home of ruin bars: derelict buildings that have been transformed into eclectic, relaxed drinking spaces.

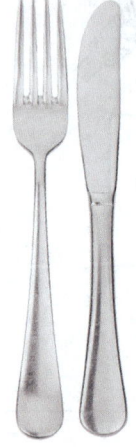

MENU DECODER

Borscht A sour ruby-red soup, typically made of beetroot.

Stuffed cabbage Cabbage rolls filled with a mixture of rice, meat and spices. Often called *holubtsi* or *sarma*.

Gulyás/Goulash Hungary's famously hearty beef and vegetable-based soup.

Burek Flaky pastry with various fillings, common in the Balkans.

Pierogi Meat- or vegetable-filled dumplings, common in Poland.

Kielbasa Polish sausages.

Latke Fried potato pancakes, popular among Eastern Europe's Jewish communities.

Pickled vegetables Fermented cucumbers, cabbage and beetroot are popular everywhere.

Baklava A sweet, flaky pastry filled with nuts and soaked in syrup or honey.

Kürtőskalács Cylindrical-shaped spiral dough baked over an open flame and rolled in sugar, cinnamon and other sweet sprinkles. Common in Hungary and Transylvania.

Medovik Russian honey cake.

Marlenka Honey cake similar to *medovik*.

HOW TO...

How to Sample Eastern Europe's Street Food

Most Eastern European countries have some sort of street food, and trying these dishes is a great way to experience the region's diverse flavours and blend in with locals. In Poland, pierogi (dumplings) are unmissable – find them at numerous *pierogarnia* on street corners. In Hungary, try *lángos*, a deep-fried disk-shaped dough topped with sour cream, shredded cheese and garlic oil. Look for it at markets. Romania loves *mici*, juicy sausages typically sold with mustard and bread; they're popular at markets in Bucharest or Cluj. In the Balkans, *burek* is king, a flaky pastry stuffed with meat, cheese or spinach; find them in bakeries from Sarajevo to Belgrade. Serbia and Bulgaria also have grilled meats like *ćevapi* or *kebapche*. For something sweet, try *kürtőskalács:* a cylindrical pastry baked over coals and rolled in sugar, cinnamon or other sweet toppings.

HOW MUCH FOR...

a pint of beer
€1.50–4

a glass of wine
€2–5

a burek
€1–2.50

an espresso
€1–2.50

a midrange meal
€10–20

a Michelin-starred meal
€100–200

a scoop of ice-cream
€1.50–3

a public transport ticket
€1–2

HOW TO...

How to Enjoy Eastern Europe's Nightlife

Eastern Europe has a lively nightlife scene, especially in big cities like Belgrade, Prague, Kraków and Budapest. Ease into the pre-game – locals usually gather at bars and pubs from 8pm onwards to eat something before a big night out. Kraków has great vodka bars, the beer cellars in Prague are unbeatable and ruin bars are a Budapest phenomenon. Go easy with traditional spirits like vodka, *pálinka* or *raki* – they kick like a mule. As Eastern Europe parties late, clubs usually don't fill up until midnight or 1am, with the biggest crowds peaking around 2am or 3am. Locals are generally welcoming to foreigners and a night out can be spontaneous, so be open to going with the flow – but always make sure to look after yourself and know your limits. Ride-sharing apps like Bolt and Uber are widely used and safer than random taxis when going home. Though rowdy stag dos are common, these are mostly comprised of foreigners; locals party in a more peaceful manner. So start slow, stay late, dress smart and embrace the unexpected – while staying aware of your surroundings. Whether you sip craft beer in Prague, toast *pálinka* with new friends in Budapest or dance the night away at a *splav* (floating bar) in Belgrade, you're in for a night you'll (hopefully) always remember – cheers!

The Grandaddy of Ruin Bars

Opened in 2004, Budapest's **Szimpla Kert** is widely regarded as a pioneer of the ruin bar concept, which involves converting abandoned buildings or old courtyards into a relaxed lounge space with mismatched furniture and eclectic decor.

SOUP CULTURE

Some travellers may be surprised by the sheer amount of soup that Eastern Europeans consume, come rain or shine. It plays a central role in everyday meals and it's always on the menu. As winters can be harsh in this part of the world, traditional soups are hot and filling, using ingredients like root vegetables, lentils, cabbages, meat and bones. In some countries like Hungary, cold fruit soups take over in summer. Soup is not considered to be an optional starter but the first course of a structured meal, especially at lunch. This comfort food is passed down through the generations – every Eastern European grandma has a signature soup recipe. Meaty soups are often consumed with bread, which you use to clean your bowl. Some of Eastern Europe's best soups are meaty goulash from Hungary, Polish *żurek*, a sour rye soup with sausages, Ukrainian *borscht*, Russian *solyanka* with meat and vegetables, and garlicky *česnečka* from Slovakia and Czechia. In many countries, especially Romania, Hungary and Poland, restaurants offer a fixed-price lunch menu, which usually consists of two or three courses for less than €10. A three-course daily menu includes soup, a main dish and a dessert, and if you opt for a two-course option, you can choose whether you'd like soup or dessert with your main dish. Eastern Europeans will also gladly share their soup recipes, so heading to a local market for ingredients and making your own soup is a special experience.

Responsible Travel

Climate Change & Travel

It's impossible to ignore the impact we have when travelling; Lonely Planet urges all travellers to engage with their travel carbon footprint, which will mainly come from air travel. While there often isn't an alternative, travellers can look to minimise the number of flights they take, opt for newer aircrafts and use cleaner ground transport, such as trains.

One proposed solution—purchasing carbon offsets—unfortunately does not cancel out the impact of individual flights. While most destinations will depend on air travel for the foreseeable future, for now, pursuing ground-based travel where possible is the best course of action.

The **UN Carbon Offset Calculator** shows how flying impacts a household's emissions

The **ICAO's carbon emissions calculator** allows visitors to analyse the CO_2 generated by point-to-point journeys

Use Public Transport

In most countries, especially in major capitals, the public transport system is well-developed and affordable. Choose buses, trams or metros over taxis or private cars.

Skip the Plane

The region has long been accessible by train and bus. Major hubs are Prague (Czechia), Budapest (Hungary), Bucharest (Romania) and Belgrade (Serbia). A few countries, like Albania, have no international train services.

Long-distance hiking and cycling trails crisscross the region, and following one isn't just good for the environment, but also provides insight into Eastern Europe's most beautiful landscapes.

Instead of going into touristy shops, buy from local artisans to support the community. Their crafts make better and more authentic gifts.

SLEEP SUSTAINABLY

Eastern Europe has private pensions and guesthouses galore, so opt for locally run accommodation over big-name hotels. Support businesses that are cutting down on single-use plastic and water waste and have sustainability certifications.

While English is widely spoken in major cities, the more rural you get, the less you'll hear. Being able to say a few words in the local language can go a long way.

Go Local

Whether you're embarking on a walking tour or hiking in a national park, try to use a local guide. Hearing stories from local people brings the region to life, plus you're supporting local businesses.

Respect Nature & Wildlife

Eastern Europe is home to beautiful landscapes and colourful flora and fauna. When hiking or visiting nature reserves, always stay on marked trails.

Travel Off-Peak

Bucket-list destinations like Budapest, Prague and Dubrovnik get crowded in summer, so plan your trip for the spring or autumn if possible to avoid contributing to (and having to deal with) overtourism.

Eat Local Food

Dine at local, eco-conscious restaurants or markets that prioritise organic produce and locally sourced ingredients. You'll find many small eateries and markets that support small-scale farmers around the region.

Opt for Eco-Friendly Tours

Eco-friendly walks and hikes are available in many Eastern European countries. When embarking on hikes in the mountains or national parks, pick tours that prioritise responsible tourism.

Bike-share schemes are common in big cities and are easy on the environment.

Many cities and towns have drinking fountains where you can refill your water bottle.

Green Capital

In 2025, Vilnius (Lithuania) was named the European Green Capital by the European Commission, recognising its commitment to sustainability, climate action and smart urban development.

RESOURCES

seat61.com
Tips on navigating Eastern Europe's rail system.

worldpackers.com
Volunteer work in eco-villages around Eastern Europe.

wwfadria.org
Region-wide outpost of the WWF, protecting natural resources.

LGBTIQ+ Travellers

Aside from a few progressive places, Eastern Europe's stance on LGBTIQ+ issues isn't all rainbows and butterflies. Highly conservative views and even homophobia still linger in some places, though attitudes are slowly changing. While life can be difficult for local LGBTIQ+ communities, travellers aren't generally affected as long as they're reasonably discreet.

An Outdated Mindset

Eastern Europe presents a complex, challenging landscape for LGBTIQ+ communities. Generally, the rights of and attitudes towards LGBTIQ+ people are less progressive when compared to Western Europe or some parts of North America. Social attitudes, legal frameworks and protections for LGBTIQ+ individuals differ greatly between countries in the region. While some countries like Czechia, Estonia and Slovenia have the best reputation for acceptance, the stance of other countries – such as Russia, Ukraine, Hungary, Belarus, Romania and Poland – are out of step with the rest of Europe.

PRIDE PARADES

Most major cities have festive annual Pride marches. Some like Prague Pride, Tallinn Pride or Ljubljana Pride are more progressive and generally safer, while others like Budapest Pride, Belgrade Pride or Warsaw Pride can face more opposition from nationalist or far-right groups, though these events are generally well-protected by police and recent parades have taken place without major incidents.

Generational Differences

In general, younger generations in Eastern Europe have greater access to more progressive ideas through social media, travel and education, making them more accepting of LGBTIQ+ communities than older generations, who may harbour homophobic or transphobic views reinforced by political parties, church authorities and state-sponsored media.

LEGAL DISCRIMINATION

While some countries like Russia or Hungary still actively impose laws against local LGBTIQ+ communities, making their lives rather difficult, this doesn't necessarily reflect the attitude of the general population and travellers aren't usually affected.

PDA

Public displays of affection may still be risky or attract negative attention in some Eastern European countries, especially outside major capitals. You may get looks and an occasional snarky comment but should not face any serious issues if you're reasonably discreet.

SMALL BUT SOLID GAY SCENE

Though perhaps not as famously open, accepting or visible as in some European capitals like Berlin or Lisbon, most major cities do have a small but active gay scene with LGBTIQ+-friendly clubs, cafes and bars – even in Moscow, St Petersburg and Budapest. However, establishments can be low-key. Outside major towns, LGBTIQ+ life may be completely invisible.

⬤ Accessible Travel

Eastern Europe can generally be challenging for travellers with disabilities, though it depends greatly on the destination. While individual museums, sights and hotels are being brought up to Western European standards of accessibility, implementation is uneven. Off the beaten track, facilities are almost non-existent and transport presents a challenge.

Cobblestones

The region has many charming old towns, where cobblestoned lanes and steps can prove extremely challenging for the mobility-impaired. Plan to tram/bus hop between sights.

Airport

Most major airports in Eastern Europe are accessible and offer assistance in terminals, the use of wheelchairs and aid with boarding. Airlines must be notified at least 48 hours in advance.

Accommodation

Accessible accommodation is widely available In major cities, especially at well-known hotel chains. Regional examples also exist, but specific research is necessary. Euan's Guide (*euansguide.com*), a disabled access review, can be handy.

RESOURCES

Accessable (*disabledaccessible travel.com*) Has a wide range of bespoke services for travellers in need of adapted solutions.

Wheelchair Traveling (*wheelchairtraveling. com*) The personal website of accessible-travel advocate John Morris, with helpful tips on wheelchair travel.

Accessible Prague (*accessibleprague. com*) A local travel agency for people living with disabilities, with useful information on accommodation, transport, tours and equipment rental.

ACCESSIBLE BEACHES

For a list of accessible beaches across Croatia, download the handy Plaja Beach Finder app (*plaja.hr*). Some, like Borak Beach near Bol, have special chair lifts to access the water.

BE MY EYES

This app connects people who are blind or have impaired vision with volunteers and companies worldwide through live video chat. You can connect to a volunteer anytime for help. Download the app at *bemyeyes.com*.

Accessible Cities

Some of Eastern Europe's most accessible cities are Warsaw (Poland), Prague (Czechia), Tallinn (Estonia), Riga (Latvia) and Bratislava (Slovakia).

Friendly Festival

One of Europe's major music events, Budapest's Sziget Festival, is accessible and home to XS Land, an interactive experience park with a focus on various disabilities.

Eastern Europe's natural attractions are often assumed to be off-limits for disabled travellers. To resolve this, projects like Access Routes (Estonia/Latvia) are creating tactile maps, digital platforms and accessible trails, while Croatia and Slovenia highlight accessible beaches and national parks.

Quirky Ways to Get Around

Getting from A to B in Eastern Europe isn't so much about the destination but the journey, especially if you factor in some of the quirky means of transport and travel conditions the region offers. Sharing a minivan – and coffee stops – with locals, speeding over the frozen Baltic Sea with seatbelts unbuckled and getting waved on by a ten-year-old signalman are all possible in Eastern Europe.

Shared Minivans

One of the most local travel experiences you can have in Eastern Europe is hopping on a shared minivan, known as a *marshrutka*, *furgon* or *kombi*, and common in Albania, Kosovo, North Macedonia, Bosnia, Montenegro, Bulgaria, Moldova, Romania and parts of the Baltics. They connect towns, villages and sometimes even city neighbourhoods and don't really have a fixed schedule – they only leave when they're full. You can find them clustered in parking lots close to stations; pay the driver with cash. On board, the driver often listens to local music, chats with passengers, and stops for cigarettes and coffee while passengers come and go. Expect people to squeeze in beyond official capacity, and to get on or off at random locations. Shared minivans are cheap, charmingly chaotic and a great way to connect with local culture.

Road Conditions & Driving Culture

Roads in the region vary from pristine highways in Poland or Slovenia to potholed obstacle courses in Moldova, Albania and Romania. In some countries, especially in the Balkans, traffic rules may not always be strictly followed, and driving can sometimes be chaotic with drivers not always staying in their lanes or obeying traffic lights. Locals drive confidently and may overtake you even on winding mountain roads – it's not for the faint of heart. In rural areas, goats and donkeys sometimes share the road, while horse-drawn carts sometimes trot alongside cars. Hitchhiking is still relatively common and safe, and in rural areas locals may offer rides to strangers as a gesture of kindness.

Ice Driving in Estonia

Unbuckle your seatbelts, unlock the doors and step on the gas. No, this is not a trailer for the latest instalment of *Fast & Furious*, but a description of what it's like to drive across the Estonian ice. Along the Baltic coast is a network of officially recognised ice roads that are open whenever it's cold enough for the sea to freeze over – generally January to late March. There are 80km of roads altogether, the longest stretching 25km between the mainland and the island of Hiiumaa. Though the main goal is to facilitate getting around, these roads continue to entice daring tourists every year. The roads are safe; it's always clearly indicated which roads are open and the ice quality and thickness is examined on a regular basis. You should know the rules, however: seatbelts are discouraged, and the doors should be unlocked in case you need to make a speedy exit. Keep a minimum distance of 250 metres from the car ahead of you in order to avoid putting too much load on the ice, and go fast or go slow – just never stop.

The officially recommended speed is either below 25 km/h or between 40 and 70 km/h.

Speeds between 25 and 40 km/h are the most dangerous, as your car can cause a wave that breaks the ice.

A RAILWAY RUN BY CHILDREN

A unique attraction in Budapest is the Children's Railway (pictured; p205), a throwback to Communist-era travel that's operated almost entirely by kids. The sweet-looking staff wear blue, white and red uniforms and hold all positions on the train, from conductors to signallers, while a little adult supervision keeps things on track (the engineers are grown-ups). The Children's Railway is the longest narrow-gauge children's railway line in the world and earned an inclusion in the Guinness World Records; working on it is considered a real honour. The quirky ride takes travellers around the prettiest excursion spots of Budapest and the staff are the loveliest in Hungary.

Trolley Buses

Electric buses running on overhead wires are common everywhere, and Soviet-built models are still in operation. They're slightly slower than regular buses but are eco-friendly and quirky.

Scenic Trams

Many Eastern European cities offer squeaky tram rides that seem like a journey from another era, and these old red-and-cream or sunflower-yellow trams still run alongside sleek modern ones. Prague has one of the best tram networks in Europe, while Budapest's line 2 is often called one of the most beautiful tram rides in the world – it doubles as a cheap sightseeing tour. While they're a part of everyday life for locals, travellers often find them photogenic.

LIFTS THAT NEVER STOP

A paternoster – named after the opening words of the Lord's Prayer for its resemblance to a giant rosary – is a series of open cubicles that rotate continuously in a loop. There's no button to push or door to open; you simply hop on when a cubicle reaches your floor level and jump out when you reach your desired floor. Though they're rare today, some are still found in government buildings and ministries in Czechia and Hungary. You can take a tour on a paternoster in Prague's City Hall.

STORYBOOK

Our writers delve deep into different aspects of Eastern European life.

A History of Eastern Europe in 15 Places

Eastern Europe has a truly tumultuous, complex and eventful history.

Kata Fári

p462

Yugoslav Modernist Architecture & Monuments

Learn the story of Yugoslavia's magnificent modernist masterpieces.

Vesna Maric

p466

Food, Music & Tradition in Northwest Balkans

A braided cultural continuity, even in difficult times.

Katherina Grace Thomas

p469

Europe on the Brink

Europe today is facing unprecedented challenges from Russian aggression and the surge of the far-right.

Anna Kaminski

p472

The Railway Unlinking the Baltics from Their Past

The infrastructure project that is redefining European connectivity and reshaping politics.

Angelo Zinna

p476

Lake Ohrid (p308), North Macedonia
SENNARELAX/SHUTTERSTOCK

HISTORY OF EASTERN EUROPE IN
15 PLACES

Conflicts between empires, fights for independence and shifting borders – Eastern Europe has a truly tumultuous, complex and eventful history. With Yugo-nostalgia very much a thing and the Soviet Union's legacy present throughout the region, the past is never too far away here. And with the ongoing Russo-Ukrainian war, history is still in the making. By Kata Fári

IN 2025, A discovery at Grăunceanu in Romania revealed evidence of human activity that was at least 1.95 million years old – currently the oldest known traces of hominins in Europe. Much has transpired since, but in a nutshell, Eastern Europe's history has mainly been characterised by fighting for territory: the Greeks and Romans in ancient times, the Magyars and Mongols in the Middle Ages, the Ottomans and Habsburgs in the early modern period, and Nazi Germany and the Soviets in the 20th century. Over the centuries, Eastern Europe's small but feisty kingdoms have constantly fought for their independence, and Ukraine is still struggling to break away from Russian repression.

Today, the Ottoman Empire, the Austro-Hungarian Empire, Yugoslavia, Czechoslovakia, the Soviet Union and the Eastern Bloc are all things of the past. The now independent and individual countries have started to navigate the challenges of democratisation, market economies and solidifying their shift towards the Western side of the continent by joining institutions like the EU and NATO. The region's resilience in maintaining its national identities, languages and cultural practices offers a profound lesson in endurance.

1. Lepenski Vir, Serbia
THE DAWN OF CIVILISATION
Evidence of human presence in Eastern Europe dates back to the Paleolithic era, with sites in Romania, Russia and the Balkans showing the earliest of human activity. What is now Đerdap National Park was once a major centre for Mesolithic- and Neolithic-era fishing communities, a past that has been wonderfully preserved in Belgrade's unsung National Museum. Religious and workaday artefacts, sculptures and skeletons dating back as far as 7000 BCE are all on display. Perhaps the most impressive is the world-famous *Foremother* and several other sculptures of fish-like idols with human faces.

For more on artefacts from Lepenski Vir, see p384.

2. Butrint, Albania
CLASSICAL ANTIQUITY
Butrint's ruins, in a fantastic natural setting, span a variety of periods over 2500 years. In the 1st millennium BCE, the Illyrian tribes dominated a chunk of the Western Balkans, and their language is considered a precursor of Albanian. Gradually, the Hellenist (Greek) tribes established colonies along the Black Sea and the Med-

iterranean coast and built the first city and later Butrint's celebrated site: the theatre. The Romans followed, building a forum, thermal baths and more. Then came the Byzantines, who built a well-kept 6th-century Great Basilica, and the Venetians, responsible for a 16th-century tower and triangular castle.

For more on Butrint, see p63.

3. Ohrid, North Macedonia
RISING SLAVIC KINGDOMS
From the 6th century on, Slavic tribes inhabited a large portion of Central and Eastern Europe. Over the next two centuries, they expanded westwards to the Elbe River and the Alps, southwards into the Balkans, and eastwards in the direction of the Volga River. Early Slavs settled around sublime Lake Ohrid, establishing the city of Ohrid and making it a significant centre of culture and missionary work. They turned the city into a hub of Slavic literacy and Christianity, especially with the establishment of the Ohrid Literary School in 886 CE, solidifying its importance in early Slavic history and culture.

For more on Ohrid, see p308.

Piran (p429), Slovenia

RUDY BALASKO/SHUTTERSTOCK

4. Budapest, Hungary
THE HUNGARIAN CONQUEST
In the late 9th and early 10th centuries, the Magyars settled in Central Europe. Grand Prince of the Hungarians, Árpád, led the Magyars into the region in 895, crushing the First Bulgarian Tsardom and settling in the Great Hungarian Plain. They soon secured the territory, and in 1000 CE established the Kingdom of Hungary, which would become a significant Christian power in Central Europe for centuries. From the crowning of Saint Stephen, the first king of Hungary, the Árpád Dynasty ruled for 300 years. Today's Millennium Monument in Budapest's Heroes' Square is a key sight related to the Hungarian Conquest.

For more on Heroes' Square, see p211.

5. Sighişoara, Romania
A SAXON FORTRESS
Starting in the 10th century, the Magyars began to expand into Transylvania, forming a fragmented feudal system that was ruled over by a military class. By the 13th century, the area became an autonomous principality under the Hungarian crown. Following devastating Tatar raids on Transylvania in 1241 and 1242, King Bela IV of Hungary persuaded ethnic Germans from around Luxembourg to settle and defend the area by offering free land and tax incentives. The 'Saxons', as they are called, built cities, churches and fortresses across the region. The most spectacular is, arguably, the Citadel at Sighişoara.

For more on the Citadel, see p359.

6. Piran, Slovenia
MINI-VENICES ALL AROUND
Beginning in the 13th century, the Venetian Republic established dominion over the coast of Istria, founding a pseudo-empire along the eastern Adriatic in modern-day Slovenia, Croatia and Albania. They shaped the region's architecture, culture and maritime trade: in Piran, for example, flourishing salt commerce fostered an economic, architectural and spiritual boom. At one point in 1797, little Piran had not only a monastery, but also more than 23 churches. To this day, the town remains a repository of Venetian Gothic architecture, and it's hard to imagine a more romantic spot anywhere.

For more on Piran, see p429.

7. Tallinn, Estonia
THE FORERUNNER OF THE EU

Meanwhile, in 13th-century Northern Europe, the Hanseatic League – an association of merchants and cities – was coming into being. For more than 400 years, it influenced the economy, trade and politics of Northern Europe, and its members spanned from England to Russia. The Baltic League component dominated trade in the region, with cities in modern-day Estonia, Latvia and Lithuania becoming key centres of commerce and influence. The Hanseatic-era shipwreck exhibited in Tallinn's Maritime Museum is an important piece of the puzzle. The 700-year-old vessel offers a rare glimpse into a chapter of European history that was written on water.

For more on Tallinn's Maritime Museum, see p183.

8. Bitola, North Macedonia
OTTOMAN RULE

In the 14th century, the Ottoman Turks began expanding into Eastern Europe and occupied much of the Balkans and parts of Hungary. Centuries of Muslim rule followed, and many people converted to Islam. The diplomatic and cultural centre of the Ottoman Empire in the Balkans was Bitola, where Ottoman influence echoes in buildings like the 16th-century Yeni, Isak and Yahdar-Kadi Mosques. The lively Stara Čaršija (Old Bazaar) was an important trade centre with more than a thousand craft shops. Wandering around the cobblestone streets is a fun experience today, and offers the opportunity to grab some bargains and authentic souvenirs.

For more on Bitola, see p311.

9. Olomouc, Czechia
FRANZ JOSEPH ASSUMES THE THRONE

Signed on 26 January 1699, the Treaty of Karlowitz was a pivotal agreement that forced the Ottomans to cede large territories including Hungary, Transylvania and Croatia to the Habsburg Monarchy, establishing the latter as the dominant power in Central Europe. For centuries, the stately college town of Olomouc served as a bastion of support for the ruling Habsburgs. During the revolution of 1848, when the emerging middle classes revolted against their rulers, the Habsburgs fled here for their personal safety. Austrian Emperor Franz Joseph I was even crowned emperor at Olomouc's Archbishop's Palace that year at the tender age of 18.

For more on Olomouc, see p168.

10. Soča Valley, Slovenia
WORLD WAR I

World War I began on 28 July 1914, when Austria-Hungary declared war on Serbia. Though the assassination of Archduke Franz Ferdinand in Sarajevo a month earlier was the catalyst, a complex system of alliances quickly drew other European nations into the conflict, turning it into a global war. The Isonzo Front in the Soča Valley saw some of the bloodiest battles of WWI. Today, a long-distance hiking trail from the Julian Alps to Trieste on the Adriatic connects Slovenia and Italy's WWI heritage sites. Museums, cemeteries, memorials and chapels record the lives lost and promote peace between nations.

For more on Soča Valley, see p427.

11. Auschwitz-Birkenau, Poland
THE HOLOCAUST

There's hardly another place that's a better example of the horrors of WWII than the Auschwitz-Birkenau complex. The Auschwitz extermination camp was established in prewar Polish army barracks on the outskirts of Oświęcim by the German occupiers in April 1940. The much larger camp at Birkenau (Brzezinka) was built 2km west of the original site in 1941 and 1942, followed by another one in Monowitz (Monowice), several kilometres to the west. Auschwitz-Birkenau is now synonymous with the Holocaust. More than a million Jews, and many Poles and Roma, were murdered here by German Nazis during WWII. It's essential to visit both to appreciate the extent and horror of the place.

For more on Auschwitz-Birkenau, see p331.

12. Tirana, Albania
SURVEILLANCE UNDER SOCIALISM

Following WWWII most of Eastern Europe was under the control of the USSR, though the countries of the Eastern Bloc all had their own homegrown tyrants. One of the most notorious was Albania's Enver Hoxha, who coordinated a vast network of spies at the House of Leaves: an interroga-

Hill of Crosses (p263), Lithuania

tion and surveillance centre, aka a place of torture. Home to the Museum of Secret Surveillance today, numerous surveillance items and quite a few graphic details suggest what happened to those considered enemies of the regime. Similar establishments functioned in other Eastern Bloc countries, too.

For more on the House of Leaves, see p59.

13. Belgrade, Serbia

A CRASH COURSE ON YUGOSLAVIA

Yugoslavia was a multinational state founded after WWWI and later a socialist federation under president-for-life Josip Broz Tito, from 1945 until 1980. Following Tito's death and the collapse of communism, rising feelings of nationalism led to Yugoslavia's disturbing and violent disintegration in the early 1990s. Visiting Serbia's Museum of Yugoslavia, which houses an invaluable collection of more than 200,000 artefacts, provides insight into the tumultuous history of Yugoslavia. There are photographs, artworks, historical documents, films, weapons and priceless treasure, while Marshal Tito's Mausoleum is located in the House of Flowers on the museum's grounds.

For more on the Museum of Yugoslavia, see p383.

14. Pristina, Kosovo

EUROPE'S YOUNGEST CAPITAL

Kosovo declared its independence from Serbia on 17 February 2008, which offi-cially makes it Europe's youngest country. Though not on most travellers' radar, the capital Pristina is a fast-changing city full of optimism and potential. While there are a couple of worthwhile museums and galleries, as well as interesting nearby sights, Pristina is a place where the atmosphere is as much an attraction as any tourist landmark. Littered with mismatched brutalist architecture and post-socialist concrete blocks, Pristina is not a conventionally pretty capital, but it is full of youthful energy and vibrancy, which gives it an especially unique feel in Europe.

For more on Pristina, see p226.

15. Hill of Crosses, Lithuania

SOLEMN COMMEMORATION

Over 100,000 crosses, crucifixes, statues, rosaries and religious icons are crammed onto a small hill 12km north of Šiauliai. The exact origins of Lithuania's Kryžių Kalnas, or Hill of Crosses, remain a mystery, though the tradition of leaving crosses on the hill is believed to have started after the 1831 uprising as a quiet act of resistance against Russian rule. Despite many attempts to destroy it over the past decades, this unusual, eerie and profoundly moving sight remains filled with commemorations. Today, the Hill of Crosses is as much a pilgrimage sight as a symbol of defiance, resilience, freedom and hope – sentiments that describe all of Eastern Europe.

For more on the Hill of Crosses, see p263.

465

YUGOSLAV MODERNIST ARCHITECTURE & MONUMENTS

Learn the story of Yugoslavia's magnificent Modernist masterpieces. By Vesna Maric

AS SOMEONE WHO grew up in Yugoslavia, I always have a warm feeling in my heart when I remember the socialist blocks we lived in and the monuments we visited: the unique designs, the beautiful light, the green spaces where we played, and the humanist, eccentric and always liveable, never exclusive, architecture of our youth.

But when I emigrated to the UK, no one believed me when I said that we had none of the 'drab Soviet tower blocks' that Westerners associated with the so-called Eastern Bloc. If I spoke of the spaces and architecture, I was regarded with a quizzical look that signified my communist brainwashing. In 2019, some 30-odd years after the 1990s war, New York's MoMA hosted the exhibition 'Towards a Concrete Utopia – Architecture in Yugoslavia 1948–1980'. The museum stated that the exhibition 'introduced the exceptional work of socialist Yugoslavia's leading architects to an international audience for the first time, high-

lighting a significant yet thus-far understudied body of Modernist architecture, whose forward-thinking contributions still resonate today.' I felt vindicated!

The Architecture

Yugoslavia sat between the West and East, politically and geographically. Its socialism was based on 'self-management', an economic model founded by Edvard Kardelj, in which workers were direct owners of their enterprise, whether it was inside the factory or within an architectural endeavour. In order for self-management to work, a massive education project had to take place in a largely agrarian society, where illiteracy in the post-WWII period was over 80%. The rebuilding effort meant that schools, kindergartens and worker universities were of the utmost architectural priority. By 1959, 129 universities had been built, with the most impressive design being Radovan Nikšić and Ninoslav Kučan's Novi Zagreb

University, whose open spaces and flexible designations were conceived entirely to be comfortably inhabited. Other examples are the surreal Museum of Contemporary Art in Belgrade, designed by Ivan Antić and Ivanka Raspopović, which resembles a space-beehive with its glass grids and angular skylights. Sarajevo's History Museum of Bosnia & Hercegovina is a marble cube resting impossibly atop a transparent, glass structure. It was the pride and joy of the city. Designed in 1963 in the International Style by Boris Magaš, with Edo Šmidihen and Radovan Horvat, it is now largely dilapidated, poorly funded and forgotten.

But despite the neglect of post-war governments across the former Yugoslavia, most of these structures are still in use and can be visited. In fact, with the Instagram-inspired resurgence of love for brutalist architecture, much of Yugoslavia's extraordinary design has become more popular and visible in recent years. Stylistic trends of the moment notwithstanding, it's essential to keep in mind that Yugoslav Modernism had important political and historical content. For example, the right to housing in Yugoslavia was enshrined in law, and most of the housing and major buildings were the result of architectural competitions. There were vast amounts of bespoke design constructed without mass production, for all of the country's population. It was a truly alternative way to organise a state and its housing and working conditions, and it reminds us that design can be a tool of social progress.

The Monuments

Part of the reason why Yugoslavia was able to build its own economic and state model – which some have termed 'market socialism' – was because it liberated its own territory in WWII, without relying on large amounts of Soviet assistance. The country's partisans, under Tito's leadership, did that work for themselves. The WWII partisan struggle was widely commemorated inside Yugoslavia by commissioning those same top-class architects to build monuments honouring landmark moments from the war. These monuments were hugely popular and often visited – not only because of their symbolic celebration of the partisan struggles and victories, but also because of their fantastical, abstract forms, which were simultaneously Modernist, organic and always set in beautiful natural landscapes.

Examples include the Battle of Sutjeska Memorial, in Bosnia & Hercegovina, once among the most visited sites in the country, and the Partisan Memorial Cemetery in Mostar, a memorial park that formed an essential part of the city. Bogdan Bogdanović designed the latter, together with many other monuments. The Jasenovac extermination camp memorial is one of the most emblematic. According to legend, Tito himself picked the design, against the wishes of other Communist Party members. Bogdanović claimed that the only reason Tito had chosen his proposal was because, unlike the other artists, he had not adopted the Soviet sculptural style of 'headless bodies, wounded figures and stretchers'. Commonly known as the Stone Flower, it is simply breathtaking.

Architects and designers often played with symbols taken from nature, used shapes of cosmic bodies and included water and other elements in their designs. As with architecture, where aesthetics and utilitarianism were major factors, local materials and the environment were always essential. The main concern was how the spaces, or the monuments, would be inhabited by human beings. Just as the housing projects provided accommodation for all (as opposed to the Western notion of 'social housing'), the monuments did not impose upon or shrink the viewer. The structures inspired awe, but were also always spaces in which to move, have a picnic and rest.

When you see Yugoslav architecture and monuments today, they seem – considering their context – quite dogma-free. Equally, keeping in mind the subsequent treatment of those structures by post-war nationalist governments (ranging from neglect to outright vandalism and destruction), you can appreciate their enduring symbolic power.

FOOD, MUSIC & TRADITION
IN THE NORTHWEST BALKANS

In Croatia and Bosnia & Hercegovina, the history of food and music has long been intertwined, creating a braided cultural continuity, even in difficult times. By Katherina Grace Thomas

CROATIA'S PALATE HAS been influenced by its layers of history, from pastoral ways of living and the Roman rule of Dalmatia to the Austro-Hungarian Empire. In Bosnia & Hercegovina, food, music and religion have converged throughout the centuries, nodding to Bosniak, Ottoman and Austro-Hungarian traditions. Without movement, migration and the merging of cultures and faiths, many of these culinary and musical treasures would not exist.

A Culinary History of Croatia

One of Croatia's oldest culinary dishes is *čobanec* (meat stew). Nobody knows its exact origin story, but this hearty, slow-cooked traditional dish from Slavonia is as old as the hills. It once kept the stomachs of shepherds *(čobani)* full during the long days spent watching their flocks. Prepared in a traditional copper cauldron, this thick stew often includes veal, pork and other kinds of meat, blended together with carrots, onions, tomatoes, celery and paprika.

Zagorski štrukli, a 'pulled pasta' dish, also goes back many centuries and is closely related to a similar traditional Slovenian dish. Made from flour, water, salt, eggs, cottage cheese and sour cream, the pastry is stretched out wide across a table before being boiled or baked into parcels of soft dough that almost resemble dumplings. One of Croatia's national dishes, in 2007 *zagorski štrukli* was added to the Ministry of Culture's list of intangible heritage.

Soparnik, a thin savoury pie stuffed with Swiss chard and onions, holds such historical significance in Dalmatia that this culinary treasure is protected by both the Croatian Ministry of Culture and the EU. It has been baked throughout the centuries, including – so the story goes – during Roman rule in 305 CE when Roman emperor Diocletian abdicated and retired to Split. While there, he and other Romans enjoyed soparnik so much that the recipe was brought back to Italy, where it became the prototype for pizza (however,

Croatia is not the only country to stake a claim to inventing pizza). Today, it is still baked in its original round shape, sliced into strips and drizzled with garlicky olive oil. Another traditional Dalmatian dish is *ispod peka* – its name, which translates as 'under the bell', refers to an ancient cooking method, a slow way of stewing beneath a dome-shaped lid among hot, glowing embers. There are many kinds of *peka* – octopus, squid, lamb – but one trait they share is that they're all usually heavy on the potatoes. Then there's *Konavoska zelena menestra*, also from Dalmatia. First mentioned in historical records from 15th-century Dubrovnik, this green stew can be made from all kinds of dried meat, including salty pig head or ribs, and is often topped with freshly grated horseradish.

Pastries, too, have stood the test of time. Legend has it that *Rapska torta*, from the Adriatic island of Rab, was first served in the 12th century to Pope Alexander III when he visited the island. Baked with finely ground almonds, lemon zest and Maraschino cherry liqueur from Zadar, its elegant spiral shape evokes the passage of time. Many people don't realise that *štrudle* – more frequently associated with Austria – has been baked in Croatia since at least the days of the Austro-Hungarian Empire. Traditional sweet fillings you'll find in bakeries include cherry or grated apple with raisins and cinnamon. Also keep an eye out for savoury varieties, including cheese, lamb, vegetables and mushrooms. During the annual Štrudlafest in Jaškovo, festival-goers have vied for several Guinness World Records, including for the longest strudel chain in the world, made up of 9000 baked strudels.

The Convergence of Food, Music and Religion in Bosnia & Hercegovina

Traditional *sevdalinka* or *sevdah* music – with its emotionally intense lyrics and melodies – is a kind of Balkan blues, an ancient form of love song and lyric poetry shaped by Islam, Turkish rule and urban displacement. It's performed everywhere from concert halls to coffee houses, accompanied by trays of hot *džezva* and *rahat lokum* (Turkish delight). *Sevdalinka* takes its name from the Ottoman Turkish term *sevda*, the idea of being in love. Over time it has evolved into a Bosnian term for bittersweet longing, similar to the Portuguese *saudade*. The genre dates back to 15th-century Ottoman Bosnia, when urban neighbourhoods known as *mahala* were built with separate gendered living spaces, prompting songs of separation and longing. It is also believed to be tied to the arrival of Sephardic refugees, Iberian Jews who resettled in the Ottoman Empire and North Africa in the wake of the Spanish Inquisition. Originally popular within Bosniak Islamic communities, *sevdalinka* are passed down orally within families and are now performed by people from all ethnic groups. The oldest documented *sevdalinka* is 'Bolest Muje Carevića' (The illness of Mujo Carević), believed to have been written in 1475.

Centuries later, around the end of the 20th century, the Austro-Hungarian era introduced Central European heritage, including musical and culinary traditions. Accordions and clarinets began appearing at concerts, sometimes sharing the stage with the traditional seven-string *saz*. At the same time, kitchen tables, especially among wealthy families, began including Central European imports like *kiflice* (sweet, crescent-shaped vanilla pastries) and *štrudle*. Cultures, histories and faiths came together despite religious and political divides.

Even a century later, during the brutal 1992–95 Bosnian War – when food became scarce, meals were built around ICRC canned beef rations and tensions between Bosniaks, Serbs and Croats reached a breaking point – this symphony of musical and culinary influences played on. Symbolic versions of dishes were created from foraged greens and rationed tins, while the Sarajevo Philharmonic Orchestra played a benefit concert in the ruins of the national library, a building designed under Austro-Hungarian rule. The orchestra still performs today, blending Western European classical music with *sevdalinka* and *hasanaganica*, honouring Bosniak cultural heritage.

Ispod peka

EUROPE ON THE BRINK

Europe today is facing unprecedented challenges, from Russian aggression and the erosion of individual liberties to the surge of the far-right. By Anna Kaminski

THIS IS EUROPE'S time of reckoning. In 2022, Russia's invasion of Ukraine brought armed conflict to the continent for the first time since WWII and exposed European vulnerabilities. Meanwhile, personal freedoms have been eroded in several European countries while migration related to climate change and political unrest has contributed to a surge in far-right politics.

On the Front Lines

In the early hours of 10 September 2025, Polish fighter jets scrambled to shoot down three of the 19 Russian drones that made an unprecedented incursion into Poland's air space. In the aftermath, France and Germany expanded air policing over Poland, while the Netherlands and Czechia deployed air defence systems, artillery and troops to help secure the Polish border. Just nine days later, on 19 September 2025, three Russian fighter jets violated Estonian airspace before being intercepted by Italian, Swedish and Finnish NATO aircraft stationed in Estonia. It wasn't the first time that Russia has provoked Poland and the Baltic States since invading Ukraine, but it is part of a brazen pattern of escalation that seems aimed at testing NATO's resolve to defend its members from Russian attack.

For Russia's immediate neighbours, the war in Ukraine feels existential. There is a sense of urgency in the Baltic States, Finland and Poland that seems to be lacking elsewhere in Europe, as well as an appreciation for the fact that Vladimir Putin respects only one thing: a show of strength. Poland is re-arming itself at a speed and on a scale not seen since the Cold War, pouring nearly 4% of its GDP into fighter jets, artillery, tanks and air defence. Poland has also been one of Ukraine's staunchest supporters, taking in over three million Ukrainian refugees and providing Ukraine with ammunition, military training and Starlink units. Long committed to neutrality, Finland abandoned its stance practically overnight, joining NATO in 2023 and effectively doubling the alliance's border with Russia.

The Baltic countries – Estonia, Latvia and Lithuania – see themselves as Russia's most likely targets after Ukraine, especially given the restive Russian-speaking populations in all three countries. The three nations have joined forces to build a collective Baltic Defence Line along their eastern borders with Russia and Belarus, incorporating trenches, anti-tank ditches, mines and other obstacles designed to slow down potential invaders. They've also

rapidly increased their military spending, invested in medium-range air-defence systems and participated in joint military exercises with other NATO troops.

Migration Challenges and the Rise of the Far Right

Russia's attack on Ukraine has shaken Europe's sense of security. Millions of Ukrainian refugees have fled the conflict, challenging countries throughout the continent to respond with compassion and resources. Yet the solidarity with which Ukrainians have been met, by and large, has not extended to migrants from beyond Europe, who have been driven from their homes by climate pressures, poverty and war. Drownings in the Mediterranean have become almost daily tragedies, and migration has fuelled calls for stricter border controls throughout Europe. In many European countries, far-right rhetoric citing 'foreign invasions' has become more acceptable in political discourse and far-right political parties have taken advantage of increasing polarisation to surge ahead in local and national elections.

The reasons behind the rise of the far right are manifold. These parties present themselves as patriotic defenders of cultural heritage and sovereignty, and speak to growing concerns over immigration, globalisation and the question of national identity, in addition to economic insecurity and the erosion of public trust in mainstream political leadership. These parties offer simplistic answers to complex social problems, and their rhetoric – which emphasises stricter border controls, scepticism of EU bureaucracy and resistance to progressive social policies – appeals to voters who feel threatened by rapid social and economic change.

In Poland feelings of solidarity with Ukraine's wartime plight sit uneasily alongside social tensions caused by this considerable influx of new arrivals – many of whom do not speak Polish, and additionally require housing, employment and access to healthcare, stretching finite social services. And even prior to the Russo-Ukrainian War, Belarus made consistent efforts to orchestrate a migration crisis in Poland and Lithuania by encouraging migrants from the Middle East and Africa to travel to Minsk with promises of easy entry to the EU, then herding them towards the frontiers with Poland and Lithuania, leading both countries to fortify their borders in response.

Personal Freedoms under Fire

In certain European countries, personal freedoms have also been subjected to mounting pressure. And in some cases, they have even been drastically curtailed – nowhere more so than in Hungary and Belarus. Since Viktor Orbán was elected prime minister of Hungary in 2010, his government has forced out experienced, impartial judges, pressured the judiciary to reduce its independence, imposed restrictions on independent media and cracked down on various NGOs, criminalising those that help migrants, for instance. At the same time, Hungary has passed laws that permit increased surveillance of its citizens, heavily restrict the rights of the LGBTIQ+ community and impose financial penalties on the govertment's critics.

Yet compared to the Belarus regime of Alexander Lukashenko – 'Europe's last dictator' and president since 1994 – Hungary is still a relatively free country, if no longer fully democratic. In 2020, Lukashenko refused to accept that his opponent Svetlana Tikhanovskaya had likely won the popular vote in the presidential election. As no impartial observers were present and vote-rigging was allegedly rife in the incumbent's favour, Lukashenko remained in power, which resulted in unprecedented mass protests. Lukashenko answered with violent crackdowns and continues to silence dissent in Belarus through mass arrests and censorship.

Hungary and Belarus are perhaps the most obvious examples in Eastern Europe, but other countries have also taken measures that infringe on individual rights. For example, Amnesty International has documented that since 2016, the right to peaceful protest in Poland has been severely curtailed by restrictive legislation and heavy-handed policing. Poland's far-right Law and Justice party – in power for eight years till 2023 – has also faced criticism for enforcing strict and unpopular abortion laws that severely limit women's reproductive rights and for undermining judicial independence. Harassment of journalists and government pressure on independent media is on the rise in Serbia and Bosnia, while Russia has sought to influence recent democratic elections in neighbouring countries such as Romania by engaging in mass propaganda efforts and other forms of election interference.

Going Forward

Russia's continued aggression and incessant provocations require a multi-faceted response, including rapid adaptation to 21st-century warfare. While NATO is already taking steps to strengthen its eastern flank by deploying multinational troops in the Baltics and Poland and investing in cyber and missile defence capabilities, it's not financially viable to mobilise multimillion-euro fighter jets every time Russian drones enter its airspace. NATO needs to learn from Ukraine, which has been repelling Russian drone attacks on a nightly basis, and to continue to support Ukraine with funding, intelligence and military aid. Whether the ongoing tension with Russia will lead to conflict elsewhere in Europe is anyone's guess. In the wake of Russian incursions, both Poland and Estonia have triggered Article 4, which requires urgent consultation between NATO members. However, there's a great reluctance to trigger Article 5 (which requires an armed response when a member state has been attacked), since the most militarily capable NATO member – the United States – has been ambivalent at best when pressed about upholding its treaty obligations to defend its allies.

While the erosion of individual freedoms across Europe is a pressing concern, there's still much that can be done to promote democratic values. On an international level, this might mean more vigorous enforcement when European governments undermine judicial independence and curtail press freedom and minority rights in their respective countries. For example, invoking Article 7 would suspend EU funding and voting rights of a persistent violator, such as Hungary. Individuals can contribute to grassroots human-rights and legal-aid NGOs, support independent media to strengthen press freedoms, and push back against repressive governments by taking part in peaceful protests in order to show solidarity with marginalised groups.

NATO badge
KARLIS DAMBRANS/SHUTTERSTOCK

The electoral success of far-right parties across Europe has sparked debate about the future of the European project, minority rights and democratic values. Is the rise of the far-right inevitable? According to the adage about the pendulum swing, this rightwards shift is a temporary occurrence, and it's only a matter of time before European societies re-embrace liberal values. Still, much can be done to slow down or counter the current trend. We can all play a part in building inclusive, resilient communities, as strong social bonds reduce the appeal of extremist groups. Education is crucial: stay informed about far-right narratives, call out hateful language and behaviour, and be vocal in debunking myths with facts. Staying engaged is also crucial: vote in local and general elections to strengthen tolerant voices and weaken repressive ones, join advocacy campaigns and challenge discriminatory policies or rhetoric in the public sphere.

Europe's future remains uncertain. But one thing is for sure: we continue to live in interesting times.

Rīga station, Latvia
VIESTURS JUGS/SHUTTERSTOCK

THE RAILWAY UNLINKING THE BALTICS FROM THEIR PAST

The Baltic nations have embarked on the largest infrastructure project of the past century, aimed at redefining European connectivity, reshaping politics and starting a new historical chapter. By Angelo Zinna

INTERNATIONAL RAIL TRAVEL across the EU is about to get much easier. Estonia, Latvia and Lithuania, supported by the EU, have initiated the largest infrastructure project of the past 100 years: the construction of a new 870km railway line that will provide seamless connectivity between the three Baltic countries, Warsaw and Western Europe. The Rail Baltica project, planned for completion in 2030, is poised to transform the way people and goods move across the continent, reducing travel times between the Baltic states and key European destinations.

Historically situated at the crossroads of trade routes, the Baltic region is now reclaiming its central role in European affairs. The move towards improved connections with the rest of the EU has obvious political implications that go well beyond the modernisation of transport infrastructure – the Baltic states are not just getting closer to their western neighbours, but also cutting ties with Russia, whose influence remains especially visible in the railway network crisscrossing Estonia, Latvia and Lithuania.

Gauge Size Matters

Let's take a step back. In the early 19th century, the Industrial Revolution was transforming the way people travelled around the world. The first railway line appeared in England in 1825 and it didn't take long before the rest of Europe– and later the planet – adopted the revolutionary technology. Within three decades, railway lines had appeared on all five continents, and by the late 1870s more than 1.3 million passengers and 700 million tons of goods were moving across the globe aboard steam-powered carriages. Jules

Verne's imagined trip around the world in 80 days had finally become a real possibility.

The Russian Empire was initially reluctant to enter the rail age. Building a network of lines that would effectively connect opposite corners of a barely industrialised empire covering a sixth of the world's landmass seemed unfeasible. Even as other European powers invested in speed, Russian transport along often frozen water courses appeared as slow as ever. It would take a German engineer, Franz Anton von Gerstner, to convince Tsar Nicholas I to construct the first 23km railway line between the then capital of St Petersburg and Tsarskoe Selo, the tsar's summer residence, in 1837.

The initial test was a success and the tsar began work to expand the Russian railway network across Eurasia. In 1843, Nicholas I appointed an American engineer, George Whistler, as the supervisor for the construction of the new St Petersburg–Moscow line, the longest double-track railway in the world, measuring 644km. Whistler promoted the use of the 1524mm train gauge, invented in England and common in the United States, which would become the norm in the entire Russian Empire in the following decades. When Russia began constructing its first railways in the 19th century, there was no universally accepted standard gauge – different countries and regions all had their own rail gauges. But things were changing. In 1846, the United Kingdom introduced a new Railway Regulation Act that enforced the use of the narrower 1435mm gauge across Great Britain and Ireland. Since the UK was Europe's main exporter of trains, the 1435mm gauge became the standard in most of Western Europe (except for Spain and Portugal).

The main issue with different gauges is that trains cannot cross from one system to the other. When, in the 1860s, the Russian Empire started building railways in the Baltics, the two networks clashed. After the collapse of the Russian Empire, the Germans regauged sections of the Baltic railway network to meet the Western European standard, but after WWII and the absorption of Estonia, Latvia and Lithuania into the USSR, the Soviets converted all the lines back to the broader 'Russian gauge' (adapted to 1520mm). It was a stra-

tegic move – by keeping the networks separated, the Soviet Union avoided the risk of enemy forces entering their territory via rail. To this day, the vast majority of rail lines within the former USSR continue to use the Russian gauge.

It's not just a matter of gauge size – the entire railway network of the three Baltic countries is oriented towards Moscow and St Petersburg. After the fall of the USSR, integration with the European Union happened relatively quickly on an institutional level – the Baltics joined NATO and the EU in 2004 – but transport infrastructure maintained its iron ties with the East, favouring trade with Russia.

Switching Tracks Westward

Discussions on decoupling from the Russian system started soon after Estonia, Latvia and Lithuania regained their independence in 1991, although it would take over a decade before concrete proposals would be put on the table, due to the immense scale of the task at hand. Rebuilding the infrastructure to integrate it with the European rail network and shifting from an east–west to a north–south orientation was an unprecedented enterprise with clear geopolitical implications. Unsurprisingly, it has received more pronounced support since the start of the war between Russia and Ukraine in 2014. The conflict heightened concerns in the Baltic states and the wider European community about regional security and stability, and the Rail Baltica project became a means to bolster regional resilience and reduce vulnerabilities.

Initial predictions of the total cost of the project set the price tag for Rail Baltica at €5.8 billion, with the EU committed to funding the large majority of the railway's construction. Far from cheap, Rail Baltica would not pay for itself in the short term, but Ernst & Young analysts estimated that the new transport infrastructure would bring in over €16 billion in indirect revenue into the Baltic countries, the result of reduced air pollution, climate change mitigation, faster freight transport and more accessible public transport for citizens. Doubts about such estimated benefits have emerged as the project moves forward, and exact calculations about short- and medium-term advantages remain ambiguous. In addition to the predicted benefits, Rail Baltica is expected to employ approximately 13,000 people in regions of Eastern Europe that have experienced heavy outward migration in recent decades.

The challenge, however, lies in keeping the costs within the estimated budget – a task that has already presented many obstacles. In 2022, Estonia made the news for being the eurozone country hit hardest by inflation, with price increases that surpassed 20% (compared to a 9% European average). Latvia and Lithuania followed at a short distance, with double-digit inflation measurements. The Baltic countries' dependency on exports made them highly vulnerable to the energy crisis that hit Europe following Russia's invasion of Ukraine – a blow reflected in increased costs of construction materials that slowed down the progress of Rail Baltica. In the summer of 2023, the EU's Connecting Europe Facility awarded an additional €928 million to the project, followed by the Latvian government, which allotted €18 million to complete the domestic section of the rail line. Yet, the Latvian Ministry of Transport has declared that funding is still falling short of covering two of Rail Baltica's key nodes, Rīga Central Station and Rīga International Airport.

The first section of the project, known as Rail Baltica I, was completed in 2015, covering the 120km distance between Kaunas and the Lithuania–Poland border. A year later, the first service between Kaunas and the Polish city of Białystok was inaugurated, allowing passengers to travel across the border without having to switch trains for the first time. Once completed, Rail Baltica will run from Tallinn to Pärnu via Rapla, and then continue along the Baltic coast all the way to Rīga. From there, trains will enter Lithuania to reach Panevėžys before reaching Kaunas, Vilnius and ultimately Warsaw. The line will avoid passing through Kaliningrad, the Russian exclave locked between Poland and Lithuania, which is connected to Russia via a direct rail link. A proposal to extend the Rail Baltica line all the way to Helsinki via a tunnel that would run through the Gulf of Finland has also been presented, although at the time of writing Estonia, Finland and the EU were still studying the feasibility of the project. If approved, the 80km Tallinn–Helsinki line would become the longest rail tunnel in the world.

As the Rail Baltica project moves closer to completion, it promises to not only transform the transportation landscape of the Baltic region but also the political dynamics of Europe as a whole.

Rail Baltica train, Lithuania

INDEX

INDEX

D–K

Map Pages **000**

"I love to wander around the Ottoman-era stone alleyways in Berat (p60), snapping photos as the light strikes its cherished windows"

JOEL BALSAM

"As spring ends and the weather warms up, Pärnu (p188) comes to life with Estonians, Finns and Latvians heading to the Baltic Sea."

ANGELO ZINNA

Mapping data sources:
© Lonely Planet
© OpenStreetMap http://openstreetmap.org/copyright

THIS BOOK

Destination Editor
Shauna Daly

Production Editor
Jeremy Toynbee

Image Researcher
Dominic Allen

Cartographer
Daniela Machová

Assisting Cartographers
Mark Griffiths, Jennifer Johnston, Valentina Kremenchutskaya, Anthony Phelan

Coordinating Editor
Christopher Pitts

Assisting Editors
Liana Cafolla, Nigel Chin, Holly Proctor, Fionnuala Twomey

Contributing Writers
Kat Barber, Shaun Busuttil, Virginia DiGaetano Becki Enright, Anthony Haywood, Isabel Putinja, Kevin Raub, Simon Richmond, Andrea Schulte-Peevers, Monica Suma, Ryan Ver Berkmoes, Barbara Woolsey

Cover Researcher
Katelyn Perry

Thanks Daniel Bolger, Kate James, Amy Lysen, Darren O'Connell, Charlotte Orr, Saralinda Turner

MIX
Paper | Supporting responsible forestry
FSC™ C021741
www.fsc.org

Paper in this book is certified against the Forest Stewardship Council™ standards. FSC™ promotes environmentally responsible, socially beneficial and economically viable management of the world's forests.

Published by Lonely Planet Global Limited
CRN 554153
17th edition – Jun 2026
ISBN 978 1 83869 386 2
© Lonely Planet 2026 Photographs © as indicated 2026
10 9 8 7 6 5 4 3 2 1
Printed in Malaysia